Get results with Mark Connelly's Get Writing: Paragraphs and Essays!

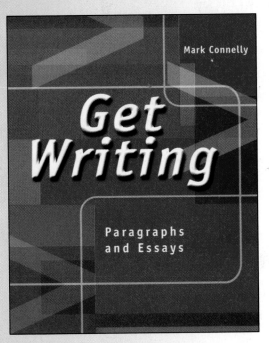

Mark Connelly

Get Writing

Paragraphs and Essays

This new developmental writing text helps students acquire skills and develop confidence as writers by engaging them in their own writing from the first page. *Get Writing* incorporates a range of writing prompts to build students' confidence in their ability to create thesis statements, draft and develop paragraphs, and write and revise their own essays. This text includes a guided questioning strategy that encourages students to examine and critique their own work and prompts students to write about real-world topics.

This exciting new text moves students from skill-based paragraph exercises to drafting, examining, and revising their own essays. *Get Writing* includes many inventive features such as:

- **Innovative writing prompts in every chapter** that inspire students to write—*see PREVIEW page 2.*

- **A colorful visual orientation and visual prompts** that encourage today's media-oriented students to write—*see PREVIEW page 3.*

- **Uniquely strong coverage of modes**—nine full chapters—*see PREVIEW page 4.*

- **A concise handbook for easy reference**—*see PREVIEW page 5.*

- **Online tools for students and instructors**—including personalized online study plans for students with ThomsonNOW for Connelly's *Get Writing: Paragraphs and Essays* as well as course management, preparation, and testing resources for instructors—*see PREVIEW pages 6 and 7.*

- **PLUS many student resources**—available for convenient packaging with this book—*see PREVIEW page 8.*

Please turn the page to begin your quick tour ▶▶▶

THOMSON

™

WADSWORTH

D1532938

1

With these writing prompts, students are eager to respond!

▶ **Get Writing prompts and activities appear throughout every chapter.**
Barely a few lines into this text, students encounter their first writing prompt. Connelly taps into their personal interests and concerns, providing topics that students want to write about—their future careers, their courses, their families, and their goals. The easy-to-spot *Get Writing* icon alerts students to these prompts.

▼ **What Are You Trying to Say?...
What Have You Written?**
Each chapter's *What Are You Trying to Say?* prompts students to express their thoughts about a subject in clear topic sentences, paragraphs, and essays. *What Have You Written?* then guides students to think critically about their paragraphs and essays—by examining word choices, topic sentence clarity, and use of details to support their thesis. This guided questioning strategy encourages students to think critically about their own work and connect what they learn about grammar with what they are trying to say.

1

Why Write?

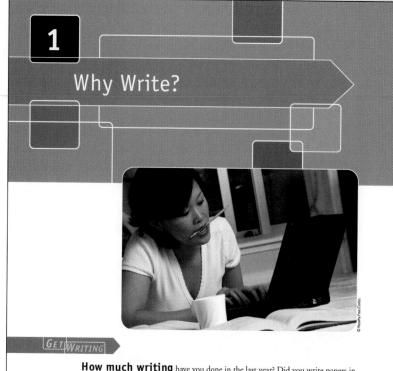

GET WRITING

How much writing have you done in the last year? Did you write papers in high school or college courses, prepare reports at work, or e-mail friends?

Write a paragraph that describes your recent writing experiences. List any problems you have faced, from organizing your thoughts to grammar and spelling.

WHAT HAVE YOU WRITTEN?

Read your paragraph carefully.

1. Underline the topic sentence. Does it express a focused controlling idea? Could it be more clearly stated?
2. Do the other sentences support the controlling idea or do they contain unrelated details?

WHAT ARE YOU TRYING TO SAY?

Select one of the topics below or develop one of your own and make a few notes before writing.

racial profiling	bloggers
health clubs	current fashions
campus parking	role models
first dates	cell phone etiquette

...nd write a paragraph that supports it with meaningful

▶ **Critical Thinking assignments**
These assignments encourage students to write about personal experiences and world issues ranging from the impact of technology on their lives to the ways the media influence their values. In *Critical Thinking* assignments, as well as throughout the book, Connelly emphasizes how good writers use critical thinking to observe, ask questions, collect facts, and test commonly held beliefs—in short, showing students that all good writing goes beyond the obvious to explore and analyze events, people, and ideas.

CRITICAL THINKING

What effects have cell and camera phones had on society? Have they improved communications, making our jobs and lives better and easier? Or have they robbed us of privacy and created a new source of annoyance in theaters, restaurants, and other public places? Write a paragraph outlining the positive and/or negative effects of cell and camera phones. Support your points with examples.

Visual prompts and collaborative exercises get students writing!

13
Developing Paragraphs Using Argument

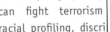

Hijacker Mohammed Atta passes through airport security, September 11, 2001

GET WRITING

What can be done to protect our nation from terrorists? The 9/11 hijackers were able to enter the country, obtain driver's licenses, take flying lessons, and board planes with weapons.

Write a paragraph arguing how to increase our security.

◀ Every chapter opens with a photo or illustration accompanied by critical thinking questions—encouraging students to examine and write about their personal viewpoints related to future career choices, school life, family, and social issues. Contrasting photos are often used to encourage analysis and comparison. Unlike other developmental writing texts, *Get Writing* uses visuals to stimulate critical thinking rather than just immediate reactions.

▼ The chapter's visual theme is revisited at the end of Chapters 1-21, where students have an opportunity to analyze a contrasting image.

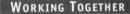

GET WRITING

In April 1942, four months after the attack on Pearl Harbor, Japanese-Americans, many of them born in the United States, were placed in internment camps. Many were forced to sell their businesses and houses at a great loss. Recognizing the unfairness of this action, Congress granted each survivor $20,000 in compensation in 1988.

Write a paragraph argu[ing]
can fight terrorism
racial profiling, discri[mination]
violations.

▶ *Working Together*—**group work that leads to stronger writing!** Throughout this book, Connelly includes collaborative writing and editing exercises that demonstrate the value of peer review and give students practice in working in groups.

WORKING TOGETHER

Working with a group of students, revise this e-mail to shorten and clarify directions. You may wish to create numbered points.

Dorm Resident Advisors:

Security guards have again reported that students are breaking the rules regarding the underground parking garage in the dorms. Remember that under no circumstances are students allowed to store gasoline cans or other flammable products in the garage. Several students with motorcycles have been placing cans of gas in their parking spaces or on homemade tool benches. Also parking spaces must be kept clear. They are getting cluttered with spare tires and toolboxes. In addition, remind students not to work on their cars in the garage, especially to change tires using jacks

Strong modes coverage, real-world examples, and more!

▶ **Nine modes chapters focusing on paragraph development and essay writing**

Connelly's *Get Writing* devotes a chapter to each of nine modes: description, narration, example, definition, comparison and contrast, division and classification, process, cause and effect, and argument. Each chapter demonstrates how a particular mode is used to build paragraphs, answer essay exam questions, and organize college essays and professional documents.

▼ **Real-world writing—students practice writing beyond the classroom**

Chapter 18, "Writing at Work," introduces students to writing and revising documents they will encounter in their careers: e-mail, résumés, letters, and reports.

EXERCISE 1 Revising E-Mail

Revise this e-mail to create a clear, concise message.

Kim:

This e-mail is about the student enrollment problems we face with online courses. Right now it seems many students sign up and cannot find the website for their course and have no idea how the class is going to be run or what is expected of causing a problem. I am getting a lot of complaints from students who seem we can do some things to improve this situation next semester. The main site should have a link to all online courses. Each online instructor must course website an expanded syllabus that explains the nature of the course, assignment due dates, readings, and online discussion groups. In additio partment website should list its online offerings.

▶ **Thorough coverage of sentence structure— connecting grammar with critical thinking**

Parts 4, 5, and 6—"Improving Style" (Chapters 19-21), "Understanding Grammar" (Chapters 22-31), and "Understanding Punctuation and Mechanics" (Chapters 32-35)—effectively explain the grammatical elements of sentences and how they work together to express thoughts. Connelly connects grammar with critical thinking so students understand that decisions about sentence structure depend on what they are trying to say.

Developing Paragraphs Using Comparison

13

Developing Paragraphs Using Argument

Hijacker Mohammed Atta passes through airport security.
September 11, 2001

What can be done to protect our nation from terrorists? The 9/11 hijackers were able to enter the country, obtain driver's licenses, take flying lessons, and board planes with weapons.

Write a paragraph arguing how to increase our security.

Part 4

Improving Style

Chapter 19 Improving Essays
Chapter 20 Improving Sentence Variety
Chapter 21 Improving Word Choice

ordination and
ma Splices
placed

Chapter 30 Pronoun Reference, Agreement, and Case
Chapter 31 Adjectives and Adverbs

PLUS a concise handbook and other tools for student writers

Handbook

◀ Connelly provides grammar and style guides in each chapter—in easy-to-spot tan boxes. In addition, he includes a *Handbook* at the end of the text with a condensed explanation of important grammar and style rules. The *Handbook* is an easy-to-read resource that covers basic sentence structure, fragments, run-ons, subject-verb agreement, verb tense and choice, pronoun agreement, dangling and misplaced modifiers, capitalization, punctuation, and spelling.

PARTS OF SPEECH

Nouns	name persons, places, things, or ideas: *teacher, attic, Italy, book, liberty*
Pronouns	take the place of nouns: *he, she, they, it, this, that, what, which, hers, their*
Verbs	express action: *buy, sell, run, walk, create, think, feel, wonder, hope, dream*
	link ideas: *is, are, was, were*
Adjectives	add information about nouns or pronouns: a *red* car, a *bright* idea, a *lost* cause

▼ *Points to Remember* boxes
Placed throughout each chapter, concise boxes summarize key concepts.

POINT TO REMEMBER

Reading out loud can help identify fragments. Ask yourself, "Does this statement express a complete thought?"

WRITING ON THE WEB

Using a search engine such as Yahoo!, Google, or AltaVista, enter terms such as *narration, writing narration, narrative techniques,* and *first-person narratives* to locate current sites of interest.

1. Review news articles in online versions of magazines like *Time* and *Newsweek* and notice how writers explain events. How do they organize paragraphs, use dialogue, and signal transitions?
2. Write an e-mail to a friend describing something you saw or experienced. Revise your paragraphs to delete minor details and highlight important points.

◀ *Writing on the Web* sections
Found in every chapter, *Writing on the Web* boxes help students effectively navigate the Internet to locate writing resources.

Turn the page to learn more about this book's exceptional online resources

Strong support for improving student writing

5

Personalized online study plans and online tutoring!

ThomsonNow for *Get Writing: Paragraphs and Essays* (formerly known as Writer'sResourcesNow)

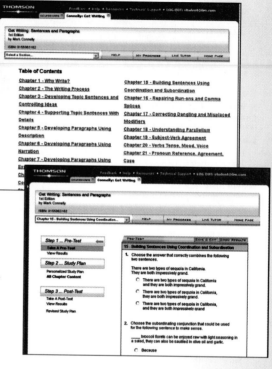

Available to your students at a reduced price when packaged with Connelly's *Get Writing: Paragraphs and Essays,* **ThomsonNOW for *Get Writing: Paragraphs and Essays*** is a Web-based, intelligent study system that provides a complete package of diagnostic quizzes, *Personalized Study Plans,* course management features, and a direct link to vMentor tutoring. After completing a chapter in Connelly's *Get Writing: Paragraphs and Essays,* students take an online Pretest to assess their proficiency in the skills covered in the chapter. Based on the results of the Pretest, the student receives a personalized *Study Plan* with links to multimedia tutorials that reinforce the skills covered in the chapter. After working through their *Study Plans,* students complete a follow-up *Posttest* to assess their mastery of the material. **ThomsonNOW for *Get Writing: Paragraphs and Essays'*** automatically generated *Study Plans* help students to prioritize their studies and to use their study time effectively. To see a demonstration of **ThomsonNOW for *Get Writing: Paragraphs and Essays,*** visit **http://developmentalenglish.wadsworth.com.** Ask your Thomson Wadsworth representative how to package **ThomsonNOW for *Get Writing: Paragraphs and Essays*** with the every new student copy of Connelly's *Get Writing. (For additional information, please consult your local Thomson representative.)*

Book Companion Website— *student resources available at no extra cost!*

http://developmentalenglish.wadsworth.com/connelly2/
This site features a wealth of resources for students, including online grammar quizzes, a quick guide to punctuation, a list of commonly misspelled and commonly confused words, and links to online resources for writers.

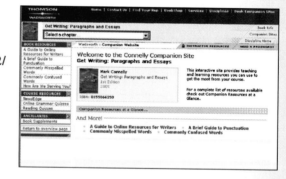

vMentor™— *Live online tutoring right at students' computers-at no additional cost!*

Available via a live link on the Book Companion Website, **vMentor** lets your students connect with subject area experts who have been trained on Connelly's text. The **vMentor** virtual classroom features several ways for students to interact with these experts-two-way audio, an interactive whiteboard for displaying presentation materials, and instant messaging.

For proprietary, college, and university adopters only. For additional information and hours of operation, please consult your local Thomson Wadsworth representative.

Great online libraries generate writing topics

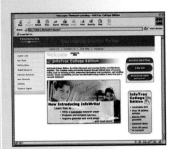

InfoTrac® College Edition—
Nearly 5,000 journals and magazines!
The access code is available upon request with your adoption order—at no additional cost.
A four-month subscription to this extensive online library is available with every new copy of Connelly's text—at no additional cost! **InfoTrac College Edition** includes innumerable articles from thousands of magazines, newsletters, respected journals, and popular periodicals. This library's full-length articles (not just excerpts) are updated daily, expertly indexed, and ready to use—24 hours a day, seven days a week! **InfoTrac College Edition** is an invaluable resource that students can use for every course they take—to conduct research for assignments, to generate writing topics, or to simply catch up on current events through publications such as *Time, Newsweek, and Forbes. For more information, consult your local Thomson Wadsworth representative.*

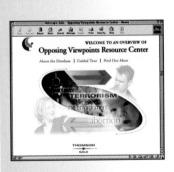

Opposing Viewpoints Resource Center—
exploring the issues!
Available with each text for a nominal fee, this extensive online library exposes students to various sides of controversial issues, giving them an opportunity to explore issues-thinking critically about the pros and cons of each position. The site includes selections from Greenhaven Press' titles in the Opposing Viewpoints series, such as "At Issue," "Contemporary Issues Companions," and "Current Controversies." Also included are full-text articles from more than 30 major newspapers and magazines, such as *The New York Times* and *U.S. News and World Report,* plus a wide variety of search features and a built-in Research Guide with analysis and critical thinking tools. Please visit http://www.gale.com/OpposingViewpoints/index.htm for a tour. Ask your Thomson Wadsworth representative how to package **Opposing Viewpoints Resource Center** with the every new student copy of Connelly's *Get Writing.*

And these exceptional course preparation and testing tools:

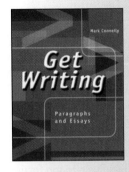

Annotated Instructor's Edition
This annotated version of Connelly's *Get Writing* contains answers to exercises in the text. (Student texts contain answers to odd-numbered exercises only.)

Instructor's Manual/Test Bank for Connelly's *Get Writing*
0-155-06633-1
Correlated with the text, this useful manual contains:

- Additional writing assignments
- Discussion of the professional and student papers included in the text's writing chapters and how the papers can be taught in class
- Sample syllabi
- Additional helpful teaching tips
- *Test Bank* questions for Chapters 1–18 (the text's writing chapters) that quiz students on the writing skills and concepts introduced in the chapters
- *Test Bank* questions for Chapters 19–35 (the text's style/grammar/punctuation chapters) that feature diagnostic and mastery tests (30 test items for each chapter)
- *Answer Key*

Also available for convenient packaging with this book!

Writer's Resources CD-ROM, Version 2.0— *Interactive multimedia that teaches all aspects of grammar and writing*

This CD-ROM is appropriate for an instructor-led classroom, a writing lab, or as an independent electronic resource for students. A complete writing course with more than 4, 500 interactive exercises, as well as audio and animation, this CD-ROM's four sections cover all the skills necessary to help students become effective writers:

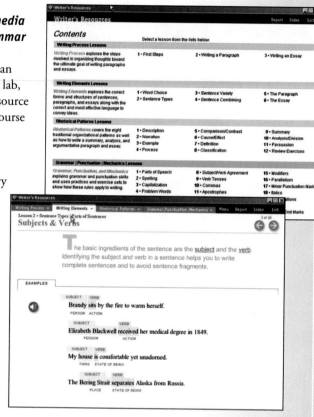

- **The Grammar, Punctuation, and Mechanics Section** covers 21 basic grammar, punctuation, and mechanics problem areas. Each lesson focuses students on one concept at a time, with animated examples and practice sessions that give detailed feedback for all student responses.
- **Writing Elements** discusses the building blocks of college writing, showing how to choose effective words, write strong sentences, develop paragraphs, and compose essays.
- **Writing Process** covers all the stages of the process, from brainstorming and pre-writing to final draft preparation.
- **Rhetorical Patterns** discusses eight traditional organizational patterns with step-by-step instructions on how to organize a piece of writing using that pattern, and features student paragraph and essay models of each pattern.

Ask your Thomson Wadsworth representative how to package **Writer's Resources CD-ROM 2.0** with the every new student copy of Connelly's *Get Writing*.

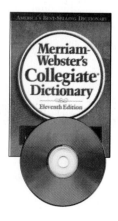

Merriam-Webster's Collegiate® Dictionary, Eleventh Edition

Available at a discounted price when packaged with Connelly's text, the new Eleventh Edition of America's best-selling dictionary merges print, CD-ROM, and Internet-based formats to deliver unprecedented accessibility and flexibility. **1,664 pages. Hardcover. Package item only.**

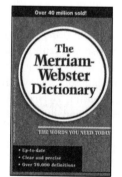

The Merriam-Webster's Dictionary

Available at a discounted price when packaged with Connelly's text. **894 pages. Paperback. Package item only.**

Annotated Instructor's Edition

Get Writing

Paragraphs and Essays

Mark Connelly

Milwaukee Area Technical College

THOMSON

WADSWORTH

Australia • Brazil • Canada • Mexico • Singapore • Spain • United Kingdom • United States

Annotated Instructor's Edition
Get Writing: Paragraphs and Essays
Mark Connelly

Publisher: Michael Rosenberg
Senior Acquisitions Editor: Steve Dalphin
Senior Development Editor: Michell Phifer
Editorial Assistant: Cheryl Forman
Technology Project Manager: Joe Gallagher
Managing Marketing Manager: Mandee Eckersley
Marketing Assistant: Dawn Giovanniello
Associate Marketing Communications Manager: Patrick Rooney
Senior Project Manager, Editorial Production: Samantha Ross
Print Buyer: Betsy Donaghey

Senior Permissions Editor: Isabel Alves
Production Service/Compositor: G&S Book Services
Text Designer: Brian Salisbury
Photo Manager: Sheri Blaney
Photo Researcher: Christina Micek
Senior Art Director: Bruce Bond
Cover Designer: Linda Beaupré
Cover Printer: Phoenix Color Corp.
Printer: Courier-Kendallville

Printed in the United States of America
1 2 3 4 5 6 7 09 08 07 06 05

Library of Congress Control Number: 2005931594

Student Edition: ISBN 0-1550-6625-0

Annotated Instructor's Edition: ISBN 1-4130-0263-3

Thomson Higher Education
25 Thomson Place
Boston, MA 02210-1202
USA

For more information about our products, contact us at:
Thomson Learning Academic Resource Center
1-800-423-0563

For permission to use material from this text or product, submit a request online at **http://www.thomsonrights.com** Any additional questions about permissions can be submitted by e-mail to **thomsonrights@thomson.com**

Credits appear on pages 675–676, which constitute a continuation of the copyright page.

Brief Contents

Contents

PART 2 DEVELOPING PARAGRAPHS 27

Chapter 3 Developing Topic Sentences and Controlling Ideas 28

Chapter 4 Supporting Topic Sentences with Details 44

Chapter 8   Developing Paragraphs Using Definition   102

Chapter 9   Developing Paragraphs Using Comparison and Contrast   113

PART 4   IMPROVING STYLE   291

PART 7 READINGS FOR WRITERS 555

HANDBOOK 611

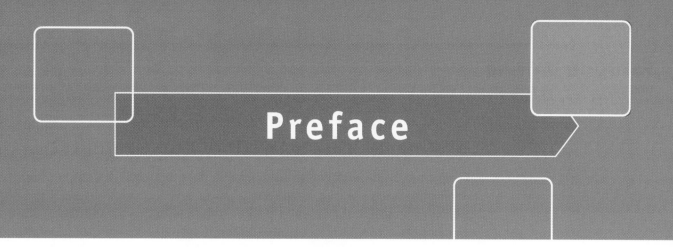

The Goals of *Get Writing: Paragraphs and Essays*

Get Writing helps students improve the writing skills needed to succeed in college and their future careers by engaging them in their own writing. *Get Writing* assumes that students have things to say about their jobs, their friends, their families, their college experience, their career goals, and the world around them. Throughout the book students are given opportunities to express themselves on a variety of issues and then examine and improve their choice of words, sentences, and paragraphs. Above all, *Get Writing* connects critical thinking (what students are trying to say) with grammar and mechanics (what they have written).

Approach

Get Writing guides students to enhance their writing skills by asking two questions:

1. **What are you trying to say?**
   Why did you select this topic?
   What do you want readers to know about it?
   What details should you include?
   What is the best way to organize your ideas?

2. **What have you written?**
   Are your words accurate and effective?
   Do your sentences clearly express what you want to say?
   Can readers follow your train of thought?
   Are there mechanical errors that detract from your message?

Get Writing meets the needs of a variety of students, including recent high school graduates, working adults returning to school, and those for whom English is not their native language. Writing exercises and prompts cover a range of interests — history, politics, popular culture, jobs, education, science, and current events.

Get Writing does not teach writing in isolation. It assists students with the writing tasks they will encounter in other courses and in their jobs. Writing assignments ask students to comment on their progress in college, to identify upcoming challenges, and to consider strategies for improving their writing skills, study habits, and time management.

Focus on Writing

Get Writing offers students a range of writing opportunities.

What Are You Trying to Say?/What Have You Written?

Chapters open by asking students to express their thoughts on a range of topics. After completing a writing assignment, they are asked to examine what they have written. By analyzing their word choices, their use of details, and their critical-thinking skills, they learn to improve their writing and link what they are studying with their own work.

Responding to Images

Visual prompts encourage students to use critical thinking to write about images depicting school life, jobs, family, social issues, and world events. Photos are often paired to encourage comparison and analysis.

Critical Thinking

Assignments direct students to write about personal experiences and express their opinions on issues ranging from national security to their favorite television show.

Real World Writing

Throughout *Get Writing* students write, revise, and edit documents they will encounter beyond the classroom: announcements, e-mail, résumés, and letters.

Working Together

Collaborative writing and editing exercises demonstrate the value of peer review and provide practice working in groups.

Organization

Get Writing consists of seven parts, which can be taught in different sequences to meet the needs of instructors and courses.

Part 1: Getting Started introduces students to the importance of writing and presents strategies for succeeding in composition courses. The writing process, from prewriting to final editing, is explained in practical steps.

Part 2: Developing Paragraphs shows students how to build paragraphs by creating clear topic sentences supported by details. These chapters cover nine patterns of development: description, narration, example, definition, comparison and contrast, division and classification, process, cause and effect, and argument.

Exam skills demonstrate how students use different patterns of development to answer essay questions.

Student paragraphs illustrate how students use a particular pattern of development to build paragraphs for personal essays, college assignments, and examinations.

Putting Paragraphs Together show how separate paragraphs work together to create a short essay.

Part 3: Writing Essays explains how to create thesis statements and develop outlines to organize supporting details and guide the first draft. Students are shown methods to create essays with clear transitions and effective introductions and conclusions. Step-by-step directions explain how to write essays in nine patterns of development: description, narration, example, definition, comparison and contrast, division and classification, process, cause and effect, and argument. Annotated student essays demonstrate how writers frequently use more than one pattern to develop an essay.

Part 4: Improving Style provides students with guidelines for enhancing the focus, consistency, and style of essays, the clarity and variety of sentences, and the effectiveness of word choices. Students are shown how to overcome shifts in person and tense, choppy or unclear sentences, wordy phrases, and errors in usage.

Parts 5 and 6: Understanding Grammar and **Understanding Punctuation and Mechanics** demonstrate that grammar is not simply a set of arbitrary rules but a tool to express ideas and prevent confusion. *Get Writing* connects grammar with critical thinking, so students understand that decisions about sentence structure depend on what they are trying to say. Students are given practical tips for detecting and repairing common sentence errors.

What Do You Know? exercises open each chapter, offering a short quiz with answers so students can test themselves to see how much they know about each unit.

Sequenced exercises direct students to identify and repair individual sentences then detect and repair errors in context.

Writing exercises guide students to develop their own sentences and paragraphs then look for and correct errors in their own writing.

Cumulative exercises combine errors from previous chapters, providing students with realistic editing and revising challenges.

What Have You Learned? exercises conclude each chapter, offering a short quiz with answers so students can test themselves, identifying areas that need continued review.

Points to Remember provide main points for quick review and reference.

Part 7: Readings for Writers outlines strategies for critical reading and presents two professional essays for each pattern of development. The annotated readings include new and classic pieces by Anna Quindlen, Janice Castro, Maya Angelou, Russell Baker, and Cornel West. The topics discussed include race relations, the environment, homelessness, and reality TV. Each reading is followed by questions that guide students to analyze the writer's meaning, strategy, and use of language. Writing prompts direct students to express their views and incorporate new techniques in their own writing.

Other Features

The **Handbook** summarizes grammar and mechanics for easy reference.

Writing at Work offers practical advice on the most common writing tasks students encounter after they leave college—writing e-mail, reports, cover letters, and resumes.

Using Sources and MLA Documentation demonstrates how to document essays to assist students not only in composition but other college courses requiring research papers.

Writing on the Web guides students to use the Internet to locate online writing resources.

ESL boxes provide help with specific writing problems encountered by students still mastering English.

Ancillaries

The *Annotated Instructor's Edition* provides answers to exercises found in the student version of the textbook.

The *Instructor's Manual/Test Bank* is an inclusive supplement written by Luis Nazario of Pueblo Community College.

The *Instructor's Manual* section contains a variety of teaching aids, including directions on how to use the integrated features of *Get Writing*, such as the Working Together activities, visual writing prompts, Critical Thinking assignments, and What Are You Trying to Say?/What Have You Written? exercises. The manual also discusses how to incorporate the professional and student model paragraphs in class and provides additional writing assignments, collaborative activities, and teaching tips for every chapter. The *Instructor's Manual* offers ESL information for many chapters as well as suggestions for teaching to various learning styles.

The *Test Bank*, which includes diagnostic and mastery tests, consists of almost six hundred items. The tests are a combination of generative testing items, which ask students to write their own sentences within guided parameters, and objective questions that cover the skills and concepts presented in the textbook.

Writer's Resources Ⓦ Now™

Writer's ResourcesNow™, available for a modest fee when purchased with the textbook, is a Web-based, intelligent study system, keyed to the text, that provides students and instructors with an integrated package of diagnostic quizzes, a personalized study plan, multimedia elements, learning modules, writing assignments, and an instructor grade book.

A free *Companion Website* features a wealth of resources for students, such as online grammar quizzes, a quick guide to punctuation, a list of commonly misspelled and confused words, and links to online resources for writers.

vMentor™ provides live, one-on-one, online tutoring from a subject-area expert. Students may interact with a tutor using two-way audio, an interactive whiteboard for illustrating the problem, and instant messaging. *vMentor* is accessible for free via a link on the Companion Website or through Writer's ResourcesNow.

Acknowledgments

All books are a collaborative effort. My special thanks goes to Michael Rosenberg, publisher; Stephen Dalphin, acquisitions editor; and Michell Phifer, development editor, for their support, vision, and enthusiasm for *Get Writing*. I would also like to thank the talented Wadsworth production team, Samantha Ross, production project manager, Joe Gallagher, technology project manager, and Sheri Blaney, photo manager, as well as Leah McAleer, production coordinator at G&S Book Services.

Get Writing: Paragraphs and Essays benefited greatly from comments and suggestions made by a dedicated group of reviewers:

Caryl Terrell-Bamiro, *Chandler-Gilbert Community College*

Jeff Carney, *Snow College*

Zoe Ann Cerny, *Horry-Georgetown Technical College*

Sandra Chumchall, *Blinn College*

Beth Conomos, *Erie Community College*

Linda Conry, *Collin County Community College*

Carol Cooper, *Jackson State University*

Catherine Decker, *Chaffey College*

Rita Delude, *New Hampshire Community Technical College*

Terese Derballa, *Asheville-Buncombe Technical Community College*

Joy Ferkel, *Terra State Community College*

Rebecca Frier, *South Georgia College*

Judy Harris, *Tomball College*

Elaine Herrick, *Temple College*

Eric Hibbison, *J. Sargeant Reynolds Community College*

Peggy Hopper, *Walters State Community College*

Deborah Johnson, *Prince George's Community College*

Ann Lewald, *Tennessee Technical University*

Joan Mauldin, *San Jacinto College*

Jack Miller, *Normandale Community College*

Raymond Orkwis, *Northern Virginia Community College*

Teresa Prosser, *Sinclair Community College*

Dee Pruitt, *Florence Darlington Technical College*

Melissa Rankin, *Richland Community College*

David Robson, *Delaware County Community College*

Lawrence Roy, *Madisonville Community College*

Virginia Smith, *Carteret Community College*

Wendy Jo Ward, *Miami-Dade College*

Janet Wasson, *Hinds Community College*

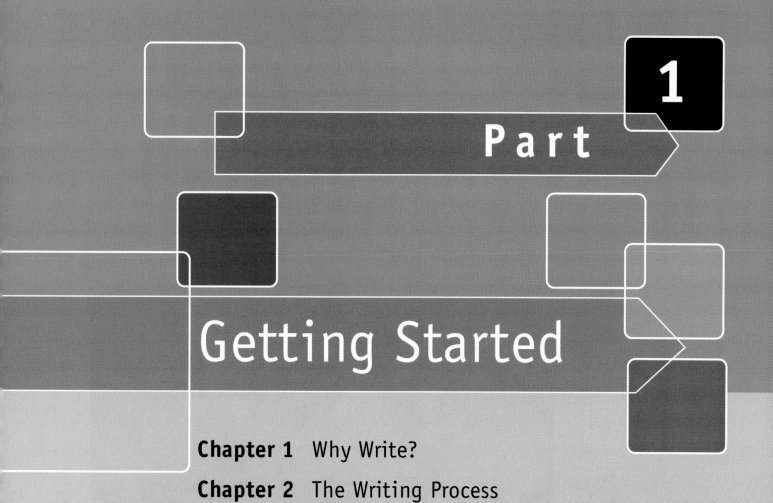

Part 1

Getting Started

Why Write?

© Royalty-Free/Corbis

GET WRITING

How much writing have you done in the last year? Did you write papers in high school or college courses, prepare reports at work, or e-mail friends?

Write a paragraph that describes your recent writing experiences. List any problems you have faced, from organizing your thoughts to grammar and spelling.

Few students plan to become writers. Most people think of writers as men and women who write for a living—reporters, screenwriters, historians, playwrights, and novelists. In the information age, however, writing is an important part of any career.

When you imagine your life after college, you probably see yourself in action—an engineer designing a new engine, a medical technician performing lab tests, a police officer investigating an accident, or a therapist counseling clients. All these professionals are writers. They do not publish books or write newspaper articles, but they communicate in writing. Engineers send reports, letters, and e-mail to investors, suppliers, customers, and managers. Medical personnel maintain detailed records and charts. Police officers record their observations in reports that may become evidence in legal proceedings. Whatever profession you enter, your success will depend on your ability to inform and persuade people by expressing your thoughts in writing.

"Put It in Writing"

In school you write papers, reports, and essay examinations to demonstrate your knowledge and skills. A badly written assignment will result in a poor grade. Outside the classroom, however, badly written documents can have more serious consequences. Agreements made in person or over the phone are difficult to prove if disputes or questions arise. Managers, supervisors, and courts base judgments on written records. The e-mail, letters, bills, contracts, and reports you write may make you liable for actions that can cost you or your employers millions of dollars. Poorly written documents can undo years of hard work. When told to "put it in writing," think carefully before committing your thoughts to paper or e-mail. Never respond to a question or complaint when angry. Make sure you revise and edit whatever you write. Ask peers to review your writing for illogical, controversial, or confusing statements. The ability to express ideas clearly and logically in writing is an essential vocational skill in the information age.

WRITING ACTIVITY   GET WRITING

What is your career goal? List situations in which people in that field write to others. Whom do they have to inform or persuade? Why is communicating information or ideas important for their success?

_____

_____

_____

_____

_____

_____

_____

_____

_____

_____

_____

Read what you have written and list the most important way writing will shape your future:

_____

_____

_____

GOALS OF THIS BOOK

Get Writing has been created to:

- increase your awareness of the importance of writing
- improve your knowledge of the writing process
- increase your understanding of paragraphs and essays
- help you overcome common writing problems
- prepare you for writing challenges in college and in your future career

Using *Get Writing*

At first glance, textbooks can be intimidating. Look through *Get Writing* to become comfortable with it. Highlight useful passages with bookmarks or Post-it notes for quick reference. Look at the handbook at the back of the book for help with common writing errors. Remember to use *Get Writing* as a resource not only in English courses, but in any writing you do in or out of school.

WORKING TOGETHER

Discuss writing with three or four other students and ask them to list problems and questions they have—from getting started to using commas. List your own top five problems:

1. _____

2. _____

3. _____

4. _____

5. _____

Examine the table of contents and the index in *Get Writing* and mark pages that address these problems.

What Is Good Writing?

You may feel unsure about what is considered "good writing." Comments by teachers and professors are sometimes contradictory. Papers that would receive good grades in high school may be viewed as unacceptable in college. English teachers urge you to use colorful words and creative language to express yourself, while business and technical instructors insist you avoid personal impressions and use objective terminology. Writing that is effective in one situation is inappropriate in another.

Good writing expresses what you want to say, meets the reader's needs, and uses the appropriate style and format.

The Writing Context

What is considered "good writing" depends on context. Writers don't work in a vacuum, but in a context shaped by four elements:

1. the writer's goal
2. the readers' needs, expectations, beliefs, and knowledge
3. the discipline, situation, occupation, or event in which the writing takes place
4. the nature of the document

Context explains why a school fund-raising letter sent to parents differs from a formal proposal presented to a foundation or government agency. A letter to people familiar with the school can explain the need for a new roof or more computers in a few paragraphs and motivate readers to write checks for fifty or a hundred dollars. A proposal seeking a million dollars from the board of directors of a foundation, on the other hand, might run twenty pages and include statistics, audited balance sheets, and a formal mission statement.

Before you write, establish the context by asking yourself four key questions:

What Is Your Goal?
Are you writing to explain an idea, complete an assignment, answer a question, or apply for a job? Do you want to inform readers or motivate them to take action?

Who Is the Reader?
Are you writing to an individual or a group? Are readers familiar with your subject or do they require background information? Are they likely to be receptive, neutral, or hostile to your point of view? What evidence will you have to include to persuade readers to accept your ideas?

What Is the Discipline or Situation?
Disciplines, professions, corporations, and communities have unique traditions, standards, and values. Humanities courses expect students to offer personal interpretations of novels, films, or paintings. Science courses, on the other hand, demand students follow uniform standards in conducting objective research. An ad agency depends on creativity, while an accounting firm demands accuracy. One company may believe the best way to increase their profits is by improving their sales, while another may concentrate on lowering costs.

What Is Expected in the Document?

When you write, make sure your message matches the document. Few people have the patience to read a ten-page e-mail. Most professors expect research papers to be more than ten pages. Résumés, ads, and brochures have to communicate at a glance and may use bulleted points to highlight important information. Scholarly books may devote several pages to fully discuss and examine a minor point.

GET WRITING ▶ **WRITING ACTIVITY**

A computer malfunction causes an airline to cancel over a hundred flights on Christmas Eve, stranding thousands of passengers in airports across the country. Following industry guidelines, the airline attempts to place passengers on other flights, provides bus and train tickets for commuters, and offers hotel rooms to those who will have to wait until the following day to get a flight.

Briefly describe the context of the following documents.

A college student sending a text message to her parents explaining why she will miss her flight:

* Writer's goal _____

* Reader _____

* Discipline _____

* Document _____

A statement posted on the airline's website informing passengers of the delays and explaining steps being taken to assist with their travel plans:

* Writer's goal _____

* Reader _____

* Discipline _____

* Document _____

Comments on the blog of a travel writer who has consistently rated this airline as one of nation's worst carriers:

* Writer's goal _____

* Reader _____

* Discipline _____

* Document _____

An airline e-mail to its employees urging them to handle passenger complaints with patience and respect:

* Writer's goal _____

* Reader _____

* Discipline _____

* Document _____

To appreciate the variety of writing contexts, examine websites, newspapers, and magazines. Notice how the writing style of *Seventeen, People,* and *Cosmopolitan* differs from that of the *New York Times, Newsweek,* and *Foreign Affairs.* How do your college textbooks differ from the ones you read in high school? How do car or computer ads in the *Wall Street Journal* differ from those in the *Star* or *National Enquirer?*

STRATEGIES FOR SUCCEEDING IN WRITING COURSES

1. *Review your syllabus and textbooks carefully.* Make sure you know the policies for missed classes, late papers, and incompletes. Note due dates on your calendar.
2. *As soon as possible, read descriptions of all assignments listed in the syllabus.* Reviewing assignments in advance allows you to think ahead and make notes for upcoming papers.
3. *Make sure you fully know what your instructor expects on each assignment.* Study the syllabus, sample papers, and handouts for guidance. If you have any questions about an upcoming paper, ask your instructor.
4. *Locate support services.* Many colleges have computer labs, tutoring facilities, and writing centers to assist students.
5. *Talk to other students about writing.* Bounce ideas off other students. Ask them to comment on your topic, main idea, or supporting arguments. Share rough drafts with others.
6. *Experiment by writing at different times and places.* If you are new on campus you may find some places easier to work in than others. The casual atmosphere of a student union may be a better writing environment than a computer lab or the library. You may find it easier to write early in the morning or after working out.
7. *If you don't already write on a computer, learn.* Most colleges offer short courses in word processing. Once you graduate you will be expected to work on a computer. Though a bit cumbersome at first, writing on a computer makes your job as a student much easier.
8. *Read your papers aloud before turning them in.* The fastest and easiest way to edit papers is to read them aloud. It is easier to "hear" than to "see" missing and misspelled words, awkward phrases, fragments, and illogical statements.
9. *Keep copies of all assignments.*
10. *Study returned papers, especially ones with poor grades.* When you get an F or a D− on an assignment, you might want to throw it away or bury it under some books. Although they are painful to look at, these papers hold the key for success. Note the instructor's comments and suggestions. List mechanical errors and note sections in *Get Writing* that can help you overcome these problems in future assignments.
11. *Never copy or use the work of others in your writing without informing your readers.*
12. *Write as often as you can.* Writing, like anything else, takes practice. Keep a journal or an online blog, e-mail friends, and take notes in class. Record your thoughts while you watch television. Any of these activities will help you get used to expressing yourself in writing.

GET THINKING
AND **WRITING**

CRITICAL THINKING

Write a paragraph describing your writing experiences in past courses or at a recent job. What assignments or tasks were the most difficult? What comments did teachers make about your writing? What work documents gave you the most trouble?

Read your paragraph and identify the most important ideas you discovered. Summarize your most important point in one sentence:

_____

_____

_____

_____

_____

_____

_____

_____

_____

_____

_____

_____

_____

_____

_____

_____

_____

_____

What two or three things would you want to change about your writing?

1. _____

2. _____

3. _____

WHAT HAVE YOU WRITTEN?

Read your statement aloud. What changes would you make if you had to turn it in for a grade?

- Are there sentences that are off the topic and should be deleted?
- Could you add more details and examples?
- Could you choose more effective words?
- Would a teacher or other readers understand your main point?

© Royalty-Free./Corbis

GET WRITING

What challenges do you face this semester? Examine your syllabi for upcoming assignments.

Write a paragraph describing your greatest challenge. Are you taking a demanding course this semester? Do you have to balance work and school? Do you need to organize your time better? How can you improve your chances of success?

WRITING ON THE WEB

Exploring Writing Resources Online

The Internet contains a constantly expanding variety of resources for student writers: dictionaries, encyclopedias, grammar exercises, databases, library catalogs, editing tips, and research strategies.

1. Review your library's electronic databases, links, and search engines. Locate online dictionaries and encyclopedias that can assist you with upcoming assignments.
2. Using a search engine such as Yahoo!, Google, or AltaVista, enter key words such as *prewriting, proofreading, thesis statement, editing strategies,* and other terms that appear throughout the book, the index, or your course syllabus. In addition to formal databases, many schools and instructors have constructed online tutorials that can improve your writing, overcome grammar problems, and help with specific assignments.

POINTS TO REMEMBER

1. Writing is important not only in college but in any career you choose.
2. Writing takes place in a context formed by the writer's goal, the reader, the discipline or situation, and the document.
3. You can improve your writing by studying past efforts.
4. Writing improves with practice. Write as often as you can.

If you use Writer's ResourcesNow, please have your students log in and view the pretest, study plan, and posttest for this chapter.   **Writer's Resources ☉ Now™**

2

The Writing Process

© Patrik Giardino/CORBIS

GET WRITING

How do you write? Do you write in longhand or on a computer? Do you make notes or outlines to organize ideas? Do you write a complete draft and then make revisions or do you work paragraph by paragraph? How do you decide what information to include? Do you edit your work for errors in grammar and spelling?

Write a paragraph describing your writing method. Identify areas you would like to improve.

This chapter explains the basic steps most writers use to choose a subject, develop supporting details, organize ideas, create a first draft, make revisions, and edit a final copy. Follow these steps in your first writing assignments, then try other methods to create your own composing style, a way of writing that works with both the way you think and the assignments you face.

THE WRITING PROCESS

Step 1   Prewrite: Use critical thinking to explore ideas.
Step 2   Plan: Establish context, develop a thesis, outline ideas.
Step 3   Write: Get your ideas on paper.
Step 4   Cool: Put your writing aside.
Step 5   Revise: Review and rewrite your paper.
Step 6   Edit: Check the final document for mechanical errors.

POINT TO REMEMBER

You can improve your writing by asking yourself two questions:

What am I trying to say?
What have I written?

Although writing can be separated into different steps, it is often a *recursive* or repeated process. Writers don't always work step-by-step but write, revise, and edit as they go along. They may edit and polish the first paragraph before starting the rest of the essay. On another assignment, they may write the conclusion first. Writing on a computer allows you to move easily from writing to editing, so you can come up with new ideas and fix errors as you work.

Step 1: Prewrite

Good writing does more than record what you "feel" or repeat what you have heard or seen on television or read in the newspaper. To write something meaningful, you first have to engage in *critical thinking*. You need to look at your subject carefully, ask questions, collect facts, test common beliefs, and consider alternative interpretations to move beyond first impressions and immediate reactions. Good writing is never "about" a topic—it has a purpose and makes a point. Good writing goes beyond the obvious to explore ideas and events and to analyze people and ideas.

STRATEGIES FOR INCREASING CRITICAL THINKING

1. *Study subjects carefully—don't rely on first impressions or make snap judgments.* If your car is stolen and your neighbor's house is broken into, you may quickly assume that crime is increasing in your community. But until you study police reports, you really only know that you are one of two victims. It could be that crime is actually dropping, but that you and your neighbor happened to fall into the shrinking pool of victims.

(continued)

2. *Distinguish between facts and opinions.* Don't mistake people's opinions, attitudes, or feelings with facts. Opinions express a point of view. They can be valid, but they are not evidence. You can factually report that your sister sleeps until ten, doesn't make her bed, and won't look for a summer job. But calling her "lazy" states an opinion, not a fact.

3. *Don't rely on limited evidence.* Isolated events and personal experiences may be interesting but lack the authority of extensive objective research. The fact that your great-grandfather smoked three packs of cigarettes a day and lived past ninety does not prove that tobacco is harmless.

4. *Avoid basing judgments on weak comparisons.* No two situations are ever identical. Because a policy works in Japan does not mean it will work in the United States. Strategies that worked in the Gulf War might not be effective in another conflict. Comparisons can be compelling arguments but only if supported by facts.

5. *Don't confuse a time relationship with cause and effect.* Events take place over time. If you develop headaches after a car crash, you might assume they were caused by the accident. But the headaches could be caused by lack of sleep or a food allergy and have nothing to do with your recent accident.

6. *Judge ideas, not personalities.* Don't be impressed by celebrity endorsements or reject an idea because the person supporting it is controversial. Judge ideas on their own merits. Unpopular people often have good ideas, and popular people can be wrong.

7. *Avoid making absolute statements.* If you make absolute statements such as "all politicians are corrupt" or "people always regret buying a used car," your argument can be dismissed if a reader can provide a single exception.

8. *Examine quotations and statistics offered as support.* People often try to influence us by offering quotations by famous people or impressive statistics. But until you know the full context of someone's statement or the origin of statistics, they have little value. Statistics may be based on biased research and easily distorted. Even accurate numbers can be misinterpreted.

9. *Above all—think before you write.*

TIPS FOR BRAINSTORMING

1. **Focus brainstorming by keeping the final paper in mind.** Review the assignment instructions.
2. **Use full sentences to write out important ideas you may forget.**
3. **Use key words for a quick Internet search.** Glancing at a list of websites may stimulate new ideas.
4. **Think of the list as a funnel leading from broad subjects to defined topics.** Avoid creating a list of random ideas.

Prewriting Techniques

Writers put critical thinking into action by engaging in *prewriting*. The goal of prewriting is not to create a rough draft of a paper but to explore a subject, discover ideas, and identify questions. Prewriting can help you save time by indicating which topics are better suited for an assignment and which ones may be too complex or require too much research.

Writers use a variety of prewriting techniques. As a writing student, experiment with as many as you can. Feel free to switch or combine methods to discover which ones you find the most productive.

Brainstorming lists ideas. A student brainstorming for an upcoming history paper starts with the title of a chapter in a textbook then lists ideas to discover a topic:

THE GREAT DEPRESSION

Stock market crash

Causes of crash

Speculation

Unregulated stock transactions

Widespread margin accounts

Congressional hearings/calls for reform/response from Big Business

TOPIC: *Birth of Security and Exchange Commission*

In **freewriting** you record ideas, observations, opinions, impressions, and feelings by writing as quickly as possible. Freewriting is not an attempt at a rough draft but a way to identify what you already know about your subject and discover new ideas. Freewriting is like talking into a tape recorder to capture everything you know about a topic. When you freewrite, don't stop to check spelling, worry about writing in complete sentences, or prevent yourself from going off topic. Remember, you are not writing an essay but exploring ideas.

To freewrite, sit with a blank page or computer screen and write as fast as you can about a subject:

> Last week I tried to buy a textbook with my credit card and was told I was over my limit. Strange because I knew I had paid my bill last month and had at least two thousand in available credit. Back at the dorm I logged on bank site and found fifteen charges to may card I never even made. Charges from stores I never heard of. Bills for plane tickets. Charges made in California and two ATM withdrawals. I immediately called my bank and they started an investigation. All day I wondered what else could have been charged against me. Was someone using my Social Security number to get loans or an ID? Could someone being using my name to get other credit cards, drivers licenses, passports, or mortgages?—(60 minutes or 20/20 story about the guy who found out he owed a million dollars in four states). All over America people getting their ID's stolen and used without there knowledge. IRS problems. Credit denials. People losing student loans. Being connected with drug deals, crime gangs, even terrorists. Government and consumer groups have to do something to stop identity theft and protect credit cards users. People use credit cards too easily to buy stuff they don't need. We waste way too much money on things we don't need or even want. We buy clothes we will never wear or CDs we will never listen to.

The paragraph contains awkward sentences and misspelled words. It ends with a series of unrelated observations. But the student has discovered a topic for an interesting paper—the need to protect consumers from identity theft.

Asking questions is an effective way to identify your existing knowledge, discover terms that need to be defined, and pinpoint ideas that require explanation. Questions prompt critical thinking because they require answers, leading you to analyze your ideas and views rather than just list them. A student describing a high school coach might develop a paper that contains only superficial and obvious facts about what he or she looked like or what teams he or she coached. Asking questions, however, can help the student create an essay that explores more interesting and significant ideas:

Why did I decide to write about Coach Reynolds?

Of all the people I know or have met, why this person?

What made Coach Reynolds so memorable?

What did Coach Reynolds teach me?

What was the coach's best advice?

TIPS FOR FREEWRITING

1. **Use freewriting for personal essays and open-topic assignments.** Freewriting allows you to explore your existing knowledge and beliefs. This method, however, may not help you respond to highly structured assignments or develop business documents.
2. **Use a question to focus freewriting.** Asking yourself "Why do kids drop out of school?" is a better starting point than a general idea of "writing a paper about public schools."
3. **Don't feel obligated to write in complete sentences.** Making lists or jotting down key words can save time.
4. **Save your freewriting for future assignments.**
5. **Highlight important ideas by underlining or circling them.**

How did Coach Reynolds inspire us?

How did the coach teach us to cope with defeat?

How did the coach help me understand my strengths and weaknesses?

What did I learn about setting goals?

Was the coach the best teacher I had in high school? Why or why not?

Questions like these spark memories and develop thoughts so the student can write a paper that does more than state minor details about what the coach looked like.

Clustering (also called **diagramming, mapping,** and **webbing**) uses symbols like circles, columns, boxes, and arrows to list and arrange ideas. If you are visually minded, this technique may be easier than freewriting or asking questions. It can be very useful if you are writing about a group of ideas or comparing subjects.

Here a student explores different terrorist threats:

Terrorism

Biological
Anthrax
Weaponized flu
Ebola virus
Crop-dusting germs
Infected suicide terrorist
*difficult to distribute
*no evidence of planning

Chemical
Nerve gas, chemical weapons
Industrial chemicals
Bombs in chemical plants or chemical railcars
*chemical plants easy targets
*evidence of terrorist plans

Dirty bombs
How dangerous?
Different effects of alpha, beta, gamma radiation?
*captured documents showing bomb plans
*Soviet "loose nukes" on black market
*real potential damage vs. public panic

Attacks on aircraft
Shoulder-fired weapons
*Africa attacks on El Al plane
*laser attacks on pilots

Car/truck bombs
1st World Trade Center attack
Oklahoma City/McVeigh
*use of limos?
*use of phony emergency vehicles?

Cyberterrorism
Hacking into govt. & corporate computers
Disrupting 911 operations
Shutting down trains, airports, phones, power plants
Generating false alarms

Notes: Write about the worst or most likely type of terrorism
Discuss causes of terrorism
Describe prevention

TIPS FOR ASKING QUESTIONS
1. **Keep the assignment in mind as you pose questions.**
2. **Avoid questions that call for simple yes or no answers.** Use questions that ask "why?" or "how?"
3. **Remember, the goal of asking questions is to identify a topic and prompt critical thinking.**

TIPS FOR CLUSTERING
1. **Clustering is helpful when you have complex or conflicting ideas.** You can group related items and place pro and con items in separate columns.
2. **Keep the artwork simple.** Don't spend too much time on the appearance of your notes. Remember, you are not creating a visual aid for a formal presentation, just a rough diagram.

By mapping ideas, the student can get an overview of a complex subject, isolating topics for a short paper.

POINTS TO REMEMBER

1. The goal of prewriting is to explore ideas, discover a topic, and organize points—not write a rough draft.
2. Consider using more than a single prewriting technique. Blend as many methods as you need to develop and organize your thoughts.
3. Save prewriting notes. Ideas that may not be appropriate for one paper may be helpful in future assignments.
4. Keep prewriting simple. Avoid elaborate notes that may be difficult to follow.

WRITING ACTIVITY   GET WRITING

Select one of the following topics or a topic from the list on pages 647–648 and prewrite for ten minutes. You may use one or more techniques. If you have an upcoming assignment in any of your classes, use this opportunity to get started.

Topics

reality TV shows	school vouchers
your first boss	first apartment
immigration	drinking age
favorite band	fad diets
women in combat	job interviews
cost of daycare	most challenging course

Step 2: Plan

Moving from Topic to Thesis

Narrowing Your Topic

After using prewriting to discover a topic, you may have to limit it further to develop one suited for your paper. It would be difficult to write anything meaningful about a broad topic like the Internet in five hundred words, but you could write something interesting about online college courses or cyberterrorism.

Developing a Thesis

After you limit the topic, the next step is developing a **thesis,** or main point. Good papers are not "about" a topic. They make a point, pose a question, express an opinion, or make a declaration. The thesis states your viewpoint and explains your intent, expressing what you want readers to understand.

Topic	choice schools
Narrowed topic	poor quality of several choice schools
Controlling idea	increased accountability is needed for choice schools
Thesis	*To provide genuine alternatives to public schools, choice schools must be held accountable to insure they provide students with a quality education.*

Topic	Jane Falco, my first boss
Narrowed topic	Jane Falco as mentor and role model
Controlling idea	first boss provided help in giving direction, guidance beyond the job
Thesis	*Jane Falco, my first boss, shaped my life by giving me a set of principles and directions that led me to pursue higher education, take responsibility for my actions, and set goals.*

POINT TO REMEMBER

Don't confuse a *thesis* with a narrowed topic. A thesis does more than focus the subject of a paper—it has to express an opinion and make a statement.

WORKING TOGETHER

Select one of the following general topics or one from the previous exercise and develop a narrowed topic, a controlling idea, and a thesis. When you are finished, share your work with other students. Make sure each person in the group develops a thesis and not just a narrowed topic.

General Topics

campus parking	part-time jobs	online shopping
downloading music	cable news	voting
gas prices	shopping malls	worst job
favorite restaurant	dream job	Social Security
health insurance	makeover shows	veterans' benefits

General topic: _____

Narrowed topic: _____

Controlling idea: _____

_____

Thesis: _____

_____

Organizing Support

After developing a thesis, you need to organize your ideas by outlining the paper's introduction, body, and conclusion. Taking a few minutes to develop an outline before you begin to write can save time in the end. In planning your paper, consider your goal, your readers, the discipline, and the nature of the document.

Your goal	What idea or opinion do you want to express? What information, facts, or observations do you need to support your thesis?
Your reader	What attitudes do your readers have about your subject? What evidence will they find most convincing? Do readers have any prejudices or misconceptions you must confront or correct?
The discipline	Will your writing use the accepted approach, style, and support expected in this discipline or profession?
The document	What is the appropriate format for this paper?

Developing an Outline

An outline does not have to use Roman numerals or capital letters. Even a rough sketch can organize ideas and save time by creating a road map of your first draft. It should list the beginning, middle, and end of your essay. It is subject to change. As you write, new thoughts will come to you, and you may decide to expand or narrow the paper.

The kind of outline you use depends on your assignment. To plan a narrative, you may only need a simple timeline to organize ideas. Other papers may be more complex and require more detailed plans to arrange your thoughts, balance conflicting ideas, organize complicated evidence, or place confusing events in a logical order. Most outlines cover three basic parts of a document: introduction, body, and conclusion.

Introduction	grabs attention presents the topic addresses reader concerns prepares readers for what follows
Body	organizes supporting details in a logical pattern
Conclusion	ends with a brief summary, a final thought or observation, question, call for action, or prediction

POINT TO REMEMBER

You can place your thesis at the beginning, middle, or end of the paper. If your audience is opposed to your opinion, you may wish to present facts or tell a story before expressing your point of view.

GET WRITING **WRITING ACTIVITY**

Develop an outline for a topic and thesis you created in the previous exercise. You may also use this opportunity to organize your next assignment.

Topic: _____

Introduction: _____

_____

Body: _____

_____

_____

_____

_____

Conclusion: _____

Step 3: Write

After going over your outline, write as much as you can in one sitting. Your goal at this point is not to attempt a final draft of your paper but to get your ideas on paper. Don't feel that you have to write complete sentences—to save time, use phrases or key words to list ideas you might forget. Don't worry about spelling or grammar at this point. If you stop to look up a word in a dictionary or check a grammar rule in a handbook, you may break your train of thought. Instead, highlight errors for future reference as you write:

Every year _____ (get figure from Newsweek article) computers are discarded by businesses, government <u>agentcies</u>, and universities. Some end up in landfills and others get contributed to schools, churches, or homless shelters. (Add quote by Nancy Sims from Internet article). In many cases sensitive data is left on hard drives that has been <u>acessed</u> (sp?) by people who not see this data. One high school senior managed to find files on her computer that listed names, addresses, and personnel (personal?) medical records. Even listing hundred of people with HIV. Some places replace hard drives but many do not. Some do not even delete files. There should be some national regulations on maintaining privacy when companies discard computers.

GET WRITING **WRITING ACTIVITY**

Write a draft of the paper you planned in the previous exercise or of an upcoming assignment.

Step 4: Cool

This is an easy—but important—step. After you finish writing, put your work aside to let it "cool." When you complete a draft, your natural impulse might be to immediately check your work for mistakes. However, it is hard to be objective about your writing at this point because the ideas are still fresh in your mind. Take a walk, run an errand, or work on another assignment. Then examine your writing. If you have an e-mail to send today, plan to write a draft in the morning so you can set it aside then read and revise it in the afternoon.

Step 5: Revise

Revising means "to see again." Revising consists of much more than simply correcting misspelled words or adding missing facts.

Revising Checklist
1. Print a copy of your draft. Revising on a computer can be difficult because the screen does not allow you to see the entire page.
2. Review the assignment and your goal. Does your draft meet the requirements and express what you want to say?
3. Examine the thesis—is it clearly and logically stated? Would it be more effective if placed in another part of the essay?
4. Does the introduction gain attention and prepare readers for the body of the essay? If you added new ideas as you wrote, the opening should include these.
5. Does the main body of the essay contain enough details to support your thesis? Are your facts and ideas clearly organized? Can readers follow your train of thought?
6. Are there any mistakes in critical thinking? Do you need to include additional evidence to support your views or restate your opinions?
7. Are there gaps in the essay? Do you need to include additional facts or ideas? Are there unrelated facts, thoughts, or details that should be deleted?
8. Does the conclusion leave readers with a fact, comment, or question they will remember or does it only repeat the introduction?

Having revised your work, you are ready to write additional drafts. Your work may need only minor changes. In other instances, it may be easier to start a new version using a different approach.

Using Peer Review

Many students develop the belief that getting help with assignments is cheating. It is not cheating to have others read something you have written, make comments, and respond to questions you ask. Never let others *write* a paper for you, but you can benefit from their criticisms and suggestions.

PEER REVIEW GUIDELINES

1. Explain the assignment to reviewers. Writing is difficult to evaluate unless people know who is going to read it or what it is supposed to accomplish. Before asking people to analyze your work, describe the assignment and show them any instructor's directions.
2. Let your paper speak for itself. Don't prompt readers by telling them what you are trying to say. Explain the assignment, then let them read your draft so they can objectively evaluate the words on the page. After hearing their initial comments, you might explain what you want to say, then ask if they think you accomplished your goals.
3. Ask for detailed responses. Questions like, "Is this any good?" or "What do you think?" may prompt only vague comments. Instead, ask readers if the thesis is clear, if the introduction is effective, if you present enough details, and if your arguments make sense.
4. Encourage readers to be critical. Too often friends and other students want to be polite and positive and may be reluctant to appear negative.
5. When reviewing other people's writing, be objective and make constructive criticisms. Don't just point out errors. Suggest ways to overcome mistakes or make improvements.

REVISING ACTIVITY

Revise the draft you have written. You may wish to share your work with other students and ask them for suggested improvements.

Step 6: Edit

The last step in the writing process is editing the final document. In editing, make sure you not only correct spelling and capitalization errors but eliminate wordy phrases and rewrite confusing or weak sentences.

Editing Checklist
1. Read your paper out loud. It is often easier to "hear" than to see errors such as misspelled or missing words, awkward phrases, clumsy sentences, and fragments (see Chapters 20 and 23).
2. Make sure your sentence structure is appropriate to the document. An e-mail should be written in short, easy-to-read sentences. A long essay or research paper, however, can include long and complex sentences (see Chapters 20 and 22).
3. Replace unnecessarily wordy phrases, for example, change "at this point in time" to "now" and "blue in color" to "blue" (see Chapter 21).
4. Make sure your final document meets the required format. Should it be single- or double-spaced? Do you need documentation such as endnotes and a works cited page?

EDITING ACTIVITY

Edit the paper you have written and revised. Share your paper with other students. Refer to the index or table of contents of this book for help with grammar problems.

AVOID PLAGIARISM

Never copy or use the work of others in your writing without informing your readers. Plagiarism is cheating. Faced with a tough assignment, you may be tempted to download an article from the Internet, copy a friend's paper, or take paragraphs from a magazine to put into your paper. Students caught copying papers are often flunked or expelled. If you use an outside source like a website or a magazine, just changing a few words does not make your writing original. You can quote important statements or use statistics and facts if you tell readers where they came from. You don't always need detailed footnotes to prove you are not stealing. Just make sure you mention sources as you use them.

> *Newsweek* reported that fourteen leading economists agree that unless something is done, the Social Security system will go bankrupt in less than forty years.

Use quotation marks when you copy word for word what someone has said or written.

> In a recent address, Senator Claire Wilson stated, "Cyberterrorists could launch an electronic attack from overseas and paralyze our economy."

Mention the author when you *paraphrase* and use your own words to express the same idea.

> According to Senator Claire Wilson, foreign terrorists could launch a cyberattack and cripple the nation's economy.

Writing under Pressure: The Essay Exam

Ideally, writing is done in stages so that you have enough time to think about what you want to say, develop a plan, write, revise, and edit over a few days. But often you will be forced to go through all these stages to answer an exam question in less than an hour. Instructors use multiple-choice and true-and-false questions to measure your memory of facts. Essay questions are designed to accomplish additional goals, such as to

- measure your understanding of facts by asking you to restate them in your own words;
- evaluate your ability to evaluate and organize information;
- test your critical-thinking skills;
- measure your ability to apply knowledge to specific or hypothetical situations;
- test your ability to apply solutions by presenting a problem and asking you to propose a solution.

Many students find essay examinations intimidating. There are, however, strategies you can follow to both study for and write essay exam questions.

STRATEGIES FOR STUDYING FOR ESSAY EXAMINATIONS

1. *Ask your instructor what the exam will cover.* You don't want to spend hours studying only to discover that you have been reviewing the wrong chapters.
2. *Ask your instructor the best way to study for the exam.* Find out if you should focus on the textbook, your lecture notes, lab material, or handouts.
3. *Begin studying at once. Don't attempt to cram the night before.* Two hours of studying spread over a week will give you more opportunity to learn and recall information than attempting to absorb the same amount of information in four hours of last-minute cramming.
4. *Talk to other students about the upcoming examination.* Discuss possible topics, methods of studying, and lecture notes. In talking to classmates, you may realize that you have forgotten or misunderstood information or failed to recall an instructor's recommendation.
5. *Consider the nature of the course.* The type of response instructors expect depends on the course. In the humanities, students are free to write personal interpretations of a work of art or historical event. Creative essays, provided they are well supported, are highly valued. However, in law, psychology, sociology, and nursing, students are expected to follow specific standards and practices that can be scientifically proven or follow well-established rules.
6. *Review your syllabus, notes, textbooks, and handouts.* Highlight important passages for a quick review just before the exam. Note significant facts, statistics, and quotes that may serve as support for your responses.
   - Take notes as you study. Essay exams require that you state ideas in your own words, not simply identify what you have read. If definitions are important, close your book and write a brief version of your own definition and then compare it to the text. *Writing about the material is the best way to prepare for an essay test.*
   - If you are taking an open-book examination, highlight passages and use Post-its so you can quickly locate information while writing. Familiarize yourself with the book's index.
7. *Recall the types of questions your instructor has asked in class.* The kinds of questions asked to prompt class discussion may provide a clue about the way the instructor will word questions on essay examinations.
   - Does your instructor focus on comparing issues, analyzing problems, or debating alternative interpretations or theories?
   - Does he or she concentrate on presenting in-depth analysis of narrow topics or on providing a sweeping, inclusive overview of the subject?
8. *Think in terms of patterns of development.* Most essay questions ask students to *define* elements, *compare* related topics, *explain* a process, or list *causes* or *effects.*
   - In reviewing your notes and textbook, consider what major items require definition, which subjects are often compared, and what ideas are presented as causes or effects.

(continued)

9. *Prewrite possible responses.* Select the key issues or topics you expect to appear on the examination and freewrite, cluster, or brainstorm possible essays. List possible thesis statements.
   - Remember that an essay test requires that you express what you know in writing. Fifteen minutes of prewriting can help you assimilate information, identify facts, generate ideas, and reveal knowledge you have overlooked more quickly than hours of reading and memorizing. *Prepare yourself to write.*
10. *Get as much rest as possible the night before.* Late-night cramming may help you identify facts and figures that appear on multiple-choice tests, but essay questions demand thinking. If you are not rested, you may find yourself unable to analyze issues, generate ideas, make connections, and present your thoughts in an organized fashion.

STRATEGIES FOR WRITING ESSAY EXAMINATIONS

Writing under pressure can frustrate even the most prepared student. If you tend to become nervous, you may wish to take a walk between classes, call a friend, eat a high-energy snack, or listen to your favorite song just before the test to put yourself in a positive mood.

1. *Come to the examination prepared to write.* Bring two pens, paper, and, unless prohibited, a dictionary and handbook.
2. *Read* all *the questions before writing.* Go over all the questions carefully before starting to write. Determine how much each question is worth. Some instructors will indicate the point value of each question.
3. *Budget your time.* Determine how much time you should devote to each question. Give yourself enough time for planning and editing each question.
4. *Answer the easiest questions first while thinking about the more difficult ones.* The easiest questions will take less time to answer and help stimulate ideas that may help you confront more challenging ones. If you run out of time, you will be skipping questions you may have been unable to answer.
5. *Read each question twice.* Students often miss points by failing to fully read the question. They respond to a word or phrase out of context and begin writing an essay that does not address the question.
6. *Study the verbs or command words that direct your response.* Most essay questions contain clues to the kind of response the instructor expects.

Question:	Desired Answer:
List reasons for the rise of labor unions in the 1930s.	A series of reasons rather than an in-depth analysis of a single factor
Distinguish the differences between gasoline and diesel engines.	A comparison/contrast, highlighting differences
What led to the collapse of the Soviet Union?	A cause-and-effect essay, perhaps related in a narrative or organized by division or classification

(continued)

Describe three common forms of depression.	Three short definitions or descriptions organized by division
Discuss the effects of global warming on the environment.	An essay consisting of cause and effect, process, description, or division

7. *Study questions that require more than a single response.* Some essay questions contain more than one command and require a two- or three-part response.

Question:	**Desired Response:**
Provide a definition of chemical dependency and explain why treatment remains problematic.	1. Define term 2. List causes for problems in treatment
Select three key economic proposals made by the president in the State of the Union address and predict how they will affect both the trade deficit and unemployment.	1. Describe or define three points 2. Discuss each point listing effects on trade deficit and unemployment

8. *Write a clear thesis statement.* Your essay should do more than just list facts and ideas. A strong thesis statement will give your response direction and can help organize points. This is very important if instructors present you with general questions or topics.

Question:
How has the concept of separation of church and state affected American society?

Possible Thesis Statements:
The separation of church and state has allowed American public schools to accommodate students from diverse religious backgrounds with little of the conflict found in other countries.

Unlike state-supported religious institutions in other nations, American churches are independent and able to take active roles in criticizing government policies regarding discrimination, capital punishment, American foreign policy, and abortion.

9. *Explain or justify your response to broad questions.* Sometimes instructors ask sweeping questions that cannot be fully addressed with a brief response.

Question:
What caused the American Civil War?

(If you write a short essay about slavery, an instructor may think you believe that it was the only cause for the conflict. If, on the other hand, you list a dozen reasons, an instructor may feel your essay is superficial and without depth. You can earn a higher grade by explaining your answer.)

There were numerous political, social, economic, philosophical, and moral causes of the Civil War. But clearly the most significant and enduring cause for the conflict was the problem of slavery. . . .

(continued)

Although most Americans cite slavery as the main reason for the Civil War, it is difficult to isolate a single factor as a cause for the conflict. To understand why the states went to war, one must appreciate the full range of social, economic, commercial, foreign policy, and moral disputes that separated North and South. . . .

10. *Keep an eye on the clock.* Pace yourself. Don't "overdo" a response simply because you are knowledgeable about the topic. Provide enough information to address the question and then move on.

11. *Keep writing.* If you become blocked or stalled on a question and can't think, move on to other questions or review what you have answered. Often rereading the response to one question will spark ideas that aid in another.

12. *Provide space for revisions.* Write on every other line of the page or leave wide margins. You will not have time to write a full second draft, but you can make neat corrections and slip in ideas if you give yourself space for changes and additions.

Chapters 5–13 contain sample essay questions and student answers.

CRITICAL THINKING

How well did your high school courses prepare you for college? Do you wish instructors devoted more time to certain subjects? Were you given the basic reading, writing, and math skills you believe you need to succeed? Write a paragraph stating your views. Use revision and editing to improve your comments.

© Jon Feingersh /CORBIS

GET WRITING

Do you consider how your words will be read? Do you try to visualize the person reading your work? In expressing something you want to say, why is it important to consider who you are writing to?

If you were assigned to create a fund-raising letter for a charity, what would you want to know about the intended readers? Write a paragraph describing why it would be important to analyze the audience to be successful in motivating people to make donations.

WRITING ON THE WEB

1. Using a search engine like Yahoo!, Google, or AltaVista, enter terms such as *writing process, writing strategies, prewriting techniques, revising papers, improving college writing,* and *proofreading skills* to locate sites that might assist you in this course.
2. Write an e-mail to a friend. Notice the writing process you use to create an informal document. How many times do you revise, edit, and rewrite a simple message?

POINTS TO REMEMBER

1. Writing is a process—it does not occur in a single burst of inspiration.
2. Good writing has a purpose, a *thesis,* or controlling idea. It is not a collection of random thoughts, first impressions, or feelings. Good writing reflects *critical thinking*—close observation, research, and analysis.
3. Prewriting techniques help explore ideas. Brainstorming, freewriting, and asking questions are useful tools to identify topics, discover new ideas, narrow a topic, and develop a thesis.
4. Outlines, whether formal or informal, organize ideas and identify missing information or unnecessary details.
5. First drafts serve to get ideas on paper—they are not expected to be flawless.
6. Reading papers aloud while revising and editing can help you detect missing details, awkward sentences, misspelled words, and grammar errors.
7. Avoid plagiarism. Never use the work of others without informing readers.

Writer's Resources ⚛ Now™   If you use Writer's ResourcesNow, please have your students log in and view the pretest, study plan, and posttest for this chapter.

Part 2

Developing Paragraphs

Developing Topic Sentences and Controlling Ideas

Paris Hilton arriving at Teen Choice Awards, 2003

GET WRITING

Write one or more paragraphs describing your reactions to this photograph. Do you believe that celebrities have too much influence on teenagers? Does the emphasis on style, fashion, and consumerism distort young people's values?

What Is a Paragraph?

Paragraphs form the building blocks of writing. Like chapters in a book, paragraphs work to emphasize important ideas and help readers follow your train of thought.

> A paragraph is a group of related sentences that express a main idea.

Writing without paragraphs is difficult to read. Important ideas are hard to identify and transactions are lost in the block of text.

```
      In 1898 a struggling author named Morgan Robertson
concocted a novel about a fabulous Atlantic liner,
far larger than any that had ever been built. Robertson
loaded his ship with rich and complacent people and
then wrecked it one cold April night on an iceberg.
This somehow showed the futility of everything, and in
fact, the book was called Futility when it appeared
that year, published by the firm of M. F. Mansfield.
Fourteen years later a British shipping company named
the White Star Line built a steamer remarkably like the
one in Robertson's novel. The new liner was 66,000 tons
displacement; Robertson's was 70,000. The real ship
was 882.5 feet long; the fictional one was 800 feet.
Both vessels were triple screw and could make 24-25
knots. Both could carry about 3000 people, and both had
enough lifeboats for only a fraction of this number.
But, then, this didn't seem to matter because both were
labeled "unsinkable." On April 10, 1912, the real ship
left Southampton on her maiden voyage to New York. Her
cargo included a priceless copy of the Rubaiyat of Omar
Khayyam and a list of passengers collectively worth two
hundred fifty million dollars. On her way over she too
struck an iceberg and went down on a cold April night.
Robertson called his ship the Titan; the White Star
Line called its ship the Titanic. This is the story
of her last night.
```

Presented in its original form, the foreword to Walter Lord's book *A Night to Remember* is far more dramatic and easier to read.

```
      In 1898 a struggling author named Morgan Robertson        introduction
concocted a novel about a fabulous Atlantic liner, far
larger than any that had ever been built. Robertson
loaded his ship with rich and complacent people and
then wrecked it one cold April night on an iceberg.
This somehow showed the futility of everything, and in
fact, the book was called Futility when it appeared
that year, published by the firm of M. F. Mansfield.
```

transition

Fourteen years later a British shipping company named the White Star Line built a steamer remarkably like the one in Robertson's novel. The new liner was 66,000 tons displacement; Robertson's was 70,000. The real ship was 882.5 feet long; the fictional one was 800 feet. Both vessels were triple screw and could make 24-25 knots. Both could carry about 3000 people, and both had enough lifeboats for only a fraction of this number. But, then, this didn't seem to matter because both were labeled "unsinkable."

transition

On April 10, 1912, the real ship left Southampton on her maiden voyage to New York. Her cargo included a priceless copy of the *Rubaiyat of Omar Khayyam* and a list of passengers collectively worth two hundred fifty million dollars. On her way over she too struck an iceberg and went down on a cold April night.

conclusion

Robertson called his ship the *Titan*; the White Star Line called its ship the *Titanic*. This is the story of her last night.

Paragraphs play an important part in organizing essays:

- Paragraphs work as building blocks.
- Paragraphs usually present a single main idea expressed in a *topic sentence.*
- Paragraph breaks signal transitions, moving readers from one main idea to another.
- Like chapters in a book, paragraph breaks provide pauses, allowing readers to absorb ideas before moving to new material.
- Paragraph breaks in dialogue indicate shifts between speakers.

WHAT DO YOU KNOW?

Answer each question about paragraphs True or False.

1. _____ Paragraphs arrange information.

2. _____ Paragraphs help readers follow a writer's ideas.

3. _____ Paragraphs must contain at least five sentences.

4. _____ Long essays about complex topics always have long paragraphs.

5. _____ Introductions and conclusions must always be placed in separate paragraphs.

Answers appear on the following page.

GET WRITING | **WHAT ARE YOU TRYING TO SAY?**

Write a two- or three-paragraph response to one of the following topics.

Compare your best and worst jobs, high school courses, cars, or apartments.

Describe the greatest challenge you face this semester and how you plan to meet it.

Review the best or worst movie you have seen in the last year.

Explain what you consider one of the most serious problems facing this country.

Describe the qualities, opportunities, and rewards of your ideal job.

_____

_____

_____

_____

_____

_____

_____

_____

_____

_____

_____

_____

_____

_____

_____

_____

_____

_____

WHAT HAVE YOU WRITTEN?

Examine what you have written. Are your ideas clearly stated and easy to follow? Are important ideas organized in paragraphs? Do paragraph breaks make logical pauses and demonstrate transitions from past to present or from one main point to another? Are there short, choppy paragraphs that could be combined to join related ideas?

ANSWERS TO WHAT DO YOU
KNOW? ON PAGE 30
1. True 2. True 3. False
(paragraphs can be of any length)
4. False (complex essays often
have short paragraphs to show
transition or dramatize an idea)
5. False (short essays may not
require whole paragraphs to
introduce or end an essay)

Topic Sentences and Controlling Ideas

Most paragraphs contain a topic sentence that expresses what the paragraph is about and conveys a _controlling idea_ that states a main point or opinion. The remaining sentences relate to the topic sentence, supporting it with facts, details, comments, and observations. Topic sentences generally open paragraphs to introduce the main idea and indicate the support to follow.

Revenue sharing has benefited professional football, allowing NFL teams to flourish in smaller cities. Unlike baseball, basketball, and hockey, professional football teams share money generated by national television and memorabilia sales. Currently each team receives some $100 million annually, allowing teams in smaller cities like Green Bay and Minneapolis to compete with teams in major markets like New York and Chicago. As a result, NFL teams are more balanced, having the funds to hire players and invest in team development and coaching. Other sports, which suffer declining ticket sales and dwindling profits in smaller media markets, may consider moving to revenue sharing to keep teams competitive and maintain fan interest.

Topic sentences can appear anywhere in a paragraph.

In Milwaukee, the castlelike brick buildings that once housed the Pabst Brewing Company are being renovated into an upscale community of shops, apartments, offices, and condominiums. In Camden, New Jersey, the mammoth RCA factory has been transformed into loft apartments. In Manhattan, old tanneries, cutting mills, and packing houses are being turned into apartments, art galleries, coffee shops, and gourmet restaurants. *Throughout the country, formerly run-down neighborhoods are being transformed into fashionable neighborhoods for young professionals who want to live in suburban comfort without a two-hour commute.*

Topic sentences serve key roles in a paragraph:

- Topic sentences explain what the paragraph is about.
- Topic sentences make a general statement supported by the rest of the paragraph.
- Topic sentences indicate the kind of detail readers should expect in the paragraph.
- Topic sentences signal shifts in the writer's train of thought.
- Topic sentences dramatize a writer's main points, making writing easier to read and remember.

EXERCISE 1 Identifying Topic Sentences in Paragraphs

Underline the topic sentences in each paragraph.

1. Now the city began to die. In most places, water and gas services had stopped. Newspapers began to close down; the last was the Nazis' own *Völkischer Beobachter,* which shut up on the twenty-sixth (it was replaced by a Goebbels-inspired four-page paper called *Der Panzerbär* [The Armored Bear], described as the "Combat Paper for the Defenders of Greater Berlin," which lasted six days). All transportation within the city was grinding to a halt as streets became impassable, gasoline scarce, and vehicles crippled. Distribution services broke down; there were almost no deliveries of any kind. Refrigeration plants no longer functioned. On April 22, the city's 100-year-old telegraph office closed down for the first time in its history. The last message it received was from Tokyo; it read: "GOOD LUCK TO YOU ALL." On the same day, the last plane left Tempelhof Airport, bound for Stockholm with nine passengers aboard, and Berlin's 1,400 fire companies were ordered to the west.

CORNELIUS RYAN, *THE LAST BATTLE*

2. The dream for many of those who find themselves owning casinos, or even working in them, is to figure exactly how to separate the count room from its loot. Over the years, the methods employed have run from owners getting their hands on drop box keys to employees grabbing fists full of cash before the boxes are even counted. There are complicated methods of misdirected fill slips and maladjusted scales that weigh only one-third of the loot coming through the count room doors. The systems for skimming casinos are as varied as the genius of the men doing the skimming.

NICHOLAS PILEGGI, CASINO

3. There were eccentric characters in the hotel. The Paris slums are a gathering-place for eccentric people — people who have fallen into solitary, half-mad grooves of life and given up trying to be normal or decent. Poverty frees them from ordinary standards of behavior, just as money frees people from work. Some of the lodgers in our hotel lived lives that were curious beyond words.

GEORGE ORWELL, DOWN AND OUT IN PARIS AND LONDON

4. Lyndon Baines Johnson, a consummate politician, was a kaleidoscopic personality, forever changing as he sought to dominate or persuade or placate or frighten his friends and foes. A gigantic figure whose extravagant moods matched his size, he could be cruel and kind, violent and gentle, petty, generous, cunning, naïve, crude, candid, and frankly dishonest. He commanded the blind loyalty of his aides, some of whom worshipped him, and he sparked bitter derision or fierce hatred that he never quite fathomed. And he oscillated between peaks of confidence and depths of doubt, constantly accommodating his lofty ideal to the struggle for influence and authority. But his excesses reflected America's drama during his lifetime, among them the dramas he himself created. Or, as Hubert Humphrey, the vice-president he both respected and abused put it, "He was an All-American president. He was really the history of this country, with all of the turmoil, the bombast, the sentiments, the passions. It was all there. All in one man."

STANLEY KARNOW, VIETNAM

READING TOPIC SENTENCES

No doubt by this point in the semester you have read textbooks in this and other courses. If you have underlined or highlighted as you studied, look at your textbooks.

1. Examine the sentences you highlighted. How many of them are topic sentences? Do they state a controlling idea supported by the rest of the paragraph?
2. Skim through a few pages in your textbooks. How important are topic sentences in communicating ideas? Would it be harder to read and remember information if authors did not use topic sentences?

When you read, notice how writers use topic sentences to emphasize important ideas.

Writing Topic Sentences

Topic sentences have to be clearly and accurately worded. Generalized or abstract statements might express a controlling idea but give little direction to paragraphs. The more clearly defined a topic sentence is, the easier it is for readers to understand what you are trying to say.

EXERCISE 2 Identifying Topic Sentences and Controlling Ideas

Select the best topic sentence in each group.

1. a. _____ Television soap operas began airing in the late 1940s.

   b. _____ Many early soap operas were based on earlier radio programs.

   c. _x_ Soap operas have remained popular for nearly sixty years because they tap into the most basic challenges humans face: finding love and overcoming obstacles to happiness.

   d. _____ Daytime dramas are called "soap operas" because early programs were sponsored by detergent companies.

2. a. _____ In 1919 Congress passed the Volstead Act, which prohibited the manufacture, sale, and distribution of alcohol.

   b. _____ Supporters of Prohibition were nicknamed "drys," and their opponents called themselves "wets."

   c. _____ Prohibition was unpopular by ethnic groups who considered wine part of household meals.

   d. _x_ Passed in a spirit of idealism that followed the First World War, Prohibition was widely ignored, gave birth to organized crime, and seemed to have little effect on the problems of alcohol abuse.

3. a. _x_ Throughout the twentieth century, the supply and price of oil had profound effects on the world economy.

   b. _____ As oil wells began to run dry in Pennsylvania, many feared a coming gasoline famine in the 1920s, driving prices up.

   c. _____ A few years later, prices collapsed when huge oil deposits were found in Oklahoma and Texas.

   d. _____ Increases in oil prices in the 1970s fueled inflation in Europe, the United States, and Japan.

4. a. _____ A tsunami is caused by an earthquake on the ocean floor.

   b. _____ "Tsunami" is a Japanese word, which is considered more accurate than the term "tidal wave."

   c. _____ Tsunamis are not associated with tides.

   d. _x_ Tsunamis are mammoth waves that can devastate low-lying coastal areas, killing thousands and destroying billions of dollars in property.

5. a. _x_ Once produced on Hollywood back lots and mammoth sound-stages, motion pictures are now made on location all over the world.

   b. _____ Modern film equipment is smaller and more mobile.

   c. _____ Today's audiences expect the natural realism of films shot on actual locations rather than sets.

   d. _____ An increasing number of filmmakers find it cheaper to make movies in Canada.

EXERCISE 3 Developing Topic Sentences

Write a topic sentence for each subject, inventing details or opinions to express a controlling idea.

EX: Subject   **Obesity in teenagers**

   Topic sentence   *Teenage obesity is becoming a national epidemic, posing a greater*

   risk to the health of young people than AIDS or drug abuse.

1. Subject   **Your favorite television show**

   Topic sentence   _____

   _____

2. Subject   **Paying for school**

   Topic sentence   _____

   _____

3. Subject   **Video phones**

   Topic sentence   _____

   _____

4. Subject   **Car insurance**

   Topic sentence   _____

   _____

5. Subject   **High school sports**

   Topic sentence   _____

   _____

Paragraphs without Topic Sentences

Not all paragraphs have a topic sentence you can underline. All paragraphs, however, should have a controlling idea or a main point.

> In October, Patton Industries was sued by a group of investors who claimed the company owed them money. Two months later, a fire destroyed its main warehouse in San Diego. Unable to meet customer demands, Patton Industries lost several highly profitable contracts. Facing the loss of commissions and lowered bonuses, nearly 20 percent of the sales force left the firm. Several leading catalog companies dropped Patton products in the fall.

The list of problems faced by Patton Industries states a clear controlling idea, so the paragraph does not need a topic sentence such as, "Patton Industries faces several serious problems."

POINT TO REMEMBER

Paragraphs may not have a topic sentence, but they must have unity and purpose. All the ideas in a paragraph should relate to a clear point readers will easily understand. *All paragraphs should have a controlling idea.*

EXERCISE 4 Identifying Controlling Ideas and Creating Topic Sentences

Read each paragraph and describe in your own words its controlling idea — its main idea. Then supply a possible topic sentence.

1. Here and there, thinly scattered across the broad land, lived the one hundred and thirty million subjects of the Tsar: not only Slavs but Balts, Jews, Germans, Georgians, Armenians, Uzbeks, and Tartars. Some were clustered in provincial cities and towns, dominated by onion-shaped church domes rising above the white-walled houses. Many more lived in straggling villages of unpainted log huts. Next to doorways, a few sunflowers might grow. Geese and pigs wandered freely through the muddy street. Both men and women worked all summer, planting and scything the high silken grain before the coming of the first September frost. For six interminable months of winter, the open country became a wasteland of freezing whiteness. Inside their huts, in an atmosphere thick with the aroma of steaming clothes and boiling tea, the peasants sat around their huge clay stoves and argued and pondered the dark mysteries of nature and God.

ROBERT K. MASSIE, *NICHOLAS AND ALEXANDRA*

Controlling idea _____

_____

Possible topic sentence _____

_____

2. Back at the hotel the aides ripped the masking tapes from the draperies and let the sunlight flood into Hughes's bedroom. The layers of paper-towel "insulation" were gathered up and run through the shredder. The movie screen, projector, and amplifier were taken down and packed. There were no other personal belongings of Hughes to be taken care of. He had no photographs, no mementoes, no favorite paintings, no cherished books, none of the sentimental impedimenta that people normally carry with them from place to place.

JAMES PHELAN, *HOWARD HUGHES: THE HIDDEN YEARS*

Controlling idea _____

_____

Possible topic sentence _____

_____

3. Doctors and lawyers frequently discuss everyday business on cellular phones. In one case, a doctor was notified that a VIP patient had tested positive for AIDS. The information was intercepted, and before long, the VIP's medical status was common knowledge. In another case, a lawyer from Ohio reviewed a client's prenuptial agreement with a second lawyer who was using a cellular telephone. A teenage neighbor of the second lawyer intercepted the conversation. "Before long, the whole damn neighborhood knew about our secret wedding and my financial situation," said the angry groom-to-be.

LOUIS R. MIZELL JR., "WHO'S LISTENING TO YOUR CELL PHONE CALLS?"

Controlling idea _____

_____

Possible topic sentence _____

_____

4. A blistering white sun beats down on the camp. Our shirts become damp. Our shoes are soon covered with dust. We walk in single file through the concrete maze, jostling our way past groups of Palestinians. Finally we are afforded a look at the dunes hugging the camp. They are dotted on top with Israeli gun emplacements, sandbagged bunkers, large concrete slabs, and a snaking electric fence. Armored green jeeps and tanks roar and clank along the fence's perimeter, throwing up clouds of dust. Knots of nervous Palestinians stand gazing in the direction of the behemoths until they pass out of sight.

CHRIS HEDGES, "GAZA DIARY"

Controlling idea _____

_____

Possible topic sentence _____

Revising Paragraphs

Even if you have created a detailed outline, you may have some trouble making logical paragraph breaks when you write the first draft. New ideas will come to you as you write. You may include new points without being sure where to place them in the text. Out of habit, you may discover that your first draft is written in a single block of text or a series of choppy two- or three-sentence paragraphs.

In revising a draft, look at your notes and consider new ideas you may have added. What ideas are the most important? What are your main points? Paragraphs should organize main points and demonstrate transitions.

WORKING TOGETHER

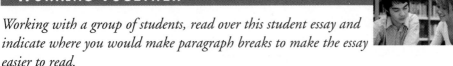

Working with a group of students, read over this student essay and indicate where you would make paragraph breaks to make the essay easier to read.

```
     The Internet has revolutionized education, busi-
ness, and personal communications. Small enterprises
can now access the global economy. Students in remote
areas or those attending small schools with limited
library sources can obtain research material once
available only in major universities. But like any new
communications tool, the Internet has been abused. In
the last ten years law enforcement officials have been
waging war on the growing problem of cyberstalking.
The Internet has been used to harass, stalk, black-
mail, and threaten a widening pool of victims. In
Indiana a young woman who didn't even own a computer
discovered that a man she had rebuffed had posted her
name, address, and photographs of her house and car on
an adult website, generating dozens of late night ob-
scene phone calls and a number of men knocking at her
door expecting sexual favors. In Florida an auto re-
pair shop discovered that a former employee, fired for
stealing cash and tools, was sending fake e-mails to
```

consumer groups, state agencies, and local media complaining about having been cheated by the shop owner. In one case a professor who made controversial political remarks at a hearing discovered that someone had taken photographs of himself, his children, his home, and his office and e-mailed them to a number of hate groups across the country. Law enforcement officials admit that the anonymity and breadth of the Internet often make it difficult to detect and prosecute cyberstalkers. Some cyberstalkers have developed sophisticated methods to elude investigators, even using overseas Internet sites to route messages and hide their identities. Until recently, many states did not have laws that specifically addressed electronic harassment. Traditional restraining orders, for example, were designed to protect someone's physical space, not their presence in an electronic universe. New laws and tracking technology may help protect the public and lead to more convictions. As technology evolves, new tools for cyberstalking will emerge. Today the popularity of video phones promises to cause similar problems, further eroding personal privacy and giving stalkers a powerful new way to harass the unsuspecting.

The Internet has revolutionized education, business, and personal communications. Small enterprises can now access the global economy. Students in remote areas or those attending small schools with limited library sources can obtain research material once available only in major universities.

But like any new communications tool, the Internet has been abused. In the last ten years law enforcement officials have been waging war on the growing problem of cyberstalking. The Internet has been used to harass, stalk, blackmail, and threaten a widening pool of victims.

In Indiana a young woman who didn't even own a computer discovered that a man she had rebuffed had posted her name, address, and photographs of her house and car on an adult website, generating dozens of late night obscene phone calls and a number of men knocking at her door expecting sexual favors. In Florida an auto repair shop discovered that a former employee, fired for stealing cash and tools, was sending fake e-mails to consumer groups, state agencies, and local media complaining about having been cheated by the shop owner. In one case a professor who made controversial political remarks at a hearing discovered that someone had taken photographs of himself, his children, his home, and his office and e-mailed them to a number of hate groups across the country.

Law enforcement officials admit that the anonymity and breadth of the Internet often make it difficult to detect and prosecute cyberstalkers. Some cyberstalkers have developed sophisticated methods to elude investigators, even using overseas Internet sites to route messages and hide their identities. Until recently, many states did not have laws that specifically addressed electronic harassment. Traditional restraining orders, for example, were designed to protect someone's physical space, not their presence in an electronic universe. New laws and tracking technology may help protect the public and lead to more convictions.

As technology evolves, new tools for cyberstalking will emerge. Today the popularity of video phones promises to cause similar problems, further eroding personal privacy and giving stalkers a powerful new way to harass the unsuspecting.

In getting your thoughts on paper, you may find yourself listing ideas in two- or three-sentence paragraphs. In revising, identify your controlling ideas and organize supporting details to create fully developed paragraphs.

EXERCISE 5 Revising Paragraphs

Examine this draft of a student essay. Identify its main ideas and then rewrite the essay in no more than six paragraphs.

Today college students have many alternatives to the traditional three-day-a-week lecture. Across the country, a growing number of students are taking advantage of new delivery systems.

Many of these students are working adults with families whose schedules prevent them from taking standard courses.

Some work during the day or travel, making it difficult to even sign up for night school courses.

Other students live at great distance from the nearest college offering the programs they need.

To meet the needs of these nontraditional students, colleges offer a variety of distance-learning opportunities.

For decades many colleges have broadcast telecourses on cable or local PBS stations, allowing students to watch educational programs and mail in assignments.

These courses are being supplemented with newer television technology that lets students interact with the instructor or other students.

The most popular new delivery system is the Internet, which allows instructors to reach a global audience. A noted professor of rare art in New York can

offer a highly specialized course to students
nationwide.

Internet courses are becoming more sophisticated
as websites now offer video.

Online courses enable students to post comments
and questions and use chat rooms for discussions.

These new delivery systems do have critics.

Some educators question if students will find it
easier to cheat because instructors cannot tell who is
e-mailing assignments or taking online tests.

Defenders of new delivery systems point out that
cheating has always been a problem in colleges.

New technology, they argue, will eliminate much of
the problem.

Internet courses are winning over many traditional
teachers who now supplement lectures with online study
guides and links to research material.

Today college students have many alternatives to the traditional three-day-a-week lecture. Across the country, a growing number of students are taking advantage of new delivery systems.

Many of these students are working adults with families whose schedules prevent them from taking standard courses. Some work during the day or travel, making it difficult to even sign up for night school courses. Other students live at great distance from the nearest college offering the programs they need.

To meet the needs of these nontraditional students, colleges offer a variety of distance-learning opportunities. For decades many colleges have broadcast telecourses on cable or local PBS stations, allowing students to watch educational programs and mail in assignments. These courses are being supplemented with newer television technology that lets students interact with the instructor or other students.

The most popular new delivery system is the Internet, which allows instructors to reach a global audience. A noted professor of rare art in New York can offer a highly specialized course to students nationwide. Internet courses are becoming more sophisticated as websites now offer video. Online courses enable students to post comments and questions and use chat rooms for discussions.

These new delivery systems do have critics. Some educators question if students will find it easier to cheat because instructors cannot tell who is e-mailing assignments or taking online tests.

Defenders of new delivery systems point out that cheating has always been a problem in colleges. New technology, they argue, will eliminate much of the problem. Internet courses are winning over many traditional teachers who now supplement lectures with online study guides and links to research material.

Using Paragraph Breaks in Dialogue

If you reproduce a conversation using direct quotations, paragraphs play a critical role in showing the back and forth nature of dialogue. Paragraph breaks show when one person stops talking and another begins.

I shall never forget the day she scolded me into reading *Beowulf*.

"But Miss Bessie," I complained, "I ain't much interested in it."

Her large brown eyes became daggerish slits. "Boy," she said, "how dare you say 'ain't' to me! I've taught you better than that."

"Miss Bessie," I pleaded, "I'm trying to make first-string end on the football team, and if I go around saying 'it isn't' and 'they aren't,' the guys are gonna laugh me off the squad."

"Boy," she responded, "you'll play football because you have guts. But do you know what *really* takes guts? Refusing to lower your standards to those of the crowd. It takes guts to say you've got to live and be somebody fifty years after all the football games are over."

CARL ROWAN, "Unforgettable Miss Bessie"

EXERCISE 6 Using Paragraph Breaks in Dialogue

Rewrite this paragraph to separate the direct quotations between the two speakers.

Last summer I had what I thought would be an ideal summer job, working at a local cable TV station. I was fascinated with the high-tech control room and seeing the reporters and sportswriters for the evening news. I even hoped to see some athletes and celebrities who did interviews on *News at Nine.* But I had no idea I would have a boss like Cynthia Peterson to work with. "Just do what I say, when I say it, and everything will work out," she told me sternly at our interview. "Great," I told her. "I've never worked in TV and want to learn as much as I can." "Good," she told me with a tight-lipped smile. "First thing, take the webcast footage down to the control room for me," she said, handing me a CD and walking out of the room. I took the CD downstairs and opened the door to the control room. Instantly, three or four people began shouting at me. "What the hell are you doing?" the floor director yelled. "Ms. Peterson told me to bring this down to the control room," I answered, shaking with embarrassment. "Didn't she tell you never to come in here during a broadcast?" "No," I replied. This would be the first of a stream of mistakes I would make trying to follow Cynthia Peterson's incomplete orders.

Last summer I had what I thought would be an ideal summer job, working at a local cable TV station. I was fascinated with the high-tech control room and seeing the reporters and sportswriters for the evening news. I even hoped to see some athletes and celebrities who did interviews on News at Nine. But I had no idea I would have a boss like Cynthia Peterson to work with.

"Just do what I say, when I say it, and everything will work out," she told me sternly at our interview.

"Great," I told her. "I've never worked in TV and want to learn as much as I can."

"Good," she told me with a tight-lipped smile. "First thing, take the webcast footage down to the control room for me," she said, handing me a CD and walking out of the room.

I took the CD downstairs and opened the door to the control room. Instantly, three or four people began shouting at me.

"What the hell are you doing?" the floor director yelled.

"Ms. Peterson told me to bring this down to the control room," I answered, shaking with embarrassment.

"Didn't she tell you never to come in here during a broadcast?"

"No," I replied. This would be the first of a stream of mistakes I would make trying to follow Cynthia Peterson's incomplete orders.

GET THINKING ▶ CRITICAL THINKING

Write two or three paragraphs describing a difficult decision you had to make in the last year. Did you decide to quit a job, return to school, sell a prized possession, quit smoking, or end a relationship?

WHAT HAVE YOU WRITTEN?

Write out the topic sentence or controlling idea for each paragraph. Is each one clearly stated? Do the details in each paragraph support the controlling idea?

Do the paragraphs clearly organize main points? Do the paragraphs demonstrate clear transitions? Should any paragraphs be separated for greater clarity? Are there any choppy paragraphs stating related ideas that should be combined?

Review your sentences for spelling errors (see Chapter 35), fragments (see Chapter 23), comma splices and run-ons (see Chapter 25), and errors in agreement (see Chapters 28 and 30).

GET WRITING

© Peter M. Fisher/CORBIS

Do you see a connection between this photograph and the one on page 28? Does the image celebrities present affect the way young people see themselves? Does the media give teenagers unrealistic and distorted views of adult life? Are teens driven to measure themselves too much on how they look and dress? Does our society stress glamour, fashion, and celebrity over knowledge, values, and spirituality?

Write one or more paragraphs describing what this image symbolizes to you. Does it simply capture a light-hearted and enjoyable part of growing up? Do you see it as evidence of a serious social problem?

WHAT HAVE YOU LEARNED?

Answer each question about paragraphs True or False.

1. _____ Every paragraph must have a controlling or main idea.

2. _____ Paragraphs usually consist of details supporting a topic sentence.

3. _____ Paragraph breaks signal transitions.

4. _____ Topic sentences always open a paragraph.

5. _____ An essay always has at least five paragraphs.

Answers appear below.

WRITING ON THE WEB

Using a search engine such as Yahoo!, Google, or AltaVista, enter terms such as *paragraphs, topic sentences, controlling ideas,* and *writing paragraphs* to locate current sites of interest.

1. Review recent articles in online journals and note how writers use topic sentences to state main ideas and paragraphs to organize articles.
2. Write an e-mail to a friend, then review your use of paragraphs. How can paragraphs make even a short e-mail easier to read? Do you use paragraph breaks to reproduce dialogue?

POINTS TO REMEMBER

1. Paragraphs are the building blocks of an essay.
2. Every paragraph must have a controlling idea supported by details.
3. Paragraph breaks signal transitions between main points.
4. Paragraph breaks are used to separate direct quotations in dialogue.
5. Precisely worded topic sentences guide writing, helping you decide what details to include in paragraphs and which details to leave out.

ANSWERS TO WHAT HAVE YOU LEARNED?
1. True (pages 31–32) **2.** True (page 32) **3.** True (page 30) **4.** False (page 32) **5.** False (page 31)

If you use Writer's ResourcesNow, please have your students log in and view the pretest, study plan, and posttest for this chapter.

Writer's Resources Now™

Supporting Topic Sentences with Details

© Peter Beck/CORBIS

GET WRITING

How have computers changed the world?

Write a paragraph describing one or more ways computers have changed society, the economy, and personal relationships.

What Are Supporting Details?

For a paragraph to be effective, the topic sentence and controlling idea must be supported by details—facts, statistics, testimony, personal experiences, and observations. Without enough support, a topic sentence is unproven. Irrelevant details can confuse and distract readers and weaken the paragraph.

WHAT DO YOU KNOW?

Underline the topic sentence in the following paragraph, then cross out sentences that do not support the controlling idea.

American students should be required to learn at least one foreign language. The United States is the greatest superpower in the world. It is the richest nation on the planet. Its power and prosperity, however, depend on maintaining good relations with other countries and participating in the global economy. With the collapse of the Soviet Union, the United States became the leading military power in the world. This has caused many people in other countries to see America as an imperial power bent on building a modern version of the British Empire. Millions of American jobs now depend on exports. Yet few American executives are able to converse in languages other than English. American forces are operating in Afghanistan and Iraq, but few military officers speak Urdu or Arabic. Surprisingly, many public schools and colleges are dropping foreign language requirements just when we must be able to communicate with the rest of the world for our survival. We must make the study of foreign languages a requirement for graduating. Computer courses should be required as well since nearly every job now requires people to send e-mail and access online data.

Answers appear on the following page.

WHAT ARE YOU TRYING TO SAY?   GET WRITING

Select one of the topics below or develop one of your own and make a few notes before writing.

job interviews	racial profiling	bloggers
talk shows	health clubs	current fashions
voting machines	campus parking	role models
underage drinking	first dates	cell phone etiquette

Write a clear topic sentence and write a paragraph that supports it with meaningful details.

_____

_____

_____

_____

_____

_____

_____

_____

_____

_____

_____

_____

_____

_____

_____

WHAT HAVE YOU WRITTEN?

Read your paragraph carefully.

1. Underline the topic sentence. Does it express a focused controlling idea? Could it be more clearly stated?
2. Do the other sentences support the controlling idea or do they contain un-related details?

Steps to Building Effective Paragraphs

Start with a Clear Topic Sentence and Focused Controlling Idea

In Chapter 3 you learned the importance of developing a topic sentence. When you revise paragraphs, examine the topic sentences to make sure they state a clear controlling idea.

Weak Topic Sentence	Improved Topic Sentence
College is tough.	My college courses are more rigorous than I expected.
High school sports benefit students.	High school sports teach students the importance of teamwork, discipline, and self-reliance.
America needs more tools to fight terrorism.	America needs greater intelligence, more cooperation from foreign governments, improved diplomatic relations with Islamic countries, and enhanced security technology to fight terrorism.

EXERCISE 1 Improving Topic Sentences

Revise each of the following weak topic sentences, adding details to create a more focused controlling idea.

EX: Exercise is important.

Regular exercise improves cardiovascular function, reduces stress, and helps those who need to lose weight.

1. Cable television can be bad for young children.

_____

_____

2. College students misuse credit cards.

_____

_____

3. Recycling is a good idea.

_____

_____

4. Communicating with teenage children is hard.

_____

_____

5. Junk e-mail is a headache.

_____

_____

Distinguish between Supporting Detail and Restating Topic Sentences

A topic sentence expresses a controlling idea. The remaining sentences in the paragraph should provide evidence that supports, explains, or proves the controlling idea, not simply repeats it. In writing a first draft, you may find yourself repeating general ideas rather than providing detailed evidence.

> The new stadium is a disappointment. After spending nearly $250 million, fans and taxpayers expected a lot more. Those who anticipated Opening Day this year were dismayed. The new stadium does not measure up to what the public wanted. More and more people are expressing their unhappiness with the situation. A quarter of a billion dollars should have given the city a landmark facility, not one that has disappointed fans and upset taxpayers. The new stadium is just a disaster.

The first sentence states a controlling idea. The following sentences, however, do not support or explain it but simply restate the idea in different words. The paragraph provides no reasons or evidence why the stadium is a disappointment.

Deleting repetitions and supporting the topic sentences with facts and observations creates a stronger, more convincing paragraph.

> The new stadium is a disappointment. After spending $250 million, taxpayers expected a state-of-the-art venue with ample parking, comfortable seating, appealing shops, and decent refreshments. Those attending Opening Day soon discovered the same parking problems they faced at the old stadium. The seats are small and uncomfortable. Several sections are poorly lit and have blocked views. Vendors operate from pushcarts rather than stores. Most of the refreshments consist of microwaved hot dogs and frozen pizza. The public expected a lot more for a quarter-billion dollars.

Support Topic Sentences with Adequate and Relevant Details

Topic sentences state an opinion or observation that requires adequate and relevant support. The other sentences should contain details that directly support the topic sentence—not simply list everything you know or can remember about the topic. A topic sentence is not a writing prompt to inspire you to write everything you can think of, but a clear statement requiring specific evidence.

Vague

> The college needs a new bookstore. The current store was built in 1967 and is outdated. It no longer meets the needs of this growing college. Two years ago the library received a ten-million-dollar renovation. But the bookstore remains unchanged since the sixties. Enrollment has increased as have the number of courses offered. The bookstore computer system is inadequate. Book orders cannot be tracked. Students can often get a book faster by ordering it on the Internet than going to the bookstore on campus. This is the same with athletic uniforms as well. The athletic department requires six weeks to order something you can have mailed to your dorm room in ten days. The bookstore causes headaches every semester. Until a new bookstore is built, getting books will remain a chore students dread.

This paragraph opens with a clearly worded topic sentence. The sentences that follow basically repeat the topic sentence, adding only minor details. Comments about the library and athletic department are interesting but provide no direct support for the need for a new bookstore. Sentences contain words like "inadequate" and "headache" but few details. Eliminating repetition and adding more specific detail can create a more effective paragraph.

Improved

> The college needs a new bookstore. Built in 1967, the current store no longer meets the needs of a college with a growing student enrollment and expanding list of course offerings. In the sixties the college needed to supply books for less than a hundred courses. Last semester the college offered over 250 separate courses, each with a unique book list. The outdated computer system cannot track book orders. Books are ordered from publishers and distributors by phone, mail, or fax. Every semester students can expect long lines, misplaced book orders, mislabeled books, and clerks who cannot help because they cannot access computer data. Students find it easier, cheaper, and faster to order their books online, denying the college a source of income. The college has renovated the library, the swimming pool, and a

faculty garage in the last two years. It is time to renovate the forty-year-old bookstore.

EXERCISE 2 Recognizing Relevant Supporting Details

After reading each topic sentence, check those sentences that provide relevant support. Ignore sentences that simply restate the topic sentence or contain irrelevant details.

1. America is unprepared for a cyberterrorist attack.

a. _____ The United States is vulnerable for a cyberattack.

b. _x_ Using supercomputers, cyberterrorists can overwhelm servers, paralyzing Internet operations.

c. _x_ Hackers could disrupt 911 centers, destroy sensitive data, trigger false alarms, knock out air traffic control computers, and shut down the nation's power grid.

d. _____ The Internet is very important to the nation's economy.

e. _____ One of the aims of terrorists is to cause economic damage.

2. Popular television shows have the power to influence social and cultural change.

a. _____ Because TV shows are popular, they can influence behavior.

b. _x_ The 1970s show *The Love Boat* is credited for the increased demand for ocean cruises.

c. _x_ A decade later, applications to law school increased after *LA Law* became a hit.

d. _____ When television started, many Hollywood stars thought appearing on the small screen would hurt their careers.

e. _x_ Italian newspapers called that country's legal reforms the Perry Mason law after the popular American TV show that led Italians to question their nation's old-fashioned justice system.

3. Global warming could have disastrous effects on agriculture, wildlife, the economy, and political stability.

a. _x_ Rising temperatures will cause droughts and famines, especially in the poorer nations of Africa.

b. _x_ Environmental change could kill rare species throughout the world.

c. _____ Climate change caused by the Earth's warming will cause economic, social, and farming problems.

d. _____ Some scientists and politicians question whether global warming is taking place at all.

e. _____ Ironically global warming may cause ocean currents to shift, making Northern Europe colder.

4. We need to develop alternative fuels to guarantee economic growth, end our dependence on imported oil, and reduce pollution.

a. _____ Using new kinds of fuel could reduce the need to get oil from overseas.

    b. _x_   Hydrogen cars, for example, release only water vapor instead of carbon monoxide and other deadly fumes.

    c. _x_   Soybeans and sunflower seeds can be made into fuels that are cleaner than gasoline.

    d. _x_   As long as industrial nations need oil from the Middle East, they risk price hikes and supply interruptions.

    e. _____   Use of public transportation could reduce the reliance on private cars.

5. Childhood obesity is becoming a major health crisis in America.

    a. _x_   Children are getting heavier, and more of them are developing health problems once associated with middle age.

    b. _____   Americans spend billions on exercise programs, diet plans, and weight-loss spas.

    c. _x_   More children are eating at fast-food restaurants.

    d. _x_   Worried about their children using drugs or joining gangs, some parents overlook poor eating habits.

    e. _____   In a desire to look like their favorite stars, some teenage girls go on binge diets and risk their health.

Types of Support

Personal Observations and Experiences

Personal observations include recollections and impressions about a person, place, thing, or situation. A paragraph about your first days of basic training would include memories of your drill instructor, the barracks, the other recruits, and training. A topic sentence that stated boot camp was tougher than you expected could be supported by focusing on how demanding the exercises were and how tired you were at the end of the day. A topic sentence that declares your apartment building needs repair could be supported by your observations about faulty wiring, uncollected trash, broken elevators, and damaged windows.

Like personal observations, experiences from your own life can supply rich details to support a topic sentence. Accounts of your experiences as a high school student, parent, resident of a particular neighborhood, or employee can humanize an issue and provide gripping evidence. Nathan McCall uses personal experiences to illustrate the problems black students faced when bused to previously all-white schools.

> The daily bus ride home brought its own set of fears. A group of white boys got on our bus regularly for the sole purpose, it seemed, of picking fights. I was scared to death of them. With older brothers to fight at home, I was confident I could whip any white boy my age and size, but many of the white guys who got on that bus were eighth graders, and they looked like giants to me. Others were older, white, leather-jacket-wearing hoods who I was certain were high school dropouts.

Makes Me Wanna Holler

TIPS FOR USING PERSONAL OBSERVATIONS AND EXPERIENCES AS SUPPORT

1. **Personal observations and experiences are best suited for personal essays.** They may not be appropriate in objective research papers or business reports.
2. **Make sure your observations and experiences directly support the topic sentence.** Your goal is not to tell a story but to provide support. Avoid including unnecessary detail or unrelated events.
3. **Because personal experiences and observations are only one person's opinion or story, balance this support with facts, statistics, or other people's experiences.** Understand the limits of personal experiences as evidence. You may have to prove that your observations or experiences are not isolated events.
4. **Use personal observations and experiences to humanize impersonal data such as numbers and statistics.**

Examples

Examples are specific people, things, places, or events that illustrate an idea or provide supporting evidence. Examples may be individual items, but they are not isolated. They represent something larger. You can support a topic sentence describing the dangers of fad diets with examples of one or more people who became sick or died attempting to lose weight. In writing about a high school teacher who gave him valuable lessons that changed his life, Carl Rowan supports his opening topic sentence with a specific example.

> Miss Bessie noticed things that had nothing to do with schoolwork, but were vital to a youngster's development. Once a few classmates made fun of my frayed, hand-me-down overcoat, calling me "Strings." As I was leaving school, Miss Bessie patted me on the back of that old overcoat and said, "Carl, never fret about what you *don't* have. Just make the most of what you *do* have—a brain."

> **"Unforgettable Miss Bessie"**

Facts

Facts are objective details that can be observed, analyzed, and documented by others. A personal observation might reflect the writer's opinion, such as "The Ramones lived in a spacious home in one of the most exclusive communities in El Paso." The terms "spacious" and "exclusive" are personal impressions, not facts. "The Ramones lived in a five-bedroom home in a subdivision where house prices begin at $800,000" is a statement of facts that can be verified. Facts are not opinions, but they serve as evidence to support opinions. Opinions reflect a personal impression, viewpoint, or attitude. Opinions can be used as support (see page 53) but should never be confused with facts.

Opinion	Fact
Sid wants too much for his '92 Mustang.	Sid wants $9,500 for his '92 Mustang.
Tredway is a great investment.	Tredway stock has risen 35% in two years.
The Aviator is a great movie.	*The Aviator* has been nominated for eleven Academy Awards.

TIPS FOR USING EXAMPLES AS SUPPORT

1. **Make sure your examples are representative—not exceptions.** Listing a half dozen smokers who lived past eighty does not adequately support the idea that tobacco is harmless.
2. **Use examples readers will recognize.** Avoid using obscure events or people that require lengthy explanations as examples.
3. **Provide more than one example, if possible.**
4. **Blend examples with factual support.** To prove that your example is not an isolated case, provide statistics or expert testimony.

Facts provide strong support for topic sentences. In some instances writers allow facts to speak for themselves and list them without a general topic sentence. To inform readers about the devastating impact of the Great Depression on New York City in the 1930s, Robert Caro developed a paragraph that includes numerous facts. Although there is no topic sentence you can underline, the paragraph has a clearly defined controlling idea.

> More than 10,000 of New York's 29,000 manufacturing firms had closed their doors. Nearly one of every three employables in the city had lost his job. An estimated 1,600,000 New Yorkers were receiving some form of public relief. Many of those fortunates who had kept their jobs were "underemployed," a euphemism for the fact that they worked two or three days a week or two weeks a month—or, if they worked full time, were paid a fraction of their former salaries; stenographers, earning $35 to $40 per week in 1928, were averaging $16 a week in 1933; Woolworth's was paying salesladies $7 a week.
>
> *The Power Broker*

Statistics

Statistics are facts stated in numbers. Statistics can provide powerful support because they are easy for readers to understand and remember.

> Eighty-five percent of our students work full or part time.
>
> One in eight trucks on the road has faulty brakes.
>
> This year 25 percent of our employees earned bonuses.

Used properly, statistics are convincing evidence to support a topic sentence. Arguing that the criminal justice system is unfair to African Americans, Manning Marable offers statistics as support.

> In criminal justice, African Americans constitute only one-seventh of all drug users. Yet we account for 35 percent of all drug arrests, 55 percent of drug convictions and 75 percent of prison admissions for drug offenses.
>
> **"An Idea Whose Time Has Come"**

Testimony (Quotations)

Testimony includes the words, experiences, opinions, ideas, and observations of others. They can be participants in an event, witnesses, or experts. Testimony can be given in direct quotations that repeat word for word what someone wrote or said or in indirect summaries. The words or observations of real people adds life to a paragraph. Stanley Karnow describes the initial optimism American soldiers had in the early days of the Vietnam War, supporting his point with the testimony of a young officer.

> All this power intoxicated the Americans who initially went to Vietnam with a proud and overwhelming sense of confidence. Whatever the objective of the war— and many could not define its purpose with any precision— they were certain that U.S. omnipotence would triumph. Philip Caputo, then a young marine lieutenant, recalled the feeling that he and his buddies shared as their battalion splashed ashore at Danang in the spring of 1965: "When we marched into the rice paddies on that damp March afternoon, we carried, along with our packs and rifles, the implicit convictions that the Vietcong would be quickly beaten."
>
> *Vietnam: A History*

TIPS FOR USING TESTIMONY AS SUPPORT

1. **Avoid using quotations from famous people unless they directly support your topic sentence.** Adding quotations by Shakespeare or Martin Luther King, no matter how impressive, will only distract readers unless they clearly support your controlling idea.
2. **Make sure you quote people accurately.** Don't rely on your memory of what someone said. Try to locate the original source and copy it exactly.
3. **Place direct quotations in quotation marks.** Remember to use quotation marks when you copy word for word what someone else has said or written (see pages 257–259).
4. **Do not take quotations out of context.** Make sure that the quotations you use reflect someone's overall attitudes and experiences, not isolated outbursts.
5. **If needed, explain who you are quoting.** Testimony will only be effective if readers understand the speaker's knowledge or value. Just adding quotes to a paragraph will not impress readers.

   The rising crime rate is ruining the Southside. Joe Long said, "I can't take it anymore, so I am moving."

   Improved

   The rising crime rate is ruining the Southside. Joe Long, who has lived here for thirty-eight years, said, "I can't take it anymore, so I am moving."

6. **Verify the accuracy and validity of opinions.** Opinions can be powerful evidence, as long as the person you are quoting is a respected expert or authority. Avoid biased opinions or those based on little factual support.

Blending Support

Because each type of support has strengths and weaknesses, writers often use more than one to provide evidence for a topic sentence.

topic sentence

facts

example

statistics

expert testimony

personal experience

Outsourcing is threatening America's middle class. In the past, manufacturing jobs were moved offshore. Today college-educated professionals are losing their jobs as the work they used to do is electronically exported to India and China. These countries are graduating well-trained engineers and accountants willing to work for a few hundred dollars a month. Federal Financial Services in Dallas has its mortgages, audits, and investment reports processed by a firm in India. Eight of the nation's largest accounting firms now have nearly 50% of their income tax work shipped overseas. Information services in the United States may see a 10–15% annual loss in jobs as more companies outsource this work to cheaper markets overseas. Timothy O'Doole, a Harvard economist, stated, "Soon doctors and lawyers will find their jobs outsourced as professionals in India review contracts and evaluate CAT-scans e-mailed to them from law firms and hospitals in the United States." For eight years I reviewed blueprints to see if they conformed with Boston building codes. That work is now being done in Shanghai by an engineer making $9,500 a year.

POINTS TO REMEMBER

In selecting support, ask yourself, "Does this support my controlling idea?"

In writing the first draft, you may remember facts or experiences. New ideas about your subject may come to mind. But unless these details directly support the topic sentence, they do not belong in the paragraph.

EXERCISE 3 Developing Supporting Details

Supply supporting details for each topic sentence. Make sure the details directly support the controlling idea expressed by the topic sentence.

1. Cars are safer than they used to be.

   a. Testimony _____

   b. Example _____

   c. Fact _____

   d. Personal observation _____

2. Young people benefit from role models.

   a. Statistics _____

   b. Testimony _____

   c. Example _____

   d. Fact _____

3. Television makeover shows give the public unrealistic expectations about cosmetic surgery.

   a. Testimony _____

   b. Fact _____

   c. Personal observation _____

   d. Example _____

4. Americans do not save enough money.

   a. Statistics _____

   b. Fact _____

   c. Example _____

   d. Personal experience _____

5. Public schools don't provide skills students need to compete in a global economy.

   a. Example _____

   b. Fact _____

   c. Statistics _____

   d. Personal observation _____

EXERCISE 4 Revising the Paragraph

Revise this paragraph, deleting repetitive and irrelevant details and adding your own ideas that support the topic sentence.

Excessive television watching can damage children's health, social development, and education. Children who watch too much TV spend their free time on a couch, often eating junk food instead of playing outside. Junk food is too easily available these days. Neighborhoods that once had one fast-food restaurant now have four or five. In addition, the servings have gotten larger. Children usually watch television in isolation. They are not learning the social development skills that come from interacting with others. They are not getting the lessons you can learn by playing and working with other children. The fast pace of television may limit children's attention spans and make it harder for them to have the concentration needed to read. Studying requires attention and concentration.

EXERCISE 5 Writing Organized Paragraphs

Write a well-organized paragraph that builds on one or more of the following topic sentences and uses one or more types of supporting details.

   1. It is difficult to quit smoking.
   2. People who use cell phones are often inconsiderate.
   3. Reality television shows are extremely popular.
   4. Many families find health insurance unaffordable.
   5. The media spends too much time focusing on celebrities.

WORKING TOGETHER

Working with a group of students, edit this paragraph from a student paper to eliminate repetition and irrelevant details. Review sentences for fragments (see Chapter 23), run-ons and comma splices (see Chapter 25), and misspelled words (see Chapter 35).

I never considered my self "prosperous" or "afluent" until I visited my father's hometown in Mexico. I grew up in a ranch house that seemed too small for four kids, my parents' cars were always second hand. No way did I feel priviledged. Last summer my Dad took us to Mexico on vacation were we usually go. But we did visit our usuall destanations like Cancun or Acapulco. Instead, he took us to the village where he was born. A village with no electricity or running water. The streets were dirt, the houses were tin shacks. The people did not have phones, never saw TV, or went to doctors. They had to wash clothes in steel tubs and cook on wood fires. I could not believe people lived like this in the 21st century. Looking at the way my cousins lived, I felt guilty. How could a eigteen-year old with a TV, DVD player, air-conditioned bedroom, camera phone, palm pilet, and a car feel he wasn't rich next to them?

I never considered myself "prosperous" or "affluent" until I visited my father's home-town in Mexico. I grew up in a ranch house that seemed too small for four kids; my par-ents' cars were always secondhand. Last summer my dad took us to Mexico on vacation, but we did not visit our usual destinations like Cancun or Acapulco. Instead, he took us to the village where he was born. The village had no electricity or running water. The streets were dirt, and the houses were tin shacks. The people did not have phones, never saw TV, and never went to doctors. They had to wash clothes in steel tubs and cook on wood fires. I could not believe people lived like this in the 21st century. Looking at the way my cousins lived, I felt guilty. How could an eighteen-year-old with a TV, DVD player, air-conditioned bedroom, camera phone, Palm Pilot, and a car feel he wasn't rich next to them?

GET THINKING
AND WRITING

CRITICAL THINKING

Would you buy a hybrid car that used less energy and caused less pollution even if it cost more than a regular car? Why or why not? Write one or more paragraphs stating your opinion supported by details.

WHAT HAVE YOU WRITTEN?

Read your paragraphs out loud. Is there a clear controlling idea? Have you stated it in a topic sentence? Do you provide enough supporting detail? Are there irrelevant details that should be deleted? Edit your sentences for run-ons and comma splices (see Chapter 25), agreement errors (see Chapter 28), and misplaced modifiers (see Chapter 26).

© Bettmann /CORBIS

ENIAC computing machine, 1946

GET WRITING

The first computers, constructed with thousands of vacuum tubes and miles of wire, cost millions of dollars and were the size of a small house. Few scientists then could imagine that computers would shrink to the size of a book and cost hundreds of dollars. How do you think computers will change in the next fifty years? Will computers improve education, expand business opportunities, and give individuals greater influence? Will they invade personal privacy, provide terrorists with new weapons, and rob people of their identity?

Write two or more paragraphs describing the positive and negative ways computers could change the world in the next fifty years.

WHAT HAVE YOU LEARNED?

Read the following paragraph carefully and underline the topic sentence; then cross out sentences that do not support the controlling idea.

The Internet has increased the amount of information students can access, but it has not made them smarter. Today a student in a small remote school can easily log on and obtain information from the most famous and well-stocked libraries in the world. The Internet lets people order clothes, invest in stocks, and buy airline tickets without leaving home. Despite all this information flashing on their computer screens, students are not getting much of an improved education. Education is essential for our kids to get good jobs in a high-tech world and global economy. There is a lot of adult material on the Internet that endangers children as well. The problem with the Internet is that it just provides raw data. Students need to develop skills to interpret, analyze, evaluate, and compare sources. They need sophisticated intellectual skills to make use of all the data at their fingertips. Schools and parents don't always face the fact that the Internet spews out information. It does not teach students how to think.

Answers appear on the following page.

WRITING ON THE WEB

Using a search engine such as Yahoo!, Google, or AltaVista, enter terms such as *paragraph design, modes of development, revising paragraphs,* and *topic sentences* to locate current sites of interest.

1. Review recent online articles and notice how writers select and organize details to support a topic sentence and express a controlling idea.

2. Note how authors use the modes of development to organize paragraphs.

POINTS TO REMEMBER

1. Paragraphs must have clearly stated controlling ideas.
2. Topic sentences must be supported with facts, statistics, personal observations and experiences, or testimony.
3. Avoid simply restating the topic sentence.
4. Details should directly support the topic sentence, not introduce new or irrelevant ideas.
5. Each type of support has limitations, so use more than one.

Writer's Resources Now™   If you use Writer's ResourcesNow, please have your students log in and view the pretest, study plan, and posttest for this chapter.

ANSWERS TO WHAT HAVE YOU LEARNED? ON PAGE 57
The Internet has increased the amount of information students can access, but it has not made them smarter.
Cross out the following: *The Internet lets people order clothes, invest in stocks, and buy airline tickets without leaving home. Education is essential for our kids to get good jobs in a high-tech world and global economy. There is a lot of adult material on the Internet that endangers children as well.*

Developing Paragraphs Using Description

© Ariel Skelley/CORBIS

Write a paragraph describing what children learn by playing sports. Consider your own experiences or those of children you know.

What Is Description?

Description presents facts, images, and impressions of people, events, things, and ideas. Description records what we see, hear, feel, taste, touch, and smell.

Description can be *objective* or *subjective. Objective* description presents factual details others can see or verify. This type of description is used in college papers, news articles, business letters, and professional reports.

> Cullen, Georgia, population four thousand, was formerly the site of four major linen mills. Since 2000 the population has dropped 35% as laid-off workers have sought jobs in Atlanta, Memphis, and Chattanooga. The current unemployment rate is 25%. Alcohol and drug-related offenses have increased 44% in five years. City and state officials have been unable to attract new industry or other development to the region. After announcing the third budget cut in a single year, the town's part-time mayor resigned.

Subjective description expresses feelings, images, and personal observations rather than facts or statistics. This type of description is found in personal letters and essays.

> In Cullen, Georgia, it's 1932 *Grapes of Wrath* America all over again— without the hope of a New Deal. The great old linen mills are silent and empty. Jobless men wander hopelessly down aching streets lined with vacant shops. Others sit in doorways and drink or take drugs. Now and then a rusty pickup or dusty SUV, its windows blocked with plastic bags full of clothes, heads north, taking another family from the dying town. The part-time mayor, a broken man, resigned in despair.

The type of description you use depends on your purpose, your readers, and the writing context. Popular books and magazine articles often blend subjective impressions with objective facts.

> Cullen, Georgia, is a relic of the nearly dead American linen industry. One by one, the crumbling nineteenth-century red-brick mills closed their doors, unable to compete with Asian imports. Hundreds of families have left the dying town, seeking jobs in the cities. The once-thriving working-class community has become a mini-ghetto with its share of drunks and drug addicts loitering around empty storefronts and Cullen's lone tavern. After announcing yet another budget cut, the town's part-time mayor announced his resignation.

GET WRITING

WHAT ARE YOU TRYING TO SAY?

Select one of the following topics:

- your first apartment
- a local restaurant or club
- a popular band
- the last movie you saw
- your first school
- your last boss
- your coworkers
- a celebrity

Write a description paragraph that includes objective, factual details about your topic.

_____

_____

_____

_____

_____

_____

_____

_____

_____

_____

Write a description paragraph that includes subjective details expressing your personal impressions and feelings about your topic.

_____

_____

_____

_____

_____

_____

_____

_____

_____

_____

_____

_____

_____

WHAT HAVE YOU WRITTEN?

Read your paragraphs carefully. Underline words that provide details about your topic. Does your objective description give readers facts and not personal impressions? Does your subjective description use words and details that reflect personal impressions and feelings?

Creating Dominant Impressions

Whether you are writing objective description for a research paper or subjective description for a personal essay, your goal is not to list every fact and detail you can remember. Good descriptions have a focus. They make a point. If you attempt to include everything you can think of to describe a restaurant, for instance, you can create a collection of trivial and obvious details.

> The Pride of Athens is located at 2844 West Greenfield Avenue between a dry cleaner and a hardware store. There is only street parking. It used to be a shoe store. There is a small oak bar that looks like something from a Wild West saloon. The kitchen doors are screened off with black and red screens with Chinese symbols on them. They came from the old Cathay House that closed last year. The booths along the bar came from a Wendy's. The second-hand menu holders have pictures of pizzas on them. The only Greek décor comes from a large homemade tacky mural of the Acropolis painted on one wall. The place is popular. The food is great. The owner plans to expand and begin catering. It's the most Greek place in town.

The paragraph provides a lot of facts and observations but fails to make a clear point. No connection is made between the non-Greek décor and the statement that it is the "most Greek place in town." The restaurant is described as being "popular" and having "great food" with little explanation. The most important ideas are not developed, while minor details about parking and menu holders are included.

A more effective description deletes minor and obvious details to create a dominant impression.

> The Pride of Athens is an unlikely place to win restaurant awards. Wedged between a hardware store and a dry cleaners, the one-time shoe store is furnished with an assortment of secondhand items from a Wendy's, a Chinese restaurant, and a bankrupt pizzeria. Cups and saucers do not match. The only décor clue to the restaurant is a tacky homemade mural behind the bar. The owner, however, spares no expense on the food. Patrons come from Chicago, ninety miles away, to savor his dishes of broiled lamb and genuine moussaka. Visiting Greek officials have asked him for his recipes. In the last two years, four national restaurant magazines have run feature articles about the Pride of Athens, which the famed *Gourmet Guide to America* rates with four stars.

By creating a dominant impression and adding specific details about why the restaurant is special, the description becomes lively and effective.

POINT TO REMEMBER

The dominant impression is the controlling idea of a description paragraph.

EXAM SKILLS

Many examination questions call for writing one or more description paragraphs. As with any exam, read the question carefully and make sure your paragraph directly responds to it.

From American History

What was the Underground Railroad?

general
description

The Underground Railroad was a system of safe houses and escape routes used by abolitionists to help slaves flee the South details

*before the Civil War. Because their actions were illegal, the aboli-
tionists had to operate in secret. They used railroad terms as a
code. The people who led the escaping slaves from point to point
were called "conductors." Hiding places, usually barns or attics
and cellars in private homes, were called "stops" or "stations."
Some people built secret rooms to hide slaves in case their
homes were searched. The work was dangerous. Slaves risked being tortured or killed. Whites caught helping escaping slaves*

general
description

*faced jail. Often their homes were burned in reprisal. The Under-
ground Railroad was loosely organized and did not keep records,
but historians believe it helped thousands of slaves flee North
to free states.*

The paragraph opens with a general description of the Underground Railroad
and adds details explaining its name and how it operated. The student closes the
paragraph noting the lack of documents and historians' estimates.

Like an encyclopedia article, the student offers a brief but thorough description
of the topic.

EXERCISE 1 Recognizing Dominant Impressions and Supporting Details

*Read the following descriptive paragraph, identify the dominant impression and
controlling idea, and list the supporting details.*

The master of River Valley Farm, Herbert William Clutter, was forty-eight years old,
and as a result of a recent medical examination for an insurance policy, knew himself to
be in first-rate condition. Though he wore rimless glasses and was of but average height,
standing just under five feet ten, Mr. Clutter cut a man's-man figure. His shoulders were
broad, his hair had held its dark color, his square-jawed, confident face retained a
healthy-hued youthfulness, and his teeth, unstained and strong enough to shatter wal-
nuts, were still intact. He weighed a hundred and fifty-four—the same as he had the
day he graduated from Kansas State University, where he had majored in agriculture.
He was not as rich as the richest man in Holcomb—Mr. Taylor Jones, a neighboring
rancher. He was, however, the community's most widely known citizen, prominent
both there and in Garden City, the close-by county seat, where he had headed the
building committee for the newly completed First Methodist Church, an eight-
hundred-thousand dollar edifice. He was currently chairman of the Kansas Conference
of Farm Organizations, and his name was everywhere respectfully recognized among
Midwestern agriculturists, as it was in certain Washington offices, where he had been a
member of the Federal Farm Credit Board during the Eisenhower Administration.

TRUMAN CAPOTE, *IN COLD BLOOD*

Dominant impression

_____

_____

Supporting details

1. _____

2. _____

3. _____

4. _____

Key words

1. _____   6. _____

2. _____   7. _____

3. _____   8. _____

4. _____   9. _____

5. _____   10. _____

EXERCISE 2 Creating Dominant Impressions

Create a dominant impression for each subject.

1. **A local shopping mall**

   _____

   _____

2. **The coach of a college or professional sports team**

   _____

   _____

3. **A local news anchor**

   _____

   _____

4. **Favorite childhood television show**

   _____

   _____

5. **The best or worst car you have had**

   _____

   _____

EXERCISE 3 Supporting Dominant Impressions

Select a topic from Exercise 2 and list examples of details that would support the dominant impression.

Dominant impression

_____

_____

Supporting details

1. _____

2. _____

3. _____

4. _____

Improving Dominant Impressions and Supporting Details

Dominant impressions are developed by details. To be effective, these details have to be precisely stated. Vague and abstract words and phrases lack impact and fail to give readers strong impressions of your topic. In writing descriptive paragraphs, avoid using general words like "great," "terrible," or "wonderful." Select words that are concrete and specific.

General Description

My mother's optimism is boundless and inspiring. Although she faced many terrible things in her life, my mother managed to always stay positive. She had to overcome many obstacles to finish her education. She worked hard, but just when things were going well, we faced both a family and economic crisis. But my mother managed to create a whole new career that allows her to balance her growing demands for childcare and desire to succeed in her career.

Improved

My mother's optimism is boundless and inspiring. After the divorce, my mother, a high school dropout, was left with three children and no income. She waited tables fifty hours a week and went to night school to get her GED and later earned an associate degree in data processing. She was hired by an insurance firm and received four promotions in two years. We had just moved into a nice condo when she was laid off, and my younger brother was diagnosed with autism. Refusing offers to move in with relatives, my mother started her own online consulting business, which allows her to pursue a growing career at home, where she can look after my brother.

EXERCISE 4 Revising Dominant Impressions and Supporting Details

Revise the following descriptions by inventing details and adding more precise and effective word choices (see pages 346–347 about word choice and connotations).

1. Bill's car is terrible to drive. The tires are in bad shape. The steering is not good, especially on icy roads. The heater does not work. The seats are old. The radio is not good. The engine makes terrible noises. The muffler is bad, and you have to keep a window open to get air even in winter.
2. The new dorms are perfect. There is plenty of space for students to store things. The desks are very modern. They are perfect for computers, monitors, and printers. The view from the windows is very nice. In fact, these dorm rooms remind many visitors of a resort hotel.
3. Last night's Hip Hop Awards were awful. The show took too long. The performers were not at their best. The presenters seemed confused. The winners gave speeches that were too long and hard to understand. There were many commercials. Some of the best groups did not even make an appearance.
4. The new women's basketball coach is great. She looks like she can take the team all the way to the state finals this season. She is an inspiring leader. She keeps the players positive by her example. Her unique training program builds on her player's strengths. She has taught players how to respond to bad situations.
5. The bridesmaids' dresses my sister chose for her wedding were awful. They had the worst colors you could imagine. They looked terrible. They looked like something

in a bad movie. Plus they were very uncomfortable. The skirts were so badly designed you had trouble sitting down. Just the expressions on their faces in the video shows how much the bridesmaids hated what my sister made them wear.

Student Paragraphs

Description of a Person

Usually the class clown is some hyperactive kid who might be bright and witty but not focused enough to pay attention to lessons or disciplined enough to study hard. Ben Mandelstein was different. He was half Einstein, half Seinfeld. He brought every class to life. In French he corrected the teacher's pronunciation, and when she reprimanded him, he would pout like Jean Paul Belmondo, puff an imaginary cigarette, and talk back to her in Parisian slang that reduced her to tears. He buzzed through geometry tests in ten minutes then spent the rest of the hour making paper airplanes. While we struggled to finish the test before class ended, he sailed off a dozen paper planes that swooped over our heads and crashed into the trash can. The day we started reading *Death of a Salesman* in English, he came to class in one of his father's old suits bearing a suitcase, which he parked by his desk and began an Oscar-worthy imitation of an exhausted Willy Loman.

Description of a Place

Café Norde, located below a florist shop on Brady Street, has been an eastside venue of the offbeat, the angry, and the artistic since its beatnik days of the late 1950s. The beatniks are long gone, as are the hippies and Gen Xers who followed them. But the coffee house still carries that air of leftwing defiance. Protest posters are taped haphazardly on the scarred wooden walls along with poems and concert flyers. The coffee is strong, the air thick with illegal cigarette smoke. The stone floor is strewn with trash. Bearded college students bend over chipped wooden tables to shout politics over the blare of reggae folk music. As the haven of the young and the hip, Café Norde, in many ways, has not changed in fifty years.

Description of a Concept

Just-in-time production, popularized by the Japanese, is now used by many companies to lower warehousing costs. Years ago factories maintained huge warehouses full of raw materials waiting to be processed and more warehouses full of finished products waiting to be shipped. With just-in-time production, raw materials are delivered as needed to the plant, and finished products are shipped out as soon as they leave the assembly line. The system is highly efficient and saves money. It is, however, very dependent on reliable transportation. Any delay in shipping at either end can shut down the whole operation. Still, many businesses believe that the overall savings can make up for any temporary interruptions.

PUTTING PARAGRAPHS TOGETHER

Pompeii

Most cities evolve over the centuries, with old buildings being torn down to make way for the new, so their history is lost. <u>Ironically, the Roman city of Pompeii was both destroyed and preserved by one of the deadliest natural disasters in history</u>. In AD 79 Mount Vesuvius erupted, spewing hot ash and cinders onto the thriving Roman city of 20,000. The torrent of hot wet ashes buried the city, smothering many in their homes. Others died from breathing poisonous fumes and collapsed in the streets, their bodies encased in ash. Soon only the tallest columns stood above sixty feet of ash covering the town.

introduction

topic sentence

supporting details

1. How does this paragraph introduce readers to the topic?
2. How does the student describe the disaster?

Survivors returned to the city to dig for valuables and personal possessions, but soon these efforts were abandoned. Later eruptions toppled those ruins protruding from the surface, and all traces of the city vanished. Over the centuries, local peasants dug tunnels to locate items of value, but few outsiders remembered the city at all. In 1500, workers discovered the lost city's amphitheater and forum. Later excavations unearthed artifacts that were placed in museums. Systematic archaeological digs began in the late 1800s and continued for over a hundred years. <u>Slowly the city that was destroyed emerged nearly intact from its protective cover of hardened ash.</u>

description of city's loss and rediscovery

topic sentence

1. How does this paragraph build on the first one?
2. What details does the student include to describe how the city vanished and was later rediscovered?
3. The student places the topic sentence last. Is this effective? Why or why not?

topic sentence

descriptive
details

    <u>Today Pompeii is a great outdoor museum that transports visitors to first-century Rome.</u> Tourists can walk the streets that were hidden from view for over a thousand years, providing remarkable glimpses into the daily life of Romans. They can visit the temples, the homes of the wealthy, the public lavatories, the sporting arenas, and the brothels. Guides point out that just before the eruption, an election was being held. Many of the ancient walls still bear campaign slogans. Artifacts like eating utensils, coins, earrings, and statues are on display in a nearby museum. Tourists, however, are easily reminded of the tragedy that preserved this city. Among the most memorable exhibits are the plaster casts taken of the ash-coated bodies of men, women, and children unearthed 2000 years after their death. The hot wet ash coated them as they died, preserving forever their last agonized expressions. Few visitors will forget the faces of those who died with their mouths open, evidently crying for help as the burning ash enveloped them.

1. How does this paragraph follow the previous ones?
2. How do the details support the topic sentence?
3. What impact does the last line have?

STEPS TO WRITING A DESCRIPTIVE PARAGRAPH

1. Study your subject and apply critical thinking by asking key questions:

   Why did I choose this subject?

   What does it mean to me?

   What is important about it?

   What do I want other people to know about it?

2. List as many details as you can, keeping your main idea in mind.
3. Review your list of details, highlighting the most important ones, especially those that create a dominant impression.
4. State a controlling idea or topic sentence for your paragraph.
5. Write a first draft of your paragraph.

6. Read your paragraph aloud and consider these questions:

Is my subject clearly described?

Do I provide enough details?

Are there minor or irrelevant ideas that can be deleted?

Do I use clear, concrete words that create an accurate picture of my subject?

Do I create a clear dominant impression?

Does my paragraph tell readers what I want them to know about my topic?

Selecting Topics

Consider the following topics for writing descriptive paragraphs:

People

your favorite relative

a celebrity you consider a role model

your supervisors or managers

fans at sports events or concerts

a homeless person

the teacher, boss, or coach who helped you make an important decision

the person you consider your exact opposite

Places

your ideal workplace

a bus stop or subway station

a place you would like to visit on vacation

the place that symbolizes what you consider right or wrong about American society or values

a favorite store or mall

a place that inspires you

a place you would take a first date

a place you want your children to see

Things

your cell phone

a musical instrument

a car, house, or other object you believe represents success

clothes you love or hate

tattoos

something in your home or car you want to replace

a lost object you wish you could replace

EXERCISE 5 Planning and Writing Paragraphs

Select a topic from the previous lists or choose one of your own and develop details and a topic sentence.

Subject: _____

Possible supporting details:

1. _____

2. _____

3. _____

4. _____

5. _____

Circle the most important details to create a dominant impression.
State your controlling idea and write a topic sentence:

_____

_____

Write your first sentence: topic sentence, first detail, or introductory statement.

_____

_____

Supporting details:

1. _____

2. _____

3. _____

4. _____

5. _____

Write your last sentence: final detail, concluding statement, or topic sentence.

_____

_____

Write out your paragraph and review it by reading it out loud.

WORKING TOGETHER

Working with a group of students, revise this description from a student paper to delete irrelevant or obvious details that do not support the dominant impression and controlling idea. Edit the paragraph for fragments (see Chapter 23), run-ons and comma splices (see Chapter 25), and spelling errors (see Chapter 35).

From a distance Riverton looks impressive. The half dozin ten-storey buildings neatly arranged around a plaza featuring play grounds and a garden. Moving closer visitors begin to notice the broken windows, graffitti, and litter. The place is ugly. Riverton is so dirty. The empty play ground being too dangerous for children. Mothers keep their kids inside to avoid gang shootings. Gang violence has risen in the city, despite the national decline of street crime. The lobbies are strewn with trash. Half the elevators being broken. The hall lights are out and the walls are peeling. The apartments are overcrowded and many have no working heat or plumbing. Riverton, once a gleaming multi-milion dollar solution for the urban housing problem, is now as bad as the slum dwellings it replaced.

From a distance, Riverton looks impressive. The half-dozen ten-story buildings are neatly arranged around a plaza featuring playgrounds and a garden. Moving closer, visitors begin to notice the broken windows, graffiti, and litter. The empty playground is too dangerous for children. Mothers keep their kids inside to avoid gang shootings. The lobbies are strewn with trash. Half the elevators are broken. The hall lights are out, and the walls are peeling. The apartments are overcrowded, and many have no working heat or plumbing. Riverton, once a gleaming multimillion-dollar solution for the urban housing problem, is now as bad as the slum dwellings it replaced.

CRITICAL THINKING

GET THINKING AND WRITING

Describe the most important skill needed to succeed in your career in one or more paragraphs.

WHAT HAVE YOU WRITTEN?

Read your paragraph(s) carefully. Do you clearly describe the skill's significance to your future? Do you include specific details? Are the supporting details clearly organized?

Write out the topic sentence or implied controlling idea.

_____

_____

List the details that support your topic sentence or implied controlling idea.

_____

_____

_____

- Do the details support your controlling idea and create a dominant impression?
- Could you improve your description by adding more details?
- Are there minor facts or trivial details that could be deleted?

Describe your reaction to this photograph in a paragraph. How does it differ from the image on page 59? Have societies used children's interest in teamwork, uniforms, recreation, and achievement to indoctrinate them in hateful ideologies? Can you think of current examples?

© Hulton-Deutsch Collection/CORBIS

Young Fascists marching in Italy, 1943

WRITING ON THE WEB

Using a search engine such as Yahoo!, Google, or AltaVista, enter terms such as *description, writing description,* or *rhetorical mode description* to locate current sites of interest.

1. Review online articles that describe a recent event, person, or situation. Notice how the writers develop controlling ideas, create dominant impressions, use supporting details, and use word choice. Examine liberal and conservative websites to read opposing descriptions of a current controversy or personality.
2. Write an e-mail to a friend describing a recent event on campus, at work, or in your life. Revise your paragraphs to create controlling ideas, build dominant impressions, and organize supporting details.

POINTS TO REMEMBER

1. Description paragraphs present images and impressions of places, people, things, and events.
2. Effective description paragraphs create dominant impressions that state the writer's most important points.
3. Dominant impressions and controlling ideas are supported with specific details.
4. Not all description paragraphs contain a topic sentence, but they should express a clear controlling idea.

Writer's Resources⬤Now™   If you use Writer's ResourcesNow, please have your students log in and view the pretest, study plan, and posttest for this chapter.

6

Developing Paragraphs Using Narration

© Royalty-Free/Corbis

Have you ever used a cell phone in an emergency? Write a paragraph about an incident where having a cell phone prevented you from becoming lost, wasting time, or missing an important appointment.

What Is Narration?

Narration tells a story or explains a chain of events. Narration can be fiction or nonfiction. Novels, short stories, fables, screenplays, and many comedy routines are narration, as are biographies, police reports, history books, and most newspaper articles. Many of the papers you write in college use narration.

English
It began snowing at ten, and the principal cancelled afternoon classes so we could get home before the blizzard blocked the roads.

Economics
The Security and Exchange Commission was established in the 1930s to regulate the stock market and prevent the wild speculation that occurred in the 1920s.

Psychology
Fifteen of the twenty-six patients treated with the new medication reported fewer symptoms of depression and anxiety.

GET WRITING **WHAT ARE YOU TRYING TO SAY?**

Write a paragraph that relates one of the following events:

- moving into your first apartment or dorm room
- the surprise ending of a favorite movie or TV show
- a key play in the best or worst game you have seen recently
- an event that led you to make a decision
- an incident that changed your opinion of someone or something

_____

_____

_____

_____

_____

_____

_____

_____

_____

_____

_____

_____

_____

_____

_____

_____

_____

_____

_____

Read your paragraph carefully. Does your narrative highlight the most important events or is it cluttered with minor details? Is your paragraph clearly and logically organized?

Writing Narration: Making a Point

Effective narratives have a clear purpose and stress significant details in order to demonstrate the importance of an event. A narrative does not have to record everything that happened. Narrative paragraphs do not always have a topic sentence, but they should have a controlling idea and dramatize a clearly focused point.

Narrative Lacking Focus

It was December 26, 2003. It was cold and snowy. The streets were icy, and there were not many places to park with all the snowbanks. It was the day I had to help my grandmother move out of her house on 28th and National. The house was being sold on the first of the year, and she was moving into a nursing home. Walking into the house was sad. It was empty. All her belongings were in boxes heading to storage. She had two bags. Her whole life was in those bags. I could see how sad she looked. I picked up her bags, and I slowly helped her down the sidewalk to my uncle's SUV. I borrowed his car because my Neon was too small for everything. I drove her away from National Avenue for the last time. She looked so sad. I hit the expressway and headed west to the nursing home. This was the hardest thing I have ever done. I could not wait for this day to be over. I just did not know what to say to her. She was so sad but never spoke.

The paragraph explains an important event in the life of the student, but its impact is weakened because it is cluttered with unimportant details such as the address, the weather, the car, and directions to the nursing home. Deleting these minor details and stressing the significance of this event can create a more moving and interesting narrative.

I was home for Christmas vacation, so the task of moving my grandmother into a nursing home fell to me. She was no longer able to maintain the house she had lived in for fifty-six years. She was leaving the small house she first entered as a young bride, the house where she raised children and visited with grandchildren. With my grandfather dead and her vision failing, she sadly accepted the fact that she had to move. I knew this was coming. We all did. But as I walked into her house that last day, the blank emptiness of the rooms hit me like a hammer. I was unprepared to see all the pictures, books, china, and souvenirs I had known since childhood packed into boxes for storage. She had only two bags and a photo album she was unable to see. I helped her to the car, and we left her home for the last time. I expected that she might want one last look, but she stared straight ahead into the winter sun, her face wet with tears.

TIPS FOR MAKING POINTS

1. **Guide your writing by keeping in mind the most important thing you want your reader to know.**
2. **Delete minor details that do not support your main point.**
3. **Focus on conflict or contrast to create tension or drama.**
4. **Organize details to create strong impressions.**
5. **Use concrete words rather than general or abstract terms to provide dramatic but accurate depictions of events.**

   Abstract
   The new student service lounge areas have become popular places for commuter students to spend time on campus between classes.

   Concrete
   The new coffee bar, salad bar, and Internet cafe have become popular places for commuter students to meet, relax, nap, and study between classes.

6. **Avoid shifting point of view (from "I" to "you" or "they") unless there is a clear change in focus.**

   Awkward Shift
   Whether *I* drive or take the bus, it takes *you* almost an hour to get to school.

   Improved
   Whether *I* drive or take the bus, it takes *me* almost an hour to get to school.
   or
   Whether *you* drive or take the bus, it takes *you* almost an hour to get to school.

   Acceptable Change in Point of View
   When *I* worked in the mail room last year, *I* never had to deal with problems *you* face every day.

7. **Use tense shifts to show logical changes between past and ongoing or current events.**

   I *drove* a cab in Manhattan, which *takes* a lot of patience.
   Sandy *sings* the songs she *wrote* when she *worked* at MGM.
   The physics lab *is* in Carroll Hall, *constructed* in 1910.

EXERCISE 1 Making a Point

Select one of the following subjects, narrow the topic, and establish a controlling idea.

an argument or scuffle you witnessed
the most dramatic event that happened in high school or at your job
the way someone delivered bad news
an accident or medical emergency

an event that changed American society
a turning point in your life or the life of a friend

Narrowed topic: _____

Point or controlling idea: _____

Now develop a narrative paragraph that uses details to support the controlling idea.

After completing your paragraph, review your subject and your main point. Does your paragraph tell readers what you want them to know? Should minor details be deleted and important details emphasized?

EXAM SKILLS

Many examination questions call for writing one or more narrative paragraphs. As with any exam, read the question carefully and make sure your paragraph directly responds to it. In writing a narrative, remember your goal is not to tell everything that happened or every detail you can remember but to concentrate on an important point. Your narrative should have a clearly stated goal and topic sentences to guide the events you select.

From *American Institutions*

What caused the rise and eventual collapse of the Know-Nothing Movement?

introduction and summary of events	*"Know-Nothing" is an unofficial term for a number of anti-immigrant secret societies that formed in the 1840s on the East Coast. Many native-born Americans feared and resented the influx of immigrants, especially Catholics, who they saw as a threat to their values. Their nickname came from the fact that*
details	*when members were questioned about their groups or activities, they claimed to "know nothing." The Know-Nothing organizations grew rapidly but were soon eclipsed by the Mexican War in 1845. The various groups regained influence when the war ended. They argued that people should only vote for people born in the United States and that immigrants should have to reside in America for 25 years before becoming citizens. The major Know-Nothing groups split over the issue of slavery, and the movement died out by the time of the Civil War. The Know-Nothing movement*
controlling idea	*was one of many anti-immigrant movements that sought to restrict the rights of people they perceived as threats to American social order. The Know-Nothings targeted Irish Catholics. Later groups would attack Asian, Jewish, and Hispanic immigrants.*

Writing Narration: Using Transitions

A narrative paragraph relates events over a period of time. To prevent readers from becoming confused and to help them follow the actions, it is important to signal shifts in time with transitional words and phrases.

Two nights ago the fire alarm went off in my building. This is the third time this has happened this year. *Last month* the alarm went off at two in the morning. I had a midterm exam *the following day* and ended up standing in the parking lot *until almost five a.m.* while the fire department searched for the cause of the alarm. *Yesterday* I ran into the manager and asked her if something could be done to fix the problem. She agreed that false alarms were a common complaint. The system the owner installed *two years ago* is very sensitive and is sometimes set off by smoke from a cigarette or even heat from a candle. She agreed false alarms were a headache but reminded me of the apartment fire in Nashville last winter that killed sixteen people while they slept. *After hearing that,* I agreed the occasional false alarm is a small price to pay for safety.

KEY TRANSITIONS

before	now	first
after	later	finally
after a while	immediately	suddenly
next	the following day	hours, days, weeks later
following	in the meantime	that morning, afternoon
while	then	

EXERCISE 2 Identifying Transitions

Underline transitional statements in the following paragraph.

The American oil industry began when Colonel Drake struck oil in Pennsylvania in 1858. Within a few decades, companies like Standard Oil became some of the richest and most powerful corporations in the country. John D. Rockefeller, who owned Standard Oil, became the first American billionaire. Just as it was reaching its peak, the oil industry faced a threat to its existence. At that time oil was mostly used to make kerosene or lamp oil. In 1876 Edison invented the lightbulb. By the turn of the century, electric lights had replaced oil lamps in the cities and larger towns. Oil companies continued to sell kerosene to farmers and people in small towns without electric power. Standard Oil exported lamp oil to China, but even in Asia electricity was beginning to shrink the demand for their product. It seemed only a matter of time before the oil industry would dwindle in significance. But just as the demand for kerosene was dropping, the demand for gasoline to power the rapidly growing number of cars rose. Oil companies once threw away gasoline as a useless by-product. Now the need for gasoline would keep them in business throughout the twentieth century.

Writing Narration: Using Dialogue

If you are explaining an event that involves people talking, using direct quotes can advance the story better than an indirect summary of a conversation.

Indirect Summary

I was taking a nap on the patio when I heard Mrs. Gomez next door screaming for help. I woke up and jumped over the small hedge between our yards. I asked her what the problem was, and she said her son had fallen into their pool. Timmy was lying on the ground. His face was puffy and bluish white. I told her to call 911 and get a blanket. I rubbed his wrists and ankles, trying to remember what I had learned in first-aid class. Mrs. Gomez asked me if he was breathing. I told her I was not sure. I turned him over, and water came out his mouth. I laid him out straight and started doing mouth to mouth. His mother kept asking me if he was breathing. I motioned with my hand, not wanting to stop. He coughed up more water and moved his legs. Mrs. Gomez began crying. As the paramedics arrived, Timmy pulled away and coughed up more water. A paramedic told us he was breathing, but they needed to take him to the hospital to be examined by doctors. Mrs. Gomez sank to her knees and kept thanking God.

Narrative with Direct Quotations

I was taking a nap on the patio when I heard Mrs. Gomez next door scream, "Help me! Help!"

I jumped over the small hedge between our yards. "What's wrong?" I asked.

"Timmy fell in the pool. I found him floating in the pool," she said, sitting next to Timmy who was lying on the ground. His face was puffy and bluish white.

"Call 911 and get a blanket!" I shouted to her. I rubbed his wrists and ankles, trying to remember what I had learned in first-aid class.

"Is he breathing?" Mrs. Gomez asked.

"I don't know. I'm not sure," I told her. I turned him over, and water came out of his mouth. I laid him out straight and started doing mouth to mouth.

"Is he breathing? Is Timmy breathing? Can he breathe?" Mrs. Gomez kept asking.

Not wanting to stop mouth to mouth, I motioned with my hand. He coughed up more water and moved his legs. Mrs. Gomez began crying. As the paramedics arrived, Timmy pulled away and coughed up more water. A paramedic said, "He's breathing on his own, but we need to get him to the hospital to be checked out. Just to make sure. But he looks good right now."

Mrs. Gomez sank to her knees, moaning, "Thank God, thank God, thank God."

- Dialogue brings people to life by having them speak directly. Their tone, attitude, and lifestyle can be demonstrated by the words they choose.
- Because dialogue is stated in short paragraphs, it is faster and easier to read than a long block of text. In addition, direct quotations can reduce the need for statements like "he said" or "she told me."

POINT TO REMEMBER

In writing dialogue, start a new paragraph each time a new person speaks. Because dialogue may include many short paragraphs, including one-word responses, your essay may appear to be longer than the assigned length. Use a computer word count. A three-page essay with dialogue is often no longer than a page and a half of description.

EXERCISE 3 Writing Narration Using Dialogue

Write a narrative paragraph that uses dialogue—direct quotes—to relate an event in which two people have an argument, someone tells friends a funny story, or a boss gives employees some bad news.

Student Paragraphs

Personal Narrative

Growing up in a Duluth suburb, I was usually seen as being Hispanic. I joined a Latino organization, took Spanish, and listened to a lot of Mexican music. Last December, however, my first visit to Mexico was an awakening. I went to visit my grandfather. Despite three years of high school Spanish, I found it almost impossible to hold a conversation. I was unprepared for the poverty of my grandfather's mountain village. The food was like nothing I ate in a Mexican restaurant in America. The villagers celebrated Christmas without carols, trees, or a Santa. I never felt so American in my life. My grandfather evidently felt the same way because he jokingly introduced me to his friends, telling them my name was George Bush.

Narrative in a History Paper

The Tet Offensive in early 1968 was the turning point in the Vietnam War. Although college students had been protesting against the draft and the war for several years, most Americans believed the United States was making progress in the fight against the Vietcong. Then during the Tet New Year's holiday, Communist forces stormed into Saigon and nearly overran the American embassy. Battles erupted throughout South Vietnam. Americans saw the fierce house-to-house fighting on TV and sensed that the war could not be won. Public opinion shifted and many famous Americans began to call for an end to the war. Facing pressure from the demonstrators and critics in his own party, President Johnson announced he would not run for reelection. Ironically, the Tet Offensive was a major defeat for the Communists, who failed to create a popular uprising and lost so many men and supplies it took them years to recover.

Narrative in an Earth Science Research Paper

In the 1770s Joseph Priestly conducted a series of experiments using bell jars. He noticed that a candle placed under a glass jar soon went out. He placed a mouse under a glass jar and watched as the mouse stopped moving and eventually died. Clearly, some substance necessary for the flame to burn and the mouse to live was being absorbed or lost. He also noticed that if he placed a green plant under the jar, the candle could be relit. A mouse placed under the jar with a green plant lived longer. Whatever substance the flame and mouse absorbed was being refreshed by the plant. Without fully realizing it, Priestly had discovered oxygen and carbon dioxide and the basic nature of the Earth's atmosphere.

PUTTING PARAGRAPHS TOGETHER

A Vital Lesson

<u>Most of us are luckier than we know.</u> Occasionally, however, we run into a reminder. Two summers ago I got a job at Victor's. I was not twenty-one and could not get a bartender's license and earn good tips. The only job I could do was wash dishes. It was hot, dirty, and depressing work. But it was the only job I could find near my house. All the jobs I wanted were too far to take the bus. It looked like it was going to be long, boring, and lonely summer. My girlfriend was taking summer courses in New York. My car was sitting in my uncle's garage with a cracked block and more oil leaks than I could count. Leaving work each night with wet clothes and sore hands, I went home to watch TV in my empty apartment, feeling very sorry for myself. Everyone else I knew seemed to be having a great time hitting the beach, cruising in cars, and partying. I felt so down sometimes I wished I was dead.

introduction

details about job

details about writer's mood

1. What is the controlling idea of this paragraph?
2. How does the student organize the details?
3. How effective is the last sentence? Is it a good place to make a break in the narrative? Why or why not?

One Friday afternoon I went to the bank to cash my measly paycheck. I was very depressed. I was angry. My whole summer was going to be a waste. I kept looking at my check. After I paid my bills, I would have thirty-six dollars to last two weeks. I'd have to use my credit card again to buy groceries, getting deeper in debt when I should be saving for college. I was getting madder and madder; then I heard a crash and a teller say, "Someone should help him."

incident at bank

1. How does this paragraph advance the narrative?
2. How does it build on the first paragraph?

I turned and saw a young man on crutches caught in the revolving door. I was the last in line and nearest the door, so I walked over and helped him. I was about to turn back, when I noticed it was Erik Thoma from high school. He had been our quarterback and class president. He was a handsome honor student who dated the head cheerleader and got a full scholarship to Yale. He had rich parents and drove a Boxster. In short, he was the kind of guy I loved to hate. Fumbling on his crutches, he said, "Thank you." Then looking up, his eyes met mine, and he nodded feebly, saying, "Hi, sorry but I . . . I don't do well with names these days." The weakness of his voice shocked me. He sounded like an old man.

1. How does this paragraph follow the preceding one?
2. What is the paragraph's controlling idea? Does the paragraph have a topic sentence? Is one needed? Why or why not?
3. What details does the student highlight? How do they differ from those in the preceding paragraphs?

After we cashed our checks, Erik offered to drive me home. "I'm just getting back to driving," he said as he painfully worked his way behind the wheel of his car. As he drove, he filled me in on what had happened. It seemed almost as if he was getting rid of something painful by talking. "It was just before Christmas. Sandy and I were making a snowman in the park. This kid on a snowmobile lost control on some ice, hit a snowbank, and flipped over right on top of us. I was in intensive care for a week and had two operations. I lost a kidney, and they had to put in a plastic hip joint. But I'm lucky. Sandy's had brain damage, and she's going to be a wheelchair the rest of her life. We were going to get married in June. But she doesn't even recognize me now."

1. How does this paragraph advance the narrative?
2. What role do direct quotations play in the paragraph?
3. What is the impact of the last line? Is it a good place to end the paragraph? Why or why not?

When I got out of the car, my knees were shaking. I was almost ready to cry, not only because of Erik but because of my childish selfishness. I went to my apartment and sent my girlfriend a long e-mail. I told her what had happened to Erik and Sandy and asked her to ignore all the whiny letters I had sent her over the weeks. We were apart. I had an unpleasant summer

job. My car was disabled. All these problems, however,
were temporary and could be overcome by gifts money
can never buy—a sound mind and healthy body.

1. How effective is this final paragraph? Does it bring the narrative to a logical close?
2. How does the last line relate to the opening line?
3. How important are final paragraphs in a narrative? How can writers highlight or demonstrate an idea or detail they want readers to remember?

STEPS TO WRITING A NARRATIVE PARAGRAPH

1. Study your topic and use critical thinking by asking key questions:

    Why did I choose this event to write about?

    What did it mean to me?

    Why do I remember it?

    What is significant about it?

    What do I want other people to know about it?

    What is my most important point?

2. List your point or message as a topic sentence to guide your writing (the topic sentence does not have to appear in the finished paragraph).
3. List supporting details that establish your point.
4. Review your list, deleting minor ones and highlighting significant ones.
5. If people speak in your narrative, consider using dialogue rather than indirect summaries of conversations. Remember to use paragraph breaks to indicate a shift in speakers (See pages 40–41).
6. Write a first draft of your paragraph.
7. Read your paragraph aloud and consider these questions:

    Does my paragraph make a clear point?

    Does it tell readers what I want them to know?

    Do I provide sufficient details?

    Are there unimportant details that could be deleted?

    Do I use concrete words, especially verbs, to create action?

    Do I avoid illogical shifts in point of view or tense?

    Do I provide clear transitions to advance the narrative and explain the passage of time?

Selecting Topics

Consider these topics for writing narrative paragraphs:

renting your first apartment

the most memorable event that happened in high school

an event that changed the life of a close friend or coworker

the best or worst party you attended

how someone you know overcame a problem

the story of how a false rumor got started

being lost

enduring a blizzard, hurricane, or some other natural disaster

an incident that placed you in danger

an event that led you to end a relationship, quit a job, or return to school

a story your parents or grandparents told you about their childhood

how you responded on September 11

the most amazing play you saw an athlete or team make recently

the history of your neighborhood, school, or employer

preparing for an unpleasant task

being caught doing something you regretted

a telephone call that changed your life

the moment you felt you became an adult

a brief history of a local scandal or sensational crime

a news story that affected you personally

EXERCISE 4 Planning and Writing Paragraphs

Select a topic from the previous list or choose one of your own and develop details and a topic sentence that states the point of your narrative.

Topic _____

Possible supporting details:

1. _____
2. _____
3. _____
4. _____
5. _____

Circle the most important details that explain the event.

State the point of your narrative and write a topic sentence:

_____

_____

Organize your supporting details chronologically using transitional statements to advance the narrative.

First sentence: topic sentence, first detail, or introductory statement

_____

_____

Supporting details:

1. _____
2. _____
3. _____
4. _____
5. _____

Last sentence: final detail, concluding statement, or topic sentence

_____

_____

Write out your paragraph and review it by reading it out loud.

WORKING TOGETHER

Working with a group of students, revise this accident report to delete irrelevant details, illogical shifts in tense and person, and awkward transitions. Edit the paper for fragments (see Chapter 23), run-ons and comma splices (see Chapter 25), and misspelled words (see Chapter 35).

March 19, 2006
Sidney Carton

RE: Accident March 19, 2006 Cherry Hill, NJ SUV #12

Dear Sidney:

I was told to send you an e-mail as soon as I could. This morning at 7:55 I had an accident on Route 70 and Breckinridge Road in Cherry Hill. I had picked up some flyers at the Kinkos on Saukville Road and stopped at the post office before heading back to Philadelphia to meet Maynard Sloate about a loan package. I am driving just under the speed limit on Route 70 (45 mph) when a white florist van pulled out of gas station and hits my rite rear fender. I skid sideways and struck a light poll that smashed in the grille and broke a headlight. No one was hurt and the police gave the driver of the florist truck a citation for reckeless driving. Witnesses on the scene backing up my version of the event. I had the SUV towed to Garden State Auto Repair at 1818 Blackhorse Pike. I contact the insurance company and I e-mailed a claim. Let me know if there anything else I should do. I can drive my own car until a company vehicle is provided, I will not miss any other sales calls.

Trinity Mitchell

I was told to send you an e-mail as soon as I could. This morning at 7:55 I had an accident on Route 70 and Breckinridge Road in Cherry Hill. I had picked up some flyers at the Kinko's on Saukville Road and stopped at the post office before heading back to Philadelphia to meet Maynard Sloate about a loan package. I was driving just under the speed limit on Route 70 (45 mph) when a white florist van pulled out of a gas station and hit my right rear fender. I skidded sideways and struck a light pole that smashed in the grille and broke a headlight. No one was hurt, and the police gave the driver of the florist truck a citation for reckless driving. Witnesses on the scene back up my version of

the event. I had the SUV towed to Garden State Auto Repair at 1818 Blackhorse Pike.

I contacted the insurance company, and I e-mailed a claim. Let me know if there is any-

thing else I should do. I can drive my own car until a company vehicle is provided; I will

not miss any other sales calls.

GET THINKING AND WRITING

CRITICAL THINKING

Write one or more paragraphs that relate an encounter you had with a stranger. Did talking to someone you sat next to on a plane or met waiting in line teach you something about people, yourself, or the world around you? Have you ever encountered racist or sexist behavior? Did anyone challenge your sense of right and wrong? Have you ever had to ask a stranger for help or had someone ask you for a favor?

Remember, you can include dialogue if you wish.

WHAT HAVE YOU WRITTEN?

Read your paragraph carefully.

Write out your topic sentence or implied controlling idea:

_____

_____

List the main supporting details in your paragraph:

_____

_____

_____

- Do these details support your controlling idea and provide evidence for your point of view?
- Could you improve your paragraph by adding more details?
- Are there minor facts or trivial details that could be deleted?

Does your paragraph explain the significance of this encounter?

WRITING ON THE WEB

Using a search engine such as Yahoo!, Google, or AltaVista, enter terms such as *narration, writing narration, narrative techniques,* and *first-person narratives* to locate current sites of interest.

1. Review news articles in online versions of magazines like *Time* and *Newsweek* and notice how writers explain events. How do they organize paragraphs, use dialogue, and signal transitions?
2. Write an e-mail to a friend describing something you saw or experienced. Revise your paragraphs to delete minor details and highlight important points.

Have you seen people talking on a cell phone while driving? Have you ever felt unsafe when the person driving the car you were riding in picked up a phone? Write a paragraph about a driver using a cell phone. Include dialogue if you wish.

POINTS TO REMEMBER

1. Narration paragraphs should make a clear point, not simply summarize events.
2. Narratives can be written in first person ("I"), second person ("you"), or third person ("they"). Avoid illogical shifts.

   I climbed to the top of the hill where *you* can see for miles.

3. Narration can be stated in past or present tense. Avoid illogical shifts.

   I *drove* to the library where I *study* all night.

4. Paragraphs should have clear transition statements to advance the narrative, indicate the passage of time, and prevent confusion.
5. Dialogue—direct quotations—can be more effective than summaries of conversations. Remember to use quotation marks and begin a new paragraph to indicate a shift in speakers.

If you use Writer's ResourcesNow, please have your students log in and view the pretest, study plan, and posttest for this chapter.   **Writer's Resources** ⍟ **Now**™

7

Developing Paragraphs Using Example

© Tony Arruza/CORBIS

What does this photograph represent? Is it an example of creative promotions, inappropriate marketing, or a growing social problem?

Write a paragraph commenting on the way companies should and should not advertise alcoholic beverages. Support your views with clear examples.

88

What Is an Example?

Examples illustrate ideas, issues, problems, situations, theories, or behaviors. Examples explain something or provide evidence to support a point of view. You can explain that a felony is "a serious crime" by giving readers examples—*murder, robbery, sexual assault.* To argue that your landlord is not taking care of your apartment building, you can list examples of uncut grass, burnt-out lights, broken pipes, missing locks, and peeling paint. Examples are specific items that represent something greater.

Colleges are cutting support to sports that generate little revenue—*track and field, swimming, boxing,* and *fencing.*

New York, Minneapolis, Milwaukee, and *San Francisco* are examples of cities that have seen a dramatic drop in violent crime.

Over-the-counter medications like *cold pills, cough syrup,* and *aspirin* are often abused.

POINT TO REMEMBER

Descriptions provide details about one subject. Examples provide details about a subject that represents a general type.

WHAT ARE YOU TRYING TO SAY?

Write a paragraph that uses one or more examples to explain an idea or support a point of view about one of the following topics:

- self-destructive behavior
- people who overcome obstacles
- television shows you consider inappropriate for children
- fad diets
- products that have made your life easier
- potential problems you will face this semester

_____

_____

_____

_____

_____

_____

_____

_____

_____

_____

_____

_____

_____

WHAT HAVE YOU WRITTEN?

Read your paragraph carefully. Underline the topic sentence. Does it clearly describe your subject? Do the examples illustrate or support your topic sentence? Will readers understand the examples you include? Can you think of better ones?

Writing Example Paragraphs

Example paragraphs provide specific illustrations for ideas or concepts readers might find abstract or confusing.

> In order to obtain a loan, applicants must have sufficient <u>collateral</u> the lender can attach in case of nonpayment. Ideally, <u>collateral</u> consists of items with fixed values that can be readily seized and used to pay for a loan in case of default. These include savings accounts, stocks, bonds, and mutual funds. Other forms of _collateral,_ such as cars, artwork, stamps, coins, and jewelry, are less desirable because their value is harder to establish and they take time to convert to cash.

The examples of _stocks, bonds,_ and _mutual funds_ illustrate what is meant by "collateral."

Writers also use examples as evidence, giving readers specific facts or incidents to support an argument.

> <u>Pacific Air is violating federal security procedures.</u> On three occasions in March, passengers were allowed to board flights out of San Jose without boarding passes. In San Antonio, Pacific Air employees allowed vendors to service aircraft without checking their credentials. In San Francisco, two Air Pacific charter jets were left untended for two hours with their cargo doors open. On a flight from Dallas to Los Angeles, an Air Pacific pilot failed to secure the cockpit door.

The list of specific security violations support the writer's claim that the airline violates federal regulations.

TIPS FOR USING EXAMPLES

1. **Create a strong topic sentence or state a clear controlling idea to prevent examples from being a list of random facts or narratives.**
2. **Choose examples readers can identify and understand.**
3. **Avoid examples readers may find controversial.**
4. **Provide more than one example to support a point of view.** A single example could be an exception and would not provide enough evidence for readers to accept your ideas.
5. **Supply additional forms of support such as statistics and facts.** Even a long list of examples does not always provide sufficient proof. Clips of a quarterback making spectacular passes does not prove he is a great player or that his team has a winning record.

Types of Examples

You can develop a paragraph using single or multiple examples.

A **single extended example** provides details about a person, place, or thing that illustrates something larger. The fact that many Americans do not have health insurance can be illustrated by one family's situation.

> Medical crises cause 46% of personal bankruptcies in the United States. Like most Americans, Erika Perez had health insurance through her employer, an Arizona trucking company. After losing that job, she found work selling lawn-care services on commission. Although she earned as much as a thousand dollars in a good week, she could not afford health insurance. Rushed to the hospital with excruciating back pains, Perez learned she needed emergency surgery to repair a slipped disc. Postoperative therapy and costly prescription drugs erased her savings and left her with $65,000 in medical expenses. No longer able to drive, she began telemarketing from home but rarely earned more than a few hundred dollars a week. After selling her car and borrowing thousands from her retired parents, Perez sought advice from a lawyer who informed her that her best option was to declare bankruptcy.

topic sentence stating a point of view

single example

TIPS FOR USING A SINGLE EXAMPLE

1. **Choose the example that best illustrates or supports your main idea.**
2. **Explain the significance of your example to prevent readers from seeing it as an isolated situation.** You can demonstrate the significance of an example by adding a fact or statistic.

    Erika Perez is just one of 2,300 Arizonians to declare bankruptcy because of a medical crisis this year.

3. **Focus on those details that directly support your point.** Delete minor items. Remember, your goal is not to tell a story but present an example.

You can also develop a paragraph using **multiple examples.**

> Product placement, the use of motion pictures to promote products, has a long history. One of the first movies ever made, an 1896 French silent film, included boxes of soap supplied by a sales rep. In the 1930s Bell

topic sentence stating general idea

example 1

example 2

example 3
example 4

example 5

Telephone supplied movie studios with their new "French phones" free of charge. They assumed the movie-going public would want to replace their old phones with the new models they saw used by Clark Gable and Jean Harlow. In the 1940s DeBeers promoted diamonds by providing movie studios with jewelry to to be worn by leading ladies. In *The Seven Year Itch,* Marilyn Monroe is seen eating a bag of Bells potato chips, then beginning a national sales campaign. Car makers have supplied vehicles for television programs and movies. Product placement has proven so successful that many companies that once supplied products without cost in exchange for free publicity are now being charged hundreds of thousands of dollars for an actor to drink their soft drink, eat their cereal, or pull into one of their gas stations on film.

TIPS FOR USING MULTIPLE EXAMPLES

1. **Choose a range of examples.** A list of specific examples can simply provide a number of exceptions and not provide significant evidence. Offer examples that include facts, statistics, or expert testimony to create a broad base of support.
2. **Avoid examples that require extensive explanations.**
3. **Choose examples readers will recognize and understand.**
4. **Place the examples in a logical order—by time or by importance.**
5. **Make sure your examples directly support your topic sentence or controlling idea.**

Using Hypothetical Examples

Most writers use real examples to illustrate an idea. In some cases, however, you can create a **hypothetical,** or fictional, example to explain a subject.

topic sentence

hypothetical example

Make sure you report all injuries, no matter how minor, to your supervisor immediately. Do not delay. For example, you fall from a stepladder and twist your knee. It feels stiff and sore but does not seem serious. You complete your shift and punch out, without informing anyone of your accident. You take some aspirin and go to bed. You wake up in the middle of the night, your swollen knee throbbing in pain. You have someone drive you to the emergency room where tests reveal you have torn ligaments and tendons that require surgery and weeks of rehabilitation. Because you failed to report the accident before leaving work, you cannot prove you injured your knee on the job and may be unable to claim benefits. Many serious injuries do not manifest themselves for hours or even days after an accident. Remember to report all work injuries immediately.

TIPS FOR USING HYPOTHETICAL EXAMPLES

1. **Hypothetical examples are useful to illustrate ideas, but, because they are not real, they are not effective support for an argument.**
2. **Use hypothetical examples that are simple and easy to understand.**
3. **Add facts or statistics to demonstrate the significance of hypothetical examples.**

Last year 45% of disputed workman's compensation claims involved unreported on-the-job injuries.

EXERCISE 1 Identifying Examples

Read the paragraph carefully and answer the questions that follow it.

The most significant threats to public health are lifestyle related. Nearly 35% of adults smoke cigarettes, placing them at greater risk of developing serious and life-threatening diseases. Alcohol abuse leads to heart and liver disease and is involved in half of all traffic fatalities. Half of adults and one-third of teenagers are overweight. Obesity, especially among the young, is responsible for the epidemic of diabetes. The population movement from Northern states to the Southwest has led to soaring rates of skin cancer because of greater exposure to the sun. The eighteen-year-old who eats junk food, smokes, and binge drinks on weekends may be starting a lifestyle that will shorten his or her life by ten years.

1. **What is the topic sentence?** _____

   _____

2. **How many examples are given?** _____

   _____

3. **Are any examples hypothetical?** _____

   _____

4. **What facts or statistics could be added to create additional support?** _____

   _____

Writing Example: Using Transitions

Paragraphs containing examples need clear transitions to keep them from becoming just lists of unrelated items. Examples have to directly support the topic sentence or main idea they are illustrating:

My new car is a lemon. One month after I bought it, *for example,* the muffler fell off.

KEY TRANSITIONS

It is helpful to introduce examples and link them to your topic sentence with transitional words or phrases.

For example, . . .	For instance, . . .
Consider the case of . . .	To illustrate, . . .
To demonstrate, . . .	Another example is . . .
Recent experiences reveal, . . .	A case in point is . . .
An example is . . .	Examples could include . . .
The best example is . . .	One of the worst cases is . . .

EXERCISE 2 Creating Examples to Explain an Idea

Select one of the following ideas and write a paragraph that uses one or more real or hypothetical examples to illustrate your topic sentence.

best ways to study for an exam	challenges parents with small
the best sitcoms	children face when traveling
overrated vacation spots	undesirable jobs
problems faced by students with jobs	people's fear of becoming old

After completing your paragraph, review the topic sentence and the example or examples you developed. Do the examples clearly illustrate your ideas or do they simply tell stories or offer descriptions?

EXERCISE 3 Creating Examples to Support a Point of View

Select one of the following ideas and write a paragraph that uses one or more factual or hypothetical examples to support your point of view.

why students drop out of high school	why a sports team is having a
why teenagers take risks	winning or losing season
why some communities are	why older people have difficulty
suspicious of the police	changing careers
why a recent movie succeeded	why trials should or should not
or failed with audiences	be televised

After completing your paragraph, review your topic sentence and the example or examples you developed. Do the examples support your point of view, or do they tell related stories or offer descriptions?

EXAM SKILLS

Many examination questions call for writing one or more example paragraphs. As with any exam, read the question carefully and make sure your paragraph directly responds to it. Create a clear topic sentence and develop one or more examples that illustrate or provide proof.

From *Abnormal Psychology*

Explain the disabling consequences of bipolar depression.

topic sentence giving explanation — *Patients with bipolar depression experience severe mood swings from elated excitement to deep depression. Both extremes can lead to behavior that can have devastating consequences. In their "high" state, patients feel all powerful and have an elevated self-esteem that leads them to make irrational and*

examples — *destructive decisions. For example, they will buy expensive gifts they cannot afford, quit their jobs to become movie stars, decide to run for office, or announce they are going to the UN*

examples

conclusion

to propose a solution to terrorism. In their "low" state, patients feel depressed, lonely, and powerless. For example, they will withdraw from friends or family, quit work or school because they feel inadequate, and abuse drugs or alcohol. Because symptoms may develop slowly, people have gone bankrupt, lost careers, and ruined families before their irrational behavior was diagnosed as bipolar depression. New drugs and therapy have helped patients cope with this disabling disorder.

Student Paragraphs

Single, Extended Example

Freshman courses are the most demanding ones students take. For example, in my Macroeconomics course I was bombarded with new terms, theories, and concepts I was totally unprepared for. I spent two to three hours a night cramming just to get B's on the ten-question quizzes the professor gave us each week. In order to write a research paper, I had to do a lot of background work before I could select a topic. When I began looking up articles on the Internet, I discovered I had to constantly refer to my dictionary of economics terms just to figure out what the article was about.

Multiple Examples

A few years ago movie studios made money primarily on ticket sales and television rights. Today there is an expanding range of ancillary markets that provide new sources of income. Video and DVD sales, for example, sometimes exceed the amount the studio makes in theaters. Cable networks like HBO and Cinemax offer studios markets for movies that might not be suited for ABC or NBC. Websites are used to sell movie memorabilia like T-shirts, coffee mugs, posters, and caps. Soundtracks and book versions of a film generate additional sources of cash. Ancillary sales can make cult films with a small but dedicated fan base highly profitable.

Hypothetical Examples

Anyone who has studied or worked with family members of addicts has probably run into what experts call "enabling." Although they are angry and hurt by the addict's behavior, family members often unconsciously allow it to continue. For example, the parents of a drug-addicted teenager who calls home asking for money because her purse was stolen send her money even though they suspect she will spend it on drugs. The wife of an alcoholic accepts her husband's excuse that he had to work late when it is obvious to her that he has been drinking. The children of a drug abuser make excuses to relatives why Mom or Dad is unable to attend a wedding or come to Thanksgiving dinner. Because they are afraid to confront the problem, people allow the addict to continue his or her life of abuse. They cover up for loved ones out of shame or embarrassment. Often they fear confrontation will only lead to arguments or the addict leaving home. In order to cope with this problem, many therapists believe that treatment must involve the whole family, not just the person with a substance abuse problem.

PUTTING PARAGRAPHS TOGETHER

Working at Home

introduction   Computers and the Internet make it possible for more and more professionals to work from home offices. Accountants, editors, analysts, lawyers, and sales people can conduct business at home, accessing corporate records online and using virtual meetings to

explanation   discuss issues with colleagues in a dozen different cities. <u>Working from home has proven to have advan-

topic sentence   tages for both employers and employees.</u>

1. What is the controlling idea of this paragraph?
2. How does the student explain why the number of people working at home has increased?

example 1
topic sentence   <u>Nearly half the claims adjusters for Great Lakes Casualty, for example, now work at home.</u> Previously, the company had eighty adjusters working in cubicles in a Chicago office tower sending e-mail, making phone calls, and filing reports on computers. Realizing most of this work could be done elsewhere, the company encouraged adjusters to work at home. Great Lakes Casualty has cut its need for office space, employee lounges, and electricity. Last year when a blizzard shut down the city, most of its key people could still get their jobs done without leaving home. Great Lakes Casualty also found it easier to recruit and retain employees, especially those with small children. The firm also believes it helps the environment by cutting back on the number of employees who drive to work.

1. What is the controlling idea of this paragraph?
2. How does it connect to the first paragraph?
3. How does the example support the writer's main idea?

<u>New companies are formed around people who expect to work at home.</u> Firms that once would rent several floors of office space, now rent space for just a few offices, work stations, and conference rooms. San Diego Design was able to save nearly a million dollars its first year by hiring employees with home offices. In some cases they were able to hire talented designers in Los Angeles and San Francisco without asking them to relocate.

example 2
topic sentence

1. What is the controlling idea of this paragraph?
2. How does the example support the topic sentence?
3. How does this paragraph build upon the preceding one?

<u>Employees find that working at home saves them both time and money.</u> Vicki Bert, a claims adjuster for Great Lakes Casualty, found that working at home saved her an hour-and-twenty-minute commute in and out of Chicago each day. By working at home she also saved sixty dollars a week in gas and parking. She used to get up at six in order to dress and hit the expressway to make it downtown by nine. She normally took an hour lunch then faced a ninety-minute commute home. Today she often gets out of bed at six, jumps behind her computer, and completes a day's worth of filing by noon. Other employees find that working at home lowers daycare costs or the need for a second car.

example 3
topic sentence

1. What is the controlling idea of this paragraph?
2. How does the example support the topic sentence?
3. How does this paragraph support the topic sentence of the first paragraph?

<u>Not all people find working at home desirable, however.</u> Some managers find it difficult to coordinate operations handled by a dozen people working different schedules in different locations. Emergency meetings are difficult to arrange. Sometimes companies have trouble responding to customer questions and complaints because employees are not in one location. Employees can find working at home isolating and lonely. Many miss the interaction and informal help they get from coworkers in a traditional workplace. Family members do not always respect the home office or resent the home worker who interrupts a meal to take a business call.

conclusion
examples

1. What is the controlling idea of this paragraph?
2. How do the examples support the topic sentence?
3. How does this paragraph contrast with the preceding ones?

STEPS TO WRITING AN EXAMPLE PARAGRAPH

1. Clearly establish your topic and describe it accurately. Examples will only work if they illustrate a precisely defined topic or provide evidence for a clearly stated point of view.
2. Consider your readers when you choose examples. Will they recognize the people, events, or situations you provide as support?
3. Avoid examples that are too complicated or require too much explanation.
4. Organize examples in a clear pattern. You might arrange events by time or group people by their age or profession. Avoid creating a jumble of examples readers may find confusing.
5. If you use a single example, delete minor details and focus on those that clearly support your main point.
6. Write a draft of your paragraph.
7. Read your paragraph aloud and ask yourself these questions:

Do I have a clear topic sentence that defines my subject?

Do the examples illustrate or represent my subject?

Will readers make the connection between my examples and the larger topic they are supposed to represent?

Can I think of better examples?

Selecting Topics

There are two ways to develop topics for an example paragraph.

One option is to select a specific person, place, thing, or idea that you think represents something greater.

A local political scandal provides a perfect example of a good person corrupted by power.

The appearance of fifty e-mails in less than an hour provides examples of spam.

A friend's loss of a job provides a perfect example of downsizing.

Another option is to select a topic or state an opinion, then think of examples that best illustrate your idea or provide evidence for your point of view.

Describe a problem in your community and provide examples.

Outline your definition of good daycare, then illustrate it with one or more examples.

Argue for a change in a law or policy, such as immigration, drinking age, airport security, bankruptcy, unemployment insurance, or health care, and support your opinion with examples.

EXERCISE 4 Planning and Writing Paragraphs

Establish a topic and define it carefully. Determine what you want readers to understand about it by listing the most important points you want to dramatize.

Topic _____

Details, things readers should know:

1. _____

2. _____

3. _____

4. _____

Example or examples that represent the topic:

1. _____

2. _____

3. _____

4. _____

First sentence: topic sentence, first example, or introductory statement:

_____

_____

Examples:

1. _____

2. _____

3. _____

4. _____

Last sentence: final example, concluding statement, or topic sentence:

_____

_____

WORKING TOGETHER

Working with a group of students, revise the following e-mail by adding examples to make it clearer. Invent any details you need.

```
Attn: South Florida Productions staff
RE: Use of company vehicles

South Florida Productions provides cars to sales and
repair personnel in order to service accounts. Company
vehicles are not meant for personal use except in some
circumstances.

It is not permissible for employees to use company
cars for non-business use on holidays or vacations.
```

Employees cannot loan company cars to others, except family members in an emergency.

To save personnel time, South Florida Productions does allow employees to use a company car for limited personal reasons on the way to or from work.

If you have any questions about the use of company cars, call Bill Hewett at (786) 555-7100.

Kelly Rodriguez

GET **THINKING**
AND **WRITING**

CRITICAL THINKING

Do you believe that movies and television programs have the power to change society? State your position and support it with examples of films or shows you feel influenced or failed to influence social change.

WHAT HAVE YOU WRITTEN?

Read your paragraph carefully. Write out your topic sentence:

_____

Is it clearly worded? Could it be revised to better state your controlling idea?

- Do your examples illustrate the topic sentence?
- Are there unrelated details that could be deleted?
- Can you supply better examples?

GET **WRITING**

What is your reaction to this image? Do you see it as an example of a social problem, law enforcement, youthful behavior, or an issue of personal responsibility? How does it relate to the photograph on page 88?

Write a few sentences or a brief paragraph to accompany this image to create an ad warning young people about drinking and driving. Use words and phrases that will grab the attention of youthful drivers.

WRITING ON THE WEB

Using a search engine such as Yahoo!, Google, or AltaVista, enter terms such as *example, writing example paragraphs,* and *example techniques* to locate current sites of interest.

1. Review news articles in online versions of magazines like *Time* and *Newsweek* and notice how writers use examples to illustrate ideas.
2. Write an e-mail to a friend and use examples to explain your ideas. If you are having problems at school, provide specific examples.

POINTS TO REMEMBER

1. Examples are *not* descriptions. Descriptions provide details about one person, place, or thing. Examples provide details about a person, place, or thing that represents a general type or supports a point of view.
2. Example paragraphs need strong, clearly worded topic sentences that identify the main idea the examples represent or support.
3. Because examples can be dismissed as exceptions, it is important to provide facts, statistics, and other evidence to support a point of view.

If you use Writer's ResourcesNow, please have your students log in and view the pretest, study plan, and posttest for this chapter.

Writer's Resources Now™

8

Developing Paragraphs Using Definition

© JIM BOURG/Reuters/Corbis

How do you define marriage? Do you believe marriage licenses should be issued to gay couples? Why or why not?

Write one or more paragraphs stating your definition of marriage and the reasons for your views.

What Is Definition?

Definition probably makes you think of a dictionary. When you hear a new word or come across a term you find confusing, you look it up in a dictionary to find out what it means. Many of your college textbooks include glossaries, which are lists of definitions of important terms. *Definitions limit or explain the meaning of a word or idea.* To communicate effectively, people must use terms with shared meanings. Doctors, lawyers, auto mechanics, stockbrokers, police officers, software designers, and engineers use specialized vocabularies to communicate with others in their field. Introductory courses in subjects like psychology, business law, sociology, or health sciences often focus on definitions of key terms.

Definition applies not only to technical terms you might learn in a physics or computer class, but to everyday words as well. If you and your landlord have different definitions of *excessive noise* or *normal wear and tear,* you may find yourself being evicted or losing your security deposit. In one company a *rush delivery* might mean a week; in another, it might mean ten minutes. One health insurance policy may consider liver transplants *standard care* and pay for them. Another policy may define liver transplants as *experimental* and deny coverage.

POINT TO REMEMBER

Descriptions provide details about a single person, place, or thing. Definitions establish details about a personality type, kind of place, or class of things.

WHAT ARE YOU TRYING TO SAY?

GET WRITING

Write a paragraph that establishes and explains your definition of one of the following topics:

- a role model
- an educated person
- an ideal job
- sexual harassment
- terrorism
- stalking

_____

_____

_____

_____

_____

_____

_____

_____

Read your paragraph carefully. Underline the topic sentence. Does it provide a clear definition of your subject or does it just list descriptive details? Do you illustrate your definition with examples?

Writing Definition: Establishing Meaning

There are different types of definition.

Standard definitions are universally accepted and usually do not change. Words like *aluminum, mammal, circle,* and *dyslexia* have exact meanings that are understood and shared by experts. Professional and technical terms in law, biology, business, and engineering generally have standard definitions.

Qualifying definitions are not as precise or as widely accepted as standard definitions. They limit the meaning of complex, abstract, or controversial words or ideas. Doctors and therapists, for example, have different definitions of *obesity* or *depression*. Economists use varying definitions for *recession*. Because qualifying definitions differ, it is important to explain which one you are using.

Personal definitions express an individual's values, views, or opinions. Your definitions of a *good parent, love,* or *success* may differ from those of your friends, classmates, or relatives. Personal definitions rely on accurate descriptions and effective examples.

Invented definitions are created by writers to identify or qualify some object, characteristic, behavior, or situation that has been previously unnamed. The term *road rage* was invented to describe a driver's overly aggressive reaction to a minor traffic incident. *Spanglish* defines a unique blend of English and Spanish spoken by bilingual people. When people began using the Internet to harass, follow, or threaten people, it was defined as *cyberstalking*. Writers often invent a definition to help readers recognize and understand a new issue. You might invent a term like *cybercourtship* to define the way people date on the Internet or *parking pig* to define drivers who take up two parking spaces in crowded garages or parking lots.

EXERCISE 1 Establishing Meanings

Select a term you have learned this semester or one of those listed on the next page and write a clear definition in your own words. You can refer to a dictionary or encyclopedia for details. After developing your definition, determine whether it is a standard, qualifying, personal, or invented definition.

smog	dirty bomb
jobs no one wants	computer virus
tsunami	air rage
obesity	cyber junkie
tornado	shopaholic

Term _____

Definition _____

_____

_____

Type _____

The Purpose of Definition

Writers use definition for two basic purposes: to explain or convince.

Definitions of technical and professional terms generally provide detailed meanings to prevent confusion. Terms like *exculpatory evidence, cirrhosis,* and *altimeter* have specific meanings for lawyers, doctors, and pilots. Writers also use definition to influence how people view issues or interpret events. The problem of drug addiction can be defined as a *crime* deserving punishment or a *disease* needing treatment. Graffiti has been defined as *vandalism* by some and *street art* by others. Some parents will define spanking as a form of *discipline* while others define it as a form of *child abuse.* For some, a *multicultural* society is one in which people of various nationalities melt and combine to create a new identity. To others a multicultural society is one in which various groups remain separate, maintaining traditional ethnic identities.

EXERCISE 2 Creating Definitions to Convince

Select one of the terms below or use one of your own and state a definition that will persuade readers to accept your interpretation of the term.

racism	rap music
binge drinking	anxiety
poverty	obesity
job security	child neglect
police brutality	capital punishment

Exam Skills

Many examination questions call for writing one or more definition paragraphs. As with any exam, read the question carefully and make sure your paragraph directly responds to it. In writing a definition, remember your goal is not simply to describe details or provide examples, but to clearly state general principles that characterize a kind or type. Your definition paragraph should have a clearly stated thesis that states a basic definition in one sentence.

From Police Science

What is an arraignment?

definition statement

details

An arraignment is an initial court appearance where charges are presented to a defendant who enters a plea or asks for a continuance to plea at a later date. During this appearance the court establishes whether the defendant has a lawyer. The judge may set bail and schedule future court appearances. Although often a formality, the arraignment is an important part in the criminal justice process. Errors made at arraignment will complicate cases later on and sometimes lead to charges being dismissed.

Student Paragraphs

Standard Definition

"Most-favored-nation status" is a term used in diplomacy and international trade relationships in which one country promises to grant another country every benefit given to any third party. If the United States granted most-favored-nation status to Mexico, then if America agreed to lower the tariff on imported beef from Argentina, Mexico would automatically qualify for lowered tariffs on beef. Most-favored-nation status gives large or wealthy countries an ability to influence negotiations with smaller, developing nations. It has often been granted as a reward to insure alliances or sway opinion in other countries.

Qualifying Definition

Experts disagree over the precise definition of what is commonly called obsessive-compulsive disorder, or OCD. Most, however, agree that it is a recognizable psychological disorder that can be managed with therapy and, in some cases, medication. Obsessive-compulsive disorder is an involuntary and overpowering need to engage in abnormally repetitive and unnecessary behaviors that in extreme cases can be socially disabling. A person who lives in a high crime area and checks the locks two or three times before going to bed is probably cautious. A person who checks the locks ten or twenty times and wakes up three or four times a night to check them again is clearly abnormal. People who wash their hands before and after meals are hygienic. People with OCD might wash their hands twenty or thirty times a day and panic when they are away from soap and water. Psychiatrists and psychologists can generally identify extreme cases but often disagree whether those with less severe symptoms have mild OCD or are simply eccentric.

Invented Definition

Today many parents have discovered that their children have become Twixters, young adults who do not leave home, either because they cannot afford a home of their own or because they refuse to give up the conveniences of living with their parents. They often have low-paying jobs or no job at all, settling into a permanent teenage existence of borrowing dad's car and expecting mom to do their laundry. This is not simply an American phenomenon. Twixters exist in Canada, where they are called "Boomerang Kids" because they bounce back home after they graduate. Germans call this generation "nesthockers" or "nest squatters." In Britain, Twixters are called KIPPERS, which stands for "Kids in Parents' Pockets Eroding Retirement Savings."

PUTTING PARAGRAPHS TOGETHER

True Heroes

The word hero is used a lot in today's society. *introduction and background* Celebrities, athletes, and elected officials have been called "heroic" for making an edgy movie, hitting home runs, or taking a stand on an issue. We see "heroes" shaking hands with the president, getting awards, and giving speeches, usually while touting some book or movie deal.

1. What is the main point of this paragraph? How does it open the essay?
2. How does the writer use examples to build the paragraph? Do they give you a clear idea of the kinds of people the student sees as being celebrated as heroes in our society?

transition contrast, what heroes
are not
examples

<u>But these people are not true heroes.</u> They may be famous and successful, but they are not heroic. The millionaire athlete who scores touchdowns or the actress who gains weight to look ugly for a controversial film may be bold or daring but not heroic. Heroes don't do things because they have their eyes on the Super Bowl or an Academy Award. We should not confuse heroism with celebrity.

> 1. What is the purpose of this paragraph? How does it relate to the previous paragraph?
> 2. How does the writer use examples to support the topic sentence?

definition statement

examples

<u>A hero is a person who risks his or her life, status, or security for others without seeking anything in return.</u> The man who runs into a burning building to save a stranger's child is a hero. The woman who volunteers to help refugees in a war-torn country is a hero. The executive or government official who refuses to participate in corruption and leaves a powerful, well-paying, high-status job to work in a factory or to teach school is a hero. Sacrifice, not success, is the mark of a hero. Heroes should not be measured by what they gain but by what they lose. The actress who refuses to play a role she feels is demeaning to women even though it would further her career and the athlete who won't use steroids and loses honestly are far more heroic than the celebrities who get headlines. The real test for heroes is their desire for anonymity and self-denial. Many of the war heroes of WWII shunned publicity and preferred to keep their acts of heroism to themselves.

> 1. How clearly stated is the definition statement? Can you express it in your own words? What key words state the writer's meaning?
> 2. How does this paragraph relate to the previous one?
> 3. What role do examples play in establishing the definition?

conclusion and final
considerations

Today, however, there seems to be too little interest in true heroes. There is a strong desire for "role models" who can inspire young people by achieving fame and success. <u>Heroes are not always going to be popular role models, especially in a consumer society.</u> True heroes sacrifice and suffer. Often their lives end tragically or in anonymity, poverty, and unhappiness with only a few aware of their good deeds.

1. What is the purpose of this paragraph? How does it relate to the previous ones?
2. Why does the writer believe that true heroes do not make popular role models?

STEPS TO WRITING A DEFINITION PARAGRAPH

1. Determine whether your goal is to explain or convince.
2. Determine whether you are writing a standard, qualifying, personal, or invented definition.
3. Make sure your paragraph has a clear definition statement, usually contained in a single topic sentence that summarizes your meaning.
4. Avoid defining a word using the same word, such as "a diffusion pump diffuses" or "a cheapskate is a person who is cheap."
5. Establish meaning by explaining what your subject is *not* to eliminate confusion or common misconceptions.

    A cheapskate is a person who refuses to spend money even when he or she has substantial sums. A poor person who cannot afford anything but necessities is not a cheapskate.

    Dyslexics are normal children who have difficulty reading. Children who are brain damaged, visually impaired, or emotionally disturbed may have trouble reading, but they are not considered dyslexic.

6. Define using description to provide details about what your subject looks, sounds, or feels like. Try to help readers visualize your subject by describing it in action.

    An airbag is a rapidly inflated cushion designed to protect the occupants of an automobile in a collision.

7. Define using examples readers can identify.

    An adjective is a word that describes nouns: a *red* car, a *new* bus, a *cold* drink, a *broken* door, or a *popular* movie.

    Examples are useful to qualify abstract terms. People are likely to have different interpretations of a term such as "minor theft." Examples can help establish your meaning of the term.

    Only inmates convicted of minor thefts, such as shoplifting items under twenty dollars, snatching a neighbor's newspaper, or stealing hubcaps, were given an early release.

8. Define using comparisons. You can explain an abstract or technical term or idea by comparing it with something more common that people can recognize.

    When picked up on radar, an airplane has a *signature* indicating its size and shape, much like a flashlight casting someone's shadow on a wall.

    Because comparisons can oversimplify a subject, use them carefully.

Selecting Topics

Consider these topics for writing definition paragraphs:

a good boss

loyalty

a healthy lifestyle

an ideal job

depression

self-respect

a best friend

beauty

civil rights

censorship

child neglect

EXERCISE 3 Planning and Writing Definition Paragraphs

Select a topic from the previous list or choose one of your own and develop details that support a clearly stated topic sentence that makes a definition statement.

Subject _____

Definition statement: _____

_____

Supporting details:

1. _____

2. _____

3. _____

4. _____

5. _____

Write out your paragraph and review it by reading it out loud. Does your paragraph state a definition or provide only descriptive details?

WORKING TOGETHER

Revise the following e-mail to make definitions clearer by adding examples.

Attn. new employees

Atlas Motors has announced a new personal day policy. The employee manual states that all employees are en-titled to receive three paid personal days a year in addition to paid holidays and vacation time. These days should not be considered extra vacation days.

Personal days are designed to assist employees in coping with major life issues. Personal days should not be taken for unimportant issues employees can resolve on their own time.

CRITICAL THINKING

Should alcoholism be defined as a "disability"? Should alcoholics who are unable to work receive disability benefits? Why or why not? Write a paragraph stating your opinion. Your paragraph should contain your definitions of both alcoholism and disability.

WHAT HAVE YOU WRITTEN?

Read your paragraph carefully. Do you establish clear definitions, then explain why alcoholism is or is not a disability?
Write out the topic sentence stating your definition:

_____
_____

List the details that support the topic sentence or further explain your definition:

_____
_____
_____

- Do these details directly support your definition?
- Could you improve your definition by adding more details?
- Are there minor or irrelevant details that should be deleted?

© Chris Farina/Corbis

How do you define patriotism? Can someone protest against the government in a time of war and be considered a patriot? Why or why not?

WRITING ON THE WEB

Using a search engine like Yahoo!, Google, or AltaVista, enter terms like *definition, writing definition paragraphs, establishing definitions,* or *controversial definitions* to locate current sites of interest.

1. Review news articles in online magazines and notice how writers use definitions of key terms to both inform and persuade readers.
2. Examine websites by groups taking sides on controversial issues like the war in Iraq, Social Security, capital punishment, and abortion, and notice how each offers different definitions of terms like *security, family values, rights,* or *justice.*
3. Select terms you have learned this semester in one or more courses and use a search engine to locate alternative definitions.

POINTS TO REMEMBER

1. Definitions are *not* descriptions. They do not provide details about one person, place, thing, or idea—they characterize a type.
2. Definition paragraphs should have a clear definition statement that summarizes your characterization of the subject.
3. Definition statements can be supported with description, examples, and comparisons.
4. There are different types of definition: *standard definitions* with universal and fixed meanings, *qualifying definitions* that limit the meaning of a complex or controversial subject, *personal definitions* that express an individual interpretation, and *invented definitions* that create a name or label for a personality type, behavior, situation, or place.
5. Definitions can be used to inform or persuade readers.

Writer's Resources ⓦ Now™   If you use Writer's ResourcesNow, please have your students log in and view the pretest, study plan, and posttest for this chapter.

9

Developing Paragraphs Using Comparison and Contrast

© Corbis /CORBIS SYGMA

Do you think men and women communicate differently? Do they use language differently? Do you see differences in the way they deliver bad news, express anger, give orders, or make suggestions?

Write a paragraph comparing the ways men and women communicate.

What Are Comparison and Contrast?

Comparison illustrates how two topics are alike. Contrast demonstrates how they are different. College courses use comparison and contrast to explain how a federal law differs from a state law, how one hybrid engine measures up against another, or how two presidents dealt with a similar crisis. You probably have used comparison and contrast to make decisions at work, determining which method to use to solve a problem, how to make a repair, or decide which supervisor to call for assistance. Consumers use comparison and contrast when they consider which car to purchase, which apartment to rent, or how to pay for a vacation. Many college papers and business documents use comparison and contrast.

> The FBI handles domestic investigations of terrorism; the CIA handles overseas counterterrorism operations.

> After World War II, the United States constructed freeways, unlike Europe, which concentrated on building public transportation.

> Midwest National provides better insurance coverage for our employees than Pacific Mutual.

GET WRITING ▶ **WHAT ARE YOU TRYING TO SAY?**

Write a paragraph that compares or contrasts one of the following pairs:

- married and single friends
- two popular comedians
- civilian and government jobs
- Democratic and Republican views on taxes, terrorism, education, or Social Security
- two football, baseball, or basketball teams, players, or coaches
- your attitudes about school, marriage, success, or jobs and those of a friend or family member

_____

_____

_____

_____

_____

_____

_____

_____

_____

_____

_____

_____

_____

_____

WHAT HAVE YOU WRITTEN?

Read your paragraph carefully. Underline your topic sentence. Does it clearly state the two topics? What are the important details you listed for the first topic?

1. _____

2. _____

3. _____

What are the important details you listed for the second topic?

1. _____

2. _____

3. _____

Can you think of better details to add? Are there any unrelated details that could be deleted?

How could you revise this paragraph to improve its impact?

The Purposes of Comparison and Contrast

Comparison and contrast is used for two reasons: to explain and to convince.

Writing to Explain

Comparisons can explain similar topics, showing the differences between high school and college, American and European laws, or warm- and cold-blooded animals. You can think of these comparisons as pairs of descriptions or definitions. The goal of these paragraphs is to teach readers something or clear up common misunderstandings.

Many people use the words "fire truck" and "fire engine" interchangeably. In fact, some dictionaries and city governments make no distinction between the two terms. But in many fire departments, including ours, there are distinct differences. Fire engines carry water and are used to fight fires, especially where hydrants are not available, such as wooded areas, expressways, and airports. Fire trucks carry ladders and other equipment used in fighting fires and other emergencies, especially rescuing people from burning buildings or vehicles. Our department has three engine companies and five ladder or truck companies. Fire engines and fire trucks have separate crews and command structures. Engine companies and ladder companies respond to separate emergencies, although they often work together on major fires or disasters.

EXERCISE 1 Using Comparison and Contrast to Explain

Write a paragraph using comparison or contrast to explain the similarities and differences of one of the following topics:

classic and punk rock	two daycare centers	two cars
credit and debit cards	two popular diets	two teachers
two fast-food restaurants	Mexican and Puerto Rican	satellite vs. cable
film and digital cameras	dialects of Spanish	television
two pension plans	two sitcoms	
football and baseball fans	two sisters	

TIPS FOR WRITING COMPARISON PARAGRAPHS TO EXPLAIN

1. **Create direct, clearly worded sentences that describe both items.**
2. **Use details and examples to illustrate each type.**
3. **Point out key similarities and key differences.**
4. **Use concrete words rather than general or abstract words.**
5. **Avoid details that require too much explanation.**

Writing to Convince

Comparison can be useful when you want to convince readers that one thing is better than another. You might convince readers to lease rather than buy their next car or support or reject a change in Social Security or tax law. Comparison paragraphs designed to convince readers need a clear topic sentence.

In order to grow, Vincennes County Community and Technical College should expand its humanities offerings rather than its technical programs. Although Vincennes began as a vocational school and built its reputation as a leading technical college, the local economy and student demand indicate that the college's future depends on teaching general education and college transfer liberal arts courses. Supporters of technical programs insist Vincennes focus on high-tech programs like fiber optics and robotics to attract students. These programs are extremely expensive to set up. The three largest manufacturing companies that once hired nearly half our technical students have closed. The biggest employers are now insurance companies, health-care facilities, and social service agencies that require college degrees. Vincennes can only maintain its enrollment by meeting the needs of students who intend to get bachelor degrees. As a two-year school, we can serve this market by offering more college-level courses in English, history, sociology, psychology, and economics. Last semester, for example, four technical programs were cancelled because of lack of enrollment, while both the English and math department filled all their classes in one week and had to turn away nearly two hundred students.

TIPS FOR WRITING COMPARISON PARAGRAPHS TO CONVINCE

1. **Create a strong topic sentence clearly stating your choice.**
2. **Provide readers with concrete evidence and examples to support your topic sentence, not just negative comments.**

Ineffective
Technical programs are a total waste. Young people today don't want to get their hands dirty or work in factories.

Improved
Technical programs are less popular. Young people today want to to develop general education skills they can use in a variety of future occupations rather than specific skills they fear may become obsolete in a few years.

3. **Support your topic sentence with examples, facts, quotes, and statistics.**

EXERCISE 2 Using Comparison and Contrast to Convince

Write a paragraph using comparison or contrast to convince readers that one option is better than another:

alternative fuels	working for yourself vs.
ways of punishing criminals	working for others
union & nonunion jobs	renting vs. owning a home
study techniques	treatments for addiction
solutions to illegal immigration	parenting styles
views of the UN	two types of daycare
online and traditional classes	ways of preventing terrorism

Organizing Comparison Paragraphs

Because comparison paragraphs contain two subjects, they must be clearly organized to prevent confusion.

Confusing

Right now the city is considering two plans to revitalize downtown and improve the city's economy and employment opportunities. Mayor Bolan advocates granting $50 million in tax breaks for corporations and developers. Aldermen Marks and Spens support building better schools, new low-income housing, job training centers, and community health centers. Bolan supporters believe you need to increase the tax base by building high-rise condos and townhouses to attract wealthy people to the city. Marks and Spens believe that without skills and daycare, few poor people will be able to fill any newly created jobs. Bolan believes that upper-income residents will shop and dine downtown, creating entry-level jobs in stores and restaurants. New housing, Marks and Spens argue, should benefit the homeless, not the rich. Bolan has said the city needs a thriving, upscale downtown to attract tourists and investors. Marks and Spens insist money spent on restoring and securing a few blocks for the rich will never help the poor. Marks and Spens believe the first step in making the city attractive is spending $200 million to clear the slums that line the river and border the expressway. Everyone agrees, however, that massive investment is needed to revitalize the city.

The paragraph contains a number of details, but it shifts back and forth between the two proposals and is hard to follow.

There are basically two methods of organizing comparison paragraphs: **subject by subject** or **point by point.**

Subject by Subject

Subject by subject divides the paragraph into two parts. The first sentences generally introduce the two topics and state the controlling idea. The paragraph describes the first subject, then the second. Most of the actual comparison occurs in the second part of the paragraph.

Right now the city is considering two plans to revitalize downtown and improve the city's economy and employment opportunities. Mayor Bolan advocates granting $50 million in tax breaks for corporations and developers. Bolan supporters believe you need to increase the tax base by building high-rise condos and townhouses to attract wealthy people to the city. They believe that upper-income residents will shop and dine downtown, creating entry-level jobs in stores and restaurants. Mayor Bolan has said the city needs a thriving, upscale downtown to attract tourists and investors. Aldermen Marks and Spens believe the first step in making the city attractive is spending $200 million to clear the slums that line the river and border the expressway. They support building better schools, new low-income housing, job training centers, and community health centers. Marks and Spens believe that without skills and daycare, few poor people will be able to fill any newly created jobs. New housing, they argue, should benefit the homeless, not the rich. Marks and Spens insist money spent on restoring and securing a few blocks for the rich will never help the poor. Everyone agrees, however, that massive investment is needed to revitalize the city.

- Subject-by-subject paragraphs are simple to organize because they divide the paragraph into two parts.
- You can avoid repetition by mentioning facts and details that are found in both subjects in a single statement:

The mayor and his opponents both agree the city must create jobs and higher revenues to overcome two decades of urban decay.

Point by Point

Point by point develops a series of comparisons, showing specific similarities and differences.

Right now the city is considering two plans to revitalize downtown and improve the city's economy and employment opportunities. Mayor Bolan advocates granting $50 million in tax breaks for corporations and developers. Aldermen Marks and Spens believe the first step in making the city attractive is spending $200 million to clear the slums that line the river and border the expressway. Bolan supporters believe you need to increase the tax base by building high-rise condos and townhouses to attract wealthy people to the city. New housing, Marks and Spens argue, should benefit the homeless not the rich. They support building better schools, new low-income housing, job training centers, and community health centers. Bolan believes that upper-income residents will shop and dine downtown, creating entry-level jobs in stores and restaurants. Marks and Spens believe that without skills and daycare, few poor people will be able to fill any newly created jobs. Bolan has said the city needs a thriving, upscale downtown to attract tourists and investors. Marks and Spens insist money spent on restoring and securing a few blocks for the rich will never help the poor. Everyone agrees, however, that massive investment is needed to revitalize the city.

- Point-by-point comparisons place specific facts, numbers, dates, or prices side by side for easier reading.
- Point-by-point comparisons are useful to demonstrate advantages and disadvantages because each point is presented separately.

Many examination questions call for writing one or more comparison paragraphs. As with any exam, read the question carefully and make sure your paragraph directly responds to it. In writing a comparison paragraph, make sure you organize details clearly using either a subject-by-subject or point-by-point approach.

From *Allied Health Occupations*

What are the main differences between bacterial and viral infections?

general comparison

first subject

second subject

The main differences between bacterial and viral infections are the agents that cause them. Both produce mild to fatal contagious and non-contagious infections. Bacterial infections are caused by single cell organisms that can be seen with a microscope. They exist throughout the environment. Most bacteria are harmless, and some aid digestion in humans and animals. Harmful bacteria invade the body and release enzymes that destroy or damage living cells. Tuberculosis, anthrax, and diphtheria are bacterial infections. Viral infections are caused by capsules of genetic material. Much smaller than bacteria, they can be seen only with electron microscopes. Unlike bacteria, viruses cannot live outside a host. After entering the body, viruses take over cells and direct them to produce the material needed for the virus to grow. The common cold, influenza, HIV, and polio are viral infections. It is important to distinguish between infections because they respond to different drugs. Overuse of antibiotics to treat viruses has been blamed on creating drug-resistant germs.

Student Paragraphs

Subject by Subject

Over the past five years I have rented both apartments and flats. Apartments have the advantage of being low maintenance. I never had to carry out trash, shovel snow, or cut the grass. Trash and recycling chutes were located on every floor, so I never had to go outside in winter to take out trash. Both buildings had heated underground parking, laundry facilities, vending machines, and a community room I could rent for parties. Apartments, however, were confining. The rooms were small, and the windows could not be fully opened. Flats, on the other hand, were spacious and homey. I lived in duplexes with spacious front lawns and backyards. I had large balconies where I could sunbathe or grill a steak. On the other hand, the flats had no garages. There was no building manager, so I had to shovel my walk, change lightbulbs in the hall, and lug trash outside. Although I enjoy the homey atmosphere of a flat, I prefer an apartment because between going to school and working two jobs, I have little time for household chores.

Point by Point

New York City and Los Angeles both have police departments with colorful and sometimes controversial histories that have made them popular subjects for movies and TV shows. There are, however, major differences in their size and organization. New York has 39,000 police officers, making it larger than some European armies. In contrast, the entire city of Los Angeles is protected by only 9,000 officers. Police officers are paid well in both cities, though New York City officers earn more. The median pay for a police sergeant in New York is about $91,000 a year; sergeants in LA receive a median pay of $84,000. Because of the density of Manhattan and the crowded streets, officers and detectives often work on foot. An officer's beat can be a few blocks or a single high-rise. In contrast, LA police officers operate out of cars and respond to calls. New York cops have been celebrated in shows like *Kojak* and *Law and Order* and shown as corrupt and violent in movies like *Serpico* and *Prince of the City*. Los Angeles officers have been depicted as heroes in programs like *Dragnet* and *Adam-12* and portrayed as racist and brutal in movies like *LA Confidential*. No doubt both departments will continue to inspire future generations of moviemakers and television writers.

Point by Point

The majority of Hispanic students at Ocala Community College are from Mexico and Cuba. Most of the Mexican students are recent immigrants, unlike the Cubans, nearly all of whom are the children or grandchildren of those who left Cuba after Castro assumed power in 1959. The majority of Mexican students are low income, and many work full time in order to pay for college. Most of the Cuban-Americans are middle class, and some come from very affluent families. For nearly all the Mexican students, English is a second language, and many are enrolled in ESL classes. For most of the Cubans, English is their primary language. Some do not speak Spanish at all, and only a few are truly fluent in both languages. Mexican students tend to support Democratic candidates and are concerned about poverty and social justice issues. Although not as fiercely anti-Castro as their parents, Cuban students generally support Republican candidates and are interested in maintaining a strong economy and low taxes.

PUTTING PARAGRAPHS TOGETHER

Shia and Sunni

Since the Iraq War, Americans have heard a lot about Shia and Sunni Muslims, but few understand what the terms mean or the events that led Muslims to split into two groups.

introduction
topic sentence

> 1. What is the goal of this paragraph?
> 2. Is a one-sentence introduction helpful or distracting?

The split between Shia and Sunnis dates back to the death of Muhammad. There was a dispute over who would assume leadership. Sunnis (Arabic for "one who follows the traditions of the Prophet") accepted Abu Bakr, one of Muhammad's most trusted advisors, as the rightful successor. Not all Muslims agreed with this position. Some believed the successor should come from Muhammad's family. They asserted that the true successor should have been Muhammad's cousin and son-in-law, Ali. Shia (Arabic for "Party of Ali") view Ali as Muhammad's true successor. Over the centuries, Sunni and Shia Muslims have developed different traditions, interpretations of the Koran, and legal systems.

topic sentence

historical explanation

definition of "Sunni"

definition of "Shia"

> 1. What are the main ideas in this paragraph?
> 2. How does the student organize this paragraph?
> 3. How does this paragraph answer questions raised in the first paragraph?

A major difference between Sunni and Shia Muslims concerns their view of imams or spiritual leaders. Sunnis believe that imams should earn the trust of the people by demonstrating skills and knowledge. Shia Muslims, on the other hand, follow a line of imams they believe were appointed by Muhammad or God. Imams are viewed as infallible and are often revered as saints. Shia Muslims make pilgrimages to shrines and tombs of imams. Sunnis reject the idea of a hereditary class of leaders and do not view them as having the power of divine intervention.

topic sentence

contrasting views of leadership

> 1. How does this paragraph build on the previous one?
> 2. How does the student organize the details?

conclusion

topic sentence

        Sunnis make up 85% of all Muslims and dominate
most Muslim nations. Shia live mostly in Iran and
Iraq, the only two countries with Shia majorities.
Although Shia and Sunni Muslims have engaged in
violent conflicts, both groups share basic Islamic
values and beliefs. Many Muslims prefer to identify
themselves simply as "Muslims" rather than belonging
to either group.

1. How does this paragraph serve to end the comparison?
2. Does the topic sentence relate to the ideas in the opening paragraph?
3. Why is the last sentence important?

STEPS TO WRITING A COMPARISON AND CONTRAST PARAGRAPH

1. Narrow your topic and identify key points by creating two lists of details.
2. Determine the goal of your paragraph. Do you plan to explain differences or argue that one subject is better or more desirable than the other?
3. Develop a topic sentence that clearly expresses your main point.
4. Determine whether to use subject by subject or point by point to organize your details, then make a rough outline.
5. Write a draft of your paragraph, then consider these questions:

    Is my topic sentence clearly stated?

    Are there minor details that should be deleted or replaced?

    Is my paragraph clearly organized?

    Do I provide enough information for readers to understand my comparison or accept my point of view?

Selecting Topics

Consider these topics for developing comparison and contrast paragraphs:

two people you have worked with

two popular talk shows, sitcoms, or soap operas

the way television, music, an industry, or neighborhood has changed over time

differences between generations

contrasting ways people confront bad news

American and Asian customs

American and Canadian health-care systems

conventional wars vs. wars against terrorism

pros and cons of welfare reform, school choice, legalizing marijuana, banning handguns, or other issues

two ways of commuting to work or school

advantages and disadvantages of buying a new car, owning a home, investing in the stock market, getting married at a young age, staying home to raise children, or owning a pet

PLANNING AND WRITING COMPARISON AND CONTRAST PARAGRAPHS

GET THINKING AND WRITING

Select a topic from the previous list or choose one of your own and develop details and a topic sentence that states the goal of your paragraph.

Topic: _____

Possible supporting details:

Subject 1	*Subject 2*
1. _____	**1.** _____
2. _____	**2.** _____
3. _____	**3.** _____
4. _____	**4.** _____

Topic sentence:

_____

Organization (Subject by Subject or Point by Point): _____

First sentence: topic sentence, first detail, or introductory statement:

_____

Supporting details in order:

1. _____

2. _____

3. _____

4. _____

Last sentence: final detail, concluding statement, or topic sentence:

_____

Write your paragraph and review it by reading it aloud. ◀

WORKING TOGETHER

Working with a group of students, revise this e-mail message to make it easier to read by organizing in a subject-by-subject or point-by-point pattern. Consider why comparison and contrast writing depends on clear organization to be effective.

District Managers:

Please remind your staff about corporate communications policies. Employees should use e-mail for ALL internal communications. Communications directed to individual employees involving pensions, medical benefits, terminations, promotions, hiring, or disciplinary actions must be sent by first-class mail to their home address. E-mail is appropriate for personnel announcements intended for all employees. Deliveries of hardcopy reports or shipments should be announced and acknowledged by e-mail. Customer questions sent by e-mail should be answered by e-mail. If managers believe the question requires a response in letter form, an e-mail should inform the customer of the letter response.

If there are any questions about the use of e-mail and first-class mail, contact Cara Malina at ex. 5656.

Shannon O'Donoghue

GET THINKING AND WRITING

CRITICAL THINKING

In past wars the government urged the public to buy bonds and accept sacrifices like rationed gasoline and higher taxes. Do you think our government should ask Americans to make sacrifices to fight the war on terrorism?

Write a paragraph stating your views.

WHAT HAVE YOU WRITTEN?

Read your paragraph carefully.

Write out your topic sentence below:

_____

_____

Could it be stated more clearly or directly?

Do the details in the rest of the paragraph support your topic sentence? Can you add more ideas? Are there irrelevant or minor details that could be deleted?

© Bettmann /CORBIS

Write a paragraph comparing and contrasting male and female attitudes about relationships. What do men value in a relationship? What do women think is important? Use either subject by subject or point by point to organize your ideas.

WRITING ON THE WEB

Using a search engine such as Yahoo!, Google, or AltaVista, enter terms such as *writing comparison, comparison contrast essays, organizing comparison essays, subject-by-subject comparison,* and *point-by-point comparison* to locate current sites of interest.

1. Search for news articles using comparison and contrast and review how writers organized their ideas.
2. Review websites hosted by organizations with opposing views on controversial issues like abortion, gun control, or the war in Iraq. Notice how their statements use comparison to influence others to share their ideas.
3. Write an e-mail to a friend using comparison to discuss how something has changed, the difference between two classes, two concerts you attended, or two jobs you are considering.

POINTS TO REMEMBER

1. Comparison points out similarities; contrast points out differences.
2. Comparison can be used to explain differences or argue that one subject is superior to another.
3. Comparison paragraphs should have a clear topic sentence expressing your goal.
4. Comparison paragraphs can be organized *subject by subject* to discuss one topic then the other or *point by point* to discuss both topics in a series of comparisons.
5. Comparison paragraphs depend on clear transitions to prevent confusion.

If you use Writer's ResourcesNow, please have your students log in and view the pretest, study plan, and posttest for this chapter.   **Writer's Resources ⓦ Now**™

10

Developing Paragraphs Using Division and Classification

© Peter Beck/CORBIS

GET WRITING

Write a paragraph explaining the careers you are interested in. What is most important to you—income, security, helping others, a sense of personal accomplishment, or owning your own business?

What Are Division and Classification?

Division separates a subject into types. **Classification** ranks subjects on a scale, such as best to worst, easiest to most difficult, least to most expensive, or youngest to oldest. Many chapters in college textbooks are organized using division and classification. Jobs frequently require employees to make decisions based on division and classification.

Division

A balanced diet should include fruits and vegetables, protein, and whole grains.
Our employees include students, homemakers, and recent immigrants.
We have three types of company vehicles: long-haul trucks, delivery vans, and SUVs.

Classification

These diets include 1200-, 1500-, and 2000-calorie-a-day programs.
Our employees are paid hourly, weekly, or monthly.
The cars have four-, six-, and eight-cylinder engines.

POINT TO REMEMBER

Division separates a subject into parts; classification ranks types on a scale.

WHAT ARE YOU TRYING TO SAY?

GET WRITING

Write a paragraph that uses division to discuss different types of one of the following subjects:

- students at your college*
- your neighbors
- cliques or groups of students at your high school
- off-campus housing
- useful websites
- local restaurants
- problems caused by poverty
- health problems related to poor diet
- ways people cope with stress
- music groups

* Example: Divide students by their major, their ethnic background, their residence, or the way they study.

or

Write a paragraph that uses classification to rank types of one of the following subjects:

- students at your college*
- bosses

- diets
- new cars
- consumers
- disabilities
- careers
- recent movies
- Internet search engines

* Example: Classify students from youngest to oldest, best to worst, those who work full time, part time, or not at all, or poorest to richest.

_____

_____

_____

_____

_____

_____

_____

_____

_____

_____

_____

_____

_____

WHAT HAVE YOU WRITTEN?

For a division paragraph:

1. What is your subject? _____

2. Underline your topic sentence. If you find it unclear, revise it.

_____

_____

3. How do you divide your topic? _____

4. What types do you discuss?

a. _____   c. _____

b. _____   d. _____

5. Could you add other types? Could some of the divisions be combined?

6. Does your paragraph clearly describe or define each type?

For a classification paragraph:

1. What is your subject? _____

2. Underline your topic sentence. If you find it unclear, revise it.

_____

_____

3. How do you classify or measure your topic?_____

4. What levels or ranks do you discuss?

    a. _____   **c.** _____

    b. _____   **d.** _____

5. Are the classifications easy to understand? Do you clearly organize the ranks in order: A, B, C; 1–10; by age; or by price range?

6. Does your paragraph clearly describe or define each level?

Writing Division Paragraphs

Division paragraphs explain a complex or abstract subject by breaking it into parts or types. Iraq can be explained as a nation consisting of Sunni, Kurdish, and Shia regions. Insurance can be divided into health, life, home, and auto coverage. Biology and medical courses make the human body easier to understand by dividing it into parts, such as the respiratory, digestive, nervous, and circulatory systems. Law schools offer courses in civil, criminal, business, and international law.

You probably encountered division in jobs that assigned workers to different tasks or to different parts of a company. Division might be used to train employees how to handle cash, credit card, and check transactions or determine which orders are sent by mail, parcel post, or special messenger.

A paragraph can explain a subject by using a **formal division** established by a college, government agency, profession, industry, or corporation.

> Triplex Data Processing has three divisions. Triplex National, headquartered in Boston, processes account information for banks, insurance companies, and mutual fund companies. It generates and distributes account statements to individual and corporate account holders. Triplex Credit, located in Houston, is the second largest data processing center for credit card companies. It uses state-of-the-art security measures to insure privacy and prevent identity theft. Triplex Atlantic works solely for government agencies. It has contracts with several cities, states, and the U.S. military to conduct audits and generate payroll and pension reports.

Paragraphs can also be organized using a **personal division** based on an individual's experience or observation.

After working at Triplex Atlantic for two years, I noticed that most of the workers fit one of three distinct groups. There were the lifers, mostly glum-looking, overweight middle-aged men and women in drab business suits who drank a lot of coffee and spent their break time talking about early retirement. There were the part-timers, nearly all of whom were college students. They generally worked second shift and considered themselves lucky to be making $20 an hour banging out computer reports while they listened to hip hop on their headphones. They drank Diet Coke and sent out for pizzas. The interns formed a small but noticeable group. These were fresh business-school graduates. They were here to work for six weeks to learn the ropes before being sent on for further training. They were the same age as the part-timers but dressed in stylish suits and took their jobs and themselves very seriously. The part-timers admired them, hoping to join their ranks someday. The lifers gave them a grudging, resentful respect, knowing these kids were on the fast track and would soon be their bosses.

TIPS FOR WRITING A DIVISION PARAGRAPH
1. **Create a clear topic sentence that explains how you are dividing your subject.**
2. **Avoid oversimplifying your subject.** Don't mislead readers by suggesting everyone or everything fits into one of three or four types. Not all music, for example, can be neatly labeled rap, rock, or pop. *Point out possible exceptions.*
3. **Make sure types fit only one category.** If you divide businesses by geographical region— North, South, East, and Midwest— where do you place a company that operates in all fifty states?
4. **Use specific examples to illustrate each type.**

EXERCISE 1 Writing Division Paragraphs

Write a paragraph using division to explain different types of one of the following topics:

movies	coworkers	college courses
teachers	hobbies	credit cards
actors or singers	talk shows	women's magazines
pet owners	drivers	student jobs

Writing Classification Paragraphs

Classification paragraphs explain differences in types by rating them on a single scale. Geologists classify rocks by their hardness. Doctors classify burns as first-, second-, and third-degree based on tissue damage. In law, homicides are classified manslaughter, second-degree murder, and first-degree murder according to standards established by each state.

At work you may have learned special classifications used in a particular business or industry. Meat, lumber, diamonds, and other products are often classified by price or quality. In many jobs, salaries and wages are set by a pay grade based on experience and years of seniority.

A paragraph can use a **formal classification** officially established by the government, a corporation, or an organization.

> Reynolds Electric produces power cords and cables in three grades. *Consumer grade* consists of extension cords, printer cables, telephone cords, and other devices designed for home or small office use. They are widely sold in hardware and wholesale outlets like Office Depot, Staples, Wal-Mart, Home Depot, and Ace Hardware. *Commercial grade* includes heavier power cords used in construction of commercial properties like restaurants, strip malls, motels, and some high-rise office and apartment buildings. *Industrial grade* consist of cables used in aircraft carriers, generator plants, and high-tension power lines.

Classification paragraphs can also be based on a **personal classification** that reflects an individual's view or opinion.

> When I worked at Reynolds, I ran into three types of supervisors. The best ones had superior knowledge about the plant, products, and industry, and had great human relations skills. Ed Norton and Sally Deptford were perfect examples. You could go to them with any problem and get not only the information you needed but some support and maybe a tip on getting a promotion. They were fun to be around, and you could learn a lot by just sharing a cup of coffee with them. The next group had superior knowledge and would help when you had a problem, but they were cold and distant. They always acted like you were interrupting something important, and they made you feel guilty for not knowing some arcane serial number or computer code. They stayed in their offices or work cubicles and never spent free time with the rank and file. The worst supervisors were either brand new and just as clueless as you were or nearing retirement and would rather calculate their pension than keep up on the new codes. Both types were useless. They may have been friendly, but they never had any answers to the questions I had.

Formal and personal classifications appear in newspaper movie listings. A motion picture might bear an R or a PG, indicating an official rating, and one or more stars, indicating the rating given by a local film critic.

Tips for Writing a Classification Paragraph

1. **Clearly define a single method of classifying your subject.**
2. **Establish clear ranks or classes that do not leave any gaps.** A grading scale, for instance, should establish clear categories for each grade to prevent confusion of what test score receives an A and what score receives a B.
3. **Illustrate each class with specific examples.**
4. **Explain possible exceptions or changes.** A C student, for example, might work harder after midterms and complete the course with an A or B, and an A student might do poorly on the final exam and finish the course with a C.

EXERCISE 2 Writing a Classification Paragraph

Write a paragraph using classification to explain different types of one of the following topics:

football or baseball standings	restaurants	addictive drugs
hotels or cruise ships	musicians	sitcoms
salary schedules	fractures or other	home security systems
car engines	injuries	health insurance plans

EXAM SKILLS

Many examination questions ask for writing one or more paragraphs that use division or classification. As with any exam, read the question carefully and make sure your paragraph directly responds to it. In writing a division paragraph, make sure you clearly explain how and why you are breaking the subject into parts. In writing a classification paragraph, remember to use a single method to measure or evaluate your subject. In both cases, explain possible exceptions or situations in which someone or something could fit more than one category or move from one to another.

From *Metal Working*

Explain the different types of stainless steel and their common uses.

topic sentence explaining four types	There are four basic kinds of stainless steel made with different alloys and carbon levels to serve different purposes.
type #1	Austenitic stainless steel has a low carbon content and contains at least 16% chromium. It is tough and resists corrosion and is used in shafts, pipes that transport salt water, and equipment used in chemical plants and dairy food production.
type #2	Ferritic stainless steel contains 10.5 to 27% chromium. It is less tough and less resistant to corrosion than austenitic steels. It is used in automotive trim and exhaust systems. Martensitic
type #3	steels have higher carbon content and contain 11.5 to 18% chromium. They are magnetic. They are hard but less resistant to corrosion. They are used to make medical instruments, knives, aircraft parts, and bearings. Precipitation-hardening steels are
type #4	similar in alloy content to austenite or martensite steels but are heat-treated to make them very strong. They are used in shafts, high-pressure pumps, fasteners, and springs.

Student Paragraphs

Division

For any group to function, its members have to have the 3 C's: cohesion, cooperation, and compromise. First, they have to be willing and able to meet. People have to show up at meetings. Today cell phones, e-mail, and online discussions allow people to overcome time and distance to communicate with each other. Group members have to cooperate; they have to be willing to work together. People might show up at the first meeting called to talk about an issue but may not be willing to invest time and resources to accomplish anything meaningful. Last, people have to be willing to compromise. They have to understand that they cannot get their way all the time. They will have to listen to other points of view and moderate or even abandon their positions. Without these three elements, groups—whether they are churches, labor unions, corporations, or charities—are bound to fail or slowly wither away.

Classification

People usually divide cars into two types, American and import. In today's global economy, however, you really have to classify cars by the degree they benefit the American economy. First, you have American/American cars, such as Buicks built in Detroit. Even though they probably contain a large portion of imported parts, these cars are made here, creating jobs for American workers, and an American corporation gets the profits. Then there are American/foreign cars, such as Chryslers assembled in Mexico or Canada. Although an American company makes a sale and gets the profits, they have outsourced jobs to foreign workers. Foreign/American cars, like Toyotas built in Tennessee, create jobs for Americans, but the profits go to a foreign company. Finally, there are the foreign/foreign cars like BMWs imported from Germany or Kias from Korea. The only Americans benefiting from these cars are sales reps and service personnel. The manufacturing jobs and profits go overseas.

Division and Classification

In most states convicted criminals are assigned to maximum-, medium-, and minimum-security facilities based on four criteria: the nature of their offense, their flight risk, past criminal behavior, and potential for violence against themselves, staff, and other inmates. In maximum-security facilities, inmates spend up to 23 hours a day in locked cells. They are given few privileges and allowed little movement within the prison. In medium-security prisons, inmates often have the ability to lock and unlock their doors. Except at night, they can freely move about within the prison. They eat in mess halls, attend classes, or work in shops. They are counted several times a day and locked in at night. Many minimum-security facilities have no high walls or even a fence. They resemble college campuses or military bases. Inmates are often allowed to go outside or even enjoy weekend passes. These convicts are usually guilty of nonviolent crimes or are deemed nonflight risks. Occasionally major crime figures serve time in these facilities because they have plea bargained, accepting a two-year sentence for testifying against others rather than facing twenty years. Fear of reprisals from other criminals make them highly unlikely to escape. In some minimum-security facilities, the dormlike facilities have no locked doors and only a white line on the lawn to indicate the boundary of the prison.

PUTTING PARAGRAPHS TOGETHER

Types of Businesses

introduction

    Like many people, you may dream of going into business for yourself. <u>Before you get started, though, it is important to understand the four basic kinds of businesses: sole proprietorship, general partnership, limited partnership, and corporation.</u> Each type has advantages and disadvantages. One issue you have to consider is just how much risk you are willing to assume.

division into
four types
classification issue

> 1. How does the student introduce the subject?
> 2. How does the paragraph use division?
> 3. Why is the opening paragraph important for division and classification essays? What must it include?

type 1
details
definition

    <u>A sole proprietorship is the simplest business and is the easiest to set up.</u> Basically, you and the business are one in the same. The business does not file taxes. As business owner, you report all income on your personal income-tax return. The main disadvantage is that as owner you have unlimited personal liability for any business losses. Sole proprietorships expose you to great risk.

> 1. How does this paragraph build upon the first paragraph?
> 2. What details does the student use to explain sole proprietorship?
> 3. Does this paragraph supply enough information? Can you define "sole proprietorship" in your own words?

type 2
definition

    <u>A general partnership is an association of two or more people engaged in making a profit.</u> It is a bit more complicated to set up. Because you work with

other people, you can benefit by adding their start-up
capital, time, energy, and talent to the business.
Like a sole proprietorship, the partnership does not
pay taxes. Profits are split among the partners who
report them on their personal income-tax returns. The
major drawback to a partnership is risk. As a partner,
you are liable not only for your own actions but for
the actions of your partners. Because of this risk, it
is essential to choose potential partners carefully.

details

1. How does this paragraph build upon the first paragraph?
2. How does the student distinguish a general partnership from a sole
   proprietorship?
3. What transitions does the student use?

In a limited partnership, you go into business
with a general partner and receive a split of the
profits, which you report on your personal income-tax
return. The general partner or partners operate the
day-to-day operations of the business while you serve
as an investor. The arrangement is more complex to set
up than a general partnership but has a clear advantage. As a limited partner, your liability is limited
to the amount of your investment.

type 3
definition

advantage of less risk

1. How does this paragraph relate to the others?
2. Why does this paragraph appear after the previous one?
3. Why does a limited partnership have less risk than a general partnership?

Corporations are the most complex businesses to
set up and usually require the services of a lawyer or
an accountant. A corporation is unlike a sole proprietorship or partnership because you and the business
are considered separate entities. You can create a
corporation and then hire yourself as an employee,
usually as the president, and set up tax-deductible
pension and benefit plans. Because the corporation is
separate from your personal finances, it exposes you
to the least personal liability. Corporations, however, must file taxes quarterly and adhere to more
regulations than other businesses. Tax advantages and
the limited personal liability, however, can make corporations attractive even if you intend to operate a
one-man or one-woman enterprise.

type 4

definition

details

1. Why does a corporation expose business owners to the least risk?
2. How does this paragraph relate to the first paragraph?
3. Why does this paragraph come last? Does it make a logical conclusion?

STEPS TO WRITING A DIVISION OR CLASSIFICATION PARAGRAPH

1. Determine whether your goal is to divide your subject into types or classify subjects on a single scale.
2. Consider your readers. Do you need to provide background information or define terms before they can understand your division or classification?
3. Clearly explain the method you are using to divide your subject into parts or measure the parts on a single scale.
4. Consider numbering types or classes. It is easier for readers to remember divisions and classifications if you state at the beginning that there are three types of students or four classes of car insurance.
5. Use examples to illustrate each type or class.
6. Explain any exceptions, especially if it is possible for a subject to belong to more than one category at the same time or change categories.
7. Write a draft of your paragraph.
8. Read your paragraph aloud and ask yourself these questions:

   Have I clearly defined my topic?

   Do I clearly explain how I am dividing or classifying my subject?

   Do I illustrate each category with clear examples my readers can understand?

   Is there anything misleading about my division or classification? Do I need to explain exceptions?

Selecting Topics

First, select a topic you are familiar with such as a subject you are studying in college, a job you have had, a sport or hobby, people you know, or a place you are familiar with.

Second, determine the best way to explain differences or complexities about this topic.

Use division to explain types of infections you studied in a nursing class or methods of auditing in an accounting course, types of sporting equipment, or groups of people you live or work with.

Use classification to rate mild to serious medical problems, simple to complex audits, price ranges of sporting equipment, or best to worst coworkers or neighbors.

EXERCISE 3 Planning and Writing Paragraphs

Select a topic and explain it using division or classification. Make sure you provide clear descriptions or examples for each category.

Topic _____

Method of division or classification: _____

_____

First sentence: topic sentence, introductory statement, or method of division and classification:

_____

_____

Types or classes:

1. _____

2. _____

3. _____

4. _____

Possible exceptions or changes: _____

_____

Last sentence: final type or class, concluding statement, comment about exceptions, or topic sentence:

_____

_____

WORKING TOGETHER

Working with a group of students, revise the following announcement by establishing clearer organization of the classifications. Invent any details you need. Develop new titles or a number or lettering system to clarify types.

Attn: Service Staff
RE: Vehicle Repair Priority

To insure that vehicles are serviced and repaired in the proper order, follow these new priority guidelines: General service vehicles such as staff cars, general delivery vans, tractors, and pickup trucks should be serviced only after all Class B emergency vehicles.

Class A emergency vehicles include ambulances, paramedic and fire vehicles, and bomb squad trucks. These must be serviced before all other vehicles.

Class B emergency vehicles include first-aid vans, general police cars, and fire trucks. These should be serviced after all Class A vehicles.

Power mowers, street cleaners, and trash trucks are serviced last.

There is one important seasonal consideration. From April 15 to November 30, snowplows are classified in the group with trash trucks. From December 1 to April 14, they are considered Class A emergency vehicles.

GET THINKING AND WRITING

CRITICAL THINKING

At any given time the United States faces a range of domestic and foreign policy problems, ranging from health care to terrorism. Write one or more classification paragraphs describing the most to least important problems you think the president and congress should concentrate on.

WHAT HAVE YOU WRITTEN?

Read your paragraph carefully. Write out your topic sentence:

_____

Is it clearly worded? Could it be revised to better state your controlling idea?

- Have you established clear classes and organized them in a logical pattern from most to least serious?
- Do you explain why you consider some problems more serious than others?
- Do you provide examples readers can understand? Can you think of additional or better examples?

GET WRITING

Write a paragraph that classifies what you consider the best to worst jobs. Establish clear classifications and provide examples of each type that clearly demonstrate why you consider them desirable or undesirable.

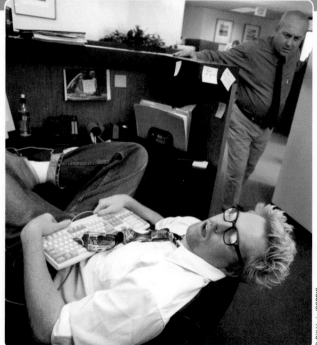

© Bill Varie/CORBIS

WRITING ON THE WEB

Using a search engine such as Yahoo!, Google, or AltaVista, enter terms such as *writing division and classification, division paragraphs,* and *classification paragraphs* to locate current sites of interest.

1. Look up online articles using search terms such as *types of* or *classification* to locate articles that use division or classification.
2. Look for articles using *types of* or *classes of* as title search terms.
3. Write an e-mail to a friend about your current experiences at college or work. Use division to discuss recent types of problems or assignments and use classification to organize them from easiest to most difficult.

POINTS TO REMEMBER

1. Division separates a subject into parts; classification ranks subjects on a scale.
2. Division and classification paragraphs need details and examples to clearly define each type or class.
3. Avoid overlapping categories.
4. Explain possible exceptions.

If you use Writer's ResourcesNow, please have your students log in and view the pretest, study plan, and posttest for this chapter.

Writer's Resources ⚘ Now™

11

Developing Paragraphs Using Process

© Charles E. Rotkin/CORBIS

What processes have you learned in previous jobs or courses? Can you describe how the heart functions, how banks process checks, how steel is made, how yeast causes bread to rise, how hurricanes form, or how a hybrid engine works?

Write a paragraph explaining step by step how a process takes place. Be sure to define terms and explain background information.

What Is Process?

Process paragraphs **explain how things work** or **give directions** to accomplish a specific task. College textbooks use process to explain how a bill becomes law, how earthquakes occur, how a disease affects the body, how a drug kills bacteria, how journalists cover a story, or how police book a criminal suspect.

Recipes, repair manuals, and instructional booklets give readers step-by-step directions to bake a cake, change a tire, install new software, or operate a power tool. Consumer magazines use process to give readers advice or suggestions on how to lose weight, choose a doctor, start an exercise program, buy a used car, or save for retirement. To be effective, a process paragraph has to be directed to specific readers, whether they are students, employees, or consumers.

Explaining How Things Work

The bacteria grows in warm wet places, then spreads to dry areas in direct sunlight.

The personnel staff examines the résumés, selects ten candidates, conducts a round of interviews, then chooses three finalists to be interviewed by the managers.

As tires lose air, they flatten, placing more of their surface on the road, which increases friction and reduces fuel efficiency.

Giving Directions

To prevent bacteria growth, clean your lab bench carefully and fully dry all cloths, test tubes, and instruments.

At the interview greet each member of the committee, provide five copies of your résumé, answer questions directly and positively, and be prepared to give a five-minute presentation on why you want to work at National Electric.

To improve gas mileage, make sure your tires are fully inflated.

WHAT ARE YOU TRYING TO SAY? GET WRITING

Write a paragraph that uses process to explain something you learned in college or at work:

- how cell phones work
- how aluminum or paper is recycled
- how blood pressure is measured
- how the NFL draft works
- how the electoral college functions
- how exercise builds muscle
- how digital cameras work
- how computer viruses are spread
- how people become citizens

or

Write a paragraph that explains how readers can accomplish a task:

- how to study for a test
- how to cook with a wok

- how to create a web page
- how to send a text message
- how to select a good daycare center
- how to operate a power tool
- how to drive in snow
- how to improve a golf swing

_____

_____

_____

_____

_____

_____

_____

_____

_____

_____

_____

_____

_____

WHAT HAVE YOU WRITTEN?

1. What is your subject? _____

2. Do you provide background information or define terms readers need to know in order to understand the process or follow directions?

3. Do you use transitional words and phrases or numbered points so readers can follow your explanation or instructions?

4. Write down the three or four most important things readers need to know about the process you describe:

   a. _____   c. _____

   b. _____   d. _____

Does your paragraph clearly explain these points? Have you forgotten details or created sentences readers may find confusing?

5. Read your paragraph aloud, then rewrite it to include any details you have forgotten and revise awkward or confusing sentences.

Writing Paragraphs That Explain

Process paragraphs explain how something works by breaking it down into a series of steps. Like a slow-motion movie, it slows down a process so readers can understand how it takes place. In explaining how something works, it is important to consider how much your readers know about the subject. Make sure you provide necessary background information, define key terms, and clear up any common misunderstandings people may have about the subject.

> Contrary to what some people think, tornados don't suddenly appear out of a clear sky. They are actually created by thunderstorms that contain updrafts of warm, moist air. This warm, humid air rises and forms clouds in the higher, colder atmosphere, creating ice crystals, which explains why hail often precedes a tornado. Downdrafts of cold air can also occur as the thunderstorm gets stronger. If the winds are powerful, the updraft of air begins to spin. Along the ground, a horizontally rotating column of air rises vertically. If the rotation becomes strong enough, a spinning cloud descends from the thunderstorm creating a funnel-shaped cloud. When this funnel-shaped cloud touches the ground, it officially becomes a tornado. Moving at speeds of 300 mph or greater, tornados can cause tremendous damage. Because they appear with little warning and can move erratically, tornados are extremely dangerous, and people should seek immediate shelter.

TIPS FOR EXPLAINING HOW THINGS HAPPEN
1. **Study the process carefully and emphasize key points.**
2. **Separate the process into logical steps.** Avoid emphasizing minor points by isolating them in single steps or crowding too much information in one stage.
3. **Alert readers to possible exceptions or variations to the process.**
4. **Use transitional words and phrases to link steps.**
5. **Stress the importance of time.** Because process explains things in slow motion, it can mislead people about the amount of time involved. You can prevent confusion by opening with a "real-time" description of the process.

> The test car struck the barrier at thirty-five miles an hour. In less than a tenth of a second, the bumper crumpled, sending shock waves through the vehicle as the fenders folded back and the hood flew off, shattering the windshield.

> The rest of the paragraph can repeat the process, slowly relating each stage in greater detail.
6. **Use images, details, and examples to explain steps.**

EXERCISE 1 Writing Paragraphs That Explain

Write a paragraph that explains one of the following processes:

how instructors determine final grades

the hiring process at your job

how children learn to walk or talk

how a certain crime is committed

how something is made, sold, or repaired

how winners are chosen for the Academy Awards, Emmys, or Grammies

how wages or salaries are set at your job

how playoffs work in the NFL

how people lose weight

a method used to complete a task at work

how a lottery operates

how people look for jobs

Writing Paragraphs That Give Directions

Directions are step-by-step instructions that tell readers how to accomplish a specific task. Process paragraphs that provide advice or suggestions can be written in a standard paragraph.

> During a tornado watch, pay attention to the sky. Tornados are formed by thunderstorms, especially those with frequent thunder and lightning. Look for an extremely dark sky highlighted with green or yellow clouds. Listen for a steady rumbling noise that might sound like a distant freight train or jet engine. If these conditions occur, do not wait for the approach of a funnel cloud; take shelter immediately.

If you are giving readers precise step-by-step instructions, consider using numbered steps or bulleted points rather than a traditional paragraph. Recipes and repair manuals are used as references while people are working at something, and numbered steps make them easier to read. Numbered steps highlight key information and eliminate the need for transitional phrases such as *the next thing you should do is* and *once this is done, now it is time to. . . .* To emphasize action, begin each numbered point with a clear action verb that tells people what to do.

> In case of a tornado warning, which means that a funnel cloud has been reported, take these steps immediately:
>
> 1. Turn off all computers and lab equipment. *Make sure all Bunsen burners and other gas flames are turned off.*
> 2. Place microscopes on the floor under the bench.
> 3. Secure all documents in lab bench drawers.
> 4. Turn out the lights, leave the lab, and close *both* doors.
> 5. Take shelter in the basement of the main building.
> 6. Do *NOT* take shelter in the cafeteria, gym, or garage.
> 7. Remain in the shelter until the warning is declared over by the principal or your teacher.

TIPS FOR GIVING DIRECTIONS

1. **Consider your readers' level of knowledge.** Define key terms.
2. **Make sure directions are self-contained.** Your paragraph should include all the information readers need.
3. **Consider using numbered steps, graphs, diagrams, and other visual aids for easier reading.**
4. **Provide precise, complete instructions.** Avoid vague directions such as "put the cake in the oven for thirty minutes or until done." Someone baking the cake for the first time will have no idea what it is supposed to look like when "done." Stating "put the cake in the oven for thirty minutes or until the center is firm and edges are dark brown" gives readers a clear idea of what to expect.
5. **Tell readers what not to do.** Give negative directions to prevent readers from making common mistakes like skipping a step or substituting cheaper materials.
6. **Inform readers of possible events they may misinterpret as mistakes.** If at some point in the process a machine can overheat or a mixture changes color or a computer slows down, let readers know this is normal.
7. **Keep sentences short and direct.**
8. **Warn readers of any hazards to their health and safety or risks to their property, other people, or the environment.**

EXERCISE 2 Writing Paragraphs That Give Directions

Write a paragraph that provides instructions to one of the following processes. You may use numbered steps if appropriate.

how to service or repair an appliance
how to plan a wedding
how to teach a child to walk
how to quit smoking
how to operate a machine
how to respond to a fire or other emergency

how to rent an apartment
how to care for a pet
how to save money
how to treat a minor injury
how to deter a mugger
how to stay on a diet

EXAM SKILLS

Many examination questions call for writing process paragraphs that either explain how something works or provide specific directions. As with any exam, read the question carefully and make sure your paragraph directly responds to it. Explain your subject step by step and provide transitional words or phrases or numbered points to organize details.

From Economics

How does the Federal Reserve set monetary policy?

general description   *The Federal Reserve System's monetary policy, which controls the supply of money, is determined by its Federal Open Market Committee or FOMC. This group has 12 voting members,*

description   *which include 7 from the Federal Reserve Board of Governors*

step-by-step process	and 5 Reserve bank presidents. The FOMC is headed by the Chairman of the Reserve Board and meets 8 times a year. At these meetings, the members determine to lower, maintain, or increase the discount rate (the rate the Reserve charges member banks for overnight loans). The FOMC can also influence the money supply by buying and selling government securities that affect the federal funds rate. These changes in interest rates cause banks, credit card companies, and other lenders to raise
effects of the process	or lower interest they charge consumers. The Federal Reserve lowers interest rates to stimulate the economy and raises them
goal of the process	to prevent inflation. The actions of the FOMC are designed to maximize employment while keeping prices stable.

Student Paragraphs

Explaining How Something Works

San Francisco cable cars operate without any steering or engines. They are propelled by a cable under the streets that moves at a constant speed of 9.5 miles an hour. To move the car, the operator uses a lever that grips the cable, much like a skier grabbing onto a towline on a ski lift. Heading downhill, operators often release the car and allow gravity to pull it forward. To slow or stop the car, the operator uses a complex system of brakes. The brake shoes are made of long blocks of soft pine that are replaced every three days. Because the cars cannot turn themselves, huge turntables at the end of each line are used to reposition the cars to head in the opposite direction.

Giving Directions

There are over 50,000 known computer viruses, with almost 500 new ones being created each month. To protect your computer from viruses, there are a number of steps you can take. First, use a good, up-to-date antivirus system that will block viruses and allow you to scan and delete potentially infected files. Make sure to scan your computer at least once a week and update your system regularly. Most viruses today are spread through e-mail. Do not open e-mail from someone you do not know. Be especially careful about opening attachments, especially if you do not know the sender. Back up your important files on discs, CDs, or an external drive.

Giving Directions Using Numbered Steps

If you fail to get the job after a good interview, you are bound to feel angry, discouraged, or depressed. Not getting a job you really wanted and felt you were perfect for can weaken your self-esteem. If you really want the job, you should send a letter or e-mail to the person who interviewed you.

1. Thank the person for the opportunity of being interviewed and express continued interest in the organization or the position.
2. Maintain a positive tone. Don't suggest that you would have been a better candidate than the person hired or that the employer made a mistake.
3. Briefly restate the strong points highlighted on your résumé and at your interview.
4. Close by saying how and where you can be contacted for future interviews.

If the firm is small and not likely to have additional openings, consider e-mailing or calling the interviewer and ask her if she knows any other employers who might be looking for someone with your skills.

PUTTING PARAGRAPHS TOGETHER

Boosting Your FICO

Most students know their SAT score and their GPA. *(introduction)* But few have even heard of a FICO score or how it can affect their lives. FICO scores (which come from a *(definition)* system created by Fair Isaac & Co) are credit ratings. Anyone who plans to borrow money to buy a car or a house should know how FICOs are determined and how to *(topic sentence)* boost his or her score. Lenders use FICO scores to determine what interest rate you should pay or even whether you deserve a loan at all.

> 1. What is the function of this paragraph?
> 2. How does the student explain what a FICO is and why it is important?

FICO scores are determined by five main factors *(explanation of how scores are determined)* that are given different values:

1. **Payment History (35%)**
   The number of accounts you have and the number of *(numbered parts of process)* late or missing payments are counted.
2. **Amounts Owed (30%)**
   The amount you owe and the types of loans or credit accounts you have are measured.
3. **Credit History (15%)**
   The length of your credit history and age of your credit accounts are measured.
4. **Types and Use of Credit (10%)**
   The number and types of accounts (mortgage, car loan, school loans, credit cards) are evaluated.

5. New Credit (10%)
    Recent requests for credit or newly opened accounts are considered.

explanation of scoring system

Because evaluations and values can vary, lenders usually use scores from three agencies and use the middle score. Scores range from 300-900. Half of American consumers have scores between 700-800. Anyone with a score lower than 620 will have problems getting credit.

---

1. What is the purpose of this paragraph? How does it explain the process?
2. How does this paragraph build upon the first paragraph?
3. Why does the student use numbered points? Would the list of factors be harder to read if placed in a standard paragraph?

---

directions to increase scores

You can boost your score by taking some important steps that will make it easier for you to get loans and save money by getting lower interest rates:

numbered steps

1. Plan ahead.
    It can take 3-6 months to change your credit rating, so start the process as soon as you can.
2. Get your credit report.
    You can order your credit report from three agencies: Equifax (www.equifax.com), Experian (www.experian.com) and TransUnion (www.transunion.com).
3. Study your report for errors.
    Report mistakes to creditors and credit agencies as soon as possible.
4. Pay bills promptly.
    Pay at least the minimum due on credit cards. Avoid late payments at all costs.
5. Avoid going over your credit limit even if your creditors automatically extend your limit without penalty.
6. Cancel cards you are not using and avoid opening new ones.
7. Pay down credit cards with high balances and don't consolidate credit cards. Having balances over 50% of your credit limit lowers your score. It is better to owe $1500 on two cards with $5000 limits than $3000 on a single card with a $5000 limit.

---

1. How do these directions relate to the explanation paragraphs?
2. Would this paragraph be effective if written without numbered steps? Why or why not?
3. How does the student highlight important points?

```
        You can obtain additional information from your
bank, credit union, and a number of nonprofit credit
organizations listed in the Yellow Pages.
```
conclusion

> **1.** What does this paragraph add? Why is it important?
> **2.** How should writers address readers' desire or need for additional information or questions?

STEPS TO WRITING A PROCESS PARAGRAPH

1. Determine whether your goal is to explain how something happens or to give readers directions to accomplish a task.
2. Consider your readers' existing knowledge. Do you need to define terms or explain background information for people to understand the process?
3. Address common misconceptions or confusions. In some cases the first thing your paragraph should do is establish clear definitions or separate fact from fiction.
4. Use examples to illustrate steps in the process.
5. Explain any exceptions or variations to the process.
6. Write a draft of your paragraph.
7. Read your paragraph aloud and ask yourself these questions:

   Have I clearly defined my topic?

   Is my description of the process self-contained? Is it complete? Did I forget any steps?

   Do I break the process into logical steps?

   Do I use numbered steps or transitional words and phrases to link steps in the process?

   Is there anything misleading in my paragraph my readers may not understand?

Selecting Topics

First, select a topic you are familiar with such as a subject you have studied, something you have worked with, or something you have learned about as a consumer.

Second, determine whether you want to explain how the process works or direct readers to accomplish a process step by step.

Third, consider your readers. Are you writing to people familiar with your topic or the general public?

EXERCISE 3 Planning and Writing Process Paragraphs

Select a topic and explain it or give directions. Make sure you divide the process into clear steps.

Topic _____

Goal: to explain or to give directions _____

First sentence: topic sentence, introduction, definition, or background information:

_____

_____

Steps in the process:

1. _____

2. _____

3. _____

4. _____

5. _____

Possible exceptions or changes: _____

_____

Potential hazards: _____

_____

Last sentence: final step, suggestions about further information, or final comment:

_____

_____

WORKING TOGETHER

Working with a group of students, revise the following e-mail by establishing clearer steps and adding missing information. List questions you have about these instructions. Refer to a car repair or car owner's manual or a website to evaluate the quality of these directions. Note missing steps and safety warnings.

```
Note to all drivers of company vehicles.

Because sales staff often travel on remote roads far
from possible assistance, all drivers should know how
to change a tire.

    1. Park the car.
    2. Remove the jack from the trunk.
    3. Loosen lug nuts.
    4. Use the jack to raise the car and remove lug nuts.
    5. Remove old tire from axle and replace with spare.
    6. Tighten lug nuts and lower car.
    7. Remove jack and firmly tighten lug nuts.
```

GET THINKING AND WRITING

CRITICAL THINKING

Write a paragraph giving suggestions to high school seniors heading to college or adults returning to school. Based on your own experiences, give them step-by-step directions that will prepare them not only for classes but also for adjustments they may have to make in their personal lives to succeed in college.

WHAT HAVE YOU WRITTEN?

Read your paragraph carefully. Write out your topic sentence or controlling idea:

_____

Is it clearly stated? Could it be revised to better state your goal?

- Have you organized the paragraph in clear steps?
- Do you number steps or use clear transitions to move readers from step to step?
- Do you emphasize your most important suggestions by placing them first or last on your list?
- Do you give people information that will really help?
- Do you give readers practical examples they can understand?
- Is there anything else you can add that would help readers prepare for college?

© Alexander Walter / Taxi / Getty

GET WRITING

Write one or more paragraphs that relate an experience in which you tried to teach someone how to do something or give directions. Why is giving instructions difficult? Looking back, can you spot errors you made?

WRITING ON THE WEB

Using a search engine such as Yahoo!, Google, or AltaVista, enter terms such as *how to, how things work, how things happen, process writing, writing explanations, writing directions,* or *writing instructions* to locate current sites of interest.

1. Read online advice articles or websites giving directions to see how writers organize instructions and explain complex or abstract ideas.
2. Explore websites about hobbies or interests you have to see how they give advice, inform readers, or state directions.
3. Write an e-mail to a friend and explain step by step something you learned at work or in college.

POINTS TO REMEMBER

1. Process explains how something happens or gives directions to accomplish a task.
2. Readers may need background information or definitions of key terms to fully understand the process.
3. Process paragraphs can include numbered steps for easy reading and reference.
4. Examples and clear details are important to explain steps.
5. Directions should inform readers of any potential hazards.
6. Peer review can detect missing steps and confusing directions.

Writer's Resources ⓥ Now™   If you use Writer's ResourcesNow, please have your students log in and view the pretest, study plan, and posttest for this chapter.

Developing Paragraphs Using Cause and Effect

GET WRITING

What causes homelessness—mental illness, domestic violence, unemployment, the lack of affordable housing, or addiction?

Write a paragraph stating what you consider to be the major causes of homelessness.

What Is Cause and Effect?

Why are reality shows popular? What motivates suicide bombers? How will global warming affect the planet? Why are health-care costs rising? How effective are crash diets? Will personal accounts strengthen or weaken Social Security? How does outsourcing affect the job market? The answers to all these questions call for cause-and-effect writing that explains **reasons why things happen** or **analyzes or predicts results.**

I dropped my evening classes because I transferred to second shift.

Hybrid cars are selling well because people fear rising gas prices and are concerned about the environment.

If you keep smoking, you will ruin your lungs.

After five years of effort, Mayor Ramon's Agenda 2000 plan to attract business to downtown created 1500 new jobs.

GET *WRITING* ▶

AND *REVISING*

WHAT ARE YOU TRYING TO SAY?

Write a paragraph that explains the causes or effects of one of the following topics.

Causes why:

- students suffer from stress
- few Americans learn foreign languages
- people immigrate to the United States
- a candidate won or lost a recent election

Effects of:

- dropping out of school
- violent video games
- terrorism
- 24-hour cable news channels

_____

_____

_____

_____

_____

_____

_____

_____

_____

_____

_____

_____

_____

What Have You Written?

Read your paragraph carefully. Underline the topic sentence. List the main causes or effects in your paragraph:

1. _____

2. _____

3. _____

Do these causes or effects logically relate to your topic sentence?
Can you think of better causes or effects? To revise this paragraph, what changes would you make?

Critical Thinking for Writing Cause-and-Effect Paragraphs

Writing about causes and effects requires careful observation and critical thinking. Experts on terrorism, for example, disagree about its causes—poverty and the lack of opportunities for young men in poor countries, American foreign policy, religious extremism, or authoritarian regimes in the Middle East. Economists argue whether cutting taxes will stimulate the economy and create jobs or lower government revenues and increase deficits. Even when you write about your own life, you may be unable to define the reasons for decisions you have made. For instance, why did you choose this college? Which factor influenced you the most: course offerings, the campus, the location, your family, or the cost?

In determining causes, it is important to look beyond first impressions and assumptions. Make sure you collect enough evidence and avoid rushing to judgment. A century ago, scientists discovered that glandular disorders could cause physical and mental illnesses. Some speculated that bad glands caused criminal behavior. To find evidence for this theory, researchers examined the throats of boys in reform schools and prep schools. Students in reform schools, they found, showed a greater incidence of inflamed tonsils than those attending prep schools. These findings appeared to support their theory that criminal behavior was caused by infected glands. They failed to consider, however, other reasons for the differences in the health of boys living in crowded, poorly heated reform schools and affluent students attending exclusive schools who saw doctors regularly, enjoyed good food, and lived in clean rooms. More recently, some politicians cited the decline in the homicide rate as evidence that violent crime was dropping in their cities. Researchers, however, suggested the decline in homicides was caused by the widespread use of cell phones and better emergency services. Paramedics and trauma surgeons were saving more shooting victims, reducing the number of homicides but not reducing the amount of violent crime. Even experts can jump to conclusions, failing to consider other explanations for what they observe.

Don't confuse a coincidence or a time relationship with a cause. The fact that your headache went away fifteen minutes after you took an aspirin does not mean the aspirin was effective. Your headache may have gone away on its own. An increase in car sales following a new ad campaign does not alone prove that the commercials were responsible. A drop in interest rates, better employment, or a recall announcement by a competitor could also explain why sales increased. The fact that someone has a heart attack a week after being laid off does not prove it was caused by the stress of losing a job. Just because one event happens before another does not establish a cause-and-effect relationship.

EXERCISE 1 Critical Thinking and Cause and Effect

Read each statement and evaluate how effectively the writer uses critical think-ing to identify a cause-and-effect relationship. Write C for a clear cause, X for a time relationship or coincidence, and P for a possible cause-and-effect relationship.

1. __X__ I flunked my math exam. I should have known something bad was going to happen today. I saw a black cat this morning.

2. __P__ SAT scores at our school have increased steadily. It must be because we opened a new library and computer lab two years ago.

3. __P__ Reading and math scores dropped greatly after 9/11 in the New York schools. Clearly the shock of the terrorist attack traumatized children, affecting their ability to concentrate.

4. __P__ Mayor Jackson should be reelected. Violent crime dropped 25% during her first term.

5. __X__ I've been having transmission trouble ever since I moved to Florida. The heat must be bad for my car.

6. __P__ Sarah's grandmother had a stroke last week. It must have been caused by those hormone shots her doctor gave her. She never had high blood pressure before.

7. __P__ Reports of sexual assault have increased in the last ten years. It must be caused by the easy availability of pornography on the Internet.

8. __P__ Movie attendance has dropped 8% this year. High ticket prices are clearly to blame.

9. __P__ Most of the girls who got pregnant in my high school dated football players. Boys who play sports are more sexually active and less responsible than other boys.

10. __C__ Losses from theft have decreased since we beefed up security. The visibility of guards is likely to be the cause.

EXERCISE 2 Identifying Causes

Read the following paragraph, then answer the questions that follow.

We can expect oil prices to increase over the next decade. First, oil reserves are steadily dwindling. As oil producers have to use more expensive technology to locate oil and bring it to the surface, it will cost more. Production will be hampered because of political instability in Iraq. Russia has large oil fields, but its pipelines are decayed and will take years to replace in order to develop an efficient delivery system. Second, demand is rising sharply throughout the world. India and China are booming. They are increasing their industrial production, and hundreds of millions of their citizens are becoming consumers. China, for example, has seen a surge in two-car families, something that was almost unheard of just ten years ago. With a growing demand for a limited amount of oil, petroleum prices will definitely rise.

1. What is the topic sentence?

2. What are the causes? Restate them in your own words:

a. _____

b. _____

c. _____

d. _____

e. _____

EXERCISE 3 Identifying Effects

Read the following paragraph, then answer the questions that follow.

The likely increase in oil prices will have dramatic effects on the economy, consumer behavior, and scientific research. First, we can expect higher fuel prices will drive up the cost of living. Almost everything that is sold in this country is shipped by truck. Airfares and bus tickets will likely rise to pay for the higher cost of fuel. Housing prices will rise because roof shingles and plastic pipes are made from petroleum. Rising gas prices will lessen demand for SUVs and spark interest in smaller, more fuel-efficient cars. Hybrid cars will no doubt increase in sales. Interest in alternative sources of energy, ranging from wind to nuclear, will increase as well. Rising transportation costs will lead businesspeople to use video conferences and e-mail to reduce the need for face-to-face meetings. Rather than fly across the country to attend conventions, more professionals may prefer to participate online. Rising oil prices will cause inflation and unemployment. As consumers have to spend more on gas and heating oil, they will have less money to spend on other goods and services. These economic problems will cause greater pressure on Congress to fund research to find new energy sources.

1. What is the topic sentence?

2. What are the effects? Restate them in your own words:

a. _____

b. _____

c. _____

d. _____

e. _____

EXAM SKILLS

Examination questions often call for cause-and-effect answers. Given the time limit of most exams, it is important to identify key causes or effects. Because any answer you give will likely be incomplete, you can qualify your answer with a strong introduction or conclusion.

From *Introduction to Literature*

Why does Willy Loman commit suicide at the end of *Death of a Salesman?*

introduction, rejects other possible causes	*Many readers assume that Willy Loman commits suicide because he is depressed over losing his job. Willy <u>is</u> a defeated and angry man, but he does not kill himself out of despair. Willy is not facing an economic crisis. His house is paid off, and his*
topic sentence	*friend Charlie offers to give him a job. <u>Instead, Willy Loman views taking his life not as an escape from his problems but a victory over them.</u> Willy imagines he will have a massive funeral that will*
cause #1	*finally prove to his son Biff that he was well-known and respected. In addition, he plans to leave his insurance money to*
cause #2	*Biff. With this money, Biff, who has been making a dollar an hour as a farm hand, will finally become a success. For Willy, suicide is not an act of desperation but his last big business deal that will prove to everyone that he was right all along.*

Student Paragraphs

Cause Paragraph

Our football team had another disappointing season. We remain a campus joke. Of course, a technical college does not draw serious players. The gifted high school players are recruited by the state universities and Big Ten schools with generous athletic programs. We do have good players. We do have a good coach. But we have a hard time fielding an effective team for two main reasons. First, most of our players are older men with jobs and families. They may love the game, but it cannot be a priority in their lives like it is for a teenager on an athletic scholarship. Second, all of our players live off campus. We don't have team housing or have players who can walk across the street between classes to hit the weight room. Some of our players have to commute fifty miles to practice and arrive tired and stressed out. We are never likely to have a winning season, but we play for one reason. We play because we love the game.

Effect Paragraph

Learning I had hypertension last May, I decided to begin exercising. I joined a health club, which I visit three times a week, and I take a morning run every day. This routine was tough at first. But after two months, I lost fifteen pounds and became firmer. I also found that my concentration and energy improved. I no longer needed a nap after I came home from work to stay awake in night school. It took me less time to complete assignments, and I remembered more of what I read. The main effect of my exercise program has been a more positive attitude. I feel more optimistic, more enthusiastic about doing new things, and more confident about my future. I no longer feel overwhelmed and no longer take comfort in junk food.

Cause-and-Effect Paragraph

In the last decade, infection has become a serious problem in our nation's hospitals. In some institutions, one-third of patients leave the hospital with an infection they did not have when they were admitted. There are many causes, but the most important two are the rise in drug-resistant germs and poor hand-washing habits. Some studies show that only 10% of doctors follow the approved sanitation standards. As a result, thousands of people die needlessly, and tens of thousands require longer hospitalization and expensive drugs to recuperate. The proper use of soap and water can shorten hospital stays, reduce complications, and save billions of dollars annually.

PUTTING PARAGRAPHS TOGETHER

Going Condo

Since 2000 over 3500 new condominium units have been completed downtown. Another 850 are under construction. Most cost an average of $500,000. The top floor units in Cathedral Square Towers range from 1.2 to 1.3 million dollars. Despite these prices, many of these new condo towers are sold out before the buildings are finished. <u>These condos are reshaping downtown and changing the lifestyle of the city.</u>

introduction

topic sentence

1. What is the purpose of this paragraph?
2. What factual details does it contain?

topic sentence

causes

supporting details

    <u>There is a high demand for expensive condos downtown because they meet the needs of affluent home buyers.</u> "Empty nesters" are selling their suburban houses to move to the city to avoid the long commutes and yard work. In addition, retirees who take long trips and business travelers have fewer worries about break-ins because condos provide 24-hour security. The condos are also in high demand by young professionals who like living downtown because they enjoy being able to walk to nightclubs, sporting events, theaters, and restaurants. They also like the condos because they feature pools, health clubs, dry cleaning services, and hair salons that save them time running errands, and sometimes eliminate the need for a couple to have a second car or even own a car at all. The growing number of people who work at home appreciate the condos with business centers that provide copiers, mailboxes, and FedEx services.

> 1. What causes does the paragraph describe?
> 2. How does this paragraph build upon the first one?
> 3. What is the purpose of this paragraph?

topic sentence

effects

details

    <u>The influx of upper-income residents to downtown is causing a business revival.</u> No longer does downtown empty after five o'clock when the office workers head home to the suburbs. With thousands of upper-income residents living downtown, there is a stable customer base for a variety of profitable shops and services. In the last year, eighteen new stores opened on Michigan Avenue. The new Metro Market, an upscale supermarket featuring gourmet and health foods, is highly successful and created 150 jobs. Piano bars, jazz clubs, and a Hard Rock Café on Water Street have helped hotels and the new convention center attract tourists.

> 1. How does this paragraph build upon the previous one?
> 2. What effects does it list?

conclusion

topic sentence

details

    <u>In just five years the rapid rise of condos has reversed the fifty-year trend of professionals living in the suburbs and taking the freeway to work downtown.</u> The growth of upper-income residents increases the city's tax base, providing more revenue for police and fire services, public transportation, and the school system.

> 1. What is the purpose of this paragraph?
> 2. How does it relate to the previous paragraphs?
> 3. What details does it include?

STEPS TO WRITING A CAUSE-AND-EFFECT PARAGRAPH

1. Study your topic and use critical thinking by asking key questions:

Am I going to explain causes or effects or both?

What is the most important cause or effect I want readers to know?

Are there any terms I need to define?

Do readers need any background information?

What evidence such as facts, examples, or quotes can support my ideas?

2. Develop a topic sentence that clearly states your controlling idea.

3. Review your list of causes or effects and delete minor or confusing details. Organize your ideas by time or by order of importance.

4. Write a draft of your paragraph.

5. Read your paragraph aloud and consider these questions:

Does my paragraph have a clear topic sentence?

Are causes or effects clearly stated and supported by facts, examples, and other evidence?

Is the paragraph clearly organized?

Selecting Topics

Consider the following topics for cause-and-effect paragraphs. Explain the causes of one of these topics:

low voter turnout

racism

student cheating

popularity of a TV show

the breakup of a band

popularity of a fad

Write a paper measuring the effects of one of the following topics:

unemployment

a death in the family

living away from home

having a baby

cost of health-care insurance

binge drinking

EXERCISE 4 Planning and Writing Cause-and-Effect Paragraphs

Select a topic from one of the previous lists or choose one of your own. Develop a topic sentence that states your point of view.

Topic: _____

Causes or effects:

1. _____

2. _____

3. _____

4. _____

First sentence: topic sentence, first cause or effect, or introductory statement:

_____

_____

Causes or effects:

1. _____

2. _____

3. _____

4. _____

Last sentence: final cause or effect, concluding statement, or topic sentence:

_____

_____

Write out your paragraph and review it by reading it aloud.

WORKING TOGETHER

Working with a group of students, revise this e-mail to shorten and clarify directions. You may wish to create numbered points.

Dorm Resident Advisors:

Security guards have again reported that students are breaking the rules regarding the underground parking garage in the dorms. Remember that under no circumstances are students allowed to store gasoline cans or other flammable products in the garage. Several students with motorcycles have been placing cans of gas in their parking spaces or on homemade tool benches. Also parking spaces must be kept clear. They are getting cluttered with spare tires and toolboxes. In addition, remind students not to work on their cars in the garage, especially to change tires using jacks or to change oil. Students are not allowed to wash cars in the garage. The hose is for maintenance use only. Remind students that for insurance reasons we cannot have students working on cars in the garage. Also it is a fire hazard to have gasoline stored in cans in an underground garage. Please make sure you

inform all students of these rules, which are listed
in the student handbook.

Cindy Rosales

GET THINKING
AND WRITING

CRITICAL THINKING

What effects have cell and camera phones had on society? Have they improved communications, making our jobs and lives better and easier? Or have they robbed us of privacy and created a new source of annoyance in theaters, restaurants, and other public places? Write a paragraph outlining the positive and/or negative effects of cell and camera phones. Support your points with examples.

WHAT HAVE YOU WRITTEN?

Read your paragraph carefully.

Write out your topic sentence or controlling idea:

_____

_____

List the effects you identify:

_____

_____

_____

- Are they significant effects? Can you think of more important ones?
- Could you place them in a different order to make your paragraph stronger and easier to read?

GET WRITING

© Peter Blakely/CORBIS SABA

What is the effect of panhandling? How do people respond when they see people begging on the streets? Can it drive away tourists and customers from local businesses? Does it anger some people? How should public officials respond to public panhandling? Do you see a difference between people asking for help and those who aggressively demand money?

Write a paragraph describing the effects panhandling has on the public and a community.

WRITING ON THE WEB

Using a search engine such as Yahoo!, Google, or AltaVista, enter terms such as *writing cause and effect, cause-and-effect essays, organizing cause-and-effect essays,* and *critical thinking and cause and effect.*

1. Search for news articles using cause and effect to examine issues like terrorism, global warming, unemployment, tax cuts, or a recent controversy in your area.
2. Write an e-mail to a friend using cause and effect to explain a decision you have made or give reasons for a problem.

POINTS TO REMEMBER

1. Cause-and-effect paragraphs need clear topic sentences.
2. Cause-and-effect paragraphs depend on critical thinking and evidence. Readers will expect you to prove your points.
3. Qualify your comments and acknowledge alternative interpretations.
4. Peer review can help detect mistakes in critical thinking like hasty generalizations or confusing time relationships for cause and effect.

Writer's Resources Now™   If you use Writer's ResourcesNow, please have your students log in and view the pretest, study plan, and posttest for this chapter.

Developing Paragraphs Using Argument

© Reuters./CORBIS

Hijacker Mohammed Atta passes through airport security, September 11, 2001

What can be done to protect our nation from terrorists? The 9/11 hijackers were able to enter the country, obtain driver's licenses, take flying lessons, and board planes with weapons.

Write a paragraph arguing how to increase our security.

What Is Argument?

Argument paragraphs are designed to convince readers to accept an idea, adopt a solution, change their opinions, or take action. Writers use reason and facts to support their arguments, often disproving or disputing conflicting theories or alternative proposals. Attorneys prepare written arguments stating why a client has a valid claim or deserves a new trial. Scientists present the results of experiments to argue for new medical treatments or question current practices. Economists collect data to support arguments to raise or lower interest rates. As a student, you develop arguments in essays and research papers to demonstrate your skills and knowledge. In your career you will have to impress clients, motivate employees, justify decisions, defend actions, and propose new ideas with well-stated arguments.

To write effective argument paragraphs, it is important to understand what an argument is *not*. First, the word *argument* does not mean a fight. Calling people names, using stereotypes, making accusations, and using facts taken out of context is not likely to be convincing.

> Alderman Angel Sanchez's plan to build a light-rail system downtown is totally insane. Only an idiot would suggest spending over $500 million to build a streetcar line. They ripped out the streetcar tracks almost a hundred years ago when they invented buses. Evidently Sanchez does not realize we already have public transportation. It is called the bus line. Maybe he could look out the window of his city limo and notice the lines of people waiting for the bus on every corner. How about spending maybe $5 or $15 million to buy a few more buses and save us all a lot of trouble? Sanchez must be on the take from the contractors bidding on the biggest waste of city money in history.
>
> *Letter to the Editor*

Effective argument is based on reason and is respectful in order to change readers' viewpoints without alienating them.

Improved

Alderman Angel Sanchez has proposed spending $500 million to build a streetcar line to reduce downtown congestion. Construction would take three years and disrupt traffic on major intersections just when the city is trying to attract major conventions to the expanded Civic Center and new Hyatt Hotel. The city already operates a highly effective bus system that carries over 25,000 riders downtown every day. We can achieve much of Alderman Sanchez's goals by simply spending $5 or $15 million on more buses.

GET WRITING ▶ ## WHAT ARE YOU TRYING TO SAY?

Write a paragraph that uses argument to state your opinion on one of the following topics. You may narrow the topic to focus on a key point. Make sure you have a strongly stated topic sentence and give readers reasons to accept your point of view.

- why a school policy should or should not be changed
- why drivers should always wear seat belts

- why illegal aliens should or should not be given driver's licenses
- why women should or should not be required to register for the draft
- why everyone should know his or her cholesterol and blood pressure
- why high schools should or should not teach sex education
- why a recent film, band, or television show is under- or overrated
- why a choice in roommate can affect your success in college
- why the state should or should not limit the number of hours high school students work

WHAT HAVE YOU WRITTEN?

Read your paragraph carefully.
What is the topic sentence or controlling idea?

_____

_____

Can you rewrite it to make it more precise or convincing?
What examples, reasons, evidence, or observations do you include to support your topic sentence?

1. _____

2. _____

3. _____

4. _____

Do these items directly support your topic sentence? Should any be deleted or revised?
Can you think of better types of support?

Critical Thinking for Writing Argument Paragraphs

Argument paragraphs require clearly stated topic sentences. Your goal is not to simply provide information or express your feelings but to direct readers to accept a specific point of view, take a particular action, or become aware of a problem or situation.

The college must increase security in the student union to curb the rash of recent purse snatchings.

Students should support the history department's demand for expanded computer lab and library hours during exam weeks.

The city must invest in new roads, sewers, and water lines if it wants to expand.

TIPS FOR WRITING TOPIC SENTENCES FOR ARGUMENT PARAGRAPHS

1. State your argument precisely; avoid vague generalized statements.

Vague
They should do something about all this trash on campus.

Improved
The maintenance department should clean the campus by removing litter and installing more trash cans.

2. Avoid emotional or inflammatory language.

Emotional
These sick child molesters should be shot on the spot.

Improved
People convicted of multiple sexual assaults against children should be given the maximum sentence the law allows.

3. Create topic sentences that can be supported with specific facts, examples, statistics, and other evidence.

The automotive services program is outdated and needs new equipment to train students to work on hybrid engines.

Topic sentences must be supported with evidence.

Facts are objective details that can be directly observed or collected from reliable sources. A student arguing for more campus security can use police reports to document an increase in thefts, assaults, and break-ins.

Testimony (quotations) are observations or statements made by witnesses, participants, or experts. A student arguing against violent video games could quote a concerned parent or a psychologist.

Examples are specific persons, events, or situations that illustrate a writer's point. The need for a traffic light could be demonstrated with examples of recent accidents.

Statistics are facts expressed in numbers. An argument to create additional sections of a course can be supported with numbers of filled classes, waiting lists, and requests for overenrollment.

TIPS FOR USING EVIDENCE

It is important to use evidence that is effective. In writing and revising an argument paragraph, ask yourself the following questions about the support you include.

1. **Is the evidence accurate?** Can you verify that the facts, statistics, and quotations you present are correct? Have facts or statements been taken out of context so their meaning has been distorted?

2. **Are the sources reliable?** Did you collect information from objective sources such as encyclopedias, recognized authorities, government

agencies, and professional journals, or did it come from gossip magazines, personal websites, or special interest groups?

3. **Does the evidence suit your topic sentence?** An argument for a change in immigration policy or tax laws requires factual or statistical support, not merely quotes from individuals stating personal opinions.

4. **Do you provide evidence your readers will understand and accept?** Quotations from unknown people or facts taken from obscure magazines may lack authority. Statements by real estate developers may not impress environmentalists.

EXERCISE 1 Identifying Topic Sentences and Supporting Evidence

Read the following student paragraph and answer the questions that follow.

Last year, President Neiman told the school paper "we must dramatically increase our enrollment or face severe cuts in state funding." He approved a $150,000 increase in television, radio, and print advertising to attract new students. To spare enrolling students from standing in endless lines, the school promoted its touchtone and online system. In theory, students can avoid a trip downtown and register by phone or online from home 24 hours a day. In reality, nearly one-third of students who registered off campus never appeared on official college rosters. Many were mailed packets of forms that arrived too late to sign up for needed courses. Twenty-six nursing students who received e-mail confirmations discovered they were never actually registered in clinical programs and had to delay graduation. The registrar claims that in-person registration is the only reliable way of signing up for classes. This is an unacceptable attitude in a technical college. Every method of registration must be equally reliable or should not be offered. The college must overhaul its obsolete registration software if it wants to serve its students, project a good image to the community, and achieve President Neiman's enrollment goals.

1. **What is the student's topic sentence?**

   _____

   _____

2. **How does the student demonstrate the need for his or her position?**

   _____

3. **What evidence does the student provide to support the topic sentence?**

   _____

   _____

   _____

   _____

4. **What additional evidence might be included to support the student's position?**

   _____

   _____

   _____

   _____

5. How does the student use the evidence to support his or her point of view?

_____

_____

6. How does the college president's quotation support the student's argument?

_____

_____

EXERCISE 2 Developing Evidence to Support Topic Sentences

Describe the evidence needed to support each of the following topic sentences.

1. **The college should offer more sections of remedial math and English.**

_____

_____

_____

_____

2. **Auto insurance must be made mandatory for all drivers in this state.**

_____

_____

_____

_____

3. **The stadium should stop beer sales after halftime.**

_____

_____

_____

_____

4. **Parents must limit their children's consumption of junk food.**

_____

_____

_____

_____

EXERCISE 3 Evaluating Evidence

To provide effective support, the evidence you present must be accurate, be reliable, and meaningfully relate to your topic sentence. Read each topic sentence carefully and rate the value of the supporting evidence.

1. *The campus fire alarm system must be repaired.* Last month classes were disrupted six times by false alarms while a fire in the chemistry building failed to trigger the sprinkler system.

   Type of evidence: _____

   Value of evidence:

   Very reliable _____ Reliable _____ Somewhat reliable _____ Unreliable _____

   Comments or suggestions for additional evidence:

   _____

   _____

   _____

2. *Smoking is harmless.* Churchill smoked cigars and lived to be ninety. My eighty-year-old grandfather smokes two packs a day and is in great shape.

   Type of evidence: _____

   Value of evidence:

   Very reliable _____ Reliable _____ Somewhat reliable _____ Unreliable _____

   Comments or suggestions for additional evidence:

   _____

   _____

   _____

3. *The government should approve plans to build a nuclear power plant on the Boyle River.* The president of Southern Power and Light says we need the electricity.

   Type of evidence: _____

   Value of evidence:

   Very reliable _____ Reliable _____ Somewhat reliable _____ Unreliable _____

   Comments or suggestions for additional evidence:

   _____

   _____

   _____

4. *The college needs additional parking.* Last year 72% of students polled complained about the lack of parking. Of 85 complaints sent to Student Services this semester, 39 concerned parking.

   Type of evidence: _____

   Value of evidence:

   Very reliable _____ Reliable _____ Somewhat reliable _____ Unreliable _____

   Comments or suggestions for additional evidence:

   _____

   _____

   _____

Understanding Your Audience

Whenever you write, you need to consider your readers. This is especially true when you write an argument. In description or narration, you are simply sharing ideas and experiences with readers. In argument, you are asking people to change the way they think or behave. To be effective, you have to target your argument to address your readers' concerns, feelings, knowledge, values, and attitudes. An argument to lower the drinking age to eighteen targeted to college students may not convince their parents, state legislators, or law enforcement professionals. They may not be impressed by student polls or quotations from eighteen-year-olds insisting they are mature enough to drink responsibly. On the other hand, they might be influenced by evidence supplied by psychologists, government reports, research studies, and statistics from experts in alcohol abuse. Above all, it is important to address readers' potential objections to your ideas.

Appealing to Hostile Readers

Perhaps the most challenging problem you can face is trying to convince a hostile audience to accept your ideas—readers you know or expect will have negative attitudes about you, the organization you represent, or the ideas you advocate. There is no way to magically make people change their beliefs and feelings, but there are techniques you can use to influence readers to consider your point of view.

TIPS FOR ADDRESSING HOSTILE READERS

1. **Openly admit differences.** Instead of trying to pretend no conflict exists, frankly state that your view may differ from that of your readers.
2. **Responsibly summarize opposing viewpoints.** By fairly restating your opponents' views, you are more likely to lead readers to agree with you and demonstrate objectivity.
3. **Avoid judgmental statements.** Don't label people with differing views with hostile or negative language. Use neutral terms to make distinctions. If you call your views "right" and your readers' "wrong," you will have trouble getting people to accept your ideas because in the process they will have to accept your insults as valid. Demeaning language will only alienate your audience.
4. **Respect reader's concerns and objections.** Don't dismiss readers' concerns as being wrong, uninformed, or stupid. If people object to building low-income housing in their neighborhood because they are concerned about crime and congestion, acknowledge and address their issues directly. Don't dismiss their objections by calling them racist or narrow minded.
5. **Ask readers to maintain an open mind.** Don't demand or expect to convert readers, but keep in mind that almost everyone will agree to try to be open minded and receptive to new ideas.
6. **Overcome negative stereotypes.** Determine what negative stereotypes your readers might have about you, the organization you represent, or your thesis. Include examples, references, evidence, and stories in your paper to counter these negative impressions.

EXERCISE 4 Overcoming Readers' Objections

Describe how the writers in the following situations could approach readers to overcome their objections. What facts, statistics, quotations, or other evidence would they need to provide to convince readers to accept their point of view? What objections would they have to address?

1. **A student group writing to alumni football fans to suggest they donate to building a new library rather than a new stadium.**

   Strategy _____

   _____

   Evidence _____

   _____

2. **A tenant urging a profit-minded landlord to spend money on security measures like a lobby camera and deadbolt locks.**

   Strategy _____

   _____

   Evidence _____

   _____

3. **An administrator of the Food and Drug Administration writing an e-mail to AIDS patients about why a new drug requires further testing before it can be approved for use in humans, even those who are terminally ill.**

   Strategy _____

   _____

   Evidence _____

   _____

4. **A student organization responding to complaints from students, parents, and the public that defends their decision to invite a controversial person to speak on campus.**

   Strategy _____

   _____

   Evidence _____

   _____

5. **The government explaining to drivers why gas taxes need to be increased to cut consumption and fund research in alternative fuels.**

   Strategy _____

   _____

   Evidence _____

   _____

EXAM SKILLS

Examination questions often call for argument paragraphs. Given the time limit of most exams, it is important to develop a clearly defined topic sentence that expresses your point of view and support it with reliable evidence. If needed, you may have to address common objections to your views.

From *Fire Science*

What is the most important way fire professionals can educate the public about fire safety?

introduction	*Many fire departments have programs to educate the public about smoke alarms, but they do little to explain the reasons why. Unlike fire professionals, most of the public has no direct*
common	*experience and little knowledge about the dynamics of fires.*
misconception	*From watching TV and movies, people have a tremendous fear of being burned in fires but little understanding how deadly smoke*
topic sentence	*is. Fire professionals must educate the public to appreciate that the true killer in most fires is smoke, not flame, in order to*
example	*prevent needless death and injury. For example, in a Chicago hotel fire in 2004, 180 people were overcome by smoke inhalation. They remained in the smoky lobby because they saw no flames*
statistics	*and felt safe. According to a survey of homeowners, only 15% knew that plastics and other building materials release poison-*
testimony	*ous chemicals when burned. Smoke killed more people than fire at the World Trade Center in 2001 according to Fire Chief Andrews. The best public service fire professionals can provide is to educate the public about the fact that when rescuers pull out burned bodies from a fire, most of the victims were killed by smoke long before flames ever touched them.*

Student Paragraphs

Argument to Accept an Idea

I only found out about the programs offered by the state's technical college system by accident. I found a website listing programs I never knew existed. Like most people, I thought people went to community college to learn to be an auto mechanic or a welder. I had no idea these colleges offered computer programming, accounting, banking and finance, business law, and travel and tourism. My high school counselor, the school's Career Week, and parent/teacher conferences only mentioned the state university system. The technical colleges now offer college transfer courses, many of which are taught by PhDs with professional experience. The same introductory courses at the university are taught by teaching assistants working on master's degrees. The tuition at a technical college is a fraction of that at the university. Unfortunately, most people only learn about the technical college by word of mouth. We have to realize that higher education is not limited to universities and that technical schools have a lot to offer.

Argument to Take Action

The U.S. Congress must address rising health-care costs not only for those without insurance but for the companies that provide it. Our corporations must compete in a global economy, and rising health-care costs are inflating the cost of doing business in this country. In 2004, for example, Ford and GM paid $9 billion on health care. These costs are reflected in the sticker price of their cars, making it harder for them to compete with imports. Politicians who worry about the 40 million Americans without health insurance have to think about the companies that have to pay billions to insure their workers. High health-care costs are making it harder for American companies to keep their prices down and is a major reason many are trying to lower their insurance costs by sending jobs overseas. Write your congressman and senators and demand they take action!

Argument to Arouse Interest

Teasing and gossip have always been a part of high school life. The Internet has given teens a new way of harassing and persecuting unpopular students. In Cincinnati, several girls started a blog that posted rumors, unflattering pictures, and obscene jokes about a student they dubbed Patty the Pig. The overweight girl was stalked in hallways by students using camera phones to take pictures of her eating or trying to squeeze into a chair. Her parents transferred her to a private school. On her first day she found a Patty the Pig cartoon taped to her locker. The school changed her e-mail address after she was bombarded with Patty the Pig jokes sent from as far away as Texas and Toronto. Gossip and taunts that once had a limited audience are now spread worldwide. The anonymity of the Internet encourages teens to be vicious while concealing their identity. Schools teach driver safety, and many have dress codes. Today they must teach Internet ethics and develop a code of online conduct.

PUTTING PARAGRAPHS TOGETHER

Credit Card Responsibility

introduction

quotation

Last year Chancellor Andros told the state senate that the goal of the university system is not to "simply teach skills so our graduates can compete in a global economy but prepare them for life." Among the "life skills" he mentioned was "learning how to be responsible in an era of temptation." This is a lesson the university must learn itself, especially when it comes to issuing credit cards. <u>The university must take greater responsibility in issuing credit cards to students and educating them as consumers.</u>

topic sentence

1. What is the purpose of this paragraph?
2. What role do the quotations play?
3. How does the student use the quotations to set up the topic sentence?

factual support

In 1999 the school made a deal with Bank Central to issue credit cards. The cards feature a picture of the stadium, and 3% of all charges goes to support the athletic program. At first, the cards were sent to alumni, which generated over $100,000 for the college. In 2002 the school decided to push these cards on students. Every incoming freshman gets a glossy application. Posters urging students to get a card line every corridor and dorm elevator. Ads in the college paper show students using their cards to buy not just books, but pizzas, DVDs, spring break trips, and pitchers of beer (even though only 22% of students are of legal drinking age). <u>The college is now not only encouraging reckless spending but profiting from it.</u> The ads boast of the 7% introductory rate but do not explain that after three months the rates on unpaid balances of $500 or more jump to 18%-21%.

topic sentence

1. What is the purpose of this paragraph?
2. How does it build upon the first paragraph?
3. What evidence does the student use to support the topic sentence?

statistics

quotation

The student crisis center that was created twenty years ago to counsel students about drugs and alcohol now reports that 40% of the calls for help regard financial problems. Half the students seeking help with their expenses have college credit cards. Last semester the crisis center handled 87 students with maxed-out cards and 16 who had filed for bankruptcy. According to Carol Chang, the center director, "Most of the

students had no idea how much interest they were paying." <u>The college has taken steps to protect students</u>
<u>from drugs and binge drinking but is blind to its role</u>
<u>in allowing students to use credit irresponsibly.</u>

topic sentence

1. How does this paragraph build upon the preceding one?
2. How does this paragraph help develop the student's argument?
3. What evidence does the student provide?

    If the college is to really teach students "life
lessons," it should educate them in the proper use of
credit cards, especially when it makes a profit from
them. Bank One has a 45-minute video and a website
that fully explains how credit works and how students
can create an online budget to make them informed consumers. <u>The college should integrate this free credit</u>
<u>awareness program into the freshman orientation *before*</u>
<u>encouraging them to apply for college credit cards.</u>

argument

topic sentence

1. How does this paragraph relate to the first paragraph?
2. What evidence does the student include?
3. How does the final topic sentence bring the argument to an end?
4. How does it depend on the previous paragraphs?

STEPS TO WRITING AN ARGUMENT PARAGRAPH

1. Determine the goal of your argument—to convince readers to accept an idea or motivate them to take action.
2. Consider your readers' existing knowledge, attitudes, and possible objections to your views.
3. Develop a precisely worded topic sentence that expresses a point of view that can be supported by logic and evidence.
4. Support your topic sentence with evidence that is accurate, reliable, and addresses your readers' needs, interests, and objections.
5. Avoid alienating readers by using inflammatory language or making emotional claims that cannot be supported with evidence.
6. Write a draft of your paragraph.
7. Read your paragraph aloud and ask yourself these questions:

   Have I developed a clearly worded topic sentence that accurately expresses my point of view?

   Do I provide enough evidence that is reliable and that readers will understand and accept?

   Do I avoid using questionable evidence or emotional statements that may alienate readers?

   Is my topic sentence placed in the best position in the paragraph? Should it come first or only after some explanation and supporting evidence?

Selecting Topics

First, select topics that you can handle. The word *argument* leads many students to think that they have to write about controversial or political issues like abortion, gun control, or the death penalty. But you can convince readers to exercise, support a change in a local law, recycle trash, wear seat belts, register to vote, or sign a petition to urge legislation to solve a social problem.

Second, consider your readers' attitudes and possible objections.

Third, develop a well-stated topic sentence and list the type of evidence needed. You may wish to conduct some library research or search the Internet for facts, statistics, examples, and expert testimony.

Consider these topics for argument paragraphs:

school uniforms

global warming

labor unions

speed dating

teenage fashion

pension plans

personal responsibility for health and fitness

cell phones in high school

violent video games and children

companies that hire illegal immigrants

campus daycare services

health-care costs

bilingual education

your company's pension plan

EXERCISE 5 Planning and Writing Argument Paragraphs

Select a topic from the preceding list or choose one of your own. Develop a topic sentence that states your point of view, addresses reader concerns, and lists supporting details.

Topic: _____

Topic sentence: _____

_____

Readers' concerns or possible objections: _____

_____

First sentence: introductory fact, topic sentence, or example:

_____

Supporting evidence: facts, quotations, statistics, or examples:

_____

_____

Last sentence: final detail, topic sentence, or concluding remark: _____

Write out your paragraph and review it by reading it out loud.

WORKING TOGETHER

Working with a group of students, revise the following e-mail asking small business owners to support the Junior Entrepreneur Program by inventing support such as quotations, facts, statistics, and examples.

Dear Ms. Sandoval:

As a Northside business owner and employer, you know the value of hard work and discipline, especially in our young people. Please consider donating this month to the Junior Entrepreneur Program. It is a good program. It helps high school students learn by running their own businesses. The students learn a lot. They work hard. Many famous people support it. It is a good idea to let students learn how to run a business. It is popular with students, but the program needs your support. Please donate generously by calling 1-800-555-9700 today. We really need your support.

CRITICAL THINKING

GET THINKING AND WRITING

Select a problem you see in your community, college, or workplace. State a clear topic sentence that convinces readers to accept your point of view or motivates them to take action. Support your topic sentence with relevant evidence such as facts, examples, statistics, or quotations.

WHAT HAVE YOU WRITTEN?

Read your paragraph carefully. Write out your topic sentence or controlling idea:

_____

Does it clearly express your point of view or direct readers to take specific actions? Could it be revised to make it clearer and more precise?

List the main supporting details:

_____

- Is this evidence relevant? Does it directly support your topic sentence?
- Is the evidence accurate and reliable? Are you relying on memory or something you saw on TV? Can you recall the source of the support?
- Do you address objections readers might have?
- Can you think of additional evidence?

If possible, conduct an Internet search to locate additional support.

GET WRITING

In April 1942, four months after the attack on Pearl Harbor, Japanese-Americans, many of them born in the United States, were placed in internment camps. Many were forced to sell their businesses and houses at a great loss. Recognizing the unfairness of this action, Congress granted each survivor $20,000 in compensation in 1988.

Japanese-Americans being searched in California, 1942

Write a paragraph arguing how the government can fight terrorism without engaging in racial profiling, discrimination, or civil rights violations.

WRITING ON THE WEB

Using a search engine like Yahoo!, Google, or AltaVista, enter terms like *writing argument, analyzing readers, argument essays, developing arguments, using evidence, reader objections,* or *hostile audiences.*

1. Search for online editorials about controversial issues and examine how writers developed topic sentences, used evidence, and addressed reader objections.
2. Write an e-mail to a friend using argument to express your point of view on a current issue.

POINTS TO REMEMBER

1. Argument paragraphs convince readers to accept an idea or motivate them to take action.
2. Argument paragraphs need clearly stated topic sentences.
3. Topic sentences must be supported with facts, examples, statistics, and quotations.
4. Readers' concerns, needs, and possible objections to your point of view must be addressed.
5. Arguments are not fights but logical assertions. Avoid inflammatory statements, insults, or emotional claims that cannot be supported with facts.
6. Peer review can help refine your topic sentence, examine the quality of evidence and suggest additional support, and identify possible reader objections.

If you use Writer's ResourcesNow, please have your students log in and view the pretest, study plan, and posttest for this chapter.   **Writer's Resources ⓦ Now**™

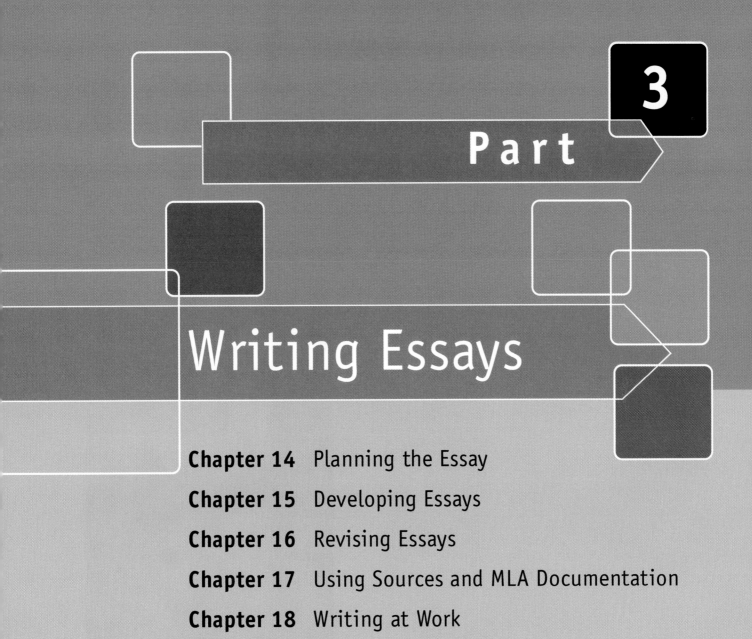

Part 3

Writing Essays

Planning the Essay

Winona Ryder enters court to face theft charges, 2002

GET WRITING

In recent years several celebrities have been charged with crimes. Do you think actors, professional athletes, and pop stars are more likely to commit crimes than other people, or do they simply attract more media attention?

Write one or more paragraphs stating your views about celebrities, crime, and the media.

What Is an Essay?

Throughout your college career you will be assigned essays or essay examinations. To develop effective essays, it is important to first know what an essay is *not*.

An essay is <u>not</u> just a collection of paragraphs.

An essay is <u>not</u> a list of everything you know about a subject.

An essay does <u>not</u> simply provide facts or ideas "about" a topic.

An essay is a multiparagraph composition that has a clear focus and a defined purpose. Formal essays inform or persuade readers to understand an issue or accept a point of view. Informal essays share a writer's personal feelings, thoughts, or experiences. Whether written to inform, entertain, motivate, or express an opinion, essays must have a clear goal, address a specific subject, and logically organize supporting details.

The Thesis Statement

The most important part of any essay is the **thesis** or main idea. Just as the topic sentence expresses the controlling idea of a paragraph, a **thesis statement** explains the controlling idea of an essay. The thesis statement presents the writer's position and serves as the essay's mission statement. A thesis is not simply a narrowed topic — a thesis expresses a point of view. It is a declaration of purpose.

Topic	Narrowed Topic	Thesis Statement
TV shows	quiz shows	Quiz shows remain popular because they allow viewers to match wits with contestants.
being a smart consumer	using credit cards wisely	Credit cards should be used for emergencies and purchases of necessities, not meals, fashion items, or impulse purposes.
public schools	charter schools	Charter schools need accurate methods to measure student performance.

ELEMENTS OF A THESIS STATEMENT

Effective thesis statements share common elements.

- *The thesis statement forms the core of the essay.* It states the writer's most important idea.
- *Thesis statements are usually stated in a single sentence.* Most writers create a single sentence to summarize their main idea.
- *Thesis statements help limit the topic.* Part of the job of a thesis statement is to focus the topic. The thesis statement "Speed dating is an effective way for busy professionals to meet each other" expresses a point of view and narrows the essay to a single method of meeting new people.
- *Thesis statements organize supporting details.* The thesis statement "Running burns calories, exercises the heart, and reduces stress" suggests the essay will be divided into three parts.
- *Thesis statements indicate the kind of support that follows.* The thesis statement "The airport must be expanded to reduce congestion" implies a cause-and-effect argument based on factual details. The thesis statement "The loneliness of road sales led me to choose a job where I could work with people" suggests an essay expressing personal observations and experiences.

EXERCISE 1 Developing a Thesis Statement

Narrow the topic and develop a thesis statement for each of the following subjects. Remember that your thesis should express a point of view and not simply narrow the topic.

1. Used cars

Narrowed topic: _____

Thesis statement: _____

_____

2. Daycare

Narrowed topic: _____

Thesis statement: _____

_____

3. Quitting smoking

Narrowed topic: _____

Thesis statement: _____

_____

4. Student loans

Narrowed topic: _____

Thesis statement: _____

_____

5. Immigration

Narrowed topic: _____

Thesis statement: _____

_____

Organizing Essays

Essays generally consist of three main parts:

title and introduction

body

conclusion

Each part is important in developing an effective essay.

The Title and Introduction

The Title

Titles play a vital role in creating effective essays. A strong title announces what the essay is about, attracts attention, can express a thesis, and prepares readers to accept your ideas. Don't think you have to decide on a title right away. As you write, you may discover an interesting word or phrase that captures the essence of your essay and can serve as an effective title.

Writers use a variety of titles.

Labels announce what the essay is about:

Education Reform in Ohio
Campus Daycare

Thesis statements declare a point of view:

We Must Stop Child Abuse
Racial Profiling Does Not Prevent Terrorism

NOTE: Even if presented in the title, thesis statements should always appear in the main text of the essay.

Questions arouse reader interest and create suspense because the writer's thesis is not expressed:

Should We Lower the Drinking Age?
Is Nuclear Terrorism a Realistic Threat?

Creative phrases generate curiosity:

Dodging the Audit Bullet
Facelifts and Mine Fields

The title you select should match your purpose, audience, and context. Creative titles and questions should be avoided in research papers and formal business reports but can be very effective to generate attention for personal essays.

The Introduction

The introduction should make a strong, clear statement that arouses the readers' attention and prepares them for the details that follow. Avoid weak introductions that serve as titles, only announcing the topic.

Weak

This paper is about identity theft. People are being victimized by this growing problem.

Open with a Thesis Statement

Consumers must protect themselves to avoid becoming one of the growing numbers of victims of identity theft.

Open with a Fact or Statistic

In 2005 more than 10,000 Americans were unable to get mortgages because their credit histories had been ruined by identity theft.

Open with a Quotation

Speaking before Congress last month, Ivan Bettelheim, president of the American Banking Association, stated, "Identity theft is the greatest threat to our financial system."

Open with a Short Example or Narrative

Tameka Jackson thought the bank made an error when her rent check bounced. She soon discovered $6,000 had been deducted from her checking account and that all her credit cards were maxed out.

The Body

The paragraphs that make up the body or main part of the essay contain details — facts, observations, personal experiences, statistics, quotations — that support the thesis statement. Just as all the sentences in a paragraph should relate to the topic sentence, all the paragraphs in an essay should support the thesis statement.

The body paragraphs may be organized by one or more patterns of development. An essay describing your first apartment, for instance, might contain a paragraph comparing living at home with living on your own and another using cause and effect to explain your reasons for moving out.

The body should present paragraphs in a logical way so readers can follow your train of thought. There are three common methods of organizing details: by time, parts, or importance.

Organize by Time

Essays can be organized as a chain of events. A formal essay could discuss the Internet by explaining its rapid growth in its first ten years. An informal essay about your sister could discuss your relationship from early childhood to the present. An essay in a history class might examine the rise of terrorism from the 1980s to the present. A psychology paper can trace the effects of a mental illness by telling the story of a single patient.

- Readers find essays organized as narratives or stories easy to follow.
- Important events in an essay can be highlighted with flashbacks and flashforwards. An essay about high school might open with your graduation,

then flash back to explain the challenges you had to overcome and flash forward to college.

Organize by Parts

The supporting details of an essay can be organized by grouping them into parts or subdivisions. An essay about professional athletes might discuss football, baseball, and basketball players. An essay analyzing job opportunities could be organized by region, industry, or starting salaries. A personal essay might classify three kinds of employees you have worked with.

- Complex issues are easier to explain part by part.
- Organizing an essay in parts helps people follow your train of thought step by step, letting them pause to understand details before moving on to the next section.

Organize by Importance

If you think some ideas or details are more significant than others, you can arrange them by order of importance. Because reader attention is greatest at the beginning and end of an essay, you should open or close your essay with your most important ideas.

- You can start with a minor point and move on to more important ideas, then end the essay with your most significant point to create a dramatic conclusion.
- You can also open with your most significant point to get your readers' attention, then follow it with additional supporting details.
- Avoid placing your most important ideas in the middle of the essay where readers may overlook them.

The Conclusion

The conclusion of an essay should state a memorable fact, final thought, or observation, pose a question, or call for action. In a short essay, there is little need to repeat or summarize what readers have just read.

Weak
    In conclusion, identity theft is a growing problem in America.

Conclude with a Significant Fact or Statistic Readers Will Remember
    Unless steps are taken to curb identity theft, it is estimated that by 2010 one in four Americans will become a victim.

End with a Meaningful Quotation
    Congress must address the problem of identity theft to prevent what Senator Harris predicts could become "the greatest threat to the economy since the savings and loan crisis of the 1980s."

Pose a Final Question
    If identity theft continues, will anyone feel safe buying anything online anymore?

End with a Call to Action
    To fight this problem, consumers must take steps by calling their Congressmen, demanding greater security from their credit card companies, and insisting courts treat perpetrators as criminals rather than hackers.

EXERCISE 2 Evaluating the Essay

Underline the thesis statement twice and each topic sentence once in the following essay, then answer the questions that follow it.

introduction

I played football in high school. I spent most of my time on the bench. I never scored a touchdown or made a play anyone will ever remember. But it changed the rest of my life. Football taught me discipline, teamwork, and maturity.

body paragraph

Until my father urged me to play football, I was disorganized and lazy. I got C's in school, spent my free time lying on the couch watching TV, and never exercised. Once on the team, however, I had to show up at practice on time and be prepared to work. The drills were tough and left me sore and exhausted. The coach put us all on a rigid schedule, which forced me to structure my time and give up TV. I stopped eating junk food and began working out at home. Football taught me how to take charge of my life and use my time and energy to accomplish goals.

body paragraph

Football made me appreciate the importance of working with others. I had been pretty much a loner before playing sports. In drills, in practice games, and on the field I learned how important it was to connect with others. We got to the point that we could communicate with a hand signal or a number and work together like a well-oiled machine. Making plays depended on each of us knowing his part. We began to think like a group and worked to keep each other motivated when someone got hurt or frustrated with a bad play.

body paragraph

Perhaps the most important thing football did was help turn me into an adult. I had always been an impulsive and emotional person. I used to blow up at minor insults or get depressed and withdrawn when something disappointed me. I played in many tough games. We often lost. In September I would throw my helmet on the ground, curse, or slam a locker door. By December, when the season ended, I had learned to control my emotions, accept my limits, recognize the strengths of others without jealousy, and take responsibility for my actions.

conclusion

Parents and teachers often criticize high school sports for stressing athletics over academics and giving teenagers false hopes of turning pro. I was a terrible football player, but football made me a better student, equipped me for the rigors of college, and prepared me for the tough decisions that come with adult life.

1. State the thesis in your own words.

_____

_____

2. What points does the student make in the introduction?

_____

_____

3. What is the main idea of the second paragraph?

_____

_____

4. What is the main idea of the third paragraph?

_____

_____

5. What is the main idea of the fourth paragraph?

_____

_____

6. What is the most important point of the conclusion?

_____

_____

Putting It All Together: Developing an Outline

The word *outline* may remind you of elaborate diagrams using Roman numerals and capital letters. These formal outlines, however, are often created as table of contents for readers to follow after something has been written. They differ from *working outlines* writers use to plan an essay and guide a first draft. Taking a few minutes to create an outline, even a rough sketch, can organize your thoughts and save you time once you start writing.

```
            Preparing for a Job Interview

Intro—Valuable tips lead to success

Par #1- Preparation
            learning about company
            reviewing past
            dry runs

Par #2 Interview
            do's and don'ts
            attitudes
            tough questions
            questions to ask

Par #3 Thank-You letter
            what to say
            what to add

Conclusion—What to do if you don't get the job
```

Topic Sentence Outlines

Topic sentence outlines are useful planning tools because they clearly establish the controlling idea of each paragraph in the essay. By writing out the thesis statement and each topic sentence before beginning to write, you establish a clear blueprint to guide the first draft.

```
            Preparing for a Job Interview

Intro/Thesis      Job applicants can improve their
                  chances of success through prepara-
                  tion, honesty, and persistence.

Par #1            Applicants should research employers,
                  rehearse for interviews, and conduct
                  a dry run to build confidence.

Par #2            Maintaining a positive attitude and
                  demonstrating genuine interest in the
```

employer as well as the job are essential to making you stand out from
other applicants.

Par #3   Although often overlooked, the thank-
                          you letter is critical to securing a
                          job offer.

Conclusion   Don't become discouraged if you don't
                          get the job.

Having written out the thesis and topic sentences, you can complete the essay by adding details to support each topic sentence.

Preparing for a Job Interview

Job applicants can improve their chances of success through preparation, honesty, and persistence.
Many talented people fail to get hired because they
make common interview errors. They arrive late, are
disorganized, appear selfish or defensive, and often
show little interest in the employer's goals or problems. Following these simple tips can help improve
your chances of getting a job.
   Applicants should research employers, rehearse for
interviews, and conduct a dry run to build confidence.
Learn as much as you can about the company you are
going to interview with. Search the Internet for
information about the company's history, products,
problems, goals, and organization. Rehearse what you
want to stress about your skills, experience, and education. Think of three or four key accomplishments you
can explain in detail. Consider making a dry run of
the interview. Make sure you know how to get to the employer's office, where to park, and what to wear. Visit
the employer a few days before, if you can, to become
familiar with the environment. The more you know about
the location, the more confident you will feel.
   Maintaining a positive attitude and demonstrating
genuine interest in the employer as well as the job
are essential in helping you stand out from other
applicants. A job interview is a sales presentation.
Don't simply discuss your skills and experience but
suggest how they can benefit the employer. Avoid being
boastful or defensive. Answer questions directly and
honestly. If you lack a skill or do not know the answer to a question, admit your lack of knowledge but
point out situations in the past that demonstrate
your ability to learn quickly. Don't focus only on the
job but show interest in the employer by asking about

the company's overall aims and current challenges. Demonstrate how your background or interests will help the company achieve its goals.

<u>Although often overlooked, the thank-you letter is critical to securing a job offer.</u> As soon as you leave the interview, plan a letter or e-mail. Thank the interviewer for taking time to meet you and stress why you believe you can benefit the company. Include any details you forgot to mention during the interview. Less than 10% of applicants send a thank-you letter, so even a brief note will make you memorable.

<u>Don't become discouraged if you don't get the job.</u> Don't allow yourself to become angry, disappointed, or depressed if a seemingly successful interview does not lead to a job offer. The job may have been filled by a transfer or promotion. The fact that you were not hired does not mean that you may not be hired in the future. Send a letter or e-mail to the employer reminding them of your skills and suggest you are willing to consider other positions. Call the employer and ask for suggestions about finding other jobs. Use this person as a contact to find other job openings you may not know about. If you don't get the job, at least use the interview to learn something.

POINT TO REMEMBER

Outlines should guide the first draft. As you write, however, new ideas may come to you. You may discover that your essay needs to be expanded or realize that you are attempting to address too many ideas in a single essay. Be willing to make changes to your outline to improve the focus of your essay. Review the assignment and your goals to make sure any changes or additions you make will improve your paper.

EXERCISE 3 Developing an Outline

Select a topic from the following list or develop one of your own and prewrite for a few minutes to develop ideas. Organize your ideas on the following form.

how high school students should prepare for college
reasons why you admire or dislike someone
the reasons you decided to attend this college
why men and women have different attitudes about relationships, marriage, or dating
two types of bosses, employees, or customers

your prediction for a sports team's success or failure next season

your worst day in the last month

a person you worry about

the hardest thing about quitting smoking, losing weight, saving money, or
   studying for exams

Topic/title _____

Introduction and thesis _____

_____

_____

Topic sentence for supporting paragraph _____

_____

_____

Topic sentence for supporting paragraph _____

_____

_____

Topic sentence for supporting paragraph _____

_____

_____

Conclusion _____

_____

WORKING TOGETHER

*Work with a small group of students and exchange outlines.
Make copies so each person can make notes. Discuss what you
want to say and ask if they think your outline makes sense. Does
your introduction arouse attention and state a clear thesis? Do the paragraphs
in the body directly support the thesis? Are they arranged in a logical order?
Does the conclusion make a final, memorable point or just repeat the introduction?*

GET THINKING
AND WRITING

CRITICAL THINKING

*If you saw a coworker stealing from your employer, would you tell your boss, confront
the employee, or look the other way?*

   *Write two or more paragraphs explaining the actions you would take. Would your
actions depend on the value of the property taken, the person involved, or the type of
job you had?*

WHAT HAVE YOU WRITTEN?

Read your paragraphs carefully. Do you clearly explain the action you would take and why?

- How effective is your opening sentence? Does it engage readers or simply announce what you are writing about?
- How do you organize your main ideas? Do you use paragraphs to signal transitions or shifts in your train of thought?
- Do all the sentences in the paragraph support the paragraph's controlling idea? Do all the paragraphs support the thesis?
- How do you end your final paragraph? Does it simply repeat what you have written or does it make a final memorable point?

© Michael Tweed/Reuters/Corbis

Robert Blake speaks to the press after being acquitted of murder, 2005

GET WRITING

Do juries treat celebrities differently? Do you think a jury would find it hard to convict a popular movie star of a serious crime? Do people excuse acts committed by celebrities they might condemn in others?

Prewrite for a few minutes to develop ideas, then create an outline to guide a short essay of three or four paragraphs. After writing a draft, review your outline. Could your plan have been easier to follow? Could it have helped organize your ideas better or save time?

WRITING ON THE WEB

Using a search engine such as Yahoo!, Google, or AltaVista, enter terms such as *writing essays, types of outlines,* and *planning essays* to locate current sites of interest.

1. Read news articles online and notice how writers develop introductions, create conclusions, and use paragraphs to organize their ideas.
2. Write a multiparagraph e-mail to a friend. Make sure your message has a clear introduction and conclusion.

POINTS TO REMEMBER

1. An essay states a main idea supported by related paragraphs that provide details.
2. Essays consist of three parts:

Title and introduction:	Grabs attention
	Announces the topic
	Addresses reader concerns
	Prepares readers for what follows
	States a clear thesis or main idea
The body:	Organizes paragraphs in a clear, logical pattern
The conclusion:	Ends with a brief summary, final thought or observation, question, call for action, or prediction

3. Essays often use different types of paragraphs — comparison, example, narration, cause and effect, and description — to support a thesis.
4. In writing essays, consider your readers in presenting ideas, selecting details, and choosing words.

Writer's Resources ⊕ Now™   If you use Writer's ResourcesNow, please have your students log in and view the pretest, study plan, and posttest for this chapter.

Developing Essays

© LWA-Stephen Welstead/CORBIS

Television commercials advertise prescription drugs that promise to cure depression, reduce anxiety, improve sexual performance, and eliminate the effects of aging. Do these ads send the wrong message to the public? Do they suggest a pill can magically reverse years of poor health habits? Do they attack the cause of disease or just mask their symptoms?

Write one or more paragraphs stating your view of the way prescription drugs are advertised. Do they inform or mislead the public?

How Do Writers Develop Essays?

College assignments and business documents often call for specific kinds of writing. An essay for an English course might *compare* two short stories, a psychology exam might ask students to *define* a mental illness, and an e-mail from the sales department might demand *causes* for delays in shipping. Chapters 5–13 show how to develop paragraphs using the *modes* or *patterns* of development. These same methods can be used to develop whole documents, such as essays, research papers, business letters, and reports. These patterns of development, however, are more than just ways of organizing material. They refer to your main purpose of writing—the goal of your essay.

The type of pattern you choose depends on what you are trying to say.

Description—Presents facts, observations, and impressions about persons, places, objects, or ideas. It records what you see, hear, feel, taste, and touch.

Narration—Tells stories or relates a series of events, usually in chronological order.

Example—Illustrates ideas, issues, events, or personality types by describing one or more specific events, objects, or people.

Definition—Explains or limits the meaning of a word or idea.

Comparison and contrast—Examines similarities and differences.

Division/classification—Separates a subject into parts or measures subjects on a scale.

Process—Explains how something occurs or provides step-by-step instructions to accomplish a specific task.

Cause and effect—Explains reasons and results.

Argument—Directs readers to accept a point of view or take action.

POINT TO REMEMBER

The type of essay you choose expresses your main purpose. Not all paragraphs in a narrative essay will contain narration. Not all paragraphs in a definition essay will include definitions. You will probably use various types of paragraphs to achieve your goal. In writing a *process* essay that explains a diet, you might first *describe* the risks of being overweight, *define* terms like "carbohydrate" and "cholesterol," and conclude the essay with *examples* of people who lost weight and try to *persuade* readers to do the same.

Description

Description presents facts, observations, and impressions about persons, places, objects, or ideas. It records what you see, hear, feel, taste, and touch.

The goal of a description essay is to explain a subject to readers by providing meaningful details. These details can be objective facts or the writer's subjective or personal impressions. Good descriptions bring people, places, and things to life by highlighting interesting details and creating dominant impressions.

STEPS TO WRITING A DESCRIPTION ESSAY

Planning

1. *Determine your purpose.* Is your goal to provide readers with facts or personal impressions? What do you want readers to know about your subject?
2. *Consider your readers.* What type of description best suits your audience? Are you writing a personal essay for an English class or an objective description for a business or technical course?
3. *Narrow your topic.* It is easier to develop interesting facts and details about one aspect of Central Park than attempt to describe New York City in a two-page essay.
4. *Select key details.* Avoid minor facts like dates, addresses, or people's height or ages, unless they are important for readers to know.
5. *Organize details in a clear pattern.* Consider using comparison, narration, or process paragraphs to arrange ideas.

Writing the First Draft

1. *Create dominant impressions.* Good descriptions do not simply list details but create an overall picture of a topic.
2. *"Show" rather than "tell."* Descriptions can be brought to life by using short narratives or examples to show people and objects in action.
3. *Include dialogue to add action to descriptions of people.* Letting people speak in their own words is an effective way of revealing their education, attitudes, and personalities.

Revising— Questions to Ask about a Description Essay

1. Does my essay have a thesis or controlling idea, or is it only a loose collection of facts and observations?
2. Do I create dominant impressions supported by interesting and accurate details?
3. Are there details that should be deleted because they are repetitive or off topic?
4. Are details clearly arranged so readers can follow my train of thought?
5. Can I add action or dialogue to bring life to my description?
6. Does my essay tell readers what I want them to know?

My Bug

My father was in first grade when my Bug rolled off an assembly line in West Germany thirty-eight years ago. I have no idea what its original color was, but it has gone from gray to rust to black during my time. My '69 VW is not just a car but a family artifact. — thesis / introduction

My grandfather bought it in May 1969 as a second car for his wife. She drove it along the Jersey shore selling real estate for six years. The car followed the family west to San Francisco in 1975. My uncle then got the car and drove it to college in New Mexico. After graduating and getting a new car, he gave it to — narration: family history of car

my dad who was just learning to drive. By now the car bore the tattoos of college bumper stickers, bent fenders, and rusted chrome. My dad had the car painted a light cream color and invested in new tires. During a ski trip his freshman year, the Bug skidded off an icy mountain road in Colorado and rolled over. He had the dents pounded out and the car painted gray. It took my parents on their honeymoon. Two years later the battered Bug carried me home from the hospital. After my parents bought a van, the Bug was relegated to being a backup vehicle. When my mom got a new car, the Bug was retired to the garage.

description: details about car

Now it is mine. The fenders, though repainted, still bear the shallow depressions from the Colorado rollover. The windshield is pitted from stones that flew off a a speeding gravel truck that nearly ran me off the road in Nevada last year. The door handles are replacements I found on eBay. The car seats are patched with tape. Rust holes in the floorboards have been covered with cookie sheets. The dashboard sports the compass my mother glued on ten years ago so she would not get lost taking me to soccer games. The glove compartment is jammed with rumpled maps and snapshots from three decades of family vacations and road trips.

conclusion

My Bug is not the most glamorous vehicle in the college parking lot, but it has to be the most loved. It looks like a rolling homeless shelter to many. But to me it is a moving family album. I love every ding and dent.

Understanding Meaning: What Is the Writer Trying to Say?

1. Can you state the student's thesis in your own words?

   _____

   _____

2. What is the student's dominant impression about the car? Does it support the thesis?

   _____

   _____

3. What details does the student select to support the dominant impression?

   _____

   _____

Evaluating Strategy: How Does the Writer Say It?

1. Which details are subjective and which are objective?

Subjective	Objective
_____	_____
_____	_____
_____	_____
_____	_____

2. How does the student use narrations to develop the description of the car? What do these stories add?

3. How does the student organize the description? How effective are the introduction and conclusion?

4. How does the student organize the body of the essay?

Appreciating Language: What Words Does the Writer Use?

1. Which words most effectively describe the car?

2. How would you describe the student's tone and style?

WORKING TOGETHER

Working with a group of students, discuss this essay and consider how you might improve it.

1. What are the essay's strong points?

2. What are the essay's weak points?

_____

_____

3. How would you revise this essay? What other information do you wish the student had added? Are there details that could be deleted? Would you rearrange or rewrite any of the paragraphs? Can you think of a more effective introduction or conclusion?

_____

_____

4. List your group's primary suggestion or a question you wish you could ask the writer.

_____

_____

GET WRITING ▶

WRITING ACTIVITY

Write a descriptive essay about one of the following topics or one your instructor suggests. Remember to build dominant impressions and include details to support your points. You may use contrast, narrative, or other methods of development to create your essay.

your first car
your room
a favorite possession
a fashion, behavior, or social
　trend you disapprove of
best or worst actor or singer
a favorite store, café, or park

a recent date
the most interesting building you
　have seen recently
best or worst neighborhood in town
most interesting person on campus
a student clique in high school
your dream home

Narration

Narration tells stories or relates a series of events, usually in chronological order.

The goal of a narration essay is to tell a story. It could relate a personal experience and highlight your thoughts and feelings or present an accurate and objective narrative of a historical event or scientific experiment. Narration essays can be written in first person ("I") or third person ("they"). As a writer, you can be the main character relating everything from your point of view or an objective reporter of events.

STEPS TO WRITING A NARRATION ESSAY

Planning

1. *Define the purpose of your narrative.* What is the point of your narrative? What do you want your readers to understand about your story?
2. *Consider your readers.* How much background information or definitions do you need to supply so readers can appreciate the significance of your narrative?
3. *Limit the scope of your narrative.* Your job in writing a narrative essay is not to recall everything that happened. If you try to describe everything that happened the day your grandmother died, for example, you might create a superficial list of events. You could, however, create a moving narrative by focusing on a single incident that occurred that day, such as greeting a mourning relative or making a difficult phone call.
4. *Select key details.* Avoid minor facts, like dates and addresses, unless they provide information readers need to know.
5. *Create a clear time pattern to organize events and details.*

Writing the First Draft

1. *Use transitional statements to show the passage of time and advance the narrative.* Phrases like "an hour later" or "the next day" help readers follow the timeline and understand the flow of events.
2. *Add dialogue to advance the narrative.* If people exchange words in your narrative, consider using direct quotations rather than summaries. Direct quotes express what people really said, revealing their attitudes, personalities, and moods.
3. *Avoid awkward shifts in tense.* Keep the narrative in past or present tense unless there is a clear change in time.

   Awkward
   I drive all night and got to Miami by noon.

   Improved
   I drove all night and got to Miami by noon.

Revising— Questions to Ask about a Narration Essay

1. Does my narration have a thesis or controlling idea, or is it only a list of events?
2. Do I spend too much time on minor incidents or fail to develop important events?
3. Am I trying to cover too much in an essay? Should I narrow the focus of the narrative?
4. Are there details that can be deleted because they are repetitive or off topic?
5. Are events clearly arranged so readers can follow my train of thought?
6. Can I add action or dialogue to bring life to my narration?
7. Does my narration create the impact I want?

Law and Order and Me

When I got a summer intern job working for a television show, I could not believe my luck. I was just out of high school and had sent in a résumé almost as a joke. But a production assistant called me back,   **introduction** and soon I was working for the hit series *Law and Order.*

description:
expectations

Learning that I would be helping the location manager, I visualized myself standing behind the cameras watching actors, stuntmen, and directors at work. I imagined the stars arriving in limos, signing autographs for tourists, and nodding at me as one of the crew.

contrast:
realities

The reality was very different. My job was to help scout and set up locations. Most of the time I held a tape measure or climbed ladders to measure ceilings for the manager who drove a battered Volvo station wagon full of secondhand tools. We spent our days checking out dumpy bars, cabstands, street corners, filthy tenement lobbies, and stuffy subway stations. We had to take measurements and set up diagrams so other crews knew what lighting equipment they would need and where to place the cameras.

narration

My summer dragged on. Every day I would squeeze into the battered Volvo with no air-conditioning and windows that couldn't open. We would rattle up to Harlem to look at a nightclub and wait for an hour for the manager to show up, only to realize his club was too classy to match the script's call for a seedy drug den. Then we would hit the second club on our list, a dingy dive in the Bronx that reeked of stale beer and bug killer. But that club wouldn't work either, so we moved on to check the third spot, a grimy tavern on Second Avenue. The next day we might be scouting a warehouse or a landfill. Later in the week I would be pacing off spots on a rooftop parking lot in 98° heat and putting down X's in masking tape.

conclusion

After a few weeks something began to bother me. I had seen enough episodes of *Law and Order* to know many of the scenes are shot in upscale clubs, art galleries, townhouses, office suites, and mansions. One day while eating our usual lunch of French fries and cheeseburgers, I asked my boss why we never visited those locations. "Oh," he said casually, "I let Lou stake out places like Tiffany's and Trump Tower. Those people expect you to dress nice, and I hate wearing ties. But Lou doesn't seem to mind."

Understanding Meaning: What Is the Writer Trying to Say?

1. What is the student's main point about the job?

_____

_____

2. How did the student's expectations contrast with the reality of the job?

_____

_____

3. What details does the student use to characterize the job?

_____

_____

4. The student does not provide a thesis statement for this narrative. Can you summarize the essay's main point in a sentence?

_____

_____

Evaluating Strategy: How Does the Writer Say It?

1. How does the student organize the essay and advance the narrative?

_____

_____

2. The student states that the reality of the job was different than what he or she expected, but the student never states what his or her feelings were. What words or details about the job suggest the student's attitude?

_____

_____

3. How effective is the conclusion? Is the dialogue effective?

_____

_____

Appreciating Language: What Words Does the Writer Use?

1. Circle the words that reflect the student's attitude about the job. What impressions do they create?

2. Do you find the tone and style of the essay effective?

_____

_____

WORKING TOGETHER

Working with a group of students, discuss this essay and consider how you might improve it.

1. What are the essay's strong points?

_____

_____

2. What are the essay's weak points?

_____

_____

3. How would you revise this essay? What other information do you wish the student had added? Are there details that could be deleted? Would you rearrange or rewrite any of the paragraphs? Can you think of a more effective introduction or conclusion? Would you add more dialogue?

_____

_____

4. List your group's primary suggestion or a question you wish you could ask the writer.

_____

_____

GET WRITING ▶ **WRITING ACTIVITY**

Write a narrative essay about one of the following topics or one your instructor suggests. Remember to use transitions and paragraph breaks to advance the narrative. You may use description, comparison, or other methods of development to create your narrative.

a job interview

a controversial event

story told by your parents or
    other relatives

an event that taught you a lesson

your first day at college

an event that changed someone's life

an emergency

plot of your favorite movie

biography of someone you admire

story behind making a tough decision

a historical event you think was
    important

Example

Example illustrates ideas, issues, events, or personality types by describing one or more specific events, objects, or people.

One way to explain a topic is to provide readers with specific items, events, or people they can recognize. You can explain that a verb is a *word that expresses action*, then illustrate it with examples—*run, buy, sell, build, drive.* The achievements of a movie director can be demonstrated by scenes from his or her films. Lawyers filing a discrimination claim will list examples of illegal actions. Students demanding greater campus security might use examples of recent crimes to support their views.

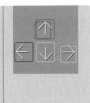

POINT TO REMEMBER

Examples differ from descriptions or narrations, which provide details about a single subject or tell one story. Examples represent something larger. The story of one coach could provide an example of a role model. The success of one business could illustrate an economic trend.

An example essay can tell a single story, describe a single person, or provide a number of examples. Examples can be real or hypothetical.

Real

The Internet has created a generation of female entrepreneurs. For example, Miranda Ocara started on online interior design service in her home that, in a single year, grew into a multimillion-dollar business with sixteen employees.

Hypothetical

The Internet has created a generation of female entrepreneurs. For example, imagine a housewife taking her knowledge of interior design and creating an online business selling her advice to homeowners all over the country.

STEPS TO WRITING AN EXAMPLE ESSAY

Planning

1. You can plan an example essay in two ways. Examine a specific person, situation, object, or event and explain how it illustrates something larger.
   - A power failure in your building illustrates our dependence on electric power.
   - A friend's dedication to a disabled child illustrates your concept of devotion.

   Select a topic and use one or more examples to illustrate it or provide evidence for your point of view.
   - You explain cyberstalking then provide one or more examples of victims.
   - You state that the college needs better student advising and support your views with examples of students being assigned the wrong classes or given the wrong schedules.
2. Consider your readers. Select examples your readers can relate to. Teenagers, for instance, may not understand historical examples from the Great Depression or World War II.
3. Determine if your essay would benefit from one extended example or a series of examples.
4. Develop a well-stated thesis statement that links the specific example with the general subject it illustrates.
5. Organize examples in a clear pattern. Consider using comparison, narration, or process paragraphs to arrange details.

Writing the First Draft

1. Create a strong thesis statement that explains the purpose of your essay and what the examples illustrate.

(continued)

2. Introduce examples with phrases such as "for example," "for instance," or "to illustrate."
3. Highlight the important details of examples and delete minor details that do not directly support your thesis such as dates, addresses, and physical descriptions of people.

Revising— Questions to Ask about an Example Essay

1. Does my essay include examples that illustrate a general idea or just describe specific subjects or tell isolated narratives?
2. Do I keep the examples in the same tense, tone, and voice? Do I shift from first to third person or past to present tense when there is no clear change in time?
3. Are there examples that can be deleted because they are repetitive or off topic?
4. Are examples clearly arranged so readers can follow my train of thought?
5. Do my examples tell readers what I want them to know?

Falling through the Cracks

introduction

narration

description

On Valentine's Day last year, Chris Day, a 58-year-old Vietnam veteran, froze to death in a cardboard box under Wacker Drive. He had been mentally ill for years and homeless for months. Day had been living in a Southside rooming house until neighbors, complaining about his disruptive behavior, demanded the landlord evict him. He was getting over a thousand dollars a month in Social Security disability and veterans benefits. His sister and mother sent him money every month. He had been visited by a social worker and was being treated at a veterans' hospital. Day stopped taking his medicine, lost or threw away the cell phone his mother gave him, and dropped out of sight.

transition

thesis

Some people think that a homeless veteran dying of exposure is a sign of an uncaring society. But I think Chris Day is an example of someone who falls through the cracks and gets lost despite the best efforts to help him. He received enough money from the government to afford a room and food. He was entitled to free medical care and received free medication. His family tried to help when he avoided social workers. But even his mother was unable to control him. He created arguments, played his boom box all night, and frightened his sister's small children. He refused or forgot to take his medication and repeatedly walked off, leaving hundreds of dollars stuffed in envelopes or old coffee cans.

transition

additional examples

Chris Day is just one of thousands of people who are not sick enough to be placed in a hospital against their will but not really able to live on their own. In Boston, a schizophrenic who lived in a halfway

house stopped taking his medication and fell or jumped
from a rooftop. Five homeless people froze to death
in 1999 on a single subzero night in Manhattan. One of
the victims, who had been sleeping in a doorway, had
three uncashed disability checks and a city hotel
voucher in her purse.

    It might sound cold to say these things happen.   conclusion
But even when people are willing to help, there are
those in need who just can't be reached.

Understanding Meaning: What Is the Writer Trying to Say?

1. State the student's thesis in your own words.

_____

_____

2. How do the examples illustrate the student's thesis?

_____

_____

3. How does the opening example illustrate the student's last line?

_____

_____

Evaluating Strategy: How Does the Writer Say It?

1. How effective is the opening example? Would you want to see more details about Chris Day?

_____

_____

2. How does the student use narration and description to develop an example essay?

_____

_____

3. Would the inclusion of facts, statistics, or quotations from experts strengthen this essay? Why or why not?

_____

_____

4. How does the student organize the essay? Are the introduction and conclusion effective?

_____

_____

Appreciating Language: What Words Does the Writer Use?

1. How would you describe the tone and style of this essay?

   _____

   _____

2. Do any words or phrases suggest the student is uncaring about the victims?

   _____

   _____

WORKING TOGETHER

Working with a group of students, discuss this essay and consider how you might improve it.

1. What are the essay's strong points?

   _____

   _____

2. What are the essay's weak points?

   _____

   _____

3. How would you revise this essay? What other information do you wish the student had added? Are there details that could be deleted? Would you re-arrange or rewrite any of the paragraphs? Can you think of a more effective introduction or conclusion?

   _____

   _____

4. List your group's primary suggestion or a question you wish you could ask the writer.

   _____

   _____

GET WRITING ▶ WRITING ACTIVITY

Write an essay using one or more examples to illustrate a point. Use one of the following topics or one suggested by your instructor. Remember that examples have to illustrate something or provide support for a point of view. Your examples can be real or hypothetical.

a role model   an environmental problem
the loss of privacy   racial profiling

the way women are portrayed   dangers posed by the Internet
    on television   job opportunities
terrorist threats   people's ability to overcome challenges
differences between men and women   bad habits

Definition

Definition explains or limits the meaning of a word or idea.

The goal of a definition essay is to establish meaning to prevent confusion or to influence the way readers interpret or understand a subject. A definition essay can take several forms.

- A *standard definition* explains a widely accepted understanding of a term or concept, much like an encyclopedia article.
- A *personal definition* expresses your individual interpretation of a subject, such as who is a "hero" or what you consider "child abuse."
- A *persuasive definition* influences readers to share your interpretation of a subject. You might suggest that violent video games be defined as "adult material" like pornography that should not be sold to anyone under eighteen or that drug addicts be seen as "victims of a disease" rather than criminals.
- An *invented definition* explains the meaning of a previously unnamed attitude, behavior, or situation that you have observed. You might define people who always seem to introduce singles to the wrong people as "toxic matchmakers" or call those who habitually gather at upscale coffee shops as "coffeeholics."

POINT TO REMEMBER

Definition is *not* description. Description provides details about one person, item, idea, or place. Definition provides details about a class or type of people, items, ideas, or places. A *description* essay might *describe* your uncle as being a cheapskate because he refuses to buy items he can easily afford. A *definition* essay, however, would *define* what a "cheapskate" is and use your uncle as an example.

STEPS TO WRITING A DEFINITION ESSAY

Planning

1. Determine your purpose. Is your goal to define a standard term, share a personal interpretation, persuade readers to accept your opinion, or create a new definition?
2. Develop a clear thesis statement summarizing your definition.
3. Consider your readers. How much do they know about the subject? Do you need to provide background information or define other terms for them to understand your essay? What is the best way to explain your definition? What examples would they be able to understand?

(continued)

4. Organize details in a clear pattern. Consider using comparison, narration, or process paragraphs to arrange ideas.

Writing the First Draft

1. Make sure you *define* and not just *describe* your topic. Remember your goal is to establish meaning about a general type not just list details about a single person, place, or thing.
2. Clear up misconceptions by explaining what your topic is not. If you write an essay defining "felonies," list crimes that are felonies, then also include examples of crimes that are not felonies.
3. Use comparisons, examples, and descriptions carefully. In establishing a definition, you can use comparisons, examples, and descriptions but be careful to point out exceptions to avoid misleading readers. In defining a computer virus, for example, you could compare it to a human infection. To be accurate, however, you would have to point out how an electronic virus is different from a human disease.

Revising— Questions to Ask about a Definition Essay

1. Does my essay have a clearly stated thesis statement summarizing my definition?
2. Do I use examples readers can understand?
3. Are there details that can be deleted because they are repetitive or off topic?
4. Are details clearly arranged so readers can follow my train of thought?
5. Does my essay tell readers what I want them to know?

Tsunami

introduction
and background

The 2004 tsunami that ravaged Southwest Asia killed 250,000 people and did billions of dollars of damage. It drew worldwide interest to this form of natural disaster. Massive destructive ocean waves were commonly called "tidal waves." But this term is misleading because these waves have nothing to do with the tides, which are controlled by the moon.

what a
tsunami is <u>not</u>

thesis stating
definition

Tsunamis are catastrophic waves caused by volcanic eruptions, landslides, or earthquakes under the ocean. Like a swimmer kicking his or her legs under the water in a pool, these underwater movements cause ripples that roll outward in concentric circles. Out at sea, tsunamis may travel over 400 miles an hour and move hundreds of miles outward in all directions. Because they are often less than three feet high, tsunami waves can pass under a ship without being noticed. As they reach land, however, tsunami waves become higher.

comparison

description

process

The first indication of a major series of tsunami waves is a sudden outrush of water. This is soon followed by the first large wave that covers the exposed beach and surges inland. Subsequent waves are often larger, forcing huge volumes of water onto the land, turning streets into rivers.

The amount of destruction tsunamis cause depends on their intensity and geography. Waves that crash against high cliffs may cause minimal damage. Similar waves striking low-level areas, however, can flood hundreds of square miles. Motion pictures often depict tsunamis as towering waves hundreds of feet high that crash down on shorelines. In reality, it is not the height of a single monster wave that causes destruction but the massive volume of water in a series of waves that pushes inland.

The death toll from tsunamis can be very high for a number of reasons. The waves can hit suddenly with little warning and can occur on a clear, sunny day. Floods caused by rainstorms give ample warning, allowing people to evacuate to higher ground. In addition, tsunamis are uncommon events. People do not always appreciate the impending danger. In 2004 many people on the beach stood and watched as the water rushed out to sea just before the first wave hit.

cause and effect

Given the terrible death toll caused by tsunamis in 2004, the international community must take steps to create warning systems in the Indian Ocean that would at least give a few hours notice of a coming disaster.

conclusion persuasion

Understanding Meaning: What Is the Writer Trying to Say?

1. Can you restate the student's definition in your own words?

2. Why is "tidal wave" an inaccurate term for tsunamis?

3. What creates tsunamis and why can they be so destructive?

Evaluating Strategy: How Does the Writer Say It?

1. How does the student use description, comparison, cause and effect, and process to develop a definition essay?

2. How does the student organize the essay?

_____

_____

3. How effective are the introduction and conclusion?

_____

_____

Appreciating Language: What Words Does the Writer Use?

1. Which words does the student use to express the force and power of tsunamis?

_____

_____

2. How would you describe the essay's tone and style?

_____

_____

WORKING TOGETHER

Working with a group of students, discuss this essay and consider how you might improve it.

1. What are the essay's strong points?

_____

_____

2. What are the essay's weak points?

_____

_____

3. How would you revise this essay? What other information do you wish the student had added? Are there details that could be deleted? Would you re-arrange or rewrite any of the paragraphs? Can you think of a more effective introduction or conclusion?

_____

_____

4. List your group's primary suggestion or a question you wish you could ask the writer.

_____

_____

Write a definition essay about one of the following topics or one suggested by your instructor. Remember that a definition essay does not describe a single subject but establishes details about a type. You may use example, narrative, comparison, or other methods of development to create your essay.

a best friend	stalking
a just society	an educated person
loyalty	wealth
responsibility	addiction
sportsmanship	a good relationship
road rage	sexism

Comparison and Contrast

Comparison and contrast examines similarities and differences.

The goal of a comparison-and-contrast essay is to point out the similarities and differences of two subjects. Your comparison essay can be informative, presenting a pair of descriptions or definitions, or persuasive, arguing that one subject is better than the other.

Because comparison essays deal with two subjects, they have to be carefully organized to prevent confusion. There are two standard patterns for organizing comparisons.

- *Subject by subject* divides the essay into two parts, fully describing the first subject, then showing how it differs from the second.
- *Point by point* divides the essay into a series of comparisons, discussing both subjects in each paragraph.

A comparison of two hotels, for example, could be organized either way.

Subject by Subject	Point by Point
Introduction	Introduction
Hyatt Hotel	Hotel size
1. Size	**1.** Hyatt Hotel
2. Location	**2.** Marriott Hotel
3. Banquet facilities	Hotel location
4. Convention facilities	**1.** Hyatt Hotel
5. Room rates	**2.** Marriott Hotel
Marriott Hotel	Banquet facilities
1. Size	**1.** Hyatt Hotel
2. Location	**2** Marriott Hotel
3. Banquet facilities	Convention facilities
4. Convention facilities	**1.** Hyatt Hotel
5. Room rates	**2.** Marriott Hotel
Conclusion	Room rates
	1. Hyatt Hotel
	2. Marriott Hotel
	Conclusion

STEPS TO WRITING A COMPARISON/CONTRAST ESSAY

Planning

1. Determine your purpose. Is your goal to explain similarities and differences or argue that one subject is better than the other?
2. Select key details about both subjects.
3. Determine the best way to organize your comparison—subject by subject or point by point.
4. Consider your readers. Define key terms and clear up any misconceptions your readers may have.

Writing the First Draft

1. Write clear, concise descriptions of both subjects.
2. Choose words carefully. Be aware how connotations can shape meaning. Make sure the words you use, whether positive or negative, reflect your meaning.
3. Use similar patterns to organize comparisons. Comparisons are easier to follow if you present facts or ideas in the same format.

   Nancy Adams is a 26-year-old lawyer from Maryland with two children who supports school vouchers. Her opponent, LaToya Green, is a 35-year-old sales manager from Delaware with one child who opposes vouchers.

4. Include a conclusion only if it adds new information or makes a final point. Your essay may not need a conclusion that simply summarizes what readers have just read.

Revising— Questions to Ask about a Comparison-and-Contrast Essay

1. Are my two topics clearly described or defined?
2. Do I devote sufficient attention to both subjects or is my essay lopsided, devoting eight paragraphs to one subject and two paragraphs to the other?
3. Is my essay easy to follow?
4. Are there details that can be deleted because they are repetitive or off topic?
5. Does my comparison essay tell readers what I want them to know?

Entrepreneurial and Family Businesses

introduction

Small businesses generate many of the entry-level jobs open to recent graduates. Entrepreneurial start-

thesis

ups and long-established family businesses both offer job seekers advantages and disadvantages, so it pays to understand how they operate. Choosing the right one can give you the career and lifestyle you seek. Choosing the wrong one can lead to constant frustration and often the need to quit and start over.

definition

Entrepreneurs are people who create a new business venture. By nature they are people with a dream. They are gamblers. They gamble that their product or service will beat the established competition. They gamble their own fortunes, their credit ratings, their

description

reputations, and their employees. They can be bold, intelligent, and inspiring. They can also be narrow-minded, selfish, and stubborn.

Working for an entrepreneur has many risks and potential rewards. If you are lucky, you may be getting in on the ground floor of a booming business and sharing in the company's growth and expansion. On the other hand, many new ventures fail, and you may find yourself looking for a job after the entrepreneur has gone bankrupt. Before working for anyone starting a new enterprise, make sure his or her business plan is realistic. Make sure your values match his or hers. In negotiating for a job, consider asking for potential shares as part of your salary. If you own stock, your boss will see you as more of a partner than an employee. If the company succeeds, a few shares of an initial stock offering could be worth several years salary.

advantages

disadvantages

process:
suggestions

Long-established family-owned businesses tend to offer greater stability. The advantage is that a family-owned business often has a greater chance of success. The partners are related and share a sense of responsibility for the company's success. They are more willing to invest personal capital or forgo a paycheck to help the business in tough times.

description

advantages

On the other hand, working for a family-owned business places you at a disadvantage. You will always be an outsider. You may find yourself working with or even supervising relatives who can easily go over your head because the boss is also their father or grandfather. Because they are accustomed to being treated as children rather than employees, they may expect special treatment.

disadvantages

It is not uncommon for workers to be fired in order to give a job to an unemployed family member. In negotiating for a job, ask if the company has promoted nonrelatives. Be honest about your concerns about working in a family-owned business.

process:
suggestions

In looking at any job opening, consider the merits of the organization and your long-term goals.

Understanding Meaning: What Is the Writer Trying to Say?

1. Can you restate the student's thesis in your own words?

_____

_____

2. What are the main advantages and disadvantages of working for an entrepreneur?

_____

_____

3. What are the main advantages and disadvantages of working for a long-established family business?

_____

_____

4. Based on what you have read, which business would better suit you when you graduate? Why?

_____

_____

Evaluating Strategy: How Does the Writer Say It?

1. How does the student use definition and description to establish the comparison?

_____

_____

2. How does the student organize the essay?

_____

_____

3. What evidence does the student provide to support the main points?

_____

_____

Appreciating Language: What Words Does the Writer Use?

1. How does the student define "entrepreneur"?

_____

_____

2. Do you detect any bias in words or phrases that suggest one form of small business is better than the other?

_____

_____

WORKING TOGETHER

Working with a group of students, discuss this essay and consider how you might improve it.

1. What are the essay's strong points?

_____

_____

2. What are the essay's weak points?

_____

_____

3. How would you revise this essay? What other information do you wish the student had added? Are there details that could be deleted? Would you re-arrange or rewrite any of the paragraphs? Can you think of a more effective introduction or conclusion?

_____

_____

4. List your group's primary suggestion or a question you wish you could ask the writer.

_____

_____

WRITING ACTIVITY

GET WRITING

Write a comparison or contrast essay about one of the following topics or one your instructor suggests. You can use either the subject-by-subject or point-by-point method to organize details. You may use the essay to explain differences or suggest that one topic is better than the other.

a difference between men and women
two sports teams
best and worst jobs
two friends
Republican and Democratic view of a
    problem or issue

high school and college
contrasting attitudes toward
    a recent controversy
best and worst bosses
buying vs. leasing cars
two popular TV shows

Division and Classification

Division and classification separates a subject into parts or measures subjects by a standard.

Division essays make complicated or abstract subjects easier to understand or work with by separating them into parts. You might write an essay about terrorism and use division to discuss different threats—biological, chemical, radiological, and hijacking; or causes—poverty, resentment of the West, and religious funda-mentalism. An essay about diets could discuss low-carbohydrate diets, low-calorie diets, and low-fat diets.

Classification essays rank subjects by one standard. You might classify terrorist risks from the most to least likely or most to least destructive. Diets could be classified by the most to least successful or most to least healthy. Remember to use a single standard to measure your subject and define each category or level clearly. You can write an essay classifying new cars by their price, their fuel efficiency, or their cost to insure. But you cannot write a classification essay that discusses expensive cars, fuel-efficient cars, and hard-to-insure cars.

STEPS TO WRITING A DIVISION OR CLASSIFICATION ESSAY

Planning

1. Determine your purpose. Is your goal to divide your subject into parts (division) or rank subjects on a scale (classification)?
2. Consider your readers. How much background information do your readers know? Are there terms you need to explain or define?
3. In writing division, establish clear types. Consider your division essay a series of short descriptions or definitions. Each item should be fully explained.
4. In writing classification, establish clear categories on a well-defined scale. Explain that you are ranking cars by those costing $20–30,000, $30–40,000, and $40–50,000 or students by those who do not work, those working part time, and those working full time.

Writing the First Draft

1. Develop a clear introduction explaining your purpose and method of division or classification.
2. Explain possible exceptions. If not all items can fit in the categories you establish, point this out to readers. Simply stating "most students belong to three types. . ." indicates that not all students fit your division or classification.
3. Explain possible changes. If it is possible for a person or situation to change over time and switch categories, point this out to readers. For example, a student classified as an "A student" might do poorly on midterms and slip into the "B student" category. A student earning A's in chemistry could receive C's in history.
4. Use examples to illustrate each type.

Revising— Questions to Ask about a Division and Classification Essay

1. Does my essay establish clear categories?
2. Is my thesis clearly stated?
3. Are there any categories that are not clearly defined or could be confused with others?
4. Are my categories clearly organized by paragraph breaks and transitional statements? Can readers follow my train of thought?
5. Do I explain possible exceptions?
6. Does my essay tell readers what I want them to know?

Blog America

introduction:
definition of
blogger

    America has become a nation of bloggers. Right now some eight million Americans blog. Some blog every day. Bloggers are people who use the Internet to share their thoughts, feelings, opinions, and experiences with the world. <u>Blogs, which come from the words "web logs," are as varied as the people who use the Internet, but four distinct types have emerged.</u>

thesis

type 1

    The cyber diary. Thousands of blogs record the thoughts, feelings, and experiences of ordinary people ranging from high school students writing about prom dates to desperate housewives detailing their latest sexual fantasy. Most go unread but some bloggers have developed fans who love to follow the lives of people like them. These blogs are a blend of reality TV and the age-old wish to read someone's diary. Most are boring, but some are witty and moving.

description

    The therapy room. For some, the blog has become an anonymous way of speaking out about some of the most troubling and devastating life situations. Blogs are maintained by parents of autistic children, addicts struggling to stay straight, battered women, downsized executives looking for work, or people with eating disorders. These blogs range from confessions to cries for help. Some become self-help networks, with readers posting responses, adding links to online resources, research, and professional help.

type 2

description

    The shadow media. Blogs have created a new form of media. Blogs are produced by amateur reporters, columnists, and researchers. An earthquake in California will generate dozens of blogs by eyewitnesses, scientists, and local reporters whose stories never made the papers. Blogs may contain more direct, accurate, and in-depth information than provided by mainstream media whose reporters are generalists limited to brief articles or sound bites. Bloggers are credited with generating major news stories and undoing the career of CBS anchor Dan Rather.

type 3

description

    The conspiracy web. Conspiracy theories are not new, but they used to be broadcast slowly by fringe publications and radio call-in shows. Now bloggers instantly respond to events, post videos and links, and broadcast to the world the latest theory about UFOs, 9/11, Iraq, global warming, or terrorism. The ability to link one fringe website to another can create an instant network of people trying to convince the world of their latest theory.

type 4

description

    Blogs are emerging all over the Middle East, creating an online democracy. As with the Internet itself, only time will tell whether blogs will be a major force shaping the politics, society, and art of the twenty-first century.

conclusion

Understanding Meaning: What Is the Writer Trying to Say?

    1. What is a blog?

_____

_____

2. What four types of blog does the student describe?

_____

_____

3. What social impact have bloggers made?

_____

_____

Evaluating Strategy: How Does the Writer Say It?

1. Which method does the student use to write about blogs—division or classification?

_____

_____

2. How does the student use description and definition to develop the essay?

_____

_____

3. What role do paragraph breaks play in organizing the essay?

_____

_____

Appreciating Language: What Words Does the Writer Use?

1. Why is it important for the student to explain "blog" and "blogger"? Are these terms clearly defined?

_____

_____

2. What do the tone, style, and word choice reveal about the student's intended readers?

_____

_____

WORKING TOGETHER

Working with a group of students, discuss this essay and consider how you might improve it.

1. What are the essay's strong points?

_____

_____

2. What are the essay's weak points?

_____

_____

3. How would you revise this essay? What other information do you wish the student had added? Are there details that could be deleted? Would you re-arrange or rewrite any of the paragraphs? Can you think of a more effective introduction or conclusion?

_____

_____

4. List your group's primary suggestion or a question you wish you could ask the writer.

_____

_____

WRITING ACTIVITY

GET WRITING

Write a division or classification essay about one of the following topics or one suggested by your instructor. Remember to clearly establish categories and provide examples to illustrate each type. You may use definition, comparison and contrast, or other methods of development to create your essay.

Division	Classification
Divide students by . . .	Classify students by . . .
ethnic background	grade point average
favorite sports	income level
majors	hours worked per week
Divide houses by . . .	Classify houses by . . .
style	price
homeowner	distance from downtown
landscaping	cost to insure
Divide TV shows by . . .	Classify TV shows by . . .
type (talk show, sitcom, soap opera)	ratings
appeal (entertainment, information)	amount of adult content
source (network, basic cable, premium channel)	education level of viewers

Process

Process explains how something occurs or provides step-by-step instructions to accomplish a specific task. The goal of a process essay is to explain how something occurs or instruct readers to accomplish a specific task.

Many textbooks use process to explain how the heart pumps blood, how a diesel engine works, how a bill becomes a law, how rising interest rates affect the economy, or how a disease affects the body.

Manuals, repair books, recipes, lab books, and first aid instructions use process to provide readers with step-by-step instructions to install software, change a tire, bake a cake, conduct an experiment, or treat a sprained ankle.

STEPS TO WRITING A PROCESS ESSAY

Planning

1. Determine your purpose. Is your goal to explain or instruct?
2. Consider your readers. Are you writing to the general public or people familiar with your subject? Do you need to provide background information or define important terms?
3. Separate the process into logical stages.
4. Consider using numbered steps, especially in giving instructions. Process essays do not have to be written in standard paragraphs. Numbered steps, paragraph breaks, and visual aids can help inform readers and make your ideas easier to follow.

Writing the First Draft

1. Create a clear introduction that announces the subject and explains your purpose.
2. Use transitional statements to advance the essay step-by-step. Statements like "after the bill passes the Senate" or "once you agree on the price" can help readers follow your train of thought.
3. Make sure instructions are self-contained. Directions should include all the information readers need to accomplish the task, not refer readers to another document to complete the process.
4. Give negative instructions. To prevent readers from making common mistakes, tell readers not only what they should do but what they should not do.
5. Provide complete instructions. Avoid vague directions. Readers should be given clear descriptions so they know when one stage ends and the next begins.

   Vague
   Place the cake in the oven at 300 degrees for 30 minutes or until it is done.

   Improved
   Place the cake in the oven at 300 degrees for 30 minutes or until the center is firm and the edges are golden brown. (Note: If the center remains soft, microwave for one minute).

6. Warn readers of any hazards to their health, safety, or property. If instructions direct people to use stoves, cleaning products, or machinery, alert them to any possible dangers.

Revising— Questions to Ask about a Process Essay

1. Does my essay clearly explain a process or provide clear instructions?
2. Would numbered steps make my essay easier to read?
3. Have I included all relevant information?
4. Have I warned readers of any possible dangers?
5. Are there details that can be deleted because they are repetitive or off topic?
6. Does my essay tell readers what I want them to know?

How to Protect Yourself against Identity Theft

My sister is very responsible with money. She was totally surprised right before the Fourth of July last year when her rent check bounced. She called her bank and found out that three thousand dollars had been deducted from her account. The bank corrected what she thought was just a computer error. But this was just the beginning. By the end of the summer, she found out someone was using her identity to buy cars, charge jewelry and plane tickets on credit cards she never applied for, and borrow ten thousand dollars from a loan company. My sister became one of the hundreds of thousands of people who become victims of identity theft. It has ruined her credit rating, cost her thousands in legal fees, and put her dream of buying a condo on hold.

introduction

example

effects

Identity theft, one of the fastest-growing crimes in America, occurs when someone uses another's name, address, date of birth, and Social Security number to take their money and charge debts and bills to their name. Anyone can become a victim. To protect yourself against becoming a victim of identity theft, there are seven steps you should take.

definition

thesis

1. **Secure checkbooks, bank books, and credit cards.** Today thieves can steal from you without taking your purse or wallet. They only have to have access to your credit card numbers, Social Security number, pay stubs, and driver's license. Never leave your purse, wallet, or financial records where others can see them.

2. **Never give out your Social Security number.** The most prized piece of ID thieves look for is a Social Security number. Never respond to e-mail or telemarketing calls that ask for a Social Security number. *Do not carry your Social Security card in your purse or wallet where it can be stolen.* Place it in a safe-deposit box or a safe place at home. It is not a form of acceptable ID, so there is no need to carry your card on your person.

3. **Check bank and credit card statements carefully.** Look for charges or deductions you did not make. Contact your bank or credit card company immediately if you suspect fraudulent transactions.

4. **If you shop online, use only one credit card for all transactions.** It is easier to track online charges made to one statement and cancel one account in case of identity theft.

5. Be wary of requests for personal information, especially online. Identity thieves send bank and Internet Service Provider customers fake warnings claiming that if they do not update their records their accounts may be closed. Always call the 800 number found on your bank statement, credit card, or phone book to check if this is a valid request. *Banks and Internet providers never ask for Social Security numbers, passwords, or ATM PIN numbers.*

6. Tell family members, relatives, and your employer never to give out your personal information without your permission.

7. Cancel credit cards and charge accounts you no longer use.

Finally, if you suspect you have been victimized, notify your bank, credit card companies, employer, credit bureaus, and police department immediately. Some states have offices that specialize in identity theft that can be found online or in the telephone book. Your bank can assist you in reestablishing your credit and recovering your identity.

Understanding Meaning: What Is the Writer Trying to Say?

1. What is identity theft?

   _____

   _____

2. What damage can identity theft have on victims?

   _____

   _____

3. Summarize the student's directions in your own words.

   1. _____   5. _____

   2. _____   6. _____

   3. _____   7. _____

   4. _____

Evaluating Strategy: How Does the Writer Say It?

1. How does the student use description and definition to develop the process essay?

   _____

   _____

2. The student uses numbered points in this essay. Is this effective in giving directions? Why or why not?

_____

_____

3. How does the student organize paragraphs? Are they easy to follow?

_____

_____

Appreciating Language: What Words Does the Writer Use?

1. Does the student clearly define "identity theft"? Can you state the definition in your own words?

_____

_____

2. What does the tone, word choice, and style suggest about the student's intended audience?

_____

_____

WORKING TOGETHER

Working with a group of students, discuss this essay and consider how you might improve it.

1. What are the essay's strong points?

_____

_____

2. What are the essay's weak points?

_____

_____

3. How would you revise this essay? What other information do you wish the student had added? Are there details that could be deleted? Would you rearrange or rewrite any of the paragraphs? Can you think of a more effective introduction or conclusion?

_____

_____

4. List your group's primary suggestion or a question you wish you could ask the writer.

_____

_____

GET WRITING ▶ **WRITING ACTIVITY**

Write a process essay about one of the following topics or one your instructor suggests. You can either explain how a process works or give readers step-by-steps instructions to accomplish a specific task. Remember, numbering directions can make them easier to follow.

how to apply for a car loan	how a machine operates
how a disease is spread	how to protect your computer
how a tornado or earthquake	against viruses
occurs	how to change a tire
how to teach something to	how to save money
small children	how to prepare for a job interview ◀

Cause and Effect

Cause and effect explains reasons and results.

Cause-and-effect essays explain the reasons why something happens or discusses the results something creates. History books explain the causes of the Great Depression and the effect of Roosevelt's New Deal programs. Medical courses discuss the causes of arthritis and effects of new treatments. Business professors present the causes of globalization and then predict its effects.

Critical thinking is important in writing cause-and-effect essays. Be sure to avoid three common errors.

- *Hasty generalizations or jumping to conclusions.* Don't make snap judgments based on what you think you know. If you hear that someone you know had a car accident, don't assume it was caused by drunken driving simply because you know this person consumes a lot of alcohol. Don't instantly assume that a fatal explosion at an army base in Iraq was caused by terrorists. Make sure you base conclusions on evidence.
- *Mistaking a time relationship for a cause-and-effect relationship.* Just because one event came before another does not mean that it was the cause. The fact that you became ill an hour after lunch does not mean it was caused by something you ate.
- *Confusing an association for a cause-and-effect relationship.* As early as the 1920s, doctors suspected that smoking caused cancer and heart disease. Many of their patients smoked, but not all smokers became ill. It took forty years of research to determine a cause-and-effect relationship between tobacco and disease.

STEPS TO WRITING A CAUSE-AND-EFFECT ESSAY

Planning

1. Determine your purpose. Your essay can discuss causes, results, or both.
2. Plan a clear thesis statement that expresses the goal of your essay.

(continued)

3. Explain the methods of establishing causes or measuring results. If you write that outsourcing causes the loss of skilled jobs, explain how you measure the loss of these jobs.
4. Organize causes or effects from least to most important or most to least important. Don't place your most important points in the middle of the essay where reader attention is weakest.
5. Offer logical, accurate evidence. Present facts, observations, examples, and statistics from standard, reliable sources readers will trust.

Writing the First Draft

1. Develop a strong introduction outlining the goal of your essay and providing background information.
2. Use example, comparison, process, and definition to explain causes and outline results.
3. Use transitional statements and paragraph breaks to signal shifts between separate causes and effects.
4. Point out possible exceptions or alternative interpretations.

Revising— Questions to Ask about a Cause-and-Effect Essay

1. Does my essay have a thesis or controlling idea?
2. Do I explain causes and results clearly with comparisons, examples, and narratives?
3. Do I provide enough evidence to convince readers?
4. Do I avoid making mistakes in critical thinking such as hasty generalizations or mistaking a time relationship for a cause?
5. Are there details that can be deleted because they are repetitive or off topic?
6. Are details clearly arranged so readers can follow my train of thought?
7. Does my essay tell readers what I want them to know?

Why Do They Hate Us?

In the months following 9/11, many shocked Americans wondered why people hated the United States. The horror of watching planes flying into buildings was matched by the disbelief and anger many felt watching people in the Middle East dancing in the streets, honking car horns, and passing out candy to children like it was a holiday. Polls taken in the Middle East revealed that vast numbers of Arabs and Muslims approved of Osama bin Laden, whose image appeared on posters and T-shirts. As President Bush prepared for war in Iraq, many people in Europe began to criticize the United States. The anti-American feeling in countries like Britain, France, and Germany troubled many Americans.

introduction

description

Why do they all seem to hate us? Scholars, reporters, and diplomats have given us many reasons. They suggest that anti-Americanism is caused by jealousy, resentment over the way American culture is eroding traditional cultures, America's support for Israel, and the exploitation of workers and resources.

suggested causes

thesis

causes

examples

comparisons

causes

effects

conclusion

But none of these reasons is new. America has been making movies that offend foreign tastes for eighty years. The United States has supported Israel since 1948.

The main cause for rising anti-Americanism, I think, is the end of the Cold War. For almost fifty years the world was controlled by two superpowers—the United States and the USSR. This conflict made America look less threatening and violent in contrast to a Communist dictatorship that killed and jailed millions.

People in West Germany may have grumbled about being under America's shadow, but they only had to look over the Berlin Wall to realize it was a lot better than being in East Germany under Communist rule. There was no comparison between living in South and North Korea, either. The Arabs may have resented America's support for Israel, but they knew the United States believed in freedom of religion. The Soviets were atheists and denounced all religion. The spread of American influence may have weakened Islamic values, but the growth of Soviet-sponsored Communist movements in Pakistan, Iran, and Egypt threatened to abolish Islam.

The Cold War made America look like the lesser of two evils. We were the good cop in the good cop/bad cop scenario. People resented American influence, but they had reasons to fear the Communists.

Now that the Cold War is over, the world has one superpower. We no longer look like the good cop or the lesser evil. To many people in other countries, the United States is a global bully, an economic giant, and a cultural titan—all of which make other nations feel intimidated and second-rate. And no one likes feeling second-rate.

Understanding Meaning: What Is the Writer Trying to Say?

1. What is the student's thesis? Can you state it in your own words?

   _____

   _____

2. Why does the student dismiss many of the causes for anti-Americanism suggested by others?

   _____

   _____

3. What does the student mean by "the good cop/bad cop scenario"?

   _____

   _____

4. How did the end of the Cold War create problems for the United States?

_____

_____

Evaluating Strategy: How Does the Writer Say It?

1. How does the student use example and comparison to develop a cause-and-effect essay?

_____

_____

2. How does the student organize the essay? What role do paragraphs play in arranging details?

_____

_____

3. How effective are the introduction and conclusion?

_____

_____

Appreciating Language: What Words Does the Writer Use?

1. Are expressions like "good cop/bad cop" appropriate in an essay about a serious subject like foreign policy? Why or why not?

_____

_____

2. What do the tone, style, and word choice suggest about the student's intended audience?

_____

_____

WORKING TOGETHER

Working with a group of students, discuss this essay and consider how you might improve it.

1. What are the essay's strong points?

_____

_____

2. What are the essay's weak points?

_____

_____

3. How would you revise this essay? What other information do you wish the student had added? Are there details that could be deleted? Would you re-arrange or rewrite any of the paragraphs? Can you think of a more effective introduction or conclusion?

_____

_____

4. List your group's primary suggestion or a question you wish you could ask the writer.

_____

_____

GET WRITING ▶ | **WRITING ACTIVITY**

Write a cause-and-effect essay about one of the following topics or one your instructor suggests. Your essay may present causes or effects or both. You may use description, example, definition, or other methods of development to create your essay.

causes for:
    teenage obesity
    high school dropouts
    drug abuse
    low voter turnout
    a team's recent victory or defeat
    divorce
    a TV show's popularity
    changes in a local neighborhood
    problems with Social Security

effects of:
    violent video games
    domestic violence
    having a child
    24-hour cable news networks
    losing a job
    online gambling
    cheap imported products
    school vouchers
    tougher child-support laws

Argument

Argument directs readers to accept a point of view or take action.

The goal of argument is to influence the way readers think about something or motivate them to change their behavior. Writers use three appeals to influence readers. Each appeal has advantages and disadvantages.

Logical Appeal—Uses facts, statistics, scientific evidence, expert opinions, surveys, and interviews.
    Advantages
        provides compelling, objective support
        offers evidence needed for major or group decisions
    Disadvantages
        requires a high degree of reader attention
        can be boring and undramatic
Emotional Appeal—Uses images, sensations, or stories to stir readers to re-spond based on their fears, loves, dislikes, biases, and hopes.

Advantages

    has instant impact

    requires little reader preparation or attention

Disadvantages

    has a temporary effect

    offers little hard evidence to support major decisions

Ethical Appeal—Uses shared values, ideals, and beliefs.

    Advantages

        provides compelling motivation

        calls upon readers' core beliefs

    Disadvantages

        depends on readers sharing the writer's values

        provides no hard evidence for major decisions

Because each appeal has limitations, writers often use more than one. An argument calling for a change in Homeland Security practices might use all three.

Emotional appeal using human-interest story of one person:

Early in 2002 Mohammed Naboti, an American citizen, was detained as a threat to national security without being charged with a crime, presented with any evidence, or given access to a lawyer. A married engineer with three children, Naboti has been unable to win his freedom. Although he has never belonged to any political or religious organization, he has been labeled a potential threat. His wife, unable to make the mortgage payments on their home, has been forced to sell their house.

Logical appeal presenting facts and evidence:

Naboti is just one of 575 American citizens who have been detained without charges after passage of the Homeland Security Act. According to an FBI study, 20% of those detained were victims of mistaken identity. Jane Newman, a New York civil rights attorney, argues, "Dozens of citizens have been denied their Constitutional rights and jailed without charges based on an anonymous tip or the complaint of a prejudiced neighbor. In one case a family of Sikhs was rounded up simply because the men arriving at a back-yard birthday party wore turbans."

Ethical appeal calling upon American values:

We must correct abuses and errors in the Homeland Security Act. As a nation trying to change the values of the Middle East and spread democracy, we cannot be seen as hypocrites. As a nation of law and order, we cannot deprive people of their rights, especially our citizens, based on ethnic stereotypes and vague suspicion.

STEPS TO WRITING AN ARGUMENT ESSAY

Planning

1. Determine your purpose—to persuade readers to accept your opinion or motivate them to take action.
2. Consider your readers' existing beliefs, attitudes, and knowledge.

(continued)

3. Determine which appeals best suit your purpose.
4. Don't confuse propaganda with persuasion. Calling people names, using inflated or biased statistics, hurling accusations, and making unfair comparisons create weak and unconvincing arguments.
5. Organize ideas from most important to least important or least important to most important. Avoid placing your most important details in the middle of the essay where reader attention is the weakest.
6. Develop an introduction that arouses attention, establishes your approach, and uses persuasive appeals that create a favorable relationship with your readers.
7. Create a conclusion that ends the essay with a final thought, meaningful fact, call to action, or thought-provoking question.

Writing the First Draft

1. Present facts in ways readers can understand. Explain what statistics mean or the qualifications of people you quote.
2. Use a variety of appeals.
3. Use paragraph breaks and transitional statements to signal shifts between main points.
4. Recognize and comment on possible alternative opinions.
5. Address possible reader objections to your views.

Revising— Questions to Ask about an Argument Essay

1. Does my essay have a clearly stated thesis?
2. Do I provide enough support to convince readers?
3. Is my argument easy to follow?
4. Are there details that can be deleted because they are repetitive or off topic?
5. Does my essay tell readers what I want them to know?

Curbing Our Enthusiasm: Cutting Down on
Off-Campus Drinking

introduction
examples

Last semester fifty-two students were charged with underage drinking at an off-campus St. Patrick's Day party at a "fraternity house." That weekend four students were seriously injured when a drunk senior ran a stop sign in the main parking lot. This fall's Homecoming Weekend saw police shutting down four illegal keg parties.

description

North Central Community College does not serve alcohol anywhere on campus. It has no dorms. But in the last few years, several duplexes on Interbay Avenue have become de facto "fraternity houses" populated by mostly male students right out of high school. In the last few years, keg parties in these houses have led to minors drinking and some students binge drinking to the point of needing the paramedics. As many as two hundred students have crowded into these houses. Photos taken at these parties show as many as fifty students crowded on flimsy wooden decks and balconies. Balconies like these have collapsed in other cities, leading to deaths and serious injuries.

In the last two years, these "fraternity houses" have posted invitations on campus and on websites urging students to buy a ten-dollar ticket that allows them to enter the house and eat and drink for free. The students evidently believe this makes the distribution of liquor legal since they are not actually "selling" it on-site.

These parties have attracted very negative media attention. Local residents have repeatedly filed complaints. Given the college's desire to expand next year, the administration cannot afford to alienate the community.   **effects**

North Central Community College must take steps to curb off-campus drinking parties. Although they don't take place on school property, students are involved and it reflects badly on the school's image.   **thesis**

First, the college must ban illegal fraternities. True fraternities are independent corporate organizations that have to have a charter from a college to operate. They have to promise to follow all college rules and local regulations. Groups calling themselves fraternities without charters should not be allowed to advertise parties on campus. The Student Union should not allow them to post ads on college bulletin boards or take out ads in the school paper.   **definition**

details

Second, the administration must work with Alderman Secora, the police, and landlords to make sure student tenants obey laws regarding alcohol, occupancy, and parking regulations. Clearly, the last few parties were fire hazards. A two-story duplex was never meant to hold hundreds of people.

Third, college organizations should offer non-alcohol activities. At Piedmont College, the Irish Club stages a St. Patrick's Day festival featuring Irish food, dancing, music, limerick contests, and sporting events, providing students with fun and recreation that has greatly reduced binge drinking. There is no reason why North Central can't stage a similar event. Cinco de Mayo, another favorite day for off-campus parties, could feature events hosted by any number of Chicano organizations.

Fourth, the college has to educate students about the dangers of drunk driving, binge drinking, and alcohol abuse in general. The National Institute of Alcohol Abuse and Alcoholism reports that each year 1,400 college students die and 500,000 are injured by hazardous drinking. No North Central student has died so far. We should not wait for a fatality and perhaps a major lawsuit to make the college take action.   **factual support**

conclusion

Understanding Meaning: What Is the Writer Trying to Say?

1. Can you state the student's thesis in your own words?

   _____

   _____

2. Why does the student believe the college must regulate off-campus student activities?

   _____

   _____

3. What steps does the student suggest the college take to reduce student drinking?

   _____

   _____

4. Why does the student call the fraternities illegal?

   _____

   _____

Evaluating Strategy: How Does the Writer Say It?

1. What reasons and support does the student provide to support the thesis? Is it effective?

   _____

   _____

2. The student includes statistics from the National Institute of Alcohol Abuse and Alcoholism. Should the essay contain more factual detail?

   _____

   _____

3. How does the student organize the essay?

   _____

   _____

Appreciating Language: What Words Does the Writer Use?

1. Many students, no doubt, consider these parties to be fun and harmless. How does the student's choice of words, tone, and style reveal the writer's attitude?

   _____

   _____

2. Why is it important for the student to define "fraternity"?

_____

_____

WORKING TOGETHER

Working with a group of students, discuss this essay and consider how you might improve it.

1. What are the essay's strong points?

_____

_____

2. What are the essay's weak points?

_____

_____

3. How would you revise this essay? What other information do you wish the student had added? Are there details that could be deleted? Would you re-arrange or rewrite any of the paragraphs? Can you think of a more effective introduction or conclusion?

_____

_____

4. List your group's primary suggestion or a question you wish you could ask the writer.

_____

_____

WRITING ACTIVITY

GET WRITING

Write a persuasive essay for or against one of the following topics or one your instructor suggests. You may use contrast, example, cause and effect, or other methods of development to create your essay.

school choice	granting driver's licenses to
raising minimum wage	undocumented workers
requiring welfare recipients to	investing in alternative energy
work for benefits	taxing online sales
tougher gun laws	censoring cable television
requiring women to register	admitting lie detector evidence in
for the draft	court
right-to-die laws	working while attending college

GET THINKING
AND WRITING

CRITICAL THINKING

The Internet and computers have allowed an increasing number of people to work from their homes. For some, this means they can schedule work around family errands, save time and money by not having to commute, and limit daycare costs. For others, working at home is lonely and isolating and erases a needed boundary between a job and personal life.

Write a short essay stating whether or not you want to work from your home. Would it make you more productive? Would you miss working with others? Would your family understand?

WHAT HAVE YOU WRITTEN?

Read your essay carefully.

- What is your thesis? Is it clearly focused and precisely worded?
- What kind of essay did you write—narration, comparison, or argument?
- What kinds of paragraphs did you use to support your thesis? What patterns of development do they represent—definition, description, or cause and effect?
- How effective is the introduction? Does it arouse attention, include your thesis, or pose a question, or does it only announce what the paper is about?
- Does the conclusion end the essay on a strong point or simply repeat what you have already stated?

If possible, use peer review to improve your essay.

GET WRITING

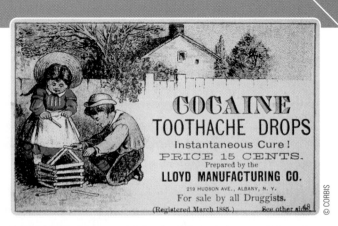

Before doctors understood its addictive properties, cocaine was used as an ingredient in over-the-counter medicines, including those given to children. Do you think there is a danger that many of the popular drugs advertised on television today may prove dangerous in the future? Do consumers assume anything endorsed by doctors is safe?

Advertisement for toothache drops containing cocaine, 1885

Write a short essay that expresses your views on drug safety. Do drugs require more testing? Do commercials fully inform people about potential side effects?

WRITING ON THE WEB

Using a search engine such as Yahoo!, Google, or AltaVista, enter terms such as *developing essays, writing essays, writing comparison, using cause and effect, argument,* and *composing essays* to locate current sites of interest.

1. Read online news articles and notice how writers use different patterns of development to organize an essay. Notice which appeals are used in persuasive essays, editorials, and opinion pieces.
2. Write a multiparagraph e-mail to a friend. Practice using different methods of development such as comparison, definition, or process in telling a story or describing a situation.

POINTS TO REMEMBER

1. An essay states a main idea supported by related paragraphs that provide details.
2. Writers generally use more than one pattern of development in creating an essay. A narration essay might include paragraphs consisting of definitions, cause and effect, or example.
3. Essays should have a defined topic and clear purpose.
4. Consider your reader's attitudes, background knowledge, and interests to define new terms, clarify misconceptions, and present evidence readers can appreciate.
5. Use peer review to detect errors and improve the quality of your essay.

If you use Writer's ResourcesNow, please have your students log in and view the pretest, study plan, and posttest for this chapter.   **Writer's Resources 🖐 Now**™

Revising Essays

© Ken James./Corbis

Arnold Schwarzenegger, an Austrian immigrant, body builder, and movie star, became governor of California. Ronald Reagan, another Hollywood actor, served as governor of California before becoming the 40th president of the United States. Do you think celebrities have an advantage when they enter politics, or do voters evaluate them the way they would any other candidate?

Write a brief essay stating your opinion whether or not celebrities have an advantage running for public office.

What Is Revision?

When you complete the draft of an essay, your first thoughts might be to check for misspelled words, verify names and facts, and look for missing punctuation. These corrections consist of *editing*—making final repairs. Before you look for minor imperfections in your essay, you should **revise** it.

Revision is different than editing. Revision means *to see again*.

Before examining your essay for minor mistakes, look at the big picture.

STRATEGIES FOR REVISING AN ESSAY

1. **Let your writing "cool."** Before you can look at your writing objectively, set it aside. Trying to revise your work just after you finish writing is hard because the ideas are still fresh in your mind. Let some time pass between writing and revising. Work on other assignments, run an errand, or check your e-mail before looking at your essay.

2. **Print your draft.** Some students can revise on a computer, but you may find it easier to work with a hard copy. Printing the draft lets you spread out the pages and see the whole essay at once. Double- or triple-space the hard copy to leave room for notes and corrections.

3. **Review your goal.** Before reading your essay, go over the assignment and any instructor guidelines.
   - Look at samples of the essay you are writing.
   - If your essay does not fit the assignment, it may be easier to review your notes, create a new outline, and write a new essay than to rewrite a failed attempt.

4. **Examine the big picture.** Revising is *not* editing. Don't immediately begin to correct spelling and punctuation. Instead, focus on the larger elements of the draft.
   - Is the thesis clearly stated?
   - Is the supporting evidence sufficient?
   - Are paragraphs logically organized?
   - Does the introduction arouse interest and prepare readers for what follows?
   - Does the conclusion leave readers with a strong final impression, question, or call to action?
   - Are sections "off topic" or repetitive?
   - Does your essay meet the requirements of the assignment?
   - What are the strong and weak points of the essay? What problems should be given priority?

5. **Read the essay with a "reader's eye."** Consider how your readers' knowledge, experiences, values, or attitudes will shape their responses to your essay.
   - Are readers likely to be supportive, indifferent, or hostile to your views?
   - Do you expect reader objections?
   - Do readers need background information to understand your ideas? Are there misconceptions that need to be cleared up? Do you need to define any terms?
   - Will readers respond favorably to your essay's style and tone?

(continued)

6. **Read your essay out loud.** Illogical statements, repeated ideas, and missing details are far easier to "hear" than read.
7. **Have others read your draft.** Many instructors encourage students to use peer review. If you have the chance to work with a group, ask other students to read your essay.
   - Let others read your essay "cold." If you tell them what you are trying to say before they read it, they will have a harder time evaluating your essay objectively.
   - If you ask people who are not in your class to read the essay, first explain the assignment. People cannot give you good advice unless they know what the essay is supposed to accomplish. The more they know about your goal and the intended audience, the more valuable their responses will be.
   - Don't be defensive. Ask for people to give you their honest opinion of your essay.
   - Ask students what they consider the paper's strong and weak points.
   - Make notes of their remarks and ask how your draft could be improved.
8. **Revise and rewrite.**
   - Revising is a continuing process. If you write on a computer, it is easy to make minor improvements every time you read your essay.
   - As you make changes to your essay, keep your goal and the assignment in mind.

STRATEGIES FOR PEER REVIEW

Many writing instructors encourage students to work in small groups and engage in peer review of writing assignments. Sharing your essay with other students can give you fresh views about your topic as well as tips for filling in missing details and repairing errors. When you read the work of other students, you become an editor. There are several things you can do to make peer review helpful for everyone in the group.

1. **Understand the role of editors.** An editor is not a writer. Your job as editor is not to tell other students how you would write their essays but to help them improve their work.
2. **Understand the writer's goal and the assignment.** It is difficult to review writing in a vacuum. If you are not familiar with the assignment, ask to see any directions the student received from the instructor. Read the directions carefully to offer valuable suggestions.
3. **Review the essay globally, then look at specifics.** Before pointing out grammar and spelling errors, focus on the big picture.
   - Does the topic suit the assignment?
   - Does it need to be more clearly focused or limited?
   - Does the paper have a clear thesis?
   - Is the thesis supported with details?
   - Are there irrelevant details that can be deleted?
   - Do paragraph breaks adequately organize the paper? Could the paragraph structure be more effective?
   - Can you detect sentences that are unclear, illogical, or awkward?

(continued)

- Does the paper need proofreading for spelling and grammar errors? As a peer editor, your job is not to correct mechanical errors, but you should indicate to the writer if the paper needs proofreading.

4. **Be positive.** Make constructive, helpful comments. Don't simply point out errors but show how they can be corrected or avoided.

5. **Ask questions.** Instead of stating that a sentence or paragraph does not make sense, ask the student what he or she was trying to say. Asking questions can prompt a writer to rethink what he or she wrote, remember missing details, or consider new alternatives.

6. **When you submit work to editors, seek their advice.** Don't be defensive. Allow editors to read and speak freely. Encourage feedback by asking targeted questions. If you simply ask, "Do you like it?" or "Is my paper any good?" you are likely to get polite compliments or vague comments that your work is "OK." To get advice you can use, ask other students specific questions.

   - Is the thesis clear?
   - Does the essay need more support?
   - Should I put in more statistics? Are the quotations effective?
   - Should I add some more details in the introduction?

Revising Elements of an Essay

Although you can correct spelling and punctuation mistakes whenever you spot them, remember your main goal in revising is examining the larger elements of your essay, especially paragraphs.

Look at the Big Picture

Review the Entire Essay

Read your essay out loud. How does it sound? What ideas or facts are missing, poorly stated, or repetitive? Highlight areas needing improvement and delete paragraphs that are off topic or repetitive.

- Does your essay meet your goal and the needs of the assignment?
- What are the most serious defects?
- Is the essay clearly organized? Would a chronological approach be better than division? Should you open with your strongest point or state it in the conclusion?

Examine the Thesis Statement

Does your essay have a clearly written thesis statement or controlling idea—or is it simply a collection of facts and observations? Does the essay have a point?

- If your essay has a thesis statement, read it aloud. Is it clearly worded? Is it too general? Can it be adequately supported?
- Where have you placed the thesis? Would it be more effective if placed before or after you presented evidence, defined a term, or explained some background information? Remember, the thesis does not have to appear in the opening paragraph.

Review Topic Sentences and Controlling Ideas of Each Paragraph

Each paragraph should have a clear purpose and support the thesis.

- Review the controlling ideas for each paragraph.
- Do all the paragraphs support the thesis?
- Are there paragraphs that are off topic? You may have developed some interesting ideas, included an important fact or quote, or told a moving story, but if they don't support the thesis, they do not belong in the essay.

Review the Order of Paragraphs

As you write, you may add new ideas or detour from your outline, changing the design of the essay. Look at the topic sentences in each paragraph to see if the order of ideas should be revised.

- Should paragraphs be rearranged to maintain a clear timeline or build greater emphasis?
- Does the order of paragraphs follow your train of thought? Should some paragraphs come after those containing definitions and background information?

Revise the Introduction

The opening sentences and paragraphs of your essay are important. They set the tone, announce the topic, get readers' attention, and establish how the rest of the essay is organized.

INTRODUCTION CHECKLIST

1. Does the introduction clearly announce the topic?
2. Does the opening paragraph arouse interest?
3. Does it limit the topic, preparing readers for what follows?
4. If the thesis appears in the opening, is it precisely stated?
5. Does the language of the opening paragraph set the proper tone for the paper?
6. Does the introduction address reader concerns, correct misconceptions, or provide background information so readers can understand and appreciate the evidence that follows?

Because you cannot always predict how you will change the body of the essay, you should always return to the introduction and examine it before writing a new draft.

Revise Body Paragraphs

The paragraphs in the body of the essay should support the thesis, develop ideas, or advance the chronology.

BODY PARAGRAPH CHECKLIST

1. Does the paragraph have a clear focus?
2. Is the topic sentence supported with enough evidence?
3. Is the evidence easy to follow? Does the paragraph follow a logical organization? Would a different pattern of development be more effective?
4. Are there irrelevant ideas that should be deleted?
5. Are there clear transitions between ideas and within paragraphs?
6. Do paragraph breaks signal major transitions? Should some paragraphs be combined and others broken up?

Revise the Conclusion

Not all essays require a separate conclusion. A narrative may end with a final event. A comparison may conclude with the last point.

CONCLUSION CHECKLIST

1. Does the conclusion end the paper on a strong note? Will it leave readers with a final image, question, quote, or fact that will challenge readers and lead them to continue thinking about your subject?
2. Does the conclusion simply repeat the introduction or main ideas? Is it necessary? Should it be shortened or deleted?
3. If your purpose is to motivate people to take action, does the conclusion provide readers with clear directions?

Revising an Essay

After attending a campus forum on legalizing drugs, a student decided to respond to one of the speakers in an argument paper for an English class.

First Draft

                    Why Legalizing Drugs Won't Work
     For thirty years various people have been saying that drugs should be legalized for a lot of reasons. They believe legalizing drugs would eliminate drug gangs and the crimes caused by desperate junkies because the legal drugs would be cheaper. These arguments make a lot of sense until you begin to think about it.
     The only way drugs would be legalized is if they were treated like alcohol so nobody under 21 could buy them. So we still would have illegal drugs. Mostly people start using drugs in high school so we would still have that problem.
     Another thing people who support legalization don't talk about is just who is going to sell legal drugs. I don't think that Walgreens or Rite Aid is going to sell grass and crack. If the idea is making drugs cheaper, then there won't be enough profit for any established business to want to sell them. Drugstores make their profit selling prescription drugs and beauty products. Customers with kids would avoid any store that would have druggies walking around.
     The whole idea of treating addicts like people with a problem and not criminals makes sense. I agree with that. So letting these people have access to cheap drugs and clean needles might help stop the spread of AIDS and lower crime a little. But people are only going to step forward for legal programs when

they are really dope sick. So for years before they did drugs and maybe stole to get money to buy them. We treat alcoholics like people with a disease but that has not stopped drunk driving from killing people. People don't wake up one day and decide to take heroin so they sign up to be legal addicts. Only after years of abuse do they hit bottom and want help.

So legalizing drugs is not going to fix every-thing. It might work. But it won't have the great results its supporters predict.

Revision Notes

Why Legalizing Drugs Won't Work

vague:
needs strong
thesis statement

For thirty years various people have been saying that drugs should be legalized for a lot of reasons. They believe legalizing drugs would eliminate drug gangs and the crimes caused by desperate junkies be-cause the legal drugs would be cheaper. These arguments make a lot of sense until you begin to think about it.

limit essay

number points
rewrite topic
sentence

The only way drugs would be legalized is if they were treated like alcohol so nobody under 21 could buy them. <u>So we still would have illegal drugs.</u> Mostly people start using drugs in high school, so we would still have that problem.

weak transition

<u>Another thing people who support legalization don't talk about is just who is going to sell legal drugs.</u> I don't think that Walgreens or Rite Aid is going to sell grass and crack. If the idea is making drugs cheaper, then there won't be enough profit for any established business to want to sell them. Drug-stores make their profit selling prescription drugs and beauty products. Customers with kids would avoid any store that would have druggies walking around.

improve wording

revise topic
sentence

The whole idea of treating addicts like people with a problem and not criminals makes sense. I agree with that. So letting these people have access to cheap drugs and clean needles might help stop the spread of AIDS and lower crime a little. But people are only going to step forward for legal programs when they are really dope sick. So for years before they did drugs and maybe stole to get money to buy them. We treat alcoholics like people with a disease but that has not stopped drunk driving from killing people. People don't wake up one day and decide to take heroin so they sign up to be legal addicts. Only after years of abuse do they hit bottom and want help.

make comparison
stronger

need stronger
conclusion

So legalizing drugs is not going to fix every-thing. It might work. But it won't have the great results its supporters predict.

Revised Essay

Why Legalizing Drugs Won't Work

For thirty years advocates of legalizing drugs have argued that legalization would make drugs cheaper, eliminating violence associated with drug gangs and crimes committed by desperate junkies. <u>Legalizing drugs, however, will have a minimal impact on crime and violence for three main reasons.</u>

thesis listing three points

First, most people who take drugs begin using them in high school. It is unlikely that any state will allow the legal sale of addictive drugs to anyone under twenty-one. We would still see drug gangs and an underground drug culture supplying drugs to minors. <u>Legalizing drugs will have no effect on teenage drug abuse.</u>

topic sentence

Second, advocates of legalization never explain how addicts will be able to buy drugs. Since the goal of legalization is to lower prices to stem crime, sales of drugs will not generate substantial profits. Drugstores like Walgreens and Rite Aid make their money selling prescription drugs and beauty supplies. They are not going to alienate their customers and community leaders by selling addictive recreational drugs. Legalizing drugs will only eliminate crime if they are easy to obtain. <u>Because it is unlikely legal businesses will want to sell them, legalizing drugs will have no impact on crime and violence.</u>

topic sentence

<u>Third, making drugs and clean needles available to addicts may help stop the spread of AIDS but will have little impact on crime and violence.</u> Advocates have suggested that drug addicts be treated like patients, not criminals, and be allowed to register for programs that would give them inexpensive or free drugs. But people do not become addicts overnight. They begin experimenting with drugs, then become casual users, then move to full-blown addiction. Along the way, under the influence of drugs, they commit crimes, abuse their partners, lose jobs, and ruin families. Only when they hit rock bottom are addicts likely to step forward to register. Alcohol is legal. Alcoholics are not treated like criminals and can obtain treatment whenever they want. Those without insurance can enter free programs or join AA. But that does not stop violence committed by those under the influence of alcohol or prevent thousands of people from being killed by drunk drivers every year.

topic sentence

<u>Legalizing drugs, despite the promises of its advocates, will realistically have only a limited impact on the problem of crime and violence caused by drug addicts.</u>

conclusion topic sentence

EXERCISE 1 Revising Essays

Improve the following essay by revising the thesis statement, topic sentences, and organization of paragraphs. Delete details that are off topic and add facts, ideas, and examples that support the thesis.

Freshman Blues

The first year of college is difficult. Most students have some problems their freshman year. In fact, nearly half the students who drop out of college leave after their first year. High schools and colleges do not do enough to prepare students for this. The transition is difficult.

In high school, students attend classes and study halls all day. Teachers take attendance and remind students to turn in late or missing homework. In college, students attend class a few hours a week and are expected to do most of the studying on their own. Professors rarely take attendance and do not chase after students' missing work. They expect students to be adults and take responsibility for their actions. For many students this freedom is something they cannot handle. They are used to being prodded and reminded. Many lack the ability to complete assignments on their own.

To overcome this problem, both high schools and colleges should prepare students for this change. High schools are usually judged by the success of their graduates, so it is in their interest to help. High school teachers should introduce seniors to what college is like. They could offer a last-semester seminar telling students how to pick a major, study, schedule their time, and budget their money. Colleges could have a one-semester program that makes students e-mail in a progress report on how they are doing every week. If a report is late, the college computer automatically e-mails parents and tells them to call their children.

Most high school students live at home where parents monitor not only their homework but their hours. They remind students to study, to go to bed early, and to spend their money carefully. Away from home for the first time, many freshmen party late into the night, run up credit card bills, hang out with friends, and find themselves, after one semester, behind in their homework and broke.

With all the money parents spend on education and all the pressure that high schools and colleges get to perform better, some of these ideas make sense and would cost very little to put into place.

EXERCISE 2 Revising Essays

Select an essay you wrote this semester. Review the assignment and your original notes, then examine your essay carefully. Determine how you could improve your writing by revising the thesis statement, topic sentences, supporting details, and organization. Pay attention to the introduction and conclusion.

WORKING TOGETHER

Work with a group of students and exchange copies of recent essays you have written. Make copies so each person can make corrections and comments. Discuss what you want to say and ask how what you have written could be improved.

CRITICAL THINKING

Should the United States reinstate the draft and require all eighteen-year-olds to serve in the military? Why or why not? If you support the draft, would you suggest any deferments? If the armed forces do not need troops, should young people be required to serve some other form of national or community service? Why or why not?

Write a short essay stating your opinion about requiring eighteen-year-olds to serve their country.

WHAT HAVE YOU WRITTEN?

1. Does your essay have a clearly written thesis expressing your opinion?
2. Does each paragraph's topic sentence support the thesis statement?
3. Do the details in each paragraph support its topic sentence?
4. Are there details that are off topic or repetitive and could be deleted?
5. Do some points require further development? Should you add facts, ideas, or examples to support your points?
6. Does the introduction arouse attention, explain background information, state your thesis, and prepare readers for what follows in the rest of the essay?
7. Are the paragraphs in the body clearly organized? Do paragraph breaks and transitional statements help readers follow your train of thought?
8. Does the conclusion bring the essay to a logical end or does it simply repeat the introduction?

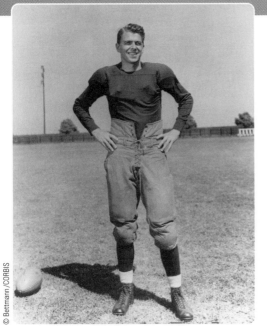

© Bettmann /CORBIS

Ronald Reagan played heroic characters in movies before entering politics. Do you think that an actor who played evil, violent, or comic characters would be taken seriously by voters? Could a standup comedian or a rap artist who made explicit music videos enter politics? Can voters separate an artist's image from his or her personal character?

Write an essay stating your views, then review your thesis, topic sentences, and paragraph structure.

WRITING ON THE WEB

Using a search engine such as Google, Yahoo!, or AltaVista, enter terms such as *revising essays, the writing process, writing essays,* or *developing essays* to locate current sites of interest.

1. Read news articles online and study how writers develop introductions, use conclusions, and organize paragraphs.
2. Write e-mails to friends. Before sending them, review the way you have used paragraphs to organize ideas. Revise your message to strengthen the introduction and conclusion, improve transitions, and add necessary details.

POINTS TO REMEMBER

1. Revision is an important part of the writing process.
2. Before revising an essay, review your plan, the needs of the assignment, and your intended readers.
3. In examining your essay, look at the "big picture" first. Determine if your essay has a clear thesis supported with sufficient details.
4. The introduction should announce your topic, arouse reader attention, supply background information, and prepare readers for what follows in the rest of the essay.
5. The paragraphs in the body of the essay should follow a clear pattern of development using clear transitions so readers can follow your train of thought.
6. The conclusion should do more than simply repeat the introduction. It should end the essay with a memorable fact, call to action, quotation, or question.
7. Peer review can help detect errors and provide suggestions for improving your essay.

Writer's Resources ⊕ Now™   If you use Writer's ResourcesNow, please have your students log in and view the pretest, study plan, and posttest for this chapter.

Using Sources and MLA Documentation

© Royalty-Free /Corbis

Lawyers support arguments they make in court with scientific evidence, documents, eyewitnesses, and expert testimony. In some cases experts are paid thousands of dollars to testify.

Write a short essay expressing your opinion about paid witnesses. If you were on a jury, would it influence your opinion of witnesses if you found out they were paid to testify?

Why Use and Document Sources?

Throughout your college career, you will probably be assigned papers that require using and documenting sources. Even if your instructor does not ask you to include outside sources, adding documented evidence can strengthen your essay.

Original
The police department needs more resources to fight gangs. There are not enough police officers. The gangs are committing more crime. They kill people and steal cars. The gangs are growing fast.

With Documented Sources
The police department needs more resources to fight gangs. There are twenty-six vacant positions on the force (Mendoza 15). According to the FBI, gangs are responsible for 25% of homicides and 45% of all car thefts in this city and have doubled their membership since 2004 (Brown 5).

Outside sources give your essay greater authority by supporting your thesis with facts, statistics, and quotations from experts.

Using Sources

Whenever you use outside sources, it is important to remember your goal. The purpose of your essay is to state *your* thesis and *your* arguments supported by additional evidence—not simply list facts and summarize what other people have written.

The sources you select should be *relevant, accurate, reliable,* and *representative.*

- **Relevant** sources relate directly to your topic, thesis, and assignment.
- **Accurate** sources provide correct, recent, and objective information. Make sure you copy quotations, numbers, and statistics carefully and avoid distorting their meaning by taking them out of context. The statement "In 2005 18 students from Marshall High School were expelled for gang activity" may be accurate but misleading if you fail to inform readers that this is the lowest number of expulsions in ten years and that the "gang activity" involves nonviolent crimes like minor vandalism and dress code violations.
- **Reliable** sources include articles, books, speeches, interviews, and websites by widely respected authors, experts, and institutions. Avoid using sources that distort facts and present questionable evidence to advance conspiracy theories or launch personal attacks.
- **Representative** sources present examples, facts, statistics, and opinions reflecting a larger truth. A list of ten homeless Harvard graduates and ten millionaire high school dropouts does not accurately represent the general truth about the value of education.

Finding and Locating Sources

You can locate sources in the library, online, or on your own.

Library Sources

College and public libraries offer a range of sources, including books, magazines, videos, and databases.

- **Encyclopedias and reference books** provide background information and offer an overview of topics. Specialized encyclopedias offer in-depth articles about people, facts, events, and terms.
- **Online and card catalogs** list books and their call numbers in the library's collection. You can search books by author, title, or subject.
- **Periodical indexes** (also called **serials holding lists**) list magazines, newspapers, and journals held by the library.
- **Databases** like InfoTrac College Edition and LexisNexis allow you to search thousands of magazines to locate articles. In most cases you can read, print, and e-mail articles.

If you have difficulty locating sources about your topic, ask the reference librarian for help. Telling the librarian about your assignment and the type of paper you are writing can help him or her direct you to the best sources.

Internet Sources

You can explore the Internet in the library or at home by using a number of search engines:

Google	www.google.com
Yahoo!	www.yahoo.com
AltaVista	www.altavista.com
Northern Light	www.northernlight.com
HotBot	www.hotbot.com

- **Check the spelling of search terms.**
- **Make search terms specific.**
- **Follow search engine directions to refine your search.**

George Bush AND Iraq War *or* George Bush + Iraq War will list sites that include both terms.

George Bush NOT Iraq War *or* George Bush − Iraq War will list sites about George Bush that do not mention the Iraq War.

"Leopold and Loeb" will list only sites that contain both names, eliminating sites about King Leopold or Loeb Realty.

POINT TO REMEMBER

Whenever you decide to use outside sources, take careful notes and be sure to record information you will need to document in your paper.

- Books – author or editor, title, city of publisher, publisher, edition, year, and page numbers of material you will use.
- Articles – author, article title, magazine or newspaper title, date, page numbers, and specific page numbers of material you will use.
- Websites – URL address (www.abc.com), owner of site, author title, date of site, date of access (date you looked at or printed the site).

Note: If you make photocopies of books or magazines, write the information on your copies to prevent confusion. Make sure if you print online material that your hardcopies contain all the information you need.

EXERCISE 1 Locating Sources

Explore sources at your library or online to find information for the following questions.

1. What is the population of Chattanooga, Tennessee?
2. Who is the current mayor of New Orleans?
3. Does the University of Wisconsin-Milwaukee have a law school?
4. What is the library call number for Herman Melville's *Moby Dick*?
5. Can you locate three articles on autism that came out in the last six months?

What Is Documentation?

Whenever you include outside sources to a paper, you must document their use. Documentation is a way of showing readers which ideas are your own and which ideas come from another source. There are several documentation methods used in college courses. Most college English courses use the MLA style developed by the Modern Language Association.

MLA documentation includes two parts:

citations that appear in the essay whenever you use an outside source

a Works Cited list that appears at the end of your essay and lists all outside sources

Using Citations

As you include outside sources, note their use with **citations.** These citations should be brief but accurate. If you mention an author or source in your text, you only need to add a page number at the end in parentheses.

Winston Hachner has noted, "The Internet has provided us with a dilemma of choice" (874).

(Note: Place the period after the parenthetical citation. It is part of the sentence.)

If you do not mention the source, include the author's last name or title with page numbers in the parentheses.

```
The Internet has given us more choices than we can
process (Hachner 874). The sheer volume of information
can overwhelm, confuse, and strangle businesses accus-
tomed to defined channels of communication ("Internet
Nation" 34-35).
```

Sources without page references do not require parenthetical citations if noted in the text.

```
During a 60 Minutes interview in 2005, George West ar-
gued, "A terrorist attack in cyberspace can cripple
our economy."
```

You can avoid long, awkward parenthetical notes by citing titles or several authors in the text.

```
As stated in the Complete Directory of Modern Communi-
cation, "The Internet has reshaped the way we think,
communicate, and see our place in the world." Jacobson
and Marley view the Internet as the greatest force in
communications since the invention of the printing
press (145-146).
```

You can shorten long titles by using one or two of the first key words. A newspaper article without an author called "The Dramatic Birth of a New Energy Source" could be cited as "Dramatic" or "Dramatic Birth."

```
The desire to reduce pollution and free the country
from Middle Eastern oil is generating a range of new
sources of power ("Dramatic" 15).
```

Do not shorten the title to "Birth" because that would lead readers to expect the full title of the article to be alphabetized under B rather than D.

Building a Works Cited List

As you write your essay, keep track of the outside sources you use. All sources that appear in the final paper will be listed alphabetically in a Works Cited list at the end of your essay.

```
Complete Dictionary of Modern Communications.
    Educational Network. 25 Apr. 2005. <http://
    www.ednetwork.com/modcom.dic./html>.

Hachner, Winston. America and the Millennium.
    New York: Atlantic, 2006.

———. "Internet Nation." Chicago Magazine Mar. 2004:
    32-41.

Jacobson, Max and Jane Marley. The Internet and the
    World. New York: Random, 2005.
```

West, George. Interview. <u>60 Minutes</u>. CBS. WCBS, New
    York. 3 Apr. 2005.

Pages 261–268 show how to cite and list books, articles, television shows, and on-line material.

POINT TO REMEMBER

When an instructor in any class assigns a paper, ask two questions:

- Do I have to document outside sources?
- What documentation style should I use?

Why Document Sources?

Using documentation achieves three important goals.

1. **Avoid plagiarism.** *Plagiarism* is using the words, ideas, or artistic work of others without giving them credit. It is considered stealing. Most colleges have strict policies about plagiarism. Instructors often fail students who plagiarize papers. Many universities expel students who submit plagiarized assignments. *Accurate documentation clearly distinguishes your work from that of others so no one can accuse you of cheating.*

2. **Support a thesis.** Citing sources not only protects you from charges of cheating but makes your writing more effective. To convince readers to accept your thesis, it is important to provide them with evidence. *The more controversial your thesis, the more readers will demand supporting evidence from reliable sources.*

3. **Help readers learn more.** Your citations show readers where they can obtain additional information by listing periodicals, books, and websites.

What *Not* to Document

Just because you include facts and statements you looked up in a book or found online does not mean they require documentation.

1. **Common expressions or famous quotations.** You don't need to list the Bible or your edition of Shakespeare if you simply check the wording of a quotation by Jesus or Hamlet. If you refer to statements readers are familiar with, such as Martin Luther King's "I have a dream" or John F. Kennedy's "Ask not what your country can do for you—ask what you can do for your country," you don't have to note their original source. *Less familiar statements, especially controversial ones, must be documented.*

2. **Common knowledge that doesn't change and is available in numerous sources.** You don't have to list *The Encyclopedia Britannica* as a source if you use it to look up where George Washington was born, when *Death of a Salesman* opened on Broadway, when Malcolm X died, or the height of Mount Everest. General facts such as these are not subject to change and are readily available in hundreds of books, almanacs, biographies,

(continued)

textbooks, and websites. No one will accuse you of stealing information that is considered standard and widely known by millions of people. *Facts subject to change or dispute, such as the population of Denver, the number of people on death row, or income tax regulations, must be documented.*

What You *Must* Document

In almost every other case, you must acknowledge the use of sources.

1. **Direct quotations.** When you copy word for word the spoken or written words of others, use quotation marks or block paragraphs to distinguish them from your own and indicate the source.
2. **Indirect quotations or paraphrases.** Even if you don't copy information but restate the author's ideas in your own words, you must list the source. Changing a few words in a quotation or summarizing several pages in a paragraph does not change the fact that you are using material from an outside source. Although you don't use quotation marks, indicate your use of other sources.
3. **Specific facts, statistics, and numbers.** Facts will only be acceptable to readers if they know where they came from. If you state, "Last year eighteen innocent men were sentenced to death for crimes they did not commit," readers will wonder where you got this figure and if it is true.
4. **Graphs, charts, photographs, and other visual aids.**

EXERCISE 2 Documenting Sources

For each of the following sources, answer True if it must be documented or False if it does not need to be documented.

1. __F__ Opening sentences of the Gettysburg Address.
2. __F__ Names of Supreme Court justices nominated by President Johnson.
3. __T__ Number of high school seniors in Chicago public schools in 2005.
4. __T__ Quote from a recent movie review in the *New York Times*.
5. __T__ Original box-office figures for *The Matrix*.

Using and Documenting Sources

There are two basic ways of including outside sources:

direct quotations that copy a source word for word

paraphrases (indirect quotations) that summarize a source in your own words

In both cases, you need to let readers know you are using outside material.

Using Direct Quotations

Direct quotations should be used sparingly. Remember, the goal of your paper is to express your thoughts and opinions, not present a collection of other people's ideas. There are times, however, when direct quotations can be powerful additions to your essay.

Use direct quotations:

1. When they present a significant statement by an authority or eyewitness.
2. When the statement is unique or memorable.
3. When the idea expressed conflicts with common views.
4. When the original statement is well written and more compelling than a paraphrase or summary.
5. When readers may question a controversial point of view or question that a certain person made the statement.

Direct quotations have to be smoothly blended into your essay.

1. Indicate short direct quotations (1–4 lines) by placing them in quotation marks followed by a parenthetical citation.

   ```
   According to Lester Armstrong, "The university
   failed to anticipate the impact of state budget
   cuts" (17).
   ```

   Indicate long direct quotations (over 4–5 lines) by placing them in indented paragraphs without quotation marks. Indent ten spaces on the left side and introduce with a colon. (Note: Place the period before the parenthetical citation.)

   ```
   According to Lester Armstrong, higher education
   suffered greatly during the recession:
               The university failed to anticipate the
               impact of state budget cuts. As a result,
               construction on the new stadium was
               halted. Twenty-five administrators were
               laid off. Plans to expand the computer
               labs, bilingual programs, and adult night
               school were scrapped. The library budget
               was slashed by 24%, and two daycare
               centers were closed. The century-old
               Main Hall, which was scheduled for an
               extensive refurbishing, was given only
               cosmetic repairs and painting. (17)
   ```

2. Link direct quotations with your text. Avoid isolated quotations.

   Incorrect
   ```
   Children are greatly affected by violence on tele-
   vision. "By the time a child graduates from high
   school, he or she has witnessed over 18,000 homi-
   cides on television" (Smith 10). Young people come
   to view violence, even murder, as a reasonable
   method of resolving conflicts.
   ```

   Blend direct quotations into your text by introducing them.

   Revised
   ```
   Children are greatly affected by violence on tele-
   vision. "By the time a child graduates from high
   school," Jane Smith notes, "he or she has wit-
   ```

```
nessed over 18,000 homicides on television" (10).
Young people come to view violence, even murder,
as a reasonable method of resolving conflict.
```

3. You may edit quotations to eliminate redundant or irrelevant material. Indicate deleted words by inserting an *ellipsis* (three spaced periods) in brackets.

Original Text

   George Washington, who was heading to New York to confer with his leading advisors, agreed to meet with Franklin in Philadelphia on June 10th.

Edited Quote

```
As Smith notes, "George Washington [. . .] agreed
to meet with Franklin in Philadelphia on June
10th" (12).
```

Deletions should only remove unnecessary information; they should not alter the meaning of the text by removing qualifications or changing a negative statement into a positive one. It is unethical to alter a quotation such as, "We should, only if everything else fails, legalize drugs" to read "We should [. . .] legalize drugs."

4. Insert words or other information to prevent confusion or avoid grammatical errors. For instance, if a direct quote refers to a Frank Bush by his last name and you are concerned readers will confuse him with President Bush, you may insert his first name, even though it does not appear in the original text.

Original Text

   Hoping to ease tensions in the Middle East, Bush called for UN peacekeepers to patrol the West Bank.

Edited Quote

```
"Hoping to ease tensions in the Middle East,
[Frank] Bush," according to Newsweek, "called for
UN peacekeepers to patrol the West Bank" (14).
```

If you delete words or phrases, you may have to insert words to prevent a grammar error.

Original Text

   Poe and other writers of his generation were influential in shaping a new, truly American literature.

Edited Quote

```
According to Sydney Falco, "Poe [. . .] [was]
influential in shaping a new, truly American
literature" (64).
```

Using Paraphrases

Paraphrases are indirect quotes. You must document your use of sources, even when you do not copy the text word for word. If you read two or three pages of a history book and summarize its points in a single paragraph, document your use of that source. Although you did not directly reproduce any words or sentences, the ideas you present are not your own and should be documented.

Original Text

More than 10,000 of New York's 29,000 manufacturing firms had closed their doors. Nearly one of every three employables in the city had lost his job. An estimated 1,600,000 New Yorkers were receiving some form of public relief. Many of those fortunates who had kept their jobs were "under-employed," a euphemism for the fact that they worked two or three days a week or two weeks a month— or, if they worked full time, were paid a fraction of their former salaries; stenographers, earning $35 to $40 per week in 1928, were averaging $16 in 1933; Woolworth's was paying full-time salesladies $6 per week.

Robert Caro, *The Power Broker*, pp. 323–24

Paraphrase

```
The Great Depression devastated New York City. A
third of the manufacturers shut down operations, and
over a million and a half New Yorkers were on re-
lief. Those with jobs saw their hours cut and their
salaries slashed (Caro 323-24). Conditions in Chi-
cago, Los Angeles, and San Francisco were similar.
```

Parenthetical references should be placed immediately after the paraphrased material at an appropriate pause or at the end of the sentence.

EXERCISE 3 Documenting Direct Quotes and Paraphrases

Write one or two paragraphs discussing terrorist threats and use at least one direct quote and one paraphrase from the following source.

THE TERRORIST MENACE   52

among others. Today the greatest terrorist threats do not involve hijacked airliners or suicide bombers. Documents captured in former terrorist camps reveal that Al-Qaeda groups have developed sophisticated plans to attack the United States in a variety of unexpected ways.

Cyberterrorism. A laptop seized in Jordan contained detailed strategies for using supercomputers in Pakistan and Egypt to launch highly sophisticated cyberattacks to disrupt banking transactions, air and rail schedules, 911 operations, and corporate e-mail. Computer viruses could shut down online communications or disable computers used to regulate power plants and emergency services.

Bioterrorism. A handful of anthrax letters mailed in 2001 caused a national panic and forced lawmakers in Washington to evacuate their offices for months. Popular media suggests that terrorists could use Ebola virus or plague to kill hundreds of thousands. Perhaps the most deadly agent would be a weaponized flu. The influenza epidemic of 1918 killed 20 million people, more than were killed throughout World War I. Testifying before Congress last year, Dr. Nancy Alcott of the CDC estimated "that a highly weaponized flu virus could sweep the United States in four to six weeks and claim 100 million lives."

Radiological terrorism. Constructing a full-scale sophisticated nuclear weapon would cost a terrorist group billions of dollars and require highly

> skilled technicians. However terrorists may be able to purchase or steal a nuclear weapon from one of the former Soviet Republics. Radioactive material can be used to create a crude "dirty bomb" in which conventional explosives are used to spread radioactive material over a large area. A radiological truck bomb detonated in Times Square might render most of Manhattan uninhabitable for decades. The immediate loss of life would be minimal, but the economic loss and psychological trauma would be devastating.

Source: *The Terrorist Menace* **by Wilson Goodman, published by Mainstream Books in New York City in 2004.**

Guidelines for Listing Sources in Works Cited and Parenthetical Notes

Books

- Write the author's last name, first name, then any initial. Copy the name as written. "C. W. Brown" would appear as:

      Brown, C. W.

  Omit any degrees or titles such as Ph.D. or Dr.

- State the full title of the book. Place a colon between the main heading and any subtitle. Underline all the words and punctuation in the title, except for the final period.

      Brown, C. W. <u>Sharks and Lambs: Wall Street in
          the Nineties</u>.

- Record the city of publication, publisher, and date of publication. If the book lists several cities, use only the first. If the city is outside the United States, add an abbreviation for the country. If an American city may be unfamiliar, you can include an abbreviation for the state. Record the main words of the publisher, deleting words like "publishing" or "press" (Monroe for Monroe Publishing Company). Use the initials "UP" for "University Press." End the citation with the last year of publication.

Works Cited entry:

      Brown, C. W. <u>Sharks and Lambs: Wall Street in
          the Nineties</u>. Kehoe, IL: Kellogg UP, 2003.

Parenthetical note:

      (Brown 12)

Book with Two or Three Authors

Works Cited entry:

      Smith, David, John Adams, and Chris Cook.
          <u>Writing On-line</u>. New York: Macmillan,
          2000.

Parenthetical note:

> (Smith, Adams, and Cook 23-24)

Books with More Than Four Authors

Works Cited entry:

> Chavez, Nancy, et al. <u>Mexico Today</u>. New York:
> Putnam, 2003.

Parenthetical note:

> (Chavez et al. 87)

Book with Corporate Author

Works Cited entry:

> National Broadcasting Company. <u>Programming
> Standards</u>. New York: National Broadcasting
> Company, 2002.

Parenthetical note:

> (National Broadcasting Company 112)

To avoid a long parenthetical note, mention the author or title in the text:

> According to the National Broadcasting Company's <u>Pro-
> gramming Standards</u>, "No single executive should be
> able to cancel a program" (214).

Book with Unnamed Authors

Works Cited entry:

> <u>New Yale Atlas</u>. New York: Random, 2003.

Parenthetical note:

> (<u>New Yale</u> 106)

Book with Multiple Volumes

Works Cited entry:

> Eisenhower, Dwight. <u>Presidential
> Correspondence</u>. Vol. 2. New York: Dutton,
> 1960. 6 vols.

Parenthetical note:

> (Eisenhower 77)

If you cite more than one volume in your paper, indicate the number.

> (Eisenhower 2:77)

Book in Second or Later Edition

Works Cited entry:

> Franklin, Marcia. <u>Modern France</u>. 3rd ed.
> Philadelphia: Comstock, 1987.

Parenthetical note:

> (Franklin 12)

Work in an Anthology

Works Cited entry:

> Ford, John M. "Preflash." <u>The Year's Best
> Fantasy</u>. Ed. Ellen Datlow and Terri
> Windling. New York: St. Martin's, 1989.
> 265-82.

Parenthetical note:

> (Ford 265-66)

Book in Translation

Works Cited entry:

> Verne, Jules. <u>Twenty Thousand Leagues Under the
> Sea</u>. Trans. Michel Michot. Boston: Pitman,
> 1992.

Parenthetical note:

> (Verne 65)

Book with Editor or Editors

Works Cited entry:

> Benson, Nancy, ed. <u>Ten Great American Plays</u>.
> New York: Columbia UP, 2002.

Parenthetical note:

> (Benson 23)

Book with Author and Editor

Works Cited entry:

> Gissing, George. <u>Workers in the Dawn</u>. Ed. Jason
> Day. London: Oxford UP, 1982.

Parenthetical note:

> (Gissing 78)

Book in a Series

Works Cited entry:

> Swessel, Karyn, ed. <u>Northern Ireland Today</u>.
> Modern Europe Ser. 3. New York: Wilson,
> 2003.

Parenthetical note:

> (Swessel 34)

Republished Book

Works Cited entry:

> Smith, Jane. <u>The Jersey Devil</u>. 1922. New York:
> Warner, 2002.

Parenthetical note:

> (Smith 23-25)

Periodicals

Newspaper Article

Works Cited entry:

> Chavez, Maria. "The Hispanic Century." <u>New York
> Times</u> 12 Mar. 2003: A13.

Parenthetical note:

> (Chavez)

Note: If an article has only one page, page numbers are not included in parenthetical notes.

Magazine Article

Works Cited entry:

> Janssen, Mary. "Iran Today." <u>Time</u> 25 Mar. 2003:
> 341.

Note: If an article appears on nonconsecutive pages, list the first page followed by a "+" sign.

Parenthetical note:

> (Janssen)

Scholarly Article

Works Cited entry:

> Grant, Edward. "The Hollywood Ten: Fighting the
> Blacklist." <u>California Film Quarterly</u> 92
> (2002): 14-32.

Parenthetical note:

> (Grant 21-23)

Newspaper or Magazine Article with Unnamed Author

Works Cited entry:

> "The Legacy of the Gulf War." <u>American History</u>
> 12 Mar. 2003: 23-41.

Parenthetical note:

>   ("Legacy" 25)

Letter to the Editor

Works Cited entry:

>   Roper, Jack. Letter. <u>Chicago Defender</u> Jan.
>   2002, sec. B: 12.

Parenthetical note:

>   (Roper)

Other Print Sources

Encyclopedia Article with Author

Works Cited entry:

>   Keller, Christopher. "Lisbon." <u>World Book
>   Encylopedia</u>. 2003.

Parenthetical note:

>   (Keller, "Lisbon")

Note: Page numbers are not used with works in which items are arranged alphabetically.

Encyclopedia Article with Unnamed Author

Works Cited entry:

>   "Lisbon." <u>Columbia Illustrated Encyclopedia</u>.
>   2002.

Parenthetical note:

>   ("Lisbon")

Pamphlet with Author

Works Cited entry:

>   Tindall, Gordon, ed. <u>Guide to New York Churches</u>.
>   New York Chamber of Commerce, 1998.

Parenthetical note:

>   (Tindall 76-78)

Pamphlet with Unnamed Author

Works Cited entry:

>   <u>Guide to New York Museums</u>. New York: Columbia U,
>   2003.

Parenthetical note:

>   (<u>Guide</u> 176-182)

The Bible

Works Cited entry:

> Holy Bible. New International Version. Grand
> Rapids, MI: Zondervan, 1988.

Note: Titles of sacred texts are not underlined.

Parenthetical note:

> (Mark 2:4-9)

Nonprint Sources

Motion Picture

Works Cited entry:

> Casino. Dir. Martin Scorsese. Universal, 1995.

Note: You may wish to include names of performers or screenwriters if they are of special interest to readers.

Television Program

Works Cited entry:

> "The Long Goodbye." Law and Order. Dir. Jane
> Hong. Writ. Peter Wren. Perf. Rita
> Colletti, Diane Nezgod, and Vicki Shimi.
> NBC. WTMJ, Milwaukee. 12 May 2003.

Videotape

Works Cited entry:

> Colonial Williamsburg. Prod. Janet Freud.
> American Home Video, 1996.

Note: You may include information about the director, performers, or screenwriters if these are important for readers.

Live Performance of a Play

Works Cited entry:

> All My Sons. By Arthur Miller. Dir. Anita Dayin.
> Lyric Theater, New York. 10 May 2003.

Speech

Works Cited entry:

> Goode, Wilmont. "America in the Next Century."
> Chicago Press Club. 12 Oct. 2003.

Personal or Telephone Interview

Works Cited entry:

> Weston, Thomas. Personal interview. 21 May
> 2003.

Parenthetical Notes for Nonprint Sources

Because nonprint sources do not have page numbers and often have long titles, parenthetical notes can be cumbersome. Most writers avoid inserting citations by mentioning the source within the text.

```
Multiple personality disorder was featured in a recent
episode of Law and Order.

In Gone with the Wind special effects were used to
re-create the burning of Atlanta.

Interviewed in the fall of 2003, Laura Dornan sug-
gested that many critics failed to see the feminist
theme in her play.
```

Electronic Sources

CD-ROM

Works Cited entry:

```
"Understanding Macbeth." Master Dramas. CD-ROM.
     Educational Media: Microsoft, 2002.
```

E-mail

Works Cited entry:

```
Ballard, Morton D. "Rental Cars." E-mail to
     Germaine Reinhardt. 21 May 2003.
```

Electronic Journal

Works Cited entry:

```
Smith, Perry. "Truman Capote and Kansas."
     Phoenix 2.7 (2003) 15 Sep. 2003 <http://
     www.englishlit./hts/phoenix/index>.
```

Article from Online Newspaper

Works Cited entry:

```
"Long Day's Journey Into Night Production
     Disappointing." New York Times on the Web
     17 Mar. 2003. 22 Apr. 2000 <http://
     www.nytimes.com/aponline/a/ap-play.html>.
```

Reference Database

Works Cited entry:

```
The Emerald Project: Irish Literature from
     1500-2000. Boston University. 21 Oct.
     2000 <http://www/bostonuniv/emerald/>.
```

Electronic Texts

Many books are available online. Because they lack page numbers, mention the title within the text to avoid long parenthetical notes.

Works Cited entry:

> Gissing, George. <u>Demos</u>. London, 1892. <u>The Electronic Text Center</u>. Ed. Jacob Korgman. Aug. 2003. U of Michigan Lib. 5 Mar. 2000 <http//etext.lib.michigan.edu>.

Web Pages

Web pages vary greatly. In general, include the name of the person or organization that created the site, the title, descriptions, the date of creation, the date of access, and the URL.

Works Cited entry:

> Chicago Irish Center. Home page. 5 Apr. 2003 10 May 2002 <http://www.chi.irish.cent .org>.

Discussion Group Posting

Works Cited entry:

> Baker, Jordan. "Golf Today." Online posting. 2 Mar. 2000. Professional Sports Discussion List. 15 Mar. 2000. <http://www.prosports.com/posting/>.

Linked Sources

MLA does not provide a method of citing hypertext links, but the following format allows readers to follow your search.

Works Cited entry:

> Trainer, Lois. "F. Scott Fitzgerald." Online posting. 4 Aug. 2003. Ansaxnet. 10 Oct. 2000 <http://www.amlit/edu>. Lkd. <http://www.yalelit.edu/biography>.

Sources and Sample Documented Essay

Read through the excerpts taken from a book, an article, and a website and note how the student uses and notes these sources.

Book Excerpt

From: *How to Survive College* by Nancy Hughes, published by Academic Press, New York City, 2005.

HOW TO SURVIVE COLLEGE   176

Today credit card companies bombard incoming freshmen with credit card offers. Card companies operate on campuses, often in student unions and dorm lobbies. Giving out free hats, T-shirts, coffee mugs, and pizza coupons, they encourage students to sign up for cards. Companies generally issue cards to any student over eighteen whether they have jobs or not. Faced with the need for books, clothes, computer supplies, and student fees, many students quickly apply for cards and ring up charges. At Northwestern University nearly 10% of incoming freshmen had maxed out at least one credit card by the end of their first semester.

Actual purchases, however, are often not the culprit. The ability to use a credit card to get cash from an ATM leads many students to live well beyond their means, getting into debt $40 or $60 at a time. Miranda Hayes, who graduated with $7,500 in credit card debts, had made only $2,000 in purchases. "I charged a computer my freshman year and all my books," she admits. "The rest was all cash from an ATM that went for movies, beer, pizzas, bus fare, my cell phone, health club dues, and interest."

Magazine Article

From: "University of Wisconsin Takes Up the Issue of Student Credit Card Debt" in *Cardline,* June 11, 2004, page 1.

Cardline June 11, 2004   1

UNIVERSITY OF WISCONSIN TAKES UP THE ISSUE OF STUDENT CREDIT CARD DEBT

The Board of Regents for the University of Wisconsin System, which operates the state's 13 four-year schools and 14 two-year schools, was expected to discuss credit card solicitation today, a spokesperson for the UW-Madison tells CardLine. The discussion was promoted by the release in May of a 15-page, UW-commissioned report, "Student Credit Card Debt and Policies on Credit Card Solicitation on the University of Wisconsin," which said that 40% of its students owe credit card balances of $1,000 or more. It's not clear what action the regents, who are meeting at the UW's Milwaukee campus, will take, but three of its campuses have adopted formal policies regarding credit card solicitations and others have informal ones. The report recommends that the regents adopt rules that are consistent system-wide. Some UW administrators take a much harsher attitude. They wanted credit card solicitation banned altogether, but the report said such a ban might violate the law. The UW commissioned the report following several national studies, including one by the General Accounting Office. Newspapers also regularly reported on the issue. The report gathered its data through telephone interviews with staff members, student surveys and anecdotal information. It found that between 62% and 71% of students had at least one credit card. A UW Student Spending and Employment Survey found that of those who responded to it, 40% of students owed credit card debts of $1,000 to $5,000, and 10% owed over $5,000. The high card debt takes a toll on some students. Although the campuses don't . . .

A Website

From: "Top Ten Student Money Mistakes" by Blythe Terrell on Young Money, updated at http://www.youngmoney.com/money_management/spending/ 020809_02, and accessed March 21, 2005.

 ✉ **MAIL**   🖨 **PRINT**

▶ careers

▶ consumer issues

▶ credit & debt

▶ entertainment

▶ entrepreneurship

▶ financial aid

▶ investing

▶ lifestyles

▶ money management

▶ technology

▶ travel

▶ wheels

Top Ten Student Money Mistakes

By Blythe Terrell, University of Missouri

For many students, college is the first major landmark on the path to independence. Moving away from home means no more curfews, no asking for permission, and no parents looking over their shoulders. It also means that the liberty-seeking college kid is now free to make his or her own mistakes.

In such an environment, money management often becomes an issue. Knowing how to avoid these problems is the key to beating them. Here are ten common mistakes students make, and how **you** can avoid them.

1. **Making poor choices about which credit cards to get.** Credit card companies set up booths on college campuses, offering T-shirts and other items to anyone who will sign up for a card. Although the deals can seem fantastic, students must look into the card's repayment terms carefully. "When students get credit cards, two things can happen," said Stephen Ferris, professor of finance at the University of Missouri–Columbia. "One, they don't read the fine print and see what they're paying. And they're paying a lot. Or they use it until it's maxed out." It is absolutely necessary to pay your credit cards on time each month, added Ferris.

2. **Letting friends pressure them into spending money.** College life is full of opportunities to spend money, finals-week smorgasbords, an evening out with friends, road trips and vacations. . . Not knowing how to say "no" can cause students to spend money they just do not have. "If you can't afford it, just say no," says David Fingerhut, a financial adviser with Pines Financial in St. Louis.

3. **Not setting up a budget.** If they have a set amount of money, they must plan ahead and know how much they can spend each month. "It has to work on paper before it works in real life," Fingerhut said.

4. **Not seeking out the best bank rates.** Banks offer many different kinds of checking and savings accounts, but some charge fees that others do not. It is essential for students to do research and not simply go with the closest, most accessible bank, Ferris said.

Student Essay

College Students and Debt

Students graduating in debt is nothing new. Few students or their parents have enough money to pay as they go. Even students with scholarships take on debts to pay for college expenses. But in recent years tens of thousands of students have added to their financial burdens by amassing credit card debts. Colleges, which allow credit card companies to operate on campus, must regulate the way they advertise and educate students on managing their money.

Arriving on campus, freshmen encounter credit card promoters in student unions and their dorms. Offering students free gifts, the various card companies urge students to sign up for credit cards. Card companies will issue cards to any college student who is at least eighteen (Hughes 176). Credit cards have become extremely popular with students. Currently 62-71% of college students have at least one credit card ("University" 1).

Many students are unsophisticated when it comes to using credit. Whether making a purchase or cash advance, they rarely calculate how interest charges or ATM fees will inflate their balance. In many cases, students get deep into debt not by making major purchases, but by withdrawing costly cash advances. Many students share the fate of Miranda Hayes, who amassed a $7,500 credit card debt, noting, "I charged a computer my freshman year and all my books. The rest was all cash from an ATM that went for movies, beer, pizzas, bus fare, my cell phone, health club dues, and interest" (qtd. Hughes 1).

The University of Wisconsin, among others, is considering establishing new policies to regulate credit card promotions on campus ("University" 1). But the real service colleges can give students is to prepare them for the responsibilities of adult life by including financial planning seminars that focus on credit cards, budgets, and loans. Stephen Ferris, a finance professor, points out that when students sign up for cards, "they don't read the fine print and see what they are paying. And they're paying a lot" (qtd. Terrell). Students don't consider interest rates, let peer pressure guide their spending, and fail to set up budgets (Terrell).

Ultimately, students are responsible. Away from home for the first time, they have to learn to manage their time, ignore distractions and peer pressure, and use credit wisely. Parents and colleges can provide information and give advice, but as adults, college students must take responsibility for the decisions they make.

Margin annotations:

- student thesis
- topic sentence
- paraphrase
- facts stating problem
- citation showing author and page
- specific fact cited
- topic sentence
- example supporting thesis
- quote within quote cited
- paraphase
- topic sentence
- quote within cited expert quotation
- paraphase
- conclusion
- restatement of thesis

```
                       Works Cited
Hughes, Nancy. How to Survive College. New York:
     Academic, 2005.

Terrell, Blythe. "Top Ten Student Money Mistakes."
     Young Money. 21 Mar. 2005 <http://
     www.youngmoney.com/money_management/spending/
     020809_02>.

"University of Wisconsin Takes Up the Issue of Student
     Credit Card Debt." Cardline 11 June 2004: 1.
```

EXERCISE 4 Writing a Documented Essay

Using the three sources on pages 269–270, write your own essay about student credit card use. You may choose another topic and locate at least two outside sources to create a documented essay. Include both in-text citations and a Works Cited page.

WORKING TOGETHER

Working with a small group of students, exchange documented essays and source material. Refer to pages 257–261 to see if you have cited quotations and paraphrases correctly. Make sure you avoid plagiarism—using but failing to cite the facts, ideas, and quotations taken from outside sources.

GET THINKING AND WRITING

CRITICAL THINKING

Select a controversial or highly debated topic like abortion, gun control, Social Security reform, immigration, terrorism, or reparations for slavery. Conduct an Internet search and locate at least three sources advocating different points of view.

Notice how different sources use facts, statistics, and quotations to support their opinions.

Develop a list of questions that would help you evaluate the strength and weaknesses of websites on the Internet. What should people consider before believing what they read in cyberspace?

WHAT HAVE YOU WRITTEN?

1. How have you defined or described the most serious concern students should have in examining online sources? Could you restate it more clearly and directly?

    _____

    _____

2. List errors in logic or critical thinking you have detected in any of the sources you located.

    _____

    _____

© Ted Soqui/Corbis

GET WRITING

Some attorneys argue that television shows like *CSI* give the public and juries misconceptions about the quality of evidence prosecutors can present in court. Do you think television dramas can mislead the public by creating unrealistic expectations of what evidence law enforcement officers use to convict criminals?

Write a short essay examining whether or not television programs educate or mislead the public about the criminal justice system. You may wish to refer to episodes you have seen on television or conduct an Internet search on DNA evidence to obtain additional sources.

WRITING ON THE WEB

Using a search engine like Yahoo!, Google, or AltaVista, enter terms such as *plagiarism, avoiding plagiarism, MLA documentation, documenting Internet sources, using online sources, writing research papers, using quotations and paraphrases,* and *Works Cited page.*

1. Locate a documented article online and notice how the author documents quotations and paraphrases.
2. Look up definitions and examples of plagiarism. Locate your college's policy on plagiarism.

POINTS TO REMEMBER

1. Outside sources strengthen essays by adding facts, statistics, and quotations to support the thesis.
2. Using outside sources without acknowledging them is plagiarism, a serious offense.
3. Documentation distinguishes your ideas from those taken from outside sources.
4. Commonly known facts like someone's birth date, the height of a mountain, or a state's capital do not have to be documented.
5. Document both direct quotations and paraphrases.
6. The goal of a documented essay is to express your thesis supported by sources. An essay is not a list of facts and quotes. Make sure the paper expresses what you think, not what others have written.

If you use Writer's ResourcesNow, please have your students log in and view the pretest, study plan, and posttest for this chapter.   **Writer's Resources ⓦ Now™**

© Gabe Palmer/CORBIS

Why is writing different on the job than in school?

Write three or four paragraphs comparing and contrasting the kind of writing you have done in college with the kinds of writing tasks you might expect in your career.

Writing at work differs greatly from writing in college. Although memos, e-mail, letters, and reports follow the same rules of grammar and spelling as school assignments, they are developed in a very different environment, have different readers, and serve different needs.

Business writing takes place in a specific context. The tone, style, wording, and format of business writing is shaped by the history and standards of the profession, organization, readers, and subject.

Business writing is directed to specific readers. In college you write to a general academic audience. In business you address customers, employees, supervisors, and investors who have specific questions, concerns, and problems.

Business writing is action-oriented. In college you write papers to present ideas. At work you are more likely to direct people to take action—to buy a product, use a service, hire an employee, or make an investment.

Business writing is sensitive to legal implications. Letters, reports, and contracts are legal documents. You must avoid statements that can expose you to legal action.

Business writing represents the views of others. In college your papers express personal ideas and opinions. At work the e-mails, letters, and reports you write should reflect the values, attitudes, and positions of your employer. Avoid writing personal opinions that may bring you into conflict with your superiors.

This chapter focuses on four of the most common business writing assignments you will face: e-mail, reports, résumés, and cover letters.

E-Mail

Today almost every job uses e-mail to communicate. Some people confuse e-mail with "instant messages" or chat room conversations. They write and answer e-mail without thinking, producing a stream of tangled ideas, missing details, grammar errors, and inappropriate comments. E-mail, like any kind of writing, takes thought and planning to be effective.

Strategies for Writing E-Mail

1. **Realize that e-mail is *real mail.*** E-mail can be stored, distributed, and printed. Unlike a note or memo that can be retrieved or corrected, e-mail, once sent, becomes permanent. *Never send e-mail when you are tired or angry. Avoid sending messages you will later regret.*
2. **Think before you write.** E-mail should have a clear goal. Consider whom you are writing to, what they need to know, and how you can persuade them to accept your ideas.
3. **Follow the prewriting, drafting, revising, and editing strategies you would use in writing a paper document.** Don't let an e-mail message simply record whatever comes into your head. E-mail should have a clear purpose and an easy-to-follow organization. Plan before you write.
4. **Understand what messages *should not* be expressed in e-mail.** E-mail is considered appropriate for short, informative messages. Do not

attempt to send a fifteen-page report by e-mail, though it might be sent as an attachment. Do not send personal or sensitive information by e-mail. E-mail is seen as too informal and too public for confidential correspondence.

5. **Respond to e-mail carefully.** Often e-mail messages will list multiple readers. Before sending a reply, determine whether you want everyone or just a few people to see your response.

6. **Make sure you use the correct e-mail address.** E-mail addresses can be complicated and oddly spelled. Often names are shortened or reversed. Donald Peterson might appear as "donald.peterson," "dpeterson," or "petersond." Double-check addresses.

7. **Clearly label your e-mail in the subject line.** Spam—unwanted e-mail messages—use misleading headings such as "Following your request" or "next week's conference" to grab attention. To prevent your e-mail from being overlooked or deleted before it is read, use specific identifying details in the subject such as "RE: April 19th health insurance reminder" or "Smithkin Supplies Annual Audit."

8. **Include your reader's full name and the date in your inside address.**

9. **Keep e-mail direct and concise.** People expect e-mail to be brief and easy to read. Avoid complicated sentences and long paragraphs. Use short paragraphs and bulleted or numbered points to increase readability.

10. **End the e-mail with a clear summary, request, or direction.** Summarize important points. If you are asking for information or help, clearly state what you need, when you need it, and how you can be reached. If you want readers to take action, provide clear directions.

11. **Ask readers for an acknowledgment if you want to make sure they received your message.**

12. **Review, edit, and double-check e-mail before sending.** Check your spelling, addresses, names, prices, or figures for accuracy. Read your e-mail aloud to catch missing words, illogical statements, confusing sentences, or awkward phrases.

13. **Print hard copies of important e-mail for future reference.**

```
January 30, 2006

From: John Rio
To:   Sales Staff
RE:   Expense Account Reports

To all sales staff:

As of March 1, 2006, Pacific Mutual will no longer
provide sales representatives with company cars or
expense accounts. Instead, sales representatives will
be given a flat monthly grant to cover office,
travel, and vehicle expenses:

Inside Sales Reps        $250 per month

District Sales Reps      $500 per month

Regional Sales Reps      $750 per month
```

```
This policy affects only regular monthly expenses.
Pacific Mutual will continue to pay all expenses
for those attending regional and national sales
conventions.

If you have any questions about the new policy
please contact me at ext. 7689.

John Rio
```

EXERCISE 1 Revising E-Mail

Revise this e-mail to create a clear, concise message.

Kim:

This e-mail is about the student enrollment problems we face with online courses. Right now it seems many students sign up and cannot find the website for their course and have no idea how the class is going to be run or what is expected of them. This is causing a problem. I am getting a lot of complaints from students who seem lost. I think we can do some things to improve this situation next semester. The main college website should have a link to all online courses. Each online instructor must place on the course website an expanded syllabus that explains the nature of the course, office hours, assignment due dates, readings, and online discussion groups. In addition, each department website should list its online offerings.

Bijan Naboti

Reports

Business reports use the same methods of development found in college papers, such as definition, process, cause and effect, and comparison. There are, however, key differences in the approach, style, and format of business reports.

Business reports emphasize facts and actions rather than thoughts. Academic reports explore ideas, advance theories, and offer personal interpretations. Business reports deal with practical day-to-day realities. They are direct and to the point.

Business reports are generally written to multiple readers. Academic reports are written for one instructor who is expected to read the entire document. Business reports often are sent to a number of people who may only read sections that deal with their concerns. In many cases, no one will read the entire report.

Business reports use subtitles or numbered points to signal transitions. Academic reports are double-spaced and might run ten pages without any breaks. Readers are expected to follow the writer's train of thought through subtle transition statements. Business reports are single-spaced and use visual markers to break up the text into labeled sections to make the document readable at a glance.

Business reports are generally objective and avoid using the first person ("I").

Business reports generally do not use formal documentation of outside sources. Instead, they may informally note sources.

```
According to Business Week, the deficit will not
affect interest rates.
```

`Recent news reports indicate growing labor unrest`
`in China.`

Business reports make greater use of visual aids such as graphs and charts.

Strategies for Writing Reports

1. **Determine a clear goal for your report.** Business reports either direct people to take action or provide them with information they will use to make decisions. Focus on facts and objective details.

2. **Focus on specific readers.** Consider the practical needs of the people who will read your report. What facts, figures, and concepts do they need to know to make decisions, resolve conflicts, prevent problems, or make money? Give readers information they can use.

3. **Include a table of contents in reports longer than three pages.**

4. **Use an informational, direct title that clearly tells readers what the report is about.** Avoid simple labels or generalized titles you might use in a college paper.

5. **Open the report with a clear statement of purpose.** Introductions in college papers may tell a story or provide an example to arouse interest. Business reports open with a direct statement of a problem or the writer's goal.

6. **Organize ideas in a logical format that is clearly labeled.** Avoid transitional statements or subtle shifts in your train of thought.

7. **Use conclusions to explain findings, summarize key points, or list recommendations.**

Boylan Electric

DATE:	January 12, 2006
TO:	Mary Liotta, Property Manager
FROM:	Saheeb Pradi, District Manager
SUBJECT:	Property at 901 West Highland Avenue, Milwaukee

RELOCATION OF SALES OFFICE/SALE OF 901 WEST HIGHLAND BLDG.

It is highly recommended that Boylan Electric sell its 901 West Highland building and rent offices near the airport to serve its sales staff.

BACKGROUND

The Boylan sales office in Milwaukee has been located at 901 West Highland Avenue since 1959. The building provided ample office and storage space and had easy freeway access. In 2005 freeway reconstruction and neighborhood redevelopment altered the environment. Freeway access is now limited. Parking, once available for a nominal fee across the street, is now limited to four spaces in front of the building and two spaces in the loading dock. The building, now nearly fifty years old, no longer serves the needs of Boylan's reduced sales staff. In 1959 Boylan manufactured small power tools widely sold in automotive, hardware, and department stores. Today this represents less than 10% of the product line, and sales are managed through catalog and online operations. Current sales representatives call on industrial accounts nationwide, 75% of whom make at least one flight from Mitchell Field a week.

RELOCATION NEEDS

The current sales and support staff of ten requires 1500 square feet of office space. Several office complexes on Layton Avenue and Airport Drive have vacancies ranging from $1100–$1950 a month. All provide sufficient parking and would reduce time and expense traveling to the airport. In addition, the majority of current employees live in the southern and western suburbs, so a relocation to this area would reduce their daily commuting time to a downtown office.

SALE OF HIGHLAND AVENUE PROPERTY

The Highland Avenue building, although in need of major roof and plumbing repairs, is currently valued at $395,000 (Shorewest estimate). Realtors report the property is highly marketable because of major rehabilitation of the former Pabst Brewery properties. Prospective buyers include merchants seeking retail or restaurant space and developers seeking to raze the building to allow expansion of neighboring buildings.

RECOMMENDATIONS

* Boylan Electric to seek advice and current estimates from three real estate agents.

* Boylan Electric to secure appropriate office space near the airport.

* Boylan Electric to allocate $5,000–$10,000 for minor repairs, landscaping, painting, and carpeting the lobby of 901 West Highland to enhance its marketability.

* Boylan Electric to prepare photographs, blueprints, and building specifications for realtors and potential buyers.

Résumés and Cover Letters

Résumés and cover letters are the first professional documents you will write in your career.

Résumés

Before starting to write a résumé, it is important to know what a résumé is and what a résumé is not.

A résumé is *not* a biography or a list of jobs—it is a ten-second ad.
Research shows the average executive spends just ten seconds looking at each résumé before rejecting it or setting it aside for further reading. A résumé does not have to list every job you have had or every school you attended. It should not be cluttered with employer addresses or names of references. It should briefly but clearly present facts, experiences, skills, and training that relate to a specific job or profession.

The goal of a résumé is to get an interview, not a job. Few people are hired based on a résumé. Résumés only show an employer that you are worth talking to. The goal of a résumé is to generate enough interest to prompt someone to call you for an interview.

You may need several résumés. Companies create different ads to sell the same product to different people. You might need three or four résumés that target specific jobs. A nurse, for example, might create one résumé highlighting her intensive-care experience and another focusing on her work with abused children. Because résumés are quickly screened, they have to communicate at a glance. A résumé that tries to cover too many areas will be vague or confusing.

Strategies for Writing Résumés

1. **Understand that there are no absolute "rules" for writing résumés, only guidelines.** You may have heard people say that a résumé should only be one page or must never include your age. Because careers vary, there are exceptions.

2. **Develop your résumé by focusing on the job description or company.** Study the wording of want ads or job announcements and highlight skills and experiences that directly match those listed in the ad.

3. **Include your full name, address, telephone number with area code, and e-mail address.**

```
                    Linda Chen
            842 California Street # A1
         San Francisco, California 94108
                  (415) 555-8989
                 l.chen@sfnet.com
```

4. **Provide a clear objective statement describing the job you seek.** Avoid vague objectives like "a position making use of my skills and abilities" or "sales, marketing, or public relations." If you have different interests, create separate resumes for each field or job.

```
OBJECTIVE    Restaurant management
```

5. **Use a brief overview or summary to highlight key skills and experience.**

```
OVERVIEW     Three years experience in restaurant
             management. Proven ability to hire,
             train, and motivate wait staff. Highly
             skilled in customer relations, menu
             design, and loss prevention.
```

```
SUMMARY      Restaurant Management
             * Assistant Restaurant Manager, Dio's
               2004-2006
             * Banquet Manager, Dio's 2004-2006
             * Banquet hostess, Lady of Shanghai,
               2003
             * Completed Hyatt management seminar,
               2003
```

You may find it easier to write the overview last, after you have identified your most important skills and accomplishments.

6. **List your most important credentials first.** If you are a college graduate with no professional experience, list education first. If a current or recent job relates to the job you seek, list experience first.

7. **Arrange education and job experience by time, beginning with the most recent.**

8. **Avoid general job descriptions.**

```
Office manager responsible for greeting visitors,
maintaining staff schedules, ordering supplies,
scheduling appointments, and processing payroll
and expense reports.
```

Focus on individual accomplishments and demonstrate the significance of your experience.

```
Office manager for 26 attorneys and paralegals in
state's largest law firm specializing in medical
malpractice. Individually responsible for sched-
uling appointments and processing payroll and ex-
pense reports. Reported directly to senior part-
ners on hiring and firing of office staff.
```

9. **List training seminars, volunteer work, hobbies, and military service only if they directly relate to the job you want.**

10. **Do not include addresses of employers, names of supervisors, or references.** These details can be supplied after you are called in for an interview.

Recent Graduate with Experience

LINDA CHEN
842 California Street #A1
San Francisco, California 94108
(415) 555-8989
l.chen@sfnet.com

GOAL	Restaurant management
OVERVIEW	Associate degree in hotel and hospitality management. Three years experience in restaurant management, supervision and training of wait staff, inventory control, loss prevention, menu design, scheduling, and vendor ordering.

EXPERIENCE
2004–2006

Assistant Manager, DIO'S, San Francisco, CA
Directly assisted manager and owner of 50-seat Italian restaurant with three banquet rooms.
* Supervised all special events and banquet operations, including business luncheons, wedding receptions, fundraisers, and annual meetings.
* Individually responsible for managing banquet staff of 15.
* Assisted owner in redesigning banquet menu, pricing, and scheduling.

2003

Banquet Hostess, LADY OF SHANGHAI, San Francisco, CA
Hosted over 50 banquets and special events, including weddings, holiday parties, fundraisers, and business seminars.

EDUCATION

CALTECH EXTENSION, San Francisco, CA
Associate Degree in Hotel and Hospitality Management, May 2006
Completed courses in business management, accounting, food service, food science, human relations, and marketing.
* 3.5 GPA
* One of six students selected to assist faculty in annual alumni fundraising dinner.

HYATT HOTEL, San Francisco, CA
Completed food service management course, 2003
* Sponsored by owner of Lady of Shanghai Restaurant.
* Toured major restaurants, banquet halls, and hotels in San Francisco.
* Participated in national online discussion group hosted by Hyatt Hotel corporation.

LANGUAGES

Fluent Chinese

References available on request

Recent Graduate with Unrelated Experience

THERESA ALBANESE
2744 South Prairie Avenue
Chicago, IL 60615
(312) 555-7862
albaneset@earthlink.net

OBJECTIVE   Property casualty insurance sales

OVERVIEW   Six years experience in direct sales and sales
management. Skilled in direct sales. Proven ability
in developing leads through cold calling and
telemarketing. Experienced in training and motivating
sales staff. Adept at developing online training and
management tools to enhance sales support and
productivity.

EDUCATION   LASALLE COMMUNITY COLLEGE, Chicago, IL
Associate Degree, Marketing, 2006
Completed courses in sales management,
telemarketing, business law, insurance law, and inland
marine insurance.
* Attended Kemper insurance seminar.
* Assisted in design and production of college ad
  campaign.

NATIONAL SALES INSTITUTE
Completed sales training program, 2004

SALES   UNITED STATES ARMY, Chicago, IL
EXPERIENCE   Sgt. in Chicago recruiting office responsible for
2000–Present   statewide recruiting.
* Supervised 29 recruiters.
* Achieved over 100% sales goal each year.
* Introduced new database system to trace prospects.
* Refined telemarketing procedures.
* Developed online training seminars for new
  recruiters.
* Reduced overhead 15% first year.

1996–2000   Sgt. Public Affairs Office, Fort Sheridan, IL
* Prepared press releases, newsletters, and personnel
  announcements.
* Trained staff in public presentations.
* Assisted in design of crisis communications policies.
* Rehearsed press conferences and media
  appearances with base commander.

References and transcripts available

Cover Letters

Cover letters can be as important as the résumés they introduce. Résumés submitted without letters are often discarded because employers assume that applicants who do not take the time to address them personally are not serious. Résumés tend to be lists of cold facts; cover letters allow applicants to present themselves in a more personalized way. The letter lets applicants explain a job change, a period of unemployment, or a lack of formal education.

Strategies for Writing Cover Letters

In most instances, cover letters are short sales letters using standard business letter formats.

1. **Avoid beginning a cover letter with a simple announcement.**

   ```
   Dear Sir or Madam:

   This letter is to apply for the job of office sup-
   ply sales rep advertised in the Times Picayune
   last week . . .
   ```

2. **Open letters on a strong point emphasizing skills or experiences.**

   ```
   Dear Sir or Madam:

   In the last two years I opened thirty-six new
   accounts, increasing sales by nearly $750,000.
   ```

3. **Use the letter to include information not listed on the résumé.**
   Volunteer work, high school experiences, or travel that might not be suited to a résumé can appear in the letter—if they are career related.

4. **Refer to the résumé, indicating how it documents your skills and abilities.**

5. **End the letter with a brief summary of notable skills and experiences and a request for an interview.** To be more assertive, state that you will call the employer in two or three days to schedule an appointment.

Cover Letter Responding to a Want Ad

LINDA CHEN
842 California Street #A1
San Francisco, California 94108
(415) 555-8989
l.chen@sfnet.com

May 25, 2006

Kim Sung
Royal Canton
835 Grant Avenue
San Francisco, CA 94108

RE: Banquet Management position advertised in *The San Francisco Chronicle,* May 24, 2006

Dear Ms. Sung:

In the past three years, I have supervised over 150 banquets and special events, including wedding parties of 500, political fund-raisers, VIP luncheons, sales meetings, and three Chinatown Improvement Association Annual Awards dinners.

For the past two years, I was the assistant manager at Dio's on Fisherman's Wharf, where I managed three banquet rooms and supervised a staff of fifteen. I am fully familiar with all aspects of banquet operations, from promotion and planning to ordering and scheduling. By working closely with special events planners, I was able to improve services and lower Dio's overhead by 10% the first year.

As my résumé shows, I have just received an Associate's Degree in Hotel and Hospitality Management. In addition, I completed a Hyatt Hotel food service management course.

Given my education in restaurant management and my experience in banquet operations, I believe I would be an effective banquet manager for Royal Canton. I look forward to the opportunity of discussing this position with you at your convenience. I can be reached at (415) 555-8989 or you can e-mail me at l.chen@sfnet.com.

I can e-mail you samples of banquet plans, employee training memos, and letters of recommendation, if you wish.

Sincerely yours,

Linda Chen

Cover Letter Responding to Personal Referral

THERESA ALBANESE
2744 South Prairie Avenue
Chicago, IL 60615
(312) 555-7862
albaneset@earthlink.net

May 25, 2006

John Stephens
Great Lakes Casualty
500 North Dearborn Ste 823
Chicago, IL 60610-4910

RE: Insurance Agent Position

Dear Mr. Stephens:

Phil Douglass mentioned to me that Great Lakes Casualty has openings
for additional insurance agents to call upon small- and medium-sized
businesses in the greater Chicago area.

As my résumé shows, I have just completed my associate degree in
marketing and have six years experience in direct sales. I am fully familiar
with all areas of sales from developing leads through cold calls and
telemarketing to closing sales.

Before deciding to go into insurance, I served with the United States
Army in the state's largest recruiting operation. I supervised 29 recruiters
who achieved over 100% of sales goals each year through advanced
training, including online sales seminars I designed, which are now used
service-wide.

Given my knowledge of current insurance law and my practical experience
in sales, I believe I could be an effective agent for Great Lakes Casualty.
I would appreciate the opportunity to discuss this position with you at your
convenience. I can be reached by phone at (312) 555-7862 or by e-mail at
albaneset@earthlink.net.

Sincerely yours,

Theresa Albanese

WORKING TOGETHER

*Working with a group of students, discuss this résumé and cover
letter and recommend changes. Delete needless information, reword
awkward phrases, eliminate repetitions, and edit for spelling and other mechanical
errors. List details you would ask the student to add to make the résumé more
impressive.*

KURT RUDEL
262 Peachtree Street
Atlanta, Georgia 30303
(404) 555-5687

GOAL	To ultimately own my own business. In the meantime seeking a position in tool and die.
EDUCATION	Westside Highschool 2851 Heath Road Macon, Georgia 31216 Graduted 2003 Was actively in band, school yearbook printing, football team. * Assisted football coach while recovering from major knee injury. Atlanta Area Technical and Community College 2500 Western Avenue Atlanta, Geogia 30320 Graduated 2006 Completed tool and die program with courses in tool and die making, machining, quality control, industral design, and shop managment.
EXPERIENCE 2006	Southern Machine and Tool 6536 North Industrial Drive Atlanta, Georgia 30320 worked part time
2003–2005	Becker & Houghton 1287 Brooklawn Road NE Atlanta, GA 30319 worked part time
References	George Adello Francine Demarest Maria Valadez (404) 555-8989 (404) 555-9090 (404) 555-8987

KURT RUDEL
262 Peachtree Street
Atlanta, Georgia 30303
(404) 555-5687

May 25, 2006

Dear Mr. Bechmann:

This letter is to reply to the ad in the *Atlanta Consitution* that appeared May 22, 2006 last week.

I think I would make an excellant employe at your company because I know a lot about tool and die even before going to school.

I worked at Becker & Houghton and Southern Machine and Tool while going to school

Please call me this week.

Thanking you for your attention,

Kurt

GET THINKING AND WRITING

CRITICAL THINKING

When you graduate and enter the job market, you will have to evaluate job offers. Consider the following offers and choose the one you feel best suits your goals and lifestyle. Write two or three paragraphs explaining your choice. If you wish, you can use classification to rank these opportunities from the most to least desirable.

a. A major organization in your hometown offers an entry-level position that provides security but limited upward mobility.

b. A major organization offers an entry-level position with excellent opportunities for promotion. The job is located five hundred miles away.

c. A newly formed organization needs someone with your skills. There may be excellent chances of heading a department in a few years and earning a substantial salary and bonus. The organization, however, is just as likely to fail.

WHAT HAVE YOU WRITTEN?

Do you clearly explain which opportunity best suits your needs? Do you use cause and effect, comparison, and description to explain why one job better suits your goals than another? Have you organized details clearly?

GET WRITING

Write three or four paragraphs comparing how readers of business documents (résumés, letters, e-mails, and business reports) differ from readers of college assignments. How will an employer examine your résumé compared to an instructor evaluating a term paper?

© Chuck Savage/CORBIS

WRITING ON THE WEB

Use a search engine like Yahoo!, Google, or AltaVista and enter terms such as *résumés, writing résumés, cover letters,* and *applying for jobs* to locate current sites of interest.

POINTS TO REMEMBER

1. Business writing occurs in a very different environment than college writing. Be sensitive to the tone, style, and format used in your field.
2. E-mail is real mail. Write e-mail messages with the professionalism you would use in writing a first-class letter.
3. E-mail should be clear, concise, and direct. Avoid long, rambling messages.
4. Realize the limits of e-mail. Longer documents should be sent as attachments.
5. Résumés should be written concisely so they can be scanned in seconds.
6. Résumés should stress important points in your career—avoid including hobbies, high school jobs, and other minor details.
7. Cover letters should emphasize skills and experience and link yourself to the job you want.
8. Cover letters give you the opportunity to explain unrelated experience and add information not suited for the résumé.

If you use Writer's ResourcesNow, please have your students log in and view the pretest, study plan, and posttest for this chapter.

Writer's Resources ⓦ Now™

Part 4

Improving Style

Improving Essays

Peter O'Toole and Anthony Quinn in *Lawrence of Arabia*

© Underwood & Underwood/CORBIS

GET WRITING

Do you think movies and television present stereotypes about Arabs?

Write a short essay analyzing the way popular culture has shaped people's attitudes toward Arabs and the Middle East. Include examples of movies, characters, images, and themes to support your point of view.

Good writing takes readers on a journey. For readers to follow your train of thought and understand what you are trying to say, your essay should use **consistent tense, consistent person, consistent organization, and clear transitions.**

WHAT ARE YOU TRYING TO SAY?

GET WRITING

Write a paragraph describing an experience that changed your life. Discuss the past event and the way it continues to shape your attitudes or behavior today.

_____

_____

_____

_____

_____

_____

_____

_____

_____

WHAT HAVE YOU WRITTEN?

Review your paragraphs for the use of tense. Do you clearly distinguish between past and present? Do you make any awkward shifts from first person ("I") to second person ("you") or third person ("they")?

Using Consistent Tense

Tense refers to time—*past, present,* or *future.* Readers depend on your use of tense to understand the events you describe.

Jean *worked* at WKTJ, which *was* the only all-jazz station in Chicago.
   [Jean was once employed at Chicago's former only all-jazz station.]

Jean *worked* at WKTJ, which *is* the only all-jazz station in Chicago.
   [Jean was once employed at Chicago's only all-jazz station.]

Jean *works* at WKTJ, which *was* the only all-jazz station in Chicago.
   [Jean is employed at Chicago's former only all-jazz station.]

Jean *works* at WKTJ, which *is* the only all-jazz station in Chicago.
   [Jean is employed at Chicago's only all-jazz station.]

Using Past and Present

In revising essays, make sure that your use of tense clearly reflects your meaning. Use past tense to describe actions or situations that occurred in the past or have been completed.

It rained yesterday.
The drug damaged my uncle's red blood cells.
Chicago dug the canal in 1912.

Use present tense to describe actions that are happening now, are ongoing, or began in the past and continue into the present.

It is raining.
Red blood cells carry oxygen.
Chicago is building a new public library.

In writing a narrative, for example, you can relate events either in past or present. Most writers relate an event that has happened in the past tense.

Ben *went* out with a twisted ankle, and Coach Jackson *called* me in. It *was* my first scrimmage of the season. The ball *snapped*. I *dodged* past the defense and *raced* down the field. The field *was* slippery with wet leaves. I *turned* to catch the ball. The impact *knocked* me off balance, and I *tripped* into the end zone, making my one and only touchdown in high school.

Writers, however, sometimes write about a past event using present tense to create a sense of immediate action. Present tense can dramatize an event by making it appear that the action is happening now rather than in the past.

Ben *goes* out with a twisted ankle, and Coach Jackson *calls* me in. It *is* my first scrimmage of the season. The ball *snaps*. I *dodge* past the defense and *race* down the field. The field *is* slippery with wet leaves. I *turn* to catch the ball. The impact *knocks* me off balance, and I *trip* into the end zone, making my one and only touchdown in high school.

You can use both tenses to show logical shifts between past and present action.

I *love* playing football. I *enjoyed* my high school experiences, even though I only *scored* one touchdown. Coach Jackson *is* one of the best coaches in the state. He *won* state honors in two of the last five years. He *has* a website that *provides* high school athletes with valuable advice about everything from getting better grades to avoiding steroids. When I *played* ball, he *encouraged* us to study hard, reminding us that our education *came* first. He *is* just as proud of his players who *have gone* onto Harvard and Yale as he *is* of the players who made it to the NFL.

Avoid confusing readers with illogical shifts between past and present.

The field *was* covered with wet leaves. Everyone *was* slipping. Somehow I *manage* to dodge past the defense, and I *was* racing toward the end zone. I *turn* and *caught* the ball. The impact *knocks* me off my balance. I *tripped* into the end zone and *make* a touchdown.

EXERCISE 1 Revising for Consistent Tense

Revise these paragraphs to avoid awkward and illogical shifts in tense by changing the tense of verbs. Remember only to shift tense when there is a logical change from past to present.

The most widely reproduced photograph in history is the flag raising on Iwo Jima taken by Joe Rosenthal on February 23, 1945. This photograph inspires the Marine Corps War Memorial in Washington, D.C. Initial confusion about how the picture is taken causes controversy that lasted to this day. Some people have discredited the photograph, insisting that the picture was posed and not really a news photo of a genuine historical event. They point out that it was not a picture of the original flag raising but a reenactment. Others insist the photograph is genuine.

Much of the confusion stemmed from the photographer's initial comments. On February 23, 1945, a small American flag is flying atop Mt. Suribachi on the embattled island of Iwo Jima. The sight of the flag rallied the Marines locked in the bloodiest campaign in their history. It was decided to replace this flag with a larger one.

Joe Rosenthal, an AP photojournalist, trudges up the mountain with military photographers, one of whom carried a color movie camera. The Marines carefully time the changing of the flags, so that the second larger one would be raised just as the smaller flag is lowered. Five Marines and a Navy corpsman began to raise the bigger flag, and Rosenthal scrambles to catch the moment. He swings his bulky camera into position and snapped a picture without having time to look through the viewfinder. Thinking he misses shooting the event, he asks the Marines to pose at the base of the flagpole. The Marines cluster around and wave at the camera.

Rosenthal sends his film to be developed. A Navy technician immediately spots the dramatic picture of the Marines raising the flag, crops off the edge to center the image, and wired it to the United States. Within days the photo appeared on the front pages of hundreds of newspapers. President Roosevelt orders millions of copies to be printed to boost morale and promote the sale of war bonds.

Some people, however, suspected the photo was a fake. It looks too dramatic and too perfect to be real. A reporter asked Rosenthal, who had no idea that his accidental picture had become nationally famous, if he posed the shot. Thinking the reporter is referring to his second photo, Rosenthal said yes. A radio program then reported that the famous photo was posed, starting a legend that the whole event is just a piece of wartime propaganda.

Sixty years later historians still debate the issue. Many agree the photograph, taken by accident, depicted a genuine event, the raising of the second flag on Iwo Jima. The heroism of the Marines raising the flag was genuine as well. Of the six flag raisers, three lose their lives on Iwo Jima.

The most widely reproduced photograph in history is the flag raising on Iwo Jima taken by Joe Rosenthal on February 23, 1945. This photograph **inspired** _the Marine Corps War Memorial in Washington, D.C. Initial confusion about how the picture_ **was** _taken_ **caused** _controversy that_ **lasts** _to this day. Some people have discredited the photograph, insisting that the picture was posed and not really a news photo of a genuine historical event. They point out that it_ **is** _not a picture of the original flag raising but a reenactment. Others insist the photograph is genuine._

*Much of the confusion **stems** from the photographer's initial comments. On February 23, 1945, a small American flag **was** flying atop Mt. Suribachi on the embattled island of Iwo Jima. The sight of the flag rallied the Marines locked in the bloodiest campaign in their history. It was decided to replace this flag with a larger one.*

*Joe Rosenthal, an AP photojournalist, **trudged** up the mountain with military photographers, one of whom carried a color movie camera. The Marines carefully **timed** the changing of the flags, so that the second larger one would be raised just as the smaller flag **was** lowered. Five Marines and a Navy corpsman began to raise the bigger flag, and Rosenthal **scrambled** to catch the moment. He **swung** his bulky camera into position and snapped a picture without having time to look through the viewfinder. Thinking he **missed** shooting the event, he **asked** the Marines to pose at the base of the flagpole. The Marines **clustered** around and **waved** at the camera.*

*Rosenthal **sent** his film to be developed. A Navy technician immediately **spotted** the dramatic picture of the Marines raising the flag, **cropped** off the edge to center the image, and wired it to the United States. Within days the photo appeared on the front pages of hundreds of newspapers. President Roosevelt **ordered** millions of copies to be printed to boost morale and promote the sale of war bonds.*

*Some people, however, suspected the photo was a fake. It **looked** too dramatic and too perfect to be real. A reporter asked Rosenthal, who had no idea that his accidental picture had become nationally famous, if he posed the shot. Thinking the reporter **was** referring to his second photo, Rosenthal said yes. A radio program then reported that the famous photo was posed, starting a legend that the whole event **was** just a piece of wartime propaganda.*

*Sixty years later historians still debate the issue. Many agree the photograph, taken by accident, **depicts** a genuine event, the raising of the second flag on Iwo Jima. The heroism of the Marines raising the flag was genuine as well. Of the six flag raisers, three **lost** their lives on Iwo Jima.*

Summaries of plays, movies, novels, and stories can be written in past or present tense.

Past

In "The Cask of Amontillado," Edgar Allan Poe presented the gleeful confession of a psychotic murderer. Montresor delighted in retelling his story of taking revenge against a friend who had insulted him. Knowing his friend's love of wine, Montresor lured his victim to his underground vaults and entombed him in a crypt.

Present

In "The Cask of Amontillado," Edgar Allan Poe presents the gleeful confession of a psychotic murderer. Montresor delights in retelling his story of taking revenge against a friend who insulted him. Knowing his friend's love of wine, Montresor lures his victim to his underground vaults and entombs him in a crypt.

In any narrative or description, you can include both past and present tense to indicate the difference between past and current or ongoing action.

In "The Cask of Amontillado," Edgar Allan Poe *presented* the gleeful confession of a psychotic murderer. Poe's character *represents* something rare in literature, a man who *kills* without remorse. Montresor *lured* his victim to an underground vault and *entombed* him in a crypt. The murder *was* never discovered. Poe's hero *celebrated* the fact that after fifty years no one *had discovered* the body. This attitude *reminds* modern readers of recent serial killers.

EXERCISE 2 Maintaining Consistency in Tense

Revise these paragraphs from a student paper to avoid awkward and illogical shifts in tense by changing the tense of verbs. Remember only to shift tense when there is a logical change from past to present.

Death of a Salesman is perhaps the most famous modern American play. The drama told the story of the last twenty-four hours in the life of Willy Loman, a struggling salesman. There was nothing heroic or noble about him. He lies, cheats on his wife, insults his friend, and gave his sons all the wrong values. He told his son Biff that he did not have to do well in school but just play football and be well-liked. Biff ends up at thirty-four working as a ranch hand. Willy's wife, Linda, insisted that although Willy never made a lot of money or had his name in the newspaper, he was still a human being and deserved attention.

Linda's comment is really the thesis statement of the play. Even a little man with a lot of faults deserved attention when he is fired after working for a company for over thirty years. Willy may have had naïve and childish dreams, but they gave his life purpose. At sixty-three he cannot accept the fact that he will never become a big shot. He is too proud to take a job from a friend and killed himself. Willy foolishly believes that his massive funeral will impress Biff. But none of his old business pals showed up, and Biff sees his father as just a bitter, lonely man who had all the wrong dreams.

~~Death of a Salesman is perhaps the most famous modern American play. The drama~~ **tells** ~~the story of the last twenty-four hours in the life of Willy Loman, a struggling sales-~~ ~~man. There~~ **is** ~~nothing heroic or noble about him. He lies, cheats on his wife, insults his~~ ~~friend, and~~ **gives** ~~his sons all the wrong values. He~~ **tells** ~~his son Biff that he~~ **does** ~~not have~~ ~~to do well in school but just play football and be well-liked. Biff ends up at thirty-four work-~~ ~~ing as a ranch hand. Willy's wife, Linda,~~ **insists** ~~that although Willy never made a lot of~~ ~~money or had his name in the newspaper, he~~ **is** ~~still a human being and~~ **deserves** ~~attention.~~

*Linda's comment is really the thesis statement of the play. Even a little man with a lot of faults **deserves** attention when he is fired after working for a company for over thirty years. Willy may have had naïve and childish dreams, but they gave his life purpose. At sixty-three he cannot accept the fact that he will never become a big shot. He is too proud to take a job from a friend and **kills** himself. Willy foolishly believes that his massive funeral will impress Biff. But none of his old business pals **show** up, and Biff sees his father as just a bitter, lonely man who had all the wrong dreams.*

Using Consistent Person

Essays can be written in first, second, or third person.

First person: *I* (singular) or *we* (plural)

Second person: *you* (singular and plural)

Third person: *he* or *she* (singular) or *they* (plural)

Use **first person** when you write about things you have seen or experienced or to state a personal opinion.

I was born in Brooklyn but grew up in Great Neck where *my* father taught high school English and *my* mother managed a bookstore.

As *we* waited to cross the street, *we* saw a cab run the stop sign and slam into a parked delivery van.

I am convinced that capital punishment does not deter criminals from committing violent crimes. After all, *I* doubt if anyone contemplating committing a crime expects to get caught.

Avoid using first person in formal reports and research papers.

Use **second person** to directly address your reader, especially when giving directions or suggestions.

You must scan computers for viruses at least once a week.

Retain *your* cancelled check as a receipt.

Avoid using second person in making general statements rather than ones directed to specific readers.

Awkward
The new show will air this fall on Comedy Central, one of *your* basic cable channels.

Her car needs a transmission overhaul, which is *your* most expensive repair job.

They forgot to file a flight plan, *your* most common pilot mistake.

Revised
The new show will air this fall on Comedy Central, a basic cable channel.

Her car needs a transmission overhaul, which is the most expensive repair job.

They forgot to file a flight plan, the most common pilot mistake.

Use **third person** to describe the actions of other people or organizations.

He drove to Philadelphia last night.

She moved to France.

They raised prices twice last year.

To prevent confusion, use one person in an essay, unless there are logical shifts.

They flew to Boston where *I* went to school.

I went to the accountant to get *your* taxes.

Awkward
Sara went to the top of the Eiffel Tower, where *you* could see for miles.

People often gain weight when *you* quit smoking.

You get a fifty-dollar discount when *customers* pay in cash.

Improved
Sara went to the top of the Eiffel Tower, where *she* could see for miles.

People often gain weight when *they* quit smoking.

You get a fifty-dollar discount when *you* pay in cash.

or

Customers get a fifty-dollar discount when *they* pay in cash.

EXERCISE 3 Revising Shifts in Person

Revise the following paragraphs to avoid awkward shifts in person.

For fifty years, television news was dominated by your network evening broadcasts. Tens of millions of Americans rushed home from work to see the day's events reported on television. With only three networks, your anchormen like Walter Cronkite and Huntley and Brinkley were popular and highly influential. Their coverage of civil rights demonstrations, assassinations, and moon landings shaped the way Americans thought of the country and themselves. The power of news anchors was summed up by President Johnson's comment, "If I've lost Cronkite, I've lost middle America." Infuriated by Cronkite's coverage of the Vietnam War, Johnson sometimes called CBS, demanding to speak to Cronkite during a commercial break. Cronkite was so powerful that he refused to take calls from the White House.

Today the influence of the network evening news has dwindled. Cronkite had as many as 22 million viewers in 1968. When Dan Rather retired in 2005, he drew only 7 million viewers. Only 8% of people under 40 now watch the network broadcasts. Today TVs carry CNN, CSPAN, or Fox News in your waiting rooms, hotel lobbies, bars, gyms, schools, and offices. We see the news as it happens throughout the day and feel no need to see it when you get home. Every time you log on to the Internet, we get headlines of breaking news stories and can easily click to online news sources to track stories in detail.

With so many news sources bombarding us all day long, some people still see the evening news as your official summary of current events.

For fifty years, television news was dominated by network evening broadcasts. Tens

of millions of Americans rushed home from work to see the day's events reported on television. With only three networks, anchormen like Walter Cronkite and Huntley and Brinkley were popular and highly influential. Their coverage of civil rights demonstrations, assassinations, and moon landings shaped the way Americans thought of the country and themselves. The power of news anchors was summed up by President Johnson's comment, "If I've lost Cronkite, I've lost middle America." Infuriated by Cronkite's coverage of the Vietnam War, Johnson sometimes called CBS, demanding to speak to Cronkite during a commercial break. Cronkite was so powerful that he refused to take calls from the White House.

Today the influence of the network evening news has dwindled. Cronkite had as many as 22 million viewers in 1968. When Dan Rather retired in 2005, he drew only 7 million viewers. Only 8% of people under 40 now watch the network broadcasts. Today TVs carry CNN, CSPAN, or FOX News in waiting rooms, hotel lobbies, bars, gyms, schools, and offices. **They** *see the news as it happens throughout the day and feel no need to see it when* **they** *get home. Every time* **they** *log on to the Internet,* **they** *get headlines of breaking news stories and can easily click to online news sources to track stories in detail.*

With so many news sources bombarding **them** *all day long, some people still see the evening news as* **their** *official summary of current events.*

EXERCISE 4 Revising Shifts in Person

Revise the following paragraph from a student paper to eliminate awkward shifts in person.

We reached San Francisco by noon and checked in to our hotel. We walked to Chinatown, where you can find silk dresses, inlaid boxes, Chinese coins, and exotic prints at great prices. We then took a cab to Fisherman's Wharf. One can take a boat to Alcatraz where you can tour the old prison, which is now a national park. The trip is so popular that you should make reservations. We were lucky because it was a weekday, and you could get tickets. The trip is worth it. The prison is one of the most fascinating places one can visit. We really felt the island was haunted by the ghosts of all the prisoners who were held there. I kept remembering the movie *Escape from Alcatraz* with Clint Eastwood. People still wonder if the prisoners depicted in the film managed to get to the mainland or were swept out to sea.

We reached San Francisco by noon and checked in to our hotel. We walked to Chinatown, where **we found** *silk dresses, inlaid boxes, Chinese coins, and exotic prints at great prices. We then took a cab to Fisherman's Wharf.* **Tourists** *can take a boat to Alcatraz where* **they** *can tour the old prison, which is now a national park. The trip is so popular that* **visitors** *should make reservations. We were lucky because it was a weekday, and* **we** *could get tickets. The trip is worth it. The prison is one of the most fascinating places*

we visited. *We really felt the island was haunted by the ghosts of all the prisoners who*

were held there. I kept remembering the movie Escape from Alcatraz with Clint Eastwood.

People still wonder if the prisoners depicted in the film managed to get to the mainland

or were swept out to sea.

Using Consistent Organization

One way to improve comparison, division, classification, and cause-and-effect essays is to use consistent organization. When you describe or define more than one
topic, you can help readers follow your train of thought and remember details by
presenting ideas in a common pattern.

> Most of our high school seniors attend one of three local community and
> technical colleges.
>
> Brixton County Technical College in Mayfield offers associate degrees in   name and location
> business, technology, and aviation mechanics. It has a faculty of 150 and an   faculty & students
> enrollment of 2,000. The college is best known for its FAA-approved aviation
> mechanic program, which trains students to service aircraft used by Delta,   most noted program
> Midwest, United, and other major airlines.
>
> Martin Luther King College in Patterson offers diplomas and associate   name and location
> degrees in business, health occupations, and social services. It has a faculty
> of 75 and an enrollment of 1,100. The college's most popular program is pre-   faculty & students
> nursing, which trains about 400 students a year who transfer to nursing pro-   most noted program
> grams at the state university.
>
> Payton Technical Institute in Plymouth provides certificates in auto   name and location
> mechanics, electronic repair, carpentry, and welding. It has a faculty of 50   faculty & students
> and 500 students. The new robotics welding program is very popular and   most noted program
> trains graduates for work in the local Ford assembly plant.

EXERCISE 5 Revising for Consistent Organization

Revise the following paragraphs to develop a consistent organization.

> Three of the most significant black leaders to emerge following the emancipation of
> the slaves were Frederick Douglass, Booker T. Washington, and W. E. B. DuBois.
>
> Frederick Douglass was best known for his impassioned oratory against slavery. He
> was born a slave in 1817 and fled to freedom in 1838. He began a career in public
> speaking, denouncing not only slavery but discrimination and segregation in the North.
> After publishing his autobiography, *Narrative of the Life of Frederick Douglass,* he went
> to England where he continued to campaign against slavery. Friends raised money to
> purchase his freedom. Douglass returned to America and founded an anti-slavery news-
> paper called *The North Star.* During the Civil War, Douglass met with Lincoln several
> times and helped recruit blacks to serve in the Union Army. He served as the U.S. Min-
> ister to Haiti from 1889 to 1891. He died in 1895.
>
> Booker T. Washington is best known for his interest in education. He founded the
> Tuskegee Institute, which stressed vocational skills, and the National Negro Business
> League, which encouraged black enterprise. Washington advised several presidents and

addressed Southern politicians, urging them to provide jobs for blacks. Washington was born a slave in 1856 and taught himself to read. His position that economic opportunities were more important than civil rights led to criticism from other black leaders. His organizations began to lose support after 1910. Washington died in 1915.

W. E. B. DuBois died in Ghana in 1961 after nearly eighty years of work dedicated to the advancement of African Americans. A Pan Africanist, he believed blacks in America should view themselves as Africans rather than Americans. He opposed Booker T. Washington's approach, which he thought kept blacks as second-class citizens. DuBois was a world traveler, visiting Russia and China, as well as several African nations. He was born in Massachusetts in 1868. In 1895 he became the first African American to receive a PhD from Harvard.

The three leaders often had divergent views, but their impact has shaped African-American culture, politics, and art into the twenty-first century.

Three of the most significant black leaders to emerge following the emancipation of the slaves were Frederick Douglass, Booker T. Washington, and W. E. B. DuBois.

Frederick Douglass was best known for his impassioned oratory against slavery. He was born a slave in 1817 and fled to freedom in 1838. He began a career in public speaking, denouncing not only slavery but discrimination and segregation in the North. After publishing his autobiography, Narrative of the Life of Frederick Douglass, he went to England where he continued to campaign against slavery. Friends raised money to purchase his freedom. Douglass returned to America and founded an anti-slavery newspaper called The North Star. During the Civil War, Douglass met with Lincoln several times and helped recruit blacks to serve in the Union Army. He served as the U.S. Minister to Haiti from 1889 to 1891. He died in 1895.

Booker T. Washington is best known for his interest in education. Washington was born a slave in 1856 and taught himself to read. He founded the Tuskegee Institute, which stressed vocational skills, and the National Negro Business League, which encouraged black enterprise. Washington advised several presidents and addressed Southern politicians, urging them to provide jobs for blacks. His position that economic opportunities were more important than civil rights led to criticism from other black leaders. His organizations began to lose support after 1910. Washington died in 1915.

W. E. B. DuBois was a major Pan Africanist who believed blacks in America should view themselves as Africans rather than Americans. He was born in Massachusetts in 1868. In 1895 he became the first African American to receive a PhD from Harvard. He opposed Booker T. Washington's approach, which he thought kept blacks as second-class citizens. DuBois was a world traveler, visiting Russia and China, as well as several African nations. Du Bois died in Ghana in 1961 after nearly eighty years of work dedicated to the advancement of African Americans.

The three leaders often had divergent views, but their impact has shaped African-

American culture, politics, and art into the twenty-first century.

Using Clear Transitions

When you write, you often make transitions, changing your train of thought by introducing examples, comparisons, references, quotations, or definitions. Make sure you fully explain examples, comparisons, and references.

Unclear

  After 9/11 many people worried that security measures were going to limit civil rights. There was a fear that racial profiling would treat Muslims like the Japanese were. The Patriot Act was criticized for the powers it gave authorities to detain people and hold them without formal charges.

Revised

  After 9/11 many people worried that security measures were going to limit civil rights. There was a fear that racial profiling would treat Muslims *the way the Japanese-Americans were treated during WWII, many of whom were placed in internment camps based solely on their ethnic status.* The Patriot Act was criticized for the powers it gave authorities to detain people and hold them without formal charges.

Unclear

  My first year of college was a shock. My English teacher assigned us ten novels to read in one semester. My psychology teacher gave a weekly quiz. Both my history and business law instructors required twenty-page research papers. This was so different than high school. I had to give up my social life and quit my part-time job just to maintain a B- average.

Revised

  My first year of college was a shock. My English teacher assigned us ten novels to read in one semester. My psychology teacher gave a weekly quiz. Both my history and business law instructors required twenty-page research papers. *In high school we read one novel a year and no teacher gave weekly quizzes or required anything longer than a five-page paper.* I had to give up my social life and quit my part-time job just to maintain a B- average.

Link quotations to your own writing.

Unclear

  Schizophrenia remains a devastating disease. "We have discovered new treatments, but we still have not found out what causes it" (Wilson 34). Many patients and their families find existing therapies only partially helpful, leading some to consider alternative medicine.

Improved

  Schizophrenia remains a devastating disease. *George Wilson, director of the National Institute of Mental Health, notes,* "We have discovered new treatments, but we still have not found out what causes it" (34). Many patients and their families find existing therapies only partially helpful, leading some to consider alternative medicine.

EXERCISE 6 Improving Essays

Take one or more of your recent essays and examine your paragraphs for awkward shifts in tense and person, inconsistent organization, and unclear transitions. Make a note of repeated errors and keep these in mind when you revise and edit future assignments.

WORKING TOGETHER

Working with a group of students, revise this announcement to eliminate awkward shifts in tense and person, inconsistent organization, and unclear transitions. Invent necessary facts or details.

Attention All Sales and Service Personnel:

City of Angels Productions will introduce a new travel/expense policy on May 1st:

Sales/Service Personnel, LA District
Employees are allowed a maximum of $50 a day travel reimbursement. Employees issued company cars can still use your corporate charge cards for gas. Meal allowances remain at a maximum of $25 a day.

Sales/Service Personnel, Western Region
Your meal allowances have been increased to $40 a day.
    Employees are allowed a maximum of $150 a day travel reimbursement. Use of company cars for out-of-state travel is discouraged.

Sales/Service Personnel, National Accounts
Employees are allowed a maximum of $250 a day travel reimbursement. Airline tickets should be charged onto your corporate charge card. Employee meal allowances have been increased to $60 a day.

If you have any questions, please contact me at ext. 7403

Jack Vincennes
City of Angels Productions

GET THINKING AND WRITING

CRITICAL THINKING

In the 1930s when President Roosevelt wanted better relations with Latin America, his administration encouraged Hollywood to avoid making films with negative stereotypes of South Americans. Today we are trying to improve our relations with Arab nations. Should Hollywood, which makes movies seen around the world, avoid negative images of Arabs and Muslims? Would you consider this a good idea or censorship? Write a short essay stating your views.

WHAT HAVE YOU WRITTEN?

Write out your thesis statement or controlling idea:

_____

_____

Does this statement accurately express your point of view? Could it be revised to be more direct or less abstract?

Do you accurately use shifts in tense to show changes between past and present?

Which person do you use—first (I/we), second (you), or third (he/she/they)?

Do you make any awkward or illogical shifts in person?

If you develop your essay with comparisons or examples, are details organized in a consistent pattern?

Read your essay aloud. Are there any unclear transitions? Do you explain references and examples so readers can follow your train of thought?

© Reuters/CORBIS

GET WRITING

What impact does American popular culture have on audiences in other countries? If all you knew about the United States came from watching American movies, television shows, and music videos, what would you think about the country? What would seem to be its values, its ethics, its attitudes toward other nations?

Think of your favorite movies, television shows, and music videos, and write an essay describing the messages they send to people who have no other knowledge of the United States.

WRITING ON THE WEB

Using a search engine like Yahoo!, Google, or AltaVista, enter terms such as *improving essays, revising essays, parallel development, shifts in tense, consistent tense, shift in person, consistent use of person,* and *awkward transitions.*

POINTS TO REMEMBER

1. You can improve your essays by making it easier for readers to follow your train of thought and by avoiding awkward shifts.
2. Use consistent tense, shift from past to present only when there is a logical change in time.
3. Use consistent person, avoiding illogical shifts from *I* to *you* or *they*.
4. Avoid unclear transitions. Fully explain examples and references and link quotations to your own text.
5. Use consistent organization to present ideas in a common pattern.

Writer's Resources Now™   If you use Writer's ResourcesNow, please have your students log in and view the pretest, study plan, and posttest for this chapter.

20

Improving Sentence Variety

© Scott de Freitas-Draper/Santa Maria Times/Corbis

GET WRITING

Do you think the news media is objective? Does it seem to take sides on many issues? Can you think of evidence of biased reporting?

Write a short essay expressing your views on the way television presents the news. Support your opinions with examples.

You can make paragraphs and essays more effective and easier to read by increasing the variety of your sentences. Changing the usual structure of sentences can more clearly express what you are trying to say and prevent your writing from becoming dull and repetitive.

GET WRITING

WHAT ARE YOU TRYING TO SAY?

Describe a car you would like to own.

_____
_____
_____
_____
_____
_____
_____
_____
_____
_____
_____
_____

WHAT HAVE YOU WRITTEN?

Read your paragraph carefully. Notice the style and length of your sentences.
Write out the shortest sentence:

_____

What idea does it express? Is it important enough to isolate in a single sentence? Could it be combined with another sentence?

Write out the longest sentence:

_____
_____

What idea does it express? Does your sentence address a complex issue or include more than one complete idea? Does it contain wordy phrases that add little meaning? Would your ideas be clearer if stated in more than one sentence?

Do many of your sentences follow a repetitive pattern, such as "It has air-conditioning. It has power steering. It has a DVD player"?

Varying Sentence Length

The length and complexity of sentences should reflect the message they are trying to express.

Short Sentences

Short sentences can be effective because they are direct and dramatic. They can stress an important fact or idea readers can easily understand and remember.

> Her career is finished.
> The jury voted guilty.
> Never swim alone.

Too many short sentences, however, can make writing choppy and hard to understand because instead of connecting ideas to create a train of thought, they become a list of separate statements.

Choppy
> Mayor Beam is running for reelection. He is seeking a third term. He faces a tough campaign. He is running against Elizabeth Holzer. She is a popular businesswoman. She owns the Hotel Metro. She built several condos downtown.

Improved
> Mayor Beam is running for reelection, seeking a third term. He faces a tough campaign against Elizabeth Holzer, a popular businesswoman. She owns the Hotel Metro and has built several condos downtown.

You can reduce choppy writing by joining short, related sentences that better demonstrate the relationship of ideas.

Choppy
> Talk shows dominate afternoon TV. Soap operas remain popular. They have had to change. The shows have to appeal to a younger generation. Soap stars now portray professional women. They also portray single mothers.

Improved
> Talk shows dominate afternoon TV, though soap operas remain popular. They have had to change to appeal to a younger generation. Soap stars now portray professional women and single mothers.

You can reduce choppiness by avoiding using complete sentences that simply add a single fact or detail that could be included in a related sentence.

Choppy
> Cara bought a mint-condition 1965 Mustang. It is a convertible.
> He was born in Chicago in 1978. His parents are Polish.
> The demonstration led to a riot. The riot killed six people.

Improved
> Cara bought a mint-condition 1965 Mustang convertible.
> He was born in Chicago to Polish parents in 1978.
> The demonstration led to a riot that killed six people.

EXERCISE 1 Increasing Sentence Variety by Reducing Choppiness

Revise the following sentences by joining related sentences. Eliminate sentences that simply add a detail that could be included in a related sentence.

1. Desi Arnaz was a band leader, singer, and actor. He was also the husband of Lucille Ball.

   Desi Arnaz was a band leader, singer, actor, and the husband of Lucille Ball.

   _____

2. In 1951, Desi and Lucy agreed to star in a TV comedy. It was called *I Love Lucy.*

   In 1951, Desi and Lucy agreed to star in a TV comedy called I Love Lucy.

   _____

3. At that time, TV comedies were broadcast live from studios. The studios were in New York.

   At that time, TV comedies were broadcast live from studios in New York.

   _____

4. Lucy and Desi wanted to stay in California. They wanted to live at home.

   Lucy and Desi wanted to live at home in California.

   _____

5. They suggested recording the show on film. It would be like a motion picture.

   They suggested recording the show on film like a motion picture.

   _____

6. The sponsor agreed with the plan but insisted on one change. They wanted a live audience.

   The sponsor agreed with the plan but insisted on having a live audience.

   _____

7. Desi helped pioneer a new way of recording a live performance. It used three cameras.

   Desi helped pioneer a new way of recording a live performance using three cameras.

8. This was expensive. CBS asked Lucy and Desi to accept a reduced salary.

   CBS asked Lucy and Desi to accept a reduced salary to cover expenses.

   _____

9. Desi agreed in exchange for something he wanted. He wanted to own the rights to the films.

   Desi agreed in exchange for owning the rights to the films.

   _____

10. **CBS accepted Desi's request. He would own the films after they were broadcast.**

   CBS accepted Desi's request to own the films after they were broadcast.

11. **Television was new. Few people understood the value of reruns.**

   Television was so new that few people understood the value of reruns.

12. **Lucy and Desi created a studio. It was called Desilu.**

   Lucy and Desi created a studio called Desilu.

13. **A few years later, Lucy and Desi sold the films back to CBS. They received four million dollars for them.**

   A few years later, Lucy and Desi sold the films back to CBS for four million dollars.

14. **Desilu grew rapidly. It produced many hit shows. It bought RKO Movie Studios.**

   Desilu grew rapidly, producing many hit shows and buying RKO Movie Studios.

15. **For a while, Desilu was the largest studio in the world. Lucy and Desi divorced in 1960. They split the company when they divorced.**

   For a while, Desilu was the largest studio in the world until Lucy and Desi divorced in 1960 and split the company.

EXERCISE 2 Improving Sentence Variety by Reducing Choppiness

Revise this paragraph by combining related sentences. Eliminate those that simply add a detail that could be included in another.

It was almost thirty years before 9/11. Samuel Byck planned to hijack a jet. He wanted to use it as a weapon. Samuel Byck was a failed salesman. He was emotionally unbalanced. He blamed President Nixon for his personal problems. He made threats against the president. He sent strange tapes to celebrities. The Secret Service took notice. He picketed the White House. He was arrested. He was denied a small business loan. Byck blamed Nixon. He tape-recorded an elaborate plan. He called it Operation Pandora's Box. He obtained a gun. He made a gasoline bomb. He planned to hijack a commercial airliner. He would force the pilot to fly over Washington. He would shoot the pilot. He would then crash the plane into the White House. He wanted to kill Nixon. On February 22, 1974, Byck drove to Baltimore/Washington International Airport. He shot a security guard. He stormed onto a Delta flight. He ordered the crew to take off. The pilots explained they could not. Byck shot them both. Police fired into the cockpit. Byck was wounded. He fell to the floor. He shot himself in the head. The assassination attempt drew little attention at the time. It was overshadowed by news about the Watergate scandal. It was almost forgotten. Byck's bizarre story did attract attention thirty years later. Historians and moviemakers were fascinated by Byck. Sean Penn played Byck in *The Assassination of Richard Nixon.* The film was released in 2004.

Almost thirty years before 9/11, Samuel Byck planned to hijack a jet and use it as a weapon. Samuel Byck was a failed salesman. Emotionally unbalanced, he blamed President Nixon for his personal problems. He made threats against the president and sent strange tapes to celebrities. The Secret Service took notice. He picketed the White House and was arrested. When he was denied a small business loan, Byck blamed Nixon. He tape-recorded an elaborate plan called Operation Pandora's Box. He obtained a gun and made a gasoline bomb. He planned to hijack a commercial airliner and force the pilot to fly over Washington. He would shoot the pilot, then crash the plane into the White House to kill Nixon. On February 22, 1974, Byck drove to Baltimore/ Washington International Airport. He shot a security guard and stormed onto a Delta flight. He ordered the crew to take off. When the pilots explained they could not, Byck shot them both. Police fired into the cockpit. Wounded, Byck fell to the floor and shot himself in the head. The assassination attempt drew little attention at the time. Overshadowed by news about the Watergate scandal, it was almost forgotten. Byck's bizarre story did attract attention thirty years later, fascinating historians and moviemakers. Sean Penn played Byck in The Assassination of Richard Nixon, released in 2004.

Long Sentences

Long sentences are useful to explain complicated ideas and demonstrate the relationship between ideas by placing them in a single sentence.

> Mayor Aronson has built a career on championing the need for low-income housing, but her challenger, June Avery, is gaining support by promising more jobs and better schools.

> In World War I, the United States fought Germany and was allied with Italy and Japan; in World War II the United States fought Germany, Italy, and Japan.

Paragraphs containing too many long sentences can become difficult to read, even if the sentences are grammatically correct.

> In the First World War, submarines, airplanes, and tanks were used for the first time in battle; however, it was not until the Second World War that their full potential was realized. The horrors of trench warfare, which saw millions killed in month-long battles of attrition, devastated armies and led generals to seek to avoid such losses in future conflicts. The French

built a line of massive underground fortresses to create a strong defensive shield while, in contrast, the Germans planned to launch a fast war with light mobile armies that would rush past defenses before an enemy could respond.

Improved

In the First World War, submarines, airplanes, and tanks were used for the first time in battle. It was not until the Second World War, however, that their full potential was realized. The horrors of trench warfare, which saw millions killed in month-long battles of attrition, devastated armies. Generals sought to avoid such losses in future conflicts. The French built a line of massive underground fortresses to create a strong defensive shield. The Germans, in contrast, planned to launch a fast war with light mobile armies that would rush past defenses before an enemy could respond.

You can increase variety by breaking up long sentences and using short dramatic sentences to highlight a single important idea.

After watching her mother suffer a series of strokes when she was only fifty, Carla decided she had to change her lifestyle and began a vigorous routine of diet and exercise, losing twenty-five pounds in a single month.

After watching her mother suffer a series of strokes when she was only fifty, Carla decided she had to change her lifestyle and began a vigorous routine of diet and exercise. **She lost twenty-five pounds in a single month.**

Eric promised his parents he would do better this semester, but he soon fell back to his old habit of sleeping late and watching television all day, never opening a single book.

Eric promised his parents he would do better this semester, but he soon fell back to his old habit of sleeping late and watching television all day. **He never opened a single book.**

EXERCISE 3 Increasing Sentence Variety by Highlighting Ideas in Separate Sentences

Revise the following long sentences by breaking them up to highlight important ideas in a separate short sentence. You may have to add words or short phrases for clarity.

1. **Science-fiction writers have imagined inventions long before they became practical realities, such as Jules Verne, who wrote about submarines and moon rockets in the nineteenth century and H. G. Wells, who described nuclear weapons in 1914.**

   Science-fiction writers have imagined inventions long before they became practical realities. Jules Verne wrote about submarines and moon rockets in the nineteenth century. H. G. Wells described nuclear weapons in 1914.

2. **In *The World Set Free,* Wells describes how scientists use a substance similar to plutonium to create a bomb that, when dropped from a small plane, destroys an**

entire city with a massive release of atomic energy at a time when the armies
of Europe relied on horses.

In The World Set Free, Wells describes how scientists use a substance similar to plutonium to create a bomb. Dropped from a small plane, it destroys an entire city with a massive release of atomic energy. At the time, the armies of Europe relied on horses.

3. **Harold Nicholson envisioned rockets, much like modern cruise missiles, delivering atomic bombs that create tidal waves causing global climate change in *Public Faces*, a novel he published in 1932.**

   In his 1932 novel Public Faces, Harold Nicholson envisioned rockets, much like modern cruise missiles, delivering atomic bombs. The blasts create tidal waves that cause global climate change.

4. **J. B. Priestly's 1938 novel *The Doomsday Men* describes a conspiracy to use a cyclotron to unleash a colossal chain reaction that would tear open the Earth's crust and end all human life; the conspirators were religious terrorists.**

   J. B. Priestly's 1938 novel The Doomsday Men describes a conspiracy to use a cyclotron to unleash a colossal chain reaction that would tear open the Earth's crust and end all human life. The conspirators were religious terrorists.

5. **In April 1944, *Astounding Science Fiction* published a story about an atom bomb that readers rated the worst story in that issue, but the story's details so closely resembled the top-secret atom bomb being developed by the Manhattan Project, the author was investigated by military intelligence.**

   In April 1944, Astounding Science Fiction published a story about an atom bomb. Readers rated it the worst story in that issue, but the story's details so closely resembled the top-secret atom bomb being developed by the Manhattan Project the author was investigated by military intelligence.

EXERCISE 4 Revising to Create Sentence Variety

Revise this paragraph by breaking up overly long sentences. Highlight important or dramatic ideas by placing them in short sentences.

Arthur Conan Doyle was born in Edinburgh, Scotland, in 1859, and studied medicine at the Royal Infirmary of Edinburgh, completing his degree in 1881. After serving as a doctor on a ship sailing to Africa, Doyle established a medical practice in Scotland, but he was unsuccessful and started to write fiction while waiting for patients. Still in his twenties, Doyle began publishing short stories, and soon his literary career flourished, leading him to pursue writing full time. Doyle became famous as the creator of Sherlock Holmes, the first modern detective, who appeared in four novels and over fifty short stories, and has been portrayed by dozens of actors in stage plays, motion pictures, and television dramas. Doyle also wrote science fiction, historical romances, plays, and poetry, though few of these works achieved the lasting fame of his Sherlock

Holmes stories. He created another character, featured in a series of novels, named Professor Challenger, who was a scientist and explorer. He first appeared in the 1912 novel *The Lost World,* which describes an expedition to a remote South American plateau where dinosaurs are found alive. The novel was made into a silent film in 1925, which featured many innovative special effects later used in movies like *King Kong,* and led to a series of remakes. The movie *Jurassic Park* and the popular television show *Lost* borrow themes from this ninety-year-old novel written by a doctor whose failed medical practice gave birth to some of the most famous literary figures in the world.

Arthur Conan Doyle was born in Edinburgh, Scotland, in 1859, and studied medicine at the Royal Infirmary of Edinburgh, completing his degree in 1881. After serving as a doctor on a ship sailing to Africa, Doyle established a medical practice in Scotland. He was unsuccessful and started to write fiction while waiting for patients. Still in his twenties, Doyle began publishing short stories. Soon his literary career flourished, leading him to pursue writing full time. Doyle became famous as the creator of Sherlock Holmes, the first modern detective. Holmes appeared in four novels and over fifty short stories and has been portrayed by dozens of actors in stage plays, motion pictures, and television dramas. Doyle also wrote science fiction, historical romances, plays, and poetry. Few of these works achieved the lasting fame of his Sherlock Holmes stories. He created another character, featured in a series of novels, named Professor Challenger, who was a scientist and explorer. He first appeared in the 1912 novel The Lost World, which describes an expedition to a remote South American plateau where dinosaurs are found alive. The novel was made into a silent film in 1925. It featured many innovative special effects later used in movies like King Kong and led to a series of remakes. The movie Jurassic Park and the popular television show Lost borrow themes from this ninety-year-old novel written by a doctor whose failed medical practice gave birth to some of the most famous literary figures in the world.

Increasing Sentence Variety with Questions and Exclamations

Most of the sentences you write are **declarative.** They make statements.

Austin is the capital of Texas.
I think it might snow tonight.
My car needs new tires.

Because most documents are written in declarative statements, you can arouse interest and create variety by using other types of sentences.

Questions engage readers by asking them to evaluate what they are reading or consider their own knowledge or attitudes.

When will we end our addiction to foreign oil?
Are you prepared for retirement?
Is your child safe?

Exclamations express strong statements and have exclamation points for emphasis.

Do it today!
After seven months of bitter campaigning and eight million dollars, Kim Sung lost the the election by six votes!
He's not raising taxes on the rich; he's raising taxes on the poor!

Because questions and exclamations are special effects, they should be used sparingly.

The name William Durant is not as well known as Henry Ford, but he was just as important to the development of the automobile industry. **Who was he?** Durant was the founder of General Motors, the largest carmaker in the world. He began his career as general manager of Buick in 1904. Four years later, he formed General Motors and acquired Oldsmobile. Over the next few years, he added Oakland (later Pontiac) and Cadillac. In 1915 he brought Louis Chevrolet's company into General Motors. Durant became a giant in the auto industry. The GM headquarters became known as the Durant Building. But Durant made reckless business decisions. In 1920 he was fired from the company he started. **Once the head of General Motors with a personal fortune of $50 million, Durant ended his career running a bowling alley!**

EXERCISE 5 Increasing Sentence Variety with Questions and Exclamations

Increase the sentence variety of this paragraph by turning one sentence into a question and one sentence into an exclamation.

Cinco de Mayo is widely celebrated by Mexican Americans throughout the United States. There is a great deal of confusion, however, about what the holiday celebrates. It is not Mexican Independence Day. Mexico's equivalent of the Fourth of July is not the Fifth of May (Cinco de Mayo) but the Sixteenth of September. Cinco de Mayo celebrates the Mexican army's 1862 victory over the French, who invaded the country after Mexico was unable to repay its European loans.

Cinco de Mayo is widely celebrated by Mexican Americans throughout the United States. **But what does it celebrate? It is not Mexican Independence Day!** Mexico's equivalent of the Fourth of July is not the Fifth of May (Cinco de Mayo) but the Sixteenth of September. Cinco de Mayo celebrates the Mexican army's 1862 victory over the French, who invaded the country after Mexico was unable to repay its European loans.

Varying Sentence Openings

An effective way to increase sentence variety is to alter the common subject-verb-object pattern of most sentences.

> Most people in Detroit are unaware of the vast network of streets a thousand feet under them. These streets are as wide as four-lane highways. Truck headlights shine eerily as they illuminate the dazzling white floors, walls, and ceilings of this strange underground city. Detroiters worked aboveground making cars. Other Detroiters toiled invisibly beneath them digging and blasting salt. Scientists estimated there is enough salt to operate the Detroit mines for millions of years. The mines closed in 1983. They were unable to compete with cheaper salt from Canada.

Opening Sentences with Adverbs

Adverbs (see Chapter 31) modify verbs, adjectives, and other adverbs. Many end in -*ly*. Because they can modify so many important words associated with the subject and verb, they can be used effectively to start a sentence.

> She **suddenly** announced she was quitting.
> **Suddenly,** she announced she was quitting.
>
> He **occasionally** played golf with old friends
> **Occasionally,** he played golf with old friends.

Opening sentences with adverbs can break up the monotony of standard sentence patterns and make writing more lively and interesting.

> Most people in Detroit are unaware of the vast network of streets a thousand feet under them. These streets are as wide as four-lane highways. **Eerily shining,** truck headlights illuminate the dazzling white floors, walls, and ceilings of this strange underground city. Detroiters worked aboveground making cars. **Invisibly** toiling beneath them, other Detroiters dug and blasted salt. Scientists estimated there is enough salt to operate the Detroit mines for millions of years. **Surprisingly,** the mines closed in 1983. They were unable to compete with cheaper salt from Canada.

EXERCISE 6 Opening Sentences with Adverbs

Underline the adverb in each sentence, then revise the sentence by placing the adverb at the beginning. Remember you may have to set off an opening adverb or adverbial phrase with a comma.

1. **Put your name at the top of the page always.**

   Always put your name at the top of the page.

2. **He carefully defused the timing mechanism of the bomb.**

   Carefully, he defused the timing mechanism of the bomb.

3. **Terry reluctantly placed her badge and gun on the chief's desk.**

   Reluctantly, Terry placed her badge and gun on the chief's desk.

4. **He foolishly dropped out of school a month before graduation.**

   Foolishly, he dropped out of school a month before graduation.

5. **He bravely clung to the raft, waiting for help.**

   Bravely, he clung to the raft, waiting for help.

6. **The team immediately lost hope of ever getting to the playoffs.**

   Immediately, the team lost hope of ever getting to the playoffs.

7. **The overloaded plane slowly lifted off the ground.**

   Slowly, the overloaded plane lifted off the ground.

8. **The students gratefully accepted the extended deadline.**

   Gratefully, the students accepted the extended deadline.

9. **The editor thoughtlessly failed to check the facts of the story.**

   Thoughtlessly, the editor failed to check the facts of the story.

10. **The mayor reacted immediately to the crisis.**

    Immediately, the mayor reacted to the crisis.

EXERCISE 7 Opening Sentences with Adverbs

Begin each sentence with an adverb. Remember to add a comma if needed.

1. _____ the parents confronted the coach.

2. _____ the Senate passed the bill after a ten-minute debate.

3. _____ we waited for the test results.

4. _____ the audience watched the last episode of *Everybody Loves Raymond*.

5. _____ the cast thanked their writers.

6. _____ the generals decided to respond to the surprise attack.

7. _____ Sandy called 911.

8. _____ crash investigators suspected sabotage.

9. _____ the coach decided to go for a touchdown.

10. _____ they bought the house without considering how much they would have to spend each month on utilities and property taxes.

Opening Sentences with Prepositions

Prepositions express the relationships between ideas, especially about time and space.

COMMON PREPOSITIONS

above	below	near	to
across	during	of	toward
after	except	off	under
along	for	over	with
around	from	past	within
before	like	since	without

Prepositions and prepositional phrases (often set off with a comma) can be used to open sentences.

He went to New York **without a dollar in his pocket.**
Without a dollar in his pocket, he went to New York.

She collapsed from exhaustion **on a public-speaking tour in New Mexico.**
On a public speaking tour in New Mexico, she collapsed from exhaustion.

He mowed lawns **during the summer.**
During the summer he mowed lawns.

Opening sentences with prepositions can make writing lively by altering the standard pattern of words and ideas.

In Detroit most of the people are unaware of the vast network of streets a thousand feet under them. These streets are as wide as four-lane highways. Truck headlights shine eerily as they illuminate the dazzling white floors, walls, and ceilings of this strange underground city. **Aboveground,** Detroiters made cars. **Underground,** other Detroiters dug and blasted salt. Scientists estimated there is enough salt to operate the Detroit mines for millions of years. **In 1983** the mines closed. They were unable to compete with cheaper salt from Canada.

EXERCISE 8 Opening Sentences with a Preposition

Underline the preposition or prepositional phrase in each sentence, then rewrite the sentence by placing the preposition at the beginning.

1. **World leaders throughout history have been concerned about their public image.**

   Throughout history, world leaders have been concerned about their public image.

2. **This has become increasingly important with the advent of photography.**

   With the advent of photography, this has become increasingly important.

3. **Stalin hid a deformed arm beneath his heavy uniforms.**

   Beneath his heavy uniforms, Stalin hid a deformed arm.

4. **Roosevelt disguised the effects of polio during public appearances.**

   During public appearances, Roosevelt disguised the effects of polio.

5. **He created the illusion that he could walk by leaning on the arm of an aide and using a cane.**

   By leaning on the arm of an aide and using a cane, he created the illusion that he could walk.

6. **Kennedy did not wish to be seen smoking his favorite cigars in public.**

   In public, Kennedy did not wish to be seen smoking his favorite cigars.

7. **He would slip the lit cigar into his pocket before leaving his car or Air Force One.**

   Before leaving his car or Air Force One, he would slip the lit cigar into his pocket.

8. **Kennedy burned many of his suit jackets in this effort to avoid being seen as a cigar-smoking politician.**

   In this effort to avoid being seen as a cigar-smoking politician, Kennedy burned many of his suit jackets.

9. **Kennedy hid his reading glasses from the public among other things because he felt they detracted from his image of youth and strength.**

   Among other things, Kennedy hid his reading glasses from the public because he felt they detracted from his image of youth and strength.

10. **Romanian dictator Nicolae Ceausescu looked taller between bodyguards selected for their short stature.**

    Between bodyguards selected for their short stature, Romanian dictator Nicolae Ceausescu looked taller.

EXERCISE 9 Opening Sentences with a Preposition

Add a preposition or prepositional phrase to the opening of each sentence. Remember to add a comma if needed.

1. _____ wars have been fought over many issues.

2. _____ actors and actresses appear glamorous and attractive.

3. _____ makeup, lighting, and camera angles are used to show stars at their best.

4. _____ the design and color of clothing can make a person look slimmer or taller.

5. _____ high school athletes can feel overwhelmed by the competition they face in college athletic programs.

6. _____ they are confronted by dozens of other athletes from across the country.

7. _____ the competition becomes intense as students work to impress recruiters from the NBA and NFL.

8. _____ some students neglect their studies.

9. _____ the stress of performing well leads some students to take steroids.

10. _____ colleges bear some responsibility for the popularity of steroids.

EXERCISE 10 Opening Sentences with Adverbs and Prepositions

Rewrite this paragraph by using adverbs and prepositions to create variety. Add words and punctuation where needed.

Every child in America has probably played with Crayola crayons. Edward Binney and Harold Smith founded the brand in 1903. They had previously developed dustless chalk that became a hit with schoolteachers and even received a gold medal at the St. Louis World's Fair. They visited schools and noticed the poor quality of wax crayons children used for coloring. They added color to industrial wax markers and created an improved crayon for artwork. Binney's wife came up with the name "Crayola" by combining the French word *craie* (chalk) and *oleaginous* (oily). Binney and Smith put eight of their oily chalks in a box and sold them for a nickel. The new crayons immediately became popular with children, teachers, and parents. The 100 billionth Crayola crayon was produced in 1996. That year the U.S. Post Office celebrated the company by issuing a stamp featuring a box of Crayola crayons.

Every child in America has probably played with Crayola crayons. Edward Binney and Harold Smith founded the brand in 1903. **Previously,** they had developed dustless chalk that became a hit with schoolteachers and even received a gold medal at the St. Louis World's Fair. They visited schools and noticed the poor quality of wax crayons children used for coloring. They added color to industrial wax markers and created an improved crayon for artwork. **By combining the French word** craie (chalk) and oleaginous (oily), Binney's wife came up with the name "Crayola." Binney and Smith put eight of their oily chalks in a box and sold them for a nickel. **Immediately,** the new crayons became popular with children, teachers, and parents. **In 1996,** the 100 billionth Crayola crayon was produced. That year the U.S. Post Office celebrated the company by issuing a stamp featuring a box of Crayola crayons.

Varying Methods of Joining Ideas

You can increase the variety of sentences by using different methods to combine ideas (see Chapter 24). You can join ideas using **present** and **past participles, compound subjects and verbs, appositives,** and **relative clauses.**

Combining Sentences with Present Participles

Present participles are *-ing* verbs like *running, standing, selling, dancing,* or *thinking.* You can join two related sentences by turning the verb of one sentence into an *-ing* verb to open a sentence combining the ideas of both. This can reduce repetition and wordiness and create a more lively sentence pattern.

I worked all night. I was exhausted by noon.
The car failed to start. The car was towed to the garage.
Sara studied for hours. She was determined to pass.

Improved
Working all night, I was exhausted by noon.
Failing to start, the car was towed to the garage.
Studying for hours, Sara was determined to pass.

EXERCISE 11 Combining Sentences with Present Participles: *-ing* Verbs

*Turn one of the verbs into an -*ing *verb and use it to open a single sentence that combines the ideas of both sentences.*

1. Carlo Ponzi gave his name to the "Ponzi scheme." He had immigrated to America in 1903.

   Having immigrated to America in 1903, Carlo Ponzi gave his name to the "Ponzi scheme."

2. He noticed immigrants needed international reply coupons to help poor European relatives send letters to America. He saw a business opportunity.

   Noticing that immigrants needed international reply coupons to help poor European relatives send letters to America, he saw a business opportunity.

3. Ponzi sought investors for a reply coupon business. He promised shareholders they could double their money in a few months.

   Seeking investors for a reply coupon business, Ponzi promised shareholders they could double their money in a few months.

4. Ponzi launched his Securities Exchange Company in 1920. He paid early investors the promised 50% interest.

   Launching his Securities Exchange Company in 1920, Ponzi paid early investors the promised 50% interest.

5. These investors urged others to share their fortune. They became a great advertisement for what seemed like a quick way to get rich.

   Urging others to share their fortune, these investors became a great advertisement for what seemed like a quick way to get rich.

6. **Within a few months, Ponzi collected millions of dollars. He bought a mansion and looked like a financial genius.**

   Collecting millions of dollars within a few months, Ponzi bought a mansion and looked like a financial genius.

7. **Ponzi's business survived on a constant flow of new money. It paid interest to old investors with money from new investors.**

   Surviving on a constant flow of new money, Ponzi's business paid interest to old investors with money from new investors.

8. **The business itself failed to generate much actual profit. It was bound to eventually collapse when it was unable to expand the supply of new investors.**

   Failing to generate much actual profit, the business was bound to eventually collapse when it was unable to expand the supply of new investors.

9. **In August 1920, federal agents shut down Ponzi's company. They found no inventory of the international reply coupons.**

   Shutting down Ponzi's company in August 1920, federal agents found no inventory of international reply coupons.

10. **The classic pyramid scheme earned a new name. It remains one of the most common frauds used to cheat investors.**

    Earning a new nickname, the classic pyramid scheme remains one of the most common frauds used to cheat investors.

Past participles are verbs in the past tense. Regular verbs end with *-ed* or *-d* such as *worked, developed, painted, collapsed,* or *created.* Irregular verbs have different forms such as *seen, bought, flown, sewn,* or *born* (see pages 450–452). Like present participles, they can be placed at the beginning of a sentence to combine ideas and eliminate wordiness and repetition.

The home office was difficult to reach. It was located in Olathe, Kansas.
The resort was devastated by Hurricane Andrew. It took years to recover.
The museum was equipped with high-tech security devices. It was very safe.

Improved
Located in Olathe, Kansas, the home office was difficult to reach.
Devastated by Hurricane Andrew, it took the resort years to recover.
Equipped with high-tech security devices, the museum was very safe.

EXERCISE 12 Combining Sentences with Past Participles

Turn one of the verbs into a past participle and use it to open a single sentence that combines the ideas of both sentences.

1. **Charles Goodyear was born in 1860. He is credited with developing vulcanization, the process that revolutionized the use of rubber.**

   Born in 1860, Charles Goodyear is credited with developing vulcanization, the process that revolutionized the use of rubber.

2. **Rubber had been known for centuries. It had been widely studied because it was elastic and airtight.**

   Known for centuries, rubber had been widely studied because it was elastic and airtight.

3. **Rubber became useless when subjected to cold or heat. It became brittle or melted.**

   Subjected to cold or heat, rubber became brittle or melted.

4. **Goodyear married at twenty-six. He started one of the first hardware stores in America.**

   Married at twenty-six, Goodyear started one of the first hardware stores in America.

5. **Goodyear was imprisoned for not paying his bills after the store failed. He sought a new venture.**

   Imprisoned for not paying bills after the store failed, Goodyear sought a new venture.

6. **A businessman showed Goodyear a warehouse full of rubber products that had become worthless goo in the heat. He realized the need to overcome this problem.**

   Shown a warehouse full or rubber products that had become worthless goo in the heat, Goodyear realized the need to overcome this problem.

7. **Goodyear became obsessed with rubber. He endured poverty and illness to devote his time to experiments.**

   Obsessed with rubber, Goodyear endured poverty and illness to devote his time to experiments.

8. **Goodyear was dedicated to finding a way of making rubber useful. Goodyear accidentally discovered that sulfur and heat could toughen rubber so it would not melt or crack.**

   Dedicated to finding a way of making rubber useful, Goodyear accidentally discovered that sulfur and heat could toughen rubber so it would not melt or crack.

9. **Goodyear was brokenhearted by the death of his daughter and legal battles over his discovery. He died deeply in debt.**

   Brokenhearted by the death of his daughter and legal battles over his discovery, Goodyear died deeply in debt.

10. **The Goodyear Tire and Rubber Company was founded by Frank Seiberling in 1898. The corporation has no tie to the Goodyear family.**

    Founded by Frank Seiberling in 1898, the Goodyear Tire and Rubber Company has no tie to the Goodyear family.

Combining Sentences Using Compound Subjects and Verbs

An effective way of increasing sentence variety and reducing repetitive statements is to create compound subjects and verbs to combine related sentences.

Yale is a famous Ivy League university. Harvard is also a famous Ivy League university.
Yale and Harvard are famous Ivy League universities. (compound subject)

The company sold computers. It also serviced copiers.
The company **sold** computers and **serviced** copiers. (compound verb)

EXERCISE 13 Combining Sentences with Compound Subjects

Rewrite the following pairs of sentences, using compound subjects to create a single sentence.

1. **The 1919 World Series became embroiled in scandal. Eight players became embroiled in scandal.**

   The 1919 World Series and eight players became embroiled in scandal.

2. **Careers were changed forever. The game of baseball was changed forever.**

   Careers and the game of baseball were changed forever.

3. **Chick Gandil, first baseman for the Chicago White Sox, decided to fix the games. Joseph Sullivan, a professional gambler, decided to fix the games.**

   Chick Gandil, first baseman for the Chicago White Sox, and Joseph Sullivan, a professional gambler, decided to fix the games.

4. **In 1919 sportswriters predicted the Chicago White Sox would easily defeat the Cincinnati Reds. Gamblers also predicted the Chicago White Sox would easily defeat the Cincinnati Reds.**

   In 1919 sportswriters and gamblers predicted the Chicago White Sox would easily defeat the Cincinnati Reds.

5. **Gandil resented White Sox owner Charles Comiskey, who was known for paying low salaries. Many other Chicago players resented White Sox owner Charles Comiskey, who was known for paying low salaries.**

   Gandil and many other Chicago players resented the White Sox owner Charles Comiskey, who was known for paying low salaries.

6. The players were motivated by greed and saw a unique opportunity. Gamblers were also motivated by greed and saw a unique opportunity.

   The players and gamblers were motivated by greed and saw a unique opportunity.

   _____

7. Eight White Sox players conspired to fix the games so the underdog Reds would win an upset victory. Gamblers conspired to fix the games so the underdog Reds would win an upset victory.

   Eight White Sox players and gamblers conspired to fix the games so the underdog
   Reds would win an upset victory.

8. After the highly favored White Sox lost, sportswriters became suspicious. Baseball officials also became suspicious.

   After the highly favored White Sox lost, sportswriters and baseball officials
   became suspicious.

9. The most famous player charged with throwing the games, Shoeless Joe Jackson, first confessed then retracted his confession. Eddie Cicotte also first confessed then retracted his confession.

   Shoeless Joe Jackson, the most famous player charged with throwing the games,
   and Eddie Cicotte first confessed then retracted their confessions.

10. Cleared of criminal charges, Shoeless Joe Jackson was banned from organized baseball for life. Seven other White Sox players were also banned from organized baseball for life.

    Cleared of criminal charges, Shoeless Joe Jackson and seven other White Sox play-
    ers were banned from baseball for life.

EXERCISE 14 Combining Sentences with Compound Verbs

Rewrite the following pairs of sentences, using compound verbs to create a single sentence.

1. Many scientific developments do not rely on a single person. They do not depend on a single discovery.

   Many scientific developments do not rely on a single person or depend on a single
   discovery.

2. For centuries doctors knew basic anatomy. They understood the body's major functions.

   For centuries doctors knew basic anatomy and understood the body's major
   functions.

3. Without a safe way of rendering a patient unconscious, however, doctors were limited to simple procedures. They had to operate fast to prevent shock.

   Without a safe way of rendering a patient unconscious, however, doctors were lim-
   ited to simple procedures and had to operate fast to prevent shock.

4. **Surgeons practiced speed rather than precision. They sought to end operations as quickly as possible.**

   Surgeons practiced speed rather than precision and sought to end operations as quickly as possible.

5. **In the 1840s the discovery of ether allowed doctors to put patients to sleep. They could take time to perform complicated operations.**

   In the 1840s the discovery of ether allowed doctors to put patients to sleep and take time to perform complicated operations.

6. **During the Civil War, surgeons could repair serious wounds. They could even replace missing skull tissue with steel plates.**

   During the Civil War, surgeons could repair serious wounds and even replace missing skull tissue with steel plates.

7. **Doctors at the time, however, had no knowledge of germs. They rarely bothered to wash their hands between operations.**

   Doctors at the time, however, had no knowledge of germs and rarely bothered to wash their hands between operations.

8. **Patients were saved by new surgical techniques. They often died from infections days or weeks later.**

   Patients were saved by new surgical techniques but often died from infections days or weeks later.

9. **Doctors began to accept the germ theory of disease in the late nineteenth century. They introduced sanitary operating room procedures. They sterilized their instruments.**

   Doctors began to accept the germ theory of disease in the late nineteenth century, introduced sanitary operating procedures, and sterilized their instruments.

10. **When the knowledge of anatomy came together with the discovery of anesthetics and understanding of germs, doctors could safely use surgery to treat disease. They could operate to repair injuries.**

    When the knowledge of anatomy came together with the discovery of anesthetics and understanding of germs, doctors could safely use surgery to treat diseases and operate to repair injuries.

Combining Sentences Using Appositives

An effective way to avoid choppy, repetitive writing is to combine sentences by turning one of them into an **appositive,** a word or phrase that describes, defines, or adds information about a noun or pronoun.

Choppy Sentences

Telly Savalas was the star of *Kojak*. He once worked for the U.S. State Department.

MIT is a major research university. It is conducting the laser experiments.

Penicillin is one of the oldest antibiotics. It is losing its ability to kill many germs.

Combined with Appositives

Telly Savalas, **star of *Kojak***, once worked for the U.S. State Department.

MIT, **a major research university**, is conducting the laser experiments.

One of the oldest antibiotics, penicillin is losing its ability to kill many germs.

POINT TO REMEMBER

Appositives are set off with commas and must come directly before or after the noun or pronoun it refers to.

George Washington, *the first president of the United States,* served two terms.

The first president of the United States, George Washington served two terms.

EXERCISE 15 Combining Sentences Using Appositives

Combine each pair of sentences by turning one of them into an appositive that describes a noun or pronoun. Remember to set the appositive off with commas and place it directly before or after the word it refers to. The appositive may appear at the beginning, middle, or end of the sentence.

1. **The Academy of Motion Pictures Arts and Sciences is a professional honorary organization. It has some 6,000 members.**

   The Academy of Motion Pictures Arts and Sciences, a professional honorary organization, has some 6,000 members.

2. **The Academy was organized as a nonprofit corporation. It was organized in 1927.**

   The Academy, a nonprofit organization, was organized in 1927.

3. **The organization is best known for awarding the Academy Award of Merit to directors, actors, writers, and technicians. The Award is known as the Oscar.**

   The organization is best known for awarding the Academy Award of Merit, the Oscar, to directors, actors, writers, and technicians.

4. **The Academy Award was designed by Cedric Gibbons in 1928. He was chief art director of MGM.**

   The Academy Award was designed by Cedric Gibbons, chief art director of MGM, in 1927.

5. **Frederic Hope was Gibbons's assistant. He designed the original black marble base.**

   Frederic Hope, Gibbons's assistant, designed the original black marble base.

6. **The Academy Award is one of the most famous awards in the world. The award weighs almost nine pounds.**

   The Academy Award, one of the most famous awards in the world, weighs almost nine pounds.

7. **There are many stories about how the Award began to be called Oscar. It was a nickname.**

   There are many stories about how the Award began to be called Oscar, a nickname.

8. **Gold was a precious metal. Gold was hard to obtain during World War II.**

   Gold, a precious metal, was hard to obtain during World War II.

9. **From 1942 to 1944 the Academy presented winners with Oscars made of plaster. This was a wartime substitute.**

   From 1942 to 1944, the Academy presented winners with Oscars made of plaster, a wartime substitute.

10. **At the end of the war, winners exchanged their plaster trophies for gold ones. They were mementos stars treasured for a lifetime.**

    At the end of the war, winners exchanged their plaster trophies for gold ones, mementos stars treasured for a lifetime.

Combining Sentences Using Relative Clauses

You can combine related sentences by turning one of them into a **relative clause.** Relative clauses begin with *which, who,* or *that* and describe or define a noun or pronoun. Relative clauses not only reduce choppy sentences but also more clearly express what you are trying to say by emphasizing main ideas.

> Kim Hsu only speaks Korean. She is nominated for a special effects award.
> George Miller was arrested just last week. He was caught shoplifting this morning.
> Brighton College is located in Maine. The college specializes in oceanography.

> Kim Hsu, **who only speaks Korean,** is nominated for a special effects award.
> George Miller, **who was arrested just last week,** was caught shoplifting this morning.
> Brighton College, **which is located in Maine,** specializes in oceanography.

POINTS TO REMEMBER

Use commas to set off a *nonrestrictive* relative clause that adds extra information about the word it modifies.

> Teddy Hughes, *who won a scholarship,* suddenly dropped out of school.

> *who won a scholarship* only adds extra information about Teddy Hughes, who is defined by his name.

Restrictive relative clauses that describe or define a word are not set off with commas.

> The student *who won a scholarship* suddenly dropped out of school.

> *who won a scholarship* restricts or limits the meaning of the general word *student* and is not simply extra information.

EXERCISE 16 Combining Sentences with Relative Clauses

Combine each pair of sentences by turning one of them into a relative clause. Remember to set off nonrestrictive clauses—those that add extra information—with commas.

1. **Daylight saving time is sometimes called Summer Time. It is designed to extend daylight during working hours.**

   Daylight saving time, which is sometimes called Summer Time, is designed to extend daylight during working hours.

2. **The idea seems simple enough. It has caused controversy all over the world.**

   The idea, which seems simple enough, has caused controversy all over the world.

3. **Advocates included economists, business leaders, and politicians. They argued that daylight saving time would help farmers and reduce traffic accidents.**

   Advocates, who included economists, business leaders, and politicians, argued that daylight saving time would help farmers and reduce traffic accidents.

4. **Opponents felt that changing clocks was unnatural and inconvenient. They consisted of ministers, parents, and transport executives.**

   Opponents, who consisted of ministers, parents, and transport executives, felt that changing clocks was unnatural and inconvenient.

5. **Daylight saving time was introduced during World War I. It was unpopular.**

   Daylight saving time, which was introduced during World War I, was unpopular.

6. **The federal daylight saving time law was signed by Woodrow Wilson. It was repealed in 1919.**

   The federal daylight saving time law, which was signed by Woodrow Wilson, was repealed in 1919.

7. **Daylight saving time was again signed into law in 1942. It was supposed to save energy for the war effort.**

   Daylight saving time, which was again signed into law in 1942, was supposed to save energy for the war effort.

8. **Daylight saving time was suspended in September 1945 in the United States. It was, however, imposed on Japan as part of the American occupation.**

   Daylight saving time, which was suspended in September 1945 in the United States, was imposed on Japan as part of the American occupation.

9. **Japanese citizens greatly resented being forced to change their clocks. They ended its use as soon as the American occupation ended.**

   Japanese citizens, who greatly resented being forced to change their clocks, ended its use as soon as the American occupation ended.

10. **The Uniform Time Act was passed in 1966. It mandated national use of daylight saving time in the United States.**

    The Uniform Time Act, which was passed in 1966, mandated the national use of daylight saving time in the United States.

EXERCISE 17 Combining Sentences

Use past and present participles, compound nouns and verbs, appositives, and relative clauses to revise the following paragraph to eliminate choppy and repetitive sentences.

     Few moviegoers have heard of Oscar Micheaux. He was a pioneer African American filmmaker. He overcame many odds. He was born in Illinois in 1884. His parents were former slaves. Micheaux moved to South Dakota. He operated a homestead farm. He began writing stories. No one was interested in publishing his work. Micheaux created his own publishing company. He sold his books door to door. He became the first African American to make a movie in 1919. His first movie was *The Homesteader*. It was based on his novel of the same name. He produced *Body and Soul* in 1924. The movie starred Paul Robeson. Over the next three decades, Micheaux made forty movies. His movies avoided the stereotyped black characters seen in Hollywood productions. Micheaux's films depicted black people positively. Micheaux's movies played in black theaters in the South. Micheaux made the first black film shown in white theaters. Micheaux died in 1951. His work had been celebrated by critics. It has been celebrated by scholars. Oscar Micheaux is now honored with a star on the Hollywood Walk of Fame.

     Few moviegoers have heard of Oscar Micheaux, a pioneer African American film-maker. Born in Illinois in 1884 to former slaves, he overcame many odds. Moving to South Dakota, Micheaux operated a homestead farm. He began writing stories. When no one was interested in publishing his work, Micheaux created his own publishing company, selling his books door to door. In 1919, he became the first African American to make a movie, The Homesteader, which was based on his novel of the same name.

In 1924 he produced Body and Soul starring Paul Robeson. Over the next three decades, Micheaux made forty movies. Avoiding the stereotyped black characters seen in Hollywood productions, Micheaux's films depicted black people positively. Micheaux's movies played in black theaters in the South. Micheaux made the first black film shown in white theaters. Micheaux died in 1951. His work had been celebrated by critics and scholars. Oscar Micheaux is now honored with a star on the Hollywood Walk of Fame.

EXERCISE 18 Improving Sentence Variety

Take one or more of the recent essays or paragraphs you have written in this book and examine the variety of your sentences. Are there choppy, dull, or repetitive sentences that could be improved with greater variety? Are there sentences that could be combined using participles, compound subjects and verbs, appositives, or relative clauses?

WORKING TOGETHER

Working with a group of students, revise this e-mail to reduce choppy and repetitive sentences.

```
Attn: Clerical Staff
RE: Patient Records

State law requires total patient confidentiality. We
do not release records to patient families. We do not
release records to insurance companies. These records
contain personal information. These records contain
sensitive material.

If people call asking for records, tell them you can
refer the request to the clinic director. If people
e-mail asking for records, tell them the same thing.

Do not answer any questions about a patient's health.
Do not answer any questions about which doctor a pa-
tient is seeing. It is important to be polite. It is
important to maintain a professional attitude. Explain
that you are not allowed to release patient informa-
tion of any kind. Explain that you can pass requests
on to the clinic director.

If you have any questions, call me at ext. 287.

Sandy LaFarve
```

CRITICAL THINKING

What do you do to stay in shape? Do you diet, exercise, or play sports? Do you find it difficult to maintain a healthy lifestyle? Does your schedule prevent you from working out? Is it difficult to find healthy meals?

    Write a paragraph describing your attempts at maintaining a healthy lifestyle.

WHAT HAVE YOU WRITTEN?

Write out your topic sentence or controlling idea:

_____

_____

Does it clearly express what you are trying to say? Could it be combined with other sentences to avoid choppy and repetitive writing?

Read the remainder of your paragraph. Can any sentences be combined using appositives, compound subjects and verbs, present and past participles, or relative clauses?

© David Paul Morris/Pool/Reuters/Corbis

Do you think the news media focuses too much on sensational murders, sex scandals, and celebrities instead of reporting on issues like Social Security, health care, and the environment?

State your views in one or more paragraphs and support your opinions with examples.

WRITING ON THE WEB

Using a search engine like Yahoo!, Google, or AltaVista, enter terms like *combining sentences, increasing sentence variety, relative clauses, appositives, choppy sentences,* and *revising sentences* to locate current sites of interest.

POINTS TO REMEMBER

1. The length of your sentences should reflect the ideas you are trying to express.
2. Short sentences make dramatic, easy-to-remember statements. Too many short sentences, however, can create choppy and dull writing.
3. Long sentences can express complicated relationships between ideas. Too many long sentences can be difficult to read and remember.
4. Avoid sentences that simply add a single word or minor idea that could be included in a related sentence.
5. Vary the way you open sentences to keep your writing lively and readers interested in what you are trying to say.
6. Combine related ideas to better express your train of thought and overcome choppy and repetitive sentences.

Writer's Resources ⊙ Now™   If you use Writer's ResourcesNow, please have your students log in and view the pretest, study plan, and posttest for this chapter.

Improving Word Choice

© Rob Lewine/CORBIS

GET WRITING

How hard is it to choose the right word?

Write a paragraph describing a situation, such as applying for a job or writing a condolence card to a friend, when you had problems finding words to express what you were trying to say.

The Power of Words

Words are the building blocks of paragraphs and essays. They have the power to inform, entertain, and persuade. When we talk, our word choices can be casual and haphazard because we also communicate through eye contact, tone of voice, and gestures. Speech is interactive. We can repeat sentences for emphasis and reword awkward phrases as we talk. If our listeners cannot understand what we are saying, they can ask questions.

"Going to that deal tonight?"
"Which deal?"
"The presentation by that computer guy."
"You mean Phil Armstrong?"
"Sure."
"Wish I could. I got to work at six."
"Six at night?"
"No, I start at six a.m. tomorrow, so I have to get to bed early tonight."

When we write, however, our readers can only react to the words on the page. They cannot ask us questions or give us a chance to restate our ideas—we have to get things right the first time. Readers have to rely on the text to understand what we are trying to express. We cannot correct false impressions, answer questions, or rephrase statements. Readers will assume our word choices will match the definitions they find in the dictionary.

WHAT DO YOU KNOW?

Choose the appropriate word in each sentence.

1. _____ The (presents/presence) of foreign troops on the street sparked a riot.

2. _____ The camp is (further/farther) up the road.

3. _____ Can you (accept/except) an out-of-state check?

4. _____ That costs more (then/than) he can afford.

5. _____ She is tired and should (lie/lay) down.

6. _____ (It's/Its) going to snow tonight.

7. _____ The brain needs a (continual/continuous) supply of oxygen.

8. _____ Her grandmother (dyed/died) of a stroke last night.

9. _____ This is (to/too) heavy for one person to carry.

10. _____ Computer hackers now have (access/excess) to our credit card files.

Answers appear on the following page.

WHAT ARE YOU TRYING TO SAY?

Write a paragraph that describes something you regret doing or not doing. Do you regret buying a car without checking its engine? Do you wish you had helped a friend who asked for a favor? Did you turn down an opportunity you wish you had taken? Did anyone ever coax you into making a decision you now regret? Write two paragraphs, the first describing the action or decision you did or did not make, the second explaining your current feelings. Choose words carefully to describe the decision you made and your present attitudes.

_____

_____

_____

_____

_____

_____

_____

_____

_____

WHAT HAVE YOU WRITTEN?

Underline the key words in your paragraphs. Do they give readers a strong impression? Could you improve your statement by choosing different words? Read your paragraphs out loud. What changes would you make to increase their impact? Will readers appreciate why you regret the decision?

Improving Word Choices

To improve the effectiveness of your paragraphs and essays, it is important to examine the words you have chosen.

GUIDELINES FOR CHOOSING WORDS

1. Use correct words—make sure you know a word's precise meaning.
2. Use effective words—use clear, concrete language your readers understand.
3. Delete "deadhead" words—eliminate words that add little meaning and wordy phrases that can be replaced with a single word.
4. Use appropriate words—use words suited to your purpose, subject, audience, and document. Be aware of connotations.

ANSWERS TO WHAT DO YOU
KNOW? ON PAGE 336:
1. presence 2. farther 3. accept
4. than 5. lie 6. It's 7. continuous
8. died 9. too 10. access

Using Correct Words

English has a number of words that are easily confused or misunderstood.

adopt	to take	They want to *adopt* a child.
adapt	to change	We will *adapt* the budget to include these new figures.
everyday	ordinary	Terrorists can make bombs from *everyday* hardware items.
every day	daily	Terri jogs six miles *every day*.
passed	successfully completed	We *passed* through the city at night.
past	history	His *past* remains a mystery.
who's	contraction of "who is"	*Who's* coming with me?
whose	possessive of "who"	*Whose* car is that?

(See pages 639–642 for other easily confused words.)

A NOTE ON SPELLING

An important part of using words is making sure you spell them correctly. Spelling errors confuse readers and make your work appear sloppy and unprofessional.

Tips for Improving Your Spelling

1. *Pronounce new words.* Reading them out loud can help you recall letters you might overlook like the *n* in "environment" or the *r* in "government."
2. *Write out new words you learn in school and at your job.*
3. *Make a list of words you repeatedly misspell and refer to it whenever you write.* Keep copies of this list in your notebook, by your desk, or in your purse or briefcase.

See Chapter 35 for further help with spelling.

EXERCISE 1 Using the Correct Word

Underline the correct word in each sentence.

1. She should (<u>wear</u>/where) more conservative clothes in the office.
2. The embossed (<u>stationery</u>/stationary) was too expensive for a mass mailing.
3. The men were arrested for selling (<u>illicit</u>/elicit) drugs.
4. Whenever I lose my temper, my (<u>conscience</u>/conscious) bothers me for days.
5. We can't (rise/<u>raise</u>) wheat during a drought.
6. (Less/<u>Fewer</u>) students are taking advanced math this semester.
7. We can't afford to (<u>lose</u>/loose) anymore games this season.
8. After inspection, the band will (precede/<u>proceed</u>) to the stadium.
9. Make sure the children are (<u>already</u>/all ready) vaccinated.
10. (Everyone/<u>Every one</u>) of the cars had bad tires.

POINT TO REMEMBER

Words sometimes have special or specific meanings. One college might define a *full-time student* as someone who takes twelve credits while another school requires students to take sixteen credits. The word *high rise* means one thing in Manhattan and another in Kenosha. *Make sure your readers understand the exact meanings of the words you use. Define terms with footnotes or a glossary at the end of your document to prevent confusion.*

EXERCISE 2 Understanding Meaning

Define each of the words, then check your answers using a college dictionary.

1. **alibi**   *explanation*   6. **irony**   *paradox*
2. **anecdotal**   *incidental evidence*   7. **marital**   *related to marriage*
3. **caustic**   *sarcastic*   8. **nonplussed**   *confused*
4. **defamation**   *slander, insult*   9. **orthodox**   *traditional*
5. **felon**   *criminal*   10. **sarcasm**   *derision, mockery*

How many words have you heard but could not define? How many did you get wrong? Which words have additional meanings you were unaware of?

LEARNING MORE ABOUT WORDS

1. Use a college dictionary to look up new or confusing words.
2. Study the glossaries in your textbooks to learn special terms and definitions.
3. Jot down unfamiliar words you hear at school or at work and look them up in dictionaries or glossaries.

DICTIONARIES FOR ESL STUDENTS

If English is your second language, refer to dictionaries like the *Longman Dictionary of American English* and the *Collins Cobuild Dictionary.* They not only give definitions but rules for combining words. If you look up *future,* for example, you learn that it often appears in phrases such as *predict the future, plan the future,* and *face the future.* These dictionaries include sample sentences to show how a word is used in context.

EXERCISE 3 Editing Your Writing

Select one or more writing responses you completed in a previous chapter or in the draft of an upcoming assignment and review your use of words. Look for errors in usage. Have you confused there *and* their *or* its *and* it's*? Have you written* affect *for* effect *or* adapt *for* adopt*? List words you have confused in the back of this book or in a notebook for future reference.*

Using Effective Words

To express your ideas effectively, choose words that are clear and concrete. Vague and general terms lack impact.

> I loved working at Lakeside Grill, one of the nicest restaurants in the Loop. It is a very attractive place with a lot of special customers. I met so many interesting people working there. The owner is nice and fun to work for. His wife is a great manager who really cares about the staff. Although they were busy, they treated employees well and made all of us feel special.

Words like *attractive* and *interesting* are abstract. The paragraph simply lets us know that a student enjoyed working at Lakeside Grill but does not really tell us why. What made the customers *special?* Why was the boss *nice* and his wife a *great manager?* Concrete words create stronger impressions.

> I loved working at Lakeside Grill, one of the most exclusive steakhouses in the Loop. Its elegant turn-of-the-century brass and woodwork are striking, as are the regular customers, who include the mayor, professional athletes, foreign leaders, and visiting entertainers. I waited on Jennifer Lopez, George Clooney, and the Italian ambassador in one week. The owner is pleasant, witty, and always willing to support his employees in a tough situation. His wife is a caring manager who makes sure our work schedules do not conflict with school. Even though they run a multimillion-dollar business catering to the rich and powerful, they never forget an employee's birthday or fail to send flowers to anyone who gets sick.

Instead of *made all of us feel special,* this paragraph offers specific details such as *never forget an employee's birthday or fail to send flowers.* Readers can understand that seeing *Jennifer Lopez, George Clooney, and the Italian ambassador* would make an after-school job interesting.

Using Concrete Nouns

Concrete nouns create strong images readers can identify and remember.

Abstract	Concrete
protective headgear	helmet
highly caloric desserts	cake and ice cream
student residence	dorm
electronic communications device	cell phone

Using Strong Verbs

Verbs should emphasize action. Avoid weak verb phrases that use several words to describe action that could be expressed with a single word.

Weak Verb Phrase	Strong Verb
make a decision	decide
effect a transfer	transfer
offer an excuse	excuse
perform a test	test

Avoiding Clichés

Clichés are overused sayings. They may have been original, striking, or colorful when first used but, like jokes that have been told too often, they have become stale and meaningless.

Cliché	Improved
ugly as sin	ugly
at a snail's pace	slowly
out cold	unconscious
dead as a doornail	dead

EXERCISE 4 Improving Word Choices

Rewrite each of the following sentences, replacing abstract nouns, weak verb phrases, and clichés.

1. **During the years of the Great Depression, people longed to find an escape from the problems of unemployment and business failures that seemed unrelenting.**

   During the Great Depression, people sought escape from unrelenting unemployment and business failures.

2. **Poverty had cut through the middle class like a knife, leaving people with few financial resources to pay for recreational endeavors.**

   Poverty devasted the middle class, leaving people with little money for recreation.

3. **Charles Darrow developed plans for a board game he called Monopoly, which allowed players to engage in fantasies about wheeling and dealing properties like the Rockefellers and Vanderbilts.**

   Charles Darrow developed a board game he called Monopoly that allowed players to fantasize about wheeling and dealing properties like the Rockefellers and Vanderbilts.

4. **Darrow made an attempt to sell his new game to Parker Brothers, who rejected it after making a determination that Monopoly had fifty-two design mistakes.**

   Darrow attempted to sell his new game to Parker Brothers, who rejected it for having fifty-two design mistakes.

5. **Not willing to give up, Darrow initiated a plan to manufacture Monopoly sets on his own, which began selling like hotcakes in a local department store.**

   Undaunted, Darrow manufactured Monopoly sets himself, which sold well in local department stores.

6. **With a success on his hands, Darrow went back to Parker Brothers, who had to eat their words and admit his game was a hit.**

   Now successful, Darrow went back to Parker Brothers, who had to admit his game was a hit.

7. **Parker Brothers made the decision to purchase Darrow's game, and soon Monopoly was being played coast to coast.**

   Parker Brothers purchased Darrow's game, and soon Monopoly was being played coast to coast.

8. **During World War II, the Allies hid real money, maps, and compasses in Monopoly sets that were made available to POWs to facilitate their plans for escape.**

   During WWII, the Allies hid real money, maps, and compasses in Monopoly sets sent to POWs to help them escape.

9. **Seventy years after its initial debut, Monopoly remains a popular way for people to pass their recreational time.**

   Seventy years after its debut, Monopoly remains a popular pastime.

10. **Today Parker Brothers manages the production of Monopoly in twenty-six languages and facilitates the printing of 50 billion dollars in Monopoly money in a single year.**

    Today Parker Brothers produces Monopoly in twenty-six languages and prints 50 billion dollars in Monopoly money a year.

Deleting "Deadhead" Words

Deadhead is an old railroad term for a nonpaying passenger, usually an employee riding along with the crew on the way to another job. Deadhead words ride along with others in a sentence but add no meaning. They are empty words that clutter a sentence and should be deleted to make your writing easier to read.

Cluttered

I went home and *started* to pack. Then *all of a sudden* George called and said he was *beginning to get* worried about missing the plane. I told him I was *going* to get ready as fast as I could so we could *start to* leave early.

Improved

I went home to pack. George called and said he was worried about missing the plane. I told him I was getting ready as fast as I could so we could leave early.

Reading your writing aloud can help spot deadhead words and phrases.

EXERCISE 5 Deleting Deadhead Words

Rewrite each sentence by deleting deadhead words and replacing wordy phrases with a single word where possible.

1. **After a long shift, I was getting tired and could not wait to be getting home so I could begin to relax and start getting dinner going.**

   After a long shift, I was tired and could not wait to get home to relax and cook

   dinner.

2. **I was trying to clean the house before my parents began to arrive.**

   I was cleaning the house before my parents arrived.

   _____

3. **Sara and Andy were working to paint the room, but they ended up running out of paint and had to quit.**

   Sara and Andy were painting the room, but they ran out of paint and had to quit.

   _____

4. **This semester the college is beginning to charge a parking fee for student events that are being held in Parker Hall.**

   This semester the college is charging a parking fee for student events in Parker Hall.

   _____

5. **They were driving along to work when they got a flat tire and had to start to hitchhike the rest of way.**

   They were driving to work when they got a flat tire and had to hitchhike the rest

   of the way.

Using Appropriate Words

The words you choose should suit your purpose, your readers, and the document. Words, like clothing, can be formal or informal, traditional or trendy. Just as you dress differently for a business meeting or a picnic, you write differently to produce a research paper, a résumé, or an e-mail to your best friend. It is important to use the right level of diction or word choice.

LEVELS OF DICTION

Formal/Technical	Terms used to communicate within a discipline or profession.
Standard	Words commonly used in books, magazines, and newspapers intended for a general audience.
Informal	Regional expressions, jargon used within specialized groups, slang, and text messaging ("u" for "you" or "brb" for "be right back").

Using the Appropriate Level of Diction

Professionals like attorneys, accountants, and physicians use *formal* or *technical* terms that most people are not likely to understand. Most college textbooks contain glossaries of technical terms. Understanding these terms is essential for people to communicate without confusion. *Standard* words are widely known and used. They are the kind of words found in popular books, magazines, and most websites. *Informal* English can include slang, jargon, and local expressions. Police officers, pilots, athletes, software developers, stockbrokers, and entertainers all have their own words and phrases.

Formal / Technical	Standard	Informal
permanent separation	termination	being canned
defense attorney	lawyer	mouthpiece
in extremis	near death	about to kick

The level of diction writers use depends on their goal, their readers, and the document. Doctors use official medical terminology to fill out insurance forms, standard English to instruct patients, and technical jargon or specialized slang to inform other physicians and medical staff.

It is important to avoid inappropriate word choices that can confuse readers or weaken the impact of your writing. Slang in a research paper or business report will make a writer appear unprofessional. Formal language can make e-mail difficult to read at a glance.

EXERCISE 6 Replacing Inappropriate Words

Revise each sentence to replace inappropriate words for a formal research paper.

1. In 1976 the Ebola virus <u>popped up</u> in the Sudan, signaling the presence of a previously unknown infectious agent.

   appeared _____

   _____

2. Economists in the early 1970s coined the term "stagflation" to describe the conflation of rising consumer prices and <u>unemployment going hog wild.</u>

   extreme unemployment _____

   _____

3. NASA engineers reported consistent computer failures in the Mars rover that will cost <u>an arm and a leg</u> to repair.

   a great deal _____

   _____

Revise each sentence to remove inappropriate words for an informal memo.

4. **Inform sales representatives that their personal <u>vehicles do not qualify for</u> <u>corporate insurance coverage.</u>**

   cars are covered by company insurance.

   _____

5. **All <u>electronic communications</u> directed to customers may be monitored for adherence to <u>corporate procedure and regulations.</u>**

   phone calls and e-mails

   company rules

Using Appropriate Idioms

Idioms are expressions or word combinations that state ideas. Idioms are not always logical. For example, you *get in a car* but *get on a plane*. You *hang up the phone* and *hang out with friends.* Idioms can be a challenge to understand for two reasons. First, some idioms like *pay respect to* can't be easily understood by looking at the meaning of each word. Second, many idioms like *break the ice, over the hill,* or *take the gloves off* don't mean what they literally suggest. Idioms are often difficult or impossible to translate word for word into other languages.

In college and business writing, you will be expected to use idioms accurately. If you are confused about the meaning of an idiom, refer to multilingual dictionaries like the *Longman Dictionary of American English* or the *Collins Cobuild Dictionary.*

Commonly Misused Idioms

Incorrect	Correct
abide **with**	abide **by**
different **than** the others	different **from** the others
in/with **regards** to	in/with **regard** to
independent **to**	independent **of**
irritated **with**	irritated **by**
on accident	**by** accident
satisfied **in**	satisfied **with**
superior **than**	superior **to**
type **of a**	type **of**

EXERCISE 7 Using the Appropriate Idioms

Write sentences using each of the following idioms correctly.

1. **drop on, drop off**

   _____

2. run up, run out

_____

3. wait for, wait on

_____

4. break away, break up

_____

5. play along, play up

_____

Being Aware of Connotations

When you choose words to express ideas, it is important to understand the role of **connotation.** All words have a **denotation** or basic, literal meaning. Connotation refers to a word's implied or suggested meaning. Connotations may be personal, cultural, psychological, or emotional. Colors, for example, all denote shades of the light spectrum. Many colors have connotations. _Blue_ is associated with boys; _pink_ is associated with girls. _Yellow_ suggests cowardice. _Red_ was once associated with communists. Today _green_ refers to environmentalists.

Connotations can be positive or negative. People living on the street can be called the _homeless, vagrants,_ or _bums._ A person with a drinking problem can be called _chemically dependent,_ an _alcoholic,_ a _drunk,_ or a _boozer._ A person who spends money cautiously can be praised for being _thrifty_ or ridiculed for being _cheap._ A book that is hard to read can be called _challenging_ or _incomprehensible._ A government investigation can be called _thorough and rigorous_ or a _witch hunt._

What we call things influences the way people respond to ideas. A group of protestors in the streets can be called a _demonstration_ or a _mob._ Teachers who strike children could be described as being _guilty of child abuse_ or _using corporal punishment._ A suspect can be subjected to an _interview_ or an _interrogation._ People accused of _lying_ may try to minimize their acts by admitting they _misspoke._

As a writer, it is important to consider the connotations of words you choose. Consider the different impact these words have:

successful	_vs._	rich	diplomatic	_vs._	indecisive
erotic	_vs._	pornographic	traditional	_vs._	old-fashioned
firm	_vs._	rigid	imaginative	_vs._	unrealistic
thin	_vs._	skinny	careless	_vs._	carefree
restraint	_vs._	cowardice	use	_vs._	exploit
direct	_vs._	simplistic	determined	_vs._	dictatorial

Connotations shape the way people perceive an event or situation.

Anticipating an attack, the soldiers _withdrew_ to _defensive positions_ in the hills.
Fearing an attack, the soldiers _ran_ to _find cover_ in the hills.

The president responded *impulsively,* ordering *reckless air strikes.*
The president responded *immediately,* directing *daring counterattacks.*

Eager to *address* the tragedy, Hollywood *quickly produced* two films *expressing* the public's *concern* about the *poignant* death of a *legendary* star.
Eager to *exploit* the tragedy, Hollywood *ground out* two films, *milking* the public's *curiosity* about the *pathetic* death of a *has-been* star.

LEARNING CONNOTATIONS

To make sure you understand a new word's connotation, study how it is used in context. If the word is used in a phrase or sentence that seems negative, the word's connotation is probably negative. If the phrase or sentence seems positive, the word's connotation is probably positive. You can also use a thesaurus to find a word's synonyms and antonyms. If you look up *stubborn,* for example, you will find it means the same as being *obstinate* and *pigheaded* and the opposite of *compliant* and *easygoing.*

WORKING TOGETHER

Working with a group of students, review the text of this e-mail to eliminate negative connotations. Write a more positive version of this message.

```
National Enterprises regrets to inform customers that
orders placed after December 10 will not be shipped
before Christmas. Because so many customers failed to
include phone numbers or e-mail addresses, we were
unable to verify orders. In the future, include your
phone number and e-mail address if you want to receive
your orders on time. We simply cannot send letters to
every customer who fails to include information neces-
sary for us to process orders.
```

CRITICAL THINKING

GET THINKING *AND* WRITING

Write a paragraph describing a situation where you could tell a person's views not by direct statements but by the choice of words. Did anyone use connotations to express an opinion of a movie, a politician, or an issue like abortion, capital punishment, or the Iraq War? Record the comments as accurately as you can and underline words whose connotations reveal the person's attitude.

GET WRITING

Examine the connotations used to word this WWI poster. Underline key words that have positive and negative connotations. Why would the government choose to use the word "liberty" to name bonds it was selling to the public? Why do the words "buy freely" suit the poster better than "buy often"?

If you were going to write a modern poster, what images and words would you use to sell bonds to the public to raise funds to secure the nation against terrorists? What image might you choose for the background? Describe your poster in a paragraph, then examine your writing for accurate word choice, its use of connotations, and presence of deadhead words.

© Swim Ink 2, LLC/CORBIS

WHAT HAVE YOU LEARNED?

Choose the appropriate word in each sentence.

1. _____ The new law will (affect/effect) the way Medicare pays doctors.

2. _____ They never (accept/except) late payments.

3. _____ (They're/There) working late again.

4. _____ Some parents are not (conscious/conscience) of their children's drug use.

5. _____ Premature infants in intensive care require (continual/continuous) monitoring.

Choose effective words and phrases in the following sentences.

6. _____ Scientists (performed tests on/tested) the Martian rock samples.

7. _____ Her new dress is (blue/blue-colored).

8. _____ If a (strike situation/strike) takes place, our shipments may be delayed for weeks.

9. _____ You should (begin to plan/plan) your summer school schedule this week.

10. _____ The city required the agency to (perform an audit/audit) its financial records.

Choose the proper level of diction for a college research paper.

11. _____ During the Depression, people were (disheartened/ticked off) by growing unemployment.

12. _____ Oil reserves cannot be (racked up/considered) as wealth if terrorism prevents oil exports.

13. _____ The demand for $50 billion was thought (way too much/ excessive) for Congress to approve.

14. _____ Consumers expected these devices would work (immediately/ from the get-go).

15. _____ Few scientists were able to (witness/eyeball) the volcano's first eruption.

Choose words with positive connotations.

16. _____ Heather Price (refused/declined) to make a statement.

17. _____ They hired the (veteran/old) stage actor Harold Green to play the lead.

18. _____ The soldiers (secured/occupied) the village.

19. _____ His popularity is based less on humor than his (antics/ gestures) on stage.

20. _____ This drug may cause (blindness/visual impairment).

Answers appear on the following page.

WRITING ON THE WEB

1. Use a database or a search engine like Yahoo!, Google, or AltaVista to look up articles from a variety of magazines. What do you notice about the level of diction, the use of words? How do styles of *The New Yorker, The Village Voice, People, Time,* and your local newspaper differ? What does this say about the writers, the publication, and the intended readers?

2. Analyze the language used in chat rooms on America Online or other Internet services. Have these electronic communities produced their own slang or jargon? Do chat rooms of car enthusiasts differ from those dedicated to childcare or investments? Do people with special interests bring their particular terminology and culture into cyberspace?

3. Use a search engine like Yahoo!, AltaVista, or Google and enter terms such as *diction, connotation, usage, word choice, slang,* and *vocabulary* to locate current sites of interest.

4. Write two or three sentences using new words you discover on the web. Determine which are technical, standard, and informal.

5. Ask your instructors for useful websites. Keep a list and update it when you find a useful source.

POINTS TO REMEMBER

1. The words you choose shape the way readers will react to your writing.
2. Choose correct words—check dictionaries to make sure you have selected the right words and spelled them correctly.
3. Choose effective words—use words that are clear and concrete; avoid wordy phrases, clichés, and abstract terms.
4. Consider connotations—be aware of the emotional or psychological impacts words may have. Choose words that reflect your message.
5. Review the lists of commonly confused and misspelled words on pages 643–647.
6. Study glossaries in your textbooks to master new terms you encounter in college.
7. Select a good college-level dictionary and get in the habit of referring to it several times a week. Use highlighters or Post-it notes to personalize your dictionary.
8. Practice using an online dictionary, especially if you write on a computer.

Writer's Resources ⓜ Now™   If you use Writer's ResourcesNow, please have your students log in and view the pretest, study plan, and posttest for this chapter.

ANSWERS TO WHAT HAVE YOU LEARNED? ON PAGE 349
1. affect 2. accept 3. They're 4. conscious 5. continuous (See Pages 338–339) 6. tested 7. blue 8. strike
9. plan 10. audit (See pages 340–343) 11. disheartened 12. considered 13. excessive 14. immediately
15. witness (See pages 343–345) 16. declined 17. veteran 18. secured 19. gestures 20. visual impairment
(See pages 346–347)

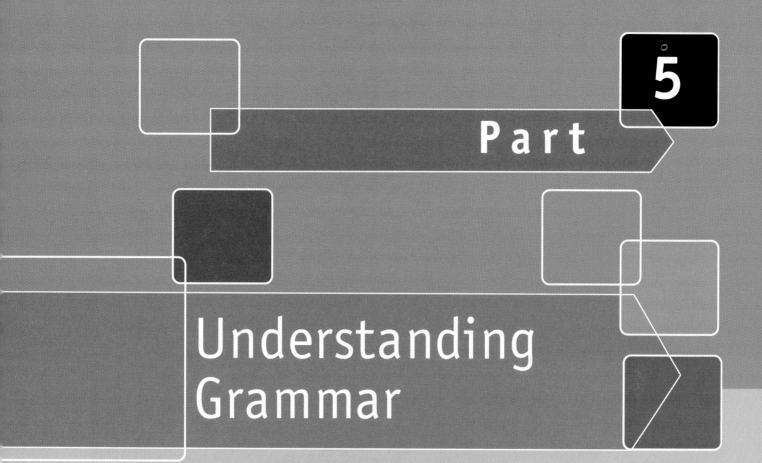

Part

5

Understanding Grammar

Understanding the Sentence

Henry Ford II at the premiere of the 1949 Ford.

The Ford Motor Company faced bankruptcy following WWII. In 1949 it introduced a streamlined model with many new features that became so popular it was called "the car that saved Ford." Over a million were produced.

Write a paragraph that describes the types of cars American companies have to produce today to compete with imports and attract buyers.

What Is a Sentence?

Everything that happens in life—natural occurrences, historical events, conflicts, thoughts, feelings, opinions, ideas, and experiences—is expressed in sentences. A main idea is connected to an action or linked with other words to state a thought. Long before they learn to read, children talk in sentences. Unwritten languages are spoken in sentences. The sentence is basic to all human communication.

Yond Cassius has a lean and hungry look.
SHAKESPEARE

We have nothing to fear but fear itself.
FRANKLIN DELANO ROOSEVELT

You can't eat the orange and throw the peel away—a man is not a piece of fruit!
ARTHUR MILLER

At last, after a long silence, women took to the streets.
NAOMI WOLF

A mind is a terrible thing to waste.
UNITED NEGRO COLLEGE FUND

> A sentence is a group of words that contains a subject and a verb and states a complete thought.

WHAT DO YOU KNOW?

Underline the subjects (main idea) and circle the verbs (action words) in each sentence.

1. Children eat too much candy.

2. The mayor signed the bill this morning.

3. You work too hard!

4. Carlos and Erica married in August.

5. Kim designs software for accounting and tests computer systems for viruses.

6. The mayor and the citizens group demanded federal aid and insisted on new state funding.

7. Although he lived in Mexico until he was seven, Hector only speaks a few words of Spanish.

8. Originally designed by NASA, this computer chip helps most airliners stay on course.

9. The director, assisted by her staff of attorneys, prepared a response to the lawsuit.

10. Las Vegas and San Jose, among other Western cities, attract new homeowners.

Answers appear on the following page.

Answers appear on the following page.

GET WRITING ▶ ## WHAT ARE YOU TRYING TO SAY?

Write a one-sentence response to each of the following questions.

1. What is the toughest course you are taking this semester?

   _____

2. Who was your best friend in high school?

   _____

3. How do you try to stay healthy?

   _____

4. What is your ideal job?

   _____

5. If you could change one thing about yourself, what would it be?

   _____

WHAT HAVE YOU WRITTEN?

Read each sentence out loud. Have you expressed a complete thought? Does your sentence make sense? Does it state what you were thinking, what you were trying to say?

This chapter explains the working parts of a basic sentence. By understanding how a sentence works, you not only avoid making mistakes but create writing that is fresh, interesting, and easy to read. To understand how sentences function, it is important to understand the parts of speech—words that have special functions.

THE PARTS OF SPEECH

Nouns	name persons, places, things, or ideas: *doctor, basement, Iraq, car, honesty*
Pronouns	take the place of nouns: *he, she, they, it, this, that, what, which, hers, his, their*
Verbs	express action: *fly, jump, consider, evaluate, swim, walk, speculate, sing* link ideas: *is, are, was, were*
Adjectives	add information about nouns or pronouns: a *new* hat, a *red* pen, a *rented* car

(continued)

Adverbs	add information about verbs:
	shouted *boldly*, *carefully* planned, *hotly* debated
	add information about adjectives:
	very old car, *poorly* edited letter
	add information about other adverbs:
	rather awkwardly stated
Prepositions	link nouns and pronouns, expressing relationships between related words:
	in the attic, *around* the house, *between* classes, *through* the tunnel
Conjunctions	link related parts of a sentence:
	Coordinating conjunctions link parts of equal value:
	and, for, or, yet, but, so, nor
	She bought a hat, *and* he bought a shirt.
	Subordinating conjunctions link dependent or less important parts:
	While she bought a hat, he bought a shirt.
Interjections	express emotion or feeling that is not part of the basic sentence and are set off with commas or used with exclamation points:
	Oh, he's fired? *Wow!*

Answers to **What Do You Know?** on Page 354:
1. Subject: *Children*, Verb: *eat*
2. Subject: *mayor*, Verb: *signed*
3. Subject: *You*, Verb: *work*
4. Subjects: *Carlos, Erica,* Verb: *married* 5. Subject: *Kim,* Verbs: *designs, tests* 6. Subjects: *mayor, citizens group,* Verbs: *demanded, insisted* 7. Subject: *Hector,* Verb: *speaks* 8. Subject: *computer chip,* Verb: *helps* 9. Subject: *director,* Verb: *prepared* 10. Subjects: *Las Vegas, San Jose,* Verb: *attract*

Words can function as different parts of speech:

I bought *oil* (noun).

I am going to *oil* (verb) those rusty hinges.

There's a leak in your *oil* (adjective) pan.

Parts of speech can be single words or phrases, groups of related words that work together:

Dr. Green and her nurses (noun phrase)

sang and danced (verb phrase)

during the evening (prepositional phrase)

Subjects and Verbs

The two most important parts of any sentence are the subject and verb. The **subject** is the actor or main topic that explains what the sentence is about. Subjects, which generally appear at the beginning of the sentence, may be a single word, several words, or a phrase.

Tanya drives a school bus.
Tanya and Eric drive school buses.
Driving a school bus requires skill.

Subjects are usually **nouns** or **pronouns.**

What Are Nouns?

Nouns are names of people, places, ideas, or things:

People	Places	Ideas	Things
doctor	basement	liberty	television
parents	valley	greed	airplane
farmer	farm	fear	nickel
pilot	plane	generosity	steel

Count Nouns may be singular or plural:

car	cars
woman	women

Spelling Note: Most nouns become plural by adding an "s" but some nouns have a plural spelling. See Chapter 35 for further information. Noncount nouns have only one form. EX: deer, gymnastics.

Nouns may be **common** or **proper.** Common nouns refer to general or abstract people, places, ideas, or things. Proper nouns refer to specific people, places, ideas, or things.

Common	Proper
college	Triton Community College
town	Westfield
actor	Alec Baldwin
drugstore	Walgreens

Note: Proper nouns are always capitalized. See pages 637–638 for guidelines on capitalization.

ARTICLES

Indefinite articles *a* and *an* are used with singular nouns to indicate a type or kind of something:

Use *a* before a consonant sound—*a* car, *a* girl, *a* loft, *a* wagon

Use *an* before a vowel sound—*an* apple, *an* error, *an* item, *an* oven

The definite article *the* is used with singular or plural nouns to indicate something specific: *the* car, *the* apple, *the* girl, *the* girls

The student borrowed *a* book. (A specific student borrowed some book.)

A student borrowed *the* book. (Some student borrowed a specific book.)

What Are Pronouns?

Pronouns take the place of a noun and can be the subject, object, or possessive of a sentence.

Noun	Pronoun
doctor	he *or* she
students	they
computer	it

There are four types of **pronouns:** *personal, indefinite, relative,* and *demonstrative.*

Personal

Personal pronouns refer to people and have three forms, depending on how they are used in a sentence: *subjective, objective,* and *possessive.*

	Subjective		Objective		Possessive	
	Singular	**Plural**	**Singular**	**Plural**	**Singular**	**Plural**
1st person	I	we	me	us	my (mine)	our (ours)
2nd person	you	you	you	you	your (yours)	your (yours)
3rd person	he	they	him	them	his (his)	their (theirs)
	she		her		her (hers)	
	it		it		it (its)	

She rented *our* cottage last summer, so *we* trusted *her* to babysit *my* son.
He rented a truck because *it* was cheaper than *your* moving company.

Relative

Relative pronouns introduce noun and adjective clauses.

who, whoever, whom, whose   which, whichever   that, what, whatever

I will help *whoever* applies for the job.
Sara was offered a promotion, *which* she refused to take.

Demonstrative

Demonstrative pronouns indicate the noun (antecedent).

this, that, these, those

That book is fascinating.
These books are hard to read.

Indefinite

Indefinite pronouns refer to abstract persons or things.

Singular				**Plural**	**Singular or Plural**		
everyone	someone	anyone	no one	both	all	more	none
everybody	somebody	anybody	nobody	few	any	most	some
everything	something	anything	nothing	many			
each	another	either	neither				

Everyone agreed to donate money, but *no one* sent a check.
Someone should do *something.*

Note: Pronouns must clearly refer to specific nouns called antecedents *and agree or match their singular or plural form.*

Incorrect

The school is a disaster. Books are missing from the library. Computer work stations are vandalized. The halls are cluttered with trash. The locker rooms in the gym are strewn with broken equipment and towels. *They* just don't care.

Who does *they* refer to? Teachers, students, administrators, or parents?

Revised

    The school is a disaster. Books are missing from the library. Computer work stations are vandalized. The halls are cluttered with trash. The locker rooms in the gym are strewn with broken equipment and towels. *The principal* just doesn't care.

Incorrect

Every student should try *their* best.

Student is a singular noun.

Correct

Every student should try *his or her* best.
Students should try *their* best.

(See Chapter 30 for further information about pronouns.)

CHOOSING SUBJECTS

In some languages, a noun and pronoun can be used together as a subject, but in English, you must choose one.

    Incorrect: My *teacher she* wrote the book for our class.

    Correct: My *teacher* wrote the book for our class.

                     OR

        She wrote the book for our class.

EXERCISE 1 Locating Subjects

Underline the subject—the main idea—in each sentence. If the subject is plural, underline it twice. If the subject is a pronoun, circle it. To identify the subject, read the sentence carefully. What is the sentence about? What part is connected to an action or linked to other words?

1. The White House is the official residence of the president of the United States.

2. It was designed by the Irish-born architect James Hoban.

3. John Adams became the first president to live in the White House.

4. Since Jefferson's time, visitors have been allowed to tour the building.

5. Built by Theodore Roosevelt, the West Wing contains staff offices.

6. These offices are well known to viewers of the popular TV show *The West Wing*.

7. Over the years, the building fell into disrepair.

8. While Harry Truman was president, a floor collapsed.

9. Steel supports were added during a major renovation in the early 1950s.

10. In 1952 a bunker was added in case of nuclear attack.

Locating "Hidden Subjects"

Subjects don't always appear at the beginning of a sentence, and at first glance they may not look like important words. *Subjects are not possessive nouns and they are not nouns in prepositional phrases.*

Inverted Sentences

In most sentences the subject comes before the verb.

> <u>Mary</u> *sold* her Miami condo.
> Last week <u>my mother</u> *bought* a new car.
> Each week <u>we</u> *mail* comment cards to all our customers.

In some sentences this pattern is inverted or reversed, so the subject follows the verb.

> There *is* <u>someone</u> waiting to see you.
> At the top of the hill *flies* an <u>American flag</u>.
> Behind too many of these successful athletes *is* <u>steroid use</u>.

Possessives

Many sentences contain a subject that is the object of a possessive.

> The school's *policy* angered both parents and students.
> Sandy's *house* needs painting.
> This spring's *designs* lack originality.

The subject in each sentence appears after a possessive. The subject is not "school" but "the school's *policy.*" One way to keep from being confused is to ask yourself who or what is doing the action or being linked to other ideas. What, for instance, "needs painting?"—"Sandy" or "Sandy's *house?*"

EXERCISE 2 Locating Subjects

Underline the subject in each sentence.

1. Your <u>wallet</u> probably contains a Social Security card.
2. There are <u>Americans</u> who are unaware of the card's history.
3. In 1936 the first <u>cards</u> were issued to track taxes and benefits.
4. The card's <u>uses</u> have expanded over the years.
5. A citizen's Social Security <u>number</u> has become a national identity number.
6. A person's <u>number</u> begins with an "area number" of three digits that indicates where the individual lives or where he or she applied for a card.
7. The highest area <u>number</u> is currently 772.
8. Perhaps because the Bible associates the number 666 with Satan, the Social Security Administration's <u>policy</u> is that 666 is not assigned as an area number.

9. The card's middle two <u>numbers</u> are called a "group number" that simply helps to break up a long number.

10. The last four <u>digits</u> are "serial numbers" issued in a straight sequence from 0001 to 9999.

Prepositional Phrases

Prepositions are words that express relationships between ideas, usually regarding time and place.

about	before	like	since
above	below	near	to
across	during	of	toward
after	except	off	under
against	for	outside	with
along	from	over	within
around	inside	past	without

Prepositions can begin phrases: *before the play, during the game, down the street, above the clouds, after class, under the sofa, inside the engine, around the house, beyond the stars.* Prepositional phrases appear frequently in English.

Before the play we talked *about the characters. In the last production* I thought the actors overlooked the potential humor *in the first scene.* The director sat *on the stage* and nodded. She agreed that the cast would try *for laughs in the next performance at eight o'clock.*

The only thing you have to remember about prepositional phrases is that *the subject of a sentence will not be found in a prepositional phrase.* The subject of the first sentence is *I,* not *play,* which is part of the prepositional phrase *before the play.*

EXERCISE 3 Locating Subjects and Prepositional Phrases

Underline prepositional phrases in the following sentences. Underline the subject of the sentence twice.

1. <u>In 1938</u> a promotional <u><u>gimmick</u></u> <u>by a wallet company</u> caused the newly formed Social Security Administration a major headache.

2. <u>By 1938</u> forty million <u><u>cards</u></u> had been issued <u>throughout the United States.</u>

3. Almost <u><u>everyone</u></u> <u>with a job</u> was now expected to carry a card <u>in his or her wallet or purse.</u>

4. The <u><u>company</u></u>, based <u>in Lockport, New York</u>, wanted to show how easily the new card would fit <u>into its wallets.</u>

5. <u><u>They</u></u> printed fake cards and put them <u>inside each wallet</u> <u>as a promotion</u> and shipped them <u>to department stores</u> <u>around the country.</u>

6. An <u><u>executive</u></u> used his secretary's real Social Security number <u>on the fake cards.</u>

7. The <u><u>word</u></u> "Specimen" was printed <u>across these cards</u> to indicate they were samples.

8. <u>Across the country</u>, however, <u>thousands</u> of people began using the secretary's number <u>as their own</u>.

9. The <u>Social Security Administration</u> ran ads <u>in major cities</u> informing the public not to use this number.

10. Forty years later, a dozen <u>people</u> in the United States still used the Social Security number they found printed <u>on a fake card</u> <u>in a wallet</u> they bought <u>in a department store</u>.

Verbs

Verbs express action, link ideas, or help other verbs.
Action verbs show what the subject is doing.

The doctor *examined* the X-rays.
We *rejected* the director's proposal.
Italy *introduced* new techniques in motion pictures.

Action verbs also express "invisible" behavior.

Sara *dreamed* of competing in the Olympics.
Brazil *contains* massive rain forests.
Sean *doubts* the plan will work.

Linking verbs connect the subject to related ideas in the sentence. Linking verbs function much like an = sign. Instead of showing action, they express a relationship between ideas:

The bus *was* late.
Ted *is* a translator.
We *are* hopeful.

Helping verbs assist the main verb by adding information:

The doctor *will* examine the X-rays.
Sara *should* win at least one medal.
You *might* assist me tonight.

Verbs also tell time, explaining when the action or relationship takes place.

Past	She *ran* two miles yesterday.	She *was* a runner.
Present	She *runs* two miles every day.	She *is* a runner.
Future	She *will run* tonight.	She *will be* a runner.

See Chapter 29 for further information on verb tense.

Verbs are either singular or plural.

| Singular | She *runs* every day. | She *is* a runner. |
| Plural | They *run* every day. | They *are* runners. |

Verbs must "agree" or match their subjects. Many subjects that look like plurals are singular:

Fifty dollars is not enough.   The *Senate is* debating the new budget.
United Technologies is a growth stock.   The *cost of oil is* increasing.

See Chapter 28 for further information on subject-verb agreement.

EXERCISE 4 Locating Action, Helping, and Linking Verbs

Underline the action verbs once, underline helping verbs twice, and circle the linking verbs in each of the following sentences.

1. Codes (are) critical for military operations.

2. Realizing Native American languages were largely unknown outside the United States, the Marines used Navajo speakers called "code talkers" in the Pacific during World War II.

3. In addition to speaking their native language, the code talkers substituted letters in the English words before translating them.

4. Even a skilled Navajo speaker would find the code talker's conversation impossible to understand.

5. The Japanese did capture a Navajo-speaking soldier in the Philippines early in the war.

6. He (was) unable to make sense of the coded messages in his native language.

7. Code talkers (were) not used in Europe.

8. Aware of the use of code talkers in World War I, Hitler ordered German anthropologists to study Native American languages.

9. The British made attempts to use Welsh speakers.

10. Soldiers often invented less sophisticated codes using slang and references to baseball, comic book heroes, radio shows, and Hollywood trivia they assumed the enemy would not be able to understand.

PHRASAL VERBS

Sometimes a verb consists of more than one word. This type of verb is called a *phrasal verb*. It consists of a verb and an *adverbial particle* such as "down," "on," or "up." The adverbial particle may explain that something is completed, as in "finish up" or "close down." Some phrasal verbs use idioms such as "She *ran up* a huge bill" or "That old building *cries out* for repairs." The literal meaning of "ran up" or "cries out" does not explain the verb's action.

Most phrasal verbs can be separated by pronouns or short noun phrases.

I *picked* Joe's uncle *up* at noon.
I *picked* him *up* at noon.

Some phrasal verbs cannot be separated.

We *went over* the paper together.

Standard dictionaries may not include phrasal verbs. If you cannot understand a phrasal verb in context, refer to a dictionary like the *Longman Dictionary of American English* or the *Collins Cobuild Dictionary*.

EXERCISE 5 Locating Subjects and Verbs

Circle the subject of each sentence. Underline action verbs once and underline linking verbs twice.

1. Despite historical links to Spain, (many) of South America's leaders <u>are</u> of non-Spanish origins.

2. (Ambrosio O'Higgins,) born in Ireland, <u>emigrated</u> to Spain and <u>served</u> as viceroy of Peru from 1796 until his death in 1801.

3. His (son,) Bernardo O'Higgins, <u>became</u> the first leader of an independent Chile in 1817.

4. (Bernardo O'Higgins) <u>created</u> the nation's military academy and <u>approved</u> the Chilean flag still in use.

5. His (attempts) to establish democratic reforms <u>were</u> opposed by wealthy landowners.

6. Overthrown by a revolt, (O'Higgins) <u>left</u> Chile and <u>died</u> years later in Peru.

7. (Alfredo Stroessner,) the son of a German immigrant, <u>ruled</u> Paraguay.

8. (Stroessner) <u><u>was</u></u> proud of his German heritage and <u>was</u> accused of turning his country into a safe haven for Nazi war criminals.

9. (Alberto Fujimori,) the son of Japanese immigrants, <u>served</u> as Peru's president from 1990 to 2000.

10. While visiting Japan in 2000, (Fujimori) <u>resigned</u> his office and <u>became</u> a Japanese citizen.

Building Sentences with Independent and Dependent Clauses

Sentences are made up of **clauses,** groups of related words that contain both a *subject* and a *verb.* There are two types of clauses: dependent and independent.

Dependent clauses contain a subject and verb but do *not* express a complete thought and are not sentences.

Because I take the bus to work.
Before Sara moved to Florida.
After they moved to San Antonio.

Dependent clauses have to be joined to an independent clause to create a sentence that expresses a complete thought.

Because I take the bus to work, I never pay for parking.
I wanted to have a party before Sara moved to Florida.
After they moved to San Antonio, Sam and Dana opened a restaurant.

Independent clauses are groups of related words with a subject and verb that express a complete thought. They are sentences.

I ride the bus.
Sara moved to Florida.
They own a restaurant in San Antonio.

Every sentence contains at least one independent clause.

Sentence Length

A sentence can consist of a single word, if it expresses a complete thought.

Run!
Stop!
Go!

In giving commands, the subject "you" is implied or understood, so it does not have to actually appear in print for a sentence to state a complete thought. Conversely, a long train of words is not necessarily a sentence.

Because the community center, funded by the city, several nonprofit agencies, and hundreds of individual donors, wants to offer daycare services, which are in high demand by local parents.

Although there is a subject ("community center") and a verb ("wants"), the words do not express a complete thought. If you read the sentence aloud, it sounds incomplete, like the introduction to an idea that does not appear. It leaves us wondering what the issue is about offering daycare services. Incomplete sentences—phrases and dependent clauses—are called *fragments.*

A NOTE ON FRAGMENTS

Incomplete sentences that fail to express a complete thought are called *fragments*—a common writing error. Although sometimes written for emphasis, fragments should be avoided in college writing.
See Chapter 23 for help on avoiding fragments.

WORKING TOGETHER

Work with a group of students and revise this e-mail to change linking verbs to action verbs.

Attn: Technical Staff

The new schedule is going to take effect May 1. All employees who are working in the main assembly plant are to start at 7:30 am instead of 8:00. First shift is set to end at 3:30 pm. Employees in the sales, training, and administration departments are going to follow the old shift schedule from 8:00 am to 4:00 pm.

Carla Fons is in charge of supervising the schedule. If you have any questions about your time or assignments, you are able to call her at ext. 5689.

Sarah Collins
District Supervisor

CRITICAL THINKING

If you could eliminate one inconvenience in your life this semester, what would it be and why? Do you need more closet space, better parking, new tires, a daycare center closer to your job, or more time to study? Write a paragraph and explain how solving this one minor inconvenience could make your life easier.

WHAT HAVE YOU WRITTEN?

Read your paragraph carefully. Circle the subjects and underline the verbs in each sentence. If you are unsure if some of your sentences are complete, see Chapter 23.

Choose one of your sentences and write it below:

Does the sentence clearly express what you were trying to say? Is the subject clearly defined? Is the verb effective? Could more concrete words or stronger verbs (see Chapter 21) improve this sentence?

Summarize your points in one sentence. What is the main reason this inconvenience troubles you so much?

Read this sentence carefully. Circle the subject and underline the verb. How effective is your word choice (see Chapter 21)?

Does this sentence fully express your ideas? Try writing a different version:

Ask a fellow student to read and comment on both sentences. Can your reader understand what you are trying to say?

WHAT HAVE YOU LEARNED?

Underline the subjects (main idea) and circle the verbs (action and linking words) in each sentence. Underline linking verbs twice.

1. My sister's wedding cost $25,000.
2. Movies glamorize violence.
3. The burden of taxes falls on the middle class.
4. Many Americans vacation in Mexico.

5. The team's last play should have worked.

6. The mayor's proposal is being examined by our lawyers.

7. Sandy is nineteen years old.

8. The computers and printers are brand new.

9. It is raining.

10. Smoking is bad for your health.

Answers appear below.

WRITING ON THE WEB

The Internet offers resources on sentence structure and style.

1. Using a search engine like Yahoo!, Google, or AltaVista, enter terms such as *sentence structure, parts of speech,* and *independent clauses* to locate current sites of interest.
2. Review past e-mails you may have sent. What changes would you make in your writing? What would make your sentences more effective?

POINTS TO REMEMBER

1. The sentence is the basic unit of written English.
2. Sentences contain a subject and verb and express a complete thought.
3. Subjects explain what the sentence is about.
4. Verbs express action or link the subject to other words.
5. Phrases are groups of related words that form parts of sentences.
6. Dependent clauses are groups of related words with a subject and a verb but do not state a complete thought.
7. Independent clauses are groups of related words that contain a subject and a verb and express a complete thought.
8. All sentences contain at least one independent clause.

Writer's Resources⊕Now™ If you use Writer's ResourcesNow, please have your students log in and view the pretest, study plan, and posttest for this chapter.

ANSWERS TO WHAT HAVE YOU LEARNED? ON PAGES 355–366
1. Subject: *wedding* Verb: *cost* 2. Subject: *Movies* Verb: *glamorize* 3. Subject: *burden* Verb: *falls* 4. Subject: *Americans* Verb: *vacation* 5. Subject: *play* Verb: *should have worked* 6. Subject: *proposal* Verb: *is being examined* 7. Subject: *Sandy* Verb: *is* 8. Subject: *computers and printers* Verb: *are* 9. Subject: *It* Verb: *is* 10. Subject: *Smoking* Verb: *is*

Avoiding Fragments

© Reuters./CORBIS

GET WRITING

Do you think television and movies glamorize crime and violence?

Write a paragraph expressing your views of the way gangsters are portrayed in popular culture. Do you think this is a dangerous influence, or do you think people are able to separate fantasy from reality?

In order to communicate, you have to express ideas in sentences—groups of words that have a subject and a verb and express a complete thought.

> The bus arrives at noon.
> Rose Fuentes teaches math.
> Should we call a cab?

Each of these sentences states a complete thought and can stand on its own. They are **independent clauses.** They make sense all by themselves. Each sentence forms a pattern in which the subject—*bus, Rose Fuentes,* and *we*—is connected to a verb expressing action—*arrives, teaches, call* (see Chapter 22).

In speaking we don't always express ourselves with complete sentences, especially when we are talking to people we know. In person, we communicate not only with words but also with gestures, tone, and facial expressions. We may stop mid-sentence and move to the next idea when we recognize that people are following our train of thought. Because our communication is interactive, listeners can interrupt us with questions if they become confused.

> "Driving to the game?"
> "Going with Al."
> "He driving?"
> "Sure."
> "New car?"
> "Got the Mustang Monday."
> "He get the red one?"
> "What else?"
> "He buy or lease?"
> "Buy."
> "OK, see you at the game."
> "Great."

When we write, however, our readers can only rely on the text we give them. If we don't write in complete sentences, we fail to express complete thoughts.

> Bought a new car.   Who bought the new car?
> Because I am working second shift.   Then what happens?
> Should Sara and Cindy?   Should they do what?

Because we often think faster than we can write, it is easy to make mistakes in expressing ideas. We skip words, shift our train of thought mid-sentence, and break off phrases. Instead of stating a complete idea, we leave our readers with partial sentences called **fragments.**

> We flew to Chattanooga last weekend. The Chicago airport was crowded. *Trying to find a place to park. Took over an hour.* We almost missed our flight.
>
> *Revised*
>
> We flew to Chattanooga last weekend. The Chicago airport was crowded. *Trying to find a place to park took over an hour.* We almost missed our flight.

WHAT DO YOU KNOW?

Label each sentence OK for a complete sentence and F for a sentence fragment.

1. _____ The team lagging in last place for the third week.

2. _____ Park behind the building.

3. _____ Attempting to maintain high grades and work overtime was too much for Sara.

4. _____ The mayor, who faces a tough reelection next month.

5. _____ On sale in stores nationwide.

   Answers appear on the following page.

What Are Fragments?

Fragments are incomplete sentences. They lack a subject or a complete verb, or fail to express a complete thought.

Subject Missing
Danced all night. [Who *danced all night*?]

Revised
She danced all night.

Verb Missing
Jean the new car. [What was Jean doing?]

Revised
Jean washed the new car.

Incomplete Verb
Jean washing the new car. [*-ing* verbs cannot stand alone.]

Revised
Jean is washing the new car.

Incomplete Thought
Although Jean washed the new car. [It has a subject and verb but fails to express a whole idea.]

Revised
Jean washed the new car.

or
Although Jean washed the new car, the fenders were streaked with dirt.

The term *fragment* is misleading because it suggests something small, but length has nothing to do with writing complete sentences. A sentence can consist of a single word:

Duck!

The subject "you" is understood. Commands express complete thoughts. A long trail of words, even those with subjects and verbs, can be a fragment if it fails to state a whole idea.

> After the team won the first game of the playoffs and appeared ready to sweep the series with little chance of facing serious competition.

Although it looks like a long sentence, these words do not express a complete thought. Readers are left wondering. After the team won the first game, then what happened?

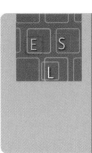

INCLUDING ALL VERBS

All parts of the verb phrase must be included to create a complete sentence. Be sure to include helping and linking verbs where needed.

Sentence needing a helping verb: The popularity of basketball *is* growing.

Sentence needing a linking verb: It *is* widespread in Latin America.

POINT TO REMEMBER

Reading aloud can help identify fragments. Ask yourself, "Does this statement express a complete thought?"

EXERCISE 1 Identifying Fragments

Label each of the following sentences OK for a correct sentence or F for a fragment. Reading a sentence aloud may help you tell whether the sentence expresses a complete idea.

1. __F__ Nikola Tesla being born in Croatia in 1856.

2. __F__ Emigrating to America in 1884 with just four cents in his pocket.

3. __OK__ Tesla worked with Thomas Alva Edison and assisted with the inventor's experiments with electricity.

4. __OK__ Tesla left the Edison organization and formed his own company in 1886.

5. __F__ Tesla conducting research on X-rays and formulating ideas about developments such as radar and radio.

6. __OK__ Tesla became friends with Mark Twain.

7. __F__ Although Tesla was a brilliant scientist who made many discoveries years before other researchers.

8. __OK__ His secretive nature and compulsive disorders led to speculations about his sanity and the nature of his research.

9. __F__ Some people claiming Tesla invented a death ray and was communicating with Martians.

10. _OK_ These stories increased in 1943 when, immediately following his death, his papers were declared top secret by the War Department.

Correcting Fragments

There are two ways to correct fragments:

1. Turn the fragment into a complete sentence by making sure it expresses a complete thought.

Fragments
Yale being the center for this research.
Public opinion surveys.
The mayor designated.

Revised
Yale is the center for this research. (complete verb added)
The new study is based on public opinion surveys. (subject and verb added)
The mayor designated Sandy Gomez to head the commission. (words added to express a complete thought)

2. Attach the fragment to a sentence to state a complete thought. Often fragments occur when you write quickly and break off part of a sentence.

Fragments
He bought a car. *While living in Florida.*
Constructed in 1873. The old church needs major repairs.

Revised
He bought a car while living in Florida.
Constructed in 1873, the old church needs major repairs.

EXERCISE 2 Identifying and Correcting Fragments

Identify and correct the fragments by adding missing words or connecting them to another fragment in the exercise. Some items may already be complete sentences.

1. Bipolar mood disorder, also known as manic depression.

Bipolar disorder is also known as manic depression.

2. Typically, sufferers experience mood swings from manic elation to depressed sadness.

Correct.

3. In their high or manic states, patients extremely confident, powerful, and energetic.

In their high or manic states, patients feel extremely confident, powerful, and
energetic.

4. In this hyper state may go on wild spending sprees, abruptly quit a job, make rash investments, or engage in high-risk behavior.

   In this hyper state, patients may go on wild spending sprees, abruptly quit a job,

   make rash investments, or engage in high-risk behavior.

5. Although patients may announce plans to open businesses, launch new careers, or discover some invention.

   _____

   _____

6. They lacking ability to concentrate and experiencing agitation when questioned about the feasibility of their plans.

   Although patients may announce plans to open businesses, launch new careers,

   or discover some new invention, they lack the ability to concentrate and experience

   agitation when questioned about the feasibility of their plans.

7. While at other times patients slide into deep depression, feeling sad, lost, lonely, and inferior.

   _____

   _____

8. Leading them to quit jobs or drop out of school believing they have no chance of success.

   At other times patients slide into deep depression, feeling sad, lost, lonely, and

   inferior, leading them to quit jobs or drop out of school, believing they have no

   chance of success.

9. Can be devastating, especially when patients make impulsive and illogical decisions in manic or depressed states.

   Bipolar disorder can be devastating, especially when patients make impulsive and

   illogical decisions in manic or depressed states.

10. Drugs and counseling are allowing many people to cope with this serious disorder.

    Correct.

    _____

EXERCISE 3 Identifying and Correcting Fragments

Identify and correct the fragments by adding missing words or connecting them to another fragment. Some items may already be complete sentences.

1. The Hollywood Walk of Fame attracting tourists visiting Los Angeles every year.

   The Hollywood Walk of Fame attracts tourists visiting Los Angeles every year.

   _____

2. **For many this is the highlight of their trip, pointing out the stars dedicated to their favorite actor or actress.**

   Correct.

3. **The first star on the Hollywood Walk of Fame honoring Joanne Woodward in 1960.**

   The first star on the Hollywood Walk of Fame honored Joanne Woodward in 1960.

4. **In the first year and a half over 1,500 stars on the walk.**

   In the first year and a half, over 1,500 stars were installed on the walk.

5. **Today there are over 2,000 stars decorating the sidewalks along Hollywood Boulevard.**

   Correct.

6. **About twenty-five new stars being added each year.**

   About twenty-five new stars are added each year.

7. **Because the stars have five categories honoring accomplishments in radio, motion pictures, television, theater, and the recording industry.**

   The stars have five categories honoring accomplishments in radio, motion pictures, television, theater, and the recording industry.

8. **Cowboy star Gene Autry the only person to have been awarded stars in all five categories.**

   Cowboy star Gene Autry is the only person to have been awarded stars in all five categories.

9. **Not all the stars are dedicated to humans.**

   Correct.

10. **Mickey Mouse and Rin Tin Tin having been honored as well.**

    Mickey Mouse and Rin Tin Tin have been honored as well.

EXERCISE 4 Correcting Fragments

Revise the following paragraph to correct fragments.

Emiliano Zapata was born in Morelos, Mexico, in 1879, to a family of independent ranchers. Although Zapata was known for wearing flashy clothing in his youth. He always maintained respect for the impoverished peasants. By thirty he had become a spokesperson for his village. Zapata championing the rights of Indians in Morelos. Assisting redistribution of land and defending the villagers' claims in property disputes with wealthy ranchers. Becoming increasingly frustrated by the government's bias in favor of wealthy landowners. Zapata began using force to seize land. Taking a leading role in the 1910 Mexican Revolution that deposed the Diaz regime. Zapata was disillusioned with the new government's failure to address the needs for effective land reform. Zapata and his followers refused to disarm. The newly reformed Mexican government attempting to bribe Zapata's followers to betray him. Placing a bounty on his head. In April 1919, Mexican General Guajardo offered to meet with Zapata. When Zapata appeared for their meeting, he was shot to death. Although the Zapata movement diminished in influence after his death. Emiliano Zapata remains an honored hero in Mexico. Where his memory still inspires organizations concerned with poverty and Indian rights.

> Emiliano Zapata was born in Morelos, Mexico, in 1879 to a family of independent ranchers. Although Zapata was known for wearing flashy clothing in his youth, he always maintained respect for the impoverished peasants. By thirty he had become a spokesperson for his village. Zapata championed the rights of Indians in Morelos. He assisted in the redistribution of land and defended the villagers' claims in property disputes with wealthy ranchers. Becoming increasingly frustrated by the government's bias in favor of wealthy landowners, Zapata began using force to seize land. He took a leading role in the 1910 Mexican Revolution that deposed the Diaz regime but was disillusioned with the new government's failure to address the needs for effective land reform. Zapata and his followers refused to disarm. The newly reformed Mexican government attempted to bribe Zapata's followers to betray him, placing a bounty on his head. In April 1919, Mexican General Guajardo offered to meet with Zapata. When Zapata appeared for their meeting, he was shot to death. Although the Zapata movement diminished in influence after his death, Emiliano Zapata remains an honored hero in Mexico. His memory still inspires organizations concerned with poverty and Indian rights.

EXERCISE 5 Correcting Fragments

Revise the following paragraph to correct fragments.

The deadliest riot in American history in New York in July 1863. Earlier that year Congress passing conscription, making men from twenty to forty-five liable for military service. The law allowing those with money to avoid the army by paying three hundred dollars. An immense sum in those days. This angered the poor. The draft was very unpopular in New York. Which had a large immigrant Irish population. Who resented fighting in a war they did not understand. In addition many feared that a Northern victory would allow freed slaves to take their jobs. Antiwar newspapers whipping up racist hatred. By mid-July, news of the high loss of life from the battle at Gettysburg reached New York. Mobs of laboring men, mostly Irish. Took to the streets and overpowered the police. Seizing weapons from the Second Avenue Armory and set fire to buildings.

Draft records were destroyed. A black orphanage was set on fire. At least eleven black men were lynched or beaten to death in the streets. Troops were rushed back from the battlefield to put down the riot. Which raged for three days. Some newspapers claimed that over a thousand people were killed in the street battles. For years, history books setting the loss of life at 300. Today most historians estimate that about 120 people were killed, with hundreds more injured and thousands displaced by fires. The actions of the mobs would fuel anti-Irish sentiment in newspaper cartoons and editorials for decades.

The deadliest riot in American history erupted in New York in July 1863. Earlier that year, Congress passed conscription, making men from twenty to forty-five liable for military service. The law allowed those with money to avoid the army by paying three hundred dollars, an immense sum in those days. This angered the poor. The draft was very unpopular in New York, which had a large immigrant Irish population who resented fighting in a war they did not understand. In addition many feared that a Northern victory would allow freed slaves to take their jobs. Antiwar newspapers whipped up racist hatred. By mid-July, news of the high loss of life from the battle at Gettysburg reached New York. Mobs of laboring men, mostly Irish, took to the streets and overpowered the police. They seized weapons from the Second Avenue Armory and set fire to buildings. Draft records were destroyed. A black orphanage was set on fire. At least eleven black men were lynched or beaten to death in the streets. Troops were rushed back from the battlefield to put down the riot, which raged for three days. Some newspapers claimed that over a thousand people were killed in the street battles. For years, history books set the loss of life at 300. Today most historians estimate that about 120 people were killed, with hundreds more injured and thousands displaced by fires. The actions of the mobs would fuel anti-Irish sentiment in newspaper cartoons and editorials for decades.

WORKING TOGETHER

Work with a group of students and revise the following e-mail to eliminate any fragments.

Attn: All technical staff

This Monday a seminar being held at Foundation Hall from 9am-3pm. Concerning the new health-care plan being offered by Empire State Insurance. All employees should plan to attend this important meeting. Medical, dental, and long-term health-care policies being discussed at this meeting. Although Passaic Union will continue to fully pay for your coverage and there will no additional fees. It is important you attend this seminar. You will have to make decisions regarding deductibles and disability options.

Kelly Koberstein
ext. 7878
koberstein.k@passaicunion.org

CRITICAL THINKING

Cheating has always been an issue in college. Today many students use the Internet to download research papers. What action should instructors and administrators take when students are caught cheating? Should the student fail the course or be expelled? Should students be given a second chance?

Write a paragraph stating your opinion of how students should be punished for cheating.

When you complete writing, identify and correct any fragments by adding missing elements or attaching the fragment to a related sentence.

1. Select one of your sentences and write it below:

   _____

   _____

2. Circle the subject and underline the verb.
3. Why does this sentence state a complete thought? What is the relationship between the subject and the verb?
4. Read the sentence aloud. Could you make the sentence more effective by replacing abstract words with concrete nouns and stronger verbs (see Chapter 21)? Try writing a different version of your sentence:

   _____

   _____

WHAT HAVE YOU WRITTEN?

Review writing exercises in this book, papers written for other courses, work you did in high school, and e-mails sent to friends for fragments. Do you have a tendency to forget words or break off phrases to create incomplete sentences? If you discover fragments or continue to make them in upcoming assignments, review this chapter. When you write, refer to pages 615–616 in the handbook.

WHAT HAVE YOU LEARNED?

Label each sentence OK for a complete sentence and F for a sentence fragment.

1. _____ Don't stand there.

2. _____ Although he was running a fever, he hit two home runs.

3. _____ While the Senate was debating the bill on stem cell research and considering nominees for the federal courts.

4. ____ Before the test, the students rushed to the library to review their notes.

5. ____ Trapped by falling debris after the earthquake struck.

Answers appear below.

WRITING ON THE WEB

Using a search engine such as Yahoo!, Google, or AltaVista, enter the terms *sentence fragment, grammar,* and *sentence structure* to locate current sites of interest.

POINTS TO REMEMBER

1. Sentences contain a subject and a verb and express a complete thought.
2. Sentence fragments are incomplete sentences—they lack a subject or a verb or fail to express a complete thought.
3. Reading a sentence aloud is the best way to detect a fragment. If a sentence sounds incomplete or like an introduction to something unstated, it is probably a fragment.
4. Fragments can be corrected in two ways:
   a. create a complete sentence by adding missing elements
   b. attach the fragment to a related sentence to state a complete thought

If you use Writer's ResourcesNow, please have your students log in and view the pretest, study plan, and posttest for this chapter.   Writer's Resources Now™

> **ANSWERS TO WHAT HAVE YOU LEARNED?**
> **1.** OK **2.** OK **3.** F **4.** OK **5.** F

Building Sentences Using Coordination and Subordination

© Les Stone/CORBIS

GET WRITING

Should women serve in combat? Why or why not?

Write one or more paragraphs stating your views.

We communicate in sentences—independent clauses that have a subject and a verb and express a complete thought. Chapter 22 explains the working parts of a *simple sentence,* a sentence with a single independent clause. We do not always write in simple sentences. In telling a story, describing a person, making a comparison, or stating an argument, we often *coordinate* ideas, creating sentences with more than one complete thought. We place two or three independent clauses in a single sentence to demonstrate how one idea affects another.

My car is in the garage, so I will take the bus to work.

The engine plant is in El Paso, and the tire factory is in Austin.

In other cases we may *subordinate* a minor idea, reducing it to a dependent clause connected to an independent clause to create a sentence.

After we lost the game, we were in no mood to go to the party.

Sidney quit smoking after his doctor told him he had high blood pressure.

Without coordination and subordination, writing can become a list of choppy and repetitive simple sentences.

```
     My parents moved to Las Vegas last year. I thought
I would hate it. I am not interested in nightlife.
I do not drink. I do not gamble. I was surprised. I
learned that Las Vegas has a lot to offer besides
casinos. I had only seen images of the Strip on tele-
vision. I had no idea Las Vegas had so many golf
courses, parks, and restaurants. I had heard of Lake
Mead. I did not know it would be only forty-five min-
utes from our house. My dad bought a boat. I love it.
For me Las Vegas means sailboats not slot machines.
```

Joining ideas with coordination and subordination creates writing that is more interesting and easier to follow.

```
     When my parents moved to Las Vegas last year,
I thought I would hate it. I am not interested in
nightlife. I do not drink, and I do not gamble. I was
surprised when I learned that Las Vegas has a lot to
offer besides casinos. Because I had only seen images
of the Strip on television, I had no idea Las Vegas had
so many golf courses, parks, and restaurants. I had
heard of Lake Mead, but I did not know it would be only
forty-five minutes from our house. My dad bought a
boat, which I love. For me Las Vegas means sailboats,
not slot machines.
```

WHAT DO YOU KNOW?

Place a C next to sentences that use coordination to join independent clauses and an S next to sentences that use subordination to join dependent clauses to independent clauses. Mark simple sentences—those with one independent clause—with an X.

1. _____ Although we ran into heavy traffic, we made it to the airport on time.

2. _____ Ted has great speed, but George has greater accuracy.

3. _____ Toronto is the capital of Ontario; Victoria is the capital of British Columbia.

4. _____ Westfield is a popular suburb in Northern New Jersey not far from Manhattan.

5. _____ Frank took the summer off, but the rest of us are going to summer school.

6. _____ It's official; we're getting married!

7. _____ The Chinese are building the biggest dam in the world, which will be the greatest single construction project in human history.

8. _____ The bus takes an hour and a half; the train takes forty-five minutes.

9. _____ Maintaining accurate records of our income and costs is essential if we want to apply for federal funding or attract charitable donations.

10. _____ After we began using recycled products, we discovered our production costs have fallen almost 15 percent.

Answers appear on the following page.

What Are Coordination and Subordination?

Coordination creates *compound sentences* that join independent clauses using semicolons or commas and coordinating conjunctions (*and, or, nor, for, yet, but, so*).

Jenna works first shift; Terry works second shift.

Jenna works first shift, and Terry works second shift.

Subordination creates *complex sentences* that join an independent clause stating a complete thought with dependent clauses that add additional information or state a less-important idea.

We cancelled the picnic because it rained.

Because it rained, we cancelled the picnic.

Note: When the dependent clause begins a sentence, it is set off with a comma.

NOTE: Subordination is a way of avoiding *fragments* (Chapter 23), by connecting dependent clauses to independent ones.

CHOOSING THE RIGHT CONJUNCTION

You can connect clauses with either a subordinating or a coordinating conjunction—but not both. Use one or the other.

Incorrect
Although we returned to campus early, *but* there were long lines at the bookstore.

Correct
Although we returned to campus early, there were long lines at the bookstore.

We returned to campus early, *but* there were long lines at the bookstore.

WHAT ARE YOU TRYING TO SAY?

GET WRITING

Write a paragraph that describes your best friend. In addition to providing details about his or her appearance, describe personality qualities you admire. Why do you consider this person important in your life? How did you meet? How does this person enrich your life?

_____

_____

_____

_____

_____

_____

_____

_____

_____

_____

_____

_____

_____

_____

_____

_____

_____

_____

ANSWERS TO WHAT DO YOU
KNOW? ON PAGE 380
1. S **2.** C **3.** C **4.** X **5.** C **6.** C **7.** X
8. C **9.** X **10.** S

WHAT HAVE YOU WRITTEN?

Underline the independent clauses in your paragraph—groups of words that have a subject and a verb and express a complete thought. Do some sentences contain more than one complete thought? Did you create any sentences that contained a dependent clause (a group of words with a subject and a verb that does not state a complete thought)?

If all the sentences are single independent clauses or simple sentences, read your paragraph out loud. Would it make your ideas clearer if some of these sentences were combined into a single statement?

Types of Sentences

Just as writers make choices about using different words to express their ideas, they also use different types of sentences. Sentence types are determined by the number and kind of clauses they contain.

A **simple sentence** consists of a single independent clause. A simple sentence is not necessarily short or "simple" to read. Although it may contain multiple subjects and verbs and numerous phrases set off with commas, it expresses a single thought.

> Paul drives.
> Paul and Nancy drive antique cars in local parades.
> Interested in advertising their real estate business, Paul and Nancy drive antique cars in local parades.

A **compound sentence** contains two or more independent clauses but no dependent clauses. You can think of compound sentences as "double" or "triple" sentences because they express two or more complete thoughts.

> Pacific Mutual sells property insurance; Atlantic Mutual sells life insurance.
> *(Two independent clauses joined by a semicolon)*

> Jim wants to stay in New York, but Nancy longs to move to California.
> *(Two independent clauses joined with a comma and coordinating conjunction)*

A **complex sentence** contains one independent clause and one or more dependent clauses.

> *James is working out twice a day* because he wants to try out for the Olympics.

> Because he wants to try out for the Olympics, *James is working out twice a day.*

> *(When a dependent clause begins a complex sentence, it is set off with a comma)*

A **compound-complex sentence** contains at least two independent clauses and one or more dependent clauses.

> Teachers buy school supplies for their students, and they often pay for class trips themselves, *because the new budget has cut funding to elementary schools.*

> *Because the new budget has cut funding to elementary schools,* teachers buy school supplies for their students, and they often pay for class trips themselves.

The type of sentence you write should reflect your thoughts. Important ideas should be stated in simple sentences to highlight their significance. Equally important ideas can be connected in compound sentences to show cause and effect, choice, or contrast. Minor ideas can be linked to complete thoughts in complex sentences as dependent clauses.

Coordination

Coordination creates *compound sentences* by linking two or more simple sentences (independent clauses). There are two methods of joining simple sentences:

1. Use a comma [,] and a coordinating conjunction (*and, or, nor, for, yet, but, so*).
2. Use a semicolon [;].

Coordinating Conjunctions

Coordinating conjunctions join simple sentences and show the relationship between the two complete thoughts.

and	adds an idea	We flew to Chicago, *and* we rented a hotel room.
or	shows choice	I will get a job, *or* I will sell the car.
nor	adds an idea when the first is negative	He was neither a scholar, *nor* was he a gentleman.
but	shows contrast	He studied hard, *but* he failed the test.
yet	shows contrast	She never studied, *yet* she got an A.
for	shows a reason	He left town, *for* he had lost his job.
so	shows cause and effect	I had a headache, *so* I left work early.

A simple diagram can demonstrate the way to use coordinating conjunctions:

INDEPENDENT CLAUSE**,** *and* INDEPENDENT CLAUSE.

> *or*
> *nor*
> *but*
> *yet*
> *for*
> *so*

NOTE: A comma always comes before the coordinating conjunction.

In some cases no coordinating conjunction is used. Parallel independent clauses can be linked with a semicolon.

Bruno writes about domestic issues; Rosa writes about foreign policy issues.

The mayor supports the plan; the city council is against it.

Semicolons are also used to join independent clauses with adverbial conjunctions (*however, meanwhile,* etc.), which are set off with commas.

Bruno writes about domestic issues; meanwhile, Rosa writes about foreign policy.

The mayor supports the plan; however, the city council is against it.

Adverbial Conjunctions

Adverbial conjunctions link independent clauses, but unlike coordinating conjunctions—*and, or, nor, for, yet, but, so*—they are set off with a comma and require a semicolon:

INDEPENDENT CLAUSE**;** *adverbial conjunction***,** INDEPENDENT CLAUSE

Common Adverbial Conjunctions

To Add Ideas

in addition	likewise	besides
moreover	furthermore	

The car needs a muffler**;** **in addition,** it needs tires.
They won't fix the roof**;** **furthermore,** they refused to paint the garage.

To Show Choice

instead	otherwise

He did not study**;** **instead,** he went for coffee.
He went on a diet**;** **otherwise,** he faced increasing hypertension.

To Show Contrast

however	nonetheless	nevertheless

We rehearsed for two weeks**;** **however,** we never got the scene right.
The weather was terrible**;** **nevertheless,** everyone loved the trip.

To Show Time

meanwhile

The teachers asked for more resources**;** **meanwhile,** the parents looked for other schools.

To Show Cause and Effect

thus	therefore	consequently
accordingly	hence	

Our house lost power**;** **hence,** we cancelled the party.
The buses are on strike**;** **therefore,** we are paying workers to take cabs.

To Show Emphasis

indeed	in fact

The students are angry about the tuition hike**;** **indeed,** several have transferred.
He did poorly during the World Series**;** **in fact,** he never got a single hit.

NOTE: You don't have to memorize all the adverbial conjunctions. Just remember you need to use a semicolon unless independent clauses are joined with *and, or, for, nor, yet, but,* or *so.*

NOTE: If you fail to join two independent clauses with a comma and a co-ordinating conjunction or a semicolon, you create errors called run-ons and comma splices.

See Chapter 25 for strategies to spot and repair run-ons and comma splices.

EXERCISE 1 Combining Simple Sentences (Independent Clauses) Using Coordinating Conjunctions and Commas

1. Write two simple sentences joined by *and*:

   _____

   _____

2. Write two simple sentences joined by *or*:

   _____

   _____

3. Write two simple sentences joined by *but*:

   _____

   _____

4. Write two simple sentences joined by *yet*:

   _____

   _____

5. Write two simple sentences joined by *so*:

   _____

   _____

EXERCISE 2 Combining Simple Sentences (Independent Clauses) Using Coordinating Conjunctions and Commas

Combine each pair of sentences using a comma and a coordinating conjunction.

1. **The Brooklyn Bridge was an engineering triumph.**

   It claimed the lives of twenty-seven workers.

   The Brooklyn Bridge was an engineering triumph, but it claimed the lives of twenty-seven workers.

2. **The bridge was dedicated with great ceremony on May 24, 1883.**

   Tragedy struck a week later.

   The bridge was dedicated with great ceremony on May 24, 1883, but tragedy struck a week later.

3. **A rumor that the bridge was about to collapse caused a panic.**

   Twelve people were trampled to death.

   A rumor that the bridge was about to collapse caused a panic, and twelve people were trampled to death.

4. Robert Odlum jumped off the bridge as a stunt in 1885.

He died of internal injuries from the fall.

Robert Odlum jumped off the bridge as a stunt in 1885, but he died of internal

injuries from the fall.

5. In 1886 Steve Brodie achieved instant fame when he claimed to have survived

a jump from the Brooklyn Bridge.

Most people believe a dummy was used in the stunt.

In 1886 Steve Brodie achieved instant fame when he claimed to have survived a jump

from the Brooklyn Bridge, but most people believe a dummy was used in the stunt.

EXERCISE 3 Combining Simple Sentences (Independent Clauses) Using Coordinating Conjunctions

Add a second independent clause using the coordinating conjunction indicated. Read the sentence aloud to make sure it makes sense.

1. The team won the first five games, *but* _____

_____

2. The mayor won an overwhelming victory, *and* _____

_____

3. The largest business in town has gone bankrupt, *so* _____

_____

4. You can fly to Chicago, *or* _____

_____

5. My car needs a lot of work, *yet* _____

_____

EXERCISE 4 Combining Simple Sentences (Independent Clauses) Using Semicolons

Write a sentence joining two independent clauses by a semicolon. Make sure the statement you add is a complete sentence.

1. _____ ;

_____

2. _____ ;

_____

3. _____ ; *therefore,*

_____

4. _____ ; *however,*

_____

5. _____ ; *in fact,*

_____

EXERCISE 5 Combining Simple Sentences (Independent Clauses) with Semicolons

Add a second independent clause to each sentence. Read each sentence aloud to make sure it makes sense.

1. I love walking to school in the fall; _____

   _____

2. The Hoover Dam is a major tourist attraction in Nevada; _____

   _____

3. The Model T Ford changed history; _____

   _____

4. Math is my toughest course this semester; _____

   _____

EXERCISE 6 Using Compound Sentences to Eliminate Choppy Sentences

Rewrite the following paragraph to eliminate choppy sentences by creating compound sentences using coordination.

The largest Japanese community outside Japan is in Brazil. There are 1.5 million Brazilians of Japanese descent. The first Japanese immigrants arrived in 1908. Brazil needed farm workers. At first most immigrants came from Europe. Later immigrants came from Asia. Japanese who immigrated to the United States became assimilated. Japanese who moved to Brazil remained loyal to their emperor. Many supported Japan during World War II. They were angered when Brazil sided with the Allies. Brazil broke off relations with Japan. It took steps to suppress its Japanese community as well. Brazil closed Japanese language schools. It banned Japanese newspapers. Japanese children had to learn Portuguese. The number of Japanese speakers dwindled. Japan and Brazil increased their economic ties in the 1980s. Thousands of Japanese-Brazilians immigrated to Japan to find jobs. They became known as *Dekasegis.*

Subordination

Subordination creates *complex* sentences by joining an independent clause with one or more dependent clauses. Dependent clauses contain a subject and a verb but cannot stand alone. They are incomplete thoughts and need to be joined to an independent clause to make sense.

Dependent Clause Stating an Incomplete Thought
Because it started to rain.
After we left the party.

Dependent clauses are *fragments* and should not stand alone (see Chapter 23).

Dependent Clause Linked to an Independent Clause Stating a Complete Thought
Because it started to rain, we moved the reception to the auditorium.
After we left the party, a fight broke out.

POINT TO REMEMBER

Place a comma after a dependent clause when it comes before an independent clause.

> Because I missed the bus, I was late for school.
> I was late for school because I missed the bus. (no comma needed)

USING SUBORDINATING CONJUNCTIONS IN DEPENDENT CLAUSES

Begin clauses with a subordinating conjunction rather than a preposition.

Incorrect
My mother's family moved to the United States *because of* they wanted a better life.

Correct
My mother's family moved to the United States *because* they wanted a better life.

Because is a subordinating conjunction. *Because of* is a two-word preposition that must be followed by a noun or pronoun.

> The flight was delayed *because of* fog.
> We were delayed *because of* him.

Subordination helps distinguish between important ideas and minor details. Without subordination, writing can be awkward and hard to follow.

> I always loved my brother's Corvette. I should never have bought it. I cannot afford it. I am only working part-time. I earn enough to pay for gas. The insurance is more than I can handle. I drive at least eighty miles a day. I will soon need new tires.

Revised

> Although I always loved my brother's Corvette, I should never have bought it. I cannot afford it because I am only working part-time. While I earn enough to pay for gas, the insurance is more than I can handle. Because I drive at least eighty miles a day, I will soon need new tires.

Dependent clauses can be placed at the beginning, within, and at the end of an independent clause. When they come first or within an independent clause, they are set off with commas.

Primary Idea	*Secondary Idea*
I learned Spanish.	I lived in Cancun.
Sid cancelled his vacation.	His mother became ill.
The sanitation workers are on strike.	Their demands have been ignored.

Complex Sentences
Because I live in Cancun, I learned Spanish.
Sid cancelled his vacation *when his mother became ill.*
The sanitation workers, *whose demands have been ignored,* are on strike.

EXERCISE 7 Combining Ideas Using Subordination

Create complex sentences by joining the dependent and independent clauses. If the dependent clause comes first, set it off with a comma.

1. **Basil Rathbone became internationally famous.**

   When he played Sherlock Holmes.

   Basil Rathbone became internationally famous when he played Sherlock Holmes.

   When he played Sherlock Holmes, Basil Rathbone became internationally famous.

2. **Although the show received good reviews.**

   ***Mean Girls* was abruptly cancelled.**

   Although the show received good reviews, Mean Girls was abruptly cancelled.

   Mean Girls was abruptly cancelled although the show received good reviews.

3. **The boardwalk restaurants do well even in bad weather.**

   Because tourists have to stay indoors when it rains.

   The boardwalk restaurants do well even in bad weather because tourists have to stay indoors when it rains.

   Because tourists have to stay indoors when it rains, the boardwalk restaurants do well even in bad weather.

4. **I take a cab to work.**

   When my sister needs the car.

   I take a cab to work when my sister needs the car.

   When my sister needs the car, I take a cab to work.

5. **Although it will be cheaper to build a new building.**

   The alumni want to restore Old Main.

   Although it will be cheaper to build a new building, the alumni want to restore Old Main.

   The alumni want to restore Old Main although it will be cheaper to build a new building.

EXERCISE 8 Combining Ideas Using Subordination

Create complex sentences by turning one of the simple sentences into a dependent clause and connecting it with the more important idea. You may change the wording of the clauses, but do not alter their basic meaning. Remember that dependent clauses that open or come in the middle of a sentence are set off with commas.

EX: **Willa Cather was born in Virginia. She grew up on a ranch in Nebraska.**

Although Willa Cather was born in Virginia, she grew up on a ranch in Nebraska.

1. **Willa Cather graduated from the University of Nebraska in 1895. She then moved to Pittsburgh.**

   After she graduated from the University of Nebraska in 1895, Willa Cather moved to Pittsburgh.

2. **Cather taught high school. She pursued a career in journalism and writing.**

   Cather taught high school while she pursued a career in journalism and writing.

   _____

3. **Her teaching experience brought her into contact with adolescents. She developed a keen insight into the minds of teenagers.**

   Because her teaching experience brought her into contact with adolescents, she developed a keen insight into the minds of teenagers.

4. **The suicide of a gifted young man made an impression on Cather. She sensed the modern industrial world was increasingly cold and hostile.**

   The suicide of a gifted young man made an impression on Cather, because she sensed the modern industrial world was increasingly cold and hostile.

5. **Pittsburgh was a city of factories and steel mills. It symbolized the modern industrialized society.**

   Because Pittsburgh was a city of factories and steel mills, it symbolized the modern industrialized society.

6. **In 1904 Cather wrote the short story "Paul's Case" based on her observations as a teacher. The character was not modeled after a specific student.**

   In 1904 Cather wrote the short story "Paul's Case" based on her observations as a teacher, although the character was not modeled after a specific student.

7. **Paul is a bright, sensitive boy who loves the arts. He does poorly in school.**

   Although Paul is a bright, sensitive boy who loves the arts, he does poorly in school.

   _____

8. **He loves working in a concert hall and visiting a young actor in his dressing room. Paul has no desire to pursue a career in the arts.**

   Even though he loves working in a concert hall and visiting a young actor in his dressing room, Paul has no desire to pursue a career in the arts.

9. **Paul steals money from his employer. He runs away to New York and enjoys a life of luxury that eludes him in Pittsburgh.**

   After Paul steals money from his employer, he runs away to New York and enjoys a life of luxury that eludes him in Pittsburgh.

10. **Paul dreads returning to the boredom of Pittsburgh. He commits suicide when his money runs out.**

    Because Paul dreads returning to the boredom of Pittsburgh, he commits suicide when his money runs out.

EXERCISE 9 Using Coordination and Subordination

The following passage is stated in simple sentences. Revise it and create compound and complex sentences to make it more interesting and easier to read.

A small North Carolina island holds a secret. It was the site of an early English colony that mysteriously disappeared. Historians and scientists have conducted research for decades. No satisfactory answer has been found. In 1585 colonists were sent to America by Sir Walter Raleigh. They established a settlement on Roanoke Island. More settlers arrived in 1587. Virginia Dare was born on the island that August. She was the first English child born in America. She was the granddaughter of John White. John White was the governor of the colony. John White sailed to England for supplies. His return trip was delayed three years. A war interrupted his plans. He reached the colony. He found it empty. The hundred colonists had disappeared. There was no sign of a battle. There was no sign of violence. The people had just vanished. There was only a single clue. The word "Croatoan" was found carved on a tree. No one could explain what happened to the settlement. It became known as "The Lost Colony." Researchers speculate that they were abducted by Native American tribes or perished during a severe drought. No accepted evidence of their fate has been discovered.

After completing your draft, read it aloud. Have you reduced choppy and awkward sentences? Does your version make the essay easier to follow?

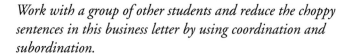

WORKING TOGETHER

Work with a group of other students and reduce the choppy sentences in this business letter by using coordination and subordination.

```
Dear Ms. Mendoza:

This year the annual convention will be held in Miami.
The Miami location is best suited for our needs. We
draw attendees from across the country. Our fastest-
growing operations are located in Florida.

I would like you to make a presentation about online
sales. Many of our new sales representatives have no
experience with Internet marketing. As of March 1st
we will no longer sell products at Wal-Mart or Target.
We will have to rely more on online sales to continue
our growth.

You have great experience in developing an online cat-
alog. This makes you a valuable asset to us. I am sure
our sales reps can learn a lot from you. They will
appreciate any insights you can give them.

Please call me this week, so we can discuss details.

Sincerely,

Sid Hussani
```

GET THINKING
AND **WRITING**

CRITICAL THINKING

The United States is a superpower that participates in a global economy. To prosper in the twenty-first century, Americans will have to conduct business in dozens of foreign countries. Do you think that every college student should be required to learn a foreign language? Why or why not? Write a paragraph stating your views.

WHAT HAVE YOU WRITTEN?

When you complete your paragraph, read over your work. Underline each independent clause once and each dependent clause twice. Did you create effective compound and complex sentences and punctuate them correctly? Read your sentences aloud. Are there missing words, awkward phrases, or confusing shifts that need revising?

1. Select one of the compound sentences and write it below:

   _____

   _____

   Are the independent clauses closely related? Do they belong in the same sentence? Could you subordinate one of the ideas to create a complex sentence? Try writing a complex sentence that logically reflects the relationship between the ideas:

   _____

   _____

   Does this complex sentence make sense—or would a compound sentence better express what you are trying to say?
   Have you used the best method to join the two ideas? If you used a comma and coordinating conjunction, rewrite the sentence using a semicolon:

   _____

   _____

   How does this version affect meaning? Does it make sense? Why are coordinating conjunctions important?

2. Select one of your complex sentences and write it below:

   _____

   _____

   Underline the independent clause. Is it the more important idea? Does the dependent clause express only additional or less-important information?
   Turn the dependent clause into an independent one and create a compound sentence—remember to use a semicolon or a comma with and, or, yet, but, *or* so *to join the two clauses:*

   _____

   _____

Does the compound sentence better express what you are trying to say or does it appear illogical or awkward?

Write the two independent clauses as separate simple sentences:

_____

_____

How does stating these ideas in two sentences alter the impact of your ideas? Does it better express what you are trying to say or only create two choppy sentences?

When you are trying to express an important or complex idea, consider writing two or more versions using simple, compound, and complex sentences. Read them aloud and select the sentences that best reflect your ideas.

WHAT HAVE YOU LEARNED?

Place a C next to sentences that use coordination to join independent clauses and an S next to sentences that use subordination to join dependent clauses to independent clauses. Mark simple sentences—those with one independent clause—with an X.

1. _____ New York is the largest city on the East Coast; Los Angeles is the largest city on the West Coast.

2. _____ Detroit is on Eastern Standard Time.

3. _____ George found that his antique car was difficult to maintain and cost too much to insure.

4. _____ The teachers are willing to donate their time, and some parents have offered money.

5. _____ The buses are slow; the cabs are hard to find.

6. _____ Because it has no calories and can ease hunger pangs, coffee is popular with dieters.

7. _____ I took Advanced Algebra after I got a perfect score on the entrance exam.

8. _____ She has a degree in business and a certificate in accounting, but Deborah lets her brother do the taxes.

9. _____ The governor angered the teachers' union when she claimed teachers only deserved part-time pay for part-time work.

10. _____ Mexico abolished slavery before the United States did.

Answers appear on the following page.

WRITING ON THE WEB

Using a search engine such as Yahoo!, Google, or AltaVista, enter terms such as *simple sentence, compound sentence, complex sentence, independent clause,* and *dependent clause* to locate current sites of interest.

POINTS TO REMEMBER

1. Simple sentences contain one independent clause and express a single complete thought.
2. Compound sentences link two or more independent clauses with a semi-colon (;) or a comma (,) and a coordinating conjunction (*and, or, yet, but, so, for, nor*).
3. Complex sentences link one or more dependent clauses with a single independent clause.
4. Compound-complex sentences link one or more dependent clauses to two or more independent clauses.
5. Use compound sentences to *coordinate* ideas of equal importance.
6. Use complex sentences to link an important idea with a dependent clause adding secondary information.
7. Use sentence structure to demonstrate the relationship between your ideas.

Writer's Resources⑨Now™   If you use Writer's ResourcesNow, please have your students log in and view the pretest, study plan, and posttest for this chapter.

ANSWERS TO WHAT HAVE YOU
LEARNED? ON PAGE 393
1. C 2. X 3. X 4. C 5. C 6. S 7. S.
8. C 9. S 10. X

Repairing Run-ons and Comma Splices

California highway sign warning drivers of illegal immigrants

How should the United States cope with illegal immigration? Do we need tighter border security? Should people who hire undocumented workers be punished more severely? Should immigration policy be changed to admit guest workers? What can be done to prevent the deaths of people trying to cross the border? Are those concerned about border security motivated by fears of terrorism or racism?

Write one or more paragraphs expressing your views about illegal immigrants, border security, or the plight of undocumented workers.

What Are Run-ons?

Run-ons are not wordy sentences that "run on" too long. Run-ons are incorrectly punctuated compound sentences. Chapter 24 explains how independent clauses are coordinated to create compound sentences that join two or more complete thoughts. You can think of them as "double" or "triple" sentences. Compound sentences demonstrate the relationship between closely related ideas that might be awkward or confusing if stated separately.

Ted served in the navy for six years.   He never learned how to swim.
Ted served in the navy for six years, but he never learned how to swim.
("but" dramatizes the irony of a sailor never learning how to swim)

Albany is the capital of New York.   Trenton is the capital of New Jersey.
Albany is the capital of New York; Trenton is the capital of New Jersey.
(the semicolon links the two matching sentences as an equal pair)

To be effective, compound sentences have to be accurately punctuated to avoid confusion. There are two methods of joining independent clauses:

Use a semicolon
independent clause; independent clause

or

Use a comma with a coordinating conjunction
independent clause, *and* independent clause

or

nor

but

yet

so

for

If you don't use the right punctuation, you create a run-on. Run-on sentences—also caused *fused sentences*—and a related error called *comma splices,* or *comma faults,* are some of the most common errors found in college writing. Because thoughts occur to us in a stream rather than a series of separate ideas, we can easily run them together in writing if we're not careful.

I always thought it would be glamorous to own a restaurant I had no idea how much work is involved. I worked at my aunt's restaurant for just two weeks last summer I could not believe how many hours she put in every day. Long before the place opened, she was there paying bills, making up schedules, calling vendors, and planning menus. *The last dishwasher left at eleven-thirty she was still at work, counting money and getting ready for the next day.*

Revised

I always thought it would be glamorous to own a restaurant, **but** I had no idea how much work is involved. I worked at my aunt's restaurant for just two weeks last summer, **and** I could not believe how many hours she put in every day. Long before the place opened, she was there paying bills, making up schedules, calling vendors, and planning menus. The last dishwasher left at eleven-thirty, **and** she was still at work, counting money and getting ready for the next day.

Run-ons can be of any length. Just as fragments can be long, run-ons can be very short.

She begged no one cared.   He lives in Paris Texas is his birthplace.

Revised
She begged, but no one cared.   He lives in Paris; Texas is his birthplace.

WHAT DO YOU KNOW?

Label each sentence OK for correct or RO for run-on.

1. _____ Carlos filed his federal taxes on time, but he forgot to submit his state return.

2. _____ Depression is a serious disease too many people dismiss it as a minor ailment.

3. _____ Although they arrived at the airport two hours early and checked in at the express counter, Carol and Steve nearly missed their flight because two of the security scanners were malfunctioning.

4. _____ The online courses are not as popular as we predicted students enjoy the classroom experience.

5. _____ The parents met with the professors, who explained how the new grading system would work.

Answers appear on the following page.

WHAT ARE YOU TRYING TO SAY?

G E T | *W R I T I N G*
AND REVISING

Describe an upcoming vacation. Do you plan to travel, work, stay at home, or spend time with your family? Explain activities using as many compound sentences as you can to show cause and effect, contrast, or choice.

Example
   Over the next break I plan to work. It's a busy time at my uncle's business, and he promised me plenty of overtime that week. I would love to go to Florida with my brother, but I really need money. I don't have much in the bank, but I can no longer put off getting a new car. My Toyota is twelve years old and has over 120,000 miles on it, so it is time to replace it. The $1500 I can make in one week at my uncle's would really help with a down payment.

_____

_____

_____

_____

_____

_____
_____
_____
_____
_____
_____
_____

WHAT HAVE YOU WRITTEN?

Read your paragraph carefully. Have you created any compound sentences—sentences that contain two or more independent clauses or two or more complete thoughts? Are the compound sentences properly punctuated? Do you join the independent clauses with commas and coordinating conjunctions (and, or, yet, but, so, for, nor)*?*

Run-ons: Fused Sentences and Comma Splices

Some writing teachers use the term "run-on" to refer to all errors in compound sentences, while others break these errors into two types: fused sentences and comma splices.

Fused Sentences

Fused sentences lack the punctuation needed to join two independent clauses. The two independent clauses are *fused* or joined without a comma or semicolon.

I quit smoking cigarettes are expensive.

Revised
I quit smoking; cigarettes are expensive.

I didn't see the movie but I read the book.

Revised
I didn't see the movie, but I read the book.

Comma Splices

Comma splices are compound sentences where a comma is used instead of a semicolon.

The book ends with a funeral, the movie ends with a wedding.

Revised
The book ends with a funeral; the movie ends with a wedding.

He goes to Vermont to ski, I go to Vermont to paint.

Revised
He goes to Vermont to ski; I go to Vermont to paint.

ANSWERS TO WHAT DO YOU KNOW? ON PAGE 397
1. RO (comma needed after *time*)
2. RO (semicolon needed after *disease*) **3.** OK **4.** RO (semicolon needed after *predicted*) **5.** OK

Identifying Run-ons

To identify run-ons, do two things:

1. Read the sentence carefully. Determine if it is a compound sentence. Ask yourself if you can divide the sentence into two or more independent clauses (simple sentences).

   Carrie moved to Manhattan but came home after two months.

   Carrie moved to Manhattan . . . [independent clause (simple sentence)]
   came home after two months . . . [not a sentence]

   Not a compound sentence

   Sara works two shifts she wants another job.

   Sara works two shifts . . . [independent clause (simple sentence)]
   she wants another job . . . [independent clause (simple sentence)]

   Compound sentence

2. If you have two or more independent clauses, determine if they should be connected. Is there a logical relationship between them? What is the best way of connecting them? Independent clauses can be joined with a comma and *and, or, nor, yet, but, so, for,* or a semicolon.

   Sara works two shifts, but she wants another job.

   But indicates a logical contrast between two ideas. Inserting the missing comma and the word *but* quickly repairs this run-on.

EXERCISE 1 Identifying Run-ons: Comma Splices and Fused Sentences

Label each item OK for correct, CS for comma splice, and RO for run-on.

1. __RO__ Many towns and states in America were named after places in Europe New York, New Jersey, New London, and Cambridge are obvious examples.

2. __OK__ There is a region in southern Illinois called Little Egypt, but no one seems exactly sure how it got this rather exotic name.

3. __OK__ Several towns in the area have Egyptian names, Cairo being the most famous.

4. __CS/RO__ Anyone who has read *Huckleberry Finn* will remember Cairo, it was Huck and Jim's original destination.

5. __RO__ Smaller towns also bear exotic names Karnak, Dongola, and Thebes are all named after cities in Egypt.

6. __OK__ An artificial lake was constructed in southern Illinois and was given the name Lake of Egypt.

7. __OK__ One explanation for the Egyptian names is geographical; the merging Ohio and Mississippi rivers reminded early settlers of the Nile Delta.

8. __CS/RO__ Another theory is Biblical, it dates back to 1831 when an early frost killed much of the harvest in northern Illinois.

9. __OK__ Grain from southern Illinois was shipped north, and the long line of wagons loaded with wheat reminded people of the Old Testament story of Jacob's sons buying grain in Egypt.

10. __RO__ The origins of the nickname may be lost to history modern residents still enjoy naming stores, schools, and athletic teams after Egyptian sources.

EXERCISE 2 Identifying Run-ons: Comma Splices and Fused Sentences

Underline the comma splices and fused sentences in the following paragraph. If your instructor prefers, you can indicate fused sentences by underlining them twice.

Booker T. Washington was born a slave he rose to become a leading African American educator and leader. He headed the Tuskegee Institute and made many speaking tours in the North to gain support for black causes. His autobiography *Up from Slavery* became an international best-seller. Washington toured European capitals and he became, after the death of Frederick Douglass, the most well-known black figure in America. Washington became the first African American to be invited by the president to visit the White House he advised Presidents Theodore Roosevelt and Howard Taft on racial issues.

Washington first received national attention and national criticism after he addressed the 1895 Atlanta Exposition his speech was later denounced as the "Atlanta Compromise." Speaking before an audience of Southern whites, Washington proposed that blacks could advance economically while like "the fingers of the hand" remain socially separate. This approach was widely supported by whites Washington was criticized by black leaders for accepting segregation.

Washington's supporters defended his position as being practical, given the political realities of the South. His emphasis on self-reliance and black business ownership stimulated the growth of African American enterprise. Washington built a powerful organization in his later years it was challenged by newer organizations like the NAACP. Booker T. Washington died in 1915 in 1940 he became the first African American to appear on a U.S. postage stamp.

Run-ons Needing Minor Repairs

A **fused sentence** or **comma splice** may only need a minor repair. Sometimes in writing quickly you can mistakenly use a comma when a semicolon is needed.

The teachers support the new principal, the parents question her methods.

Revised
The teachers support the new principal; the parents question her methods.

In other cases you may forget a comma or drop one of the coordinating conjunctions.

The teachers support the new principal but the parents question her methods.

Teachers like the new principal, parents have reservations.

Revised

The teachers support the new principal, but the parents question her methods.

Teachers like the new principal, but parents have reservations.

Run-ons Needing Major Repairs

In other cases run-ons require more extensive repairs. Sometimes you create run-ons when your ideas are not clearly stated or fully thought out.

George Bush became president in 2001 terrorists attacked the World Trade Center.

Adding the needed semicolon eliminates a punctuation error but leaves the sentence awkward and unclear.

George Bush became president in 2001; terrorists attacked the World Trade Center.

Repairing this kind of run-on requires critical thinking. A compound sentence joins two complete thoughts, and there should be a clear relationship between them. It may be better to revise the entire sentence, changing it from a compound to a complex sentence.

Revised

George Bush was president when terrorists attacked the World Trade Center in 2001.

In some instances you may find it easier to break the run-on into two simple sentences, especially if there is no strong relationship between the main ideas.

George Murphy was an actor and singer and he later served in the U.S. Senate.

Revised

George Murphy was an actor and singer. He later served in the U.S. Senate.

POINT TO REMEMBER

A compound sentence should join independent clauses that state ideas of equal importance. Avoid using an independent clause to state a minor detail that could be contained in a dependent clause or a phrase.

My sister lives in Chicago, and she is a teacher.

Revised

My sister, who lives in Chicago, is a teacher.　　My sister is a teacher in Chicago.

Methods of Repairing Run-ons

There are several methods of repairing run-ons.

1. Put a period between the sentences.

   Sometimes in first drafts we connect ideas that have no logical relationship.

   Ken graduated from Salinas Community College, and the school had a famous football team.

   Revised
   Ken graduated from Salinas Community College. The school had a famous football team.

   Even if the two sentences are closely related, your thoughts might be clearer if they were stated in two simple sentences. Blending two sentences into one can weaken the impact of an idea you may want to stress.

   The manager asked for more security guards, but the owner refused.

   Revised
   The manager asked for more security guards. The owner refused.

2. Insert a semicolon between the sentences to show a balanced relationship between closely related ideas.

   Los Angeles is the largest city in California; Las Vegas is the largest city in Nevada.

   Commuters demand more roads; residents demand less traffic.

3. Connect the sentences with a comma and *and, or, nor, yet, but, so,* or *for* to show a logical relationship between them.

Ted is tired, *so* he is leaving early.	[indicates that one idea causes another]
Ted is tired, *but* he will work overtime. Ted is tired, *yet* he stays late.	[shows unexpected contrast between ideas]
Ted is tired, *and* he feels very weak.	[adds two similar ideas]
Ted will work late tonight, *or* he will come in early tomorrow.	[indicates one of two alternatives]

4. Rewrite the run-on, making it a simple or complex sentence to reduce wordiness or show a clearer relationship between ideas.

   Wendy bought an SUV and she later sold it to her cousin.

   Carlos took flying lessons in college he hoped to become an airline pilot.

   Revised
   Wendy bought an SUV she later sold to her cousin.
   [simple sentence]

   Carlos took flying lessons in college because he hoped to become an airline pilot.
   [complex sentence]

POINTS TO REMEMBER

Often in revising a paper, you may wonder, "Should this comma be a semi-colon?" To determine which mark of punctuation is correct, apply this simple test:

1. Read the sentence aloud. Ask yourself if you can divide the sentence into independent clauses (simple sentences that can stand alone).
2. Where the independent clauses are joined, you should see a semicolon or a comma with *and, or, nor, yet, but, so,* or *for.*
3. If *and, or, nor, yet, but, so,* or *for* are missing, the comma should be a semicolon.

Remember, a semicolon is a period over a comma—it signals a connection between two complete sentences.

WORKING TOGETHER

Work with a group of students to correct the fused sentences using each method. Have each member provide four solutions, then share your responses. Determine who came up with the most logical, easy-to-read sentence.

1. Our school may have to suspend its athletic programs the sudden rise in the liability insurance exceeds the budget.

    Two simple sentences:

    _____

    _____

    Two types of compound sentences:

    _____

    _____

    One complex sentence:

    _____

    _____

2. The police asked local TV stations to show the photo of a missing girl she is a diabetic and requires immediate medical attention.

    Two simple sentences:

    _____

    _____

    Two types of compound sentences:

    _____

    _____

One complex sentence:

_____

_____

3. Construction of new housing and a shopping mall have increased the need for expanded public transportation the bus company is announcing additional routes this fall.

Two simple sentences:

_____

_____

Two types of compound sentences:

_____

_____

One complex sentence:

_____

_____

EXERCISE 3 Revising Run-ons: Fused Sentences

Rewrite fused sentences, creating correctly punctuated compound, complex, or simple sentences.

1. America's first war against terrorism was launched in 1801 in North Africa pirates had been hijacking American ships and taking hostages since the 1780s.

_____

_____

2. The small American navy was unable to protect merchant ships far from home they were easy targets for the Barbary pirates who no longer had to face the British navy to raid ships coming from Boston or New York.

_____

_____

3. Thomas Jefferson refused to pay money demanded by the pasha of Tripoli he ordered American warships to blockade Mediterranean ports and attack the pirate fleet.

_____

_____

4. **William Eaton led a force of U.S. Marines and Arab fighters in a surprise assault on the town of Derna the pasha, fearing an advance on Tripoli, signed a treaty to end hostilities in 1805.**

_____

_____

5. **The war did not fully stop pirate attacks against America the young country did prove it could respond to terrorism halfway around the world.**

_____

_____

EXERCISE 4 Repairing Comma Splices and Fused Sentences with Commas and Semicolons

Revise each of the following sentences to correct run-ons by inserting commas and semicolons.

1. Before leaving home, millions of people slip cell phones into their pockets or purses;they are almost as common as credit cards and car keys.

2. Young people have grown up with cell phones,and they cannot imagine life without them.

3. The first American cell phone went on the market in 1983;it weighed two pounds and cost four thousand dollars.

4. Today, many companies make money on monthly fees,and they give the phones away for free.

5. Cell phones are actually two-way radios;they broadcast and receive messages.

6. The term "cell" does not describe the phone;it refers to the system that allows low-power radios to communicate over vast distances.

7. A city, for example, is divided into overlapping cells;each cell has a base station with a sending and receiving tower.

8. As a cell phone user drives a car, he or she moves from cell to cell,and the signal is passed from one to another.

9. Cell phones can now send text messages and pictures; like computers, they can become infected with viruses that steal passwords and address books.

10. The cell phone, which so many people use daily, highlights the differences between rich and poor; according to the UN, half the people in the world will never make or receive a telephone call in their lives.

EXERCISE 5 Repairing Comma Splices and Fused Sentences

Edit the following passage for comma splices and fused sentences.

On March 11, 1918, a soldier at Fort Riley, Kansas, went to the base hospital complaining of fever and a sore throat;within hours, a hundred other soldiers reported the same symptoms. During the next few days, hundreds more were stricken with high fever, muscle and joint pain, and extreme fatigue. Many died. The disease then appeared in other army camps;in California hundreds of prisoners in San Quentin fell ill. The death toll mounted,at an army base near Boston, sixty soldiers died in one day.   [.A]

By the summer, the disease was spreading across the country,and the government became alarmed. The sudden deaths of young men preparing to go to war led to wild rumors;many believed German submarines had brought the disease to America. Others blamed terrorists;they claimed spies were dispersing germs in movie theaters.

Soon the disease, now named Spanish influenza, infected the civilian population. In Philadelphia 300 people died in a single day;in New York the daily death toll reached 700. Hospitals were swamped with patients;funeral homes ran out of coffins. Doctors urged people to wear masks and avoid crowds. Schools, churches, and theaters were closed. Parades, sporting events, and bond drives were cancelled. Newspapers printed warnings and advertisements for patent medicines. Desperate to avoid the deadly disease, people gargled with strange concoctions made with sugar and kerosene.

As infected American soldiers boarded troop ships bound for Europe, the disease became global. Earlier in the war it was feared that many soldiers would be lost in transit to U-boat attacks. The use of convoys eliminated the U-boat threat,and not a single American soldier lost his life to a torpedo,thousands would be felled by the flu they , but contracted in the tightly packed ships. Within months the flu spread throughout war-ravaged Europe;it eventually reached India where millions were infected.

World War I killed 126,000 Americans;the Spanish flu killed 675,000. The war that lasted four years and saw some of the deadliest battles in history killed 15 million people,but in a single year the flu killed over 20 million. The horror of World War I and political events like the Russian Revolution overshadowed the deadly epidemic. Today, however, bioterrorism experts view this forgotten epidemic as a warning. The deadliest terrorist weapon is not a nuclear bomb but a flu that could kill 50 million people in a few months.

WORKING TOGETHER

Working with a group of students, revise this e-mail to eliminate fused sentences and comma splices.

```
Attention part-time employees:

As of March 15, part-time employees who work at least
twenty hours a week are eligible for health insurance.
Atlantic Health Services is holding informational sem-
inars meetings are scheduled every day next week at
4:30 in A220. To enroll you must bring your most
recent pay stub and your work schedule. Your supervisor
must sign your schedule, you need to supply information
about any existing health coverage you may have. This
benefit is part of the new contract, it has been sup-
plied to reduce discrepancy in wages and benefits be-
tween full- and part-time personnel. Make sure to at-
tend one of the seminars next week, additional
information is available on the company website.

Brett Chase
Benefits Manager
```

CRITICAL THINKING

Some nonprofit organizations sell lists of their donors to other charities. Do you think this is fair? When you contribute to an organization, do you think it should sell your name to others? Do you think your record of donations should be kept private? Why or why not?

Write one or more paragraphs expressing your views on the practice of selling donor lists.

WHAT HAVE YOU WRITTEN?

Read your response carefully and underline the compound sentences—those containing two or more independent clauses. Did you avoid run-ons? Did you join the independent clauses with a semicolon or a comma with and, or, nor, yet, but, so, for?

Select one of your compound sentences and write it out below:

_____

_____

1. Why did you place more than one complete idea in this sentence? Are the independent clauses logically related? Does your compound sentence link ideas of equal importance, show cause and effect, demonstrate a choice, or highlight a contrast? Could you improve the impact of your sentence by using a different coordinating conjunction?

2. If the ideas are not of equal importance, would it be better to subordinate one of them?

   My sister lives in Montana, and she won an Olympic medal in skiing.

   Revised
   My sister, who lives in Montana, won an Olympic medal in skiing.

   Select a simple sentence—a single independent clause—and write it out below:

   _____

   Think about the main idea you were trying to express and write another sentence about the same topic:

   _____

3. Read the two sentences. Should these ideas remain separate or would it be more effective to join them in a compound sentence to demonstrate their relationship?

   When you are trying to express an important or complex idea, consider writing two or more versions using simple, compound, and complex sentences. Read them aloud and select the sentence that best reflects your ideas.

WHAT HAVE YOU LEARNED?

Label each sentence OK for correct or RO for run-on.

1. _____ They rented a small apartment, they wanted to save money to buy a house.

2. _____ San Francisco is chilly in the summer but it remains a popular tourist destination.

3. _____ Sandy plays piano and has begun composing her own songs.

4. _____ The cabin lost power during the blizzard we had no heat.

5. _____ Fans surrounded her limo and they demanded autographs.

Answers appear below.

WRITING ON THE WEB

Using a search engine such as Yahoo!, Google, or AltaVista, enter terms such as *run-on, comma splice, comma fault, compound sentence, complex sentence,* and *sentence types* to locate current sites of interest.

POINTS TO REMEMBER

1. Run-ons are common writing errors.
2. A run-on is an incorrectly punctuated compound sentence.
3. Compound sentences join two or more related independent clauses using semicolons or commas with *and, or, nor, yet, but, so,* or *for.*
4. Run-ons can be corrected in two ways:
   a. If the sentence makes sense when you read it out loud and if the independent clauses are related, add the missing words or punctuation.

   Independent Clause; Independent Clause

   or

   Independent Clause, *and* Independent Clause
   or
   nor
   yet
   but
   for
   so

   b. If the sentence does not make sense, reword it or break it into separate simple or complex sentences.

Writer's Resources 🖐 Now™   If you use Writer's ResourcesNow, please have your students log in and view the pretest, study plan, and posttest for this chapter.

26

Correcting Dangling and Misplaced Modifiers

© Paul Barton/CORBIS

GET WRITING

Is owning a home a basic part of the American Dream?

Write a paragraph stating your views. Do you want to own a home? Is housing affordable in your region?

409

What Are Dangling and Misplaced Modifiers?

Modifiers describe words and phrases. Whether they are adjectives (*cold, red, old, inventive, fresh, clear, awkward*), adverbs (*quickly, freshly, clearly, awkwardly*), or participial phrases (*walking to work, speaking to the angry students, winning the game by one run*), they must be clearly linked to what they modify. Changing the position of a modifier in a sentence alters the meaning.

Sentence	*Meaning*
Only Karen takes cabs to work.	Karen is the one person to use a cab to commute to work.
Karen *only* takes cabs to work.	Karen uses cabs as her sole way of commuting to work.
Karen takes cabs *only* to work.	Karen uses cabs to commute to work and uses other means to travel elsewhere.

Dangling Modifiers

A **dangling modifier** is a modifier attached to the beginning or end of a sentence that is not clearly linked to what it is supposed to describe.

Dangling Modifier
Running into the street, the truck hit a small boy.   [who ran into the street—the truck?]

Correct
Running into the street, a small boy was hit by the truck.

Dangling Modifier
Hidden by fog, we could not see the island.   [What was hidden by fog—we?]

Correct
We could not see the island hidden by fog.

WHAT DO YOU KNOW?

Mark an X next to each sentence with a dangling or misplaced modifier and OK for each correct sentence.

1. _____ Losing by three touchdowns, the dejected fans tore up their programs and went home.

2. _____ Elected four times, Franklin Roosevelt became the most influential president since Lincoln.

3. _____ Fulfilling Kennedy's promise to reach the moon before the 1960s ended, the public watched astronauts land on the lunar surface in July 1969.

4. _____ Jogging four miles a day, Karen's cholesterol level began to drop.

5. _____ Running into sleet and poor visibility, the pilot requested a new course.

6. _____ I missed *American Idol* last night because I was stuck at the airport, which I looked forward to all week.

7. _____ I met the mayor who just resigned in the elevator.

8. _____ I was pulled over and given a speeding ticket by a cop rushing to the final exam.

9. _____ Concerned about the environment, the agency bought a fleet of hybrid cars.

10. _____ Built in 2001, the engineers were shocked by the rust and decay they found under the overpass.

Answers appear on the following page.

WHAT ARE YOU TRYING TO SAY?   *GET* WRITING

Write a paragraph describing the best teacher or boss you have had. How did this person affect your life? What events do you remember most? What lessons did you learn from this person? Provide adjectives that describe this person's characteristics and provide adverbs to describe this person's actions.

_____

_____

_____

_____

_____

_____

_____

_____

_____

_____

_____

_____

_____

_____

_____

_____

_____

Avoiding Dangling Modifiers

We frequently start or end sentences with modifying words, phrases, or clauses.

Created by a team of NASA scientists . . .
Located just outside of Chicago . . .
Discovered by a passing hiker . . .

These modifiers only make sense if they are correctly linked with what they are supposed to modify.

Created by a team of NASA scientists, the <u>lightweight plastic</u> is stronger than steel.
Tourists often visit the <u>poet's farm</u>, *located just outside of Chicago.*
Discovered by a passing hiker, <u>the wreckage</u> is believed by the FAA to be the remains of a research balloon lost almost thirty years ago.

In writing, however, it is easy to create sentences that are confusing or illogical.

Created by a team of NASA scientists, GM wants to use the lightweight plastic in its cars.
The poet's farm is popular with tourists *located just outside of Chicago.*
Discovered by a passing hiker, the FAA believes the wreckage to be the remains of a research balloon lost almost thirty years ago.

Because the ideas are clear in your mind, even reading your sentences aloud may not help you spot a dangling modifier. Keep this simple diagram in mind:

modifier, main sentence

Think of the comma as a hook or hinge that links the modifier with what it describes.

Costing just three dollars, <u>these DVDs</u> are becoming best-sellers.
We stayed at the <u>Piedmont Hotel,</u> *first opened in 1876.*

The comma links *Costing just three dollars* with *DVDs* and links *first opened in 1876* with *Piedmont Hotel.*

TESTING FOR DANGLING MODIFIERS

Dangling modifiers can be easily missed in routine editing. When you find a sentence that opens or ends with a modifier, apply this simple test:

1. Read the sentence, then turn the modifier into a question, asking *who* or *what is being described?*

   Question, Answer

(continued)

2. The answer to the question follows the comma. If the answer makes sense, the sentence is probably correct. If the answer does not make sense, the sentence likely contains a dangling modifier and requires revision.

Examples:

Working from noon to midnight, I was tired and hungry.

Question: *Who worked from noon to midnight?*   Answer: *I*

Correct

Working double shifts for a month, my check was enormous.

Question: *Who worked double shifts?*   Answer: *my check*

Incorrect and needs revision

Working double shifts for a month, I could not believe how enormous my check was.

My check was enormous because I worked double shifts for a month.

EXERCISE 1 Detecting Dangling Modifiers

Write OK for each correct sentence and DM to indicate those with dangling modifiers.

1. __DM__ Born to an unwed mother, Eva Peron's career as a radio and movie actress helped her rise from poverty to become a prominent figure in Buenos Aires society.

2. __OK__ Having married Juan Peron in 1945, she became the First Lady of Argentina when her husband assumed the presidency.

3. __OK__ Although known for her glamorous appearance, she championed the rights of the poor, especially women, who adoringly called her Evita.

4. __DM__ Although popular with working people, the aristocratic families of Buenos Aires resented her public adulation and humble origins.

5. __DM__ Seeking the vice presidency in 1951, the country's military leaders grew increasingly hostile to what they considered her amateurish meddling in state affairs.

6. __OK__ Bowing to heavy pressure, Juan Peron withdrew his wife's nomination.

7. __DM__ Stricken with uterine cancer a year later, the public was shocked when their beloved Evita died at thirty-three.

8. __OK__ Rising to cult status in death, Evita became a symbol of both Argentina and the aspirations of the poor of Latin America.

9. __OK__ Pointing to her business dealings with former Nazis, many historians are critical of her role in making Argentina a haven for war criminals.

10. __OK__ Distressed by allegations that some of the jewelry Eva Peron wore in public may have been stolen from Holocaust victims, some journalists urged theater-goers to boycott the popular musical *Evita*.

EXERCISE 2 Opening Sentences with Modifiers

Create a complete sentence by adding an independent clause to logically follow the opening modifying phrase. Test each sentence to make sure you avoid a dangling modifier. Make sure you create a complete sentence and not a fragment (see Chapter 23).

1. Rising in price, _____

   _____

2. Seen by millions on television, _____

   _____

3. Exercising every day, _____

   _____

4. Refusing to change his mind, _____

   _____

5. Facing a tough election, _____

   _____

EXERCISE 3 Ending Sentences with Modifiers

Create a complete sentence by adding an independent clause to logically precede the modifying phrase. Test each sentence to make sure you avoid a dangling modifier. Make sure you create a complete sentence and not a fragment (see Chapter 23).

1. _____

   _____, waiting in the rain.

2. _____

   _____, suffering from a bad cold.

3. _____

   _____, starring Jennifer Lopez.

4. _____

   _____, unable to find a place to park.

5. _____

   _____, written in just ten minutes.

EXERCISE 4 Eliminating Dangling Modifiers

Rewrite each of the following sentences to eliminate dangling modifiers. Add needed words or phrases but do not alter the basic meaning of the sentence.

1. Running out of medical supplies, the UN received calls for an emergency airlift by aid workers.

   _____

   _____

2. Failing to hit a single home run in thirty-five games, sportswriters and comedians began calling him the "Ten Million Dollar Mistake."

_____

_____

3. Known as spaghetti Westerns, many American movie stars got their start acting in low-budget cowboy movies shot in Italy.

_____

_____

4. Facing rising gas prices, it was harder to get part-time employees to drive all the way to the city for a two-hour shift.

_____

_____

5. Having taught deaf children for years, the daycare center was happy to hire Nadine to work with Shelby and Catherine.

_____

_____

Misplaced Modifiers

Misplaced modifiers can occur anywhere in a sentence. Because they are not always set off by commas, they can be harder to detect.

> I fixed the frame of my bicycle that was hit by a car *in the basement* last night.

> We tried to win approval for the new stadium at the board meeting *the public wants constructed next year.*

Reading sentences out loud can help you detect some misplaced modifiers, but even this may not help you avoid some of them. Because the ideas are clear in your mind, you may have a hard time recognizing the confusion your sentence creates. You know that you fixed the bicycle in the basement, not that a car hit your bicycle in the basement. You know that the public wants the stadium not a board meeting constructed next year. Readers, however, can only rely on the way your words appear on the page.

EXERCISE 5 Detecting Misplaced Modifiers

Mark OK for each correct sentence and MM for sentences containing a misplaced modifier.

1. __MM__ The Jersey Devil is a legendary creature said to live in the desolate pine barrens region of southern New Jersey which has terrified and amused residents of the Garden State for over two hundred years.

2. __MM__ People first sighted the creature in the 1700s said to have large bat-like wings, hoofs, a long neck, and a horselike head.

3. __MM__ According to one tale, the being was created when a woman cursed her unwanted thirteenth baby worn out from childbirth by saying, "Let it be a devil."

4. __OK__ This curse instantly transformed the newborn into a winged beast that flew up the chimney.

5. __MM__ In the 1840s the Jersey Devil was blamed for livestock killings by farmers.

6. __MM__ In 1909 hysteria swept New Jersey when thousands of people reported seeing the devil throughout Philadelphia suburbs flying over rooftops.

7. __MM__ Businesses and schools closed, and armed guards were placed on street cars panicked by stories of attacks.

8. __OK__ The sightings finally stopped, but fifty years later children claimed seeing the devil and hearing the anguished cries of its victims.

9. __MM__ In 1991 a driver reported seeing the Jersey Devil delivering a pizza.

10. __MM__ The Jersey Devil inspired the name of the state's hockey team that generated so much hysteria in the Garden State.

EXERCISE 6 Correcting Misplaced Modifiers

Rewrite each of the following sentences to eliminate misplaced modifiers. Add needed words or phrases but do not alter the basic meaning of the sentence.

1. The coach tried to rally the team after their staggering loss in the locker room by reminding them of last year's upset victory in the play-offs.

   _____

   _____

2. The manager who was caught shoplifting wrestled the man to the floor until the police arrived.

   _____

   _____

3. This year my parents wanted their taxes done by an accountant not knowing how to report profits from selling a home.

   _____

   _____

4. The principal met with the parents whose children vandalized the playground in a parent-teacher conference this afternoon.

   _____

   _____

5. The hostess served ice cream to her guests dripping with hot chocolate sauce on the patio.

   _____

   _____

EXERCISE 7 Detecting Dangling and Misplaced Modifiers in Context

Underline dangling and misplaced modifiers in the following passage.

In the 1770s, Joseph Priestly, a minister and scientist, conducted experiments with a glass bell jar. Placing a candle under the jar, the flame flickered out, Priestly observed. A mouse placed under the jar suffocated. The candle and mouse, Priestly reasoned, consumed something in the air they needed to stay alive. Placing a sprig of mint under the jar, something interesting happened. The candle could be relit. If placed under the jar with a mouse, the mouse stayed alive. Whatever vital substance the candle and the mouse used up was restored by the plant. Without fully realizing it, the experiment revealed a basic natural process. Animals and burning fossil fuels consume oxygen and give off carbon dioxide. Plants absorb carbon dioxide and give off oxygen.

Used to explain the problem of global warming, the earth is like one big jar. The natural balance of gases that Priestly discovered in the atmosphere has been upset. Burning oil and coal, large amounts of carbon are released into the atmosphere by cars, power plants, and factories. Producing 12,000 pounds of carbon a year per person, the United States is the world's largest polluter. By clearing forests to build cities and harvest timber, the planet's ability to absorb carbon is reduced by human activity. The extra carbon dioxide collects like the roof of a greenhouse in the atmosphere, raising the temperature of the earth.

Concerned about the effects of continued global warming, alternative fuels and hybrid cars are advocated by many scientists. Environmentalists call for preserving rainforests in the Amazon that absorb much of the earth's carbon. Some suggest planting trees on a large scale. To prevent erosion that led to floods, in the 1970s millions of trees were planted in China. These trees have since absorbed millions of tons of carbon. Doubting that new forests alone will solve the problem, consumers and corporations will have to make major changes in their lifestyles to prevent climate changes.

EXERCISE 8 Using Modifiers Correctly

Insert the modifier into each sentence by placing it next to the word or words it describes.

1. **Frank drives Karla to the beach every morning.**

   INSERT: *who is a lifeguard* **to refer to Karla**

   Frank drives Karla, who is a lifeguard, to the beach every morning.

2. **The deans met with faculty members this morning to discuss new course offerings.**

   INSERT: *who are concerned about falling enrollments* **to refer to the deans**

   The deans, who are concerned about falling enrollments, met with faculty members this morning to discuss new course offerings.

3. **The landlord met with the tenant.**

   INSERT: *who was angry about the broken windows* **to refer to the landlord.**

   The landlord, who was angry about the broken windows, met with the tenant.

4. **Larry David stars in the HBO hit show** *Curb Your Enthusiasm.*

   INSERT: *who created* **Seinfeld.**

   Larry David, who created Seinfeld, stars in the HBO hit show Curb Your Enthusiasm.

   _____

5. **The insurance adjusters met with the homeowners.**

   INSERT: *who refused to pay any repair bills* **to refer to insurance adjusters.**

   The insurance adjusters, who refused to pay any repair bills, met with the

   homeowners.

WORKING TOGETHER

Working with a group of students, revise this notice to eliminate dangling and misplaced modifiers.

New Payroll Policies

Beginning March 15, only payroll checks will be issued to employees presenting picture IDs. Direct deposit is available by filling out a request form signed by your supervisor to electronically receive your check. Checks will be sent to the post office if not picked up by 4pm.

Employees can contact supervisors who may have questions about these policies.

EXERCISE 9 Cumulative Exercise

Revise each sentence for dangling or misplaced modifiers, fragments, and run-ons.

1. **Carefully taped together, the police could read the note the killer had torn to shreds.**

   _____

   _____

2. **The union decided to strike management's final offer did not meet their minimum demands.**

   _____

   _____

3. **Shot in just eighteen days, the public loved the low-budget comedy.**

   _____

   _____

4. **The airline is paying more for fuel but it continues to make a profit because of lucrative government contracts.**

   _____

   _____

5. Because the power has still not been restored to the main building.

_____

_____

CRITICAL THINKING

GET THINKING

AND WRITING

Today's children grow up in a world of constant electronic communication through Internet chat rooms, cell phones, and PDAs. How will this influence the way they communicate later in life? Will it prepare them for jobs in the global economy, or just lead them to have short attention spans? How will it make them different from previous generations?

Write a paragraph stating your views.

WHAT HAVE YOU WRITTEN?

Underline the modifiers in each sentence. Are they properly placed? Are there any sentences that are confusing or could be interpreted in two ways?

WHAT HAVE YOU LEARNED?

Mark an X next to each sentence with a dangling or misplaced modifier and OK for each correct sentence.

1. _____ Noticing puddles of oil under the car, the mechanic examined the engine for leaks.

2. _____ Caught cheating, the teacher sent the students to the principal's office.

3. _____ Grounded by the blizzard, the agent issued hotel vouchers to the stranded passengers.

4. _____ Driving cross-country in a small car, the five of us were uncomfortable filled with luggage.

5. _____ Suffering from a severe shoulder injury, the quarterback completed only two passes.

6. _____ Having lost her cell phone, Sally had to flag down a passing car to get help.

7. _____ Trying to quit smoking, gaining weight was her greatest fear.

8. _____ She tried to get her children to eat fruits and vegetables concerned about their health.

9. _____ Sealed in plastic, the flood did little damage to the studio's collection of rare audiotapes.

10. _____ Realizing her job was going to be eliminated, Shelly applied for a transfer.

Answers appear on the following page.

WRITING ON THE WEB

Using a search engine such as Yahoo!, Google, or AltaVista, enter terms such as *dangling modifiers* and *misplaced modifier* to locate current sites of interest.

1. Review current online journals or newspapers to see how writers place modifying words and phrases in sentences.
2. Write an e-mail to a friend, then review it for dangling and misplaced modifiers and other errors.

POINTS TO REMEMBER

1. Modifiers are words or phrases that describe other words. To prevent confusion, they must be placed next to what they modify.
2. If sentences begin or end with a modifier, apply this simple test:

   Read the sentence, then turn the modifier into a question, asking who or what is being described.
   Question, Answer

   If the answer makes sense, the sentence is probably correct.

   > Born on Christmas, I never have a birthday party.
   > *Q: Who was born on Christmas?   A: I*

   Correct

   If the sentence does not make sense, it probably contains a dangling modifier and needs revision.

   > Filmed in Iraq, critics praise the movie for its realism.
   > *Q: What was filmed in Iraq?   A: critics*

   Incorrect

   Revisions:
   Filmed in Iraq, the movie was praised by critics for its realism.
   Critics praised the movie, filmed in Iraq, for its realism.

3. In revising papers, underline modifying words and phrases and circle the words or ideas they are supposed to modify to test for clear connections.

Writer's Resources ⓦ Now™   If you use Writer's ResourcesNow, please have your students log in and view the pretest, study plan, and posttest for this chapter.

Understanding Parallelism

© Jon Feingersh /Zefa /Corbis

GET WRITING

Would you ever consider having cosmetic surgery? Why or why not?

Explain your reasons in one or more paragraphs.

What Is Parallelism?

To make sentences easy to understand, pairs and lists of words have to be *parallel,* or *match*—they have to be all nouns, all adjectives, all adverbs, or all verbs in the same form. To be balanced, pairs and lists should be phrases or clauses with matching word patterns. In most instances, you use parallelism without problem. When you write a shopping list, you automatically write in parallel form.

We need *oil filters, antifreeze,* and *brake fluid.* [all nouns]

It is easy, however, to make errors when, instead of listing single nouns, you list phrases.

The assistant manager must approve menu changes, schedule waiters, order supplies, and when the manager is unavailable handle customer complaints.

The last item *when the manager is unavailable handle customer complaints* does not match the other items in the list.

The assistant manager must . . . *approve* menu changes
. . . *schedule* waiters
. . . *order* supplies
. . . *when the manager* is unavailable handle customer complaints

Revised
The assistant manager <u>must</u> *approve* menu changes, *schedule* waiters, *order* supplies, and *handle* customer complaints when the manager is unavailable.

Not Parallel	*Parallel*
Both *writing* and *to read* are important skills.	Both *writing* and *reading* are important skills.
He spoke *softly, precisely,* and *with authority.*	He spoke *softly, precisely,* and *authoritatively.*
Hunger, cold, and *fearing more earthquakes* drove the refugees farther south.	*Hunger, cold,* and *the fear of more earthquakes* drove the refugees farther south.
Students can *register for classes, apply for financial aid,* and *textbooks can be ordered* online.	Students can *register for classes, apply for financial aid,* and *order textbooks* online.

WHAT DO YOU KNOW?

Label each sentence OK for correct and FP for faulty parallelism.

1. _____ The movie is fast-paced, colorful, and offers a lot of drama.

2. _____ The car has two flat tires, a missing fender, and a cracked windshield.

3. _____ New Orleans is noted for its history, jazz, shopping, and Mardi Gras celebrations.

4. _____ Providing security and the respect for civil liberties is a difficult balance.

5. _____ She was trained to operate heavy machinery, read blueprints, and supervision of work crews.

Answers appear on the following page.

Describe someone you know well—a friend, coworker, neighbor, or relative—by writing sentences that list his or her skills, characteristics, or habits.

_____

_____

_____

_____

_____

_____

_____

_____

_____

_____

_____

_____

_____

_____

_____

_____

◄

WHAT HAVE YOU WRITTEN?

Read your sentences aloud. Did you create sentences that contain pairs of words or phrases or lists? If so, are the items parallel—do they match each other? ◄

Overcoming Parallelism Errors

Mistakes in parallelism are easy to make. If you are describing your favorite television show, many ideas, words, or phrases may come to mind. Some may be nouns, adjectives, or verbs.

funny   creative dialogue   great characters

In putting these ideas together, make sure they are parallel.

Not Parallel
King of Queens has creative dialogue, great characters, and is funny.

Parallel
King of Queens has creative dialogue, great characters, and funny situations.

TESTING FOR PARALLELISM

The simplest way of determining if a sentence is parallel is to test each element to see if it matches the base sentence.

Example: The car is new, well-maintained, and costs very little.

The car is *new*.
The car is *well-maintained*.
The car is *costs very little*.

The last item does not match and should be revised.

The car is new, well-maintained, and inexpensive.

The car is *new*.
The car is *well-maintained*.
The car is *inexpensive*.

A TIP ON REVISING FAULTY PARALLELISM

Sometimes you may find it difficult to make all the items in a sentence match. You might not be able to think of a suitable noun form of an adjective. In making the sentence parallel, you may find yourself having to change a phrase you like or create something that sounds awkward. In some cases you may have simply been trying to put too many ideas in a single sentence.

It may be easier, in some instances, to break up an unparallel sentence. It is easier to make two short sentences parallel than one long one.

Not Parallel
Example: The new dean will be responsible for scheduling courses, expanding student services, upgrading the computer labs, and most important, become a strong advocate for students.

Parallel

The new dean will be responsible for *scheduling* courses, *expanding* student services, and *upgrading* the computer labs. Most important, she must become a strong advocate for students.

EXERCISE 1 Detecting Faulty Parallelism

Write OK by each correct sentence and NP by each sentence that is not parallel.

1. __OK__ Ignaz Semmelweis was a young physician in Vienna in the 1840s whose observations would change medical history, influence scientific thinking, and save the lives of millions.

2. __NP__ He noticed new mothers attended by doctors were more likely to become infected and dying than those aided by midwives.

3. __OK__ At that time, physicians would examine patients, perform operations, conduct autopsies, and deliver babies without washing their hands.

4. __NP__ He theorized that doctors were transmitting something on their hands that caused infections and leading to the high death rate of new mothers.

5. __NP__ Semmelweis ordered caregivers to wash their hands before treating women or examined their newborns.

6. __OK__ This simple practice greatly reduced infections, and dramatic drops in the death rate of new mothers occurred.

7. __NP__ Other doctors, however, were unimpressed; they considered hand washing a needless chore and feeling insulted by the suggestion that they could be responsible for the spread of disease.

8. __NP__ A conference of leading physicians and natural scientists rejected Semmelweis's theories, and he was criticized, ridiculed, and many considered him a subject of mockery.

9. __OK__ Discredited and distraught, Semmelweis died in a mental institution at the age of forty-seven.

10. __NP__ Semmelweis's views are now universally accepted, although patients are still infected by busy doctors who move from patient to patient and failing to wash their hands.

EXERCISE 2 Revising Sentences to Eliminate Faulty Parallelism

Rewrite each sentence to eliminate faulty parallelism. You may have to add words or invent phrases, but do not alter the meaning of the sentence. In some cases, you may create two sentences.

1. **Every forest has five layers that help maintain its survival and providing a habitat for a variety of wildlife.**

   Every forest has five layers that help maintain its survival and provide a habitat for a variety of wildlife.

2. **The highest layer is the canopy, which consists of the top leaves and branches of the tallest trees that receive the most sunshine and homes for birds are provided.**

   The highest layer is the canopy, which consists of the top leaves and branches of the tallest trees that receive the most sunshine and provide homes for birds.

3. The understory contains shorter trees that grow under the canopy; they receive less sunlight and their production of food is less.

   The understory contains shorter trees that grow under the canopy; they receive less sunlight and produce less food.

4. Shrubs and bushes grow at the shrub level beneath the understory, producing fruits and seeds for animals and make homes for a variety of birds and insects.

   Shrubs and bushes grow at the shrub level beneath the understory, producing fruits and seeds for animals and making homes for a variety of birds and insects.

5. Grasses and small plants grow at the herb level, which provide food for animals ranging from mice to large bears and producing exotic flowers.

   Grasses and small plants grow at the herb level, which provide food for animals ranging from mice to large bears and produce exotic flowers.

6. The forest floor collects waste produced by the forest, including fallen leaves, broken branches, animals that have died, seeds, and rotting fruit.

   The forest floor collects the waste produced by the forest, including fallen leaves, broken branches, dead animals, seeds, and rotting fruit.

7. Spiders, insects, earthworms, and bacteria thrive on the forest floor, consuming waste material, breaking it down, and deposits they make in the soil needed for continued forest growth.

   Spiders, insects, earthworms, and bacteria thrive on the forest floor, consuming waste material, breaking it down, and making deposits in the soil needed for continued forest growth.

8. The forest system is intricate and has great fragility.

   The forest system is intricate and fragile.

9. Chopping down tall trees exposes lower levels of the forest to full sunlight, burning leaves, drying out moist soil, and many animals die.

   Chopping down tall trees exposes lower levels of the forest to full sunlight, burning leaves, drying out moist soil, and killing many animals.

10. Clearing the forest floor robs the soil of nutrients and eventually starvation of the tall trees occurs.

    Clearing the forest floor robs the soil of nutrients and eventually starves the tall trees.

EXERCISE 3 Writing Parallel Sentences

Complete each sentence by adding missing elements, making sure they create a matched pair or list of matching words or phrases in order to be parallel.

1. The loss of a job leads people to feel depressed, bitter, angry, and _____ .

2. Experts say such emotional reactions are normal, but that it is important for people to move on with their lives, take stock of their skills and abilities, and _____.

3. They should make a list of their skills, job experiences, and _____.

4. They should then ask themselves what they want to do, who they want to work with, and _____.

5. Friends, former coworkers, and _____ can be sources of information about new job openings.

6. People can look at newspaper want ads, scan the business sections of local newspapers, and _____ to see which businesses are growing in their area.

7. Looking for a job requires a good résumé that should list education, job skills, and _____.

8. _____ and patience are important in any job search.

9. To prepare for a job interview, an applicant should dress appropriately, arrive promptly, and _____.

10. During the interview, applicants should speak directly, answer questions honestly, and _____.

WORKING TOGETHER

Working with a group of students, revise the following announcement to eliminate errors in parallelism. Notice how collaborative editing can help detect errors you may have missed.

```
            Student Grant

Calmex Corporation has announced it will award five
ten-thousand-dollar grants to students enrolled in
business or technical programs. To be eligible, you
must be a full-time student, a resident of California,
and U.S. citizenship is required. In order to apply,
you need to fill out the required form, submit a
current transcript, and two letters of recommendation
from instructors or former employers must be
obtained. To learn more, view the grant website at
www.calmexcorp/studentgrant.com.
```

CRITICAL THINKING

GET THINKING
AND WRITING

Write a list of tips to help people lose weight and get in better shape. Create at least five recommendations.

  When you complete your writing, review each item in your list for faulty parallelism.

WHAT HAVE YOU LEARNED?

Label each sentence OK for correct and FP for faulty parallelism.

1. _____ The trip was long, hot, and dusty.

2. _____ The plan was rejected for three reasons: it cost the city too much, the engineers could not guarantee it would resolve the problems, and refusal by the public to pay more taxes.

3. _____ Dedication, persistence, and being creative helped her keep the business going during the recession.

4. _____ The children lacked warm clothing, clean drinking water, and their diet was not adequate.

5. _____ The riots were blamed on rising tensions between the community and the police and unemployment increased.

Answers appear on the following page.

WRITING ON THE WEB

Using a search engine such as Yahoo!, Google, or AltaVista, enter terms such as *faulty parallelism* and *writing parallel sentences* to locate current sites of interest.

1. Review some current online journals or newspapers to see how writers state ideas in parallel form.
2. Write a brief e-mail to a friend describing some recent activities or a person you have met. Review your sentences to see if pairs and lists of words and phrases are parallel.

POINTS TO REMEMBER

1. Words and phrases that appear as pairs or lists must be parallel—they must match and be nouns, adverbs, adjectives, or verbs in the same form.

Parallel	*Not Parallel*
Swimming and *fishing* are fun.	*Swimming* and *to fish* are fun.
She is *bright, witty,* and *charming*.	She is *bright, witty,* and *has charm*.
He must *design* the building, *establish* the budget, and *hire* the workers.	He must *design* the building, *establish* the budget, and *workers* must be hired.

2. You can discover errors in parallelism by testing each element in the pair or series with the rest of the sentence to see if it matches.

   Whoever we hire will have to collect the mail, file reports, answer the phone, update the website, and accurate records must be maintained.

   Whoever we hire will have to . . . *collect the mail.*
   file reports.
   answer the phone.
   update the website.
   accurate records must be maintained.

The last item does not match *will have to* and needs to be revised to be parallel with the other phrases in the list.

Whoever we hire will have to collect the mail, file reports, answer the phone, update the website, and *maintain accurate records*.

3. If you find it difficult to make a long or complicated sentence parallel, consider creating two sentences. In some instances, it is easier to write two short parallel lists than a single long one.

If you use Writer's ResourcesNow, please have your students log in and view the pretest, study plan, and posttest for this chapter.

Writer's Resources ⓦ Now™

ANSWERS TO WHAT HAVE YOU LEARNED? ON PAGE 428
1. OK **2.** FP (see page 422) **3.** FP (see page 422) **4.** FP (see page 422) **5.** FP (see page 422)

Subject-Verb Agreement

© Paul J. Sutton/Duomo/Corbis

Do you think the baseball records broken in recent years will be tarnished by allegations that players were using steroids? Do high school and college athletes feel pressured to take substances to improve their performance?

Write one or more paragraphs expressing your view on how steroids have affected sports.

What Is Subject-Verb Agreement?

The most important parts of any sentence are the *subject*—the main idea—and the *verb*—a word or words that express action (*buy, swim, sing*) or link the subject with other ideas (*is, are, was, were*). Both the subject and verb work together to state a *complete thought* and create a sentence.

Suzi *jogs* four miles a day.   Suzi *is* in great shape.

For sentences to clearly express ideas, their subjects and verbs must agree—they must match in number. *Singular subjects require singular verbs; plural subjects require plural verbs.*

Singular	*Plural*
The coach *directs* plays.*	The coaches *direct* plays.*
The plane *was* grounded.	The planes *were* grounded.
The book *is* on your desk.	The books *are* on your desk.

* In most cases you add an *-s* or *-es* to a noun to make it plural and add an *-s* or *-es* to a verb to make it singular.

> NOTE: Singular and plural verbs only occur in first and third person.
>
> | | Singular | Plural |
> |---|---|---|
> | First person: | I *am* | We *are* |
> | Third person: | He *was* | They *were* |
>
> In second person, only the plural verb is used.
>
> You *are* a person I can trust.   You *are* people I can trust.

WHAT DO YOU KNOW?

Select the correct verb in each sentence.

1. _____ The lawyer, supported by angry homeowners, (talk/talks) to the press at every opportunity.

2. _____ Two hundred dollars (is/are) more than I want to spend.

3. _____ Where (is/are) the letter signed by the teachers and parents?

4. _____ One of our players (is/are) being drafted by the NFL.

5. _____ Henderson Motors (doesn't/don't) deny the allegations.

   Answers appear on the following page.

WHAT ARE YOU TRYING TO SAY?   *GET WRITING*

Write a paragraph describing how you prepare for exams.

_____

_____

_____

_____

_____

_____

_____

_____

_____

_____

_____

_____

_____

_____

_____

WHAT HAVE YOU WRITTEN?

Circle the subjects and underline the verbs in each sentence. Do the subjects and verbs match so that your sentences clearly identify which study methods are singular and which are plural?

Grammar Choices and Meaning

Changing a verb from singular to plural changes the meaning of a sentence.

Sentence	**Meaning**
Singular	
My trainer and manager *arranges my schedule.*	*One person is both a trainer and manager.*
Plural	
My trainer and manager *arrange* my schedule.	*The trainer and manager are two people.*
Singular	
The boat and trailer *goes* on sale Monday.	*The boat and trailer are sold as one item.*
Plural	
The boat and trailer *go* on sale Monday.	*The boat and trailer are sold separately.*
Singular	
His speed and accuracy *is* amazing.	*His blend of two skills is amazing.*
Plural	
His speed and accuracy *are* amazing.	*He has two amazing skills.*

EXERCISE 1 Choosing the Correct Verb

Write out the subject and correct verb in each sentence.

	Subject	Verb

1. Job applicants (use/uses) a number of methods to find employment. — *applicants* / *use*

2. Looking at want ads, however, (is/are) not as effective as many think. — *Looking at want ads* / *is*

3. A leading expert in jobs and employment trends (estimates/estimate) that 80% of the jobs, especially the best jobs, are never advertised. — *expert* / *estimates*

4. A large corporation, like General Motors or United Airlines, (is/are) likely to use recruiters or employment agencies rather than place want ads. — *corporation* / *is*

5. A leading recruiter or headhunter (charge/charges) tens of thousands to locate the right person for the right job. — *recruiter or headhunter* / *charges*

6. A person with skills in high demand (use/uses) a recruiter as an agent to locate the best job. — *person* / *uses*

7. The method that all employment advisors (recommend/recommends) for anyone looking for a job is networking. — *advisors* / *recommend*

8. Rather than look for jobs, networking (direct/directs) applicants to look for people and organizations that could use their skills or know others who can. — *networking* / *directs*

9. One way advisors suggest using networking as a starting point (is/are) by calling friends who have the kind of job you want or know someone who does. — *one way* / *is*

10. If this person (do/does) not know of an opening, he or she may suggest another person who can help. — *person* / *does*

Special Nouns and Pronouns

In most cases it is easy to tell whether a noun is singular or plural. Most nouns add an -s to become plural, but some nouns have separate plural forms.

men   mice   teeth

1. Some nouns that end in -s and look like plurals are singular.

   gymnastics   physics   mathematics

   Athletics *takes* discipline.   Economics *relies* on accurate data.

2. Some nouns that may refer to one item are plural.

   pants   gloves   fireworks

   My pants *are* torn.   The fireworks *were* cancelled.

3. Proper nouns that look plural are singular if they are names of companies, organizations, or titles of books, movies, television shows, or works of art.

   United Nations   *Eight Men Out*   The Teamsters

   The United Nations *attempts* to prevent war.   *Eight Men Out tells* the story of a legendary sports scandal.

4. Units of time and amounts of money are generally singular.

   Sixty dollars *is* a nice bonus.   Two hours *is* more than enough time.

   They appear as plurals to indicate separate items.

   The dollars *were* lying on the street. My first hours in school *were* tough.

Group Nouns

Group nouns—nouns that describe something with more than one unit or member—can be singular or plural, depending on the meaning of the sentence.

COMMON GROUP NOUNS

audience	committee	faculty	number
board	company	family	public
class	crowd	jury	team

In most sentences, group nouns are singular because they describe a group working as a unit.

"Jury Declares Smith Guilty"   [headline describing jury working as a group]

Group nouns are plural when they describe a group working independently.

"Jury Fight Over Evidence"   [headline describing jurors acting individually]

Some group nouns are used as plurals because we think of them as individuals rather than as a single unit.

The Beatles *are* still popular.   The Yankees *are* in first place.

EXERCISE 2 Choosing the Correct Verb with Special and Group Nouns

Circle the correct verb in each sentence.

1. These scissors (is/are) very sharp.

2. *Two and a Half Men* (star/stars) Charlie Sheen.

3. The American Federation of Teachers (open/opens) a seminar on distance learning next week.

4. After days of debate, the rules committee (refuses/refuse) to discuss his membership.

5. Thirty thousand dollars (was/were) awarded to each victim by the courts.

6. (Is/Are) your gloves on the table?

7. She was convicted on drug charges, but the public (seem/seems) willing to forgive her.

8. The Lakers (head/heads) to the arena expecting another victory.

9. Thermodynamics (explain/explains) how the process works.

10. The number of students taking online courses (is/are) growing.

Hidden Subjects

In some sentences, the subject is not obvious, so that choosing the right verb requires critical thinking. You have to determine what you are trying to say.

- Subjects followed by prepositional phrases:

Incorrect
One of the players have the flu.

Correct
One of the players *has* the flu.

[*Players* is plural, but it is not the subject of the sentence; the subject is *One*, which is singular]

Incorrect
Creation of new products and new markets keep us growing.

Correct
Creation of new products and new markets *keeps* us growing.

[*Products* and *markets* are plural, but the subject is *Creation*, which is singular]

Remember, the subject of a sentence does not appear in a prepositional phrase. Make sure that you identify the key word of a subject and determine whether it is singular or plural:

The *price* of oil and petroleum products *is* rising.   [singular]
The *prices* of jewelry *are* rising.   [plural]

Prepositions are words that express relationships between ideas, usually regarding time and place:

above	below	near	to
across	during	of	toward
after	except	off	under
against	for	outside	with
along	from	over	within
around	inside	past	without
before	like	since	

- *Subjects followed by subordinate words and phrases:*
  In many sentences, the subject is followed by words or phrases set off by commas. These additional words are subordinate—extra information that is not part of the main sentence. They should not be mistaken for compound subjects.

  The landlord **and** his tenants *are* suing the contractor for property damage.
  [**Plural:** *and* links "landlord" + "tenants" to create a compound subject]

  The landlord, backed by tenants, *is* suing the contractor for property damage.
  [**Singular:** *is* indicates the subject *landlord* is singular; the tenants, set off by commas, are subordinate and not part of the subject]

- *Subjects following possessives:*
  It can be easy to choose the wrong verb if the subject follows a possessive noun.

  Incorrect
  The team's best players is injured.

  Correct
  The team's best players *are* injured.
  [The subject is not *team* but *players,* which is plural]

  Incorrect
  The parents' demand ignore the role their children played in the incident.

  Correct
  The parents' demand *ignores* the role their children played in the incident.
  [The subject is not *parents* but their *demand,* which is singular]

POINT TO REMEMBER

The subject is never the word with the apostrophe but what follows it.

- *Inverted subjects and verbs:*
  In some sentences, the usual subject-verb order is inverted or reversed, so the subject follows the verb.

Singular	**Plural**
There *is* <u>someone</u> looking for you.	There *are* <u>people</u> looking for you.
Here *is* your final <u>exam.</u>	Here *are* your final <u>exams.</u>
Over the hill *lies* a refugee <u>camp.</u>	Over the hill *lie* <u>refugees.</u>

EXERCISE 3 Choosing the Correct Verb with Hidden or Complex Subjects

Circle the correct verb in each sentence.

1. The loss of high-paying factory jobs offering benefits and pensions (lead/**leads**) workers to pursue new careers.

2. Beyond the reach of our most powerful telescopes (lies/**lie**) distant planets that may contain life.

3. The mayor, backed by local business leaders, (**demands**/demand) the governor explain the sudden changes in the highway proposal.

4. Here (**lie**/lies) the ruins of the old castle.

5. Who (**wants**/want) to save money on a new house?

6. During the hurricane, the loss of radio and telephone communications (**was**/were) frustrating.

7. Voters who supported the mayor's proposal (**were**/was) stunned by the election results.

8. There (is/**are**) no recommendations or policies about online courses in the dean's annual report.

9. Why (is/**are**) your bills always late?

10. The car's sales (is/**are**) higher than anyone predicted.

"Either . . . or" Subjects

More than one subject may appear in a sentence, but that does not automatically mean that the verb is plural.

The coach *and* the manager *are* meeting with reporters.   [coach + manager = two people (plural)]

The coach *or* the manager *is* meeting with reporters.   [coach OR manager = one person (singular)]

Remember, the conjunctions *or* and *nor* mean "one or the other but not both."

- If both subjects are singular, the verb is singular:

  Neither the book *nor* the website *helps* me study for the test.
  The car *or* the truck *is* available.
  My brother *or* my cousin *signs* for the deliveries.

- If both subjects are plural, the verb is plural:

  Neither the players *nor* the owners *are* happy about the NFL ruling.
  Cars *or* trucks *are* available.
  Our teachers *or* our parents *take* us on field trips.

- If one subject is singular and one subject is plural, the subject closer to the verb determines whether it is singular or plural:

  Neither the players *nor* the owner *is* happy   [*owner* is singular]
  about the NFL ruling.

Cars or a truck *is* available.   [*truck* is singular]
Our teacher or our parents *take* us on field trips.   [*parents* is plural]

Pay attention to special and group nouns in "either . . . or" sentences.

Neither the dean nor the faculty *wants*   [*faculty* is singular]
to confront the students.
The president or the Senate *has* to take action.   [*Senate* is singular]
Neither the lawyers nor the jury *understands*   [*jury* is singular]
the judge's rulings.

Indefinite Pronouns

Indefinite pronouns can be singular or plural, but most are singular.

INDEFINITE PRONOUNS

Singular Indefinite Pronouns

another	each	everything	nothing
anybody	either	neither	somebody
anyone	everybody	nobody	someone
anything	everyone	no one	something

Everyone *is* invited.   **Something** *seems* wrong.   **Nothing** *was* taken.

Plural Indefinite Pronouns

both	few	many	several

Both *are* late.   **Few** *are* interested.   **Many** *were* broken.

Indefinite Pronouns That Can Be Singular or Plural Depending on Meaning

all	more	none	some
any	most		

Money was stolen. **Some** *was* recovered.   [*Some* refers to *money* (singular)]
The houses burned. **Some** *are* destroyed.   [*Some* refers to *houses* (plural)]

EXERCISE 4 Choosing the Right Verb with Either/Or and Indefinite Pronouns

Circle the correct verb in each sentence.

1. Filmmakers have always embraced new technologies but some (is/**are**) threatening their industry.

2. Anyone who sees movies these days (know/**knows**) how expensive they are to produce.

3. High-priced stars or a high-tech special effect (**drives**/drive) up production costs.

4. In order to undertake such costly projects, a producer or a studio (want/**wants**) exclusive control over sales of the finished product.

5. Since the early 1980s, illegal videotapes have troubled producers, but few (was/**were**) worried they would pose a major threat to profits.

6. Bootleg videos were costly to produce and bulky to transport, and most (was/were) of such poor quality, people were willing to pay more for studio-produced versions.

7. Digital technology and the Internet, however, have changed everything, and many (sees/see) a major threat to their income.

8. Studio executives or a movie critic given advance copies of films on DVD (is/are) often targeted by thieves.

9. A DVD stolen from a messenger or bought from a dishonest employee (is/are) used to make thousands of high-quality copies that are sold illegally all over the world.

10. As computer technology improves, some (fears/fear) new movies, like music, will be downloaded on personal computers, robbing moviemakers of their ability to make money on their most expensive films.

Relative Pronouns: *Who, Which,* and *That*

The words *who, which,* and *that* can be singular or plural, depending on the noun they replace.

Who
Craig is a comedian who *uses* wit.   [*who* refers to "a comedian" = singular]
They are comedians who *use* wit.   [*who* refers to "comedians" = plural]

Which
He sold a car, which *needs* new tires. [*which* refers to "a car" = singular]
He sold cars, which *need* new tires.   [*which* refers to "cars" = plural]

That
We love a movie that *has* a   [*that* refers to "a movie" = singular]
surprise ending.
We love movies that *have* surprise   [*that* refers to "movies" = plural]
endings.

It is important to locate the exact noun these words refer to in order to avoid making errors.

Incorrect
The SUV is among the cars that   [*that* refers to "cars" not "SUV"]
needs new brakes.

Correct
The SUV is among the cars that *need* [plural]
new brakes.

Incorrect
General Motors or Ford is joining the [*that* refers to "companies" not
companies that *is* supporting   "General Motors or Ford"]
tax reform.

Correct
General Motors or Ford is joining the [plural]
companies that *are* supporting tax
reform.

EXERCISE 5 Choosing the Right Verb with *Who, Which,* and *That*

Underline the correct verb in each sentence.

1. Mulholland Drive is one of several Los Angeles streets that (is/<u>are</u>) well-known to moviegoers around the world.

2. Anyone who (watch/<u>watches</u>) police dramas set in L.A. may recall a detective getting a radio call to follow a car turning onto Mulholland.

3. The drive is a major street in the city, which (<u>is</u>/are) named after William Mulholland, who was born in Belfast in 1855.

4. Mulholland was among a large number of Irish immigrants who (was/<u>were</u>) interested in seeking a better life in the United States.

5. After working in San Francisco and Arizona, he moved to Los Angeles and got a job with the many laborers who (was/<u>were</u>) digging ditches for the city's water department.

6. Although he had no formal education, Mulholland rose from digging ditches to running the Department of Water and Power, which (<u>was</u>/were) a powerful agency for a growing city.

7. Los Angeles is one of several Western cities that (has/<u>have</u>) little water.

8. Mulholland directed one of the largest public works projects that (<u>was</u>/were) attempted at that time, a massive 233-mile-long aqueduct that included construction of over a hundred and fifty tunnels.

9. The project drained water from Owen Valley, and farmers who (was/<u>were</u>) in opposition to the aqueduct protested against Mulholland and dynamited installations.

10. Civic leaders and businessowners in Los Angeles, however, supported Mulholland's tactics, which (was/<u>were</u>) seen as necessary to supply the city with water.

EXERCISE 6 Making Subjects and Verbs Agree

Complete each of the following sentences, making sure that the verb matches the subject. Write in the present tense—walk/walks, sing/sings, *etc.*

1. One of my friends _____

   _____

2. Two of the students _____

   _____

3. Either the parents or the teacher _____

   _____

4. The cost of car repairs _____

_____

5. The mayor, supported by community leaders, _____

_____

CRITICAL THINKING

GET THINKING
AND WRITING

Do you think schools prepare their students for the job market? Do high schools, technical and community colleges, and universities provide their graduates with enough information about finding job openings, preparing résumés, and interviewing? Consider your own experiences and write one or more paragraphs stating your views.

WHAT HAVE YOU WRITTEN?

1. _Select two sentences with singular verbs and write them below:_

_____

_____

Read the sentences out loud. Have you identified the right word or words as the subject? Is the subject singular?

2. _Select two sentences with plural verbs and write them below:_

_____

_____

Read the sentences out loud. Have you identified the right word or words as the subject? Is the subject plural?

3. _Edit your paragraph for fragments (see Chapter 23), comma splices, and run-ons (see Chapter 25)._

EXERCISE 7 Cumulative Exercise

Rewrite this passage to eliminate errors in subject/verb agreement, fragments, and run-ons.

The NAACP being formed in 1909 by seven whites and one African American who was concerned about the epidemic of lynching. The organization grew out of the Niagara Movement headed by W. E. B. DuBois he was opposed to Booker T. Washington's beliefs that was seen as passive and outmoded. DuBois serving as editor of the organization's main publication _The Crisis_ for almost twenty-five years. The NAACP achieved national attention when it organized boycotts of _Birth of a Nation,_ a movie they criticized for its racist portrayals of blacks. The NAACP played a major role during the civil rights movement of the 1950s and 1960s, it sponsored demonstrations and provided legal support for protestors who was arrested. In the 1960s some members suggested changing the name of the organization because of the words "colored people" many people found these terms offensive and old-fashioned. More radical groups, such as the Black Panthers, was challenging the fifty-year-old organization, accusing it of being out of step with the times. The NAACP, however, wishing to honor its early roots in the struggle for equality decided to maintain the original name. Although the organization has faced declining membership, financial problems, and allegations of being too closely tied to certain politicians. It remains the most well-known and influential civil rights organization in the United States.

The NAACP was formed in 1909 by seven whites and one African American who were concerned about the epidemic of lynching. The organization grew out of the Niagara Movement headed by W. E. B. DuBois, who was opposed to Booker T. Washington's beliefs that were seen as passive and outmoded. DuBois served as editor of the organization's main publication The Crisis for almost twenty-five years. The NAACP achieved national attention when it organized boycotts of Birth of a Nation, a movie they criticized for its racist portrayals of blacks. The NAACP played a major role during the civil rights movement of the 1950s and 1960s; it sponsored demonstrations and provided legal support for protestors who were arrested. In the 1960s some members suggested changing the name of the organization because of the words "colored people"; many people found these terms offensive and old-fashioned. More radical groups, such as the Black Panthers, were challenging the fifty-year-old organization, accusing it of being out of step with the times. The NAACP, however, wishing to honor its early roots in the struggle for equality decided to maintain the original name. Although the organization has faced declining membership, financial problems, and allegations of being too closely tied to certain politicians, it remains the most well-known and influential civil rights organization in the United States.

WORKING TOGETHER

Working with a group of students, read this letter and circle any errors in subject-verb agreement. Note how collaborative editing can help detect errors you may have missed on your own.

Dear Ms. Clark:

The hiring committee of the Human Services Department have received your résumé and application. George Peterson, selected by the student body, members of the faculty, and the school board, head the interview team. The team plan to conduct initial interviews April 25-May 3.

Initial interviews are designed to last no more than
an hour and a half. We feel that ninety minutes
provide enough time for candidates to make a general
presentation of their credentials.

Ten candidates have been selected for the initial
round of interviews. Three finalists will be chosen to
interview with the full board. Each of those who meets
with the full board may submit work samples, letters
of recommendation, or other written documentation.
Powerpoint presentations of less than thirty minutes
is also allowed.

To schedule your first interview, please call me no
later than April 25.

Sincerely yours,

Carmen Hernandez

WHAT HAVE YOU LEARNED?

Select the correct verb in each sentence.

1. Each of the parent's requests (demand/demands) a detailed response.

2. The tenants or the landlord (has/have) to be held accountable for the condition of the building.

3. Where (is/are) the committee going to meet this week?

4. The cars that (needs/need) repairs should be parked behind the garage.

5. The price of rare coins (remain/remains) stable.

   Answers appear on page 445.

WRITING ON THE WEB

Using a search engine such as Yahoo!, Google, or AltaVista, enter terms such
as *subject verb agreement, verbs,* and *verb agreement* to locate current sites of
interest.

1. Read online articles from magazines or newspapers and notice the number of group words such as *committee, jury,* or *Senate.*

2. Send an e-mail to a friend and make sure you choose the right verbs in
   sentences containing "either-or" and "which."

POINTS TO REMEMBER

1. Subjects and verb agree—or match—in number:

   Singular subjects take singular verbs:

   > The boy *walks* to school.
   > The bus *is* late.

   Plural subjects take plural verbs:

   > The boys *walk* to school.
   > The buses *are* late.

2. Verb choice affects meaning:

   > The desk and chair *is* on sale.   Singular— both items sold as a set
   > The desk and chair *are* on sale.   Plural— items are sold separately

3. Group nouns, units of time and money, and some words that appear plural are singular:

   > The jury *is* deliberating.
   > Fifty dollars *is* not enough.

4. Some nouns that refer to a single item are plural:

   > My scissors *are* dull.
   > The fireworks *are* starting.

5. *Here* and *There* can precede singular or plural verbs depending on the subject:

   > There *is* a girl who wants to join the team.
   > Here *are* three girls who want to join the team.

6. The subject of a sentence never appears in a prepositional phrase:

   > One of my friends *lives* in Brooklyn.   *One* is the subject, not *friends*
   > The prices of oil *are* rising.   *prices* is the subject, not *oil*

7. Nouns set off by commas following the subject are not part of the subject:

   > The teacher, supported by students, *is* protesting.   Singular

8. The subject may follow a possessive:

   > Tom's cars *are* brand-new.   *cars* is the subject
   > The children's playground *is* open.   *playground* is the subject

9. *Either . . . or* constructions can be singular or plural:

   If both subjects are singular, the verb is singular:

   > Either my aunt or my sister *is* taking me to the airport.

   If both subjects are plural, the verb is plural:

   > Either the boys or the girls *are* hosting the party.

   If one subject is singular and the other is plural, the subject closer to the verb determines whether it is singular or plural:

   > Either the boy or the girls *are* hosting the party.
   > Either the girls or the boy *is* hosting the party.

(continued)

10. Some indefinite pronouns are singular:

another	each	everything	nothing
anybody	either	neither	somebody
anyone	everybody	nobody	someone
anything	everyone	no one	something

Anything *is* possible. Nothing *is* missing.

Some indefinite pronouns are plural:

both	few	many	several

Both *are* missing. Few *are* available.

Some indefinite pronouns can be singular or plural:

all	more	none	some
any	most		

All the money *is* gone. All the children *are* gone.

If you use Writer's ResourcesNow, please have your students log in and view the pretest, study plan, and posttest for this chapter.

Writer's Resources ⊕ Now™

> **ANSWERS TO WHAT HAVE YOU LEARNED? ON PAGE 443**
> **1.** demands (see page 438)
> **2.** has (see page 437) **3.** is (see page 436) **4.** need (see page 439)
> **5.** remains (see page 443)

Verbs: Tense, Mood, and Voice

Sign showing the former edge of a melting glacier in Alaska

© Ashley Cooper/Picimpact/Corbis

Since 1978 the Exit Glacier in Alaska has retreated half a mile. When it was first discovered, Glacier National Park in Montana had 150 glaciers. Today there are fewer than fifty. Some scientists predict that by 2030 the rest will have melted. Do you think our country is doing enough to prevent global warming?

Write one or more paragraphs stating your views.

What Is Tense?

Tense refers to time. In addition to showing action or linking the subject to other words, verbs tell time. All action, events, and conditions take place in time. To communicate effectively, time relationships have to be stated accurately. A doctor treating an accident victim would pay strict attention to the timing of events. Did the patient collapse and injure his head in the fall, or was he struck first? Has he had fainting spells before? When did he last eat? Does he have any medical conditions? How long has he been unconscious?

Timing is critical in many sentences. Explaining *when* something happened can be just as important as telling readers *what* happened.

WHAT DO YOU KNOW?

Select the correct verb in each sentence

1. Is the city going to (rise/raise) property taxes this year?

2. I was born on Long Island, which (is/was) the site of the 1964 World's Fair.

3. If she (was/were) hired tomorrow, we might finish the job on time.

4. He (lain/laid) his keys on the desk and left the room.

5. Please (set/sit) on the porch where it is cooler.

Answers appear on the following page.

WHAT ARE YOU TRYING TO SAY?   GET WRITING

Write a brief paragraph that describes a change you have observed in a friend, at school or work, in a neighborhood, or in a society. How have television shows changed since you were a child? Has a neighborhood gotten better or worse? How did 9/11 change the United States? Explain what is different and what has remained the same.

_____

_____

_____

_____

_____

_____

_____

_____

_____

_____
_____
_____
_____
_____

WHAT HAVE YOU WRITTEN?

Read your paragraph aloud and underline the verbs. How did you use verbs to tell time? Is it clear what events or actions took place in the past, which began in the past and continue into the present, and which actions take place only in the present?

Helping Verbs

Verb *tenses* tell when events or actions occur. *Helping verbs*—also called *auxiliary verbs*—often appear with verbs to create tense. Common helping verbs are *be, do, have, can, could, may, might, must, shall, should, will, would.*

Tenses

Tense	Use	Example
present	shows current and ongoing actions	I *run* two miles a day.
simple past	shows actions that occurred in the past and do not continue into the present	I *ran* two miles a day in high school.
future	shows future actions	I *will run* two miles a day when I go to college.
present perfect	shows actions that began in the past and concluded in the present	I *have* just *run* two miles.
past perfect	shows actions concluded in the past before another action occurred	I *had run* two miles before going to practice last Monday.
future perfect	shows future actions preceding an action or event further in the future	I *will have run* 5,000 miles by the time I graduate next May.
present progressive	shows ongoing action	I *am running* two miles a day now.
past progressive	shows actions that were in progress in the past	I *was running* two miles a day in those days.
future progressive	shows ongoing future actions	Next year I *will be running* two miles everyday.

present perfect progressive	shows actions that began in the past and continue in the present	I *have been running* two miles a day this semester.
past perfect progressive	shows actions in progress in the past before another past action	I *had been running* two miles a day until I joined the team last fall.
future perfect progressive	shows future ongoing actions taking place before a future event	I *will have been running* two miles a day for a year by the time they reopen the jogging track.

This chart may seem complicated, but we use tense every day to express ourselves. Consider the difference in responses to the question about a friend's travel plans:

She *was* in New York	past tense	indicates she has returned
She *is* in New York	present tense	indicates she is currently in New York
She *has been* in New York	past perfect	indicates several trips to New York, suggesting she may be home or still out of town
She *will be* in New York	future	indicates she will visit New York in the future

We use perfect tenses to explain the differences between events in the recent past and distant past or between the near and far future.

Sid had been looking for a welding job for two years when he was hired last month.
Cara will owe twenty thousand dollars when she finishes school next year.

PROGRESSIVE TENSE

Some verbs express actions: *run, buy, sell, paint, create, drive.* Other verbs express conditions, emotions, relationships, or thoughts: *cost, believe, belong, contain, know, prefer, want.* These verbs don't generally use the progressive form.

Citizens of developing countries *are wanting* a higher standard of living.

Revised
Citizens of developing countries *want* a higher standard of living.

Regular and Irregular Verbs

Most verbs are called "regular" because they follow a regular or standard form to show tense changes. They add *-ed* to words ending with consonants and *-d* to words ending with an *-e.*

Present	Past	Past Participle
charge	charged	charged
count	counted	counted

Present	Past	Past Participle
spoil	spoiled	spoiled
wash	washed	washed
watch	watched	watched
work	worked	worked

VERB ENDINGS

The verb endings *-s* and *-ed* may be hard to hear when added to words that end in similar sounds. Some people don't pronounce these verb endings in speaking. Make sure to add them when you are writing.

They were *suppose* to give their presentation yesterday.
She *learn* quickly.

Revised
They were *supposed* to give their presentation yesterday.
She *learns* quickly.

Irregular verbs do not follow the *-ed* pattern.

• Some irregular verbs make no spelling change to indicate shifts in tense.

Present	Past	Past Participle
cut	cut	cut
hit	hit	hit
hurt	hurt	hurt
put	put	put
quit	quit	quit
read	read	read
set	set	set

• Most irregular verbs make a spelling change rather than adding *-ed*.

Present	Past	Past Participle
awake	awoke	awoken
be	was, were	been
bear	bore	borne (not *born*)
become	became	become
begin	began	begun
blow	blew	blown
break	broke	broken
bring	brought	brought
build	built	built
buy	bought	bought
catch	caught	caught
choose	chose	chosen
come	came	come
dive	dove (dived)	dived
do	did	done
draw	drew	drawn
drink	drank	drunk

Present	Past	Past Participle
drive	drove	driven
eat	ate	eaten
feed	fed	fed
feel	felt	felt
fight	fought	fought
fly	flew	flown
forget	forgot	forgotten
forgive	forgave	forgiven
freeze	froze	frozen
get	got	gotten
go	went	gone
grow	grew	grown
hang (objects)	hung	hung
hang (people)	hanged	hanged
have	had	had
hold	held	held
know	knew	known
lay (place)	laid	laid
lead	led	led
leave	left	left
lie (recline)	lay	lain
lose	lost	lost
make	made	made
mean	meant	meant
meet	met	met
pay	paid	paid
ride	rode	ridden
ring	rang	rung
rise	rose	risen
run	ran	run
say	said	said
see	saw	seen
seek	sought	sought
sell	sold	sold
shine	shone	shone
shoot	shot	shot
sing	sang	sung
sink	sank	sunk
sleep	slept	slept
sneak	sneaked (not *snuck*)	sneaked
speak	spoke	spoken
spend	spent	spent
steal	stole	stolen
sting	stung	stung
strike	struck	struck
strive	strove	striven
swear	swore	sworn
sweep	swept	swept

Present	Past	Past Participle
swim	swam	swum
swing	swung	swung
take	took	taken
teach	taught	taught
tear	tore	torn
tell	told	told
think	thought	thought
throw	threw	thrown
understand	understood	understood
wake	woke	woken
weave	wove	woven
win	won	won
write	wrote	written

EXERCISE 1 Supplying the Right Verb

Complete the following sentences by supplying the correct verb form.

1. **Present** I sing in San Antonio clubs.

   Past I ___*sang*___ in San Antonio clubs.

   Past participle I have ___*sung*___ in San Antonio clubs.

2. **Present** I hurt my knee working out.

   Past I ___*hurt*___ my knee working out.

   Past participle I have ___*hurt*___ my knee working out.

3. **Present** They lie in the sun.

   Past They ___*lay*___ in the sun.

   Past participle They have ___*lain*___ in the sun.

4. **Present** The clothes sell well.

   Past The clothes ___*sold*___ well.

   Past participle The clothes have ___*sold*___ well.

5. **Present** They teach Spanish.

   Past They ___*taught*___ Spanish.

   Past participle They have ___*taught*___ Spanish.

EXERCISE 2 Choosing the Correct Verb

Underline the correct verb form in each sentence.

1. Most accounts of the Civil War (focus/focused) on the battles that occurred in the South.

2. Few people today (are/were) aware of the impact the war had on California.

3. Though today it (is/was) the most populous state, a hundred and fifty years ago, California only (had/has) a population of 250,000 and was not yet linked with the rest of the country by rail.

4. California's early settlers (mirror/<u>mirrored</u>) the conflict in the rest of the country.

5. The residents of commercial San Francisco identified with Northern business interests, while Californians in the agricultural south (<u>felt</u>/feel) strong ties to the Confederacy.

6. Conflicts between Northern and Southern California (were brewing/<u>had been brewing</u>) for years when war was declared in 1861.

7. Southern sympathizers in California (<u>planned</u>/had planned) to secede from the United States and form an independent republic by convincing the general in charge of Union troops in the state to support their venture.

8. General Johnston, though he supported the Southern cause, could not bring himself to oppose the Constitution he (swore/<u>had sworn</u>) to defend.

9. The plot to secede failed, but California (<u>became</u>/become) the site of over eighty Civil War battles.

10. Most of the battles consisted of skirmishes and raids by guerillas who (seek/<u>sought</u>) gold to support the Confederacy.

Problem Verbs: *Lie/Lay, Rise/Raise, Set/Sit*

Some verbs are easily confused. Because they are spelled alike and express similar actions, they are commonly misused. In each pair, only one verb can take direct objects. The verbs *lay, raise,* and *set* take direct objects; *lie, rise,* and *sit* do not.

Lie/Lay

To lie means to rest or recline. You "lie in bed" or "lie on the floor." *To lay* means to put something down or set something into position. You "lay tile" or "lay cards on a table."

Present	Past	Past Participle
lie	lay	lain
lay	laid	laid

To Lie	*To Lay*
I hate to lie in the sun.	I hate to lay tile floors.
They are lying on the beach.	They are laying new sod in the yard.
Yesterday, I lay in bed all day with a cold.	Yesterday, I laid my keys on the counter.
I have lain on that sofa.	We have laid sod like that in the past.

Remember: Lie expresses action done by someone or something.

Sid took aspirin, then *lay* on the sofa hoping the headache would go away.

Lay expresses action done to someone or something.

We *laid* Sid on the sofa and gave him aspirin.

Rise/Raise

To rise means to get up or move up on your own. You "rise and shine" or "rise to the occasion." *To raise* means to lift something or grow something. You "raise a window" or "raise children."

Present	Past	Past Participle
rise	rose	risen
raise	raised	raised

To Rise	To Raise
They don't rise until ten.	They raise the sail as soon as they leave the dock.
She is rising to greet us.	Tom is raising show horses.
They have risen from their naps.	The agents have raised insurance rates again.
He rose to attention.	She raised her arms.

Remember: Rise can refer to objects as well as people.

The dough rises in the oven.   Gold prices are rising.

Set/Sit

To set means to put something in position or arrange in place. "You set down a cup" or "set down some ideas." *Set* always takes a direct object. *To sit* means to assume a sitting position. You "sit on a sofa" or "sit on a committee."

Present	Past	Past Participle
set	set	set
sit	sat	sat

To Set	To Sit
We set the menu prices.	We sit on the menu committee.
He is setting a new policy.	She is sitting by the window.

EXERCISE 3 Choosing the Correct Verb

Underline the correct verb in each sentence.

1. Without more rain we cannot hope to (<u>raise</u>/rise) any wheat.

2. You will get a bad burn if you (set/<u>sit</u>) in the sun too long.

3. Don't (<u>set</u>/sit) those plants in direct sunlight.

4. After a brief ceremony she was (lain/<u>laid</u>) to rest beside her husband.

5. I need to (lay/<u>lie</u>) down for a while.

6. I can't (<u>lay</u>/lie) all the responsibility on your shoulders.

7. She is going (to rise/to <u>raise</u>) the flag herself.

8. Let me (<u>raise</u>/rise) the blinds to let in more light.

9. I was so tired I (laid/<u>lay</u>) in bed until noon.

10. The people (<u>rose</u>/raised) when the mayor entered.

Shifts in Tense

Events happen in time. In writing, it is important to avoid awkward or illogical shifts in time and write in a consistent tense.

> *Awkward*
> I *took* the midterm and *miss* only two questions.
>   past   present

> *Consistent*
> I *took* the midterm and *missed* only two questions.
>   past   past
>
>   or
>
> I *take* the midterm and *miss* only two questions.
>   present   present

You can change tenses to show a logical shift or change in time.

> I *was born* in Fort Worth but *live* in Austin. Next year I *will move* to Denver.
>   past   present   future

You can shift tense to distinguish between past events and subjects that are permanent or still operating.

> I *stayed* at the York Hotel, which *is* one of the largest in Toronto.
>   past   present

(Using past tense "was" to refer to the York Hotel might lead readers to believe the hotel no longer exists.)

Changing shifts in tense change meaning.

> Cindy *worked* for United Express, which *is* the only delivery service used by
>   past   present
> the FBI.
>> [Meaning: Cindy once worked for the only delivery service used by the FBI.]

> Cindy *works* for United Express, which *was* the only delivery service used by
>   present   past
> the FBI.
>> [Meaning: Cindy is working for a delivery service that used to be the only one used by the FBI.]

> Cindy *worked* for United Express, which *was* the only delivery service used by
>   past   past
> the FBI.
>> [Meaning: Cindy once worked for a delivery service that used to be the only one used by the FBI.]

In writing about literature and film, you can relate the plot's events in either past or present tense, as long as you are consistent.

Present	*Past*
In *A Separate Peace,* the hero *is* a shy sixteen-year-old boy at an elite prep school who *feels* a mix of admiration and jealousy for Finny, his roommate. Finny *is* bold, witty, and athletic.	In *A Separate Peace,* the hero *was* a shy sixteen-year-old boy at an elite prep school who *felt* a mix of admiration and jealousy for Finny, his roommate. Finny *was* bold, witty, and athletic.

One of the most common errors student writers make is beginning a passage in one tense then shifting when there is no change in time.

present

past

present

The phone *rings* and I *wake* up. It *is* only five a.m. I *pick* up the phone, expecting bad news about my grandmother who is sick. But it is Larry. He tells me to meet him at the airport at seven. I *hung* up the phone, *took* a shower, and *got* dressed. I *got* into my car and *was* just pulling out of the driveway, when I *remember* he never told me what his flight number is or even what airline he is on. I pick up my cell phone but get no response. I realize the best thing to do is just wait by baggage claim.

Revised—Present Tense

The phone rings and I wake up. It is only five a.m. I pick up the phone, expecting bad news about my grandmother who is sick. But it is Larry. He tells me to meet him at the airport at seven. I *hang* up the phone, *take* a shower, and *get* dressed. I *get* into my car and *am* just pulling out of the driveway, when I *remember* he never told me what his flight number is or even what airline he is on. I pick up my cell phone but get no response. I realize the best thing to do is just wait by baggage claim.

Revised—Past Tense

The phone *rang* and I *woke* up. It *was* only five a.m. I *picked* up the phone, expecting bad news about my grandmother who *was* sick. But it *was* Larry. He *told* me to meet him at the airport at seven. I *hung* up the phone, *took* a shower, and *got* dressed. I *got* into my car and *was* just pulling out of the driveway, when I *remembered* he never told me what his flight number *was* or even what airline he *was* on. I *picked* up my cell phone but *got* no response. I *realized* the best thing to do *was* just wait by baggage claim.

Note: The best way to check your work for awkward shifts in tense is to read your essay aloud. It is often easier to hear than see awkward shifts. Remember to shift tense only where there is a clear change in time.

EXERCISE 4 Revising Errors in Tense

Revise this passage from a student essay to eliminate awkward and illogical shifts in tense. NOTE: Some shifts in this passage logically distinguish between past events and current or ongoing conditions or situations.

```
    I was born in Philadelphia, but I grew up in
Haddonfield where my parents move when I was two. In
high school I get a job working on the Jersey shore
helping an old guy sell trinkets on the boardwalk. It
was a great job because on my lunch hour I go swimming
and hang out with my friends on the beach. Being six-
teen or seventeen, I felt invincible and never worry
about sunscreen and got a bad sunburn about once a
month.
    I went to college in San Jose, and my friends and
I took weekend trips to Vegas or the beach. I began to
use sunscreen but still forget now and then. At that
```

time all I worried about was never letting any of my
friends drive drunk.

I only begin to worry about the sun when I found
out two years ago that my aunt, who never lie out in
the sun, was diagnosed with a serious form of skin
cancer. Now I make sure I protect myself with sunscreen. I always keep some in my car because I live in
Southern California and never know when an errand or a
call from a friend will expose me to a killer.

I was born in Philadelphia, but I grew up in Haddonfield where my parents moved when I was two. In high school I got a job working on the Jersey shore helping an old guy sell trinkets on the boardwalk. It was a great job because on my lunch hour I went swimming and hung out with my friends on the beach. Being sixteen or seventeen, I felt invincible and never worried about sunscreen and got a bad sunburn about once a month.

I went to college in San Jose, and my friends and I took weekend trips to Vegas or the beach. I began to use sunscreen but still forgot now and then. At that time all I worried about was never letting any of my friends drive drunk.

I only began to worry about the sun when I found out two years ago that my aunt, who never laid out in the sun, was diagnosed with a serious form of skin cancer. Now I make sure I protect myself with sunscreen. I always keep some in my car because I live in Southern California and never know when an errand or a call from a friend will expose me to a killer.

Subjunctive Mood

Subjunctive refers to something that has not happened—a possible future event, imagined situation, or desired outcome. There are three verb forms used in the subjunctive.

- Imaginary situations stated with *if* or *wish* use *were*:

  If she *were* the boss, things would change.   [*not* she was]
  If I *were* the boss, I would raise wages.   [*not* I was]

- Clauses that begin with *that* following verbs such as *ask, call, command, demand, direct, insist,* or *order* use the base form of the verb:

  They *asked* that she *be seated*.
  We *ordered* that the city *be* responsible.
  The mayor *demanded* that the council *remain* in session.

- Clauses that begin with *that* following adjectives expressing urgency, such as *essential, imperative, important,* or *urgent,* use the base form of the verb:

  It is *important* that you be prompt.
  It is *essential* that the trucks arrive early.

Active and Passive Voice

English has two voices—*active* and *passive*. *Active voice* emphasizes the subject—who did the act. *Passive voice* emphasizes to whom or to what an act was done.

Active	*Passive*
The teacher chose the books.	The books were chosen by the teacher.
The city repaved the street.	The street was repaved by the city.
My aunt sold the old house.	The old house was sold by my aunt.

Grammar Choices and Meaning

It is important to understand that using active or passive voice is not so much a matter of being right or wrong, but in the meaning you want to express. Active voice is preferred because it is direct, strong, and clear.

Active
Atlas Electronics developed the new sensor.
Lisa Montone will direct the film.
A federal judge authorized the wiretap.

Passive voice tends to reverse the order, emphasizing the object over the subject, sometimes creating a sentence that reports an action without naming a subject.

Passive
The new sensor was developed by Atlas Electronics.
The film will be directed by Lisa Montone.
The wiretap was approved.

Passive voice is used when the act is more significant than its cause.

Passive
The missing plane was flown by a veteran pilot.
The museum was destroyed by fire.
My car was stolen.

Police officers and other investigators are trained to use passive voice in writing reports to avoid jumping to conclusions. Since active voice makes a strong connection between subject and verb, it can lead writers to make assumptions. By writing in the passive voice, reporting can be made more objective. Facts are presented and events related without stressing cause and effect or assigning responsibility.

Passive
   The security alarm was activated at 3:15 a.m. The window to the rear office was broken. Nothing was reported stolen. The owner, however, has suggested that data could have been taken from computers. No employees have been fired recently. The company has received no threats. The company's insurance company has been informed of the break-in.

Passive voice, however, can be used to avoid taking responsibility.

Passive
Attempts to repair the roof failed.
The pump was inspected last year.
Complaints were made against her.

In all these questions, the "who" is missing. Who attempted to repair the roof? Who inspected the pump? Who made complaints?

EXERCISE 5 Changing Passive to Active Voice

Rewrite these sentences to change them from passive to active voice. NOTE: In some cases you will have to invent a missing subject.

1. ***Dawn to Dusk* was released by Paramount last week.**

   Paramount released Dawn to Dusk last week.

2. **The bond issue was rejected by the voters.**

   The voters rejected the bond issue.

3. **The show was cancelled by studio executives after the ratings came out.**

   Studio executives cancelled the show after the ratings came out.

4. **The diet was criticized by several doctors and nutritionists.**

   Several doctors and nutritionists criticized the diet.

5. **The airport was repaired by the county.**

   The county repaired the airport.

Other Verb Problems

Could Have, Must Have, Should Have, Would Have

Because *have* and *of* sound alike when speaking, it is easy to mistakenly write "could *of*" instead of "could *have*." *Have* is used in verb phrases. *Of* is a preposition showing a relationship.

Have	*Of*
She could *have* taken a cab.	The price *of* cabs is rising.
They might *have* called us.	She is the secretary *of* state.
The college should *have* offered tutoring.	I lost my proof *of* purchase.

Double Negatives

Use only one negative to express a negative idea. Don't create *double negatives* with words like *hardly, scarcely, no, not,* or *never.*

Double negative	*Correct*
I never have no homework.	I never have homework.
She won't never take a plane.	She will never take a plane.
I didn't take nothing.	I didn't take anything.

AVOIDING DOUBLE NEGATIVES

Double negatives are common in some languages and in some English dialects. If you are a native speaker of one of these languages or dialects, be careful to use only one negative word in each clause.

EXERCISE 6 Eliminating Common Verb Problems and Double Negatives

Rewrite the following sentences to eliminate common verb problems or double negatives.

1. **We should of made a reservation.**

   We should have made a reservation.

2. **You should of never signed that contract.**

   You should have never signed that contract.

3. **I never got no bills.**

   I never got any bills.

4. **We hardly had no time to pack.**

   We hardly had any time to pack.

5. **The machinery was so old we could hardly make no adjustments.**

   The machinery was so old we could hardly make adjustments.

WORKING TOGETHER

Working with a group of students, revise this announcement for verb errors.

```
Notice to All Employees:

As of March 1, all employees who are working for at
least five years will be eligible for inclusion in the
expanded benefits program. Federated Insurance, how-
ever, has the right to limit coverage with employees
who are rejected for health insurance in the last two
years because of preexisting conditions. If you are
rejected, there is an appeal process. No employee will
never lose their basic existing benefits.

Karen Delgado
Human Services Director
```

CRITICAL THINKING

Write a paragraph describing how your career plans have changed since you were in high school. What did you want to be when you were sixteen or seventeen? Did your goals stay the same, or did they change? What career do you dream of pursuing now?

WHAT HAVE YOU WRITTEN?

When you finish writing, review your use of tense, mood, and voice.

1. Write out one of your sentences stated in past tense:

_____

Have you used the proper verb to show past tense?

2. Write out one of your sentences stated in present tense:

_____

Does the verb state the present tense? Does it match the subject?

3. Have you avoided errors with verbs such as *lie* and *lay, raise* and *rise, set* and *sit*?

_____

4. Have you written *of* instead of *have* in *should have* or *would have*?

WHAT HAVE YOU LEARNED?

Select the correct verb in each sentence.

1. If I (was/were) driving, I would have a map.

2. The guests (rose/raised) questions once the cruise started.

3. We could (of/have) rented a limo for the price of a cab.

4. I (lay/laid) the baby down for a nap.

5. The children (spread/spreaded) the blankets for a picnic.

Answers appear on the following page.

WRITING ON THE WEB

Using a search engine such as Yahoo!, Google, or AltaVista, enter terms such as *verb tense, past tense, past perfect tense, present progressive tense, irregular verbs, subjunctive,* and *passive voice* to locate current sites of interest.

1. Read online newspaper and magazine articles about an issue that interests you and notice how writers use tense to show shifts from past to present.
2. Write an e-mail to a friend about what you did last week. Choose verbs carefully to distinguish past events from ongoing ones.

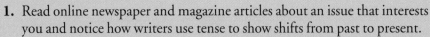

POINTS TO REMEMBER

1. Explaining *when* something happens is as important as explaining *what* happens.

2. Regular verbs add *-d* or *-ed* to show past tense.

call	called	show	showed
talk	talked	want	wanted

3. Irregular verbs do not add *-d* or *-ed* to show past tense.

set	set	thrust	thrust
get	got	make	made

4. *Lie/lay, rise/raise,* and *set/sit* are often confused.

	To lie means "to rest or recline."		*To lay* means "to place."	
present	lie	*lie down*	lay	*lay tile*
past	lay		laid	
past participle	lain		laid	

	To raise means "to lift."		*To rise* means "to get up."	
present	raise	*raise prices*	rise	*rise up!*
past	raised		rose	
past participle	raised		risen	

	To set means "to place."		*To sit* means "to recline."	
present	set	*set prices*	sit	*sit down!*
past	set		sat	
past participle	set		sat	

5. Avoid awkward shifts in tense or time.

   Awkward
   We *drove* to the pier and *see* the whales.

   Correct
   We *drove* to the pier and *saw* the whales.

6. Avoid mistaking *of* for *have* in *should have* and *could have.*

   I could *have* passed.   **not**   I could *of* passed.

7. Avoid double negatives.

   I don't have any cash.   **not**   I don't have no cash.

Writer's Resources ⓦ Now™   If you use Writer's Resources Now, please have your students log in and view the pretest, study plan, and posttest for this chapter.

ANSWERS TO WHAT HAVE YOU LEARNED? ON PAGE 461
1. were (see page 457) **2.** raised (see page 454) **3.** have (see page 459) **4.** laid (see page 453) **5.** spread (page 450)

Pronoun Reference, Agreement, and Case

© Jutta Klee/CORBIS

Write one or more paragraphs describing a situation in which you had to work as part of a group. What responsibilities were assigned to individuals? What assignments were undertaken by the whole group? Did you find the experience rewarding or frustrating?

What Are Pronouns?

Pronouns take the place of nouns. Without pronouns, your writing would be awkward.

> Frank gave Frank's presentation to the new employees yesterday. Frank hopes that Frank's system will boost productivity and increase Frank's chances for a promotion.

> Having worked in the same job for six years, Frank feels that Frank needs a change in order to make full use of Frank's skills.

Pronouns eliminate needless repetition.

> Frank gave *his* presentation to the new employees yesterday. Frank hopes that *his* system will boost productivity and increase *his* chances for a promotion.

> Having worked in the same job for six years, Frank feels that *he* needs a change in order to make full use of *his* skills.

WHAT DO YOU KNOW?

Select the correct pronoun in each sentence.

1. _____ Nancy and (he/him) are working all summer.

2. _____ Carmen or Maria will lend you (their/her) coat.

3. _____ We objected to (him/his) voting record.

4. _____ When I went to high school, the only language (I/you) could take was Spanish.

5. _____ The committee votes on (its/their) budget today.

6. _____ It's only (I/me).

7. _____ Give (this/these) discs to Rick.

8. _____ (Who/Whom) is coming to the party?

9. _____ It is (who/whom)?

10. _____ We gave the money to Frank, Jenny, Chris, and (she/her).

Answers appear on the following page.

GET WRITING ▸ **WHAT ARE YOU TRYING TO SAY?**

Describe a historical event that you think changed America. Summarize what happened and explain why you think it was significant.

_____

_____

_____

_____

_____

_____

_____

_____

_____

_____

_____

_____

_____

_____

_____

WHAT HAVE YOU WRITTEN?

Underline all the pronouns in your paragraphs.

1. Can you circle the noun (antecedent) each pronoun represents?
2. Are plural nouns represented by plural pronouns? Are singular nouns represented by singular pronouns?
3. Are the pronouns in the right case? Do you use _I, we, he, she, they,_ and _it_ as subjects? Do you use _me, us, him, her,_ and _them_ as objects? Do you use _my, our, his, hers, their,_ and _its_ to show possession?

TYPES OF PRONOUNS

There are four types of **pronouns:** _personal, indefinite, relative,_ and _demonstrative._

Personal pronouns refer to people and have three forms, depending on how they are used in a sentence: _subjective, objective,_ and _possessive._

	Subjective Singular	Plural	Objective Singular	Plural	Possessive Singular	Plural
1st person	I	we	me	us	my (mine)	our (ours)
2nd person	you	you	you	you	your (yours)	your (yours)
3rd person	he	they	him	them	his (his)	their (theirs)
	she		her		her (hers)	
	it		it		it (its)	

She bought _our_ house, so _we_ gave _her_ the keys.
They sold the car because _it_ was older than _mine._

(continued)

ANSWERS TO WHAT DO YOU KNOW? ON PAGE 464
1. he (subjective form needed)
2. her (possessive singular form needed) 3. his (possessive singular form needed) 4. I (first person singular form needed)
5. its (_committee_ is singular)
6. I (subjective form needed)
7. these (_discs_ is plural) 8. Who (subjective form needed) 9. who (subjective form needed) 10. her (objective form needed)

Relative pronouns introduce noun and adjective clauses:

who, whoever, whom, whose   which, whichever   that, what, whatever

> I will help *whoever* asks.
> Tom has a new camera, *which* he won in a contest.

Demonstrative pronouns indicate the noun (antecedent):

this, that, these, those

> *That* book is interesting.
> *These* books are interesting.

Indefinite pronouns refer to abstract persons or things.

Singular				Plural	Singular or Plural		
everyone	someone	anyone	no one	both	all	more	none
everybody	somebody	anybody	nobody	few	any	most	some
everything	something	anything	nothing	many			
each	another	either	neither				

> *Everyone* should cast his or her vote.   *More* security is needed.
> *Both* girls are attending summer school.   *More* security guards are needed.

Using Pronouns

To prevent confusion, pronouns have to be precisely used.

- Pronouns must be clearly linked to **antecedents**—the nouns or other pronouns they represent.

Unclear Reference
The classrooms are half-empty. Test scores are bad. The dropout rate is growing. *They* just didn't care.
> [Whom does *they* refer to—students, teachers, parents?]

Clear Reference
The students skip class, score poorly on tests, and drop out. *They* just don't care.
> [*They* refers to *students*]

Unclear Reference
Eric asked George to read *his* book.
> [Whose book is it—Eric's or George's?]

Clear Reference
Eric gave *his* book to George and asked *him* to read it.
Eric looked at George's book, then asked *him* to read it.

- Pronouns must agree, or match, the antecedent in number.

Incorrect
Every taxpayer must bring *their* notice to the hearing.
> [*taxpayer* is singular; *their* is plural]

Singular
Every taxpayer should bring *his or her* notice to the hearing.
> [singular *his or her* refers to singular *taxpayer*]

Plural
Taxpayers should bring *their* notices to the hearing.
   [plural *their* refers to plural *taxpayers*]

- Pronouns have to agree or match in person.

Incorrect
We went to the museum where *you* can see the Picasso collection.
   [awkward shift between *we* (first person) and *you* (second person)]

Revised
We went to the museum where *we* saw the Picasso collection.

- Pronouns have to be used in the right case.

Subjective
They took the train to Chicago.

Objective
We gave *them* the tickets.

Possessive
Ted and Carmen want to visit *their* uncle.

Reflexive
They are traveling by *themselves*.

- Unnecessary pronouns should be eliminated.

Unnecessary Pronouns
Carlos *he* should learn to drive.
The movie *it* makes no sense.
The parents *they* are angry.

Revised
Carlos should learn to drive.
The movie makes no sense.
The parents are angry.

Pronoun Reference

To express your ideas clearly, you have to use pronouns accurately. Because you know what you want to say, it is very easy to write sentences that make sense to you but will confuse your readers. The pronoun *he,* for example, can refer to any single male. It is easy to create sentences in which the word could refer to more than one person.

Jack bought a condo last year. When his brother Ted got out of the navy, he moved in to split expenses. At first they got along and enjoyed each other's company. But after a few months, he found it hard to live with a roommate.

Who does the "he" in the last sentence refer to—Jack or Ted? Inserting the **antecedent** or proper name eliminates confusion.

Jack bought a condo last year. When his brother Ted got out of the navy, he moved in to split expenses. At first they got along and enjoyed each other's company. But after a few months, *Jack* found it hard to live with a roommate.

Without a clear link between the pronoun (*I, we, you, he, she, they,* and *it*) and the antecedent or noun it represents, sentences can be misleading.

Confusing
The managers met with the employees to discuss their proposal.

Revised
The managers met with the employees to discuss the company's proposal.
The employees discussed their proposal at a meeting with the managers.

In order to correct reference errors, you may have to the reword sentences.

Unclear Reference
Jack gave Ted his keys.

Clear Reference
Jack gave his keys to Ted.

USING *THEY* WITHOUT AN ANTECEDENT

The pronoun *they* is often used without a clear antecedent. In conversation, we frequently use *they* as an abstract reference to people with authority or power.

"*They* put too much sex and violence on TV."
"Can you believe what *they* are paying pro athletes these days?"
"Why don't *they* fix this road?"

In writing, you should be more precise. Make sure every time *they* appears in your paper it is clearly linked to a specific plural noun. Replace unlinked *they*'s with concrete nouns.

Networks put too much sex and violence on TV.
Too much sex and violence appears on TV.

Can you believe what owners are paying pro athletes these days?
Can you believe what pro athletes are paid these days?

Why doesn't the county fix this road?
Why isn't this road fixed?

In editing papers, read them aloud. Pause when you see *they* and determine if it clearly refers to a noun. Revise sentences with unlinked *they*'s to eliminate confusion.

EXERCISE 1 Eliminate Unclear Pronoun References

Rewrite the following sentences to eliminate unclear pronoun references. You can revise the sentence to create a clear antecedent (noun) for they *or eliminate the pronoun by supplying a noun.*

1. **Carmen suggested that Cindy fix her bicycle.**

   Carmen showed her bicycle to Cindy and suggested she fix it.

2. **The teachers met with the parents to discuss their concerns.**

   The teachers discussed their concerns with the parents.

3. They should repair this street.

This street needs repairs.

4. My sister worked with Karen until she went to college.

Until she went to college, Karen worked with my sister.

5. Why don't they make movies I can take my kids to see?

Why doesn't Hollywood make movies I can take my kids to see?

Pronoun Agreement

Just as singular subjects take singular verbs, singular nouns take singular pronouns.

visitor	he *or* she
car	it
Ms. Essex	she
Erica	she
the halfback	he
the nun	she
voter	he *or* she

Ms. Essex left early so *she* would not miss her flight.
The car won't start because *it* needs a battery.
The voter plays an important social role when *he or she* casts a ballot.

Plural nouns take plural pronouns.

visitors	they
cars	they
the Essexes	they
the halfbacks	they
the nuns	they
voters	they

The visitors arrived early because *they* wanted to see the new exhibit.
The cars are ten years old, but *they* are in great condition.
Voters play an important role in shaping society. *They* choose our leaders.

Singular and Plural Nouns and Pronouns

- Indefinite pronouns refer to no specific person, idea, or object and are always singular:

another	either	nobody	somebody
anybody	everybody	no one	someone
anyone	everyone	none	something
anything	everything	nothing	
each	neither	one	

Another house was sold, and *it* was on the market for only two days.
Someone left *his or her* books in the classroom.
Neither boy is going to get *his* money on time.

- Some nouns that end in *-s* and look like plurals are singular:

    economics   mathematics   athletics   physics

    Economics is tough. *It* demands a lot of math skills.

- Some nouns that may refer to one item are plural:

    pants   scissors   fireworks   binoculars

    My pants are blue. *They* are made of denim.

- Proper nouns that look plural are singular if they are names of companies, organizations, or titles of books, movies, television shows, or works of art:

    United Technologies   *Two Women*   Alcoholics Anonymous

    I applied for a job at United Technologies because *it* offers great benefits.

- Units of time and amounts of money are generally singular:

    Sixty dollars *is* a fair price; *it* is more than I expected.

    They appear as plurals to indicate separate items:

    Sixty dollars *were* spread on the table. *They* were worn and tattered.

Avoiding Sexism

Because singular pronouns refer to only one sex or the other—*he* or *she*—it can be easy to create sentences that fail to include both males and females. It is acceptable, however, to use only *he* or *she* when writing about a single person or a group of people of the same sex.

Sam left work early because *he* has a cold.
Each of the women took *her* children to the clinic.
Kelly is going to night school because *she* wants an associate degree.
The best player in the NFL is one who puts *his* heart into the game.

When writing about people in general, it is important to avoid sexist pronoun use.

Sexist
Every student should do *his* best.   Aren't women students?
A doctor must use *his* judgment.   What about female doctors?

Methods to Avoid Sexism

1. Provide both male and female singular pronouns.
    Every student should do *his or her* best.

2. Use plural antecedents.
    Students should do *their* best.

3. Reword the sentence to eliminate the need for pronouns.
    Every student must excel.

USING *THEY* TO AVOID SEXISM

In speaking, people often use *they* rather than *he or she* to save time.

> Every student should do *their* best.
> Each employee is required to meet *their* supervisor before *they* can apply for a raise.
> A good teacher knows *their* students.

This agreement error is often accepted in speech, but writing requires more formal methods of eliminating sexism. If you find yourself using *they* to refer to a singular noun or pronoun, use these methods to both avoid sexism and an error in agreement.

1. Use plural nouns and pronouns to match *they*:

> All *students* should do *their* best.
> All *employees* are required to meet *their* supervisors before *they* can apply for raises.
> Good *teachers* know *their* students.

2. Eliminate the need for pronouns:

> A student should study hard.
> Every employee must have approval from a supervisor to apply for a raise.
> A good teacher knows students.

3. State as commands:

> Employees—meet with your supervisor before applying for a raise.

EXERCISE 2 Selecting the Right Pronoun

Underline the correct pronoun in each sentence.

1. A chess-playing automaton or a robot called the Turk caused a sensation when (they/<u>it</u>) first appeared in Europe in the 1770s.

2. The machine, which consisted of a large cabinet containing complex gears and wheels and the upper body of a wooden figure dressed like a Turk with moving arms, was able to play chess, and (<u>it</u>/they) defeated many human opponents.

3. The Turk was constructed by Wolfgang von Kempelen, a court official, and (<u>he</u>/they) exhibited his device throughout Europe.

4. Benjamin Franklin and Napoleon played the Turk, and (he/<u>they</u>) both lost to the mechanical chess master.

5. Players and observers were amazed when (it/<u>they</u>) saw the machine in action.

6. Johann Maelzel took the Turk on an American tour in the 1800s, where the machine impressed crowds, and many a visitor could not believe (their/<u>his or her</u>) eyes.

7. There were many skeptics, including Edgar Allan Poe, who wrote a popular article detailing (their/<u>his</u>) reasons for believing the machine was a hoax.

8. In fact, the intricate clockwork in the cabinet was just for show, and (they/<u>it</u>) left plenty of room for a human operator to sit inside the machine and operate the Turk.

9. The public gradually lost interest the Turk as (their/<u>its</u>) suspicions grew.

10. The Turk and many other exhibits were destroyed when (it/<u>they</u>) were lost in a museum fire in 1854.

Avoiding Shifts in Point of View

Pronouns express three persons:

	First	Second	Third
Singular	I, me, my	you, you, your	he, him, his/she, her, her
Plural	we, us, our	you, you, your	they, them, their

Avoid making illogical shifts when writing. Maintain consistent point of view.

Shift
We went to the beach, but *you* couldn't find a place to park.
When *he* went to college, *you* could pay tuition with a part-time job.

Revised
We went to the beach, but *we* couldn't find a place to park.
  [consistent use of plural first person]
When *he* went to college, *students* could pay tuition with a part-time job.
  [use of *students* eliminates need for second pronoun]

EXERCISE 3 Eliminating Pronoun Shifts in Point of View

Revise the following sentences to eliminate illogical pronoun shifts in point of view.

1. **Visitors to Chipilo, Mexico, may be surprised when you hear the residents talk.**

   Visitors to Chipilo, Mexico, may be surprised when they hear the residents talk.

2. **A tourist trying to speak to them in Spanish may find yourself greeted in Venet, an Italian dialect.**

   A tourist trying to speak to them in Spanish may find himself or herself greeted in Venet, an Italian dialect.

3. **Many of the people in this town descended from Italian immigrants who lived in Venice, where you still can hear a distinct dialect.**

   Many of the people in this town descended from Italian immigrants who lived in Venice, where a distinct dialect is still spoken.

4. **Venet is studied by linguists because you rarely hear it anymore.**

   Venet is studied by linguists because it is rarely heard anymore.

5. **The language has no official written form, but you can try to write Venet using the Spanish they learn in school.**

   The language has no official written form, but people try to write Venet using the Spanish they learn in school.

Using the Right Case

Nouns serve different functions in sentences. They can be subjects or objects, and they can be possessive. Pronouns appear in different forms to show how they function.

They sold *her* car to *me*.
Subject   possessive   object

These different forms are called "cases."

PRONOUN CASES

	Subjective	Objective	Possessive	Reflexive/Intensive
Singular	I	me	my, mine	myself
	you	you	you, yours	yourself
	he	him	his	himself
	she	her	her	herself
	it	it	its	itself
Plural	we	us	our, ours	ourselves
	you	you	your, yours	yourselves
	they	them	their, theirs	themselves
Singular or Plural	who	whom	whose	

In most sentences we automatically use pronouns in the right case, telling our readers the role the pronoun plays.

Subjective pronouns serve as the subject of a verb.

We are flying to Chicago tonight.
This month *she* works every other weekend.

Objective pronouns serve as objects:

The hostess made a reservation for *us.*
Help *him* pay the bill.

Possessive pronouns demonstrate the pronoun owns something:

Our house needs a new roof.
The school changed *her* grades.

Note: Because these pronouns already indicate possession, no apostrophes are needed.

USING POSSESSIVE PRONOUNS

In English, possessive pronouns—*my, your, his, her, our, their*—must agree with the nouns they represent, not the words they modify.

The club members advertised *its* bake sale on TV.

Revised
The club members advertised *their* bake sale on TV.

The possessive pronoun *their* agrees with *club members* not *bake sale.*

Reflexive pronouns refer to other pronouns:

She moved the furniture *herself.*

Intensive pronouns add emphasis:

I myself ran the fund drive.

There are, however, some pronoun uses that can be confusing, including plurals, comparisons, and sentences using certain words.

Plural Constructions

Using a single pronoun as a subject or object is generally easy.

She helped *him* study.
Sam gave the money to *her.*

However, when pronouns are part of plural subjects and objects, many writers make mistakes.

Incorrect
Phil, the teachers, the parents, and *him* met with the principal.
The principal met with Phil, the teachers, the parents, and *he.*

Correct
Phil, the teachers, the parents, and *he* met with the principal. [subjective case]

The principal met with Phil, the teachers, the parents, and *him*. [objective case]

When editing, the quickest method of checking case is to simplify the sentence by eliminating the other nouns.

. . . *he* met with the principal.
The principal met with . . . *him*.

Between

Pronouns that serve as objects of prepositions use the objective case—*him, her, me, them*. Most constructions give writers few problems—to *him*, for *them*, with *her*. However, the preposition *between* is often misused.

Incorrect (Subjective Case)	Correct (Objective Case)
between you and *I*	between you and *me*
between you and *he*	between you and *him*
between you and *she*	between you and *her*
between *he* and *she*	between *him* and *her*
between *they* and the teachers	between *them* and the teachers.

Although people often used the subjective case with *between* in speaking, the objective case is correct and should be used in writing.

Comparisons

Comparisons using *than* or *as* use the subjective case.

| She is taller than *I*. | **not** | She is taller than *me*. |
| Tina is smarter than *he*. | **not** | Tina is smarter than *him*. |

These constructions are confusing because the second verb is usually omitted. To test which pronoun to use, add the missing verb to see which pronoun sounds correct.

| She is taller than *I am*. | **not** | *me am* |
| Tina is smarter than *he is*. | **not** | *him is* |

The Verb *to Be*

Subjective pronouns follow *to be* verbs.

Is it *she* on the phone?	**not**	Is it *her* on the phone?
It is *I*.	**not**	It is *me*.
Was it *they* in the car?	**not**	Was it *them* in the car?

Because we often use phrases like "It's me" or "Is that her talking?" when we speak, the correct forms can sound awkward. The subjective case is correct and should be used in writing.

If your sentences still sound awkward, rewrite them to alter the *to be* pronoun form.

She is on the phone.
I am at the door.
Did *they* take the car?

Who and Whom

Who and *whom* are easily confused because they are generally used in questions and change the usual word pattern.

Who is subjective and serves as the subject of a verb.

Who is coming?	*Who* bought the house?	*Who* is going to the concert?

Whom is objective and serves as the object of a verb or a preposition.

Give the books to *whom*?	To *whom* it may concern.	For *whom* is this intended?

To help choose the right word, substitute *he* and *him*. If *he* sounds better, use *who*. If *him* sounds better, use *whom*.

(Who/Whom) called?
(*He*/Him) called.   [Use who— *Who called?*]

Take it from (whoever/whomever)
can help.
(*He*/Him) can help.   [Use whoever— *whoever can help*]

For (who/whom) are you looking?
For (he/*him*).   [Use whom— *For whom*]

This and That, These and Those

This and *that* are singular.

This inspection is not official.	*That* car needs work.	*This* is a fine film.

These and *those* are plural.

These inspections are not official.	*Those* cars need work.	*These* are fine films.

They and Them

They is subjective and used when it is a subject to a verb.

They are working tonight.	You know *they* don't work on weekends.

Them is objective and used as objects of prepositions or verbs.

Give the papers to *them*.	We can't get *them to* work on weekends.

UNNECESSARY PRONOUNS

Although in speaking, people sometimes insert a pronoun directly after a noun, they are unnecessary and should be eliminated.

Unnecessary
Marsha *she* is going to retire early.
The children *they* won't listen.
The book *it* doesn't make sense.

Revised
Marsha is going to retire early.
The children won't listen.
The book doesn't make sense.

EXERCISE 4 Selecting the Right Pronoun

Select the correct pronoun in each sentence.

1. Sandy and (I/me) are going to the concert next week.

2. The supervisor scheduled Sandy and (I/me) to work overtime.

3. That prevents (we/us) from leaving early.

4. I wanted to ask Ted, Carmen, Simon, Sheri, and (she/her) to drive us.

5. But (whom/who) can I ask to get up at four a.m.?

6. (This/These) things happen, I guess.

7. Dion and Carla might be able to help (we/us) out.

8. They get up very early, and we have asked (they/them) for help in the past.

9. I hate to ask Dion and (she/her) for another favor.

10. But Sandy and (I/me) are going to get there one way or another.

WORKING TOGETHER

Working with a group of students, revise the pronoun errors in the following e-mail.

Attention New Employees:

Every new employee must submit their insurance application to me no later than March 15. Anyone who fails to submit your forms by the deadline risks losing health insurance coverage. Employees who are issued a company car must also fill out his or her vehicle registration slip to make sure you are covered in case of an accident. Great Lakes Mutual representatives will be holding benefits seminars next week. I encourage all new employees to attend one of this seminars so you can get answers to any questions employees may have.

Miranda Rojak
Benefits Manager

EXERCISE 5 Cumulative Exercise

Rewrite each of the sentences for errors in pronoun use, subject-verb agreement, and run-ons.

1. **Sandy or me working all weekend.**

   Sandy or I am working all weekend.

2. **The principal met with the parents but them could not reach a decision.**

   The principal met with the parents, but they could not reach a decision.

3. **The parents were disturbed by the film it featured graphic violence.**

   The parents were disturbed by the film; it featured graphic violence.

4. **The pool was closed after cracks were found the facility needs repairs.**

   The pool was closed after cracks were found; the facility needs repairs.

5. **Whom was willing to work on the weekend?**

   Who was willing to work on the weekend?

GET THINKING AND WRITING

CRITICAL THINKING

Who is the bravest person you know? Write a paragraph describing this person and his or her actions.

WHAT HAVE YOU WRITTEN?

1. Underline all the pronouns and circle their antecedents. Is there a clear link between pronouns and the nouns or pronouns they represent? Pay attention to uses of *they.*
2. Do nouns and pronouns agree in number? Do plural nouns have plural pronouns? Do singular nouns have singular pronouns?

- Pay attention to nouns that look plural but are singular, such as *economics, committee, jury.*
- Remember that indefinite pronouns like *each, everyone, anyone, someone,* and *somebody* are singular.

3. Review your use of case.
- Use subjective case in comparisons and with pronouns following *to be* verbs: *taller than I* or *It is I.*
- Use objective case with between: *between him and me.*

WHAT HAVE YOU LEARNED?

Select the correct pronoun in each sentence.

1. _____ (Who/Whom) can help me change this tire?

2. _____ Kelly, Sandy, Terry, and (she/her) went to practice.

3. _____ (This/These) books are fascinating.

4. _____ Each driver should always carry (his or her/their) license at all times.

5. _____ The teacher told (we/us) students to work harder.

6. _____ How can these systems help the teachers and (we/us) do a better job?

7. _____ Seat (whomever/whoever) arrives first.

8. _____ Between you and (I/me), this budget makes no sense.

9. _____ Take a seat between George and (he/him).

10. _____ I can't pay you and (she/her) until next week.

Answers appear on the following page.

WRITING ON THE WEB

Using a search engine such as Yahoo!, Google, or AltaVista, enter terms such as *pronoun, pronoun agreement, using pronouns,* and *pronoun cases* to locate current sites of interest.

Review e-mails you have sent and look at your past use of pronouns. Can you locate errors in your writing? Which pronoun constructions have given you the most trouble in the past? Mark pages in this chapter for future reference.

POINTS TO REMEMBER

Pronouns have to be used with precision to prevent confusion.

1. Pronouns must clearly refer to a noun.

   Unclear Reference
   Sandy gave Vicki *her* keys.

   Clear Reference
   Sandy gave *her* keys to Vicki.

2. Pronouns and nouns match in number.

Each girl took *her* car.	**singular**
The *girls* took *their* cars.	**plural**

3. Pronouns use consistent point of view.

   Inconsistent
   When *one* visits New York, *you* have to dine at Sardis.
   When *I* work overtime, *it* gets boring.

   Consistent
   When *you* visit New York, *you* have to dine at Sardis.
   When *I* work overtime, *I* get bored.

4. Pronouns must appear in the right case.

   Subjective Case
   Who is at the door?
   She is smarter than *I.*
   It is *I.*
   Was that *she* on the phone?

   Objective Case
   To *whom* it may concern.
   Between you and *me,* the film is too long.

5. Pronouns directly following nouns they represent are unnecessary.

   Unnecessary
   The school *it* closed last week.
   Frank *he* works weekends.

   Revised
   The school closed last week.
   Frank works weekends.

ANSWERS TO WHAT HAVE YOU LEARNED? ON PAGE 479
1. Who (see page 476) **2.** she (see page 474) **3.** These (see page 476) **4.** his or her (see page 469) **5.** us (see page 465) **6.** us (see page 465) **7.** whoever (see page 476) **8.** me (see page 475) **9.** him (see page 475) **10.** her (see page 474)

Writer's Resources Now™   If you use Writer's ResourcesNow, please have your students log in and view the pretest, study plan, and posttest for this chapter.

31

Adjectives and Adverbs

© James Marshall /CORBIS

GET WRITING

Fewer employers now provide pensions. More and more workers have to manage their own retirement savings. Do you think that most people know enough about the stock market to make smart decisions? Should schools teach young people about financial planning? Do you feel prepared to save for your retirement?

Write one or more paragraphs explaining how much you know about investing.

What Are Adjectives and Adverbs?

The most important words in any sentence are the subject—the main idea or topic—and the verb—which connects the subject to action or other words. Adjectives and adverbs add meaning to a sentence by telling us more about nouns and verbs.

Adjectives are words and phrases that describe nouns and pronouns.

a *new* shirt   he was *tall*   a *unique old* car

Adverbs are words and phrases that describe verbs, adjectives, and other adverbs. They generally end in *-ly*.

she walked *quickly*   *fiercely* debated   a *freshly* painted room

Both add meaning to basic sentences.

Basic Sentence
George bought a car.

Basic Sentence Enhanced with Adjectives
George bought a *battered old* car that was *cheap* and *easy to repair*.

Basic Sentence Enhanced with Adjectives and Adverbs
George *recently* bought a *severely* battered old car that was cheap and *very* easy to repair.

WHAT DO YOU KNOW?

Identify the modifiers in each sentence by underlining adjectives and circling adverbs.

1. The former mayor stunned her dedicated supporters by suddenly announcing she was dropping out of the heated Senate race to pursue an acting career.

2. We drove carefully through the thick fog looking for the small cottage.

3. She sang softly while her brother conducted the newly reorganized band.

4. The players cautiously followed the coach's radical training techniques.

5. The old taxi bounced loudly down the winding road.

   Answers appear on the following page.

GET WRITING

WHAT ARE YOU TRYING TO SAY?

Describe a person you admire in action, such as a quarterback throwing a touchdown pass, a singer performing a hit song, a politician giving a speech, or a parent helping a small child.

_____

_____

_____

_____

_____

_____

_____

_____

_____

_____

_____

_____

_____

_____

WHAT HAVE YOU WRITTEN?

Read through your description and underline each adjective and circle each adverb. Notice how important modifiers are in expressing your ideas. If you eliminated the adjectives and adverbs, would your writing have the same effect? Would readers be able to appreciate what you are trying to say?

Understanding Adjectives

Some words are clearly adjectives because they describe other words. They add information about nouns and pronouns, telling us about their age, shape, color, quality, quantity, or character.

old	rectangular	green	wealthy	plentiful
new	straight	blue	impoverished	rare
unique	round	violet	firm	few
futuristic	square	orange	broken	numerous

Some adjectives are formed from nouns and verbs and have distinct endings.

Noun Form	Adjective	Verb Form	Adjective
North	Northern	rent	rented
law	legal	practice	practiced
navy	naval	slice	sliced
Bible	Biblical	reserve	reserved

Past participles (past-tense verbs) are adjectives—*stolen* cars, *ripped* skirt, *chosen* one, *known* felon, *forgotten* keys.

Other nouns and verbs appear as adjectives with no spelling change. You can tell they are adjectives only by context, their position in a sentence.

We bought *house* insurance.　　Put that in the *book* display.
George gave me a *steel* lock.　　We put in a *tile* floor.
They wear *plastic* helmets.　　It was found on the *ocean* floor.

> **ANSWERS TO WHAT DO YOU KNOW? ON PAGE 482**
> **1.** adj: former, dedicated, heated, Senate, acting; adv: suddenly
> **2.** adj: thick, small; adv: carefully
> **3.** adj: reorganized; adv: softly, newly **4.** adj: radical, training; adv: cautiously **5.** adj: old, winding; adv: loudly

These words serve as adjectives because they add meaning to nouns.

What kind of insurance?	*house* insurance	Which display?	*book* display
What kind of lock?	*steel* lock	What kind of floor?	*tile* floor
What kind of helmet?	*plastic* helmet	What kind of floor?	*ocean* floor

ADJECTIVES AND PLURAL NOUNS

In many languages, such as Spanish, adjectives must agree with the nouns they modify. In English there is only one noun form for both singular and plural nouns.

Singular
He wore an *old* suit.

Plural
He wore *old* suits.

EXERCISE 1 Identifying Adjectives

Underline the adjectives in each sentence.

1. The Green Bay Packers is one of the oldest teams in the NFL and perhaps the most unique.

2. All other teams have a single owner, but the Packers organization is a public company with over 100,000 shareholders.

3. Formed in 1919, the Packers became a professional franchise in 1921.

4. Financial problems forced the team to seek additional support.

5. The new backers, nicknamed "The Hungry Five," created the Green Bay Packers Football Corporation.

6. The Packers achieved their greatest fame in the 1960s under the firm leadership of Vince Lombardi, who guided the team to win the first two Superbowls.

7. Devoted fans have bought shares of stock in the team, even though the stock pays no dividends and does not increase in value.

8. Packer fans also show their devotion by filling the stadium for every game, whether the team is having a good or bad season.

9. There is a thirty-five-year waiting list for season tickets.

10. Season tickets are often included in fan wills and are often the subject of bitter divorce disputes.

EXERCISE 2 Using Adjectives

Add adjectives in each sentence.

1. I took an exercise class, which was _____ and _____.

2. The _____ dorm was closed for _____ repairs.

3. We stayed at a _____ hotel in the _____ section of the _____ city.

4. Her _____ stories inspired _____ directors to make _____ movies.

5. The _____ car was hard to sell because it was _____.

EXERCISE 3 Using Participles

Past participles are adjectives. Often in speaking, however, people drop the -ed *endings and forget to add them in writing. In each sentence, underline the misused past participle and write out the correct adjective form.*

1. We made sandwiches with <u>slice</u> cheese and <u>dice</u> ham.   *sliced, diced*

2. I had to wear a <u>borrow</u> suit to the prom.   *borrowed*

3. They served <u>corn</u> beef and cabbage and <u>mash</u> potatoes.   *corned, mashed*

4. We have coffee, soda, lemonade, and <u>ice</u> tea.   *iced*

5. We swam in the *heat* pool all day.   *heated*

COMMAS AND ADJECTIVES

Place a comma between two unrelated adjectives describing one noun or pronoun.

> We saw a new, fascinating film.   They offered us a nutritious, inexpensive meal.

Do not place a comma between two related adjectives describing one noun or pronoun.

> We saw a new Woody Allen film.   They offered us hot apple pie.

Apply this simple test to see if you need commas:

1. Read the sentence aloud and place the word *and* between the two adjectives. If the sentence sounds OK, ADD a comma.

> We saw a new *and* fascinating film.   =   sounds OK, add comma

2. If the sentence sounds awkward, DO NOT ADD a comma.

> We saw a new *and* Woody Allen film   =   sounds awkward, no comma needed

ORDER OF MULTIPLE ADJECTIVES

When using two or more adjectives to modify the same noun, you must arrange them according to their meanings. Follow the order indicated below:

- Evaluation   *charming, painful, valid*
- Size   *enormous, large, tiny*
- Shape   *rectangular, round, square*
- Age   *youthful, middle-aged, ancient*
- Color   *orange, blue, brown*
- Nationality   *Libyan, Chinese, Canadian*
- Religion   *Hindu, Catholic, Muslim*
- Material   *concrete, stone, adobe*

Examples:
We rented rooms in a *charming old Spanish* castle.
A *tall young African* gentleman stood behind the pulpit.

Understanding Adverbs

Adverbs describe verbs, adjectives, and other adverbs. They usually add *-ly* to the adjective form:

Adjective	+ *ly*	=	Adverb	Adjective	+ *ly*	=	Adverb
fine	*ly*		finely	intricate	*ly*		intricately
cold	*ly*		coldly	firm	*ly*		firmly
legal	*ly*		legally	scientific	*ly*		scientifically

Other adverbs do not end in *-ly*:

fast	hard	just	right	straight

EXERCISE 4 Identifying Adverbs

Underline the adverbs in each sentence.

1. Charles Babbage is <u>widely</u> regarded as a <u>very</u> significant figure in the history of computers.

2. He planned and <u>partially</u> constructed the first mechanical computing machine in the 1830s.

3. Babbage <u>boldly</u> envisioned a calculating machine operating with <u>precisely</u> punched cards.

4. This remarkable machine would be programmable and have a memory, making it <u>strikingly</u> similar to the electronic machines developed a century later.

5. He demonstrated an early version of what he called his "difference engine" and received a <u>very</u> generous government grant.

6. Babbage traveled <u>widely</u> throughout Europe, visiting factories and universities to learn more about manufacturing.

7. Babbage worked <u>intensely</u>, inventing tools needed to create <u>finely</u> machined parts for his intricate device.

8. Babbage worked <u>tirelessly</u>, facing financial ruin and hostility from critics who <u>increasingly</u> accused him of wasting government funds.

9. Babbage never <u>fully</u> assembled his machine but did develop working parts that allowed researchers to <u>finally</u> create a working model of his invention in 1991.

10. Babbage did <u>successfully</u> create many less-complex inventions, including a speedometer, the skeleton key, and the ophthalmoscope.

EXERCISE 5 Using Adverbs

Add adverbs in each sentence.

1. He sang so _____ and _____ that the audience applauded _____.

2. The _____ controversial policy was _____ debated by the school board.

3. Despite all her hard work, the committee _____ rejected her plan and

_____ refused to pay for her services.

4. The coach _____ taught the new players to follow the _____ successful

techniques that brought her team a/an _____ long string of victories.

5. We drove _____ through the _____ crowded streets on the way to

Tiger Stadium.

Grammar Choices and Meaning

Because both adjectives and adverbs modify other words, they can be easily confused. Changing an adjective to an adverb changes meaning.

Form		*Meaning*
adjective + adjective		
slow rusting car	=	a car that is both slow and rusting
adverb + adjective		
slowly rusting car	=	a car that is gradually rusting
adjective + adjective		
new waxed car	=	a car that is both new and waxed
adverb + adjective		
newly waxed car	=	a car (new or old) that has just been waxed
adjective + adjective		
large fiberglass car	=	a car that is large and made of fiberglass
adverb + adjective		
largely fiberglass car	=	a car (of any size) that is mostly fiberglass

Use adjectives and adverbs precisely in modifying verbs of sense—*see, hear, feel,
smell, touch,* and *taste.*

Adjective:	I feel poor after the accident.	[*poor* modifies the noun *I*, suggesting the writer feels broke or financially distressed by the accident]
Adverb:	I feel poorly after the accident.	[*poorly* modifies the verb *feel*, suggesting the writer is injured or in ill health following the accident]

POINT TO REMEMBER

When speaking, people commonly use the shorter adjective form when an
adverb is needed:

"Drive careful, now"	instead of	"Drive careful*ly*, now"
"Do the tax work accurate."		"Do the tax work accurate*ly*."
"That's real good coffee."		"That's real*ly* good coffee."
"He drove real slow."		"He drove real*ly* slow*ly*."
"She acted crazy."		"She acted crazi*ly*."

In writing, make sure you use adverbs (which often end in *-ly*) to modify
verbs, adjectives, and other adverbs.

Good and *Well*/*Bad* and *Badly*

Two adjective/adverb pairs are commonly confused:

Good and *bad* are adjectives	*Well* and *badly* are adverbs
You look good. [you appear attractive]	You look well. [you appear healthy]
I feel bad. [I am depressed or sick]	I feel badly. [I have difficulty sensing touch]

Good and *bad* modify nouns and pronouns	*Well* and *badly* modify verbs, adjectives, and other adverbs
She looked *good* despite her recent accident.	She walked *well* despite injuring her leg.
She had a *bad* fracture in her right arm.	Her right arm was *badly* fractured.

Good and *bad* and *well* and *badly* have special comparative and superlative forms.

Basic	Comparative	Superlative
good	better	best
bad	worse	worst
well	better	best
badly	worse	worst

This coffee is *good*, but the *best* coffee is served at Rio's.
The traffic is *bad* this morning, but yesterday it was *worse*.
Keri swims *well*, but Nancy is the *best* swimmer on the team.
That is a *badly* directed movie, but the *worst* has to be *Return to Yonkers*.

EXERCISE 6 Selecting the Correct Adjectives and Adverbs

Select the correct adjective or adverb in each sentence.

1. Operation Bernhardt was an (extreme/<u>extremely</u>) devious plan developed by the Nazis to undermine the British economy during World War II.

2. Bernhardt Kruger, an SS major, assembled engravers, forgers, and printers imprisoned in concentration camps and ordered them to begin the (<u>intricate</u>/intricately) task of forging British pounds.

3. The work was (<u>unbelievably</u>/unbelievable) difficult; the inmates had to make (accurately/<u>accurate</u>) engravings, imitate detailed watermarks, and create special papers.

4. The notes they produced were the (<u>best</u>/better) forgeries ever attempted.

5. The Nazi plan was (devilishly/<u>devilish</u>) and simple.

6. The Germans planned to drop pound notes over English towns, assuming that even the most patriotic Britons would keep the bills and (<u>eventually</u>/eventual) spend them, inflating the British economy.

7. Over a 100 million pounds worth of currency was counterfeited, but it was not ready until the last months of the war when it was (<u>extremely</u>/extreme) difficult for the Germans to introduce the money into Britain.

8. With the Nazi Reich (<u>totally</u>/total) collapsing, the Germans dumped the currency in a lake, where divers recovered the bills in 1959.

9. Although most of the phony pounds were hidden, some made their way into circulation and (<u>mysteriously</u>/mysterious) appeared in Britain long after the war.

10. SS Major Kruger was imprisoned after the war by the French, who put him to work (secret/<u>secretly</u>) forging documents for France's intelligence agents.

Comparisons

Adjectives and adverbs are often used in comparing two things. There are three basic rules for showing comparisons:

1. Add -er for adjectives and adverbs with one syllable.

Adjectives
Bill is *smart*.	Bill is *smarter* than Ted.
The car is *old*.	The car is *older* than mine.
The house is *cold*.	The house is *colder* than the garage.

Adverbs
She sang *loudly*.	He sang *louder* than Jane.
She worked *hard*.	She worked *harder* than Ted.
They drive *fast*.	They drive *faster* than I would.

2. Use *more* for adjectives with more than one syllable that do not end in -y.

The damage is *extensive*.	The damage is *more extensive* than we expected.
He is *talented*.	He is *more talented* than critics think.

Use *more* for adverbs, sometimes adding -er to the positive form.

He drove *recklessly*.	He drove *more recklessly* than ever.
They worked *fast*.	They worked *faster*.

3. Add -ier after dropping the -y for adjectives and adverbs ending in -y.

Adjective
The store is *busy*.	The store is *busier* on weekends.

Adverb
He felt *sleepy*.	He felt *sleepier* after his nap.

EXERCISE 7 Using Adjectives and Adverbs in Comparisons

Write out the proper comparative form of each adjective and adverb, then use it in a sentence.

1. **tired** *more tired*

2. **warmly** *more warmly*

3. **hotly** *more hotly*

4. cold *colder*

_____

5. happy *happier*

_____

AVOIDING DOUBLE COMPARISONS

When speaking, some people use double comparisons.

> Sara is *more smarter* than Beth.
> This car is *more older* than mine.
> The final is *more harder* than the midterm.

Because both *more* and *-er* indicate something greater, only one is needed.

> Sara is *smarter* than Beth.
> This car is *older* than mine.
> The final is *harder* than the midterm.

Superlatives

Comparisons show a difference between two items.

> Sam is *taller* than Sean.

To show differences between three or more items, use superlative forms.

> Sam is the *tallest* boy in class.

There are three basic rules for creating superlative adjectives and adverbs:

1. Add *-est* to adjectives and adverbs with one syllable.

Basic	Comparative	Superlative
cold	colder	coldest
slow	slower	slowest
cheap	cheaper	cheapest

2. Add *-iest* after dropping the *y* in adjectives and adverbs that end in *-y*.

Basic	Comparative	Superlative
witty	wittier	wittiest
easy	easier	easiest
icy	icier	iciest

3. Use *most* for adjectives and adverbs with two or more syllables that do not end in *-y*.

Basic	Comparative	Superlative
affordable	more affordable	most affordable
cordial	more cordial	most cordial
depressing	more depressing	most depressing

POINTS TO REMEMBER

Remember that superlatives—which usually end in *-est*—are used only when writing about three or more items. Many people mistakenly use superlatives instead of comparisons when writing about only two items.

Incorrect Use of Superlatives
Sara is the *eldest* of our two daughters.
In comparing New York and Chicago, New York is the *biggest*.

Correct Use of Comparison
Sara is the *elder* of our two daughters.
In comparing New York and Chicago, New York is *bigger*.

Do not use superlatives with absolute words such as *impossible, perfect, round, destroyed,* or *demolished.* These terms have no degree. If something is *impossible*, it means that it is not possible, not just difficult. If a building is *destroyed*, it is damaged beyond all repair. To say it is "completely destroyed" is repetitive, like saying someone is "completely dead."

Incorrect
The house was completely demolished.
The room was perfectly round.

Correct
The house was demolished.
The room was round.

EXERCISE 8 Eliminating Adjective and Adverb Errors

Revise each of the following sentences to eliminate errors in using adjectives and adverbs.

1. **Born in Alabama, Zora Neale Hurston grew up in Florida and later traveled north to attend Barnard College and Columbia University in the 1920s when most black women had extreme limited educational opportunities.**

   Born in Alabama, Zora Neale Hurston grew up in Florida and later traveled north to attend Barnard College and Columbia University in the 1920s when most black women had extremely limited educational opportunities.

2. **Hurston collected African American folklore and became one of the most wide published black writers in the 1930s and 1940s.**

   Hurston collected African American folklore and became one of the most widely published black writers in the 1930s and 1940s.

3. **Generous supported by patrons, Hurston traveled extensive throughout the South, as well as Haiti, Jamaica, and the Bahamas to conduct research.**

   Generously supported by patrons, Hurston traveled extensively throughout the South, as well as Haiti, Jamaica, and the Bahamas to conduct research.

4. Hurston became a leading figure in the Harlem Renaissance, making many influential friends and demonstrating her remarkably knowledge of African American folk culture and language.

   Hurston became a leading figure in the Harlem Renaissance, making many influential friends and demonstrating her remarkable knowledge of African American folk culture and language.

5. Some critics, however, found her homey stories about dialect-speaking African Americans unacceptable sentimental.

   Some critics, however, found her homey stories about dialect-speaking African Americans unacceptably sentimental.

6. They firmly believed that black writers should address the poorly conditions African Americans faced and that it was more better to focus on current political issues rather than old folktales.

   They firmly believed that black writers should address the poor conditions African Americans faced and that it was better to focus on current political issues rather than old folktales.

7. Hurston's objections to some aspects of the civil rights movement more further alienated her critics.

   Hurston's objections to some aspects of the civil rights movement further alienated her critics.

8. She died poorly and largely forgotten in 1960, her books having gone out of print.

   She died poor and largely forgotten in 1960, her books having gone out of print.

9. Fifteen years later, an article by Alice Walker sparked interest in Hurston, and many scholars began to read this new rediscovered author.

   Fifteen years later, an article by Alice Walker sparked interest in Hurston, and many scholars began to read this newly rediscovered author.

10. Hurston's books, once wide dismissed for being superficial, are now seen as serious works that very accurate captured the life and language of an era.

    Hurston's books, once widely dismissed for being superficial, are now seen as serious works that very accurately captured the life and language of an era.

WORKING TOGETHER

Working with a group of students, review this e-mail for errors in adjective and adverb use. Underline mistakes and discuss corrections. Note how changing modifiers changes meaning.

Dear Kayla:

I read your report today. I agree we must take immediately action. I was not aware that it was so remarkable easy for people to access our customers' personal data. I feel very badly about any potential loss of extreme sensitive data.

Cindy Diamond in the legal department says that we could face an immensely liability if any data were stolen and our customers became victims of identity theft.

I think the most best thing you can do is talk to Frank Harrison and Sandy Berger tomorrow when you are in New York. I will send them an e-mail tonight and attach your notes. Frank and Sandy have the authority to upgrade security systems throughout the company.

I appreciate you bringing this to my attention so quick.

Dayton Cooper

CRITICAL THINKING

GET THINKING
AND WRITING

In most states, nearly half the inmates who complete their sentences commit crimes when they return to society and end up back in prison. What do you think could make prisons more effective—more job training, drug and alcohol counseling, or tougher policies? Write one or more paragraphs stating your views.

WHAT HAVE YOU WRITTEN?

Read your paragraphs, underlining each adjective and circling each adverb. Review the rules explained in this chapter. Have you used modifiers correctly?

WHAT HAVE YOU LEARNED?

Select the correct adjective or adverb in each sentence.

1. I tripped on the (loose / loosely) gravel on the (bad / badly) maintained driveway.

2. This is the (worse / worst) restaurant in town!

3. California Pacific is the (best / better) of the two insurance companies.

4. It was (impossible / totally impossible) to get to the airport on time.

5. I bought the (new waxed / newly waxed) '87 Corvette.

> **ANSWERS TO WHAT HAVE YOU LEARNED?**
> **1.** loose (see page 482), badly (see page 488) **2.** worst (see page 490) **3.** better (see page 489) **4.** impossible (see page 491) **5.** newly waxed (see page 487)

WRITING ON THE WEB

Using a search engine such as Yahoo!, Google, or AltaVista, enter terms such as *adjective, adverb,* and *modifier* to locate current sites of interest.

POINTS TO REMEMBER

1. *Adjectives* modify nouns and pronouns; *adverbs* modify verbs, adjectives, and other adverbs.

   Note: Use adjectives and adverbs carefully when referring to verbs like *see, hear, feel, smell, touch, and taste*:

   adjective: I see *good* coming from this. = I predict good results.
   adverb: I see *well*. = I have good eyesight.

2. Past participles are adjectives:

   a *rented* car   a *broken* window   *mashed* potatoes

   Note: In speaking, many people drop the *-ed* ending, but it should always be used in writing. Write "mashed potatoes" *not* "mash potatoes."

3. Most adverbs end in *-ly* with some exceptions:

   hard   fast   right   just   straight

   Note: In speaking, many people commonly drop adverb endings, but they should always be used in writing. Write "drive carefully" *not* "drive careful."

4. Adjective and adverb use affect meaning:

   fresh sliced bread = sliced bread that is fresh
   freshly sliced bread = bread (fresh or stale) that has just been sliced

5. *Good* and *bad* are adjectives that describe nouns and pronouns:

   I feel good = I am healthy or happy   I feel bad = I am sad

   Well and *badly* are adverbs that describe verbs, adjectives, or other adverbs:

   I feel well = I have a good   I feel badly = I have a poor
   sense of touch   sense of touch

6. Use proper comparative form to discuss two items:

   Tom is *taller* than Barry.   My car is *more* expensive than hers.

   Note: Avoid using double comparisons, such as "more better."

7. Use proper superlative form to discuss three or more items:

   Tom is the *tallest* boy.   My car is the *most expensive*.

   Note: Avoid using superlatives to compare only two items, such as "eldest of my two girls."

8. Do not use superlatives with words like *impossible, destroyed, perfect, demolished*, or *round*:

Incorrect	*Correct*
The house was completely destroyed.	The house was destroyed.
That is totally impossible.	That is impossible.
The room was perfectly round.	The room was round.

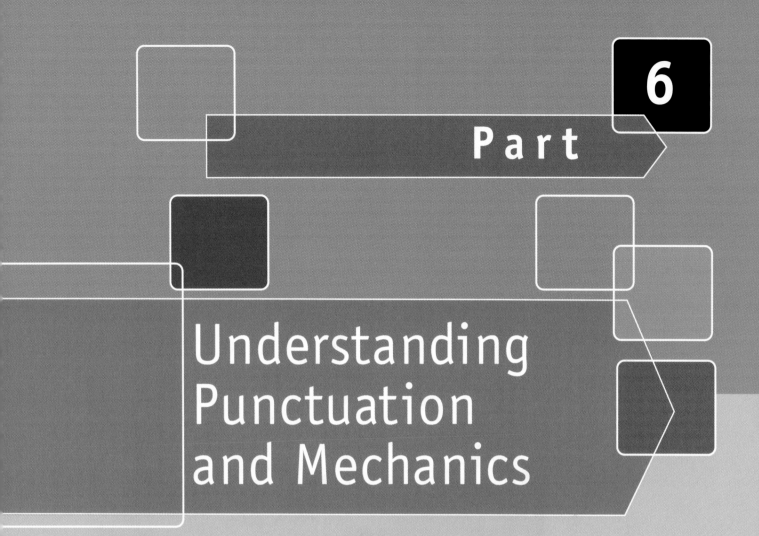

Part

6

Understanding Punctuation and Mechanics

Commas and Semicolons

© Peter Morgan / Reuters / Corbis

Do you think that the justice system treats rich and poor defendants differently? Are white-collar criminals treated differently than street criminals?

Write one or more paragraphs expressing your views.

What Are Commas and Semicolons?

Commas [,] and semicolons [;] are two of the most common—and often misused—marks of punctuation. Because they function like road signs, directing the way we read sentences, they are very important.

WHAT DO YOU KNOW?

Insert commas and semicolons where needed in the following sentences.

1. Anyone who wants to quit smoking should consider hypnosis.

2. My brother who wants to quit smoking has tried the patch.

3. On April 15 2005 the Akron Ohio office announced it was merging with the offices in Canton Ohio and La Crosse Wisconsin.

4. First we have to start saving money.

5. Washington Lincoln Roosevelt and Reagan were among the most influential and for some the most controversial presidents.

6. Education I have long argued is a lifelong process.

7. Iran exports oil China imports oil.

8. Tom got a job in San Jose Karen got a job in La Jolla.

9. The seminar on countering terrorism included Taylor Gray a former FBI agent Brooke Stefani a security consultant and Sandy Shimi an Iranian dissident.

10. Because a blizzard is predicted for tomorrow we are postponing the board meeting until next Monday.

   Answers appear on the following page.

WHAT ARE YOU TRYING TO SAY?　　　　　　　　　*GET WRITING*

Write a paragraph describing your favorite restaurant. Include details about the atmosphere, the clientele, and the menu.

_____

_____

_____

_____

_____

_____

_____

_____

_____

_____

_____

_____

_____

_____

_____

_____

WHAT HAVE YOU WRITTEN?

Circle the commas and semicolons that appear in your paragraph.

1. Can you provide a reason for inserting each comma?
2. Do you insert commas almost on reflex, without thought?
3. Do you sometimes think you miss needed commas or put them where they don't belong?
4. Do you know if any of your commas should be semicolons?

ANSWERS TO WHAT DO YOU KNOW? ON PAGE 497

1. Anyone who wants to quit smoking should consider hypnosis.
2. My brother, who wants to quit smoking, has tried the patch.
3. On April 15, 2005, the Akron, Ohio, office announced it was merging with the offices in Canton, Ohio, and La Crosse, Wisconsin.
4. First, we have to start saving money.
5. Washington, Lincoln, Roosevelt, and Reagan were among the most influential and, for some, the most controversial presidents.
6. Education, I have long argued, is a lifelong process.
7. Iran exports oil; China imports oil.
8. Tom got a job in San Jose; Karen got a job in La Jolla.
9. The seminar on countering terrorism included Taylor Gray, a former FBI agent; Brooke Stefani, a security consultant; and Sandy Shimi, an Iranian dissident.
10. Because a blizzard is predicted for tomorrow, we are postponing the board meeting until next Monday.

The Comma **,**

When we talk, we pause to separate ideas or create emphasis. In writing, we use commas to signal pauses and shifts in sentences. Commas are the most common mark of punctuation used within sentences. By habit you may automatically insert the commas correctly, just as you remember to capitalize a person's name or place a period at the end of a sentence. However, there are probably times when you are confused about where you should put commas.

Commas work like hooks that attach extra ideas to a basic sentence:

Kim became a citizen.
After studying American history and English, **Kim,** who was born in Korea, **became a citizen,** which enables him to get an American passport.

(Read this sentence aloud and notice the pauses you instinctively make to signal shifts in the flow of ideas.)

Comma mistakes, like spelling errors, can seem like minor flaws, but they weaken your writing and make your ideas hard to understand. Remember, when you are writing you are taking your readers on a journey. If you use commas correctly, they will be able to follow your train of thought without getting lost. Consider how commas change the meaning of these sentences:

The teachers say the students don't care.
The teachers, say the students, don't care.

Let's eat candy.
Let's eat, Candy.

We need coffee, tea, ice water, and soft drinks.
We need coffee, tea, ice, water, and soft drinks.

Saddling up to leave, Nevada Smith took all the gold.
Saddling up to leave Nevada, Smith took all the gold.

The best way to master comma use is to first review all the rules, then concentrate on the ones you do not understand or find confusing.

Comma Uses

Commas have ten basic uses.

1. **Use commas with *and, or, nor, yet, but, for,* or *so* to join independent clauses to create compound sentences and avoid run-ons** (see Chapter 25). When you join two independent clauses (simple sentences), use a comma and the appropriate coordinating conjunction:

   China is a land of ancient culture, **and** it is an emerging industrial power.

   We have to buy a new car, **or** we have to fix the old one.

   Gas prices increased, **yet** sales of SUVs soared.

   She was immensely popular, **but** she decided not to run for reelection.

   I have a headache, **so** I am leaving early.

   Note: In informal writing, some writers omit commas in very short compound sentences:

   I flew but she drove.   Carla jogs and she lifts weights.

POINT TO REMEMBER

Use commas with *and, or, nor, yet, but, for,* or *so* only to join two independent clauses not pairs of words or phrases.

Unnecessary Commas:
They served coffee, and tea.

Outsourcing manufacturing jobs, and declining profits in the banking industry hurt the town's economy.

Ted was in poor shape when he moved here, but began jogging and lost thirty pounds.

Correct
They served coffee and tea.

Outsourcing manufacturing jobs and declining profits in the banking industry hurt the town's economy.

Ted was in poor shape when he moved here but began jogging and lost thirty pounds.

To see if you need a comma with *and, or, nor, yet, but, for,* or *so,* apply this test:

1. Place a period just before the coordinating conjunction. If there is a complete sentence on the left and the right, *add* the comma.
2. If placing a period creates a fragment, *omit* the comma.

---

2. **Use a comma after a dependent clause that opens a complex sentence.**

    Because the school lost power, classes were cancelled.
    After she registered for classes, Juanita applied for financial aid.
    While we waited for our flight, we rehearsed our presentations.

    If the dependent clause follows the independent clause, the comma is usually omitted:

    Classes were cancelled because the school lost power.
    Juanita applied for financial aid after she registered for classes.
    We rehearsed our presentations while we waited for our flight.

    Writers often omit commas if the opening clause is short and commas are not needed to prevent confusion:

    After he left we celebrated.   Before I run I stretch.

3. **Use a comma after a long phrase or introductory word.** To prevent confusion, commas should follow long phrases that open sentences. There is no clear definition of a "long phrase," so use your judgment. A short opening phrase may not require a comma to prevent confusion:

    After lunch let's go to the beach.

    Longer phrases should be set off with commas to prevent confusion and signal the shift in ideas:

    After lunch with our parents and the new counselors, let's go to the beach.

    Introductory words such as interjections or transitions are set off with commas to prevent confusion and dramatize a shift in ideas:

    No, I can't take your check.   Amazingly, no one was injured in the accident.

    First, we have to make a plan.   Wait, you forgot your keys!

4. **Use commas to separate words, phrases, and clauses in a series:**

> *Words*
> I bought gas, oil, and tires.

> *Note:* Many writers omit the final comma before the conjunction:
> I bought gas, oil and tires.

> Most editors add the final comma to prevent possible confusion:
> We needed salads, soup, ham and cheese sandwiches.
> [Do you need ham and sandwiches made with cheese or ham and cheese sandwiches?]

> *Phrases*
> I bought gas, changed the oil, and rotated the tires.

> *Clauses*
> I bought gas, Sandy changed the oil, and Jim rotated the tires.

> *Note:* If clauses contain commas, separate them with semicolons (see pages 507–509).

EXERCISE 1 Add Commas Where Needed in Complex and Compound Sentences and to Separate Items in a Series

Add commas where needed to set off elements in a series.

1. Ambrose Bierce, Judge Crater, and Jimmy Hoffa are among the most famous missing persons of the twentieth century.

2. Ambrose Bierce was a newspaper columnist, an editor, a short story writer and critic, and he became a noted social figure and friend of Mark Twain.

3. In 1913 he went to Mexico, and he rode along with Pancho Villa's soldiers.

4. In December he sent a friend a letter predicting he might be shot, and Bierce then vanished without a trace, and his disappearance led to endless failed investigations.

5. In August 1930, Judge Crater left a Manhattan restaurant, got into a taxi, and was never seen again.

6. People speculated that he had run off with another woman, been killed by gangsters, or fled the country before he could be exposed in a scandal.

7. Although it was discovered that he cleaned out his office and cashed several checks before he left, little more was learned about Judge Crater, and he was declared dead in 1939.

8. Jimmy Hoffa was president of the powerful Teamsters Union in the 1960s, but he was sent to prison for fraud and jury tampering.

9. After he was released on parole, Hoffa sought to regain control over the Teamsters, and he agreed to meet two Mafia leaders for lunch to discuss his situation.

10. On July 30, 1975, Hoffa went to a restaurant in suburban Detroit, and he was never seen again, although many speculated he was murdered.

5. **Use commas to set off nonrestrictive or parenthetical words or phrases.** In some sentences you will notice a phrase such as *who is my friend* set off with commas, then see the same phrase in another sentence without commas. Whether or not a word or phrase is set off with commas depends on whether it is *nonrestrictive* or *restrictive*. When a word or words simply describe or add extra information about a noun, they are **nonrestrictive** and set off with commas. *Nonrestrictive* words are parenthetical and can be taken out of the sentence without changing the meaning of the noun they describe. If the words limit or define the noun, they are **restrictive** and *not* set off with commas. *Restrictive* words tells us more about a general or abstract noun like *anyone, someone, student, person,* or *parent:*

> Anyone *who wants to lose weight* . . .
> Someone *who exercises daily* . . .
> The citizen *who fails to vote* . . .
> Any student *who takes too many courses* . . .
> Each homeowner *who complains about traffic* . . .

These phrases limit or define the subject. Without them the nouns lose much of their meaning. These *restrictive* phrases are part of the noun and therefore are not set off with commas. These same words could be *nonrestrictive* and set off with commas if they followed more specific nouns:

> George, *who wants to lose weight* . . .
> Jenna, *who exercises daily* . . .
> My sister, *who fails to vote* . . .

In each case the phrase only adds extra information about a clearly defined noun. Removing the phrase from the sentence does not change the meaning of the noun:

Nonrestrictive	*Restrictive*
Adds extra information about a noun; commas needed	Defines or limits the noun; no commas
My father, who wants to quit smoking, should try hypnosis.	**Anyone who wants to quit smoking should try hypnosis.**
My father can only refer to one person; *who wants to quit smoking* only adds EXTRA information about him.	*Anyone* refers to any person; *who wants to quit smoking* defines which person should try hypnosis.
Tina Brown, who hosts a TV show, will moderate the debate.	**The editor who hosts a TV show will moderate the debate.**
Tina Brown clearly defines the noun, so her hosting a TV show only adds an extra detail about her.	*who hosts a TV show* defines which editor will moderate.

POINT TO REMEMBER

To determine whether a phrase or clause is *restrictive* or *nonrestrictive*, just think of the term "ID." If the phrase or clause "IDs" or identifies the noun, it is *restrictive* and should *not* be set off with commas.

> Will the student who missed the test see me after class?
> Which student? *the student who missed the test*
> The phrase *who missed the test* IDs which student.   *no commas*

If the phrase or clause does *not* "ID" the noun but only adds *extra* information, it is nonrestrictive and should be set off with commas.

> Will Sam, who missed the test, see me after class?
> Which student? *Sam*
> The phrase *who missed the test* only adds *extra* information about
> *Sam,* who is defined by his name.   *add commas*

If the phrase or clause IDs the noun—no commas
If the phrase or clause is *extra*—add commas

EXERCISE 2 Restrictive and Nonrestrictive Elements

Insert commas where needed to set off nonrestrictive phrases and clauses. Remember, no commas are needed if the phrase or clause defines or IDs the noun.

1. Iran, which was known as Persia until 1935, is an important nation in the Middle East.

2. The Iranians, who speak Farsi, are Persians and not Arabs.

3. The country, which is a major oil producer, has had complex and often conflicting relations with the West.

4. The United States, which sought to contain communism in the 1950s, assisted the exiled Shah to regain power in Iran.

5. The Shah, who saw himself destined to lead his country onto the international stage, launched the White Revolution, which expanded women's rights, redistributed land, and built schools.

6. Many Iranians who objected to the Shah's reforms, pro-Western policies, and repressive police force supported the Islamic leader Ayatollah Khomeini.

7. The Shah was forced to leave Iran in 1979 by the Islamic Revolution, which led to the formation of an Islamic Republic that was extremely hostile to the United States.

8. Iranians who did not want to live in a nation ruled by strict Muslim principles fled the country, and many settled in the United States.

9. Many Iranians who live in the United States have nicknamed Los Angeles, which is now home to as many as half a million Iranian-Americans, "Tehrangeles."

10. Catherine Bell, who appeared on the TV show *JAG*, and the entrepreneur who founded eBay are among the growing population of Iranian-Americans.

6. **Use commas to set off contrasted elements.** To prevent confusion and highlight contrast, set off words and phrases with commas to signal abrupt or important shifts in a sentence:

> The children, not the parents, want better schools.
> Our dean, unlike the other administrators, wants to limit enrollment.

7. **Use commas after interjections, words used in direct address, and around direct quotations:**

> Hey, you dropped your keys.
> Karen, did you get my e-mail?
> Carlos shouted, "Help, call an ambulance," to Melissa as she came into the room.

8. **Use commas to separate city and state or city and country, items in dates, and every three numerals above 1,000:**

> Cindy was born in Atco, New Jersey, on November 24, 1986, and moved to London, England, where she earned over $100,000 in January 2006 singing in nightclubs.

Note: A comma goes after states, countries, or dates if followed by other words. No comma is needed if only the month and year are given.

9. **Use commas to set off absolute phrases.** Absolute phrases are groups of words that are not grammatically connected to other parts of sentences. To prevent confusion, they are attached to the main sentence with a comma:

> Unable to compete with discount stores, Housegoods USA increased its catalog operations.
> Frank painted the lobby and trimmed the lawn, hoping to attract more renters.

10. **Use commas where needed to prevent confusion or add emphasis.** Writers add commas to create pauses and signal shifts in the flow of words to prevent readers from becoming confused:

> *Confusing*
> Wherever they ate free coffee was served.
> For Karen Hughes Tool was a great place to work.
> To help the homeless people donate clothes.

Improved
Wherever they ate, free coffee was served.
For Karen, Hughes Tool was a great place to work.
To help the homeless, people donate clothes.

Note: Reading sentences aloud can help you spot sentences that need commas to prevent confusion. Listen to where you make pauses.

Writers often use commas for special effect, not to prevent confusion but to emphasize words, phrases, and ideas. Because readers pause when they see a comma, it forces them to slow down and pay additional attention to a word or phrase:

Without Comma	*With Comma for Emphasis*
Today I start my diet.	Today, I start my diet.

EXERCISE 3 Comma Use

Insert commas where needed in each sentence.

1. The Great Wall of China consists of 1,500 miles of fortifications, walls, guard towers, and barracks in northern China.

2. The wall, which was built over a thousand years, was not a single project but a series of separate defensive fortifications that were connected.

3. Local residents were forced to build the wall, and many of them were killed by gangs of attacking bandits.

4. Because so many laborers died during its construction, the Great Wall earned a grim nickname, "the longest cemetery in the world."

5. The wall was made of mostly stone and brick, although some portions in desert regions were constructed of wooden fences and earthworks.

6. Although parts of the Great Wall have been carefully restored, much of it has deteriorated over the years.

7. Developers have bulldozed sections to make way for new construction, and farmers have taken stones for building materials.

8. It has been often stated that the Great Wall of China is the only man-made object visible from the moon.

9. In fact, shuttle astronauts have reported that they could make out the Wall when in orbit a hundred miles or so above the earth.

10. Since the moon is over 200,000 miles from earth, however, it is impossible to see the Great Wall, or any other man-made object, from its surface without the use of high-powered telescopes.

Avoiding Unnecessary Commas

Because commas have so many uses, it is easy to place them where they are not needed. After reviewing all the rules, you may find yourself putting commas where they don't belong.

GUIDE TO ELIMINATING UNNECESSARY COMMAS

1. Don't put a comma between a subject and verb unless setting off non-restrictive elements or a series:

   The old car, was stolen.

   Correct
   The car, which was old, was stolen.

2. Don't use commas to separate prepositional phrases from what they modify:

   The van, in the driveway, needs new tires.

   Correct
   The van in the driveway needs new tires.

3. Don't use commas to separate two items in a compound verb:

   They sang, and danced at the party.

   Correct
   They sang and danced at the party.

4. Don't put commas around titles:

   The film opens with, "Love Me Tender," and shots of Elvis.

   Correct
   The film opens with "Love Me Tender" and shots of Elvis.

5. Don't put commas after a series unless it ends a clause that has to be set off from the rest of the sentence:

   They donated computers, printers, and telephones, to our office.

   Correct
   They donated computers, printers, and telephones, and we provided office space.

6. Don't set off a dependent clause with a comma when it ends a sentence:

   The game was cancelled, because the referees went on strike.

   Correct
   The game was cancelled because the referees went on strike.

   Note: A comma is needed if a dependent clause opens the sentence:
   Because the referees went on strike, the game was cancelled.

EXERCISE 4 Comma Use

Correct comma use in the following passage, adding missing commas where needed and deleting unnecessary commas.

While watching an indoor soccer game, in 1981 Jim Foster a former NFL executive got an idea. If soccer usually an outdoor sport could be played inside why not American football? Foster changed standard football rules played experimental games and finally in 1990 patented what he called arena football. The game follows the basic rules of NFL football with some key exceptions. The field for example is only 50 yards long and teams consist of 8 instead of 11 players. Most players have to play both offense and defense except for the quarterback kickers one offensive specialist and two defensive specialists. Because there are fewer time-outs and rebounded balls stay in play the game is faster paced than traditional football. Arena football, is gaining fans not only because of its speed, but its lower ticket prices.

While watching an indoor soccer game in 1981, Jim Foster, a former NFL executive, got an idea. If soccer, usually an outdoor sport, could be played inside, why not American football? Foster changed standard football rules, played experimental games, and, finally in 1990, patented what he called arena football. The game follows the basic rules of NFL football with some key exceptions. The field, for example, is only 50 yards long, and teams consist of 8 instead of 11 players. Most players have to play both offense and defense, except for the quarterback, kickers, one offensive specialist, and two defensive specialists. Because there are fewer time-outs and rebounded balls stay in play, the game is faster paced than traditional football. Arena football is gaining fans, not only because of its speed but its lower ticket prices.

Semicolons ;

What Are Semicolons?

You can think of semicolons as capitalized commas. They are used to connect larger items—clauses and complex items in a list.
Semicolons have two uses.

1. **Use semicolons to join independent clauses when *and, or, nor, yet, but, for,* or *so* are not present:**

   We flew to San Diego; Jack and Jean drove.
   Florida is a popular winter resort; Maine attracts summer visitors.

   Note: Remember to use semicolons even when you use words such as *nevertheless, moreover,* and *however:*

   We missed our flight; however, we arrived at the wedding on time.

   The invention increases fuel efficiency; moreover, it is easy to install.

2. **Use semicolons to separate items in a series that contain commas.** Normally commas separate items in a list:

   They will arrive in limos, buses, taxis, and rented cars.

However, if items in the list contain commas, it is difficult to tell which commas are separating items and which commas are separating elements within a single item:

> The governor will meet with Dr. Mendoza, dean of the law school, Dr. Carol Nezgod, dean of health sciences, Professor George Richter, the dean of the business school, and the college auditor.

How many people will the governor meet? Is Dr. Mendoza the dean of the law school or are Dr. Mendoza and the dean two different people? To prevent confusion, semicolons are inserted to separate items in the series:

> The governor will meet with Dr. Mendoza, dean of the law school; Dr. Carol Nezgod, dean of health sciences; Professor George Richter; the dean of the business school; and the college auditor.

The governor will meet with five people:

1. Dr. Mendoza, dean of the law school
2. Dr. Carol Nezgod, dean of health sciences
3. Professor George Richter
4. the dean of the business school
5. the college auditor

EXERCISE 5 Understanding Semicolons

Underline the items in each list and enter the number in the right column.

1. The school hired a math teacher; Ted Hines, a web designer; Jan Price; and a reading specialist. # 4

2. We read *Death of a Salesman*; *The Great Gatsby*, the novel by F. Scott Fitzgerald; a novel by Camus; a poem by Frost; "The Swimmer," an interesting story by John Cheever; and my favorite, "The Cask of Amontillado" by Edgar Allan Poe. # 6

3. The class included my sister; Candy, her roommate; Tom Drake; Don Bernstein; Tom Price; Tom's sister; Carlos Abrams, an exchange student from Chile; a student from France; and myself. # 9

4. This summer the college will repair the men's dorm; Wilson Hall, the senior women's dorm; Tara Hall, the Irish genealogy library; the math lab; and Osgood Hall, the oldest building on campus. # 5

5. We considered our all-time favorite TV shows and came up with a long list, including my favorite soap opera; *Streets of San Francisco*, Sandy's favorite show; *Saturday Night Live* with Eddie Murphy; *LA Law*; *All in the Family*; the original *Twilight Zone*, Sid's choice; and of course, *Star Trek*. # 7

EXERCISE 6 Comma and Semicolon Use

Insert commas and semicolons where needed in each sentence.

1. The names Harry Horwitz, Jerry Horwitz, and Louis Feinberg are not well known; however, their stage names, Moe, Curly, and Larry, are famous the world over.

2. As the Three Stooges, the Horwitz brothers and their friend created a comedy team that, with some cast changes, would produce almost two hundred comedy films from the early 1930s to the late 1950s.

3. The act got its name from Ted Healy, who originally billed them as "Ted Healy and his Stooges" in vaudeville houses.

4. In the early days, Moe and Curly's brother Samuel, who used the name Shemp, was part of the act, but he left to pursue a movie career.

5. The Stooges were immensely popular; audiences loved their slapstick comedy, wild stage antics, and colorful language.

6. Troubled by Healy's drinking and managing style, the Stooges left vaudeville to sign a contract with Columbia Pictures, which hired the team to make a series of shorts.

7. The Stooges began a long run, making films on low budgets within a few days.

8. When the demand for short films dwindled in the 1950s, Columbia stopped producing the Stooge films, and the comedians were out of work.

9. Columbia, however, found a new market for their library of old Stooge shorts; they sold them to television.

10. Although the Three Stooges made no money when their films appeared on television, the renewed interest created a fan base; the comics profited from a new career of making public appearances, working nightclubs, and performing on variety shows.

WORKING TOGETHER

Working with a group of students, edit this e-mail and add commas and semicolons where needed. Note how adding correct punctuation makes the message easier to read.

Dear Stan:

We are planning next year's convention which will be held July 7-9 in San Diego California. I am putting together the initial plans early next week and I would appreciate your input.

Right now we are anticipating that the main presenters will be George Sims Nancy Houghton and Ted Jackson.

According to Frank Taylor all three will be willing to make a general presentation for $4500 apiece and conduct individual seminars for $1500. Because of possible scheduling conflicts George Sims must receive a confirmation by May 30 2006.

Last year's convention drew 12568 attendees and guests this year we expect to draw at least 15000. I am convinced this is a realistic estimate our sales and technical reps are anxious to learn about our new product line.

Stan I look forward to your call. Let's hope we make this convention the best ever.

Lili Holden

CRITICAL THINKING

The president of the United States can only serve two terms. Do you think there should also be term limits for Congress? Would limiting senators and representatives to a few terms allow more people to serve in Washington and open up positions for women and minorities? Would term limits prevent successful politicians from serving again even if they were popular with voters? Write a paragraph stating your views.

Review your writing for comma and semicolon use and other errors. Read your paragraphs aloud. Does this help you discover comma errors, misspelled words, fragments, and awkward phrases?

WHAT HAVE YOU LEARNED?

Insert commas and semicolons where needed in the following sentences.

1. In April 1912 the *Titanic* struck an iceberg and sank on April 27 1912 my great-grandmother was officially listed as lost at sea.

2. The museum will sell the painting for $175000 but insists that payments must be in cash money order or bank draft.

3. I grew up in Westfield New Jersey but we moved to Milwaukee Wisconsin when I was sixteen.

4. The player who gets the most votes will be placed in the hall of fame.

5. The president made a quick tour of Latin America hoping to improve trade relationships his visits to Rio Mexico City La Paz and Buenos Aires were highly successful.

6. Africa exports oil wood carvings cocoa beans and handicrafts.

7. Because interest rates and property taxes are difficult to predict the actual cost of this house is hard to estimate.

8. The police FBI and National Guard searched Manhattan the Bronx Staten Island Queens and Brooklyn for the missing diplomat.

9. Well if the summer is hot we may have to raise prices just to pay for the air-conditioning or we may have to eliminate free deliveries.

10. High school students say that dating and parties are their greatest distractions college students report that job and family responsibilities are their greatest distractions.

Answers appear on the following page.

WRITING ON THE WEB

Using a search engine such as Yahoo!, Google, or AltaVista, enter terms such as *commas, semicolons, using commas, comma drills, comma rules, understanding commas,* and *punctuation* to locate current sites of interest.

POINTS TO REMEMBER

Commas are used for ten reasons:

1. Use commas with *and, or, yet, but,* or *so* to join independent clauses to create compound sentences and avoid run-ons.

   I went to the fair, but Margaret drove to the beach.

2. Use a comma after a dependent clause that opens a complex sentence.

   Before the game began, the coach spoke to her players.

3. Use a comma after a long phrase or introductory word.

   Having waited in the rain for hours, I caught a cold.
   Furthermore, I caught a cold waiting in the rain.

4. Use commas to separate words, phrases, and clauses in a series.

   She bought a battered, rusted, and windowless Model A Ford.
   They dug wells, planted crops, and erected new silos.

5. Use commas to set off nonrestrictive or parenthetical words or phrases.

   Sid, who lives in Chicago, should know a lot about Illinois politics.
   Anyone who lives in Chicago should know a lot about Illinois politics.

6. Use commas to set off contrasted elements.

   Children, not parents, should make this decision.

7. Use commas after interjections, words used in direct address, and around direct quotations.

   Nancy, can you work this Saturday?
   Wait, you forgot your keys.
   Rick said, "We must pay cash," every time we wanted to buy something.

8. Use commas to separate city and state and city and country, items in dates, and every three numerals above 1,000.

   He moved to Topeka, Kansas, on October 15, 2003, and bought a $125,000 house.

9. Use commas to set off absolutes.

   Their plane grounded by fog, the passengers became restless.

10. Use commas where needed to prevent confusion or add emphasis.

    Every time I drive, home is my final destination.
    This morning, we play to win.

Semicolons are used for two reasons:

1. Use semicolons to join independent clauses when *and, or, yet, for, nor, but,* or *so* are not present.

   We walked to school; they took a limo.

2. Use a semicolon to separate items in a series that contain commas.

   I asked Frank, the field manager; Candace, the sales representative; Karla, our attorney; and Erica, the city manager, to attend the budget meeting.

ANSWERS TO WHAT HAVE YOU LEARNED? ON PAGES 510–511.

1. In April 1912, the *Titanic* struck an iceberg and sank; on April 27, 1912, my great-grandmother was officially listed as lost at sea.
2. The museum will sell the painting for $175,000 but insists that payments must be in cash, money order, or bank draft.
3. I grew up in Westfield, New Jersey, but we moved to Milwaukee, Wisconsin, when I was sixteen.
4. The player who gets the most votes will be placed in the hall of fame.
5. The president made a quick tour of Latin America, hoping to improve trade relationships; his visits to Rio, Mexico City, La Paz, and Buenos Aires were highly successful.
6. Africa exports oil, wood carvings, cocoa beans, and handicrafts.
7. Because interest rates and property taxes are difficult to predict, the actual cost of this house is hard to estimate.
8. The police, FBI, and National Guard searched Manhattan, the Bronx, Staten Island, Queens, and Brooklyn for the missing diplomat.
9. Well, if the summer is hot, we may have to raise prices just to pay for the air-conditioning, or we may have to eliminate free deliveries.
10. High school students say that dating and parties are their greatest distractions; college students report that job and family responsibilities are their greatest distractions.

Writer's Resources Now™ If you use Writer's ResourcesNow, please have your students log in and view the pretest, study plan, and posttest for this chapter.

33

Other Marks of Punctuation

© Sagel & Kranefeld/Zefa/Corbis

GET WRITING

Security cameras are now placed in airports, offices, and public spaces all over the world. In Britain, for example, it is estimated that the average citizen is video-taped thirty times a day—walking down a street, driving into a parking lot, entering an office building, or getting onto a train. Do you think cameras designed to protect the public can be misused? Do you think we are losing our privacy?

Write one or more paragraphs stating your views. When you see cameras in a public place, do you feel you are being protected or spied on?

513

What Are the Other Marks of Punctuation?

Writers use punctuation to show when they are quoting other people, presenting parenthetical ideas, posing a question, or creating a contraction. Most students know when to use a question mark or an exclamation point. Other punctuation marks, however, can be confusing, so they are worth looking at in detail.

WHAT DO YOU KNOW?

Add apostrophes, quotation marks, italics, parentheses, question marks, colons, and exclamation points where needed in the following sentences.

1. Alice screamed, Call 911 right now as soon as she saw Tim collapse.

2. Can this really cost $45,000.

3. We need office supplies computer paper, ink, pencils, and stamps.

4. Did you see Miss Saigon on Broadway.

5. Ted and Nancys car wont start because its battery is dead.

6. The mens sale is a big disappointment unless you can wear 48s or 50s.

7. I found her purse on the floor near the womens room.

8. Did you read Can We Save Social Security in Newsweek.

9. I found a boys hat in the childrens library.

10. We drove to Pikes Peak in Sids old Buick.

    Answers appear on the following page.

WHAT ARE YOU TRYING TO SAY?

Write a paragraph listing what you consider to be the best and worst television shows, movies, and songs to appear in the last few years. Provide examples of both types.

_____

_____

_____

_____

_____

_____

_____

_____

_____

_____

_____

_____

Review the punctuation in your paragraph and circle items you think are wrong. ◄

The Apostrophe '

Apostrophes are used for three reasons.

1. **Use apostrophes to indicate possession.** The standard way of showing possession, that someone or something owns something else, is to add an apostrophe and an *-s:*

Noun	Tim's house is two miles away.
Acronym	The NFL's rules will change next season.
Indefinite pronoun	Everyone's ticket is cancelled.
Endings of *s, x,* or *z* sound	Hollis' book is here. [Do not repeat *-s*]

Note: Apostrophes are deleted from geographical names:

Dobsons Creek   Taylors Pond   Warners Crossing

Note: Apostrophes may or may not appear in possessive names or businesses or organizations:

Marshall Field's   Sears   Tigers Stadium   Sean's Pub

Follow the spelling used on signs, stationery, and business cards.
Because an *-s* is added to make many words plural, apostrophes have to be placed carefully to show whether the noun is singular or plural:

Singular	*Plural*
a boy's bike	the boys' bikes
my girl's hat	my girls' hats
her sister's house	her sisters' house (two or more sisters own one house)
a child's book	children's books*
the woman's coat	women's coats*

*Because *children* and *women* already indicate plurals, the apostrophe is placed before the *-s.*

Compound nouns can indicate joint or individual possession. Jim and Erica, for example, could own and share one car, share the use of several vehicles, or own separate cars they drive individually. The placement of apostrophes demonstrates what you mean:

Jim and Erica's car.	Jim and Erica both own one car.
Jim and Erica's cars,	Jim and Erica both own several vehicles.
Jim's and Erica's cars.	Jim and Erica individually own cars.

2. **Use apostrophes to signal missing letters and numbers in contractions.**
   When speaking we often shorten and combine words, so that we say "don't" for "do not" and "could've" for "could have." We also shorten numbers, particularly years, so that we talk about "the Spirit of '76" or refer to a car as a "'99 Mustang." Apostrophes show that letters or numerals have been eliminated to prevent confusion:

shell = an outer casing	she'll = "she will"
well = source of water	we'll = "we will"
cant = trite opinions	can't = "can not"

   Note: Only one apostrophe is used, even if more than one letter is omitted.
   Apostrophes are placed over the missing letter or letters, not where the words are joined:

do not = don't	*NOT*	do'nt.

   Deleted numbers are indicated with a single apostrophe:

   The roof was damaged in the storm of '97.
   He hit two home runs in the '99 World Series.
   She is still driving that '82 Toyota.

3. **Use apostrophes to indicate plurals of letters, numbers, or symbols.**
   Words do not need apostrophes to indicate plurals. An added *-s* or other spelling changes indicate that a noun has been made plural. However, because adding an *-s* could lead to confusion when dealing with individual letters, numbers, or symbols, apostrophes are used to create plurals:

   I got all B's last semester and A's this semester.
   Do we have any size 7's or 8's left?
   We can sell all the 2005's at half price.

   Note: Apostrophes are optional in referring to decades, but be consistent:

   Inconsistent
   The studio was built in the 1970s but was never used until the 1990's.

   Consistent
   The studio was built in the 1970's but was never used until the 1990's.
   or
   The studio was built in the 1970s but was never used until the 1990s.

   Note: Common abbreviations such as TV and DVD do not need apostrophes to indicate plurals:

   We bought new TVs and several DVDs.

POINT TO REMEMBER

it's = contraction of "it is"
>   It's raining.
>   I know it's going to be a long day.

its = possessive of "it"
>   My car won't start. Its battery is dead.
>   The house lost its roof in the storm.

In editing, use this test to see if you need an apostrophe:

1. Read the sentence out loud, substituting *it is* for *its/it's.*
2. If the sentence sounds OK, use *it's:*
>   *It is* going to be hot.
>   It's going to be hot.
3. If the sentence sounds awkward, use *its:*
>   I like *it is* style.
>   I like its style.

EXERCISE 1 Using Apostrophes to Show Possession

Use apostrophes to create possessive forms of nouns.

1. **a book belonging to one boy** — *a boy's book*

2. **money belonging to the people** — *the people's money*

3. **the songs of Frank Sinatra** — *Frank Sinatra's songs*

4. **a fair run by the county** — *the county's fair*

5. **research conducted by NASA** — *NASA's research*

6. **cars owned by my brother-in-law** — *my brother-in-law's cars*

7. **clothing owned by children** — *children's clothing*

8. **stories written by Carla Jones** — *Carla Jones' stories*

9. **a store owned by two women** — *two women's store*

10. **a house owned by Ted and Jill Jackson** — *Ted and Jill Jackson's house*

EXERCISE 2 Using Apostrophes to Show Contractions

Use apostrophes to create contractions of each pair of words.

1. **he is** — *he's*

2. **have not** — *haven't*

3. **he did** — *he'd*

4. **who is** — *who's*

5. **could not** — *couldn't*

6. **does not** — *doesn't*

7. **I will** — *I'll*

8. they are   *they're*

9. should have   *should've*

10. have not   *haven't*

EXERCISE 3 Using Apostrophes

Revise this essay, adding apostrophes where needed.

One of the cold war's most visible symbols was the Berlin Wall, which separated Germany's former capital for almost thirty years. At the end of World War II, the Allies' postwar plans included dividing Germany into different zones of occupation. Berlin lay inside the Soviet sector, but the city itself was divided among the Allies, so that West Berlin became the West's democratic island inside Communist East Germany.

Throughout the 1950s and into the 1960s, East Germans escaped to the West by simply taking a bus or a train to one of the city's western neighborhoods. As many as two thousand people a day fled to the West. East Germany's struggling economy suffered by the country's steady loss of workers and professionals seeking freedom and better-paying jobs. Walter Ulbricht, East Germany's Communist leader, received permission from the Soviet Union's leader Nikita Khrushchev to build a barrier across the border to stop the refugees' flight from East Germany. Khrushchev didn't want to create a crisis, so he ordered East Germany to first build a barrier of barbed wire that could be quickly dismantled if America's forces challenged its plans.

On the night of August 13, 1961, East German troops sealed the border dividing the city's two regions and supervised the erection of a barbed-wire barrier. Over the years, the original barrier's wire was replaced with high walls topped with guard towers and a wide death strip containing land mines. Desperate to escape, East Germans attempted to cross the barrier, and many were shot by border guards. The East German government called the wall its "antifascist protection barrier" and claimed the wall's purpose was to prevent an American invasion.

The Berlin Wall became a highly visible symbol of Communism's oppressive system. President Kennedy used it as a backdrop for a memorable speech that included his famous statement, "*Ich bin ein* Berliner." Ronald Reagan's speech in front of the wall in 1987 contained the challenging statement, "Mr. Gorbachev, tear down this wall!"

Nearly two hundred people were killed trying to cross the wall. Thousands escaped by digging tunnels or hiding in cars and trucks permitted to cross the border. One man's plan was ingenious. He sped under a road barrier in a low-slung sports car. In the late 1980s two men flew over the wall in an ultralight plane.

As Communist governments collapsed in 1989, East Germans began to demonstrate against their government's travel restrictions. A confused statement on East German television in 1989 led the country's citizens to believe the government's restrictions had been lifted. On November 9, 1989, thousands of people stormed the wall. Overwhelmed by the crowds, the border guards stood passively as people began to tear down the wall. With Germany's unification, the Berlin Wall was torn down. Today pieces of it are found around the world as historical relics from the cold war.

Quotation Marks " "

Quotation marks—always used in pairs—enclose direct quotations, titles of short works, and highlighted words.

1. **Use quotation marks in direct quotations.** When you copy word for word what someone has said or written, enclose the statement in quotation marks:

   Martin Luther King said, "I have a dream."

   Note: The final mark of punctuation precedes the final quotation mark, unless it does not appear in the original text:

   Did Martin Luther King say, "I have a dream"?

   Remember: Set off identifying phrases with commas:

   Sid argued, "We should ask everyone to vote."
   "It won't be fair," Sid insisted, "unless we all have a chance to decide."
   "Without a fair election, no one will accept the outcome," Sid argued.

   Note: Commas are not used if the quotation is blended into the sentence:

   They suggest we adopt a "go slow" approach to urban renewal.

   Quotations within quotations are indicated by use of single quotation marks:

   Shelly said, "I was only ten when I heard Martin Luther King proclaim, 'I have a dream.'"

   Long quotations are indented and not placed in quotation marks:

   > For generations, colleges and universities were accustomed to serving single eighteen- to twenty-two-year-olds whose only responsibility was attending class and getting good grades. This began to change in the 1980s:
   >
   > > An increasing number of adult students enrolled in college. Women seeking to reenter the workforce sought new skills. Downsized executives and displaced factory workers returned to school to secure jobs in new industries. Others returned to school to learn new skills to secure promotions. To serve the needs of this growing pool of older students, colleges built more parking lots, opened daycare centers, built satellite teaching centers in the suburbs, and offered weekend courses. (Jones 15)

   Final commas are placed inside quotation marks:

   The e-mail announced, "we will lower prices," but few believed it.

   Colons and semicolons are placed outside quotation marks:

   The e-mail announced, "The college will lower fees"; few students believed it.

   Indirect quotations do not require quotation marks:

   Martin Luther King said that he had a dream.

2. **Use quotation marks in titles of short works.** The titles of poems, short stories, chapters, essays, songs, episodes of television shows, and any named

section of a longer work are placed in quotation marks. Longer works are underlined or placed in italics:

Did you read "The Bells" by Poe?

Note: Do not capitalize articles, prepositions, or coordinating conjunctions (*and, or, yet, for, nor, but, so*) unless they are the first or last words.

Quotation marks and italics (or underlining) distinguish between shorter and longer works with the same title. Many anthologies and albums have title works. Quotation marks and italics indicate whether you are referring to a song or an entire album:

His new CD *Call My Bluff* has two good songs: "Going Home" and "Call My Bluff."

3. **Use quotation marks to highlight words.** Words are placed in quotation marks to draw extra attention:

Instead of laying off employees, the company placed a thousand workers on "unpaid leave."

EXERCISE 4 Quotation Marks and Apostrophes

Add quotation marks and apostrophes where needed.

1. Audrey told us she was getting married in June.
2. "I promise I will not raise property taxes," Karen Jackson told voters last night.
3. The course's new reading list includes John Cheever's "The Swimmer" and Albert Camus' "The Guest."
4. The crowd could not resist booing when the mayor announced, "There is nothing I can do until I receive a final ruling from the court that says, 'You can proceed.'"
5. Did you read Jane Manton's story "We Can't Go On"?
6. Carlos' favorite songs are Sinatra's "My Way" and Madonna's "Like a Virgin."
7. Frank's comments included the remark, "We're going to see if he's willing to help us."
8. "Building a New World" is the first essay in our textbook.
9. "I'm going to retire," Tom Watson told us, reminding us of his promise. "I will step aside as soon as my daughter's internship is completed."
10. Tom told us, "We're going to invest when all the economists' predictions give us a clear picture where to spend our clients' money."

Colon :

Colons are placed after independent clauses to introduce elements and separate items in numerals, ratios, titles, and time references:

Lists	Karen looked for three things in new employees: creativity, discipline, and loyalty.

Note: Colons are placed only after independent clauses to introduce lists:

Incorrect
We need: tires, oil, batteries, and air filters.

Correct
We need auto supplies: tires, oil, batteries, and air filters.

Phrases	The student council saw only one way to deal with Jane: immediate expulsion.
Time references	The plane left at 8:45 this morning.
Ratio	They have a 3:1 advantage.
Title and subtitle	I am reading *Pink Ghetto: Women in the Workplace.*
After salutations in a business letter	Dear Ms. Mendezo:
Scripture reference	Romans 12:1–5
Introduction of block quotations	Karen Meadows remembers the uneasiness the defense workers felt when the radio announced the war was over:

> Nancy and I dropped our tools and hugged and kissed. We danced around the engine we were assembling. Older workers were subdued. Some cried. They were glad their sons were coming home, but they were concerned about the future. They feared losing their jobs. They remembered the bread lines of the Depression. Many were convinced that the end of the war would end the few years of prosperity they had seen.

Parentheses ( )

Parentheses ( ) set off nonessential details and explanations and enclose letters and numbers used for enumeration:

Nonessential detail	The rules committee (established at last year's convention) will supervise the election of new officers.
First-time use of acronym	The diagnosis of obsessive compulsive disorder (OCD) is sometimes difficult to make.
Enumeration	She told us we should (1) paint the bedrooms, (2) carpet the living and dining rooms, and (3) install a new heating system.

Brackets [ ]

Brackets [ ] set off interpolations or clarifications in quotations and replace parentheses within parentheses.

Sometimes quotations taken out of context can be confusing because readers may misunderstand a word or reference. A quotation using the word "Kennedy" in a biography of Robert Kennedy would be clear in context. But if you use this quote in a paper, readers could easily assume it referred to John, not Robert, Kennedy. If you have to add clarifications or corrections, place them in brackets:

Interpolations to prevent confusion	On the eve of the primary, Lou Harris predicted, "It looks like [Robert] Kennedy will win tonight."
	Time noted, "President Bush told Frank Bush [no relation] that he agreed with his tax policies."
	The coach said, "I won't talk to them [suspended players] until they apologize."
Corrections	Larry Felber claimed, "I only owe $5,000 [$175,000 according to IRS records] in back taxes."
Parentheses within parentheses	The mayor's committee (headed by Hughes and Habib [both hoping to win city contracts]) will review the budget.

Dash —

Dashes mark a break in thought, set off a parenthetical element for emphasis, and set off an introduction to a series:

Sudden break in thought	She was shocked by the news—who could blame her?
Parenthetical element	The team—which lost ten games straight—became a local joke.
Introduction	She has everything people need to make it in Hollywood—looks, charm, talent, and a good agent.

Note: Create dashes by a continuous line or hit your hyphen key twice. No spaces separate dashes from the words they connect.

Hyphen -

A hyphen is a short line used to separate or join words and other items.

1. Use hyphens to break words:

> She was born in Phila-
> delphia in 1951.

Note: Only break words between syllables.

2. Use hyphens to connect words to create adjectives:

> They made a last-minute proposal to save the old school.

Do *NOT* use hyphens with adverbs ending in *-ly:*

> The city found the hastily written proposal confusing and impractical.

3. Use hyphens to connect words forming numbers:

> The school enrolled only twenty-seven students last year.

4. Use hyphens after some prefixes:

> Kim's self-reliance astounded her critics.

5. Use hyphens between combinations of numbers and words:

> How can it pull a 50-ton airplane?

Ellipsis . . .

An ellipsis, composed of three spaced periods [. . .], indicates that words have been deleted from quoted material:

Original text   The report stated, "All schools, including those founded under charter and choice programs, must be held to the highest standards."

With ellipsis   The report stated, "All schools . . . must be held to the highest standards."

Note: Only delete minor ideas or details—never change the basic meaning of a sentence by deleting key words. Don't eliminate a negative word like "not" to create a positive statement or remove qualifying words:

Original
We must never abandon our support for the public schools.

Incorrect Use of Ellipsis
He said, "We must . . . abandon our support for the public schools."

Note: When deleting words at the end of a sentence, add a period to the ellipsis so that four spaced periods are used:

> The report stated, "We depend on schools to build the future. . . ."

Note: Ellipses are not used if words are deleted at the opening of a quotation:

> The report stated that "building the future depends on good schools."

Note: If deleting words will create a grammar mistake, insert corrections with brackets:

Original   "Washington, Lincoln, and Roosevelt were among the greatest presidents."

With ellipsis   "Lincoln . . . [was] among the greatest presidents."

Slash /

Slashes separate words when both apply and separate lines in poetry in quotations:

Every citizen should cast his/her vote.
The poem began, "They play / They sing / They dance."

Question Mark ?

Question marks are placed after direct quotations if they are not included in the original quote and are used to note questionable items:

When are we leaving?
Did you read, "Who Can Save Us?" in *Time* last week?

Note: Question marks that appear in the original title are placed within quotation marks. If the title does not ask a question, the question mark is placed outside the quotation marks:

Did you like "The Swimmer"?

Question marks in parentheses are used to indicate that the writer questions the accuracy of a fact, number, idea, or quotation:

The report claimed it would cost taxpayers only $50,000 (?) to repair the bridge.

Exclamation Point !

Exclamation points are placed at the end of emphatic statements:

Help!
You are two hours late!

Note: Exclamation points should be used as special effects. They lose their impact if used too often.

Period .

Periods are used after sentences, in abbreviations, and as decimals:

She went home.
I talked to Ms. Green who works for Dr. Wilson.
On Jan. 30 the price will be cut from $9.95 to $7.95.

Note: When an abbreviation ends a sentence, only one period is used.

Note: Widely used abbreviations such as FBI, CIA, ABC, BBC, and UCLA do not require periods.

EXERCISE 5 Punctuation

Add missing punctuation in each sentence.

1. The Aug.15 flight will leave at 10:25 a.m.

2. The women's center is expanding its services to meet the needs of the school's growing number of part-time students.

3. The college saw three challenges: declining enrollments, reduced funding from the state, and rising health-care costs.

4. "The Look of Love" is her favorite song.

5. Can I park here?

6. Don't bother waiting because she won't be off work until 9:30.

7. Jane Bush [no relation to the president] went to Iraq on behalf of the White House.

8. To win this game we have to accomplish three goals: (1) stop turnovers, (2) complete more passes, and (3) stay focused.

9. Tim and Nan's house was the only one damaged by the storm.

10. The team made a last-ditch attempt to score a touchdown.

WORKING TOGETHER

Working with a group of students, correct the punctuation in the following announcement.

New Dorm Policy

Beginning Jan 15, the new dorm policy will go into effect. It calls for three major changes

1. Overnight guests under twentyone must be students. Residents guests must be registered by 900 pm at the dorms front desk.
2. Students are not allowed to operate large appliances refrigerators microwave ovens air conditioners or space heaters.
3. Its no longer acceptable for students vehicles (including motorcycles) to be parked overnight in the librarys north parking lot.

Anyone with questions should speak with hisher resident advisor.

EXERCISE 6 Cumulative Exercise: Punctuation and Coordination and Subordination

Rewrite this passage to correct errors in punctuation and reduce awkward and repetitive phrasing through coordination and subordination. You may have to reword some sentences, adding or deleting phrases. If you have difficulty revising some of the sentences, review pages 380–384 and 387–388.

Josh Gibson was born on December 21 1911. He was one of the greatest baseball players in history. He was often called the Babe Ruth of the Negro Leagues. Because of segregation Gibson could not try out for major league teams. He became a star player in black baseball and he broke many records. Lacking accurate statistics historians question some claims made about Gibsons career though most agree he had a lifetime batting average of 350 hit nearly 800 home runs and scored over eighty runs in a single season. Gibsons career contains many legendary moments. Some claim that he was the only player to hit a fair ball out of Yankee Stadium. Although Gibson was one of the players being considered to move into the major leagues along with Jackie Robinson he never made the transition. On January 20 1947 in Pittsburgh Pennsylvania Gibson died at the age of thirty five.

Josh Gibson, who was one of the greatest baseball players in history, was born on December 21, 1911. He was often called the "Babe Ruth of the Negro Leagues." Because of segregation, Gibson could not try out for major league teams. He became a star player in black baseball, and he broke many records. Lacking accurate statistics, historians question some claims made about Gibson's career, though most agree he had a lifetime batting average of .350, hit nearly 800 home runs, and scored over eighty runs in a single season. Gibson's career contains many legendary moments. Some claim that he was the only player to hit a fair ball out of Yankee Stadium. Although Gibson was one of the players being considered to move into the major leagues, along with Jackie Robinson, he never made the transition. On January 20, 1947, in Pittsburgh, Pennsylvania, Gibson died at the age of thirty-five.

GET THINKING AND WRITING

CRITICAL THINKING

Do you think that democracy is the best form of government for all countries in the world? Are there exceptions? Write a paragraph stating your views.

WHAT HAVE YOU WRITTEN?

Review your paper for mistakes in punctuation and other errors.

WHAT HAVE YOU LEARNED?

Add apostrophes, quotation marks, italics, parentheses, question marks, colons, and exclamation points where needed in the following sentences.

1. Ted and Ellens favorite car is their 67 VW bug.

2. Its going to rain according to the 800 am weather report.

3. I turn thirty three on Nov 25.

4. Tom asked Can anyone loan me a dime

5. His Time article Why We Love TV is very interesting.

6. Womens shoes are designed for style mens shoes are designed for comfort.

7. Ms Owens dealership sold 4500 cars last year.

8. Im getting tired of waiting for the deans call.

9. We need to stock winter clothing mens coats childrens mittens and womens gloves.

10. Dont park there because theyre going to spray paint the building.

Answers appear on following page.

WRITING ON THE WEB

Using a search engine such as Yahoo!, Google, or AltaVista, enter terms such as *colons, slashes, brackets, parenthesis, ellipsis, question marks, exclamation points, punctuation, understanding punctuation, using punctuation,* and *punctuation rules* to locate current sites of interest.

POINTS TO REMEMBER

1. Apostrophes show possession:

   Erica's car   NASA's rocket   someone's hat
   Ted and Nancy's cars.   [mutual ownership]
   Ted's and Nancy's cars.   [individual ownership]

   Apostrophes indicate missing letters or numbers:

   Didn't you sell the '97 Thunderbird?
   its = possessive of it   it's = it is

   Apostrophes indicate plurals of letters, numbers, or symbols:

   She got all A's this year.   Get the W-2's at the payroll office.

2. Quotation marks enclose direct quotations, titles of short works, and highlighted words:

   He said, "I'll be there."   Can you sing   Is he "sick"
                                         "Blue Eyes"?   again?

3. Colons are placed after independent clauses to introduce elements and separate items in numerals, titles, ratios, and time references:

   We need supplies: gas, oil, and spark plugs.   It is now 10:17 a.m.

4. Parentheses set off nonessential details and explanations and enclose letters and numbers used for enumeration:

   We got an apartment ($950 a month) because our State Loan Application (SLA) had not been approved for three reasons: (1) we needed more references, (2) we needed a bigger down payment, and (3) we owed too much on credit cards.

5. Brackets set off interpolations or clarifications in quotations and replace parentheses within parentheses:

   Time notes, "Frank Bush [no relation to the president] will work for the White House next fall.

6. Dashes mark breaks in thought, set off parenthetical elements, and set off introductions to a series:

> She expected help—wouldn't you?

7. Hyphens separate and join words and other items:

> He wrote a fast-paced soundtrack for the action film.
> You still owe twenty-eight dollars.

8. Ellipsis indicates words have been deleted from a direct quotation:

> The Senator stated, "Our country . . . needs new leadership."

9. Question marks are placed within quotation marks if they appear in the original title or quotation:

> Her article is called, "Can Anyone Lose Weight?"

Question marks are placed outside quotation marks if they are not part of the original:

> Did you read "The Gold Bug"?

ANSWERS TO WHAT HAVE YOU LEARNED? ON PAGES 526–527

1. Ted and Ellen's favorite car is their '67 VW bug.
2. It's going to rain according to the 8:00 a.m. weather report.
3. I turn thirty-three on Nov. 25.
4. Tom asked, "Can anyone loan me a dime?"
5. His *Time* article "Why We Love TV" is very interesting.
6. Women's shoes are designed for style; men's shoes are designed for comfort.
7. Ms. Owens' dealership sold 4,500 cars last year.
8. I'm getting tired of waiting for the dean's call.
9. We need to stock winter clothing: men's coats, children's mittens, and women's gloves.
10. Don't park there because they're going to spray paint the building.

Writer's Resources Now™   If you use Writer's ResourcesNow, please have your students log in and view the pretest, study plan, and posttest for this chapter.

Capitalization

**Marilyn Monroe after announcing her divorce from
Joe DiMaggio, 1954**

© Bettmann/CORBIS

GET WRITING

The average marriage now lasts eight years. Why do so many couples
divorce? What causes most marriages to fail?

Write a paragraph stating your views, supporting your points with examples. ◄■

What Is Capitalization?

Capital letters are used to begin sentences, indicate special meanings, and prevent confusion.

Words are capitalized to indicate proper nouns and prevent confusion. The word "earth" means soil; "Earth" is the name of a planet. The word "ford" means to cross a river; "Ford" refers to a car or a family name. An "apple" is a fruit; "Apple" is a computer. The word "polish" can be a verb meaning to shine or a noun meaning a protective substance as in "shoe polish"; "Polish" refers to Poland.

Capitalizing words changes their meaning.

Sam likes modern opera.	*indicates an interest in recent opera*
Sam likes Modern Opera.	*indicates an interest in a specific music class*
We flew European airlines.	*indicates several different airlines in Europe*
We flew European Airlines.	*indicates a single airline named European Airlines*
Will used a Dodge to escape.	*indicates using a car to escape*
Will used a dodge to escape.	*indicates using a trick to escape*

WHAT DO YOU KNOW?

Underline the letters in each sentence that should be capitalized.

1. He bought a toyota corolla last year because he planned to move south to florida, where he expected to do a lot of driving.

2. He saw a doctor who referred him to dr. green for more tests.

3. She ordered a salad with french dressing, but I stuck with chinese food.

4. I got a's in algebra, history, spanish, and introduction to psychology 101.

5. He spoke at the national bankers association convention last fourth of july.

   Answers appear on the following page.

GET WRITING ▶ **WHAT ARE YOU TRYING TO SAY?**

Write a list of things you would like own—cars, clothes, sound systems, or CDs.

_____

_____

_____

_____

_____

_____

_____

_____

_____

WHAT HAVE YOU WRITTEN?

_Review your list for capitalization. Did you capitalize proper nouns, such as names
of stores or product brand names? Review the rules on the following pages, then edit
your list._

Rules for Capitalization

There are a dozen main rules for capitalizing words. At first the list may seem overwhelming, but if you remember a simple guideline, you can avoid most problems. Capitalize words that refer to something specific or special—proper names or specific places or things.

1. **Capitalize the first word of every sentence:**

    They worked hard all week.

2. **Capitalize the first word in direct quotations:**

    Jim said, "We want overtime pay."

3. **Capitalize the first word and all important words in titles of articles, books, plays, movies, television shows, seminars, and courses:**

"TV Today"	_Survivor_	_Chorus Line_
War of the Worlds	_Monday Night Football_	Modern History II

4. **Capitalize the names of nationalities, languages, races, religions, deities, and sacred terms:**

Many Chinese speak English.	The Bible inspires many Catholics.
I bought a German car.	She was the city's first Latina mayor.

5. **Capitalize the days of the week, months of the years, and holidays:**

We celebrate Bastille Day every July 14th.	The party on Saturday is cancelled.
Muslims celebrate Ramadan.	I went home for Christmas last year.

    Note: The seasons of the year are not capitalized:

We loved the fall colors.	This summer is very hot.

6. **Capitalize special historical events, documents, and eras:**

the Civil War	the Monroe Doctrine
World War I	the Bill of Rights
the Whisky Rebellion	the French Revolution

7. **Capitalize names of planets, continents, nations, states, provinces, counties, towns and cities, mountains, lakes, rivers, and other geographical features:**

Neptune	South America	Mexico	Ottawa
Lake Erie	Mount McKinley	Michigan	Jersey
the Badlands	Rocky Mountains	Nile	Iraq

8. **Capitalize *north, south, east,* and *west* when they refer to geographical regions:**

   Oil was discovered in the South.
   He wears Western clothes.
   We grew up in the East.

   Note: Do not capitalize *north, south, east,* and *west* when used as directions:

   We drove west for an hour.
   The store is northwest of Albany.

9. **Capitalize brand names:**

Coca-Cola	Pontiac Firebird	Parker pen

   Note: Some common brand names like *Kleenex, Xerox,* and *Coke* sometimes appear in lowercase, but this generic use of brand names should be avoided in writing.

10. **Capitalize names of specific corporations, organizations, institutions, and buildings:**

    This plane was built by Boeing.
    The lecture is in Statler Hall at noon.
    We toured the United Nations.
    She works for the Urban League.

11. **Capitalize abbreviations, acronyms, or shortened forms of capitalized words when used as proper nouns:**

FBI	CNN	FOX	ABC
IRA	JFK	LAX	NBC
NRA	GM	IRS	OPEC

12. **Capitalize people's names and nicknames:**

Janet Rossi	Timmy Allen

    Note: Capitalize professional titles when used with proper names:

    Doctor Jackson gave a speech last night.
    We accepted Mayor Wilson's budget.
    Our school president met with President Bush.
    He has to see the president now!

    Note: Capitalize words like *father, mother, brother, aunt, cousin,* and *uncle* only when used with or in place of proper names:

My father and I went to see Aunt Jean.
After the game, I took Father to meet our aunt.

POINT TO REMEMBER

The rules of capitalization sometimes vary. Some publications always capitalize *President* when it refers to the president of the United States; other publications do not. *African American* is always capitalized, but editors vary whether *blacks* should be capitalized. Some writers capitalize *AM* and *PM*, while others do not.

Follow the standard used in your discipline or career and be consistent.

EXERCISE 1 Capitalization

Underline letters that should be capitalized.

1. Known to many as the <u>m</u>ad <u>m</u>onk, grigory <u>r</u>asputin became one of the most mysterious and fascinating figures of the <u>r</u>ussian <u>r</u>evolution.

2. Born in an obscure <u>s</u>iberian village along the <u>t</u>ula <u>r</u>iver in 1869, Rasputin developed an early reputation as a drinker and womanizer.

3. He joined a strange sect in the <u>r</u>ussian <u>o</u>rthodox <u>c</u>hurch called the "skopsty," which believed that engaging in sin was necessary in order to achieve forgiveness.

4. Rasputin became a wandering pilgrim, traveling to <u>g</u>reece and <u>j</u>erusalem before reaching <u>s</u>t. petersburg, the <u>r</u>ussian capital.

5. A tall, bearded figure with penetrating eyes, he made an impression on many who accepted him as a man of <u>g</u>od with special powers who could heal the sick and predict the future.

6. He managed to gain access to the salons of the rich and powerful; many saw the <u>s</u>iberian holy man as an amusing character, while others fell under his spell.

7. Historians disagree how he was introduced to <u>c</u>zar Nicholas II's court, but Rasputin did become an intimate figure in the royal household.

8. The czar and his wife, the czarina, were keeping a family secret; their only son and heir to the <u>r</u>omanov throne had hemophilia, a bleeding disorder that threatened to shorten his life.

9. Doctors at the time could do little but treat the symptoms of this disease, and the czarina, who was deeply religious, turned to Rasputin, whom she saw as a simple man of <u>g</u>od.

10. On several occasions, Rasputin appears to have provided relief and aided the boy's recovery when the best doctors in <u>r</u>ussia were helpless.

11. The czarina believed Rasputin had the power to heal her son through prayer, though most doctors and historians who have studied the accounts written by members of the <u>r</u>omanov court believe he may have used hypnosis.

12. In <u>n</u>icholas and <u>a</u>lexandra, biographer <u>r</u>obert <u>k</u>. <u>m</u>assie argues Rasputin's healing powers may have been quite accidental.

13. By ordering the doctors to stay away from the boy, Rasputin ended the physicians' poking and probing, which had only aggravated his condition and prevented the <u>r</u>omanov heir's blood from clotting.

14. After <u>r</u>ussia suffered a series of major losses during the <u>f</u>irst <u>w</u>orld <u>w</u>ar, discontent against the royal family grew, and the <u>c</u>ommunists gained support.

15. <u>r</u>asputin began to appear in antigovernment propaganda leaflets, many suggesting the drunken, lecherous "holy man" had become the czarina's lover.

16. Being of <u>g</u>erman origin, the czar's wife was already viewed with hostility by many <u>r</u>ussians.

17. Government officials and members of royalty saw Rasputin as a threat and wanted to eliminate him, especially <u>p</u>rince <u>y</u>ussupov, who plotted to kill the holy man.

18. In December 1916, <u>p</u>rince <u>f</u>elix <u>y</u>ussupov and the czar's cousin, <u>g</u>rand <u>d</u>uke <u>d</u>imitri, invited Rasputin to a palace, where they gave him wine and cakes containing cyanide.

19. When the poison had no effect, they shot him three times, beat him with heavy objects, and threw his body into a hole chopped into the frozen <u>n</u>eva <u>r</u>iver, where Rasputin, still alive, struggled to free himself under the ice.

20. The assassination failed to save the <u>r</u>omanov family, all of whom were executed in 1918 by the <u>b</u>olsheviks.

EXERCISE 2 Capitalization

Underline letters that should be capitalized.

1. On <u>o</u>ctober 16, 1869, workmen digging a well in <u>c</u>ardiff, <u>n</u>ew <u>y</u>ork, made an amazing discovery.

2. They informed the farm owner <u>w</u>illiam <u>n</u>ewell that they had found a a giant figure in the earth.

3. Visitors came from all over <u>n</u>ew <u>y</u>ork to see the ten-foot-high statue carved from stone.

4. Newell began charging tourists to look at the mysterious artifact that some saw as evidence of the giants mentioned in <u>g</u>enesis.

5. Some believed the statue was carved by a <u>j</u>esuit missionary to teach the <u>b</u>ible to <u>n</u>ative <u>a</u>mericans.

6. Businessmen paid newell for the statue, now called the "cardiff giant" and took it to syracuse, new york, where they planned to charge admission.

7. A yale professor examined the giant, discovered fresh chisel marks, and announced it was a phony.

8. A businessman named hull came forward and explained he had paid stonecutters to make a statue that he buried on the newell farm a year before.

9. Newell, who conspired with hull, then directed workers to dig a well, engineering the giant's "accidental" discovery.

10. The public was so fascinated by the cardiff giant, they paid to seek the fake, now nicknamed "old hoaxy."

11. Always eager to make money with a new exhibit, p. t. barnum offered to lease the giant to display in his museum.

12. When the giant's owners refused, barnum made a plaster replica of the cardiff giant, and people paid to see a copy of a fake.

13. A hundred years later, another great showman, david merrick, came up with another hoax that made broadway history.

14. He was producing a play called *subways are for sleeping,* a show that got poor reviews and sold few tickets.

15. Merrick placed an ad in the *new york herald tribune* announcing that seven of new york's leading critics raved about his play.

16. The ad featured the names of famous critics and their comments stating how great the show was.

17. The ad was a stunt; the quotes were real but misleading.

18. Merrick found seven new yorkers who shared the same name as seven leading critics and gave them free tickets and treated them to dinner.

19. After enjoying themselves with the famous producer, the seven new yorkers praised his show and agreed to let him use their names and quote their favorable comments.

20. The ad only appeared once but generated enough publicity to keep *subways are for sleeping* running for months and helped phyllis newman win a tony award.

EXERCISE 3 Capitalization

Underline letters that require capitalization.

Although there are now longer bridges in the world, the golden gate bridge remains one of the most famous structures in the world. Visitors to san francisco marvel at the way fog rolls off the cold pacific waters to bathe the tall orange structure in fog. The american society of civil engineers lists the bridge as one of the modern wonders of the world. The bridge connects san francisco with marin county to the north. Construction on the bridge began in january 1933 when the great depression was gripping the american economy. The construction of an engineering marvel inspired not only people in california but the whole country. Newsreels followed the development of this mammoth project, which along with other wpa projects helped give people hope for a better future. The bridge created well-paying but dangerous jobs. Twenty-seven workers were killed during the four years it took to complete the bridge. A safety net saved the lives of nineteen men who fell from the bridge. They called themselves members of the halfway to hell club. In may 1937, president roosevelt opened the bridge by pressing a telegraph key in the white house. Fifty years later, the bridge was closed for a celebration. Three hundred thousand people stood on the bridge at one time, causing the golden gate bridge to temporarily sag.

WORKING TOGETHER

Work with a group of students to determine the definition of each word. What difference does capitalization make? You may use a dictionary to check your answers.

1. Bronco _____
   bronco _____

2. Patriots _____
   patriots _____

3. CARE _____
   care _____

4. general motors _____
   General Motors _____

5. prohibition _____
   Prohibition _____

6. new year _____
   New Year _____

7. dial _____
   Dial _____

8. the Gulf _____
   the gulf _____

9. Rolling Stones _____
   rolling stones _____

10. civil war _____
    Civil War _____

GET THINKING AND WRITING

CRITICAL THINKING

Write a short paragraph describing recent errands you've run or shopping trips you've been on.

WHAT HAVE YOU WRITTEN?

Review your writing for capitalization. Did you remember to capitalize proper nouns—names of people, streets, stores, malls, and specific brands?

WHAT HAVE YOU LEARNED?

Underline letters in each sentence that should be capitalized.

1. I read the article on the internet before the march meeting.

2. The governor met with mayor wilson and suggested homeland security should assist with protecting the harbor along with the coast guard.

3. I remember her saying, "we must save our public schools" at the pta meeting.

4. We walked south along the hudson river until we reached west point.

5. I hope i get at least a b in dr. smith's introduction to sociology course this spring.

Answers appear below.

WRITING ON THE WEB

Using a search engine such as Yahoo!, Google, or AltaVista, enter terms such as *capitalization rules, using capitals,* and *proper nouns* to locate current sites of interest.

POINTS TO REMEMBER

1. Capitalize the first word in each sentence and direct quotation.
2. Capitalize first and important words in titles of books, articles, movies, and works of art.
3. Capitalize names of nationalities, languages, races, and religions.
4. Capitalize days of the weeks, months, holidays, historical events, documents, and eras.
5. Capitalize proper names and nicknames of people, places, products, organizations, and institutions.
6. Capitalize abbreviations such as FBI and NAACP.
7. Capitalize a person's title only when it precedes a name or is used in place of a name:

   "I took Mother to see Dr. Grant."

8. Do not capitalize seasons such as *spring* and *fall* or *north, south, east,* and *west* when used as directions.

ANSWERS TO WHAT HAVE YOU LEARNED?
1. I read the article on the **I**nternet before the **M**arch meeting.
2. The governor met with **M**ayor **W**ilson and suggested **H**omeland **S**ecurity should assist with protecting the harbor along with the **C**oast **G**uard.
3. I remember her saying, "**W**e must save our public schools" at the **PTA** meeting.
4. We walked south along the **H**udson **R**iver until we reached **W**est **P**oint.
5. I hope **I** get at least a **B** in **Dr. S**mith's **I**ntroduction to **S**ociology course this spring.

If you use Writer's ResourcesNow, please have your students log in and view the pretest, study plan, and posttest for this chapter.

Writer's Resources ⓦ Now™

© Philip Gould/CORBIS

GET WRITING

Many people advocate that public school students wear uniforms to limit the differences between rich and poor and lessen the focus on fashion they believe distracts young people from their studies. Opponents argue that uniforms inhibit creativity and personal expression. Do you believe public schools should require students to wear uniforms? Why or why not? Would you advocate stricter dress codes instead?

Write a paragraph stating your views.

Spelling influences the way people look at your writing. Consider the impression made by this e-mail:

```
Dear Mr. Lee:

I heard your talk about oppurtunities in cable telvi-
sion in northern California and was very struck by the
comments you made. I am compeleting my associate de-
gree this semsester and have two years experince work-
ing for to FM radio stations in the Bay Area. I am now
seeking a full time job and would interested in meat-
ing with you at your convenence to see if you're firm
has any openings. You can e-mail me or call me at
(415) 555-5442.

Sincerly,

Sid Sadoff
```

All the student's education and hard work are overshadowed by spelling errors, which make any writer appear careless and uneducated. Not every reader can detect a dangling modifier or faulty parallelism, but almost everyone can identify a misspelled word.

Some people have a photographic memory and need only see a word once to remember its exact spelling. Others, even highly educated professional writers, have difficulty with words. If English is your second language or if you have trouble with spelling, make it a priority. It can be the easiest, most dramatic way of improving your writing and your grades. Make sure you reserve enough time in the writing process to edit papers to correct spelling mistakes.

WHAT DO YOU KNOW?

Underline the misspelled or misused words in each sentence.

1. Your not conscience of the capitol the bank is loosing, are you?

2. Its starting to snow, so we should leave before it is to late.

3. How will flunking this quiz effect my final grade?

4. It is too quit here.

5. Please except my apology.

6. This problem seems insolveable.

7. She exercices on paralell bars and lifts wieghts.

8. He was sited for fialing to yeild.

9. Her arguements make no cents to me or anyone else.

10. We cannot recieve e-mail for some reason.

   Answers appear on page 541.

GET WRITING | WHAT ARE YOU TRYING TO SAY?

Do you object to the amount of profanity used in current movies and cable television shows? Directors and writers argue that they are striving for realism by including the language their characters would speak in real life. Critics insist profanity, especially in popular culture, is unnecessary and cheapens society. Write a paragraph stating your views. Do you think, for instance, that network and cable television shows should have different standards? Why or why not?

_____

_____

_____

_____

_____

_____

_____

_____

_____

_____

_____

_____

_____

WHAT HAVE YOU WRITTEN?

Review what you have written and check with a dictionary to see if you have misspelled any words.

1. Review assignments you have written in this or any other course for spelling errors. Do see any patterns or any words you repeatedly misspell?
2. List any words you find confusing or have doubts about:

_____   _____

_____   _____

_____   _____

_____   _____

_____   _____

STEPS TO IMPROVING SPELLING

1. Make spelling a priority, especially in editing your papers.
2. Look up new words in a dictionary for correct spelling and meaning. Write them out a few times to help memorize them.
3. Study the glossaries in your textbooks to master new terms.
4. Review lists of commonly misspelled words (see page 541) and commonly confused words (see page 542).
5. Create a list of words you have trouble with. Keep copies of the list next to your computer and in your notebook. Each week try to memorize three or four of these words. Update your list by adding new terms you encounter.
6. Read your writing out loud when editing. Some spelling errors are easier to hear than see.
7. Remember *i* before *e* except after *c*, or when it sounds like *a* as in *neighbor* and *weigh:*

i before e

achieve	field	niece	shield
brief	grievance	piece	yield

Except after c

ceiling	deceive	perceive	receipt

When it sounds like a

eight	freight	rein	vein

Exceptions: either, height, leisure, seize, weird

8. Review rules for adding word endings (see page 548).
9. Learn to use computer spell-checks and understand their limitations. Although spell-checks can easily spot typos and commonly misspelled words, not every program will alert you to confusing "there" for "their" or "affect" for "effect" (see pages 543–544).
10. If you are a poor speller, eliminating spelling errors is the fastest and easiest way to improve your grades.

ANSWERS TO WHAT DO YOU
KNOW? ON PAGE 539
1. You're; conscious; capital;
losing 2. It's; too 3. affect
4. quiet 5. accept 6. insolvable
7. exercises; parallel; weights
8. cited; failing; yield
9. arguments; sense 10. receive

Commonly Misspelled Words

Many words are commonly misspelled. They may be foreign words, contain silent letters, or have unusual letter combinations. When speaking, people often slur sounds and fail to pronounce every letter. Because you are accustomed to hearing words mispronounced, you may misspell them when you write.

Incorrect	*Correct*
goverment	gove*rn*ment
suppose (past tense)	suppose*d*
ice tea	ice*d* tea

FORTY COMMONLY MISSPELLED WORDS

absence	belief	generous	mortgage
achieve	benefit	grammar	necessary
acquire	challenge	guard	obvious
address	committee	height	opinion
among	control	heroes	parallel
analyze	decision	identity	persuade
argument	dying	label	possess
athletic	embarrass	license	privilege
beautiful	enough	marriage	separate
becoming	familiar	material	vacuum

See pages 642–643 for additional words.

EXERCISE 1 Commonly Misspelled Words

Underline the correctly spelled word in each pair.

1. <u>grateful</u>/greatful
2. avalanch/<u>avalanche</u>
3. <u>safety</u>/safty
4. lonelyness/<u>loneliness</u>
5. colum/<u>column</u>
6. <u>disappear</u>/disapear
7. preceed/<u>precede</u>
8. sterotype/<u>stereotype</u>
9. dependant/<u>dependent</u>
10. <u>similar</u>/similiar

Commonly Confused Words

In addition to easily misspelled words, there are easily confused words. The word you put on the page is correctly spelled, but it is the wrong word and has a different meaning than what you are trying to say. Many words look and sound alike but have clearly different meanings:

everyday	ordinary or common	"She wore *everyday* clothes."
every day	each day	"Take vitamins *every day*."
any one	a single person, idea, or item	"*Any one* of the rooms is open."
anyone	anybody	"Can *anyone* help us?"

roll	to turn over/a small bread loaf	"Let the ball *roll* down the hill."
role	a part in a play or event/expected behavior	"He played no *role* in the scandal."

Using the wrong word not only creates a spelling error but also creates confusion by making a statement that means something very different than what you intended:

She will *adopt* our proposal. = She will *accept* our proposal.
She will *adapt* our proposal. = She will *change* our proposal.

He gave a speech about the *eminent* trial. = He gave a speech about the *famous* trial.
He gave a speech about the *imminent* trial. = He gave a speech about the *upcoming* trial.

We want to see the *sites*. = We want to see *specific places* (ex: construction sites).
We want to see the *sights*. = We want to see *interesting places* (ex: tourist attractions).

TEN MOST COMMONLY CONFUSED WORDS

accept/except

accept	to take	"Please *accept* my apology."
except	but/to exclude	"Everyone *except* Tom attended."

affect/effect

affect	to change or influence	"Will this *affect* my grade?"
effect	a result	"What *effect* did the drug have?"

farther/further

farther	geographical distance	"The farm is ten miles *farther* on."
further	in addition	"*Further* negotiations proved useless."

hear/here

hear	to listen	"Did you *hear* her new song?"
here	a place or direction	"Put it over *here*."

its/it's

its	possessive of *it*	"My car won't start. *Its* battery died."
it's	"it is"	"Looks like *it's* going to rain."

lay/lie

lay	to put or place	"*Lay* the boxes on the table."
lie	to recline	"*Lie* down. You look tired."

principal/principle

principal	main/school leader	"Oil is the *principal* product of Kuwait."
principle	basic law	"This violates all ethical *principles*."

than/then		
than	used in comparisons	"Bill is taller *than* Tom."
then	refers to time	"He took the test *then* went home."
there/their/they're		
there	direction/a place	"*There* he goes." "Put it *there*."
their	possessive of *they*	"*Their* car won't start."
they're	"they are"	"*They're* taking the bus home."
to/too/two		
to	preposition/infinitive	"Walk *to* school." "He likes *to* dance."
too	excessive/in addition	"It's *too* hot." "I want to go, *too*."
two	a number	"The dress costs *two* hundred dollars."

See pages 643–646 for a complete list

EXERCISE 2 Commonly Confused Words

Underline and correct misspelled words in each sentence.

1. He tries <u>to</u> hard to impress people.
   too

2. She was so <u>quite</u> we didn't even <u>now</u> she was there.
   quiet   know

3. The employees have little <u>excess</u> to medical care.
   access

4. They were upset when <u>there</u> reservation was cancelled.
   their

5. The recent loss really <u>effected</u> the team's <u>moral</u>.
   affected   morale

6. I have a great <u>ideal</u> for raising money for the school.
   idea

7. The <u>plane</u> truth is I just don't like to see people <u>loose</u> their jobs.
   plain   lose

8. The campsite is <u>further</u> from here <u>then</u> I thought.
   farther   than

9. I did not mean my e-mail to <u>infer</u> that you were not working hard enough.
   imply

10. We <u>past</u> the gas station half an hour ago.
    passed

EXERCISE 3 Commonly Misspelled and Confused Words

Underline each misspelled or misused word and write the correct spelling over it.

The Grammy Award is the most famous of <u>for discreet</u> music awards in the United
                                          four   discrete
States. The Grammy gets <u>it's</u> name from the award <u>isself</u>, which is a <u>minature</u> replica of
                         its   itself   miniature
an <u>old-fashion</u> gramophone. The award is presented by the Recording Academy, an
   old-fashioned
<u>assocation</u> of professionals in the music industry. Awards are given in thirty <u>generes</u>, in-
association   genres
cluding rock, pop, rap, and gospel. These are <u>seperated</u> into over a hundred <u>catagories</u>.
                                               separated   categories
Unlike other music awards, the Grammy winners are chosen by voting members of the
academy rather <u>then</u> fans. Winners are chosen by <u>there piers</u> in the music industry.
                than   their peers

The annual awards ceremony is shown on television and <u>recieves</u> very high ratings. Like

receives

the Academy Awards, the Grammy Awards have <u>there</u> critics. Some fans <u>belief</u> that <u>its</u>

their   believe   it's

not <u>fare</u> that artists like Elvis and groups like the Rolling Stones received fewer Gram-

fair

mys <u>then</u> Pat Metheny.

than

Forming Plurals

Words change their spelling to indicate when they are plural. Most nouns simply add an *-s*:

Singular	Plural
pen	pens
coin	coins
paper	papers
bill	bills
cardiologist	cardiologists

However, many nouns use different spellings to indicate plurals. In order to avoid making spelling errors, it is important to understand which words require more than an added *-s* to become plural.

1. For words ending in *-s, -ss, -x, -z, -sh,* or *-ch,* add *-es:*

Singular	Plural
hiss	hisses
church	churches
dish	dishes
box	boxes

2. For words ending in an *-o* preceded by a vowel, add *-s:*

Singular	Plural
stereo	stereos
studio	studios
zoo	zoos
rodeo	rodeos

3. For words ending in an *-o* preceded by a consonant, add *-es:*

Singular	Plural
hero	heroes
zero	zeroes
echo	echoes
tomato	tomatoes

Exceptions

Singular	Plural
motto	mottos
photo	photos
solo	solos
piano	pianos

4. For words ending in *-f* or *-fe,* change the *f* to *v* and add *-es:*

Singular	*Plural*
shelf	shelves
wife	wives
half	halves
thief	thieves

Exceptions

Singular	*Plural*
safe	safes
roof	roofs
proof	proofs
chief	chiefs

5. For words ending in *-y* preceded by a consonant, change the *y* to *i* and add *-es:*

Singular	*Plural*
city	cities
story	stories
baby	babies
celebrity	celebrities

6. For some words, the plural form is irregular:

Singular	*Plural*
tooth	teeth
child	children
person	people
woman	women

7. For some words, the singular and plural spelling are the same:

Singular	*Plural*
deer	deer
fish	fish
sheep	sheep
series	series

8. For Greek and Latin nouns, there are special spellings:

Singular	*Plural*
memorandum	memoranda
datum	data
thesis	theses
alumnus	alumni

9. For compound nouns—made up of two or more words—make the needed change to the main word. For compound nouns written as one word, make the ending plural:

Singular	*Plural*
mother-in-law	mothers-in-law
stepchild	stepchildren
bookshelf	bookshelves

Exceptions

Singular	Plural
passerby	passersby

For compound nouns that appear as separate words or connected by hyphens, make the main word plural:

Singular	Plural
music store	music stores
icebox	iceboxes
water tank	water tanks
brother-in-law	brothers-in-law

EXERCISE 4 Creating Plurals

Write out the correct plural form of each noun.

1. reef — *reefs*

2. book — *books*

3. pop star — *pop stars*

4. toss — *tosses*

5. wolf — *wolves*

6. grandchild — *grandchildren*

7. flurry — *flurries*

8. employee of the month — *employees of the month*

9. tax — *taxes*

10. stereo — *stereos*

EXERCISE 5 Plural Spellings

Correct errors in plurals in each sentence.

1. The attorney generals of sixteen states met with representatives of companys concerned about rising bankruptcys.

   The attorneys general of sixteen states met with representatives of companies concerned about rising bankruptcies.

2. Your cholesterol ratioes would be better if you ate more fishes.

   Your cholesterol ratios would be better if you ate more fish.

3. Consumer worrys about rising prices are hurting many industrys.

   Consumer worries about rising prices are hurting many industries.

4. These powerful radioes are popular with peoples living in remote areas.

   These powerful radios are popular with people living in remote areas.

5. These safety features could save many lifes.

   These safety features could save many lives.

Adding Endings

In most instances, suffixes or word endings follow simple rules to indicate past tense or to create an adjective or adverb.

Past-Tense Spellings

Most verbs are called "regular" because they simply add *-ed* or *-d* if the word ends with an *-e:*

Regular Verbs

Present	Past
talk	talked
disintegrate	disintegrated
vote	voted
print	printed

1. If a verb ends in *-y*, change the *y* to *i* + *-ed:*

cry	cried
spy	spied
try	tried

2. If a one-syllable verb ends in a consonant preceded by a vowel, double the last letter + *-ed:*

pin	pinned
plan	planned
stop	stopped
grab	grabbed

Other verbs, called "irregular," have different spellings to indicate past tense:

Irregular Verbs

Present	Past
teach	taught
sing	sang
write	wrote
swim	swam
buy	bought

See pages 450–452 for a complete list.

Spelling Other Endings

Endings are added to words to create adjectives, adverbs, or nouns:

sad (adjective)	sadly (adverb)	sadness (noun)
create (verb)	creative (adjective)	creatively (adverb)
motivate (verb)	motivation (noun)	motivated (adjective)
happy (adjective)	happily (adverb)	happiness (noun)

1. For words ending with a silent *-e*, drop the *-e* if the ending begins with a vowel:

   arrive + al = arrival
   come + ing = coming
   fame + ous = famous
   create + ion = creation

   Exceptions: mileage, dyeing

2. For words ending with a silent *-e*, retain the *-e* if the ending begins with a consonant:

   elope + ment = elopement
   safe + ty = safety
   like + ness = likeness
   complete + ly = completely

3. Double the last consonant of one-syllable words if the ending begins with a vowel:

   rob + ing = robbing
   spot + ed = spotted
   spin + ing = spinning

4. Double the last consonant of words accented on the last syllable if the ending begins with a vowel:

   refer + ing = referring
   admit + ed = admitted
   technical + ly = technically

NOTE

Prefixes do not change spelling of base words. When you add letters before a word, no letters are dropped or added:

un + natural = unnatural   dis + able = disable
pre + judge = prejudge   il + legal = illegal
im + moral = immoral   de + mobilize = demobilize

EXERCISE 6 Past-Tense Spellings

Write the correct past-tense form of each verb.

1. **weigh**   *weighed*

2. **walk**   *walked*

3. **stand**   *stood*

4. **ram**   *rammed*

5. **capitalize**   *capitalized*

6. **think**   *thought*

7. **double**   *doubled*

8. rest   *rested*

9. sleep   *slept*

10. broil   *broiled*

EXERCISE 7 Adding Endings

Combine the following words and endings.

1. debate	+	able	*debatable*
2. legal	+	ly	*legally*
3. regret	+	fully	*regretfully*
4. force	+	ing	*forcing*
5. attend	+	ance	*attendance*
6. doubt	+	less	*doubtless*
7. win	+	ing	*winning*
8. recycle	+	able	*recyclable*
9. make	+	ing	*making*
10. fit	+	ness	*fitness*

EXERCISE 8 Identifying and Correcting Misspelled Words

Underline misspelled and misused words and write the correct spelling below them.

One of the most memorerable peaces of America's passed is the Liberty Bell. More
memorable   *pieces*   *past*
then any other relic of the Revolutionary War, it is immediatly recognized as a symbol
than   *immediately*
of freedom around the world. The bell was cast in England in 1752 and shipped to
America to hang in the Pennsylvana State House, later known as Independance Hall.
Pennsylvania   *Independence*
The first time the bell was rang in 1753, it cracked. It was recast twice then hanged
rung   *hung*
in the State House. The bell was used to summon members of the Continental Congress
in 1775 and 1776. When British solders neared Philadelphia, patriots moved the bell to
soldiers
Allentown and hid it under a church. The bell was returned to Philadelphia in 1778.

The bell tolled at the deaths of Washington, Franklin, Hamilton, Adams, Jefferson,
and Lafayette. It was not, however, offically called the Liberty Bell until the 1830s when
officially
it became a symbol of the antislavery movement. The bell's Biblical inscription, which
promised liberty to all, was seen as the perfect emblemn for the abolitionist cause.
emblem

The Liberty Bell split when it was rung to celebrate Washington's birthday in 1846.
The bell was rung in later years with a rubber mallat. On June 6, 1944, the mayor of
mallet
Philadelphia tapped the bell twelve times, which was broadcasted on radioes nation-
broadcast   *radios*
wide, to celebrate the liberation of Europe. In 1962 the bell was tapped on the first an-
niversary of the erection of the Berlin Wall to honor the people of East Germany.

In 2002 the decision to relocate the Liberty Bell <u>stired</u> controversy when it was dis-
stirred
covered that the entrance to the new exhibit hall would be placed on the <u>sight</u> of quar-
site
ters once used to house George Washington's slaves.

EXERCISE 9 Cumulative Exercise

_Rewrite these paragraphs to correct spelling errors and missing capitalization and to
eliminate fragments and run-ons. To check your revision, see page 573._

Her name was Ann and we met in the port authority bus terminal several januarys
ago. I was doing a story on homeless people. She said I wasting my time talking to her
she was just passing though, although she'd been passing though for more then too
weeks. To prove too me that this was true, she rummaged through a tote bag and
a manila envelop and finally unfolded a sheet of typeing paper and bought out her
photographs.

They were not pictures of family, or friends, or even a dog or cat, it's eyes brown-red
in the flashbulb's light. They were pictures of a house. It was like a thousand houses in
a hundred towns, not suburb, not city, but somewhere in between, with aluminun side-
ing and a chain-link fence, a narrow driveway running up to a one-car garage and a
patch of backyard. The house was yellow. I looked on the back for a date or a name
but neither was their. There was no need for discussion. I new what what she was trying to tell me for it was something I had often felt. She was not adrift, alone, anonymous, although her bags and her raincoat with the grime shadowing it's creases had
made me belief she was. She had a house or at least once upon a time had had one.
Inside were curtains, a couch, a stove, potholders. You are where you live. She was
somebody.

WORKING TOGETHER

_Working with a group of students, correct this ad for spelling errors.
Have each member underline misspelled words, then work as a
group. Note how collaborative editing helps detect errors you may miss on
your own._

COMING THIS SUMMER!

Save you're money . . .
Save time on droped calls . . .
Enjoy the best calling plan in the county . . .

On July 1, American Horizon starts it's latest and best national calling
plan do date.

7 Cents a Minute Anytime All the Time!

Call 1-800-555-7000 or visit us online at www.americanhorizon.com for
details and a free upgrade!

GET THINKING
AND WRITING

CRITICAL THINKING

How has your writing improved over the semester? What areas of writing still pose challenges? Write a paragraph describing your progress and areas you would like to improve.

WHAT HAVE YOU WRITTEN?

Examine your paragraph for spelling errors. If you have listed any areas you would like to improve, bookmark pages in Get Writing *you can use for review and reference on future writing assignments.*

WHAT HAVE YOU LEARNED?

Underline and correct the misspelled or misused words in each sentence.

1. Its later then you think!

2. I stoped there car before it rolled of the ramp.

3. That red-stripped dress is to expensive.

4. The pills had no affect on her blood pressure.

5. Several companys are relocating to Southern California.

6. This will be a causal party, so where every day cloths.

7. We now he is coming later.

8. The principle product of Saudi Arabia is oil.

9. The knew movie casts aging stars in very predictable rolls.

10. You're boxes are in the garage were I left them.

    (Check a dictionary to make sure you have successfully identified and corrected all twenty errors.)

WRITING ON THE WEB

Using a search engine such as Yahoo!, Google, or AltaVista, enter terms such as *spelling, improving spelling, spelling rules,* and *using spell check* to locate current sites of interest.

POINTS TO REMEMBER

1. Edit your papers carefully for commonly misspelled words such as *library, yield, opinion, opportunity,* and *separate.* (See list on pages 642–643.)
2. Edit your papers carefully for commonly confused words such as *anyone* and *any one* or *implicit* and *explicit.* (See list on pages 639–642.)

3. Remember, *i* before *e* except after *c*, or when it sounds like *a* such as in *neighbor* and *weigh*:

   achieve   ceiling   freight
   Exceptions: either, height, leisure, seize

4. Follow the guidelines for creating plurals.

   For words ending in -*s*, -*ss*, -*x*, -*z*, -*sh*, or -*ch*, add -*es*:

   misses   boxes   churches

   For words ending in -*o* preceded by a vowel, add -*s*.
   For words ending in -*o* preceded by a consonant, add -*es*:

   zoos   radios   heroes   zeroes
   Exceptions: mottos, photos, pianos, solos

   For words ending in -*f* or -*fe*, change the *f* to *v* and add -*es*:

   shelves   halves   thieves
   Exceptions: safes, roofs, proofs, chiefs

   Some plural words have irregular forms:

   teeth   children   people

   Some words have no plural spelling:

   sheep   fish   series

   Greek and Latin nouns have special plural spellings:

   memoranda   data   theses

   For compound nouns, make the needed change to the main word:

   bookshelves   stepchildren   boyfriends

   For compound nouns that appear as separate words, change the main word:

   brothers-in-law   beer taps   water tanks

5. Follow guidelines for creating past-tense endings.

   For regular verbs, add -*ed* or -*d* if the word ends in -*e*:

   walked   created   painted

   For verbs ending in -*y*, change the *y* to *i* + -*ed*:

   cried   spied   tried

   For a one-syllable verb ending with a consonant preceded by a vowel, double the last letter + -*ed*:

   pinned   stopped   grabbed

   Some verbs have irregular past-tense forms:

   taught   sang   swam

6. Follow guidelines for adding suffixes.

   For words ending with a silent -*e*, drop the -*e* if the ending begins with a vowel:

   arrival   coming   creation

For words ending with a silent -e, keep the -e if the ending begins with a consonant:

safety   likeness   completely

Double the last consonant of one-syllable words if the ending begins with a vowel:

robbing   spotted   spinning

Double the last consonant of words accented on the last syllable if the ending begins with a vowel:

referring   admitted   technically

7. Make and review lists of words you commonly misspell.

8. Always budget enough time in the writing process to edit your papers for spelling errors.

IMPROVING SPELLING

Review writing exercises you have completed in this book and papers you have written in this or other courses for errors in spelling. List each word. Add words that you frequently misspell or are unsure of. Check a dictionary and carefully write out each word correctly. Add definitions to words that are easily confused such as "conscious" and "conscience" or "then" and "than."

1. _____   11. _____

2. _____   12. _____

3. _____   13. _____

4. _____   14. _____

5. _____   15. _____

6. _____   16. _____

7. _____   17. _____

8. _____   18. _____

9. _____   19. _____

10. _____   20. _____

Writer's Resources ⓦ Now™   If you use Writer's ResourcesNow, please have your students log in and view the pretest, study plan, and posttest for this chapter.

Part

7

Readings
for Writers

Strategies for Reading

Reading essays can help you improve as a writer because they demonstrate different ways to develop topics, explore ideas, create a thesis, organize paragraphs, write sentences, and choose words.

When you read for enjoyment, you generally start with the first sentence and let the writer take you on a journey. You allow the writer's words, sentences, and images to tell a story or develop an argument. As a writing student, however, you should read with a "writer's eye." You should examine a reading assignment critically to see what it can teach you about developing ideas, using words, and presenting ideas. Like writing, effective reading takes place in stages.

First Reading

1. **Look ahead and skim entries.** Don't wait for the night before class to read an assignment. Skim upcoming readings to become familiar with them.

2. **Study the title.** Authors often use titles to state a thesis or pose a question. Titles can also give you a clue about the type of essay it is. Titles with the word "how" may indicate a process essay, and titles that present pairs of words may suggest a comparison.

3. **Read the entire work.** Try to get the big picture by reading the entire essay to study its main ideas and organization.

4. **Focus on understanding the writer's main point.** Try to summarize the thesis in your own words.

5. **Jot down your first impressions.** What do you think of this essay? Do you like it? Why or why not? Do you agree with the writer's observations? If you find it dull, silly, or disturbing, ask yourself why. What is missing? How did the author succeed or fail in your view?

6. **Put the essay aside.** If possible, let two or three days pass before returning to the assignment. If the assignment is due tomorrow, try to read the essay in the morning, then return to it in the evening.

Second Reading

1. **Review your first impressions.** Determine if your views are based on your personal reactions or the writer's ability. Don't let personal opinions cloud your critical thinking. Even if you don't like what a writer has to say, you can learn something about writing.

2. **Read with a pen or pencil in your hand.** Make notes in the margin and underline sentences that express important ideas or make statements you find interesting, puzzling, or troubling. Writing as you read can make reading an active rather than a passive activity.

3. **Look up unfamiliar words.**

4. **Analyze passages you found difficult or confusing during the first reading.** A second reading can help you understand complex passages. If you still have difficulty understanding part of the essay, ask why. Does the writer use references you do not understand? Search the Internet to find information about phrases, names, or events the writer uses.

5. **Review the questions at the end of the essay. The questions are arranged in three types:**
   - *Understanding Meaning: What Is the Writer Trying to Say?*
     What is the writer's goal?
     What is the thesis?
     What readers is the writer addressing?
     What is the writer trying to share with readers?

   - *Evaluating Strategy: How Does the Writer Say It?*
     How effective is the title?
     How does the writer open the essay?
     What evidence does the writer use?
     How is the essay organized?
     How does the writer end the essay?

   - *Appreciating Language: What Words Does the Writer Use?*
     How does the writer use words?
     Are the words positive or negative?
     How do the words create the writer's tone or express his or her attitude toward the subject?

6. **Summarize your responses in a sentence or two for class discussion.**
7. **Focus on what this essay can teach you about writing.** Noticing how an author states a thesis, organizes details, and presents evidence can help you strengthen your own writing.

Read the following essay by Emily Prager. Notice how a student marked it for a class discussion and made notes for possible writing assignments.

OUR BARBIES, OURSELVES

EMILY PRAGER

Emily Prager is an actress and writer; her books include A Visit from the Footbinder *and Other Stories and* Eve's Tattoo. *In this essay, she analyzes the significance of the Barbie doll.*

AS YOU READ
Notice how Prager uses several patterns of development, including description, narration, and cause and effect, to develop her essay.

Introduction (obituary as writing prompt)

I read an astounding obituary in the *New York Times* not too long ago. It concerned the death of one Jack Ryan. A former husband of Zsa Zsa Gabor, it said, Mr. Ryan had been an inventor and designer during his lifetime. A man of eclectic creativity, he designed Sparrow and Hawk missiles when he worked for the Raytheon Company, and the notice said, when he consulted for Mattel he designed Barbie.

1

2   If Barbie was designed by a man, suddenly a lot of things made sense to me, things I'd wondered about for years. I used to look at Barbie and wonder, What's wrong with this picture? What kind of woman designed this doll? Let's be honest: Barbie looks like someone who got her start at the Playboy Mansion. She could be a regular guest on *The Howard Stern Show*. It is a fact of Barbie's design that her breasts are so out of proportion to the rest of her body that if she were a human woman, she'd fall flat on her face.

description WHY?

female/feminist reaction?

3   If it's true that a woman didn't design Barbie, you don't know how much saner that makes me feel. Of course, that doesn't ameliorate the damage. There are millions of women who are subliminally sure that a thirty-nine-inch bust and a twenty-three-inch waist are the epitome of lovability. Could this account for the popularity of breast implant surgery?

questions cause and effect

4   I don't mean to step on anyone's toes here. I loved my Barbie. Secretly, I still believe that neon pink and turquoise blue are the only colors in which to decorate a duplex condo. And like so many others of my generation, I've never married, simply because I cannot find a man who looks as good in clam diggers as Ken.

5   The question that comes to mind is, of course, Did Mr. Ryan design Barbie as a weapon? Because it *is* odd that Barbie appeared about the same time in my consciousness as the feminist movement— a time when women sought equality and small breasts were king. Or is Barbie the dream date of a weapons designer? Or perhaps it's simpler than that: Perhaps Barbie is Zsa Zsa if she were eleven inches tall. No matter what, my discovery of Jack Ryan confirms what I have always felt: There is something indescribably masculine about Barbie— dare I say it, phallic. For all her giant breasts and high-heeled feet, she lacks a certain softness. If you asked a little girl what kind of doll she wanted for Christmas, I just don't think she'd reply, "Please, Santa, I want a hardbody."

Barbie as a weapon?
cause and effect

(modern ideal of a hard body!)

6   On the other hand, you could say that Barbie, in feminist terms, is definitely her own person. With her condos and fashion plazas and pools and beauty salons, she is definitely a liberated woman, a gal on the move. And she has always been sexual, even totemic. Before Barbie, American dolls were flat-footed and breastless, and ineffably dignified. They were created in the image of little girls or babies. Madame Alexander was the queen of doll makers in the '50s, and her dollies looked like Elizabeth Taylor in *National Velvet.* They represented the kind of girls who looked perfect in jodhpurs, whose hair was never out of place, who grew up to be Jackie Kennedy— before she married Onassis. Her dolls' boyfriends were figments of the imagination, figments with large portfolios and three-piece suits and presidential aspirations, figments who could keep dolly in the style to which little girls of the '50s were programmed to become accustomed; perhaps what accounts for Barbie's vast popularity is that she was also a '60s woman: into free love and fun colors, anti-class, and possessed a real, molded boyfriend, Ken, with whom she could chant a mantra.

Barbie as role model?

Barbie = adult doll not a baby or child

comparison

Ken sexless? comparison

But there were problems with Ken. <u>I always felt weird about him.</u> He had no genitals, and, even at age ten, I found that ominous. I mean, here was Barbie with these humongous breasts, and that was O.K. with the toy company. And then, there was Ken, with that truncated, unidentifiable lump at his groin. I sensed injustice at work. Why, I wondered, was Barbie designed with such obvious sexual equipment and Ken not? Why was he treated as if it were more mysterious than hers? Did the fact that it was treated as such indicate that somehow his equipment, his essential maleness, was considered more powerful than hers, more worthy of the dignity of concealment? And if the issue in the mind of the toy company was obscenity and its possible damage to children, I still object. How do they think I felt, knowing that no matter how many water beds they slept in, or hot tubs they romped in, or swimming pools they lounged by under the stars, Barbie and Ken could never make love? No matter how much sexuality Barbie possessed, she would never turn Ken on. He would be forever withholding, forever detached. There was a <u>loneliness about Barbie's situation that was always disturbing.</u> And twenty-five years later, movies and videos are still filled with topless women and covered men. <u>As if we're all trapped in Barbie's world and can never escape.</u> ∎

questions

Barbie's fate
conclusion

final observation

7

Student Notes
First Reading

Barbie as symbol of male domination?

What about GI Joe and boys?

Is Prager really serious about this?

Barbie as paradox — a toy that presents a sexist *Playboy* image of women but a toy that is independent and more "liberated" than traditional baby dolls.

Tone: witty but serious in spots, raises a lot of issues but doesn't really discuss many.

Second Reading

Thesis: The Barbie doll, the creation of a male weapons designer, has shaped the way a generation of women defined themselves. (Get other opinions)

Body: spins off a number of topics and observations, a list of associations, suited for general readers.

Approach: a mix of serious and witty commentary, writer appears to entertain as much as inform or persuade.

Organization: use of modes critical to keeping the essay from becoming a rambling list of contradictory ideas. Good use of description, comparison, cause and effect.

Conclusion—"trapped in Barbie's world" good ending.

Prewriting—Possible Topics

Description—childhood toys—models of cars and planes? games— Monopoly (preparing kids for capitalism?)

Comparison/contrast—boy and girl toys and games, playing house vs. playing ball (social roles vs. competition, teamwork)

Cause and effect—we are socialized by our toys and games in childhood, affecting how men and women develop (needs support—Psych class notes)
Example—my daughter's Beanie Baby?

STRATEGIES FOR CRITICAL READING

As you read the entries in this chapter, ask yourself these questions:

1. **What is the writer's goal?** What is the purpose of the essay — to raise questions, motivate readers to take action, or change people's opinions?
2. **What is the thesis?** What is the writer's main idea? Can you state the thesis in your own words?
3. **What evidence does the writer provide to support the thesis?** Does the writer use personal observations, narratives, facts, statistics, or examples to support his or her conclusions?
4. **How does the writer organize the essay?** How does he or she introduce readers to the topic, develop ideas, arrange information, and conclude the essay? How does the writer use patterns of development?
5. **Who are the intended readers?** What does the original source of the document tell you about its intended audience? Does the writer direct the essay to a particular group or to a general readership? What terms or references are used? Are technical or uncommon terms defined? What does the writer seem to expect readers to know?
6. **How successful is the writing—in context?** Does the writer achieve his or her goals while respecting the needs of the reader and the conventions of the discipline or situation? Are there particular considerations that cause the writer to break the rules of "good writing"? Why?
7. **What can you learn about writing?** What does this writer teach you about using words, writing sentences, and developing paragraphs? Are there any techniques you can use in future assignments?

Description

Description presents details about persons, places, objects, or ideas. It records what you see, hear, feel, taste, and touch.

THE BOMB

LANSING LAMONT

In this section from his book Trinity, *Lansing Lamont describes the first atomic bomb shortly before it was detonated in New Mexico in July 1945.*

AS YOU READ

Notice how Lamont includes both objective details about the bomb—its size, weight, and cost—with subjective details that compare the bomb to some kind of animal—a squid with tentacles and a "monster."

Words to Know

conflagration fire

The bomb rested in its cradle.   1

It slept upon a steel-supported oakwood platform, inside a sheet-metal shack 103 feet above the ground: a bloated black squid girdled with cables and leechlike detonators, each tamped with enough explosive to spark simultaneously, within a millionth of a second, the final conflagration. Tentacles emerged from the squid in a harness of wires connecting the detonators to a shiny aluminum tank, the firing unit.   2

ingot block

Stripped of its coils, the bomb weighed 10,000 pounds. Its teardrop dimensions were 4½ feet wide, 10½ feet long. Its guts contained two layers of wedge-shaped high-explosive blocks surrounding an inner core of precisely machined nuclear ingots that lay, as one scientist described them, like diamonds in an immense wad of cotton. These ingots were made from a metal called plutonium.   3

At the heart of the bomb, buried inside the layers of explosive and plutonium, lay the ultimate key to its success or failure, a metallic sphere no bigger than a ping-pong ball that even twenty years later would still be regarded a state secret: the initiator.   4

christen give birth to

Within five seconds the initiator would trigger the sequence that hundreds of shadows had gathered to watch that dawn. The bomb would either fizzle to a premature death or shatteringly christen a new era on earth.   5

Weeks, months, years of toil had gone into it.   6

The nation's finest brains and leadership, the cream of its scientific and engineering force, plus two billion dollars from the taxpayers had built the squat monster on the tower for this very moment. Yet it had been no labor of love. There was not the mildest affection for it.   7

blitzed bombed

Superfortress B-29, a WWII four-engine bomber

spawn offspring

welter flurry

Other instruments of war bore dashing or maidenly names: Britain's "Spitfires"; the "Flying Tigers"; the "Gravel Gerties" and "Gypsy Rose Lees" that clanked across North Africa or blitzed bridgeheads on the Rhine; even the Germans' "Big Bertha" of World War I; and, soon, the Superfortress "Enola Gay" of Hiroshima, deliverer of an atomic bundle called "Little Boy."   8

The test bomb had no colorful nickname. One day its spawn would be known as "Fat Man" (after Churchill). But now its identity was cloaked in a welter of impersonal terms: "the thing," "the beast," "the device" and its Washington pseudonym, "S-1." The scientists, most of whom called it simply "the gadget," had handled it gently and daintily, like the baby it was— but out of respect, not fondness. One wrong jolt of the volatile melon inside its Duralumin frame could precipitate the collision of radioactive masses and a slow, agonizing death from radiation. Or instant vaporization.   9

precipitate to bring about abruptly

vaporization complete destruction

The monster engendered the sort of fear that had caused one young scientist to break down the evening before and be escorted promptly from the site to a psychiatric ward; and another, far older and wiser, a Nobel Prize winner, to murmur, as he waited in his trench, "I'm scared witless, absolutely witless." ■   10

CRITICAL THINKING AND DISCUSSION

GET THINKING AND WRITING

Understanding Meaning: What Is the Writer Trying to Say?

1. What dominant impression does Lamont create?
2. How did the scientists feel about the bomb they created?
3. What impact did the bomb have on the men who worked on it?

Evaluating Strategy: How Does the Writer Say It?

1. How does Lamont blend objective and subjective details to describe the bomb?
2. What does the fact that, unlike other weapons, the bomb had no clever nickname reveal about the attitudes of its inventors?
3. What impact does the final quotation have? Why is it helpful to include direct quotations from participants or eyewitnesses in a description?

Appreciating Language: What Words Does the Writer Use?

1. Underline words that create Lamont's dominant impression.
2. What role does animal imagery play in shaping Lamont's view of the bomb?

Writing Suggestions

1. Write a short essay in which you bring an object like a car, house, or computer to life by comparing it to a person or an animal. You might refer to a van or truck you drove as a "beast" or describe a guitar as a "best friend."
2. *Collaborative writing:* Work with a group of students and write a brief essay describing the threat nuclear terrorism poses. What could happen if terrorists were able to place a nuclear weapon in a large American city?

UNFORGETTABLE MISS BESSIE

CARL ROWAN

Carl Rowan (1925–2000) was born in Tennessee and received degrees from Oberlin College and the University of Minnesota. He worked as a newspaper columnist for over thirty years and served as the ambassador to Finland.

AS YOU READ

In this article, published in Reader's Digest, *Rowan recalls a teacher who changed his life. Notice that he describes not only what Miss Bessie looked like, but also the influence she had on her students.*

1   She was only about five feet tall and probably never weighed more than 110 pounds, but Miss Bessie was a towering presence in the classroom.

Words to Know

Beowulf eighth-century
English epic poem

She was the only woman tough enough to make me read *Beowulf* and think for a few foolish days that I liked it. From 1938 to 1942, when I attended Bernard High School in McMinnville, Tenn., she taught me English, history, civics— and a lot more than I realized.

I shall never forget the day she scolded me into reading *Beowulf*. 2

"But Miss Bessie," I complained, "I ain't much interested in it." 3

Her large brown eyes became daggerish slits. "Boy," she said, "how dare you say 'ain't' to me! I've taught you better than that." 4

"Miss Bessie," I pleaded, "I'm trying to make first-string end on the football team, and if I go around saying 'it isn't' and 'they aren't,' the guys are gonna laugh me off the squad." 5

"Boy," she responded, "you'll play football because you have guts. But do you know what *really* takes guts? Refusing to lower your standards to those of the crowd. It takes guts to say you've got to live and be somebody fifty years after all the football games are over." 6

I started saying "it isn't" and "they aren't," and I still made first-string end— and class valedictorian— without losing my buddies' respect. 7

valedictorian student
with the highest
grades chosen to speak
at graduation

During her remarkable 44-year career, Mrs. Bessie Taylor Gwynn taught hundreds of economically deprived black youngsters— including my mother, my brother, my sisters, and me. I remember her now with gratitude and affection— especially in this era when Americans are so wrought-up about a "rising tide of mediocrity" in public education and the problems of finding competent, caring teachers. Miss Bessie was an example of an informed, dedicated teacher, a blessing to children and an asset to the nation. 8

Born in 1895, in poverty, she grew up in Athens, Ala., where there was no public school for blacks. She attended Trinity School, a private institution for blacks run by the American Missionary Association, and in 1911 graduated from the Normal School (a "super" high school) at Fisk University in Nashville. Mrs. Gwynn, the essence of pride and privacy, never talked about her years in Athens; only in the months before her death did she reveal that she had never attended Fisk University itself because she could not afford the four-year course. 9

At Normal School she learned a lot about Shakespeare, but most of all about the profound importance of education— especially, for a people trying to move up from slavery. "What you put in your head, boy," she once said, "can never be pulled out by the Ku Klux Klan, the Congress, or anybody." 10

Miss Bessie's bearing of dignity told anyone who met her that she was "educated" in the best sense of the word. There was never a discipline problem in her classes. We didn't dare mess with a woman who knew about the Battle of Hastings, the Magna Carta, and the Bill of Rights— and who could also play the piano. 11

This frail-looking woman could make sense of Shakespeare, Milton, Voltaire, and bring to life Booker T. Washington and W. E. B. DuBois. Believing that it was important to know who the officials were that spent taxpayers' money and made public policy, she made us memorize the names of everyone on the Supreme Court and in the President's Cabinet. 12

It could be embarrassing to be unprepared when Miss Bessie said, "Get up and tell the class who Frances Perkins is and what you think about her."

13   Miss Bessie knew that my family, like so many others during the Depression, couldn't afford to subscribe to a newspaper. She knew we didn't even own a radio. Still, she prodded me to "look out for your future and find some way to keep up with what's going on in the world." So I became a delivery boy for the Chattanooga *Times*. I rarely made a dollar a week, but I got to read a newspaper every day.

14   Miss Bessie noticed things that had nothing to do with schoolwork, but were vital to a youngster's development. Once a few classmates made fun of my frayed, hand-me-down overcoat, calling me "Strings." As I was leaving school, Miss Bessie patted me on the back of that old overcoat and said, "Carl, never fret about what you *don't* have. Just make the most of what you *do* have—a brain."

15   Among the things that I did not have was electricity in the little frame house that my father had built for $400 with his World War I bonus. But because of her inspiration, I spent many hours squinting beside a kerosene lamp reading Shakespeare and Thoreau, Samuel Pepys and William Cullen Bryant.

16   No one in my family had ever graduated from high school, so there was no tradition of commitment to learning for me to lean on. Like millions of youngsters in today's ghettos and barrios, I needed the push and stimulation of a teacher who truly cared. Miss Bessie gave plenty of both, as she immersed me in a wonderful world of similes, metaphors and even onomatopoeia. She led me to believe that I could write sonnets as well as Shakespeare, or iambic-pentameter verse to put Alexander Pope to shame.

17   In those days the McMinnville school system was rigidly "Jim Crow," and poor black children had to struggle to put anything in their heads. Our high school was only slightly larger than the once-typical little red schoolhouse, and its library was outrageously inadequate—so small, I like to say, that if two students were in it and one wanted to turn a page, the other one had to step outside.

Jim Crow reference to racial segregation in the South

18   Negroes, as we were called then, were not allowed in the town library, except to mop floors or dust tables. But through one of those secret Old South arrangements between whites of conscience and blacks of stature, Miss Bessie kept getting books smuggled out of the white library. That is how she introduced me to the Brontës, Byron, Coleridge, Keats, and Tennyson. "If you don't read, you can't write, and if you can't write, you might as well stop dreaming," Miss Bessie once told me.

19   So I read whatever Miss Bessie told me to, and tried to remember the things she insisted that I store away. Forty-five years later, I can still recite her "truths to live by," such as Henry Wadsworth Longfellow's lines from "The Ladder of St. Augustine":

> The heights by great men reached and kept
> Were not attained by sudden flight.
> But they, while their companions slept,
> Were toiling upward in the night.

20   Years later, her inspiration, prodding, anger, cajoling, and almost os-
motic infusion of learning finally led to that lovely day when Miss Bessie
dropped me a note saying, "I'm so proud to read your column in the
Nashville *Tennessean*."

21   Miss Bessie was a spry 80 when I went back to McMinnville and visited her in a senior citizens' apartment building. Pointing out proudly
that her building was racially integrated, she reached for two glasses and
a pint of bourbon. I was momentarily shocked, because it would have
been scandalous in the 1930s and '40s for word to get out that a teacher
drank, and nobody had ever raised a rumor that Miss Bessie did.

22   I felt a new sense of equality as she lifted her glass to mine. Then
she revealed a softness and compassion that I had never known as a
student.

23   "I've never forgotten that examination day," she said, "when Buster
Martin held up seven fingers, obviously asking you for help with question number seven, 'Name a common carrier.' I can still picture you looking at your exam paper and humming a few bars of 'Chattanooga Choo
Choo.' I was so tickled, I couldn't punish either of you."

24   Miss Bessie was telling me, with bourbon-laced grace, that I never
fooled her for a moment.

25   When Miss Bessie died in 1980, at age 85, hundreds of her former students mourned. They knew the measure of a great teacher: love and moti-
vation. Her wisdom and influence had rippled out across generations.

26   Some of her students who might normally have been doomed to poverty went on to become doctors, dentists, and college professors. Many,
guided by Miss Bessie's example, became public-school teachers.

27   "The memory of Miss Bessie and how she conducted her classroom did
more for me than anything I learned in college," recalls Gladys Wood of
Knoxville, Tenn., a highly respected English teacher who spent 43 years
in the state's school system. "So many times, when I faced a difficult
classroom problem, I asked myself, *How would Miss Bessie deal with this?*
And I'd remember that she would handle it with laughter and love."

28   No child can get all the necessary support at home, and millions of
poor children get *no* support at all. This is what makes a wise, educated,
warmhearted teacher like Miss Bessie so vital to the minds, hearts, and
souls of this country's children. ■

GET THINKING
AND WRITING

CRITICAL THINKING AND DISCUSSION

Understanding Meaning: What Is the Writer Trying to Say?

1. What is Rowan's purpose in describing Miss Bessie? What is he trying to share with readers?
2. What qualities of Miss Bessie's does Rowan admire?
3. How did Miss Bessie influence Rowan and other students?
4. Why do you think so many former students attended her funeral? Why does Rowan describe their professions? How does that support his point?

5. *Critical thinking:* Do you think Rowan sees her as a role model? Could teachers like Miss Bessie change the lives of poor schoolchildren in today's schools? Why or why not?

Evaluating Strategy: How Does the Writer Say It?

1. Rowan opens the description with details about Miss Bessie's appearance. How does this serve his purpose?
2. What dominant impressions does Rowan create about Miss Bessie?
3. How does Rowan blend descriptions of his own life into the essay to demonstrate the effect of Miss Bessie's lessons?

Appreciating Language: What Words Does the Writer Use?

1. Rowan calls Miss Bessie an *asset to the nation.* What does he mean by this phrase?
2. Rowan includes dialogue in his description. What do you notice about Miss Bessie's language? What does this add to the essay?

Writing Suggestions

1. Describe a person you know by focusing on a single positive or negative characteristic or quality. Use brief narratives to illustrate the person's behavior. Include your own reactions to this person's behavior.
2. *Collaborative writing:* Discuss Rowan's description with other students. How did Miss Bessie help generations of disadvantaged children overcome their circumstances? Could her approach help students today? Why or why not? Write a description of how teachers can help at-risk children succeed in life. Your group could write a process essay with numbered suggestions.

Narration

Narration tells stories or relates a series of events, usually in chronological order.

TRUTH AND BEAUTY

Lucy Grealy

Lucy Grealy (1963–2002) was born in Ireland but spent most of her life in New York. When she was nine, she was diagnosed with cancer of the jaw and endured a series of operations and chemotherapy treatments. In this passage from her book An Autobiography of a Face, *Grealy recounts what happened when she went outside without the hat she wore to cover her baldness.*

AS YOU READ

Notice how Grealy invents a game to catch the people staring at her, making them feel nervous or embarrassed, reversing the way people usually looked at her.

One day, when I had a full three or four inches of hair, I was leaving the house with Susie. At the last minute I turned and ran back up the stairs, calling out, "Just a minute while I get my hat." 1

"You don't need it anymore, Lucy, your hair is fine, come on already," she called back to me, frustrated that we were going to be late. 2

I stopped in the middle of the stairs and, genuinely surprised, considered what she had said. Running my fingers through my hair, I had to admit she was more or less right. It wasn't nearly as long as it used to be, but I wasn't bald. I went out with her into the world, bareheaded for the first time in years. A warm and gusty breeze parted my hair and stroked it like a caress. We went to the store, and people gave me second looks as they always did, but not one person called me Baldy. 3

The next day I went to school bareheaded, and no one mentioned it. Had I been wrong in thinking that I needed to hide behind my hat, had it all been a mistake on my part? Except people still looked at me. Though I had given up eating in the lunchroom, there were plenty of relentless daily attacks of teasing in the hallways. Girls never teased me, but out of the corner of my eye I could see them staring at me, and when I turned toward them, they glanced away quickly, trying to pretend they were concentrating on something else. Outside of school I'd catch adults staring at me all the time. I played games with them in stores, positioning myself just so and pretending I was absorbed in examining some piece of merchandise, only to turn my head quickly and trap them as they averted their embarrassed stares. Groups of boys were what I most feared, and I gladly ducked into an empty doorway if I saw a group coming my way that looked like trouble. It was easy to spot potential offenders: they walked with a certain swagger, a certain sway. ■ 4

GET THINKING
AND WRITING

CRITICAL THINKING AND DISCUSSION

Understanding Meaning: What Is the Writer Trying to Say?

1. How did people react to Grealy when she did not wear a hat? How did boys and girls behave differently? How did adults treat her?
2. Whom did she fear the most and why?
3. What game did she play with adults? What was the point of her game?
4. *Critical thinking:* What does Grealy's story reveal about the way people respond to those who are ill, disabled, or different?

Evaluating Strategy: How Does the Writer Say It?

1. Grealy mentions that she gave up eating in the lunchroom. What does this detail suggest about her isolation at school?
2. Grealy points out that she had worn a hat for years in public. Why is this fact important? How might having to hide hair loss affect a child's self-esteem?

Appreciating Language: What Words Does the Writer Use?

1. What words does Grealy use to describe the boys she fears the most? What do these words suggest about their attitudes? Why might she view them as "potential offenders"?
2. Grealy mentions that in the past people called her "Baldy." What impact would a nickname like this have on a young girl? What does it reveal about the power words can have on the way people view themselves?

Writing Suggestions

1. Write a short essay relating an incident in which you had problems dealing with the public, such as facing angry customers, working with new employees, or confronting teammates after making a bad play.
2. *Collaborative writing:* Discuss Grealy's essay with other students and write a hypothetical narrative about how children with disabilities or illnesses should be treated by others.

CHAMPION OF THE WORLD

MAYA ANGELOU

Maya Angelou (1928–) was a dancer and actress who became best known for her poetry and autobiographical books. In this section from I Know Why the Caged Bird Sings, *Angelou recounts listening to a Joe Louis prizefight on the radio. Known as the Brown Bomber, Joe Louis was the heavyweight champion from 1937–1949.*

AS YOU READ

Notice how Angelou uses dialogue to move the plot of her story. By presenting the words of others, she can show rather explain how important the fight was. She also demonstrates the importance of Joe Louis by including examples of past racism (paragraph 16).

1 The last inch of space was filled, yet people continued to wedge themselves along the walls of the Store. Uncle Willie had turned the radio up to its last notch so that youngsters on the porch wouldn't miss a word. Women sat on kitchen chairs, dining room chairs, stools and upturned wooden boxes. Small children and babies perched on every lap available and men leaned on the shelves or each other.

2 The apprehensive mood was shot through with shafts of gaiety, as a black sky is streaked with lightning.

3 "I ain't worried 'bout this fight. Joe's gonna whip that cracker like it's open season."

4 "He gone whip him till that white boy call him Momma."

5 At last the talking was finished and the string-along songs about razor blades were over and the fight began.

Words to Know

apprehensive fearful

contender challenger

assent approval

"master's voice" reference to RCA radios

accusations charges

"A quick jab to the head." In the Store the crowd grunted. "A left to the head and a right and another left." One of the listeners cackled like a hen and was quieted.   6

"They're in a clench, Louis is trying to fight his way out."   7

Some bitter comedian on the porch said, "That white man don't mind hugging that niggah now, I betcha."   8

"The referee is moving in to break them up, but Louis finally pushed the contender away and it's an uppercut to the chin. The contender is hanging on, now he's backing away. Louis catches him with a short left to the jaw."   9

A tide of murmuring assent poured out the doors and into the yard.   10

"Another left and another left. Louis is saving that mighty right. . . ." The mutter in the Store had grown into a baby roar and it was pierced by the clang of a bell and the announcer's "That's the bell for round three, ladies and gentlemen."   11

As I pushed my way into the Store I wondered if the announcer gave any thought to the fact that he was addressing as "ladies and gentlemen" all the Negroes around the world who sat sweating and praying, glued to their "master's voice."   12

There were only a few calls for RC Colas, Dr. Peppers, and Hire's root beer. The real festivities would begin after the fight. Then even the old Christian ladies who taught their children and tried themselves to practice turning the other cheek would buy soft drinks, and if the Brown Bomber's victory was a particularly bloody one they would order peanut patties and Baby Ruths also.   13

Bailey and I lay the coins on top of the cash register. Uncle Willie didn't allow us to ring up sales during a fight. It was too noisy and might shake up the atmosphere. When the gong rang for the next round we pushed through the near-sacred quiet to the herd of children outside.   14

"He's got Louis against the ropes and now it's a left to the body and a right to the ribs. Another right to the body, it looks like it was low. . . . Yes, ladies and gentlemen, the referee is signaling, but the contender keeps raining the blows on Louis. It's another to the body, and it looks like Louis is going down."   15

My race groaned. It was our people falling. It was another lynching, yet another Black man hanging on a tree. One more woman ambushed and raped. A Black boy whipped and maimed. It was hounds on the trail of a man running through slimy swamps. It was a white woman slapping her maid for being forgetful.   16

The men in the Store stood away from the walls and at attention. Women greedily clutched the babes on their laps while on the porch the shufflings and smiles, flirtings and pinching of a few minutes before were gone. This might be the end of the world. If Joe lost we were back in slavery and beyond help. It would all be true, the accusations that we were lower types of human beings. Only a little higher than the apes. True that we were stupid and ugly and lazy and dirty and   17 unlucky and, worst of all, that God Himself hated us and <u>ordained</u> us to be <u>hewers</u> of wood and <u>drawers</u> of water, forever and ever, world without end.

18 We didn't breathe. We didn't hope. We waited.

19 "He's off the ropes, ladies and gentlemen. He's moving towards the center of the ring." There was no time to be relieved. The worst might still happen.

20 "And now it looks like Joe is mad. He's caught <u>Carnera</u> with a left hook to the head and a right to the head. It's a left jab to the body and another left to the head. There's a left cross and a right to the head. The contender's right eye is bleeding and he can't seem to keep his block up. Louis is penetrating every block. The referee is moving in, but Louis sends a left to the body and it's the uppercut to the chin and the contender is dropping. He's on the canvas, ladies and gentlemen."

21 Babies slid to the floor as women stood up and men leaned toward the radio.

22 "Here's the referee. He's counting. One, two, three, four, five, six, seven . . . Is the contender trying to get up again?"

23 All the men in the Store shouted, "NO."

24 " —eight, nine, ten." There were a few sounds from the audience, but they seemed to be holding themselves in against tremendous pressure.

25 "The fight is all over, ladies and gentlemen. Let's get the microphone over to the referee. . . . Here he is. He's got the Brown Bomber's hand, he's holding it up. . . . Here he is. . . ."

26 Then the voice, husky and familiar, came to wash over us — "The winnah, and still heavyweight champeen of the world . . . Joe Louis."

27 Champion of the world. A Black boy. Some Black mother's son. He was the strongest man in the world. People drank Coca-Colas like <u>ambrosia</u> and ate candy bars like Christmas. Some of the men went behind the Store and poured <u>white lightning</u> in their soft-drink bottles, and a few of the bigger boys followed them. Those who were not chased away came back blowing their breath in front of themselves like proud smokers.

28 It would take an hour or more before the people would leave the Store and head for home. Those who lived too far had made arrangements to stay in town. It wouldn't do for a Black man and his family to be caught on a lonely country road on a night when Joe Louis had proved that we were the strongest people in the world. ■

ordained ordered by God
hewers cutters
drawers carriers

Carnera Primo Carnera, Louis's opponent

ambrosia food of the gods
white lightning homemade whiskey

CRITICAL THINKING AND DISCUSSION

GET THINKING AND WRITING

Understanding Meaning: What Is the Writer Trying to Say?

1. What is the thesis of Angelou's narrative? Why was this fight more than a sporting event?
2. How did Joe Louis's struggle appear to represent the struggle of a people rather than that of a single athlete?
3. How did the people in the store react to the fight?

4. Why did many people decide to stay in town rather than travel home that night?

5. *Critical thinking:* Do you think any athletes today have the same impact on minorities? Why or why not?

Evaluating Strategy: How Does the Writer Say It?

1. How does Angelou use dialogue to advance the narrative and support her main point?

2. How does Angelou re-create the broadcast? Do direct quotations of the announcer work better than summaries or paraphrases? Why or why not?

3. What impact does the last sentence have? How does it reinforce her main point?

Appreciating Language: What Words Does the Writer Use?

1. How does Angelou use the advertising slogan his "master's voice" in this essay? How does it ironically suit a story about race?

2. Angelou uses short sentences in some places: "We didn't breathe. We didn't hope. We waited." What effect do they have? Can a writer use too many short sentences? Why or why not?

Writing Suggestions

1. Using Angelou's essay as a model, write a narrative about an experience when you were part of a group responding to a common experience, such as watching a football game, news broadcast, or movie. Did everyone react the same way or did people behave differently? Try to capture people's responses by using direct quotes or details about their behavior.

2. *Collaborative writing:* Work with a group of students and write a brief essay about the role athletes play in society today. Do they represent anything more than success in sports? Are they role models? Could any modern athlete have the same significance as Joe Louis did seventy years ago? Why or why not?

Example

Example illustrates ideas, issues, events, or personality types by describing one or more specific events, objects, or people.

HOMELESS

ANNA QUINDLEN

Anna Quindlen (1952–) has written a column for the New York Times *and published several books, including* Living Out Loud, Object Lessons, One True Thing, *and* Black and Blue.

Example **573**

AS YOU READ

Quindlen uses a single woman to represent the plight of the homeless, whom, she states, are not really homeless but "people without homes."

1   Her name was Ann, and we met in the Port Authority Bus Terminal several Januarys ago. I was doing a story on homeless people. She said I was wasting my time talking to her; she was just passing through, although she'd been passing through for more than two weeks. To prove to me that this was true, she rummaged through a tote bag and a manila envelope and finally unfolded a sheet of typing paper and brought out her photographs.

2   They were not pictures of family, or friends, or even a dog or cat, its eyes brown-red in the flashbulb's light. They were pictures of a house. It was like a thousand houses in a hundred towns, not suburb, not city, but somewhere in between, with aluminum siding and a chain-link fence, a narrow driveway running up to a one-car garage and a patch of backyard. The house was yellow. I looked on the back for a date or a name, but neither was there. There was no need for discussion. I knew what she was trying to tell me, for it was something I had often felt. She was not adrift, alone, anonymous, although her bags and her raincoat with the grime shadowing its creases had made me believe she was. She had a house, or at least once upon a time had had one. Inside were curtains, a couch, a stove, potholders. You are where you live. She was somebody.

3   I've never been very good at looking at the big picture, taking the global view, and I've always been a person with an overactive sense of place, the legacy of an Irish grandfather. So it is natural that the thing that seems most wrong with the world to me right now is that there are so many people with no homes. I'm not simply talking about shelter from the <u>elements</u>, or three square meals a day or a mailing address to which the welfare people can send the check — although I know that all these are important for survival. I'm talking about a home, about precisely those kinds of feelings that have wound up in cross-stitch and French knots on <u>samplers</u> over the years.

4   Home is where the heart is. There's no place like it. I love my home with a <u>ferocity</u> totally out of proportion to its appearance or location. I love dumb things about it: the hot-water heater, the plastic rack you drain dishes in, the roof over my head, which occasionally leaks. And yet it is precisely those dumb things that make it what it is — a place of <u>certainty</u>, stability, predictability, privacy, for me and for my family. It is where I live. What more can you say about a place than that? That is everything.

5   Yet it is something that we have been edging away from gradually during my lifetime and the lifetimes of my parents and grandparents. There was a time when where you lived often was where you worked and where you grew the food you ate and even where you were buried. When that era passed, where you lived at least was where your parents had lived and where you would live with your children when you became <u>enfeebled</u>. Then, suddenly where you lived was where you lived for three years, until you could move on to something else and something else again.

Words to Know

elements weather

samplers embroidered pictures

ferocity intensity

certainty confidence

enfeebled weakened, disabled

And so we have come to something else again, to children who do **6**
not understand what it means to go to their rooms because they have
never had a room, to men and women whose fantasy is a wall they can
paint a color of their own choosing, to old people reduced to sitting on
molded plastic chairs, their skin blue-white in the lights of a bus station,
who pull pictures of houses out of their bags. Homes have stopped being
homes. Now they are real estate.

People find it curious that those without homes would rather sleep **7**
sitting up on benches or huddled in doorways than go to shelters. Cer-
tainly some prefer to do so because they are emotionally ill, because
they have been locked in before and they are damned if they will be
locked in again. Others are afraid of the violence and trouble they may
find there. But some seem to want something that is not available in
shelters, and they will not compromise, not for a cot, or oatmeal, or a
shower with special soap that kills the bugs. "One room," a woman with
a baby who was sleeping on her sister's floor once told me, "painted
blue." That was the <u>crux</u> of it; not size or location, but pride of ownership. Painted blue.

crux bottom-line, core

This is a difficult problem, and some wise and compassionate people **8**
are working hard at it. But in the main I think we work around it, just as
we walk around it when it is lying on the sidewalk or sitting in the bus
terminal— the problem, that is. It has been customary to take people's
pain and lessen our own participation in it by turning it into an issue,
not a collection of human beings. We turn an adjective into a noun: the
poor, not poor people; the homeless, not Ann or the man who lives in
the box or the woman who sleeps on the subway grate.

Sometimes I think we would be better off if we forgot about the **9**
broad strokes and concentrated on the details. Here is a woman without
a bureau. There is a man with no mirror, no wall to hang it on. They are
not the homeless. They are people who have no homes. No drawer that
holds the spoons. No window to look out upon the world. My God. That
is everything. ∎

GET THINKING AND WRITING ▸ CRITICAL THINKING AND DISCUSSION

Understanding Meaning: What Is the Writer Trying to Say?

1. What is Quindlen's thesis? Can you express it in your own words?
2. What does Quindlen want people to know about the homeless?
3. What kind of person is Ann, the homeless woman Quindlen meets in the bus terminal?

Evaluating Strategy: How Does the Writer Say It?

1. How does Quindlen use the single example of Ann to explain the plight of the homeless? Would an essay without a personal example be as effective?
2. Quindlen focuses on Ann's photo of her old home. Why is this detail important? What does it reveal?

Example **575**

Appreciating Language: What Words Does the Writer Use?

1. What connotations does the word "home" have? What does it mean to be "homeless" besides simply lacking shelter?
2. What does Quindlen mean by the statement, "You are where you live"?

Writing Suggestions

1. Use one or more people you have met to serve as examples of a social issue or problem. Your essay could discuss high school dropouts, single parents, people who have overcome a disability, role models, television addicts, or Good Samaritans.
2. *Collaborative writing:* Working with a group of students, develop an essay providing examples of how communities or individuals could assist the homeless.

DEATH OF A DREAM

TONY BROWN

Tony Brown (1933–) is best known for his long-running public television program Tony Brown's Journal *and his book* Black Lies, White Lies: The Truth According to Tony Brown.

AS YOU READ
Note how Brown uses the failure of a single black-owned supermarket to illustrate his theory "that the most successful economic boycott ever conducted in America is the boycott by Blacks of their own businesses."

Up! Up! You mighty race. You can accomplish what you will.

— MARCUS GARVEY

1   It was a day of celebration when Rick Singletary opened the largest Black-owned supermarket in the country in Columbus, Ohio — a spectacular $4.4 million operation. He had worked for a major grocery chain for fourteen years and started his own store with his life savings, those of his mother, and a government-insured loan from the Reagan administration. He located Singletary Plaza Mart in the Black community because he knew there was a need for a grocery store there, and because he wanted to create jobs for Blacks.

2   The <u>entrepreneur</u> needed only a $200,000-a-week volume to keep 130 Black people working. And yet, in a tragedy that <u>exemplifies</u> the real reason why Black America has never been able to compete with White America, Singletary's store failed. Although his research had shown that Blacks in Columbus spent $2.5 million per week on groceries, he could not get them to spend even $200,000 of it in the store he had built for them in their own neighborhood.

Words to Know

entrepreneur independent business owner

exemplifies represents

I am familiar with the details because I tried to help Singletary, and I tried to help the Blacks in his community realize what was happening. For three days, I joined others in the Buy Freedom campaign of Black economic empowerment in Columbus. But, sadly, we failed to save his store. **3**

This is not simply a neighborhood issue, it is a national disgrace. Rick Singletary, a good man who banked on his community, went bankrupt. He lost his life savings and his mother's savings, and 130 Black people lost their jobs. *This story is repeated somewhere in the Black community every day.* This gives <u>credence</u> to my theory that the most successful economic boycott ever conducted in America is the boycott by Blacks of their own businesses. **4**

credence acceptance as true

Making Blacks Competitive

The key to making Black America competitive with White America is really quite simple. Black Americans now earn nearly $500 billion annually, according to economist Andrew F. Brommer. This is roughly <u>equivalent</u> to the gross domestic product of Canada or Australia. And yet Blacks spend only 3 percent of their income with a Black business or Black professional. By spending 97 percent of their money outside of their racial community, they <u>exacerbate</u> their own social and economic problems. **5**

equivalent equal

exacerbate make worse

This is the reason that Blacks do not keep pace economically or socially with the rest of the country. Since 80 percent of Americans are employed in small businesses, it is common sense that if businesses in the Black neighborhoods do not flourish, job opportunities will be greatly reduced. **6**

To succeed as a people, Blacks have to invest in and build their community. Other ethnic groups turn their money over multiple times within their communities. If money turns over ten times, it means that for every $100 spent by an individual, nine other individuals or businesses will have access to that same $100. This investment increases the community's economic strength by $1,000 instead of just $100. **7**

It works this way. You earn $100 a week and I earn $100 a week. You give me ninety-seven of your dollars. I'm living on $197 and you're living on $3. How can your house be as big as mine? How can your car be as new as mine? How, even, can your IQ be as high as mine? Income affects nearly all aspects of life. A higher paycheck means you can afford to live in a better neighborhood with better schools and more opportunities for intellectual development. Studies have found that the group in America with the highest income is the group with the highest IQ. The group with the second-highest income is the group with the second-highest IQ. The overall IQ of Blacks is low in part because the income retained by Blacks is at the bottom. **8**

Take Back Your Mind

Rick Singletary knows this all too well. The problem is not that Blacks don't have money. The problem is what we do with it, or don't do with **9**

Example 577

it. Just as we waste our votes by not demanding anything in return, we don't spend our money where it pays off.

10   Over the last twenty-five years, the Black community has had a major thrust in politics and civil rights. We have staged Freedom Marches, but we have never stopped to think about what really buys freedom. It isn't worn-out shoes, and it isn't even civil rights legislation. True freedom springs from economic <u>parity</u> with other Americans.

parity equivalence

11   Money is not everything, but I rate it right up there with oxygen. After almost one hundred years of social engineering, Blacks can sit next to White people in classrooms and restaurants and on airplanes, but can they afford it? *The bottom line is that the only color of freedom is green.* Pride, education, and economic self-sufficiency were the message of Marcus Garvey and Booker T. Washington. But those two great Black men were <u>vilified</u> by the self-serving, self-hating <u>elitists</u> among their own people, and their vital message of <u>self-reliance</u> was blocked. Instead Blacks have spent decades with their arms extended and their hands out, doing the economic death dance to the tune of integration. ■

vilified slandered, criticized

elitists those with a sense of superiority

self-reliance depending on oneself

CRITICAL THINKING AND DISCUSSION

GET THINKING AND WRITING

Understanding Meaning: What Is the Writer Trying to Say?

1. What does the failure of one black business represent to Brown? What makes it significant?
2. Why, in Brown's view, is it important for African Americans to support black-owned businesses?
3. In Brown's view, how can blacks achieve economic parity with the rest of American society?
4. Why do blacks, in Brown's view, boycott their own businesses?
5. *Critical thinking:* Where, in Brown's view, has the civil rights movement failed black Americans?

Evaluating Strategy: How Does the Writer Say It?

1. How effective is the example of Singletary's failed supermarket? Would the essay benefit from other examples?
2. Would a hypothetical example be as effective as a real one?
3. Brown includes facts and statistics. Why is this important, especially in an essay with a single example?
4. Where does Brown place the thesis? Is this an effective location in your view?

Appreciating Language: What Words Does the Writer Use?

1. What words and phrases does Brown use to describe Singletary? Does he appear as a hero or role model?
2. Brown uses phrases such as *the color of freedom is green* and *economic death dance.* Are they effective? Why or why not?

Writing Suggestions

1. Write an essay about a person you see as a role model illustrating behavior that other people should imitate or support. Provide details explaining the significance of this person's contribution.
2. *Collaborative writing:* Work with other students and discuss Brown's essay. Brainstorm and suggest writing a process essay that explains how attitudes can be changed so that minority communities support minority-owned businesses.

Definition

Definition explains or limits the meaning of a word or idea.

SPANGLISH

JANICE CASTRO

Janice Castro (1949–) is a journalist who became Time *magazine's first health-policy reporter. This essay appeared as part of a* Time *cover story about Hispanics.*

AS YOU READ

Castro provides a clear definition statement that explains what Spanglish *means and illustrates it with several examples.*

Words to Know

bemused confused or puzzled

In Manhattan a first-grader greets her visiting grandparents, happily exclaiming, "Come here, *siéntate*!" Her bemused grandfather, who does not speak Spanish, nevertheless knows she is asking him to sit down. A Miami personnel officer understands what a job applicant means when he says, *"Quiero un* part time." Nor do drivers miss a beat reading a billboard alongside a Los Angeles street advertising CERVEZA— SIX PACK! 1

This free-form blend of Spanish and English, known as Spanglish, is common linguistic currency wherever concentrations of Hispanic Americans are found in the U.S. In Los Angeles, where 55% of the city's 3 million inhabitants speak Spanish, Spanglish is as much a part of daily life as sunglasses. Unlike the broken-English efforts of earlier immigrants from Europe, Asia, and other regions, Spanglish has become a widely accepted conversational mode used casually— even playfully— by Spanish-speaking immigrants and native-born Americans alike. 2

Consisting of one part Hispanicized English, one part Americanized Spanish and more than a little fractured syntax, Spanglish is a bit like a Robin Williams comedy routine: a crackling line of cross-cultural patter straight from the melting pot. Often it enters Anglo homes and families through the children, who pick it up at school or at play with their young Hispanic contemporaries. In other cases, it comes from watching TV; 3

many an Anglo child watching *Sesame Street* has learned *"uno dos tres"* almost as quickly as "one two three."

4   Spanglish takes a variety of forms, from the Southern California Anglos who bid farewell with the utterly silly *"hasta la* bye-bye" to the Cuban-American drivers in Miami who *parquean* their *carros.* Some Spanglish sentences are mostly Spanish, with a quick detour for an English word or two. A Latino friend may cut short a conversation by glancing at his watch and excusing himself with the explanation that he must *"ir al supermarket."*

5   Many of the English words transplanted in this way are simply handier than their Spanish counterparts. No matter how distasteful the subject, for example, it is still easier to say "income tax" than *impuesto sobre la renta.* At the same time, many Spanish-speaking immigrants have adopted such terms as VCR, microwave, and dishwasher for what they view as largely American phenomena. Still other English words convey a cultural context that is not implicit in the Spanish. A friend who invites you to a *lonche* most likely has in mind the brisk American custom of "doing lunch" rather than the languorous afternoon break traditionally implied by *almuerzo.*

6   Mainstream Americans exposed to similar <u>hybrids</u> of German, Chinese, or Hindi might be mystified. But even Anglos who speak little or no Spanish are somewhat familiar with Spanglish. Living among them, for one thing, are 19 million Hispanics. In addition, more American high school and university students sign up for Spanish than for any other foreign language.

hybrids blends

7   Only in the past ten years, though, has Spanglish begun to turn into a national slang. Its popularity has grown with the explosive increases in U.S. immigration from Latin American countries. English has increasingly collided with Spanish in retail stores, offices and classrooms, in pop music and on street corners. Anglos whose ancestors picked up such Spanish words as *rancho, bronco, tornado* and *incommunicado,* for instance, now freely use such Spanish words as *gracias, bueno, amigo* and *por favor.*

8   Among Latinos, Spanglish conversations often flow more easily from Spanish into several sentences of English and back.

9   Spanglish is a sort of code for Latinos: the speakers know Spanish, but their hybrid language reflects the American culture in which they live. Many lean to shorter, clipped phrases in place of the longer, more graceful expressions their parents used. Says Leonel de la Cuesta, an assistant professor of modern languages at Florida International University in Miami: "In the U.S., time is money, and that is showing up in Spanglish as an economy of language." Conversational examples: *taipiar* (type) and *winshi-wiper* (windshield wiper) replace *escribir a máquina* and *limpiaparabrisas.*

10   Major advertisers, eager to tap the estimated $134 billion in spending power wielded by Spanish-speaking Americans, have ventured into Spanglish to promote their products. In some cases, attempts to sprin-

gaffes mistakes

inadvertently accidentally

fractured mangled or inaccurate

kle Spanish through commercials have produced embarrassing gaffes. A Braniff airlines ad that sought to tell Spanish-speaking audiences they could settle back *en* (in) luxuriant *cuero* (leather) seats, for example, inadvertently said they could fly without clothes (*encuero*). A fractured translation of the Miller Lite slogan told readers the beer was "Filling, and less delicious." Similar blunders are often made by Anglos trying to impress Spanish-speaking pals. But if Latinos are amused by mangled Spanglish, they also recognize these goofs as a sort of friendly acceptance. As they might put it, *no problema*. ■

GET THINKING AND WRITING

CRITICAL THINKING AND DISCUSSION

Understanding Meaning: What Is the Writer Trying to Say?

1. How does Castro define *Spanglish*? Can you define it in your own words and give examples?
2. How does Spanglish differ from broken English spoken by other immigrants?
3. Who speaks Spanglish?
4. *Critical thinking:* What does the growth of Spanglish say about changes in American society and the influence of Hispanics?

Evaluating Strategy: How Does the Writer Say It?

1. How does Castro use examples to explain her definition?
2. Are the opening and closing paragraphs effective?
3. How does Castro organize details?

Appreciating Language: What Words Does the Writer Use?

1. What does the tone and style of Castro's essay suggest about her attitude toward Spanglish?
2. Castro calls Spanglish *slang*. What does *slang* suggest to you?

Writing Suggestions

1. Invent a term that defines a behavior, attitude, object, or situation you have observed such as *blind datism, partyholics, cable TV withdrawal,* or *workphobia*. Develop an essay that explains your term and provide examples.
2. *Collaborative writing:* Work with other students to invent a term for something you have noticed on campus. Write an essay that explains your term and illustrates it with one or more examples.

store to ask for some nails. He put two fingers together on the counter and made hammering motions with the other hand. The clerk brought him a hammer. He shook his head and pointed to the two fingers he was hammering. The clerk brought him nails. He picked out the sizes he wanted, and left. Well doc, the next guy who came in was a blind man. He wanted scissors. How do you suppose he asked for them?"

Indulgently, I lifted my right hand and made a scissoring motion with my first two fingers. Whereupon my auto-repair man laughed <u>rau-cously</u> and said, "Why you dumb jerk, he used his *voice* and asked for them." Then he said, smugly, "I've been trying that on my customers today." "Did you catch many?" I asked. "Quite a few," he said, "but I knew for sure I'd catch *you*." "Why is that?" I asked. "Because you're so goddamned educated, doc, I *knew* you couldn't be very smart."

And I have an uneasy feeling he had something there. ■ 7

ously loudly — (margin gloss)

6

CRITICAL THINKING AND DISCUSSION

THINKING WRITING

Understanding Meaning: What Is the Writer Trying to Say?

1. What is Asimov's thesis?
2. Asimov points out that even though he achieved 160 on an army intelligence test, he was assigned to work in the kitchen. What point is he making about the way society views intelligence?
3. What did the auto-repair man teach Asimov about intelligence?
4. Why does Asimov believe that intelligence tests do not really measure how smart people are? What do they measure in his view?

Evaluating Strategy: How Does the Writer Say It?

1. How does Asimov use the auto-repair man to illustrate his view of intelligence?
2. How does Asimov use example and comparison to develop his essay?
3. How effective is Asimov's conclusion? How does a one-sentence paragraph highlight his last point?

Appreciating Language: What Words Does the Writer Use?

1. Look up the word *arbiter* in a dictionary. What does it mean? Who are the arbiters of intelligence in our society? Would intelligence be measured differently if other professionals developed the tests?
2. Asimov uses the word *moron* in his essay. Do words that have powerful positive and negative meanings like *smart, dumb, stupid,* and *brilliant* make it difficult to define intelligence objectively?

Writing Suggestions

1. Write an essay that explores the definition of another quality like *bravery, strength, beauty,* or *humor.* Use examples and comparisons to show your

WHAT IS INTELLIGENCE?

ISAAC ASIMOV

Isaac Asimov (1923–1992) received three degrees from Columbia University and published over five hundred books. In this essay, Asimov considers how to define intelligence.

AS YOU READ

Notice that rather than declaring what intelligence is, Asimov uses questions to get readers to think about the way we traditionally define intelligence. Before reading the essay, consider how you define it. Who is intelligent in your view?

1   What is intelligence, anyway? When I was in the army I received a kind of aptitude test that soldiers took and, against a norm of 100, scored 160. No one at the base had ever seen a figure like that, and for two hours they made a big fuss over me. (It didn't mean anything. The next day I was still a buck private with KP[1] as my highest duty.)

2   All my life I've been registering scores like that, so that I have the complacent feeling that I'm highly intelligent, and I expect other people to think so, too. Actually, though, don't such scores simply mean that I am very good at answering the type of academic questions that are considered worthy of answers by the people who make up the intelligence tests— people with intellectual bents similar to mine?

3   For instance, I had an auto-repair man once, who, on these intelligence tests, could not possibly have scored more than 80, by my estimate. I always took it for granted that I was far more intelligent than he was. Yet, when anything went wrong with my car I hastened to him with it, watched him anxiously as he explored its vitals, and listened to his pronouncements as though they were divine oracles— and he always fixed my car.

4   Well, then, suppose my auto-repair man devised questions for an intelligence test. Or suppose a carpenter did, or a farmer, or, indeed, almost anyone but an academician. By every one of those tests, I'd prove myself a moron. And I'd *be* a moron, too. In a world where I could not use my academic training and my verbal talents but had to do something intricate or hard, working with my hands, I would do poorly. My intelligence, then, is not absolute but is a function of the society I live in and of the fact that a small subsection of that society has managed to foist itself on the rest as an arbiter of such matters.

5   Consider my auto-repair man, again. He had a habit of telling me jokes whenever he saw me. One time he raised his head from under the automobile hood to say: "Doc, a deaf-and-dumb guy went into a hardware

---

[1] *KP*: abbreviation for the military term *kitchen police*. [Eds.]

Words to I

aptitude a

norm aver:

complacen

pronounce
    declarat
    stateme

divine ora
    prophes
    predicti

intricate c

absolute t
    unquest

subsectioi

raucously loudly

store to ask for some nails. He put two fingers together on the counter and made hammering motions with the other hand. The clerk brought him a hammer. He shook his head and pointed to the two fingers he was hammering. The clerk brought him nails. He picked out the sizes he wanted, and left. Well doc, the next guy who came in was a blind man. He wanted scissors. How do you suppose he asked for them?"

Indulgently, I lifted my right hand and made a scissoring motion with my first two fingers. Whereupon my auto-repair man laughed raucously and said, "Why you dumb jerk, he used his *voice* and asked for them." Then he said, smugly, "I've been trying that on my customers today." "Did you catch many?" I asked. "Quite a few," he said, "but I knew for sure I'd catch *you*." "Why is that?" I asked. "Because you're so goddamned educated, doc, I *knew* you couldn't be very smart."   6

And I have an uneasy feeling he had something there. ■   7

GET THINKING
AND WRITING

CRITICAL THINKING AND DISCUSSION

Understanding Meaning: What Is the Writer Trying to Say?

1. What is Asimov's thesis?
2. Asimov points out that even though he achieved 160 on an army intelligence test, he was assigned to work in the kitchen. What point is he making about the way society views intelligence?
3. What did the auto-repair man teach Asimov about intelligence?
4. Why does Asimov believe that intelligence tests do not really measure how smart people are? What do they measure in his view?

Evaluating Strategy: How Does the Writer Say It?

1. How does Asimov use the auto-repair man to illustrate his view of intelligence?
2. How does Asimov use example and comparison to develop his essay?
3. How effective is Asimov's conclusion? How does a one-sentence paragraph highlight his last point?

Appreciating Language: What Words Does the Writer Use?

1. Look up the word *arbiter* in a dictionary. What does it mean? Who are the arbiters of intelligence in our society? Would intelligence be measured differently if other professionals developed the tests?
2. Asimov uses the word *moron* in his essay. Do words that have powerful positive and negative meanings like *smart, dumb, stupid,* and *brilliant* make it difficult to define intelligence objectively?

Writing Suggestions

1. Write an essay that explores the definition of another quality like *bravery, strength, beauty,* or *humor.* Use examples and comparisons to show your

WHAT IS INTELLIGENCE?

ISAAC ASIMOV

Isaac Asimov (1923–1992) received three degrees from Columbia University and published over five hundred books. In this essay, Asimov considers how to define intelligence.

AS YOU READ

Notice that rather than declaring what intelligence is, Asimov uses questions to get readers to think about the way we traditionally define intelligence. Before reading the essay, consider how you define it. Who is intelligent in your view?

1   What is intelligence, anyway? When I was in the army I received a kind of aptitude test that soldiers took and, against a norm of 100, scored 160. No one at the base had ever seen a figure like that, and for two hours they made a big fuss over me. (It didn't mean anything. The next day I was still a buck private with KP[1] as my highest duty.)

2   All my life I've been registering scores like that, so that I have the complacent feeling that I'm highly intelligent, and I expect other people to think so, too. Actually, though, don't such scores simply mean that I am very good at answering the type of academic questions that are considered worthy of answers by the people who make up the intelligence tests — people with intellectual bents similar to mine?

3   For instance, I had an auto-repair man once, who, on these intelligence tests, could not possibly have scored more than 80, by my estimate. I always took it for granted that I was far more intelligent than he was. Yet, when anything went wrong with my car I hastened to him with it, watched him anxiously as he explored its vitals, and listened to his pronouncements as though they were divine oracles — and he always fixed my car.

4   Well, then, suppose my auto-repair man devised questions for an intelligence test. Or suppose a carpenter did, or a farmer, or, indeed, almost anyone but an academician. By every one of those tests, I'd prove myself a moron. And I'd *be* a moron, too. In a world where I could not use my academic training and my verbal talents but had to do something intricate or hard, working with my hands, I would do poorly. My intelligence, then, is not absolute but is a function of the society I live in and of the fact that a small subsection of that society has managed to foist itself on the rest as an arbiter of such matters.

5   Consider my auto-repair man, again. He had a habit of telling me jokes whenever he saw me. One time he raised his head from under the automobile hood to say: "Doc, a deaf-and-dumb guy went into a hardware

----

[1] *KP*: abbreviation for the military term *kitchen police*. [Eds.]

Words to Know

aptitude ability

norm average

complacent self-satisfied

pronouncement declaration or statement

divine oracles godlike prophesies or predictions

intricate complicated

absolute total or unquestioned

subsection small part

opinion of what bravery or beauty is and is not. Consider the standard ways these qualities are measured in our society.

2. *Collaborative writing:* Working with a group of other students, write an essay that defines your group's view of intelligence and suggest ways it should be measured.

Comparison and Contrast

Comparison and contrast examines similarities and differences.

A FABLE FOR TOMORROW

RACHEL CARSON

Rachel Carson (1907–1964) was a pioneer environmentalist, best known for her 1962 book Silent Spring. *In this section of the book, she uses contrast to demonstrate the effect pesticides can have on the environment.*

AS YOU READ

Notice how Carson uses comparison and contrast to create a "before and after" view to highlight her concerns about the impact of harmful chemicals.

1   There was once a town in the heart of America where all life seemed to live in harmony with its surroundings. The town lay in the midst of a checkerboard of <u>prosperous</u> farms, with fields of grain and hillsides of orchards where, in spring, white clouds of bloom drifted above the green fields. In autumn, oak and maple and birch set up a blaze of color that flamed and flickered across a backdrop of pines. Then foxes barked in the hills and deer silently crossed the fields, half hidden in the mists of the fall mornings.

2   Along the roads, laurel, <u>viburnum and alder</u>, great ferns and wildflowers delighted the traveler's eye through much of the year. Even in winter the roadsides were places of beauty, where countless birds came to feed on the berries and on the seed heads of the dried weeds rising above the snow. The countryside was, in fact, famous for the <u>abundance</u> and variety of its bird life, and when the flood of migrants was pouring through in spring and fall, people traveled from great distances to observe them. Others came to fish the streams, which flowed clear and cold out of the hills and contained shady pools where trout lay. So it had been from the days many years ago when the first settlers raised their houses, sank their wells, and built their barns.

3   Then a strange blight crept over the area and everything began to change. Some evil spell had settled on the community: mysterious <u>maladies</u> swept the flocks of chickens; the cattle and sheep sickened and

Words to Know

prosperous wealthy, well-off

viburnum and alder shrubs and trees

abundance large quantity

maladies diseases

died. Everywhere was a shadow of death. The farmers spoke of much illness among their families. In the town the doctors had become more and more puzzled by new kinds of sickness appearing among their patients. There had been several sudden and unexplained deaths, not only among adults but even among children, who would be stricken suddenly while at play and die within a few hours.

There was a strange stillness. The birds, for example— where had they gone? Many people spoke of them, puzzled and disturbed. The feeding stations in the backyards were deserted. The few birds seen anywhere were moribund; they trembled violently and could not fly. It was a spring without voices. On the mornings that had once throbbed with the dawn chorus of robins, catbirds, doves, jays, wrens, and scores of other bird voices there was now no sound; only silence lay over the fields and woods and marsh.

moribund dying

On the farms the hens brooded, but no chicks hatched. The farmers complained that they were unable to raise any pigs— the litters were small and the young survived only a few days. The apple trees were coming into bloom but no bees droned among the blossoms, so there was no pollination and there would be no fruit.

The roadsides, once so attractive, were now lined with browned and withered vegetation as though swept by fire. These, too, were silent, deserted by all living things. Even the streams were now lifeless. Anglers no longer visited them, for all the fish had died.

withered wasted, shrunken
anglers fishermen

In the gutters under the eaves and between the shingles of the roofs, a white granular powder still showed a few patches; some weeks before it had fallen like snow upon the roofs and the lawns, the fields and streams.

granular coarse

No witchcraft, no enemy action had silenced the rebirth of new life in this stricken world. The people had done it themselves.

This town does not actually exist, but it might easily have a thousand counterparts in America or elsewhere in the world. I know of no community that has experienced all the misfortunes I describe. Yet every one of these disasters has actually happened somewhere, and many real communities have already suffered a substantial number of them. A grim specter has crept upon us almost unnoticed, and this imagined tragedy may easily become a stark reality we all shall know. ■

specter ghost

4

5

6

7

8

9

GET THINKING
AND WRITING

CRITICAL THINKING AND DISCUSSION

Understanding Meaning: What Is the Writer Trying to Say?

1. What is Carson trying to explain to her readers? What is the point of her comparison?
2. Can you briefly summarize the before-and-after contrast in your own words? What has happened to this community?
3. What are the major effects of the blight Carson describes?
4. Who is responsible for the changes that occur?

5. *Critical thinking:* Carson published her book over forty years ago when many people were not aware of environmental problems. How effective is this comparison in arousing interest in pollution?

Evaluating Strategy: How Does the Writer Say It?

1. Carson basically tells a story of mysterious ailments and problems, then announces at the end the people did it to themselves. Do you think this is an effective approach? Why or why not?
2. How does Carson use a before-and-after contrast to highlight her points?

Appreciating Language: What Words Does the Writer Use?

1. Carson uses words like *strange blight, mysterious maladies,* and *evil spell.* What impact do these have?
2. Carson uses the words *silent* and *silence* several times in this short passage. What does *silence* suggest when you think of nature, especially in springtime?

Writing Suggestions

1. Write an essay that uses a before-and-after contrast to show changes in a neighborhood, your workplace, a group of friends, an athletic team, a band, or your college. The changes can be positive or negative.
2. *Collaborative writing:* Work with a group of students and, using Carson's fable as an example, write a similar before-and-after fable to dramatize another problem in a community or single person. You could offer before and after views of a person who becomes addicted to drugs, a community after a major employer shuts down, a team after a major victory or defeat, a person who gets a big promotion, or politicians after winning or losing an election.

MAMAN AND AMERICA

Azadeh Moaveni

Azadeh Moaveni, whose parents left Iran following the fall of the Shah in 1979, was born in Palo Alto, California. She describes the complex identity she developed as someone growing up in a community of exiles trying to make lives in a new country in her book Lipstick Jihad: A Memoir of Growing Up Iranian in America and American in Iran.

AS YOU READ

In this passage from Lipstick Jihad, *Moaveni uses comparison and contrast to dramatize the differences between her divorced parents, her teenage conflicts with her mother, whom she calls Maman, and her mother's conflicting opinions of American culture.*

Words to Know

embraced accepted

derived taken from

pilfering stealing

flaunted boldly displayed

disproportionate unequal, exaggerated

allegiance loyalty

prescient prophetic

regressive backward

consistent constant, logical

compromised weakened

physiologically biologically

deprivation going without

When it served her purposes, Maman <u>embraced</u> America and lovingly recited all the qualities that made it superior to our backward-looking Iranian culture. That Americans were honest, never made promises they didn't intend to keep, were open to therapy, believed a divorced woman was still a whole person worthy of respect and a place in society— all this earned them vast respect in Maman's book. It seemed never to occur to her that values do not exist in a cultural vacuum but are knit into a society's fabric; they earn their place, <u>derived</u> from other related beliefs. Maman thought values were like groceries; you'd cruise through the aisles, toss the ones you fancied into your cart, and leave the unappealing ones on the shelf. When I was a teenager we constantly fought over her <u>pilfering</u> through Iranian and American values at random, assigning a particular behavior or habit she felt like promoting to the culture she could peg it to most convincingly. 1

Our earliest battle on this territory was over Madonna. Maman called her *jendeh,* a prostitute, which I considered an offensive way to describe the singer of "La Isla Bonita." On what grounds, I argued, was she being condemned? Was it because she <u>flaunted</u> her sexuality, and if so, did that make out-of-wedlock sexuality a bad thing? My defense of Madonna seemed to infuriate Maman; her eyes flashed, and her bearing radiated a grave, ominous disappointment. It was the same <u>disproportionate</u> reaction she'd show when I would forget which elder in a room full of aging relatives I should have served tea to first, or when I'd refuse to interrupt an afternoon with a friend to take vitamins to an elderly Iranian lady who couldn't drive. Certain conversations or requests, unbeknownst to me, would become symbolic tests of my <u>allegiance</u> to that Iranian world, and the wrong response would plunge Maman into dark feelings of failure and regret. 2

At the <u>prescient</u> age of thirteen, I realized our Madonna arguments signaled far more serious confrontations to come. Maman's contempt for Madonna seemed like sheer hypocrisy to me. Was this the same woman who thought it <u>regressive</u> and awful that Iranian culture valued women through their marital status, and rated their respectability according to the success or failure of their marriage? The woman who denounced a culture that considered divorced women criminals? She believed it was only modern to consider women fully equal to men, independent beings with a sacred right to everything men were entitled. Somehow, it became clear through her designation of Madonna as whore, that she also thought it fully <u>consistent</u> to believe premarital sex (for women) was wrong, and that women who practiced it were morally <u>compromised</u>. The men she forgave, offering an explanation worthy of an Iranian villager: "They can't help themselves." Women, it seemed, were <u>physiologically</u> better equipped for <u>deprivation</u>. Often our fights would end with me collapsing in tears, her bitterly condemning my unquestioning acceptance of "this decadent culture's corrupt ways," and my usual finale: "It's all your fault for raising me here; what did you expect?" 3

4   In Maman's view, America was responsible for most that had gone wrong in the world. *Een gavhah,* these cows, was her synonym for Americans. She'd established her criticisms early on, and repeated them so often that to this day they are <u>seared</u> on my brain: "Americans have no social skills. . . . They prefer their pets to people. . . . Shopping and sex, sex and shopping; that's all Americans think about. . . . They've figured out how corrupt they are, and rather than fix themselves, they want to force their sick culture on the rest of the world." Since she mostly wheeled out these attitudes to justify why I couldn't be friends with Adam-the-long-haired-guitarist or why I couldn't go to the movies twice in one week, or why I couldn't wear short skirts, I wondered whether they were <u>sincere</u>, or <u>tactical</u>.

5   Her restrictions were futile, and only turned me into a highly skilled liar with a suspiciously heavy backpack. Every morning she would drop me off at a friend's house, <u>ostensibly</u> so we could walk to school together. Once inside I traded the Maman-approved outfit for something tighter, smeared some cherry gloss on my lips, and headed off to class.

6   Knowing I could secretly <u>evade</u> her restrictions helped me endure the sermons, but sometimes the injustice of her moralizing would provoke me, and I would fling <u>jingoistic</u> clichés designed to infuriate her: "Love it or leave it. . . . These colors don't run. . . . No one's keeping you here." At hearing these words come out of my mouth she'd hurl a piece of fruit at me, dissolve into angry tears, and suddenly the fact that I was torturing my poor, exiled single mother filled me with terrible grief, and I would apologize <u>profusely</u>, begging forgiveness in the formal, <u>filial</u> <u>Farsi</u> I knew she craved to hear. In the style of a traditional Iranian mother, she would pretend, for five days, that I did not exist; thaw on the sixth; and by the seventh have forgotten the episode entirely, privately convinced that my rude friends, who didn't even say *salaam* to her when they came over, were responsible for ruining my manners.

7   When we encountered other second-generation Iranians at Persian parties, I was struck by how much less conflicted they seemed over their dueling cultural identities. I decided my own neurotic messiness in this area was the fault of my divorced parents. The only thing they agreed on was the safety record of the Volvo, and how they should both drive one until I finished junior high. But when it came to anything that mattered, for instance how I should be raised, they didn't even bother to carve out an agreement, so vast was the gulf that separated their beliefs. My father was an atheist (Marx said God was dead) who called the Prophet Mohammad a <u>pedophile</u> for marrying a nine-year-old girl. He thought the defining characteristics of Iranian culture—<u>fatalism</u>, political paranoia, social obligations, an enthusiasm for guilt—were responsible for the failures of modern Iran. He wouldn't even <u>condescend</u> to use the term "Iranian culture," preferring to refer, to this day, to "that stinking culture"; he refused to return to Iran, even for his mother's funeral, and wouldn't help me with my Persian homework, a language, he pronounced direly "you will

seared scorched

sincere genuine

tactical used as a strategy

ostensibly supposedly

evade avoid

jingoistic overly patriotic

profusely abundantly, liberally

filial child/parent relationship

Farsi the language of Iran

salaam traditional greeting

pedophile child molester

fatalism belief that humans are powerless over their destiny

condescend lower oneself, stoop down

never use." When I announced my decision to move to Iran, his greatest fear, I think, was that something sufficiently awful would happen to me that it would require *his* going back. That he had married Maman, a hyper-ideologue, a reactionary as high-strung as they come, was baffling; little wonder they divorced when I was an infant. Daddy was the benevolent father personified; he couldn't have cared less about curfews, dating, a fifth ear piercing, or whether my hair was purple or not. ▪

hyperideologue
extremely politically minded person

GET THINKING AND WRITING

CRITICAL THINKING AND DISCUSSION

Understanding Meaning: What Is the Writer Trying to Say?

1. How does Moaveni use comparison and contrast to explain her mother's conflicted attitude toward America?
2. How does Moaveni use comparison and contrast to explain the arguments she had with her mother?
3. Why did they fight over Madonna? What did she represent to Moaveni and her mother?
4. How did Moaveni's mother view men and women?
5. How do Moaveni's parents differ?
6. *Critical thinking:* Do all immigrant parents and their American-born children have clashes over cultural values and identity? Could similar arguments between mothers and daughters occur in a Mexican, Korean, or Vietnamese family?

Evaluating Strategy: How Does the Writer Say It?

1. What role does Madonna play in symbolizing the contrast in Moaveni's attitudes and her mother's?
2. Moaveni states that her mother thought of values like products on a store shelf. Is this an effective comparison? Why or why not?
3. How do her parents' attitudes toward Farsi, the language of Iran, differ? How does Moaveni use this to dramatize their contrasting views of their homeland?

Appreciating Language: What Words Does the Writer Use?

1. What words does Moaveni use to describe her parents?
2. What words does Maman use when she praises America? What words does she use when she condemns it? Do you see anything in common? Are they positive and negative ways of describing the same thing, such as personal freedom?

Writing Suggestions

1. Write a comparison essay that describes one or more of your own adolescent conflicts with one or both of your parents. What were points of

conflict or challenge? Were the arguments about traditions, values, or parental authority?

2. *Collaborative writing:* Work with other students and develop an essay comparing attitudes immigrants have about America and their own culture. Do some abandon their old values and become fully Americanized while others seek to maintain traditions in a new country?

Division and Classification

Division and classification separates a subject into parts or measures subjects on a scale.

BLACK POLITICAL LEADERSHIP

CORNEL WEST

Cornel West was a religion professor and director of Afro-American studies at Princeton University before being appointed to the faculty of Harvard University. In this passage from his book Race Matters, *West divides black leaders into three distinct types.*

AS YOU READ

West uses division to discuss types of current black leaders and comparison to suggest they lack the quality of previous ones.

1 Present-day black political leaders can be grouped under three types: race-effacing managerial leaders, race-identifying protest leaders, and race-transcending prophetic leaders. The first type is growing rapidly. The Thomas Bradleys and Wilson Goodes of black America have become a model for many black leaders trying to reach a large white constituency and keep a loyal black one. This type survives on sheer political savvy and thrives on personal diplomacy. This kind of candidate is the lesser of two evils in a political situation where the only other electoral choice is a conservative (usually white) politician. Yet this type of leader tends to stunt progressive development and silence the prophetic voices in the black community by casting the practical mainstream as the only game in town.

2 The second type of black political leader— race-identifying protest leaders— often view themselves in the tradition of Malcolm X, Martin Luther King, Jr., Ella Baker, and Fannie Lou Hamer. Yet they are usually self-deluded. They actually operate more in the tradition of Booker T. Washington, by confining themselves to the black turf, vowing to protect their leadership status over it, and serving as power brokers with

Words to Know

Thomas Bradley former mayor of Los Angeles

Wilson Goode former mayor of Philadelphia

constituency voters

self-deluded fooling themselves

enhance improve

transracial across racial
lines

appease soothe, give into

Marion Barry former mayor
of Washington, DC

Harold Washington former
mayor of Chicago

opportunism taking
advantage

prudential wise

Adam Clayton Powell, Jr.
former U.S.
Congressman

Ronald Dellums former
U.S. Congressman

powerful nonblack elites (usually white economic or political elites, though in Louis Farrakhan's case it may be Libyan) to "enhance" this black turf. It is crucial to remember that even in the fifties, Malcolm X's vision and practice were international in scope, and that after 1964 his project was transracial— though grounded in the black turf. King never confined himself to being solely the leader of black America— even though the white press attempted to do so. And Fannie Lou Hamer led the National Welfare Rights Organization, not the Black Welfare Rights Organization. In short, race-identifying protest leaders in the post–Civil Rights era function as figures who white Americans must appease so that the plight of the black poor is overlooked and forgotten. When such leaders move successfully into elected office— as with Marion Barry— they usually become managerial types with large black constituencies, flashy styles, flowery rhetoric, and Booker T. Washington–like patronage operations within the public sphere.

Race-transcending prophetic leaders are rare in contemporary black America. Harold Washington was one. The Jesse Jackson of 1988 was attempting to be another— yet the opportunism of his past weighed heavily on him. To be an elected official and prophetic leader requires personal integrity and political savvy, moral vision and prudential judgment, courageous defiance and organizational patience. The present generation has yet to produce such a figure. We have neither an Adam Clayton Powell, Jr., nor a Ronald Dellums. This void sits like a festering sore at the center of the crisis of black leadership— and the predicament of the disadvantaged in the United States and abroad worsens. ■

3

GET THINKING AND WRITING

CRITICAL THINKING AND DISCUSSION

Understanding Meaning: What Is the Writer Trying to Say?

1. What three types of black leaders does West identify? Can you describe each type in your own words?
2. What does West find lacking in the first two types he describes?
3. What type of leader is rare? Why?
4. Why does West view race-identifying protest leaders as being self-deluded?
5. *Critical thinking:* Can these types of leaders be found in other communities?

Evaluating Strategy: How Does the Writer Say It?

1. In the first paragraph, West announces there are three types of leaders. Is this an effective way to open a division essay? Does giving readers a specific number help them understand important points?
2. How does West use paragraph breaks to organize his essay?
3. How does West define each type of leader? Why is clear definition important in a division essay?

Appreciating Language: What Words Does the Writer Use?

1. What words does West use to describe each leadership type? Can you find positive and negative terms?
2. Look up the word *patronage* in a dictionary. What does West suggest about race-identifying protest leaders when he uses this term?

Writing Suggestions

1. Describe three types of teachers, coaches, neighbors, roommates, or coworkers. Develop a definition and supply descriptive details and examples to illustrate each type.
2. *Collaborative writing:* Work with other students and develop an essay that describes three or more types of current local or national political leaders, business leaders, entertainers, or talk show hosts.

THE PLOT AGAINST PEOPLE

RUSSELL BAKER

Russell Baker (1925–) has been writing newspaper columns for over forty years and has published two popular autobiographies, Growing Up *and* The Good Times. *In this essay, Baker describes three categories of common objects that frustrate their owners.*

AS YOU READ

Note Baker's use of a clear thesis statement in the first paragraph and specific examples to illustrate each type.

Words to Know

1   Inanimate objects are classified into three major categories— those that don't work, those that break down and those that get lost.

inanimate not living

2   The goal of all inanimate objects is to resist man and ultimately to defeat him, and the three major classifications are based on the method each object uses to achieve its purpose. As a general rule any object capable of breaking down at the moment when it is needed most will do so. The automobile is typical of the category.

3   With the cunning typical of its breed, the automobile never breaks down while entering a filling station with a large staff of idle mechanics. It waits until it reaches a downtown intersection in the middle of the rush hour, or until it is fully loaded with family and luggage on the Ohio Turnpike.

cunning craftiness

4   Thus it creates maximum misery, inconvenience, frustration and irritability among its human cargo, thereby reducing its owner's life span.

5   Washing machines, garbage disposals, lawn mowers, light bulbs, automatic laundry dryers, water pipes, furnaces, electrical fuses, television tubes, hose nozzles, tape recorders, slide projectors— all are in league with the automobile to take their turn at breaking down whenever life threatens to flow smoothly for their human enemies.

6   Many inanimate objects, of course, find it extremely difficult to break down. Pliers, for example, and gloves and keys are almost totally

incapable of breaking down. Therefore, they have had to evolve a different technique for resisting man.

They get lost. Science has still not solved the mystery of how they do it, and no man has ever caught one of them in the act of getting lost. The most <u>plausible</u> theory is that they have developed a secret method of <u>locomotion</u> which they are able to conceal the instant a human eye falls upon them. — 7

plausible likely
locomotion movement

It is not uncommon for a pair of pliers to climb all the way from the cellar to the attic in its single-minded determination to raise its owner's blood pressure. Keys have been known to burrow three feet under mattresses. Women's purses, despite their great weight, frequently travel through six or seven rooms to find a hiding space under a couch. — 8

Scientists have been struck by the fact that things that break down virtually never get lost, while things that get lost hardly ever break down. — 9

A furnace, for example, will invariably break down at the depth of the first winter cold wave, but it will never get lost. A woman's purse, which after all does have some <u>inherent</u> capacity for breaking down, hardly ever does; it almost invariably chooses to get lost. — 10

inherent inborn

Some persons believe this constitutes evidence that inanimate objects are not entirely hostile to man, and that a negotiated peace is possible. After all, they point out, a furnace could infuriate a man even more thoroughly by getting lost than by breaking down, just as a glove could upset him far more by breaking down than by getting lost. — 11

Not everyone agrees, however, that this indicates a <u>conciliatory</u> attitude among inanimate objects. Many say it merely proves that furnaces, gloves and pliers are incredibly stupid. — 12

conciliatory peace-making

The third class of objects — those that don't work — is the most curious of all. These include such objects as barometers, car clocks, cigarette lighters, flashlights, and toy train locomotives. It is inaccurate, of course, to say that they never work. They work once, usually for the first few hours after being brought home, and then quit. Thereafter, they never work again. — 13

In fact, it is widely assumed that they are built for the purpose of not working. Some people have reached advanced ages without ever seeing some of these objects — barometers, for example — in working order. — 14

Science is utterly baffled by the entire category. There are many theories about it. The most interesting holds that the things that don't work have attained the highest state possible for an inanimate object, the state to which things that break down and things that get lost can still only <u>aspire</u>. — 15

aspire desire

They have truly defeated man by conditioning him never to expect anything of them, and in return they have given man the only peace he receives from inanimate society. He does not expect his barometer to work, his electric locomotive to run, his cigarette lighter to light or his flashlight to illuminate, and when they don't, it does not raise his blood pressure. — 16

He cannot attain that peace with furnaces and keys and cars and women's purses as long as he demands that they work for their keep. ■ — 17

CRITICAL THINKING AND DISCUSSION

Understanding Meaning: What Is the Writer Trying to Say?

1. What is Baker's goal?
2. How have objects defeated people?
3. What is the real reason why objects seem to move? What does this say about the people who own them?
4. *Critical thinking:* Is there a serious side to Baker's observations? Are people too dependent on objects? Do we measure happiness in owning things that only complicate our lives rather than making them better?

Evaluating Strategy: How Does the Writer Say It?

1. How does the first paragraph introduce the subject and set up the rest of the essay?
2. What examples does Baker supply to illustrate each type?
3. Baker creates three categories for this humorous essay. Would developing five or six categories be just as effective or would it wear thin and begin to bore readers?

Appreciating Language: What Words Does the Writer Use?

1. Which words indicate that Baker is taking a humorous view of his subject?
2. How does Baker use words and phrases to bring objects to life?

Writing Suggestions

1. Write a short humorous essay that classifies three or more types of college courses, students, stores, radio stations, clubs, or entertainers.
2. *Collaborative writing:* Work with other students and develop an essay that describes three or more types of websites, Internet search engines, or Internet service providers that frustrate people.

Process

Process explains how something occurs or provides step-by-step instructions to accomplish a specific task.

TALKING TO PEOPLE

LARRY KING

Larry King is best known for his nightly interview program on CNN. Over the years, he has spoken with thousands of politicians, celebrities, newsmakers, and ordinary people. In this essay, he tells readers how to use listening skills to improve conversation.

AS YOU READ

Notice that King uses several examples to demonstrate why it is important to listen in order to become a better talker.

1 My first rule of conversation is this: I never learn a thing while I'm talking. I realize every morning that nothing *I* say today will teach me anything, so if I'm going to learn a lot today, I'll have to do it by listening.

2 As obvious as this sounds, you run across proof every day that people simply do not listen. Tell your family or friends your plane will arrive at eight and before the conversation ends they'll ask, "What time did you say your plane is coming in?" And try to estimate the number of times you have heard someone say, "I forgot what you told me."

3 If you don't listen any better than that to someone, you cannot expect them to listen any better to you. I try to remember the signs you see at railroad crossings in small towns and rural areas: "Stop— Look— Listen." Show the people you talk to that you're interested in what they're saying. They will show you the same.

4 To be a good talker, you must be a good listener. This is more than just a matter of showing an interest in your conversation partner. Careful listening makes you better able to respond— to be a good talker when it's your turn. Good follow-up questions are the mark of a good conversationalist.

5 When I watch Barbara Walters' interviews I'm often disappointed, because I think she asks too many "so what" questions, like "If you could come back, what would you like to be?" In my opinion Barbara would be much better if she asked less <u>frivolous</u> questions and better follow-ups, logical extensions of the answer to her previous question. That comes from listening.

6 I was pleased by something Ted Koppel said to *Time* magazine a few years ago. "Larry listens to his guests," he said. "He pays attention to what they say. Too few interviewers do that." Even though I'm known as a "talking head," I think my success comes first and foremost from listening.

7 When I interview guests on the air, I make notes ahead of time about the kinds of questions I will ask them. But often I'll hear something in one of their responses that leads me into an unexpected question— and a surprising answer.

8 Example: When Vice President Dan Quayle was my guest during the 1992 presidential campaign, we talked about the laws governing abortion. He said it made no sense at all for his daughter's school to require his or his wife's permission for their daughter to miss a day of school, but not to get an abortion. As soon as he said that, I was curious about Quayle's personal angle on this political topic. So I asked what his attitude would be if his daughter said she was going to have an abortion. He said he would support her in whatever decision she made.

9 Quayle's reply made news. Abortion was a white-hot issue in that campaign, and here was President Bush's very conservative running mate, the national Republican spokesman for his conservative wing's

Words to Know

frivolous playful, not
   serious

<u>unalterable</u> opposition to abortion, suddenly saying he would support his daughter if she decided to have one.

unalterable unchangeable, strongly held

10   Regardless of your views on that issue, the point here is that I got the response from Quayle because I wasn't just going through a list of questions. I was listening to what he was saying. That was what led me to the newsworthy answer.

11   The same thing happened when Ross Perot came on my show on February 20, 1992, and denied several times that he was interested in running for president. I kept hearing that his denials were less than complete, and when I put the question differently near the end of the show — bang! Perot said he'd run if his supporters succeeded in registering him on the ballot in all fifty states.

12   All of that happened not because of what I said, but because of what I *heard*. I was listening.

13   The late Jim Bishop, the popular writer, columnist, and author, was another New Yorker who spent a lot of time in Miami when I was there. He told me once that one of his pet peeves was people who ask you how you are but then don't listen to your answer. One man in particular was a repeat offender on this subject, so Jim decided to test just how poor a listener this fellow was.

14   The man called Jim one morning and began the conversation the way he always did: "Jim, how are ya?"

15   Jim says, "I have lung cancer."

16   "Wonderful. Say, Jim . . . "

17   Bishop had proved his point.

18   Dale Carnegie put it effectively in his book *How to Win Friends and Influence People,* which has now sold fifteen million copies: "To be interesting, be interested."

19   He added, "Ask questions that other persons will enjoy answering. Encourage them to talk about themselves and their accomplishments. Remember that the people you are talking to are a hundred times more interested in themselves and their wants and problems than they are in you and your problems. A person's toothache means more to that person than a famine in China which kills a million people. A boil on one's neck interests one more than forty earthquakes in Africa. Think of that the next time you start a conversation." ■

CRITICAL THINKING AND DISCUSSION

GET THINKING AND WRITING

Understanding Meaning: What Is the Writer Trying to Say?

1. Why does King stress listening when talking?
2. What mistakes do most people make in talking?
3. How can listening help develop questions you should ask during a conversation?
4. What advice does Dale Carnegie give in the passage King quotes at the end of the essay?
5. *Critical thinking:* How can the skills King explains help job applicants at interviews?

Evaluating Strategy: How Does the Writer Say It?

1. How does King use examples to illustrate his points?
2. King uses quotations from Jim Bishop and Dale Carnegie to support his view. What can outside sources add?
3. King closes with a long quotation. Is this an effective device? Why or why not?

Appreciating Language: What Words Does the Writer Use?

1. What is a *talking head*? Is it a positive or negative term? Why does King place it in quotation marks?
2. How is being *interested* in other people different from *showing an interest* in others?

Writing Suggestions

1. Write a similar essay explaining to readers how to talk on a cell phone or write e-mail. What common mistakes do people make? How can they overcome them?
2. *Collaborative writing:* Work with other students to develop an essay that gives advice on improving reading or study skills, taking notes in class, preparing for an exam, or answering questions at a job interview.

FENDER BENDERS: LEGAL DO'S AND DON'TS

ARMOND D. BUDISH

Armond D. Budish is an attorney and consumer law reporter. He writes a column on consumer issues for the Cleveland Plain Dealer. *In this article, he explains step by step what drivers should do if they are involved in a minor accident.*

AS YOU READ

Note that Budish uses numbered steps and bold print to organize his points and present ideas in a way that readers can easily remember.

1   The car ahead of you stops suddenly. You hit the brakes, but you just can't stop in time. Your front bumper meets the rear end of the other car. *Ouch!*

2   There doesn't seem to be any damage, and it must be your lucky day because the driver you hit agrees that it's not worth hassling with insurance claims and risking a <u>premium</u> increase. So after exchanging addresses, you go your separate ways.

3   Imagine your surprise when you open the mail a few weeks later only to discover a letter from your "victim's" lawyer demanding $10,000 to cover car repairs, pain, and suffering. Apparently the agreeable gentleman decided to disagree, then went ahead and filed a police report blaming you for the incident and for his damages.

Words to Know

premium insurance payments

4   When automobiles meet by accident, do you know how to respond? Here are 10 practical tips that can help you avoid costly legal and insurance hassles.

1. Stop! It's the Law.

5   No matter how serious or minor the accident, stop immediately. If possible, don't move your car— especially if someone has been injured. Leaving the cars as they were when the accident occurred helps the police determine what happened. Of course, if your car is blocking traffic or will cause another accident where it is, then move it to the nearest safe location.

6   For every rule there are exceptions, though. If, for example, you are rear-ended at night in an unsafe area, it's wisest to keep on going and notify the police later. There have been cases in which people were robbed or assaulted when they got out of their cars.

2. Zip Loose Lips.

7   Watch what you say after an accident. Although this may sound harsh, even an innocent "I'm sorry" could later be <u>construed</u> as an admission of fault. Also be sure not to accuse the other driver of causing the accident. Since you don't know how a stranger will react to your remarks, you run the risk of making a bad situation worse.

    construed interpreted

8   Remember, you are not the judge or jury; it's not up to you to decide who is or is not at fault. Even if you think you caused the accident, you might be wrong. For example: Assume you were driving 15 miles over the speed limit. What you probably were not aware of is that the other driver's blood-alcohol level exceeded the legal limits, so he was at least equally at fault.

3. Provide Required Information.

9   If you are involved in an accident, you are required in most states to give your name, address and car registration number to: any person injured in the accident; the owner, driver or passenger in any car that was damaged in the accident; a police officer on the scene. If you don't own the car (say it belongs to a friend or your parents), you should provide the name and address of the owner.

10   You must produce this information even if there are no apparent injuries or damages and even if you didn't cause the accident. Most states don't require you to provide the name of your insurance company, although it's usually a good idea to do so. However, *don't* discuss the amount of your coverage— that might inspire the other person to "realize" his injuries are more serious than he originally thought.

11   What should you do if you hit a parked car and the owner is not around? The law requires you to leave a note with your name, and the other identifying information previously mentioned, in a secure place on the car (such as under the windshield wiper).

4. Get Required Information.

You should obtain from the others involved in the accident the same information that you provide them with. However, if the other driver refuses to cooperate, at least get the license number and the make and model of the car to help police track down the owner.

12

5. Call the Police.

It's obvious that if it's a serious accident in which someone is injured, the police should be called immediately. That's both the law and common sense. But what if the accident seems minor? Say you're stopped, another car taps you in the rear. If it's absolutely clear to both drivers that there is no damage or injury, you each can go your merry way. But that's the exception.

13

substantiate prove

Normally, you should call the police to substantiate what occurred. In most cities police officers will come to the scene, even for minor accidents, but if they won't, you and the other driver should go to the station (of the city where the accident occurred) to file a report. Ask to have an officer check out both cars.

14

If you are not at fault, be wary of accepting the other driver's suggestion that you leave the police out of it and arrange a private settlement. When you submit your $500 car-repair estimate several weeks later, you could discover that the other driver has developed "amnesia" and denies being anywhere near the accident. If the police weren't present on the scene, you may not have a legal leg to stand on.

15

inflate increase

Even if you *are* at fault, it's a good idea to involve the police. Why? Because a police officer will note the extent of the other driver's damages in his or her report, limiting your liability. Without police presence the other driver can easily inflate the amount of the damages.

16

6. Identify Witnesses.

Get the names and addresses of any witnesses, in case there's a legal battle some time in the future. Ask bystanders or other motorists who stop whether they saw the accident; if they answer "yes," get their identifying information. It is also helpful to note the names and badge numbers of all police officers on the scene.

17

7. Go to the Hospital.

jeopardize endanger or risk

reimbursed repaid

If there's a chance that you've been injured, go directly to a hospital emergency room or to your doctor. The longer you wait, the more you may jeopardize your health and the more difficult it may be to get reimbursed for your injuries if they turn out to be serious.

18

8. File a Report.

Every driver who is involved in an automobile incident in which injuries occur must fill out an accident report. Even if the property damage is only in the range of $200 to $1,000, most states require that an accident report be filed. You must do this fairly quickly, usually in 1 to

19

30 days. Forms may be obtained and filed with the local motor vehicle department or police station in the city where the accident occurred.

9. Consider Filing an Insurance Claim.

20 Talk with your insurance agent as soon as possible after an accident. He or she can help you decide if you should file an insurance claim or pay out of your own pocket.

21 For example, let's say you caused an accident and the damages totaled $800. You carry a $250 deductible, leaving you with a possible $550 insurance claim. If you do submit a claim, your insurance rates are likely to go up, an increase that will probably continue for about three years. You should compare that figure to the $550 claim to determine whether to file a claim or to pay the cost yourself. (Also keep in mind that multiple claims sometimes make it harder to renew your coverage.)

deductible costs not covered by insurance

10. Don't Be Too Quick to Accept a Settlement.

22 If the other driver is at fault and there's any chance you've been injured, don't rush to accept a settlement from that person's insurance company. You may not know the extent of your injuries for some time, and once you accept a settlement, it's difficult to get an "upgrade." Before settling, consult with a lawyer who handles personal injury cases.

23 When you *haven't* been injured and you receive a fair offer to cover the damage to your car, you can go ahead and accept it. ■

CRITICAL THINKING AND DISCUSSION

GET THINKING AND WRITING

Understanding Meaning: What Is the Writer Trying to Say?

1. What problems can drivers run into if they are careless in responding to a minor accident?
2. What are the most important things you should do if involved in a fender bender?
3. Why does Budish say that you should not offer an apology, even if you believe the accident is your fault?
4. *Critical thinking:* Do you believe most people know what to do if they have a minor accident? Should this article be published as a pamphlet and distributed at service stations, insurance offices, car rental counters, and drivers' training courses?

Evaluating Strategy: How Does the Writer Say It?

1. How does Budish use an opening example to dramatize his point and arouse interest?
2. What techniques does Budish use to make his process easy to read and remember?
3. Would this essay be less effective if written in standard paragraphs without numbers? Why or why not?

Appreciating Language: What Words Does the Writer Use?

1. This article first appeared in *Family Circle.* Does this help explain its tone and style?
2. Why does Budish, a lawyer, avoid legal terms?

Writing Suggestions

1. Using this article as a model, write an essay that uses numbered steps to explain how people can avoid heart disease, quit smoking, prepare for a job interview, prevent identity theft, or remove a computer virus.
2. *Collaborative writing:* Work with a group of students and develop a process essay that tells readers how to respond to a specific emergency.

Cause and Effect

Cause and effect explains reasons and results.

WHO KILLED BENNY PARET?

NORMAN COUSINS

Norman Cousins (1915–1990) was a popular journalist and public speaker who discussed a range of social issues. In this 1962 essay, Cousins examines a televised boxing match that resulted in a fighter's death.

AS YOU READ

Notice that Cousins explores and dismisses several possible causes for the fighter's death before assigning responsibility to the fans.

Words to Know

fledgling literally, a baby bird, a novice or beginner

colossus giant

adroit skillful
feinting tricking
parrying dodging

Sometime about 1935 or 1936 I had an interview with Mike Jacobs, the prize-fight promoter. I was a <u>fledgling</u> reporter at that time; my beat was education but during the vacation season I found myself on varied assignments, all the way from ship news to sports reporting. In this way I found myself sitting opposite the most powerful figure in the boxing world.   1

There was nothing spectacular in Mr. Jacobs' manner or appearance; but when he spoke about prize fights, he was no longer a bland little man but a <u>colossus</u> who sounded the way Napoleon must have sounded when he reviewed a battle. You knew you were listening to Number One. His saying something made it true.   2

We discussed what to him was the only important element in successful promoting— how to please the crowd. So far as he was concerned, there was no mystery to it. You put killers in the ring and the people filled your arena. You hire boxing artists— men who are <u>adroit</u> at <u>feinting</u>, <u>parrying</u>, weaving, jabbing, and dancing, but who don't pack   3 dynamite in their fists— and you wind up counting your empty seats. So you searched for the killers and sluggers and maulers— fellows who could hit with the force of a baseball bat.

4   I asked Mr. Jacobs if he was speaking literally when he said people came out to see the killer.

5   "They don't come out to see a tea party," he said evenly. "They come out to see the knockout. They come out to see a man hurt. If they think anything else, they're kidding themselves."

6   Recently, a young man by the name of Benny Paret was killed in the ring. The killing was seen by millions; it was on television. In the twelfth round, he was hit hard in the head several times, went down, was counted out, and never came out of the coma.

7   The Paret fight produced a flurry of investigations. Governor Rockefeller was shocked by what happened and appointed a committee to assess the responsibility. The New York State Boxing Commission decided to find out what was wrong. The District Attorney's office expressed its concern. One question that was solemnly studied in all three probes concerned the action of the referee. Did he act in time to stop the fight? Another question had to do with the role of the examining doctors who certified the physical fitness of the fighters before the bout. Still another question involved Mr. Paret's manager; did he rush his boy into the fight without adequate time to recuperate from the previous one?

8   In short, the investigators looked into every possible cause except the real one. Benny Paret was killed because the human fist delivers enough impact, when directed against the head, to produce a massive hemorrhage in the brain. The human brain is the most delicate and complex mechanism in all creation. It has a lacework of millions of highly fragile nerve connections. Nature attempts to protect this exquisitely intricate machinery by encasing it in a hard shell. Fortunately, the shell is thick enough to withstand a great deal of pounding. Nature, however, can protect a man against everything except man himself. Not every blow to the head will kill a man— but there is always the risk of concussion and damage to the brain. A prize fighter may be able to survive even repeated brain concussions and go on fighting, but the damage to his brain may be permanent.

9   In any event, it is futile to investigate the referee's role and seek to determine whether he should have intervened to stop the fight earlier. That is not where the primary responsibility lies. The primary responsibility lies with the people who pay to see a man hurt. The referee who stops a fight too soon from the crowd's viewpoint can expect to be booed. The crowd wants the knockout; it wants to see a man stretched out on the canvas. This is the supreme moment in boxing. It is nonsense to talk about prize fighting as a test of boxing skills. No crowd was ever brought to its feet screaming and cheering at the sight of two men beautifully dodging and weaving out of each other's jabs. The time the crowd comes alive is when a man is hit hard over the heart or the head, when his mouthpiece flies out, when the blood squirts out of his nose or eyes,

assess determine

solemnly seriously

recuperate recover

exquisitely delicately

futile useless
intervened interrupted

prevailing common or
popular

mores customs

when he wobbles under the attack and his pursuer continues to smash at him with pole-axe impact.

Don't blame it on the referee. Don't even blame it on the fight man- 10 agers. Put the blame where it belongs— on the prevailing mores that regard prize fighting as a perfectly proper enterprise and vehicle of entertainment. No one doubts that many people enjoy prize fighting and will miss it if it should be thrown out. And that is precisely the point. ∎

GET *THINKING*
AND WRITING

CRITICAL THINKING AND DISCUSSION

Understanding Meaning: What Is the Writer Trying to Say?

1. What is the author's thesis?
2. What did the famous boxing promoter tell Cousins about boxing fans?
3. What damage does a blow to the head inflict?
4. Who does Cousins ultimately hold responsible for the boxer's death?
5. *Critical thinking:* Can the public also be blamed for pornography, illegal drugs, and gun violence? Why or why not?

Evaluating Strategy: How Does the Writer Say It?

1. Before discussing Benny Paret's death, Cousins tells readers what a famous boxing promoter told him as a young reporter. Is this an effective opening?
2. Cousins points out that crowds boo a referee who stops a fight. How does this support his point that fans are ultimately responsible for a fighter's death?
3. Cousins presents and dismisses several causes before he announces the real cause. Is this an effective device? Why or why not?

Appreciating Language: What Words Does the Writer Use?

1. What words does Cousins use to describe the human brain? How do they work to support his point that boxing is dangerous?
2. What words does Cousins use in paragraph 3 to compare boxing artists with fighters who are *killers, sluggers,* and *maulers?*

Writing Suggestions

1. Write a similar essay in which you identify what you feel is the "real cause" for a problem. Who is really to blame for underage drinking on campus, unemployment, outsourcing, terrorism, or gangs?
2. *Collaborative writing:* Work with other students to write an essay that discusses the responsibility fans have at sporting events or concerts. Who is responsible for rowdy behavior, drug use, and violence in stadiums and clubs?

WHY AMERICA LOVES REALITY TV

STEVEN REISS AND JAMES WILTZ

Steven Reiss teaches at The Ohio State University, where James Wiltz is working on his doctorate. In this essay they discuss results of a survey they conducted to discover why people watch reality TV programs.

AS YOU READ

First, consider your own experiences and those of your friends. Do you watch reality television shows? Which ones do you like the most? Why do you find them interesting?

1 Even if you don't watch reality television, it's becoming increasingly hard to avoid. The <u>salacious</u> *Temptation Island* was featured on the cover of *People* magazine. *Big Brother* aired five days a week and could be viewed on the Web 24 hours a day. And the *Survivor* finale dominated the front page of the *New York Post* after gaining ratings that rivaled those of the Super Bowl.

2 Is the popularity of shows such as *Survivor, Big Brother* and *Temptation Island* a sign that the country has degenerated into a nation of <u>voyeurs</u>? Americans seem hooked on so-called reality television— programs in which ordinary people compete in week-long contests while being filmed 24 hours a day. Some commentators contend the shows peddle <u>blatant</u> voyeurism, with shameless exhibitionists as contestants. Others believe that the show's secret to ratings success may be as simple and harmless as the desire to seem part of the in crowd.

3 Rather than just debate the point, we wanted to get some answers. So we conducted a detailed survey of 239 people, asking them about not only their television viewing habits but also their values and desires through the Reiss Profile, a standardized test of 16 basic desires and values. We found that the self-appointed experts were often wrong about why people watch reality TV.

4 Two of the most commonly repeated "truths" about reality TV viewers are that they watch in order to talk to friends and coworkers about the show, and that they are not as smart as other viewers. But our survey results show that both of these ideas are incorrect. Although some people may watch because it helps them <u>participate</u> in the next day's office chat, fans and nonfans score almost equally when tested on their sociability. And people who say they enjoy intellectual activities are no less likely to watch reality TV than are those who say they dislike intellectual activities.

5 Another common misconception about *Temptation Island,* a reality program in which couples were <u>enticed</u> to cheat on their partners, is that the audience was watching to see scenes of illicit sex. Some critics were surprised that the show remained popular when it turned out to be much

Words to Know

salacious scandalous

voyeurs people who get pleasure from watching others
blatant obvious

participate take part

enticed lured

expedience using shortcuts to achieve a goal

vying competing

tirade outburst

tamer than advertised. In fact, our survey suggests that one of the main differences between fans of the show and everyone else is not an interest in sex but a lack of interest in personal honor— they value <u>expedience</u>, not morality. What made *Temptation Island* popular was not the possibility of watching adultery, but the ethical slips that lead to adultery.

One aspect that all of the reality TV shows had in common was their competitive nature: contestants were <u>vying</u> with one another for a cash prize and were engaged in building alliances and betraying allies. The first *Survivor* series climaxed with one contestant, Susan Hawk, launching into a vengeful <u>tirade</u> against a one-time friend and ally before casting the vote that deprived her of the million-dollar prize. It makes sense, then, that fans of both *Survivor* and *Temptation Island* tend to be competitive— and that they are more likely to place a very high value on revenge than are other people. The *Survivor* formula of challenges and voting would seem to embody both of these desired qualities: the spirit of competition paired with the opportunity for payback.

6

But the attitude that best separated the regular viewers of reality television from everyone else is the desire for status. Fans of the shows are much more likely to agree with statements such as, "Prestige is important to me" and "I am impressed with designer clothes" than are other people. We have studied similar phenomena before and found that the desire for status is just a means to get attention. And more attention increases one's sense of importance: We think we are important if others pay attention to us and unimportant if ignored.

7

Reality TV allows Americans to fantasize about gaining status through automatic fame. Ordinary people can watch the shows, see people like themselves and imagine that they too could become celebrities by being on television. It does not matter as much that the contestants often are shown in unfavorable light; the fact that millions of Americans are paying attention means that the contestants are important.

8

And, in fact, some of the contestants have capitalized on their short-term celebrity: Colleen Haskell, from the first *Survivor* series, has a major role in the movie *The Animal,* and Richard Hatch, the scheming contestant who won the game, has been hired to host his own game show. If these former nobodies can become stars, then who couldn't?

9

The message of reality television is that ordinary people can become so important that millions will watch them. And the secret thrill of many of those viewers is the thought that perhaps next time, the new celebrities might be them. ■

10

GET THINKING AND WRITING

CRITICAL THINKING AND DISCUSSION

Understanding Meaning: What Is the Writer Trying to Say?

1. What did the survey reveal about why people watch reality TV?
2. What misconceptions do people have about the reasons for the popularity of reality TV programs?

3. What type of people watch reality TV? What is important to them?

4. *Critical thinking:* If you or your friends enjoy reality TV, what reasons can you give for the popularity of these shows?

Evaluating Strategy: How Does the Writer Say It?

1. How do the authors explain the way they conducted their survey?

2. The authors first present misconceptions, then their own findings. Is this effective?

Appreciating Language: What Words Does the Writer Use?

1. What words do the authors use to describe the viewers of reality TV?

2. What words do the authors use to describe the reality shows? What do terms like *alliance* and *contestant* suggest about their appeal?

Writing Suggestions

1. Write an essay that gives reasons why you like another kind of TV program, such as soap operas or sitcoms. Why do you watch them? What appeal do they have?

2. *Collaborative writing:* Discuss reality TV with other students. Do they see other causes for their popularity? For example, did the birth of CNN and other cable news channels create an interest in watching real events rather than fictional dramas? Write an essay summarizing the group's views.

Argument and Persuasion

Argument and persuasion encourages readers to accept a point of view or take action.

WHY I CHANGED MY MIND ON THE DEATH PENALTY

LANCE MORROW

Lance Morrow (1935–) has been a regular contributor to Time *magazine since 1965. In this essay, published in* Time *in 2000, he explains why he now opposes the death penalty.*

AS YOU READ

Morrow first explains his previous support for the death penalty, then presents his reasons for changing his opinion. The death penalty, he argues, no longer serves a moral purpose, so it has become immoral.

1 Christina Marie Riggs, a nurse in Arkansas and a single mother, killed her two children — Justin, 5, and Shelby Alexis, 2 — by giving them injections

Words to Know

potassium chloride a poison

of potassium chloride and then smothering them with a pillow. She wrote a suicide note, and apparently tried to kill herself with an overdose of 28 antidepressant tablets. She survived.

Or she did until last night, when the state of Arkansas put Riggs to death by lethal injection at the state prison in Varner. She was the first woman to be executed in Arkansas since 1845.

Jack Kevorkian a doctor who assisted the terminally ill to commit suicide

The state of Arkansas played the part of Jack Kevorkian in a case of assisted suicide. Christina Riggs said she wanted to die. She had dropped all legal appeals. She wanted to be with her children in heaven. Just before Riggs died, she said, "I love you, my babies." Some people said she had killed them because she was severely depressed. The prosecutor, on the other hand, called her "a self-centered, selfish, premeditated killer who did the unspeakable act of taking her own children's lives."

premeditated planned

So where do we stand on capital punishment now? (And, incidentally, isn't it grand that we seem to be overcoming, at the speed of light, our reluctance to execute women? Bless you, Gloria Steinem.)

Gloria Steinem feminist who championed equal rights for women

Review the state of play:

- Deterrence is an unreliable argument for the death penalty, I think because deterrence is unprovable.
- The fear of executing the wrong man (a more popular line of demurral these days) is an unreliable argument against all capital punishment. What if there are many witnesses to a murder? What if it's Hitler? Is capital punishment OK in cases of unmistakable guilt? George W. Bush says that he reviews each case to make sure he is absolutely certain a person did it before he allows a Texas execution to go ahead.

demurral hesitation

forgo give up

deferring accepting

I have argued in the past that the death penalty was justified, in certain brutal cases, on the basis of the social contract. That is: Some hideous crimes demand the ultimate punishment in order to satisfy the essentially civilizing deal that we make with one another as citizens. We forgo individual revenge, deferring to the law, but depend upon a certainty that the law will give us a justice that must include appropriate harshness. I favored the Texas folk wisdom: "He needs killing." If the law fails in that task, I said, and people see that evil is fecklessly tolerated, then the social contract disintegrates. Society needs a measure of homeopathic revenge.

homeopathic referring to a school of medicine that believes a little of what makes one sick can treat or cure

But I have changed my mind about capital punishment.

I think the American atmosphere, the American imagination (news, movies, books, music, fact, fiction, entertainment, culture, life in the streets, zeitgeist) is now so filled with murder and violence (gang wars, random shootings not just in housing projects but in offices and malls and schools) that violence of any kind— including solemn execution— has become merely a part of our cultural routine and joins, in our minds, the passing parade of stupidity/psychosis/chaos/entertainment that Americans seem to like, or have come to deserve. In Freudian terms, the

Freudian referring to Sigmund Freud, pioneer psychologist

2

3

4

5

6

7

8

once forceful (and patriarchal) American <u>Superego</u> (arguably including the authority of law, of the presidency, of the military, etc.) has collapsed into a great dismal swamp of <u>Id</u>.

9　　And in the Swamp, I have come to think, capital punishment has lost whatever cautionary social force it had—its <u>exemplary</u> meaning, its power to proclaim, as it once arguably did, that some deeds are, in our fine and virtuous company, intolerable.

10　　I think those arguing in favor of capital punishment now are indulging in a form of <u>nostalgia</u>. Capital punishment no longer works as a morality play. Each execution (divorced from its moral meaning, including its capacity to shock and to warn the young) simply becomes part of the great messy pageant, the vast and <u>voracious</u> stupidity, the Jerry Springer show of American life.

11　　Maybe most of our moral opinions are formed by emotions and <u>aesthetic</u> reactions. My opinion is this: Capital punishment has lost its moral meaning. Having lost its moral meaning, it has become as immoral as any other expression of violence. And therefore we should stop doing it.　■

Superego Freud's term for people's sense of social order and rules

Id Freud's term for instinctual drives and urges

exemplary excellent

nostalgia love of the past

voracious greedy

aesthetic concerning art or beauty

CRITICAL THINKING AND DISCUSSION

GET THINKING AND WRITING

Understanding Meaning: What Is the Writer Trying to Say?

1. What reasons does Morrow give for changing his opinion about the death penalty?
2. Why does Morrow believe that capital punishment does not serve any useful purpose?
3. Morrow opens his essay with the example of Christina Marie Riggs, who was executed for killing her children. Why is this case important in his view?
4. *Critical thinking:* Do you share Morrow's view that our culture has become obsessed with death and violence? If violent crimes and executions become frequent, does capital punishment lose its ability to make a strong statement about the value of life and the severe punishment murderers deserve?

Evaluating Strategy: How Does the Writer Say It?

1. Why is it effective when trying to persuade people about a controversial issue to explain the merits of both sides?
2. Morrow uses a one-sentence paragraph transition (paragraph 7). Is this effective? Why or why not?
3. Morrow places his thesis in the last sentence rather than the beginning of his essay. Is this effective? Why or why not?

Appreciating Language: What Words Does the Writer Use?

1. What does Morrow mean by the word *swamp*? What does the swamp contain?
2. How does Morrow explain that capital punishment moved from being *moral* to *immoral*? How does he define these terms?

Writing Suggestions

1. Write a persuasive essay about an issue you have changed your mind about. Explain your original views and what led you to change them.

2. *Collaborative writing:* Discuss Morrow's essay with other students and ask members of the group their opinions of the death penalty. If you are in agreement, develop an essay expressing your views. If members disagree, consider developing opposing essays.

IN PRAISE OF THE F WORD

MARY SHERRY

Mary Sherry, who teaches basic grammar and writing to adults, wrote this essay for Newsweek *that criticizes the public schools for graduating semiliterate students.*

AS YOU READ

Notice how Sherry uses her own son as evidence to support her view that flunking or threatening to flunk students is a positive teaching tool.

Words to Know

validity authority or value

Tens of thousands of eighteen-year-olds will graduate this year and be handed meaningless diplomas. These diplomas won't look any different from those awarded their luckier classmates. Their <u>validity</u> will be questioned only when their employers discover that these graduates are semi-literate. **1**

Eventually a fortunate few will find their way into educational-repair shops— adult-literacy programs, such as the one where I teach basic grammar and writing. There, high-school graduates and high-school dropouts pursuing graduate-equivalency certificates will learn the skills they should have learned in school. They will also discover they have been cheated by our educational system. **2**

As I teach, I learn a lot about our schools. Early in each session I ask my students to write about an unpleasant experience they had in school. No writers' block here! "I wish someone would have had made me stop doing drugs and made me study." "I liked to party and no one seemed to care." "I was a good kid and didn't cause any trouble, so they just passed me along even though I didn't read well and couldn't write." And so on. **3**

impediments barriers

I am your basic do-gooder, and prior to teaching this class I blamed the poor academic skills our kids have today on drugs, divorce and other <u>impediments</u> to concentration necessary for doing well in school. But, as I rediscover each time I walk into the classroom, before a teacher can expect students to concentrate, he has to get their attention, no matter what distractions may be at hand. There are many ways to do this, and they have much to do with teaching style. However, if style alone won't **4** do it, there is another way to show who holds the winning hand in the classroom. That is to reveal the trump card of failure.

trump card valuable playing card held until needed

5   I will never forget a teacher who played that card to get the attention of one of my children. Our youngest, a world-class charmer, did little to develop his intellectual talents but always got by. Until Mrs. Stifter.

6   Our son was a high-school senior when he had her for English. "He sits in the back of the room talking to his friends," she told me. "Why don't you move him to the front row?" I urged, believing the embarrassment would get him to settle down. Mrs. Stifter looked at me steely-eyed over her glasses. "I don't move seniors," she said. "I flunk them." I was flustered. Our son's academic life flashed before my eyes. No teacher had ever threatened him with that before. I regained my composure and managed to say that I thought she was right. By the time I got home I was feeling pretty good about this. It was a radical approach for these times, but, well, why not? "She's going to flunk you," I told my son. I did not discuss it any further. Suddenly English became a priority in his life. He finished out the semester with an A.

composure calmness

7   I know one example doesn't make a case, but at night I see a parade of students who are angry and resentful for having been passed along until they could no longer even pretend to keep up. Of average intelligence or better, they eventually quit school, concluding they were too dumb to finish. "I should have been held back," is a comment I hear frequently. Even sadder are those students who are high-school graduates who say to me after a few weeks of class, "I don't know how I ever got a high-school diploma."

8   Passing students who have not mastered the work cheats them and the employers who expect graduates to have basic skills. We excuse this dishonest behavior by saying kids can't learn if they come from terrible environments. No one seems to stop to think that— no matter what environments they come from— most kids don't put school first on their list unless they perceive something is at stake. They'd rather be sailing.

perceive see

9   Many students I see at night could give expert testimony on unemployment, chemical dependency, abusive relationships. In spite of these difficulties, they have decided to make education a priority. They are motivated by the desire for a better job or the need to hang on to the one they've got. They have a healthy fear of failure.

10   People of all ages can rise above their problems, but they need to have a reason to do so. Young people generally don't have the maturity to value education in the same way my adult students value it. But fear of failure, whether economic or academic, can motivate both.

11   Flunking as a regular policy has just as much merit today as it did two generations ago. We must review the threat of flunking and see it as it really is— a positive teaching tool. It is an expression of confidence by both teachers and parents that the students have the ability to learn the material presented to them. However, making it work again would take a dedicated, caring conspiracy between teachers and parents. It would mean facing the tough reality that passing kids who haven't

learned the material— while it might save them grief for the short term— dooms them to long-term illiteracy. It would mean that teachers would have to follow through on their threats, and parents would have to stand behind them, knowing their children's best interests are indeed at stake. This means no more doing Scott's assignments for him because he might fail. No more passing Jodi because she's such a nice kid.

This is a policy that worked in the past and can work today. A wise teacher . . . gave our son the opportunity to succeed— or fail. It's time we return this choice to all students. ■   12

GET THINKING AND WRITING

CRITICAL THINKING AND DISCUSSION

Understanding Meaning: What Is the Writer Trying to Say?

1. Why does Sherry view flunking as a valuable teaching tool?
2. How do her students recall their high school experiences?
3. How have schools, in Sherry's view, failed students and society?
4. *Critical thinking:* Why does Sherry view flunking as "positive"? What does flunking suggest about student potential? How can it motivate students?

Evaluating Strategy: How Does the Writer Say It?

1. Sherry presents herself both as a teacher and a parent of a student threatened with flunking. Why is this important in persuading readers who might object to flunking students?
2. How does Sherry use her son as evidence for her argument?

Appreciating Language: What Words Does the Writer Use?

1. Sherry calls herself a "do-gooder." What does this term imply?
2. Sherry suggests what is needed is a "caring conspiracy between teachers and parents." Is "conspiracy" an odd term to use? Do we usually associate it with evil or criminal plots? What impact does this word have?

Writing Suggestions

1. Write an essay about flunking that agrees or disagrees with Sherry's thesis. Use examples from your own high school experiences.
2. *Collaborative writing:* Work with a group of students and develop an essay that persuades readers of other changes that should be made in public schools to motivate students to learn.

Handbook

A WRITER'S GUIDE TO OVERCOMING COMMON ERRORS

Basic Sentence Structure

A sentence is a group of words that contains a subject and verb and states a complete thought.

Phrases and Clauses

Phrases are groups of related words that form parts of a sentence:

After the game	Ted and Carlos	are willing to help distribute	decorations for the party.

Clauses consist of related words that contain both a subject and a verb:

- **Independent clauses** contain a subject and verb and express a complete thought. They are sentences:

    I waited for the bus.   It began to rain.

- **Dependent clauses** contain a subject and verb but do *not* express a complete thought. They are not sentences:

    While I waited for the bus

    Dependent clauses have to be connected to an independent clause to create a sentence that expresses a complete thought:

    While I waited for the bus, it began to rain.

Types of Sentences

Sentence types are determined by the number and kind of clauses they contain. A **simple sentence** consists of a single independent clause:

Jim sings.
Jim and Nancy sing and dance at the newly opened El Morocco.
Seeking to reenter show business, Jim and Nancy sing and dance at the newly opened El Morocco, located at 55th and Second Avenue.

A **compound sentence** contains two or more independent clauses but no dependent clauses:

Jim studied dance at Columbia; Nancy studied music at Juilliard.
    [two independent clauses joined by a semicolon]

Jim wants to stay in New York, but Nancy longs to move to California.
    [two independent clauses joined with a comma and coordinating conjunction]

A **complex sentence** contains one independent clause and one or more dependent clauses:

Jim and Nancy are studying drama because they want to act on Broadway.
Because they want to act on Broadway, *Jim and Nancy are studying drama*.
    [When a dependent clause begins a complex sentence, it is set off with a comma.]

A **compound-complex sentence** contains at least two independent clauses and one or more dependent clauses:

Jim and Nancy perform Sinatra classics, and they often dress in forties clothing *because the El Morocco draws an older crowd.*

Because the El Morocco draws an older crowd, Jim and Nancy perform Sinatra classics, and they often dress in forties clothing.

PARTS OF SPEECH

Nouns	name persons, places, things, or ideas: *teacher, attic, Italy, book, liberty*
Pronouns	take the place of nouns: *he, she, they, it, this, that, what, which, hers, their*
Verbs	express action: *buy, sell, run, walk, create, think, feel, wonder, hope, dream* link ideas: *is, are, was, were*
Adjectives	add information about nouns or pronouns: a *red* car, a *bright* idea, a *lost* cause
Adverbs	add information about verbs: drove *recklessly,* sell *quickly, angrily* denounced add information about adjectives: *very* old teacher, *sadly* dejected leader add information about other adverbs: *rather* hesitantly remarked
Prepositions	link nouns and pronouns, expressing relationships between related words: *in* the house, *around* the corner, *between* the acts, *through* the evening
Conjunctions	link related parts of a sentence: **Coordinating conjunctions** link parts of equal value: *and, or, yet, but, so, for, nor* He went to college, *and* she got a job. **Subordinating conjunctions** link dependent or less important parts: *When* he went to college, she got a job.
Interjections	express emotion or feeling that is not part of the basic sentence and are set off with commas or used with exclamation points: *Oh,* he's leaving? *Wow*!

(continued)

Words can function as different parts of speech:

> I bought more *paint* [noun].
> I am going to *paint* [verb] the bedroom.
> Those supplies are stored in the *paint* [adjective] room.

Parts of speech can be single words or phrases or groups of related words that work together:

> Tom and his entire staff [noun phrase]
> wrote and edited [verb phrase]
> throughout the night. [prepositional phrase]

Sentence Errors

Fragments

Fragments are incomplete sentences. They lack a subject, a complete verb, or fail to express a complete thought:

Subject Missing
Worked all night. [Who worked *all night*?]

Revised
He worked all night.

Verb Missing
Juan the new building. [What was Juan doing?]

Revised
Juan designed the new building.

Incomplete Verb
Juan designing the new building. [*-ing* verbs cannot stand alone.]

Revised
Juan is designing the new building.

Incomplete Thought
Although Juan designed the building. [It has a subject and verb but fails to express a whole idea.]

Revised
Juan designed the building.

or

Although Juan designed the building, he did not receive any recognition.

Correcting Fragments

There are two ways of correcting fragments.

1. Turn the fragment into a complete sentence by making sure it expresses a complete thought:

   Fragments
   Yale being the center for this research
   Based on public opinion surveys
   The mayor designated

Revised

Yale is the center for this research. [complete verb added]

The new study is based on public opinion surveys. [subject and verb added]

The mayor designated Sandy Gomez to head the commission. [words added to express a complete thought]

2. Attach the fragment to a sentence to state a complete thought. (Often fragments occur when you write quickly and break off part of a sentence.)

Fragments

He bought a car. *While living in Florida.*

Constructed in 1873. The old church needs major repairs.

Revised

He bought a car while living in Florida.

Constructed in 1873, the old church needs major repairs.

POINT TO REMEMBER

Reading out loud can help identify fragments. Ask yourself, "Does this statement express a complete thought?"

Run-ons

Fused Sentences

Fused sentences lack the punctuation needed to join two independent clauses. The two independent clauses are *fused,* or joined, without a comma and a coordinating conjunction or a semicolon:

Travis entered the contest he won first prize.

Nancy speaks Spanish she has trouble reading it.

Revised

Travis entered the contest; he won first prize.

Nancy speaks Spanish, but she has trouble reading it.

Comma Splices

Comma splices are compound sentences where a comma is used instead of a semicolon:

My sister lives in Chicago, my brother lives in New York.

The lake is frozen solid, it is safe to drive on.

Revised

My sister lives in Chicago; my brother lives in New York.

The lake is frozen solid; it is safe to drive on.

Identifying Run-ons

To identify run-ons, do two things:

1. Read the sentence carefully. Determine if it is a compound sentence. Ask yourself if you can divide the sentence into two or more independent clauses (simple sentences).

Sam entered college but dropped out after six months.

Sam entered college . . . [independent clause (simple sentence)]
dropped out after six months. [not a sentence]

[not a compound sentence]

Nancy graduated in May she signed up for summer courses.

Nancy graduated in May . . .   [independent clause (simple sentence)]
she signed up for summer courses. [independent clause (simple
sentence)]

[compound sentence]

2. If you have two complete sentences, determine if they should be joined. Is
there a logical relationship between them? What is the best way of connecting them? Independent clauses can be joined with a comma and *and, or,
yet, but, so, for, nor,* or with a semicolon.

Nancy graduated in May, but she signed up for summer courses.

But indicates a contrast between two ideas. Be sure to insert a comma to
quickly repair this run-on.

Repairing Run-ons: Minor Repairs

A fused sentence or comma splice may need only a minor repair. Sometimes in
writing quickly, we mistakenly use a comma when a semicolon is needed:

The Senate likes the president's budget, the House still has questions.

Revised
The Senate likes the president's budget; the House still has questions.

In other cases we may forget a coordinating conjunction:

The Senate likes the president's budget, the House still has questions.

Senators approve of the budget, they want to meet with the president's staff.

Revised
The Senate likes the president's budget, but the House still has questions.

Senators approve of the budget, and they want to meet with the president's
staff.

Repairing Run-ons: Major Repairs

Some run-ons require major repairs. Sometimes we create run-ons when our ideas
are not clearly stated or fully thought out:

Truman was president at the end of the war the United States dropped the
atomic bomb.

Adding the necessary comma and coordinating conjunction eliminates a mechanical error but leaves the sentence awkward and unclear:

Truman was president at the end of the war, and the United States dropped
the atomic bomb.

Repairing this kind of run-on requires critical thinking. A compound sentence
joins two complete thoughts, and there should be a clear relationship between

them. It may be better to revise the entire sentence, changing it from a compound to a complex sentence:

Revised
Truman was president at the end of the war when the United States dropped the atomic bomb.

In some instances you may find it easier to break the run-on into two simple sentences, especially if there is no strong relationship between the main ideas:

Swansea is a port city in Wales that was severely bombed in World War II Dylan Thomas was born there in 1914.

Revised
Swansea is a port city in Wales that was severely bombed in World War II. Dylan Thomas was born there in 1914.

POINT TO REMEMBER

A compound sentence should join independent clauses that state ideas of equal importance. Avoid using an independent clause to state a minor detail that could be contained in a dependent clause or a phrase:

Awkward

My brother lives in Boston, and he is an architect.

Revised

My brother, who lives in Boston, is an architect.
My brother in Boston is an architect.

Modifiers

Dangling Modifiers

Modifiers that serve as introductions must describe what follows the comma. When they do not, they "dangle," so it is unclear what they modify:

Grounded by fog, airport officials ordered passengers to deplane.
    [Were airport officials *grounded by fog*?]

Revised
Grounded by fog, the passengers were ordered by airport officials to deplane.
Airport officials ordered passengers to deplane the aircraft grounded by fog.

STRATEGY TO DETECT DANGLING MODIFIERS

Sentences with opening modifiers set off by commas fit this pattern:
    Modifier, main sentence

To make sure the sentence is correct, use the following test:

(continued)

1. Read the sentence, then turn the modifier into a question, asking who or what in the main sentence is performing the action:

    question, answer

2. What follows the comma forms the answer. If the answer is appropriate, the construction is correct:

    Hastily constructed, the bridge deteriorated in less than a year.

    Question: What was *hastily constructed*?
    Answer: the bridge
    This sentence is <u>correct</u>.

    Suspected of insanity, the defense attorney asked that her client be examined by psychiatrists.

    Question: Who was *suspected of insanity*?
    Answer: the defense attorney
    This sentence is <u>incorrect</u>.

    Revised: Suspecting her client to be insane, the defense attorney asked that he be examined by psychiatrists.

Misplaced Modifiers

Place modifying words, phrases, and clauses as near as possible to the words they describe:

Confusing
Scientists developed new chips for laptop computers *that cost less than fifty cents*.

   [Do laptop computers cost *less than fifty cents*?]

Revised
Scientists developed laptop computer chips that cost less than fifty cents.

Faulty Parallelism

When you create pairs or lists, the words or phrases must match—they have to be all nouns, all adjectives, all adverbs, or all verbs in the same form:

Nancy is *bright, creative,* and *funny*. [adjectives]
Mary writes *clearly, directly,* and *forcefully*. [adverbs]
Reading and *calculating* are critical skills for my students. [gerunds]
She should *lose* weight, *stop* smoking, and *limit* her intake of alcohol.
   [verbs matching with *should*]

The following sentences are not parallel:

The concert was loud, colorful, and many people attended.
   [*many people attended* does not match with the adjectives *loud* and *colorful*]
John failed to take notes, refused to attend class, and his final exam is unreadable.
   [*his final exam is* does not match the verb phrases *failed to take* and *refused to attend*]

Quitting smoking and daily exercise are important.
   [*Quitting,* a gerund, does not match with *daily exercise.*]

Revised

The concert was *loud, colorful,* and *well attended.* [all adjectives]
John *failed* to take notes, *refused* to attend class, and *wrote* an almost unreadable final exam. [all verbs]
Quitting smoking and *exercising* daily are important.
   [both gerunds or *-ing* nouns]

Strategies for Detecting and Revising Faulty Parallelism

Apply this simple test to any sentences that include pairs or lists of words or phrases to make sure they are parallel:

1. Read the sentence and locate the pair or list.
2. Make sure each item matches the format of the basic sentence by testing each item.

Example:

Students should read directions carefully, write down assignments accurately, and take notes.

Students should read directions.
Students should write down assignments accurately.
Students should take notes.

   [Each item matches *Students should* . . .]
                    This sentence is <u>parallel</u>.

Computer experts will have to make more precise predictions in the future to reduce waste, create more accurate budgets, and public support must be maintained.

Computer experts will have to make more precise . . .
Computer experts will have to create more accurate . . .
Computer experts will have to public support must be . . .

         [The last item does not link with *will have to.*]
                    This sentence is <u>not parallel</u>.

A TIP ON PARALLELISM

In many cases it is difficult to revise long sentences that are not parallel:

To build her company, Shireen Naboti is a careful planner, skilled supervisor, recruits talent carefully, monitors quality control, and is a lobbyist for legal reform.

If you have trouble making all the elements match, it may be simpler to break it up into two or even three separate sentences:

To build her company, Shireen Naboti is a careful planner, skilled supervisor, and lobbyist for legal reform. In addition, she recruits talent carefully and monitors quality control.

(continued)

The first sentence contains the noun phrases; the second consists of the two verb phrases. It is easier to create two short parallel lists than one long one.

Verbs

Subject-Verb Agreement

Singular subjects require singular verbs:

The <u>boy</u> *walks* to school.
Your <u>bill</u> *is* overdue.

Plural subjects require plural verbs:

The <u>boys</u> *walk* to school.
Your <u>bills</u> *are* overdue.

Changing a verb from singular to plural changes the meaning of a sentence:

Singular
The desk and chair *is* on sale.   [The desk and chair is sold as one item.]

Plural
The desk and chair *are* on sale.   [The desk and chair are sold separately.]

RULES

- Not all nouns add an -*s* to become plural:
  The deer run across the road.   The women play cards.

- Some nouns that end in -*s* and look like plurals are singular:
  Mathematics *is* my toughest course.   Economics *demands* accurate data.

- Some nouns that may refer to one item are plural:
  My scissors *are* dull.   *Are* these your pants?

- Proper nouns that look plural are singular if they are names of companies, organizations, or titles of books, movies, television shows, or works of art:
  General Motors *is* building   *The Three Musketeers is* funny.
  a new engine.

- Units of time and amounts of money are generally singular:
  Twenty-five dollars *is* a lot for   Two weeks *is* not enough time.
  a T-shirt.

  They appear as plurals to indicate separate items:
  Three dollars *were* lying on   My last weeks at camp *were*
  the table.   unbearable.

(continued)

- Group nouns—*audience, board, class, committee, jury, number, team,* and so on—are singular when they describe a group working together:

"Faculty Accepts School Board Offer"	[headline describing teachers acting as a group]
"Faculty Protest School Board Offer"	[headline describing teachers acting individually]

- Verbs in "either . . . or" sentences can be singular or plural. If both subjects are singular, the verb is singular:

  Either the <u>father</u> or the <u>mother</u> *is* required to appear in court.

  If both subjects are plural, the verb is plural:

  Either the <u>parents</u> or the <u>attorneys</u> *are* required to appear in court.

  If one subject is plural and one is singular, the subject closer to the verb determines whether it is singular or plural:

  Either the parent or the <u>attorneys</u> *are* required to appear in court.
  Either the parents or the <u>attorney</u> *is* required to appear in court.

- Indefinite pronouns can be singular or plural.

  Singular indefinite pronouns:

another	each	everything	nothing
anybody	either	neither	somebody
anyone	everybody	nobody	someone

  Anything is possible.   *Someone* is coming.

  Plural indefinite pronouns:

both	few	many	several

  Both are here.   *Many* are missing.

  Indefinite pronouns that can be singular or plural:

all	some	more	most

Snow fell last night, but <u>most</u> *has* melted.	[*Most* refers to the singular "snow."]
Passengers were injured, but <u>most</u> *have* recovered.	[*Most* refers to plural "passengers."]

Verb Tense

Regular Verbs

Most verbs show tense changes by adding *-ed* to words ending with consonants and *-d* to words ending with an *e:*

Present	Past	Past Participle
walk	walked	walked
create	created	created
cap	capped	capped

Irregular Verbs

Irregular verbs do not follow the *-ed* pattern.

Some irregular verbs make no spelling change to indicate shifts in tense:

Present	Past	Past Participle
cost	cost	cost
cut	cut	cut
fit	fit	fit
hit	hit	hit
hurt	hurt	hurt
put	put	put

Most irregular verbs make a spelling change rather than adding *-ed:*

Present	Past	Past Participle
arise	arose	arisen
awake	awoke	awoken
be	was, were	been
bear	bore	borne (not *born*)
become	became	become
break	broke	broken
bring	brought	brought
build	built	built
choose	chose	chosen
come	came	come
dive	dove (dived)	dived
do	did	done
draw	drew	drawn
eat	ate	eaten
feed	fed	fed
fly	flew	flown
forgive	forgave	forgiven
freeze	froze	frozen
get	got	gotten
grow	grew	grown
hang (objects)	hung	hung
hang (people)	hanged	hanged
have	had	had
lay (place)	laid	laid
lead	led	led
leave	left	left
lie (recline)	lay	lain
lose	lost	lost
make	made	made
mean	meant	meant
meet	met	met
pay	paid	paid
ride	rode	ridden
ring	rang	rung
rise	rose	risen
run	ran	run
say	said	said

Present	Past	Past Participle
see	saw	seen
sell	sold	sold
shake	shook	shaken
shine	shone	shone
shoot	shot	shot
sing	sang	sung
sink	sank	sunk
sleep	slept	slept
speak	spoke	spoken
spend	spent	spent
steal	stole	stolen
sting	stung	stung
strike	struck	struck
swim	swam	swum
swing	swung	swung
take	took	taken
teach	taught	taught
think	thought	thought
throw	threw	thrown
understand	understood	understood
wake	woke	woken
write	wrote	written

Problem Verbs: Lie/Lay, Rise/Raise, Set/Sit

Lie/Lay

To lie = to rest or recline: "lie down for nap"

To lay = to put something down or place into position: "lay a book on a table"

Present	Past	Past Participle
lie	lay	lain
lay	laid	laid

Remember: *Lie* expresses action done *by* someone or something:

Tom called 911, then *lay* on the sofa waiting for the paramedics.

Lay expresses action done *to* someone or something:

The paramedics *laid* Tom on the floor to administer CPR.

Rise/Raise

To rise = to get up or move up on your own: "rise and shine" or "rise to the occasion"

To raise = to lift or grow something: "raise a window" or "raise children"

Present	Past	Past Participle
rise	rose	risen
raise	raised	raised

Remember: *Rise* can refer to objects as well as people.

> The bread rises in the oven.   Oil prices are rising.

Set/Sit

To set = to put something in position or arrange in place: "set down a glass" or "set down some notes"

To sit = to assume a sitting position: "sit in a chair" or "sit on a committee"

Present	Past	Past Participle
set	set	set
sit	sat	sat

Remember: *Set* always takes a direct object.

Shifts in Tense

Avoid awkward or illogical shifts in time and write in a consistent tense:

Awkward
I *drove* to the beach and *see* Karen working out with Jim.
 past   present

Consistent
I *drove* to the beach and *saw* Karen working out with Jim.
 past   past

or

I *drive* to the beach and *see* Karen working out with Jim.
 present   present

Change tenses to show a logical change in time:

I *was born* in Chicago but *live* in Milwaukee. Next year I *will move* to New York.
 past   present   future

Change tense to distinguish between past events and subjects that are permanent or still operating:

He *was born* in Trenton, which *is* the capital of New Jersey.

Pronouns

Reference

Pronouns should clearly refer to specific antecedents. Avoid unclear references.

- Make sure pronouns are clearly linked to **antecedents**—the nouns or other pronouns they represent. Avoid constructions in which a pronoun could refer to more than one noun or pronoun:

    Unclear
    Nancy was with Sharon when *she* got the news.
      [Who received the news— Nancy or Sharon?]

    Revised
    When Sharon received the news, *she* was with Nancy.

- Replace pronouns with nouns for clearer references:

  Unclear
  The teachers explained to the students why *they* couldn't attend the ceremony.
  [Who cannot attend the ceremony— teachers or students?]

  Revised
  The teachers explained to the students why *faculty* couldn't attend the ceremony.
  The teachers explained to the students why *children* couldn't attend the ceremony.

- State "*either . . . or*" constructions carefully.

  Either George or Jim can lend you *their* key.
  [George and Jim share one key.]

  Either George or Jim can lend you *his* key.
  [Both George and Jim have keys.]

  Either George or Anna can lend you *a* key.
  [avoids the need for *his or her*]

- Avoid unclear references with *this, that, it, which,* and *such:*

  Unclear
  Many people think that diets are the only way to lose weight. *This* is wrong.

  Revised
  Many people mistakenly think that diets are the only way to lose weight.

- Avoid unnecessary pronouns after nouns:

  Unnecessary
  Thomas Jefferson *he* wrote the Declaration of Independence.

  Revised
  Thomas Jefferson wrote the Declaration of Independence.

- Avoid awkward use of *you. You* is acceptable for directly addressing readers. Avoid making awkward shifts in general statements:

  Awkward
  Freeway congestion can give you stress.

  Revised
  Freeway congestion can be stressful.

Agreement

- Pronouns agree in number and gender with antecedents:

  Bill took *his* time.   *Nancy* rode *her* bicycle.   The *children* called *their* mother.

- Compound nouns require plural pronouns:

Both the *students and the teachers* argue that *their* views are not heard.
Tom and Nancy announced *they* plan to move to Colorado next year.

- Collective nouns use singular or plural pronouns:

    Singular
    The *cast* played *its* last performance.
    [The cast acts as one unit.]

    Plural
    The *cast* had trouble remembering *their* lines.
    [Cast members act independently.]

- *Either . . . or* constructions can be singular or plural. If both nouns are singular, the pronoun is singular:

    Either the city council *or* the county board will present *its* budget.
    [Only one group will present a budget.]

    If both nouns are plural, the pronoun is plural:

    The board members or *the city attorneys* will present *their* report.
    [In both instances, several individuals present a report.]

    If one noun is singular and the other is plural, the pronoun agrees with the nearer noun:

    Either the teacher or students will present *their* findings to the principal.

    Place the plural noun last to avoid awkward statements or having to represent both genders with *he and she, his or her,* or *him and her.*

- Pronouns should maintain the same person or point of view in a sentence, avoiding awkward shifts:

    Awkward Shift
    To save money, *consumers* should monitor *their* [third person] use of credit cards to avoid getting in over *your* [second person] head in debt.

    Revised
    To save money, *consumers* should monitor *their* use of credit cards to avoid getting in over *their* heads in debt.

- In speaking, people often use the plural pronouns *they, them,* and *their* to include both males and females. In formal writing, make sure singular indefinite pronouns agree with singular pronouns.

    Singular

anybody	either	neither	one
anyone	everybody	nobody	somebody
each	everyone	no one	someone

    Anybody can bring *his or her* tax return in for review.
    Everybody is required to do the test *himself or herself.*

    Plural
    If *many* are unable to attend the orientation, make sure to call *them.*

Indefinite pronouns like *some* may be singular or plural depending on context:

Singular
Some of the ice is losing *its* brilliance.

Plural
Some of the children are missing *their* coats.

AVOID SEXISM IN PRONOUN USE

Singular nouns and many indefinite pronouns refer to individuals who may be male or female. Trying to include both men and women, however, often creates awkward constructions:

If a student has a problem, *he or she* should contact *his or her* adviser.

In editing your writing, try these strategies to eliminate both sexism and awkward pronoun use:

- Use plurals:

  If students have problems, *they* should contact *their* advisors.

- Revise the sentence to limit or eliminate the need for pronouns:

  Students with problems should contact advisers.
  Advisers assist students with problems.

Adjectives and Adverbs

- Understand differences between adjectives and adverbs:

  She gave us *freshly sliced* peaches.
  [The adverb *freshly* modifies the adjective *sliced,* meaning that the peaches, whatever their freshness, have just been sliced.]

  She gave us *fresh sliced* peaches.
  [The adjectives *fresh* and *sliced* both describe the noun *peaches,* meaning the peaches are both fresh and sliced.]

- Review sentences to select the most effective adjectives and adverbs. Adjectives and adverbs add meaning. Avoid vague modifiers:

  Vague
  The concert hall was *totally inappropriate* for our group.

  Revised
  The concert hall was *too informal* for our group.
  The concert hall was *too large* for our group.

- Use adverbs with verbs:

  Incorrect
  Drive *careful.* [adjective]

  Revised
  Drive *carefully.*

- Avoid unnecessary adjectives and adverbs:

  Unnecessary
  We drove down the *old, winding, potholed, dirt* road.

  Revised
  We drove down the *winding, potholed* road.

- Use *good* and *well*, and *bad* and *badly* accurately. *Good* and *bad* are adjectives and modify nouns and pronouns:

  The cookies taste *good*. [*Good* modifies the noun *cookies*.]
  The wine is *bad*. [*Bad* modifies the noun *wine*.]

  Well and *badly* are adverbs and modify verbs, adjectives, and adverbs:

  She sings *well*. [*Well* modifies the verb *sings*.]
  He paid for *badly* needed repairs. [*Badly* modifies the adjective *needed*.]

Comma ,

- Use commas with *and, or, yet, but, for, nor,* or *so* to join independent clauses to create compound sentences and avoid run-ons:

  Chinatown is a popular tourist attraction, <u>and</u> it serves as an important cultural center.

- Use a comma after a dependent clause that opens a complex sentence:

  Because the parade was canceled, we decided to go to the shore.

  If the dependent clause follows the independent clause, the comma is usually deleted:

  We decided to go to the shore because the parade was canceled.

- Use a comma after a long phrase or an introductory word:

  After breakfast with the new students and guest faculty, we are going to the museum.
  Yes, I am cashing your check today.

- Use commas to separate words, phrases, and clauses in a series:

  Words
  We purchased computer paper, ink, pens, and pencils.

  Phrases
  We purchased computer paper, ordered fax supplies, and photocopied the records.

  Clauses
  We purchased computer paper, Sarah ordered fax supplies, and Tim photocopied the records.

  If clauses contain commas, separate them with semicolons (see page 632).

- Use commas to set off nonrestrictive or parenthetical words or phrases. *Nonrestrictive* words or phrases describe or add extra information about a noun and are set off with commas:

    George Wilson, who loves football, can't wait for the Superbowl.

    Restrictive words or phrases limit or restrict the meaning of abstract nouns and are not set off with commas:

    Anyone who loves football can't wait for the Superbowl.

- Use commas to set off contrasted elements:

    The teachers, not the students, argue the tests are too difficult.

- Use commas after interjections, words used in direct address, and around direct quotations:

    Hey, get a life.
    Paul, help Sandy with the mail.
    George said, "Welcome to the disaster," to everyone arriving at the party.

- Use commas to separate city and state or city and country, items in dates, and every three numerals 1,000 and above:

    I used to work in Rockford, Illinois, until I was transferred to Paris, France.
      [A comma goes after the state or country if followed by other words.]
    She was born on July 7, 1986, and graduated high school in May 2004.
      [A comma goes after the date if followed by other words. No comma needed if only month and year are given.]

    The new bridge will cost the state 52,250,000 dollars.

- Use commas to set off absolute phrases:

    Her car unable to operate in deep snow, Sarah borrowed Tim's Jeep.
    Wilson raced down the field and caught the ball on one knee, his heart pounding.

- Use commas where needed to prevent confusion or add emphasis:

    Confusing
    Whenever they hunted people ran for cover.
    To Sally Madison was a good place to live.
    To help feed the hungry Jim donated bread.

    Improved
    Whenever they hunted, people ran for cover.
    To Sally, Madison was a good place to live.
    To help feed the hungry, Jim donated bread.

    Reading sentences out loud can help you spot sentences that need commas to prevent confusion.

GUIDE TO ELIMINATING UNNECESSARY COMMAS

1. Don't put a comma between a subject and verb unless setting off nonrestrictive elements or a series:

   Incorrect
   The old, car was stolen.

   Correct
   The car, which was old, was stolen.

2. Don't use commas to separate prepositional phrases from what they modify:

   Incorrect
   The van, in the driveway, needs new tires.

   Correct
   The van in the driveway needs new tires.

3. Don't use commas to separate two items in a compound verb:

   Incorrect
   They sang, and danced at the party.

   Correct
   They sang and danced at the party.

4. Don't put commas around titles:

   Incorrect
   The film opens with, "Love Me Tender," and shots of Elvis.

   Correct
   The film opens with "Love Me Tender" and shots of Elvis.

5. Don't put commas after a series unless it ends a clause that has to be set off from the rest of the sentence:

   Incorrect
   They donated computers, printers, and telephones, to our office.

   Correct
   They donated computers, printers, and telephones, and we provided office space.

6. Don't set off a dependent clause with a comma when it ends a sentence:

   Incorrect
   The game was canceled, because the referees went on strike.

   Correct
   The game was canceled because the referees went on strike.

   A comma is needed if a dependent clause opens the sentence:

   Because the referees went on strike, the game was canceled.

Semicolon ;

Semicolons have two uses.

1. Use semicolons to join independent clauses when *and, or, yet, but, for, nor,* or *so* are not present:

    > Olympia is the capital of Washington; Salem is the capital of Oregon.

    Remember to use semicolons even when you use words such as *nevertheless, moreover,* and *however:*

    > They barely had time to rehearse; however, opening night was a success.

2. Use semicolons to separate items in a series that contain commas:

    > The governor will meet with Vicki Shimi, the mayor of Bayview; Sandy Bert, the new city manager; the district attorney; Peter Plesmid; and Al Leone, an engineering consultant.

Apostrophe '

Apostrophes are used for three reasons:

1. Apostrophes indicate possession:

Noun	Erica's car broke down.
Acronym	NASA's new space vehicle will launch on Monday.
Indefinite pronoun	Someone's car has its lights on.
Endings of *s, x,* or *z* sound	Phyllis' car is stalled. [or *Phyllis's*]

    Apostrophes are deleted from geographical names:

Pikes Peak	Taylors Meadows	Warners Pond

    Apostrophes may or may not appear in possessive names of businesses or organizations:

Marshall Field's	Sears	Tigers Stadium	Sean's Pub

    Follow the spelling used on signs, stationery, and business cards.

2. Apostrophes signal missing letters and numbers in contractions:

    > Ted can't restore my '67 VW.

3. Apostrophes indicate plurals of letters, numbers, or symbols:

    > I got all B's last semester and A's this semester.
    > Do we have any size 7's or 8's left?
    > We can sell all the 2003's at half price.

    Apostrophes are optional in referring to decades, but be consistent:

She went to high school in the 1990's but loved the music
of the 1960's.

or

She went to high school in the 1990s but loved the music
of the 1960s.

Common abbreviations such as *TV* and *UFO* do not need apostrophes to indicate plurals:

We bought new TVs and several DVDs.

POINT TO REMEMBER

it's   =   contraction of "it is"

It's raining.

its   =   possessive of "it"

My car won't start. Its battery is dead.

Quotation Marks " "

Quotation marks—always used in pairs—enclose direct quotations, titles of short works, and highlighted words:

- For direct quotations:

    Martin Luther King said, "I have a dream."

The final mark of punctuation precedes the final quotation mark, unless it does not appear in the original text:

    Did Martin Luther King say, "I have a dream"?

Set off identifying phrases with commas:

    Shelly insisted, "We cannot win unless we practice."
    "We cannot win," Shelly insisted, "unless we practice."
    "We cannot win unless we practice," Shelly insisted.

Commas are not used if the quotation is blended into the sentence:

    They exploited the "cheaper by the dozen" technique to save a fortune.

Quotations within quotations are indicated by use of single quotation marks:

    Shelly said, "I was only ten when I heard Martin Luther King proclaim,
    'I have a dream.'"

Final commas are placed inside quotation marks:

    The letter stated, "The college will lower fees," but few students
    believed it.

Colons and semicolons are placed outside quotation marks:

> The letter stated, "The college will lower fees"; few students believed it.

Indirect quotations do not require quotation marks:

> Martin Luther King said that he had a dream.

- For titles of short works:
  Titles of short works—poems, stories, articles, and songs—are placed in quotation marks:

  > Did you read "When Are We Going to Mars?" in *Time* this week?

  Do not capitalize articles, prepositions, or coordinating conjunctions (*and, or, yet, but, so, for, nor*) unless they are the first or last words. (Titles of longer works—books, films, magazines, and albums—are underlined or placed in italics.)

- To highlight words:
  Highlighted words are placed in quotation marks to draw extra attention:

  > I still don't know what "traffic abatement" is supposed to mean.
  > This is the fifth time this month Martha has been "sick" when we needed her.

Colon :

Colons are placed after independent clauses to introduce elements and separate items in numerals, ratios, titles, and time references:

> The coach demanded three things from his players: loyalty, devotion, and teamwork.
> The coach demanded one quality above all others: attention to detail.
> The coach says the team has a 3:1 advantage.
> I am reading *Arthur Miller: Playwright of the Century*.
> The play started at 8:15.

Parentheses ( )

Parentheses set off nonessential details and explanations and enclose letters and numbers used for enumeration:

> The Senate committee (originally headed by Warner) will submit a report to the White House.
> The Federal Aviation Administration (FAA) has new security policies.
> The report stated we must (1) improve services, (2) provide housing, and (3) increase funding.

Brackets [ ]

Brackets set off interpolations or clarifications in quotations and replace parentheses within parentheses:

Eric Hartman observed, "I think [Theodore] Roosevelt was the greatest president."

Time noted, "President Bush told Frank Bush [no relation] that he agreed with his tax policies."

The ambassador stated, "We will give them [the Iraqi National Congress] all the help they need."

Dash —

Dashes mark a break in thought, set off a parenthetical element for emphasis, and set off an introduction to a series:

Ted was angry after his car was stolen— who wouldn't be?

The movie studio— which faced bankruptcy— desperately needed a hit.

They had everything needed to succeed—ideas, money, marketing, and cutting-edge technology.

Hyphen -

A hyphen is a short line used to separate or join words and other items.

- Use hyphens to break words:

    We saw her on tele-
    vision last night.

    Only break words between syllables.

- Use hyphens to connect words to create compound adjectives:

    We made a last-ditch attempt to score a touchdown.

    Do *not* use hyphens with adverbs ending in *-ly:*

    We issued a quickly drafted statement to the press.

- Use hyphens to connect words forming numbers:

    The firm owes nearly thirty-eight million dollars in back taxes.

- Use hyphens after some prefixes:

    His self-diagnosis was misleading.

- Use hyphens between combinations of numbers and words:

    She drove a 2.5-ton truck.

Ellipsis . . .

An ellipsis, three spaced periods [. . .], indicates that words are deleted from quoted material:

Original Text
The mayor said, "Our city, which is one of the country's most progressive, deserves a high-tech light-rail system."

With Ellipsis
The mayor said, "Our city . . . deserves a high-tech light-rail system."

Delete only minor ideas or details—never change the basic meaning of a sentence by deleting key words. Don't eliminate a negative word like "not" to create a positive statement or remove qualifying words:

Original
We must, only as a last resort, consider legalizing drugs.

Incorrect
He said, "We must . . . consider legalizing drugs."

When deleting words at the end of a sentence, add a period before the ellipsis:

The governor said, "I agree we need a new rail system. . . ."

An ellipsis is not used if words are deleted at the opening of a quotation:

The mayor said "the city deserves a high-tech light-rail system."

If deleting words will create a grammar mistake, insert corrections with brackets:

Original
"Poe, Emerson, and Whitman were among our greatest writers."

With Ellipsis
"Poe . . . [was] among our greatest writers."

Slash /

Slashes separate words when both apply and show line breaks when quoting poetry:

The student should study his/her lessons.
Her poem read in part, "We hope / We dream / We pray."

Question Mark ?

Question marks are placed after direct questions and are used to note questionable items:

Did Adrian Carsini attend the auction?
Did you read "Can We Defeat Hunger?" in *Newsweek* last week?

Question marks that appear in the original title are placed within quotation marks. If the title does not ask a question, the question mark is placed outside the quotation marks:

Did you read "The Raven"?

Question marks in parentheses are used to indicate that the writer questions the accuracy of a fact, number, idea, or quotation:

The children claimed they waited two hours (?) for help to arrive.

Exclamation Point !

Exclamation points are placed at the end of emphatic statements:

Help!
We owe her over ten million dollars!

Exclamation points should be used as special effects. They lose their impact if overused.

Period .

Periods are used after sentences, in abbreviations, and as decimals:

I bought a car.
We gave the car to Ms. Chavez who starts working for Dr. Gomez on Jan. 15.
The book sells for $29.95 in hardcover and $12.95 in paperback.

When an abbreviation ends a sentence, only one period is used. Common abbreviations such as FBI, CIA, ABC, BBC, and UCLA do not require periods.

Capitalization

- Capitalize the first word of every sentence:

  We studied all weekend.

- Capitalize the first word in direct quotations:

  Felix said, "The school should buy new computers."

- Capitalize the first word and all important words in titles of articles, books, plays, movies, television shows, seminars, and courses:

  "Terrorism Today"   *Gone with the Wind*   *Death of a Salesman*

- Capitalize the names of nationalities, languages, races, religions, deities, and sacred terms:

  Many Germans speak English.
  The Koran is the basic text in Islam.

- Capitalize the days of the week, months of the year, and holidays:

  We celebrate Flag Day every June 14.
  The test scheduled for Monday is canceled.
  Some people celebrate Christmas in January.
  We observed Passover with her parents.

  The seasons of the year are not capitalized:

  We loved the spring fashions.   Last winter was mild.

- Capitalize special historical events, documents, and eras:

  Battle of the Bulge   Declaration of Independence

- Capitalize names of planets, continents, nations, states, provinces, counties, towns and cities, mountains, lakes, rivers, and other geographic features:

    Mars   North America   Canada   Ontario

- Capitalize *north, south, east,* and *west* when they refer to geographic regions:

    The convention will be held in the Southwest.

    Do not capitalize *north, south, east,* and *west* when used as directions:

    The farm is southwest of Rockford.

- Capitalize brand names:

    Coca-Cola   Ford Thunderbird   Cross pen

- Capitalize names of specific corporations, organizations, institutions, and buildings:

    This engine was developed by General Motors.
    After high school, he attended Carroll College.
    We visited the site of the former World Trade Center.

- Capitalize abbreviations, acronyms, or shortened forms of capitalized words when used as proper nouns:

    FBI   CIA   NOW   ERA
    IRA   JFK   LAX   NBC

- Capitalize people's names and nicknames:

    Barbara Roth   Timmy Arnold

    Capitalize professional titles when used with proper names:

    Last week Doctor Ryan suggested I see an eye doctor.
    Our college president once worked for President Carter.
    This report must be seen by the president.
    [The word *president* is often capitalized to refer to the president of the United States.]

    Capitalize words like *father, mother, brother, aunt, cousin,* and *uncle* only when used with or in place of proper names:

    My mother and I went to see Uncle Al.
    After the game, I took Mother to meet my uncle.

POINT TO REMEMBER

A few capitalization rules vary. *African American* is always capitalized, but editors vary whether *blacks* should be capitalized. Some writers capitalize *a.m.* and *p.m.,* while others do not. Follow the standard used in your discipline or career and be consistent.

Spelling

Commonly Confused Words

accept	to take	Do you *accept* checks?
except	but/to exclude	Everyone *except* Joe went home.
adapt	to change	We will *adapt* the army helicopter for civilian use.
adopt	to take possession of	They want to *adopt* a child.
adverse	unfavorable	*Adverse* publicity ruined his reputation.
averse	opposed to	I was *averse* to buying a new car.
advice	a noun	Take my *advice*.
advise	a verb	Let me *advise* you.
affect	to influence	Will this *affect* my grade?
effect	a result	What is the *effect* of the drug?
all ready	prepared	We were *all ready* for the trip.
already	by a certain time	You are *already* approved.
allusion	a reference	She made a biblical *allusion*.
illusion	imaginary vision	The mirage was an optical *illusion*.
all together	unity	The teachers stood *all together*.
altogether	totally	*Altogether,* that will cost $50.
among	relationship of three or more	This outfit is popular *among* college students.
between	relationship of two	This was a dispute *between* Kim and Nancy.
amount	for items that are measured	A small *amount* of oil has leaked.
number	for items that are counted	A large *number* of cars are stalled.
any one	a person, idea, item	*Any one* of the books will do.
anyone	anybody	Can *anyone* help me?
brake	to halt/a stopping	Can you fix the *brakes*?
break	an interruption	Take a coffee *break*.
	to destroy	Don't *break* the window.
capital	money	She needs venture *capital*.
	government center	Trenton is the *capital* of New Jersey.

capitol	legislative building	He toured the U.S. *Capitol.*
cite	to note or refer to	He *cited* several figures in his speech.
site	a location	We inspected the *site* of the crash.
sight	a view, ability to see	The *sight* from the hill was tremendous.
complement	to complete	The jet had a full *complement* of spare parts.
compliment	express praise, a gift	The host paid us a nice *compliment.*
conscience	moral sensibility	He was a prisoner of *conscience.*
conscious	aware of/awake	Is he *conscious* of these debts? Is the patient *conscious?*
continual	now and again	We have *continual* financial problems.
continuous	uninterrupted	The brain needs a *continuous* supply of blood.
council	a group	A student *council* will meet Tuesday.
counsel	to advise/advisor	He sought legal *counsel.*
discreet	tactful	He made a *discreet* hint.
discrete	separate/distinct	The war had three *discrete* phases.
elicit	evoke/persuade	His hateful remarks will *elicit* protest.
illicit	illegal	Her use of *illicit* drugs ruined her career.
emigrate	to leave a country	They tried to *emigrate* from Germany.
immigrate	to enter a country	They were allowed to *immigrate* to America.
eminent	famous	She was an *eminent* eye specialist.
imminent	impending	Disaster was *imminent.*
everyday	ordinary	Wear *everyday* clothes to the party.
every day	daily	We exercise *every day.*
farther	distance	How much *farther* is it?
further	in addition	He demanded *further* investigation.
fewer	for items counted	There are *fewer* security guards this year.
less	for items measured	There is *less* security this year.

good	an adjective	She has *good* eyesight.
well	an adverb	She sees *well*.
hear	to listen	Can you *hear* the music?
here	a place/direction	Put the table *here*.
imply	to suggest	The president *implied* he might raise taxes.
infer	to interpret	The reporters *inferred* from his comments that the president might raise taxes.
its	possessive of *it*	The car won't start because *its* battery is dead.
it's	contraction of *it is*	*It's* snowing.
lay	to put/to place	*Lay* the books on my desk.
lie	to rest	*Lie* down for a nap.
loose	not tight	He has a *loose* belt or *loose* change.
lose	to misplace	Don't *lose* your keys.
moral	dealing with values	She made a *moral* decision to report the crime.
morale	mood	After the loss, the team's *morale* fell.
passed	successfully completed	She *passed* the test.
past	history	That was in my *past*.
personal	private/intimate	She left a *personal* note.
personnel	employees	Send your résumé to the *personnel* office.
plain	simple/open space	She wore a *plain* dress.
plane	airplane/geometric form	They took a *plane* to Chicago.
precede	to go before	A film will *precede* the lecture.
proceed	go forward	Let the parade *proceed*.
principal	main/school leader	Oil is the *principal* product of Kuwait.
principle	basic law	I understand the *principle* of law.
raise	to lift	*Raise* the window!
rise	to get up	*Rise* and shine!
right	direction/correct	Turn *right*. That's *right*.
rite	a ritual	She was given last *rites*.

write	to inscribe	They *write* essays every week.
stationary	unmoving	The disabled train remained *stationary*.
stationery	writing paper	The hotel *stationery* was edged in gold.
than	used to compare	I am taller *than* Helen.
then	concerning time	We *then* headed to class.
their	possessive of *they*	*Their* car is stalled.
there	direction/place	Put the chair over *there*.
they're	contraction of *they are*	*They're* coming to dinner.
there're	contraction of *there are*	*There're* two seats left.
to	preposition/infinitive	I went *to* school *to* study law.
too	in excess/also	It was *too* cold to swim.
two	a number	We bought *two* computers.
wear	concerns clothes/damage	We *wear* our shoes until they *wear* out.
where	a place in question	*Where* is the post office?
weather	climatic conditions	*Weather* forecasts predict rain.
whether	alternatives/no matter what	You must register, *whether* or not you want to audit the class.
who's	contraction of *who is*	*Who's* on first?
whose	possessive of *who*	*Whose* book is that?

Commonly Misspelled Words

absence	analyze	beautiful	column	definite
accept	annual	becoming	coming	deliberate
accident	anonymous	beginning	commitment	dependent
accommodate	apparent	belief	committee	description
accumulate	appreciate	believe	competition	difficult
achieve	approach	benefit	completely	disappear
achievement	arctic	breakfast	complexion	disappoint
acquaint	argument	business	conceive	discipline
acquire	article	calendar	consistent	discuss
across	assassination	candidate	continually	dominant
address	assistance	career	control	dying
adolescence	athletic	carrying	controversial	efficient
advertisement	attention	celebrate	criticism	eighth
a lot	attitude	cemetery	curious	eligible
amateur	basically	challenge	dealt	embarrass
analysis	basis	characteristic	decision	enough

environment
equipment
essential
exaggerate
excellent
existence
experience
explanation
extremely
fallacy
familiar
fantasy
fascination
favorite
February
feminine
field
finally
foreign
forgotten
forty
fourth
frequent
friend
frighten
fulfill
fundamental
further
generally
generous
government
gradually
grammar
grateful
guarantee
guard
guidance
happiness
height
heroes
holocaust
huge
humorous
hypocrite

identically
identity
immediately
importance
incidental
independence
influence
intelligence
interest
interpret
interrupt
involvement
irrelevant
irresistible
irresponsible
judgment
judicial
judicious
knowledge
label
laboratory
language
leisure
libel
library
license
lightning
loneliness
luxury
lying
magazine
maintenance
maneuver
marriage
martial
material
mathematics
meant
mechanical
medieval
mere
miniature
mischief
misspell

mortgage
necessary
ninety
noticeable
obligation
obvious
occasionally
occupation
occurred
omit
operate
opinion
opportunity
oppose
optimism
ordinarily
original
paid
pamphlet
parallel
particularly
perform
permanent
permission
persistent
persuade
persuasion
philosophy
physical
playwright
politician
positive
possession
possible
precede
preference
prejudice
presence
primitive
probably
procedure
prominent
psychic
psychology

publicly
qualify
quality
quantity
query
quiet
quizzes
realize
recede
receive
reception
recognition
recommend
refer
regulation
relation
religious
remember
repetition
responsible
restaurant
rhythm
ridicule
roommate
sacrifice
safety
scene
schedule
seize
separate
sergeant
severely
significance
significant
similar
simplify
sincerely
situation
skillfully
sociology
sophisticated
sophomore
special
specimen

stereotype
straight
strict
studying
success
summary
surprise
synonymous
technique
temperament
tenable
tendency
thorough
thought
throughout
tomorrow
tragedy
tremendous
truly
unfortunate
uniform
unique
until
unusual
useful
using
usually
vacillate
vacillation
vacuum
valuable
various
vengeance
villain
violence
vulnerable
weird
whole
writing
yield

List other words you often misspell:

_____

_____

_____

_____

_____

_____

_____

_____

_____

_____

_____

_____

_____

_____

Two Hundred Topics for College Writing

best friends	AIDS	outsourcing jobs	steroids
gangs	cults	labor unions	binge drinking
fad diets	lawsuits	married priests	single parents
job interviews	sweatshops	nightclubs	summer jobs
athletes as role	chat rooms	gas prices	animal testing
models	drunk drivers	car repairs	life after death
bad habits	school prayer	plea bargaining	Hollywood
child support	commercials	banks	school choice
NBA salaries	student housing	lying	hate speech
doctors	wearing fur	fast food	suburbs
terrorism	work ethic	cable TV	public schools
military	eating disorders	fatherhood	birth control
spending	insanity defense	racism	credit cards
solar power	Internet	study skills	funerals
right to die	voting	immigration	toughest course
best teacher	adoption	the Olympics	working out
car insurance	celebrity justice	cell phones	Social Security
health clubs	favorite movie	property taxes	talk shows
shopping malls	teen eating habits	bilingual	heating bills
fashion models	cable TV bills	education	drug testing
hobbies	minimum wage	world hunger	aging population
foreign aid	the president	slavery	summer jobs
airport security	health insurance	reparations	stereotypes
cruise ships	images of women	worst boss	car prices
blind dates	taking the bus	binge drinking	affirmative action
exploring Mars	discrimination	the pope	moving
being "in"	TV moms	college	animal rights
used cars	the Superbowl	instructors	living wills
Osama bin	pensions	cyberspace	marriage vows
Laden	welfare reform	best restaurant	reading
democracy	the UN	profanity in	grandparents
being religious	being downsized	public	plastic surgery
freeways	favorite singer	reporters	passion
televised trials	prenatal care	your mayor	dreams
sitcoms	workaholics	Wall Street	family values
cheating	cable news	shopping till you	hospitals
today's comics	parties	drop	best jobs
drug prevention	reality TV	overcoming	stalking
ethnic	school loans	depression	gay marriage
stereotypes	women in	fraternities and	NFL
lotteries	combat	sororities	public schools
euthanasia	secondhand	racial profiling	pets
goal for this year	smoke	casinos	divorce
SAT	spring break	prisons	domestic
daycare	drinking age	family values	violence
taxes	coffee bars	online dating	Iraq

gay bashing	being in debt	world hunger	sexist or racist
MTV	relationships	right to privacy	jokes
Islam	dorm life	Internet	definition of
sex on television	person you	pornography	success
hip-hop music	admire	biological	drug busts
glass ceiling	surveillance	weapons	final exams
remembering	cameras	downloading	raising boys
9/11	sexual	music	and girls
gun control	harassment	teaching	
the homeless	Letterman or	methods	
soap operas	Leno	coping with	
learning English	rape shield laws	illness	

Odd-Numbered and Partial-Paragraph Answers to the Exercises in Chapters 3–35

CHAPTER 3

Exercise 1

1. Now the city began to die.

3. There were eccentric characters in the hotel.

Exercise 2

1. c

3. a

5. a

Exercise 3

Answers vary

Exercise 4

Answers vary

Exercise 5

Today college students have many alternatives to the traditional three-day-a-week lecture. Across the country, a growing number of students are taking advantage of new delivery systems.

Many of these students are working adults with families whose schedules prevent them from taking standard courses. Some work during the day or travel, making it difficult to even sign up for night school courses. Other students live at great distance from the nearest college offering the programs they need.

To meet the needs of these nontraditional students, colleges offer a variety of distance-learning opportunities. For decades many colleges have broadcast telecourses on cable or local PBS stations, allowing students to watch educational programs and mail in assignments. These courses are being supplemented with newer television technology that lets students interact with the instructor or other students. . . .

Exercise 6

Last summer I had what I thought would be an ideal summer job, working at a local cable TV station.

I was fascinated with the high-tech control room and seeing the reporters and sportswriters for the evening news. I even hoped to see some athletes and celebrities who did interviews on *News at Nine*. But I had no idea I would have a boss like Cynthia Peterson to work with.

"Just do what I say, when I say it, and everything will work out," she told me sternly at our interview.

"Great," I told her. "I've never worked in TV and want to learn as much as I can."

"Good," she told me with a tight-lipped smile. "First thing, take the webcast footage down to the control room for me," she said, handing me a CD and walking out of the room. . . .

CHAPTER 4

Exercise 1
Answers vary

Exercise 2
1. b, c
3. a, b
5. a, c, d

Exercise 3
Answers vary

Exercise 4
Answers vary

Exercise 5
Answers vary

CHAPTER 5

Exercise 1
Answers vary

Exercise 2
Answers vary

Exercise 3
Answers vary

Exercise 4
Answers vary

Exercise 5
Answers vary

CHAPTER 6

Exercise 1
Answers vary

Exercise 2
Within a few decades . . . as it was reaching its peak . . .
At that time . . . By the turn of the century . . .

Exercise 3
Answers vary

Exercise 4
Answers vary

CHAPTER 7

Exercise 1
1. The most significant threats to public health are lifestyle related.
2. 6
3. The eighteen-year-old who . . .
4. Answers vary

Exercise 2
Answers vary

Exercise 3
Answers vary

Exercise 4
Answers vary

CHAPTER 8

Exercise 1
Answers vary

Exercise 2
Answers vary

Exercise 3
Answers vary

CHAPTER 9

Exercise 1
Answers vary

Exercise 2
Answers vary

Chapter 10

Exercise 1
Answers vary

Exercise 2
Answers vary

Exercise 3
Answers vary

Chapter 11

Exercise 1
Answers vary

Exercise 2
Answers vary

Exercise 3
Answers vary

Chapter 12

Exercise 1
1. X

3. P

5. X

7. P

9. P

Exercise 2
1. We can expect oil prices to increase over the next decade.

Exercise 3
1. The likely increase in oil prices will have dramatic effects on the economy, consumer behavior, and scientific research.

Exercise 4
Answers vary

Chapter 13

Exercise 1
1. The college must overhaul its obsolete registration software if it wants to serve its students, project a good image to the community, and achieve President Neiman's enrollment goals.

3. a. nearly one-third of students who registered off campus never appeared on official college rosters.

b. Many were mailed packets of forms that arrived too late to sign up for needed courses.

c. Twenty-six nursing students who received e-mail confirmations discovered they were never actually registered in clinical programs and had to delay graduation.

5. Student provides evidence that off-campus registration defeats President Neiman's enrollment goals.

Exercise 2

Answers vary

Exercise 3

1. Facts, examples. Very reliable.
3. Testimony. Somewhat reliable. Lacks objectivity, biased.

Exercise 4

Answers vary

Exercise 5

Answers vary

CHAPTER 14

Exercise 1

Answers vary

Exercise 2

1. High school football benefited the writer and made him a better student.
3. Provides evidence that football improved his health habits, taught him discipline, and increased his energy.
5. Most valuable lesson football taught him was maturity and responsibility.

Exercise 3

Answers vary

CHAPTER 16

Exercise 1

Answers vary

Exercise 2

Answers vary

CHAPTER 17

Exercise 1

1. 155,554 (U.S. Census, 2000)
3. No. www.uwm.edu
5. Answers vary

Exercise 2

1. F
3. T
5. T

Exercise 3

Answers vary

Exercise 4

Answers vary

CHAPTER 18

Exercise 1

1. Answers vary

CHAPTER 19

Exercise 1

The most widely reproduced photograph in history is the flag raising on Iwo Jima taken by Joe Rosenthal on February 23, 1945. This photograph **inspired** the Marine Corps War Memorial in Washington, D.C. Initial confusion about how the picture **was** taken **caused** controversy that **lasts** to this day. Some people have discredited the photograph, insisting that the picture was posed and not really a news photo of a genuine historical event. They point out that it **is** not a picture of the original flag raising but a reenactment. Others insist the photograph is genuine.

Much of the confusion **stems** from the photographer's initial comments. On February 23, 1945, a small American flag **was** flying atop Mt. Suribachi on the embattled island of Iwo Jima. The sight of the flag rallied the Marines locked in the bloodiest campaign in their history. It was decided to replace this flag with a larger one.

Joe Rosenthal, an AP photojournalist, **trudged** up the mountain with military photographers, one of whom carried a color movie camera. The Marines carefully **timed** the changing of the flags so that the second larger one would be raised just as the smaller flag **was** lowered. Five Marines and a Navy corpsman began to raise the bigger flag, and Rosenthal **scrambled** to catch the moment. He **swung** his bulky camera into position and snapped a picture without having time to look through the viewfinder. Thinking he **missed** shooting the event, he **asked** the Marines to pose at the base of the flagpole. The Marines **clustered** around and **waved** at the camera. . . .

Exercise 3

For fifty years, television news was dominated by network evening broadcasts. Tens of millions of Americans rushed home from work to see the day's events reported on television. With only three networks, anchormen like Walter Cronkite and Huntley and Brinkley were popular and highly influential. Their coverage of civil rights demonstrations, assassinations, and moon landings shaped the way Americans thought of the country and of themselves. The power of news anchors was summed up by President Johnson's comment, "If I've lost Cronkite, I've lost middle America." Infuriated by Cronkite's coverage of the Vietnam War, Johnson sometimes called CBS, demanding to speak to Cronkite during a commercial break. Cronkite was so powerful that he refused to take calls from the White House. . . .

Exercise 5

Three of the most significant black leaders to emerge following the emancipation of the slaves were Frederick Douglass, Booker T. Washington, and W. E. B. DuBois.

Frederick Douglass was best known for his impassioned oratory against slavery. He was born a slave in 1817 and fled to freedom in 1838. He began a career in public speaking, denouncing not only slavery but discrimination and segregation in the North. After publishing his autobiography, *Narrative of the Life of Frederick Douglass,* he went to England where he continued to campaign against slavery. Friends raised money to purchase his freedom. Douglass returned to America and founded an antislavery newspaper called *The North Star.* During the Civil War, Douglass met with Lincoln several times and helped recruit blacks to serve in the Union Army. He served as the U.S. Minister to Haiti from 1889 to 1891. He died in 1895.

Booker T. Washington is best known for his interest in education. Washington was born a slave in 1856 and taught himself to read. He founded the Tuskegee Institute, which stressed vocational skills, and the National Negro Business League, which encouraged black enterprise. Washington advised several presidents and addressed Southern politicians, urging them to provide jobs for blacks. His position that economic opportunities were more important than civil rights led to criticism from other black leaders. His organizations began to lose support after 1910. Washington died in 1915. . . . .

CHAPTER 20

Exercise 1

1. Desi Arnaz was a band leader, a singer, an actor, and the husband of Lucille Ball.
3. At that time, TV comedies were broadcast live from studios in New York.
5. They suggested recording the show on film like a motion picture.
7. Desi helped pioneer a new way of recording a live performance using three cameras.
9. Desi agreed in exchange for owning the rights to the films.
11. Television was so new, few people understood the value of reruns.
13. A few years later, Lucy and Desi sold the films back to CBS for four million dollars.
15. For a while, Desilu was the largest studio in the world until Lucy and Desi divorced in 1960 and split the company.

Exercise 2

Almost thirty years before 9/11, Samuel Byck planned to hijack a jet and use it as a weapon. Samuel Byck was a failed salesman. Emotionally unbalanced, he blamed President Nixon for his personal problems. He made threats against the president and sent strange tapes to celebrities. The Secret Service took notice. He picketed the White House and was arrested. When he was denied a small business loan, Byck blamed Nixon. He tape-recorded an elaborate plan called Operation Pandora's Box. He obtained a gun and made a gasoline bomb. He planned to hijack a commercial airliner and force the pilot to fly over Washington. . . .

Exercise 3

1. Science-fiction writers have imagined inventions long before they became practical realities. Jules Verne wrote about submarines and moon rockets in the nineteenth century. H. G. Wells described nuclear weapons in 1914.
3. In his 1932 novel *Public Faces,* Harold Nicholson envisioned rockets, much like modern cruise missiles, delivering atomic bombs. The blasts create tidal waves that cause climate change.
5. In April 1944, *Astounding Science Fiction* published a story about an atom bomb. Readers rated it the worst story in that issue, but the story's details so closely resembled the top-secret atom bomb being developed by the Manhattan Project that the author was investigated by military intelligence.

Exercise 4

Arthur Conan Doyle was born in Edinburgh, Scotland, in 1859, and studied medicine at the Royal Infirmary of Edinburgh, completing his degree in 1881. After serving as a doctor on a ship sailing to Africa, Doyle established a medical practice in Scotland. He was unsuccessful and started to write fiction while waiting for patients. Still in his twenties, Doyle began publishing short stories. Soon his literary career flourished, leading him to pursue writing full time. Doyle became famous as the creator of Sherlock Holmes, the first modern detective. Holmes appeared in four novels and over fifty short stories and has been portrayed by dozens of actors in stage plays, motion pictures, and television dramas. Doyle also wrote science fiction, historical romances, plays, and poetry. Few of these works achieved the lasting fame of his Sherlock Holmes stories. . . .

Exercise 5

Cinco de Mayo is widely celebrated by Mexican Americans throughout the United States. **But what does it celebrate? It is not Mexican Independence Day!** Mexico's equivalent of the Fourth of July is not the Fifth of May (Cinco de Mayo) but the Sixteenth of September. . . .

Exercise 6

1. Always put your name at the top of the page.
3. Reluctantly, Terry placed her badge and gun on the chief's desk.
5. Bravely, he clung to the raft, waiting for help.
7. Slowly, the overloaded plane lifted off the ground.
9. Thoughtlessly, the editor failed to check the facts of the story.

Exercise 7

Answers vary

Exercise 8

1. Throughout history, world leaders have been concerned about their public image.
3. Beneath his heavy uniforms, Stalin hid a deformed arm.
5. By leaning on the arm of an aide and using a cane, he created the illusion that he could walk.
7. Before leaving his car or Air Force One, he would slip the lit cigar into his pocket.
9. Among other things, Kennedy hid his reading glasses from the public because he felt they detracted from his image of youth and strength.

Exercise 9

Answers vary

Exercise 10

Every child in America has probably played with Crayola crayons. Edward Binney and Harold Smith founded the brand in 1903. **Previously,** they had developed dustless chalk that became a hit with schoolteachers and even received a gold medal at the St. Louis World's Fair. They visited schools and noticed the poor quality

```
of wax crayons children used for coloring. They
added color to industrial wax markers and created
an improved crayon for artwork. By combining the
French word craie (chalk) and oleaginous (oily),
Binney's wife came up with the name "Crayola.". . .
```

Exercise 11

1. Having immigrated to America in 1903, Carlo Ponzi gave his name to the "Ponzi scheme."

3. Seeking investors for a reply coupon business, Ponzi promised shareholders they could double their money in a few months.

5. Urging others to share their fortune, these investors became a great advertisement for what seemed like a quick way to get rich.

7. Surviving on a constant flow of new money, Ponzi's business paid interest to old investors with money from new investors.

9. Shutting down Ponzi's company in August 1920, federal agents found no inventory of international reply coupons.

Exercise 12

1. Born in 1860, Charles Goodyear is credited with developing vulcanization, the process that revolutionized the use of rubber.

3. Subjected to cold or heat, rubber became brittle or melted.

5. Imprisoned for not paying bills after the store failed, Goodyear sought a new venture.

7. Obsessed with rubber, Goodyear endured poverty and illness to devote his time to experiments.

9. Brokenhearted by the death of his daughter and legal battles over his discovery, Goodyear died deeply in debt.

Exercise 13

1. The 1919 World Series and eight players became embroiled in scandal.

3. Chick Gandil, the first baseman for the Chicago White Sox, and Joseph Sullivan, a professional gambler, decided to fix the games.

5. Gandil and many other Chicago players resented the White Sox owner Charles Comiskey, who was known for paying low salaries.

7. Eight White Sox players and gamblers conspired to fix the games so the underdog Reds would win an upset victory.

9. Shoeless Joe Jackson, the most famous player charged with throwing the games, and Eddie Cicotte first confessed, then retracted their confessions.

Exercise 14

1. Many scientific developments do not rely on a single person or depend on a single discovery.

3. Without a safe way of rendering a patient unconscious, however, doctors were limited to simple procedures and had to operate fast to prevent shock.

5. In the 1840s the discovery of ether allowed doctors to put patients to sleep and take time to perform complicated operations.

7. Doctors at the time, however, had no knowledge of germs and rarely bothered to wash their hands between operations.

9. Doctors began to accept the germ theory of disease in the late nineteenth century, introduced sanitary operating procedures, and sterilized their instruments.

Exercise 15

1. The Academy of Motion Pictures Arts and Sciences, a professional honorary organization, has some 6,000 members.

3. The organization is best known for awarding the Academy Award of Merit, the Oscar, to directors, actors, writers, and technicians.

5. Frederic Hope, Gibbons's assistant, designed the original black marble base.

7. There are many stories about how the Award began to be called Oscar, a nickname.

9. From 1942 to 1944, the Academy presented winners with Oscars made of plaster, a wartime substitute.

Exercise 16

1. Daylight Saving Time, which is sometimes called Summer Time, is designed to extend daylight during working hours.

3. Advocates, who included economists, business leaders, and politicians, argued that daylight saving time would help farmers and reduce traffic accidents.

5. Daylight saving time, which was introduced during World War I, was unpopular.

7. Daylight saving time, which was again signed into law in 1942, was supposed to save energy for the war effort.

9. Japanese citizens, who greatly resented being forced to change their clocks, ended its use as soon as the American occupation ended.

Exercise 17

Few moviegoers have heard of Oscar Micheaux, a pioneer African American filmmaker. Born in Illinois in 1884 to former slaves, he overcame many odds. Moving to South Dakota, Micheaux operated a homestead farm. He began writing stories. When no one was interested in publishing his work, Micheaux created his own publishing company, selling his books door to door. In 1919, he became the first African American to make a movie, *The Homesteader,* which was based on his novel of the same name. In 1924 he produced *Body and Soul* starring Paul Robeson. Over the next three decades, Micheaux made forty movies. . . .

CHAPTER 21

Exercise 1

1. wear
3. illicit

5. raise

7. lose

9. already

Exercise 2

1. *alibi*   explanation   *irony*   paradox

3. *caustic*   sarcastic   *nonplussed*   confused

5. *felon*   criminal   *sarcasm*   derision, mockery

Exercise 3

Answers vary

Exercise 4

1. During the Great Depression, people sought escape from unrelenting unemployment and business failures.

3. Charles Darrow developed a board game he called Monopoly that allowed players to fantasize about wheeling and dealing properties like the Rockefellers and Vanderbilts.

5. Undaunted, Darrow manufactured Monopoly sets himself, which sold well in local department stores.

7. Parker Brothers purchased Darrow's game, and soon Monopoly was being played coast to coast.

9. Seventy years after its debut, Monopoly remains a popular pastime.

Exercise 5

1. After a long shift, I was tired and could not wait to get home to relax and cook dinner.

3. Sara and Andy were painting the room, but they ran out of paint and had to quit.

5. They were driving to work when they got a flat tire and had to hitchhike the rest of the way.

Exercise 6

1. In 1976 the Ebola virus appeared in the Sudan, signaling the presence of a previously unknown infectious agent.

3. NASA engineers reported consistent computer failures in the Mars rover that will cost a great deal to repair.

5. All phone calls and e-mail to customers may be monitored for adherence to company rules.

Exercise 7

Answers vary

CHAPTER 22

Exercise 1

1. White House

3. John Adams

5. West Wing

7. building

9. Steel supports (plural)

Exercise 2

1. wallet
3. cards
5. number
7. number
9. numbers

Exercise 3

1. In 1938 . . . gimmick (subject) by a wallet company.
3. everyone (subject) . . . with a job . . . in his or her wallet or purse.
5. They (subject) inside each wallet . . . as a promotion . . . to department stores . . . around the country.
7. "Specimen" (subject) . . . across these cards.
9. The Social Security Administration (subject) . . . in major cities.

Exercise 4

1. are (linking verb)
3. substituted (action verb)
5. did (helping verb) capture (action verb)
7. were (linking verb)
9. made (action verb)

Exercise 5

1. many (subject) are (linking verb)
3. son (subject) became (verb)
5. Attempts (subject) were (linking verb)
7. Alfredo Stroessner (subject) ruled (verb)
9. Alverto Fujimori (subject) served (verb)

CHAPTER 23

Exercise 1

1. F
3. OK
5. F
7. F
9. F

Exercise 2

1. Bipolar disorder is also known as manic depression.
3. In their high or manic states, patients feel extremely confident, powerful, and energetic.
5. Correct
7. Correct
9. Bipolar disorder can be devastating, especially when patients make impulsive and illogical decisions in manic or depressed states.

Exercise 3

1. The Hollywood Walk of Fame attracts tourists visiting Los Angeles every year.

3. The first star on the Hollywood Walk of Fame honored Joanne Woodward in 1960.

5. Correct

7. The stars have five categories honoring accomplishments in radio, motion pictures, television, theater, and the recording industry.

9. Correct

Exercise 4

Emiliano Zapata was born in Morelos, Mexico, in 1879 to a family of independent ranchers. Although Zapata was known for wearing flashy clothing in his youth, he always maintained respect for the impoverished peasants. By thirty he had become a spokesperson for his village. Zapata championed the rights of Indians in Morelos. He assisted in the redistribution of land and defended the villagers' claims in property disputes with wealthy ranchers. Becoming increasingly frustrated by the government's bias in favor of wealthy landowners, Zapata began using force to seize land. He took a leading role in the 1910 Mexican Revolution that deposed the Diaz regime but was disillusioned with the new government's failure to address the needs for effective land reform. . . .

Exercise 5

The deadliest riot in American history erupted in New York in July 1863. Earlier that year, Congress passed conscription, making men from twenty to forty-five liable for military service. The law allowed those with money to avoid the army by paying three hundred dollars, an immense sum in those days. This angered the poor. The draft was very unpopular in New York, which had a large immigrant Irish population who resented fighting in a war they did not understand. In addition, many feared that a Northern victory would allow freed slaves to take their jobs. Anti-war newspapers whipped up racist hatred. By mid-July news of the high loss of life from the battle at Gettysburg reached New York. . . .

Chapter 24

Exercise 1

Answers vary

Exercise 2

1. The Brooklyn Bridge was an engineering triumph, but it claimed the lives of twenty-seven workers.

3. A rumor that the bridge was about to collapse caused a panic, and twelve people were trampled to death.

5. In 1886 Steve Brodie achieved instant fame when he claimed to have survived a jump from the Brooklyn Bridge, but most people believe a dummy was used in the stunt.

Exercise 3

Answers vary

Exercise 4

Answers vary

Exercise 5

Answers vary

Exercise 6

Answers vary

Exercise 7

1. Basil Rathbone became internationally famous when he played Sherlock Holmes.
   When he played Sherlock Holmes, Basil Rathbone became internationally famous.
3. The boardwalk restaurants do well even in bad weather because tourists have to stay indoors when it rains.
   Because tourists have to stay indoors when it rains, the boardwalk restaurants do well even in bad weather.
5. Although it will be cheaper to build a new building, the alumni want to restore Old Main.
   The alumni want to restore Old Main although it will be cheaper to build a new building.

Exercise 8

1. After graduating from the University of Nebraska in 1895, Willa Cather moved to Pittsburgh.
3. Because her teaching experience brought her into contact with adolescents, she developed a keen insight into the minds of teenagers.
5. Because Pittsburgh was a city of factories and steel mills, it symbolized the modern industrialized society.
7. Although Paul is a bright, sensitive boy who loves the arts, he does poorly in school.
9. After Paul steals money from his employer, he runs away to New York and enjoys a life of luxury that eludes him in Pittsburgh.

Exercise 9

Answers vary

CHAPTER 25

Exercise 1

1. RO
3. OK
5. RO
7. OK
9. OK

Exercise 2

<u>Booker T. Washington was born a slave, but he rose to become a leading African American educator and leader.</u> He headed the Tuskegee Institute and made many speaking tours in the North to gain support for black causes. His autobiography *Up from Slavery* became an international bestseller. <u>Washington toured European capitals, and he became, after the death of Frederick Douglass, the most well-known black figure in America.</u> <u>Washington became the first African American to be invited by the president to visit the White House, he advised Presidents Theodore Roosevelt and Howard Taft on racial issues.</u> . . .

Exercise 3

Answers vary

Exercise 4

1. Before leaving home, millions of people slip cell phones into their pockets or purses; they are almost as common as credit cards and car keys.
3. The first American cell phone went on the market in 1983; it weighed two pounds and cost four thousand dollars.
5. Cell phones are actually two-way radios; they broadcast and receive messages.
7. A city, for example, is divided into overlapping cells; each cell has a base station with a sending and receiving tower.
9. Cell phones can now send text messages and pictures; like computers, they can become infected with viruses that steal passwords and address books.

Exercise 5

On March 11, 1918, a soldier at Fort Riley, Kansas, went to the base hospital complaining of fever and a sore throat; within hours, a hundred other soldiers reported the same symptoms. During the next few days, hundreds more were stricken with high fever, muscle and joint pain, and extreme fatigue. Many died. The disease then appeared in other army camps; in California hundreds of prisoners in San Quentin fell ill. The death toll mounted. At an army base near Boston, sixty soldiers died in one day.

By the summer, the disease was spreading across the country, and the government became alarmed. The sudden deaths of young men preparing to go to war led to wild rumors; many believed German submarines had brought the disease to America. Others blamed terrorists; they claimed spies were dispersing germs in movie theaters. . . .

Chapter 26

Exercise 1

1. DM
3. OK
5. DM
7. DM
9. OK

Exercise 2

Answers vary

Exercise 3

Answers vary

Exercise 4

Answers vary

Exercise 5

1. MM
3. MM
5. MM
7. MM
9. MM

Exercise 6

Answers vary

Exercise 7

    In the 1770s, Joseph Priestly, a minister and scientist, conducted experiments with a glass bell jar. <u>Placing a candle under the jar,</u> the flame flickered out, Priestly observed. A mouse placed under the jar suffocated. The candle and mouse, Priestly reasoned, consumed something in the air they needed to stay alive. <u>Placing a sprig of mint under the jar,</u> something interesting happened. The candle could be relit. <u>If placed under the jar with a mouse,</u> the mouse stayed alive. Whatever vital substance the candle and the mouse used up was restored by the plant. <u>Without fully realizing it,</u> the experiment revealed a basic natural process. Animals and burning fossil fuels consume oxygen and give off carbon dioxide. Plants absorb carbon dioxide and give off oxygen.

    <u>Used to explain the problem of global warming,</u> the earth is like one big jar. The natural balance of gases that Priestly discovered <u>in the atmosphere</u> has been upset. <u>Burning oil and coal,</u> large amounts of carbon are released into the atmosphere by cars,

```
power plants, and factories. Producing 12,000 pounds
of carbon a year per person, the United States is the
world's largest polluter. . . .
```

Exercise 8

1. Frank drives Karla, who is a lifeguard, to the beach every morning.

3. The landlord, who was angry about the broken windows, met with the tenant.

5. The insurance adjusters, who refused to pay any repair bills, met with the homeowners.

CHAPTER 27

Exercise 1

1. OK

3. OK

5. NP

7. NP

9. OK

Exercise 2

1. Every forest has five layers that help maintain its survival and provide a habitat for a variety of wildlife.

3. The understory contains shorter trees that grow under the canopy; they receive less sunlight and produce less food.

5. Grasses and small plants grow at the herb level, which provide food for animals ranging from mice to large bears and produce exotic flowers.

7. Spiders, insects, earthworms, and bacteria thrive on the forest floor, consuming waste material, breaking it down, and making deposits in the soil needed for continued forest growth.

9. Chopping down tall trees exposes lower levels of the forest to full sunlight, burning leaves, drying out moist soil, and killing many animals.

Exercise 3

Answers vary

CHAPTER 28

Exercise 1

1. applicants (subject)   use (verb)

3. expert (subject)   estimates (verb)

5. recruiter or headhunter (subject)   charges (verb)

7. advisors (subject)   recommend (verb)

9. one way (subject)   is (verb)

Exercise 2

1. are

3. opens

5. was

7. seems

9. explains

Exercise 3

1. leads

3. demands

5. wants

7. were

9. are

Exercise 4

1. are

3. drives

5. were

7. see

9. is

Exercise 5

1. are

3. is

5. were

7. have

9. were

Exercise 6

Answers vary

Exercise 7

The NAACP was formed in 1909 by seven whites and one African American who were concerned about the epidemic of lynching. The organization grew out of the Niagara Movement headed by W. E. B. DuBois, who was opposed to Booker T. Washington's beliefs that were seen as passive and outmoded. DuBois served as editor of the organization's main publication *The Crisis* for almost twenty-five years. The NAACP achieved national attention when it organized boycotts of *Birth of a Nation,* a movie they criticized for its racist portrayals of blacks. The NAACP played a major role during the civil rights movement of the 1950s and 1960s; it sponsored demonstrations and provided legal support for protestors who were arrested. . . .

CHAPTER 29

Exercise 1

1. sang, sung

3. lay, lain

5. taught, taught

Exercise 2

1. focus

3. is, had

5. felt

7. planned

9. became

Exercise 3

1. raise

3. set

5. lie

7. to raise

9. lay

Exercise 4

I was born in Philadelphia, but I grew up in Haddonfield where my parents moved when I was two. In high school I got a job working on the Jersey shore helping an old guy sell trinkets on the boardwalk. It was a great job because on my lunch hour I went swimming and hung out with my friends on the beach. Being sixteen or seventeen, I felt invincible and never worried about sunscreen and got a bad sunburn about once a month.

I went to college in San Jose, and my friends and I took weekend trips to Vegas or the beach. I began to use sunscreen but still forgot now and then. At that time all I worried about was never letting any of my friends drive drunk. . . .

Exercise 5

1. Paramount released *Dawn to Dusk* last week.

3. Studio executives cancelled the show after the ratings came out.

5. The county repaired the airport.

Exercise 6

1. We should have made a reservation.

3. I never got any bills.

5. The machinery was so old we could hardly make adjustments.

CHAPTER 30

Exercise 1

1. Carmen showed her bicycle to Cindy and suggested she fix it.

3. This street needs repairs.

5. Why doesn't Hollywood make movies I can take my kids to see?

Exercise 2

1. it

3. he

5. they

7. his

9. its

Exercise 3

1. Visitors to Chipilo, Mexico, may be surprised when they hear the residents talk.

3. Many of the people in this town descended from Italian immigrants who lived in Venice, where a distinct dialect is still spoken.

5. The language has no official written form, but people try to write Venet using the Spanish they learn in school.

Exercise 4

1. I

3. us

5. whom

7. us

9. her

Exercise 5

1. Sandy or I am working all weekend.

3. The parents were disturbed by the film; it featured graphic violence.

5. Who was willing to work on the weekend?

CHAPTER 31

Exercise 1

1. oldest, unique

3. professional

5. new, Hungry

7. Devoted

9. thirty-five year, waiting, season

Exercise 2

Answers vary

Exercise 3

1. sliced, diced

3. corned, mashed

5. heated

Exercise 4

1. widely, very

3. boldly, precisely

5. very

7. intensely, finely

9. fully, finally

Exercise 5

Answers vary

Exercise 6

1. extremely

3. unbelievably, accurate

5. devilish

7. extremely

9. mysteriously

Exercise 7

1. more tired

3. more hotly

5. happier

Exercise 8

1. Born in Alabama, Zora Neale Hurston grew up in Florida and later traveled north to attend Barnard College and Columbia University in the 1920s when most black women had extremely limited educational opportunities.

3. Generously supported by patrons, Hurston traveled extensively throughout the South, as well as Haiti, Jamaica, and the Bahamas to conduct research.

5. Some critics, however, found her homey stories about dialect-speaking African Americans unacceptably sentimental.

7. Hurston's objections to some aspects of the civil rights movement further alienated her critics.

9. Fifteen years later, an article by Alice Walker sparked interest in Hurston, and many scholars began to read this newly rediscovered author.

CHAPTER 32

Exercise 1

1. Ambrose Bierce, Judge Crater, and Jimmy Hoffa are among the most famous missing persons of the twentieth century.

3. In 1913 he went to Mexico, and he rode along with Pancho Villa's soldiers.

5. In August 1930 Judge Crater left a Manhattan restaurant, got into a taxi, and was never seen again.

7. Although it was discovered that he cleaned out his office and cashed several checks before he left, little more was learned about Judge Crater, and he was declared dead in 1939.

9. After he was released on parole, Hoffa sought to regain control over the Teamsters, and he agreed to meet two Mafia leaders for lunch to discuss his situation.

Exercise 2

1. Iran, which was known as Persia until 1935, is an important nation in the Middle East.

3. The country, which is a major oil producer, has had complex and often conflicting relations with the West.

5. The Shah, who saw himself destined to lead his country onto the international stage, launched the White Revolution, which expanded women's rights, redistributed land, and built schools.

7. The Shah was forced to leave Iran in 1979 by the Islamic Revolution, which led to the formation of an Islamic Republic that was extremely hostile to the United States.

9. Many Iranians who live in the United States have nicknamed Los Angeles, which is now home to as many as half a million Iranian-Americans, "Tehrangeles."

Exercise 3

1. The Great Wall of China consists of 1,500 miles of fortifications, walls, guard towers, and barracks in northern China.

3. Local residents were forced to build the wall, and many of them were killed by gangs of attacking bandits.

5. The wall was made of mostly stone and brick, although some portions in desert regions were constructed of wooden fences and earthworks.

7. Developers have bulldozed sections to make way for new construction, and farmers have taken stones for building materials.

9. In fact, shuttle astronauts have reported that they could make out the Wall when in orbit a hundred miles or so above the Earth.

Exercise 4

```
     While watching an indoor soccer game in 1981, Jim
Foster, a former NFL executive, got an idea. If soc-
cer, usually an outdoor sport, could be played
inside, why not American football? Foster changed
standard football rules, played experimental games,
and, finally in 1990, patented what he called arena
football. The game follows the basic rules of NFL
football with some key exceptions. The field, for
example, is only 50 yards long, and teams consist of
8 instead of 11 players. . . .
```

Exercise 5

1. The school hired <u>a math teacher</u>; <u>Ted Hines</u>, a web designer; <u>Jan Price</u>; and <u>a reading specialist</u>.   #____4____

3. The class included <u>my sister</u>; <u>Candy</u>, her roommate; <u>Tom Drake</u>; <u>Don Bernstein</u>; <u>Tom Price</u>; <u>Tom's sister</u>; <u>Carlos Abrams</u>, an exchange student from Chile; <u>a student from France</u>; and <u>myself</u>.   #____9____

5. We considered our all-time favorite TV shows and came up with a long list, including <u>my favorite soap opera</u>; <u>*Streets of San Francisco*</u>, Sandy's favorite show; <u>*Saturday Night Live*</u> with Eddie Murphy; <u>*LA Law*</u>; <u>*All in the Family*</u>; the original <u>*Twilight Zone*</u>, Sid's choice; and of course, <u>*Star Trek*</u>.   #____7____

Exercise 6

1. The names Harry Horwitz, Jerry Horwitz, and Louis Feinberg are not well known; however, their stage names, Moe, Curly, and Larry are famous the world over.

3. The act got its name from Ted Healy, who originally billed them as "Ted Healy and his Stooges" in vaudeville houses.

5. The Stooges were immensely popular; audiences loved their slapstick comedy, wild stage antics, and colorful language.

7. The Stooges began a long run, making films on low budgets within a few days.

9. Columbia, however, found a new market for their library of old Stooge shorts; they sold them to television.

CHAPTER 33

Exercise 1

1. a boy's book
3. Frank Sinatra's songs
5. NASA's research
7. children's clothing
9. two women's store

Exercise 2

1. he's
3. he'd
5. couldn't
7. I'll
9. should've

Exercise 3

One of the cold war's most visible symbols was the Berlin Wall, which separated Germany's former capital for almost thirty years. At the end of World War II, the Allies' postwar plans included dividing Germany into different zones of occupation. Berlin lay inside the Soviet sector, but the city itself was divided among the Allies, so that West Berlin became the West's democratic island inside Communist East Germany.

Throughout the 1950s and into the 1960s East Germans escaped to the West by simply taking a bus or a train to one of the city's western neighborhoods. As many as two thousand people a day fled to the West. East Germany's struggling economy suffered by the country's steady loss of workers and professionals seeking freedom and better-paying jobs. Walter Ulbricht, East Germany's Communist leader, received permission from the Soviet Union's leader Nikita Khrushchev to build a barrier across the border to stop the refugees' flight from East Germany. Khrushchev didn't want to create a crisis, so he ordered East Germany to first build a barrier of barbed wire that could be quickly dismantled if America's forces challenged its plans. . . .

Exercise 4

1. Audrey told us she was getting married in June.
3. The course's new reading list includes John Cheever's "The Swimmer" and Albert Camus' "The Guest."
5. Did you read Jane Manton's story "We Can't Go On"?
7. Frank's comments included the remark, "We're going to see if he's willing to help us."

9. "I'm going to retire," Tom Watson told us, reminding us of his promise. "I will step aside as soon as my daughter's internship is completed."

Exercise 5

1. The Aug. 15 flight will leave at 10:25 a m.
3. The college saw three challenges: declining enrollments, reduced funding from the state, and rising health-care costs.
5. Can I park here?
7. Jane Bush [no relation to the president] went to Iraq on behalf of the White House.
9. Tim and Nan's house was the only one damaged by the storm.

Exercise 6

```
      Josh Gibson, who was one of the greatest base-
ball players in history, was born on December 21,
1911. He was often called the "Babe Ruth of the Negro
Leagues." Because of segregation, Gibson could not
try out for major league teams. He became a star
player in black baseball, and he broke many records.
Lacking accurate statistics, historians question some
claims made about Gibson's career, though most agree
he had a lifetime batting average of .350, hit nearly
800 homeruns, and scored over eighty runs in a single
season. . . .
```

CHAPTER 34

Exercise 1

1. Known to many as the <u>m</u>ad <u>m</u>onk, <u>g</u>rigory <u>r</u>asputin became one of the most mysterious and fascinating figures of the <u>r</u>ussian <u>r</u>evolution.
3. He joined a strange sect in the <u>r</u>ussian <u>o</u>rthodox <u>c</u>hurch called the <u>s</u>kopsty, which believed that engaging in sin was necessary in order to achieve forgiveness.
5. A tall, bearded figure with penetrating eyes, he made an impression on many who accepted him as a man of <u>g</u>od with special powers who could heal the sick and predict the future.
7. Historians disagree how he was introduced to <u>c</u>zar Nicholas II's court, but Rasputin did become an intimate figure in the royal household.
9. Doctors at the time could do little but treat the symptoms of this disease, and the czarina, who was deeply religious, turned to Rasputin, whom she saw as a simple man of <u>g</u>od.
11. The czarina believed Rasputin had the power to heal her son through prayer, though most doctors and historians who have studied the accounts written by members of the <u>r</u>omanov court believe he may have used hypnosis.
13. By ordering the doctors to stay away from the boy, Rasputin ended the physicians' poking and probing, which only aggravated his condition and prevented the <u>r</u>omanov heir's blood from clotting.

15. rasputin began to appear in antigovernment propaganda leaflets, many suggesting the drunken, lecherous "holy man" had become the czarina's lover.

17. Government officials and members of royalty saw Rasputin as a threat and wanted to eliminate him, especially prince yussupov, who plotted to kill the holy man.

19. When the poison had no effect, they shot him three times, beat him with heavy objects, and threw his body into a hole chopped into the frozen neva river, where Rasputin, still alive, struggled to free himself under the ice.

Exercise 2

1. On october 16, 1869, workmen digging a well in cardiff, new york, made an amazing discovery.

3. Visitors came from all over new york to see the ten-foot-high statue carved from stone.

5. Some believed the statue was carved by a jesuit missionary to teach the bible to native americans.

7. A yale professor examined the giant, discovered fresh chisel marks, and announced it was a phony.

9. Newell, who conspired with hull, then directed workers to dig a well, engineering the giant's "accidental" discovery.

11. Always eager to make money with a new exhibit, p. t. barnum offered to lease the giant to display in his museum.

13. A hundred years later, another great showman, david merrick, came up with another hoax that made broadway history.

15. Merrick placed an ad in the *new york herald tribune* announcing that seven of new york's leading critics raved about his play.

17. The ad was a stunt; the quotes were real but misleading.

19. After enjoying themselves with the famous producer, the seven new yorkers praised his show and agreed to let him use their names and quote their favorable comments.

Exercise 3

Although there are now longer bridges in the world, the golden gate bridge remains one of the most famous structures in the world. Visitors to san francisco marvel at the way fog rolls off the cold pacific waters to bathe the tall orange structure in fog. The american society of civil engineers lists the bridge as one of the modern wonders of the world. The bridge connects san francisco with marin county to the north. Construction on the bridge began in january 1933 when the great depression was gripping the american economy. The construction of an engineering marvel inspired not only people in california but the whole country. Newsreels followed the development of this mammoth project, which along with other wpa projects helped give people hope for a better future. . . .

CHAPTER 35

Exercise 1

1. grateful
3. safety
5. column
7. precede
9. dependent

Exercise 2

1. too
3. access
5. affected, morale
7. plain, lose
9. imply

Exercise 3

The Grammy Award is the most famous of <u>for</u> [four] <u>discreet</u> [discrete] music awards in the United States. The Grammy gets <u>it's</u> [its] name from the award <u>isself</u> [itself], which is a <u>minature</u> [miniature] replica of an <u>old-fashion</u> [old-fashioned] gramophone. The award is presented by the Recording Academy, an <u>assocation</u> [association] of professionals in the music industry. Awards are given in thirty <u>generes</u> [genres], including rock, pop, rap, and gospel. These are <u>seperated</u> [separated] into over a hundred <u>catagories</u> [categories]. Unlike other music awards, the Grammy winners are chosen by voting members of the academy rather <u>then</u> [than] by fans. . . .

Exercise 4

1. reefs
3. pop stars
5. wolves
7. flurries
9. taxes

Exercise 5

1. The attorneys general of sixteen states met with representatives of companies concerned about rising bankruptcies.
3. Consumer worries about rising prices are hurting many industries.
5. These safety features could save many lives.

Exercise 6

1. weighed
3. stood
5. capitalized
7. doubled
9. slept

Exercise 7

1. debatable
3. regretfully
5. attendance
7. winning
9. making

Exercise 8

One of the most <u>memorerable</u> [memorable] <u>peaces</u> [pieces] of America's <u>passed</u> [past] is the Liberty Bell. More <u>then</u> [than] any other relic of the Revolutionary War, it is <u>immediatly</u> [immediately] recognized as a symbol of freedom around the world. The bell was cast in England in 1752 and shipped to America to hang in the <u>Pennsylvana</u> [Pennsylvania] State House, later known as <u>Independance</u> [Independence] Hall.

The first time the bell was <u>rang</u> [rung] in 1753, it cracked. It was recast twice, then <u>hanged</u> [hung] in the State House. The bell was used to summon members of the Continental Congress in 1775 and 1776. When British <u>solders</u> [soldiers] neared Philadelphia, patriots moved the bell to Allentown and hid it under a church. The bell was returned to Philadelphia in 1778. . . .

Exercise 9

See page 572.

Credits

This page constitutes an extension of the copyright page. We have made every effort to trace the ownership of all copyrighted material and to secure permission from copyright holders. In the event of any question arising as to the use of any material, we will be pleased to make the necessary corrections in future printings. Thanks are due to the following authors, publishers, and agents for permission to use the material indicated.

Photo Credits

2: © Royalty-Free/CORBIS; **8:** © Tom Grill/RF/CORBIS; **10:** © Patrik Giardino/CORBIS; **25:** © Jon Feingersh/CORBIS; **28:** © Frank Trapper/CORBIS; **42:** © Peter M. Fisher/CORBIS; **44:** © Peter Beck/CORBIS; **57:** © Bettmann/CORBIS; **59:** © Ariel Skelley/CORBIS; **72:** © Hulton-Deutsch Collection/CORBIS; **72:** © Royalty-Free/CORBIS; **87:** © Michael A. Keller Studios, Ltd./CORBIS; **100:** © Hutchings Stock Photography/CORBIS; **102:** © JIM BOURG/Reuters/CORBIS; **111:** © Chris Farina/CORBIS; **113:** © CORBIS SYGMA; **125:** © Bettmann/CORBIS; **126:** © Peter Beck/CORBIS; **138:** © Bill Varie/CORBIS; **140:** © Charles E. Rotkin/CORBIS; **151:** © Alexander Walter/GETTY; **153:** © Viviane Moos/CORBIS; **163:** © Peter Blakely/CORBIS SABA; **165:** © Reuters/CORBIS; **180:** © CORBIS; **184:** © Reuters/CORBIS; **195:** © Michael Tweed/Reuters/CORBIS; **197:** © LWA/Stephen Welstead/CORBIS; **238:** © CORBIS; **240:** © Ken James/CORBIS; **249:** © Bettmann/CORBIS; **251:** © Royalty-Free/CORBIS; **273:** © Ted Soqui/CORBIS; **274:** © Gabe Palmer/Mug Shots/CORBIS; **288:** © Chuck Savage/CORBIS; **292:** © Underwood & Underwood/CORBIS; **305:** © Reuters/CORBIS; **307:** © Scott de Freitas-Draper /Santa Maria Times/CORBIS; **333:** © David Paul Morris/Pool/Reuters/CORBIS; **335:** © Rob Lewine/CORBIS; **348:** © Swim Ink, LLC/CORBIS; **352:** © Bettmann/CORBIS; **367:** © Reuters/CORBIS; **378:** © Les Stone/CORBIS; **395:** © Lichtenstein Andrew/CORBIS SYGMA; **409:** © Paul Barton/CORBIS; **421:** © Jon Feingersh/Zefa/CORBIS; **430:** © Paul J. Sutton/Duomo/CORBIS; **446:** © Ashley Cooper/Picimpact/CORBIS; **463:** © Jutta Klee/CORBIS; **481:** © James Marshall/CORBIS; **496:** © Peter Morgan/Reuters/CORBIS; **513:** © Sagel & Kranefeld/Zefa/CORBIS; **529:** © Bettmann/CORBIS; **538:** © Phillip Gould/CORBIS; **Working Together icon:** © Photodisc/Getty

Text Credits

32: From *The Last Battle* by Cornelius Ryan; **33:** From *Casino* by Nicholas Pileggi; **33:** From "Down and Out in Paris and London" by George Orwell; **33:** From *"Vietnam: A History* by Stanley Karnow; **36:** From *The Hidden Years* by James Phelan; **36:** From "Who's Listening to Your Cell Phone Calls?" by Louis R. Mizzell, Jr.; **36:** From *Nicholas and Alexandra* by Robert K. Massie; **37:** From

Index